W9-ACA-423

SCOTT FORESMAN · ADDISON WESLEY

Mathematics

Authors

Randall I. Charles
Janet H. Caldwell
Mary Cavanagh
Dinah Chancellor
Alma B. Ramirez

Warren Crown
Jeanne F. Ramos
Kay Sammons
Jane F. Schielack

Francis (Skip) Fennell
William Tate
Mary Thompson
John A. Van de Walle

Consulting Mathematicians

Edward J. Barbeau
Professor of Mathematics
University of Toronto
Toronto, Ontario, Canada

David M. Bressoud
DeWitt Wallace Professor of
  Mathematics
Macalester College
Saint Paul, Minnesota

Gary Lippman
Professor of Mathematics
  and Computer Science
California State University
  Hayward
Hayward, California

PEARSON

Scott
Foresman

Glenview, Illinois • Parsippany, New Jersey • New York, New York

Sales Offices: Parsippany, New Jersey • Duluth, Georgia • Glenview, Illinois
Coppell, Texas • Ontario, California • Mesa, Arizona

Reading Consultants

Peter Afflerbach
Professor and Director of The Reading Center
University of Maryland
College Park, Maryland

Donald J. Leu
John and Maria Neag
 Endowed Chair in Literacy and Technology
University of Connecticut
Storrs, Connecticut

Reviewers

Mary Bacon
Mathematics Specialist
East Baton Rouge Parish School
 System
Baton Rouge, Louisiana

Cheryl Baker
Mathematics Teacher
Norton Middle School
Norton, Ohio

Marcelline A. Barron
Curriculum Leader Math and
 Science, K–5
Fairfield Public Schools
Fairfield, Connecticut

Mary Connery-Simmons
Mathematics Specialist
Springfield Massachusetts
 Public Schools
Springfield, Massachusetts

Anthony C. Dentino
Supervisor of Curriculum
Brick Township Schools
Brick, New Jersey

Dawn Evans
Mathematics Teacher
Bret Harte Elementary School
Chicago, Illinois

Sam Hanson
Teacher
Totem Falls Elementary
Snohomish, Washington

Allison Harris
Professional Development
 School Coach
Seattle Public Schools
Seattle, Washington

Pamela Renee Hill
Teacher
Durham Public Schools
Durham, North Carolina

Catherine Kuhns
Teacher
Country Hills Elementary
Coral Springs, Florida

Madeleine A. Madsen
District Curriculum Resource
Community Consolidated
 School District 59
Arlington Heights, Illinois

Lynda M. Penry
Teacher
Wright Elementary
Ft. Walton Beach, Florida

Deanna P. Rigdon
District Math Curriculum
 Specialist, Grades 3–4
Granite School District
Salt Lake City, Utah

Thomas Romero
Principal
Adams Elementary
Wapato, Washington

Wendy Siegel
Mathematics Coordinator K–12
Orchard Park Middle School
Orchard Park, New York

Sandra Smith
Teacher
Cheat Lake Elementary
Morgantown, West Virginia

Rochelle A. Solomon
Mathematics Resource Teacher
Cleveland Municipal School
 District
Cleveland, Ohio

Frank L. Sparks
Curriculum Design and Support
 Specialist, Secondary
 Mathematics
New Orleans Public Schools
New Orleans, Louisiana

Beth L. Spivey
Lead Teacher, Elementary
 Mathematics
Wake County Public
 School System
Raleigh, North Carolina

Paula Spomer
Teacher
Chisholm Elementary
Edmond, Oklahoma

Robert Trammel
Math Consultant
Fort Wayne Community Schools
Fort Wayne, Indiana

Annemarie Tuffner
Mathematics Lead Teacher,
 K–12
Neshaminy School District
Langhorne, Pennsylvania

Judy L. Wright
Curriculum and Staff
 Development Specialist
Columbus Public Schools
Columbus, Ohio

Theresa Zieles
Teacher
Indianapolis Public School 88
Indianapolis, Indiana

ISBN: 0-328-11709-9

1

Place Value, Adding, and Subtracting

Instant Check System
- Diagnosing Readiness, 2
- Warm Up, daily
- Talk About It, daily
- Check, daily
- Diagnostic Checkpoint, 21, 35, 47

Test Prep
- Mixed Review and Test Prep, daily
- Test Talk, daily, 48
- Cumulative Review and Test Prep, 54

Reading For Math Success

Reading Helps!
- Reading Helps, 18, 32, 42
- Key Vocabulary and Concept Review, 50

Writing in Math
- Writing in Math exercises, daily

Problem-Solving Applications, 44

Discovery CHANNEL
SCHOOL
Discover Math in Your World, 31

Additional Resources
- Learning with Technology, 11
- Practice Game, 25
- Enrichment, 17
- Chapter 1 Test, 52
- Reteaching, 56
- More Practice, 60

Multiplying Whole Numbers and Decimals

Dividing with One-Digit Divisors

4

Dividing with Two-Digit Divisors

 Instant Check System
- Diagnosing Readiness, 200
- Warm Up, daily
- Talk About It, daily
- Check, daily
- Diagnostic Checkpoint, 213, 229, 241

 Test Prep
- Mixed Review and Test Prep, daily
- Test Talk, daily, 242
- Cumulative Review and Test Prep, 248

Reading For Math Success
Reading Helps!
- Reading for Math Success, 208
- Reading Helps, 210, 226
- Key Vocabulary and Concept Review, 244

Writing in Math
- Writing in Math exercises, daily

Problem-Solving Applications, 238

Discovery Discover Math
in Your World, 221

Additional Resources
- Learning with Technology, 221
- Practice Game, 217
- Enrichment, 207, 237
- Chapter 4 Test, 246
- Reteaching, 250
- More Practice, 254

5 Data, Graphs, and Probability

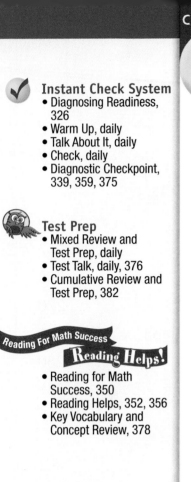

6 Geometry

Instant Check System
• Diagnosing Readiness, 326
• Warm Up, daily
• Talk About It, daily
• Check, daily
• Diagnostic Checkpoint, 339, 359, 375

Test Prep
• Mixed Review and Test Prep, daily
• Test Talk, daily, 376
• Cumulative Review and Test Prep, 382

Reading For Math Success
Reading Helps!
• Reading for Math Success, 350
• Reading Helps, 352, 356
• Key Vocabulary and Concept Review, 378

Writing in Math
• Writing in Math exercises, daily
• Writing to Describe, 356

 Problem-Solving Applications, 372

Discovery SCHOOL Discover Math in Your World, 345

Additional Resources
• Learning with Technology, 367
• Practice Game, 335
• Enrichment, 331, 349, 363, 371
• Chapter 6 Test, 380
• Reteaching, 384
• More Practice, 388

Fraction Concepts

8 Fraction Operations

 Instant Check System
- Diagnosing Readiness, 458
- Warm Up, daily
- Talk About It, daily
- Check, daily
- Diagnostic Checkpoint, 471, 489, 509

 **Test Prep**
- Mixed Review and Test Prep, daily
- Test Talk, daily, 510
- Cumulative Review and Test Prep, 516

Reading For Math Success
Reading Helps!
- Reading for Math Success, 482
- Reading Helps, 484, 504
- Key Vocabulary and Concept Review, 512

Writing in Math
- Writing in Math exercises, daily

 Problem-Solving Applications, 506

 Discovery CHANNEL SCHOOL Discover Math in Your World, 499

Additional Resources
- Learning with Technology, 481
- Practice Game, 469
- Enrichment, 493
- Chapter 8 Test, 514
- Reteaching, 518
- More Practice, 522

9 Measurement

Measuring Solids

Sidebar

 Instant Check System
- Diagnosing Readiness, 592
- Warm Up, daily
- Talk About It, daily
- Check, daily
- Diagnostic Checkpoint, 609, 619, 629

 Test Prep
- Mixed Review and Test Prep, daily
- Test Talk, daily, 630
- Cumulative Review and Test Prep, 636

Reading For Math Success
Reading Helps!
- Reading for Math Success, 604
- Reading Helps, 606, 624
- Key Vocabulary and Concept Review, 632

Writing in Math
- Writing in Math exercises, daily

 Problem-Solving Applications, 626

 Discover Math in Your World, 597

Additional Resources
- Learning with Technology, 601
- Enrichment, 613
- Chapter 10 Test, 634
- Reteaching, 638
- More Practice, 641

Ratio, Proportion, and Percent

12

Algebra: Integers, Equations, and Graphing

Instant Check System
- Diagnosing Readiness, 694
- Warm Up, daily
- Talk About It, daily
- Check, daily
- Diagnostic Checkpoint, 711, 723, 733

Test Prep
- Mixed Review and Test Prep, daily
- Test Talk, daily, 734
- Cumulative Review and Test Prep, 740

Reading For Math Success
Reading Helps!
- Reading for Math Success, 704
- Reading Helps, 706, 720
- Key Vocabulary and Concept Review, 736

Writing in Math
- Writing in Math exercises, daily
- Writing to Compare, 720

 Problem-Solving Applications, 730

 Discover Math in Your World, 727

Additional Resources
- Learning with Technology, 715
- Practice Game, 699
- Chapter 12 Test, 738
- Reteaching, 742
- More Practice, 745

What can help you get higher test scores?

Turn the page to find out.

Test-Taking Strategies

Remember these six test-taking strategies that will help you do well on tests. These strategies are also taught in the Test Talk before each chapter test.

Understand the Question

- **Look for important words.**
- **Turn the question into a statement: "I need to find out..."**

1. Which figure does NOT have a line of symmetry?

   A.

   B.

   C.

   D.

1. What are some important words in the problem that tell you what the problem is about?

2. What important word in the problem is highlighted using capital letters?

3. Turn the question into a statement that begins with "I need to find out . . .."

Get Information for the Answers

- **Get information from text.**
- **Get information from pictures, maps, diagrams, tables, graphs.**

2. Van is ordering a sandwich for lunch. He needs to pick the type of bread he wants and a filling. How many possible combinations of one type of bread and one filling does he have to choose from? Explain.

The Sandwich Shack

Bread Choices	Filling Choices
Rye	Tuna salad
Wheat	Egg salad

_____

_____

_____

_____

4. What information from the picture is needed to solve the problem?

5. What information in the text is needed to solve the problem?

Plan How to Find the Answer

- **Think about problem-solving skills and strategies.**
- **Choose computation methods.**

3. Bruce is wrapping presents for a party. He bought 4 bows and a spool of ribbon that contains 12 yards. How many inches of ribbon are on the spool? (Remember, there are 36 inches in a yard.)

   A. 3 inches

   B. 48 inches

   C. 432 inches

   D. 436 inches

6. Tell how you would use the following problem-solving skills and strategies as you solve the problem.

   - Identify extra or missing information.
   - Choose an operation.
   - Draw a picture.

7. Which of the following computation methods would you use to solve this problem?

   - Mental math
   - Paper and pencil
   - Calculator

Make Smart Choices

- **Eliminate wrong answers.**
- **Try working backward from an answer.**
- **Check answers for reasonableness; estimate.**

4. Mrs. Corrin's class collected 242 pinecones and put them in a large box. Mrs. Corrin wants each child to get the same number of pinecones to use for an art project. There are 22 children in the class. How many pinecones will each child receive?

   A. 11 pinecones

   B. 17 pinecones

   C. 110 pinecones

   D. 220 pinecones

8. Which answer choices can you eliminate because you are sure they are wrong answers? Explain.

9. How could you use multiplication to work backward from an answer to see if it is correct?

10. How could you estimate the answer? Is the correct answer close to the estimate?

Use these two strategies when you have to write an answer.

Use Writing in Math

- Make your answer brief but complete.
- Use words from the problem and use math terms accurately.
- Describe steps in order.
- Draw pictures if they help you to explain your thinking.

5. Laurie has a square vegetable garden 2.5 meters by 2.5 meters. The garage runs along one side of the garden. Laurie wants to use fencing to enclose the other three sides. How many meters of fencing does Laurie need? Explain how you found your answer.

Work space

11. What words from the problem will you use in your response?

12. What steps could you describe in your response?

13. How can drawing a picture help you explain your thinking?

Improve Written Answers

- Check if your answer is complete.
- Check if your answer is clear and easy to follow.
- Check if your answer makes sense.

6. Will's grandfather is a wallpaper hanger. Will is helping his grandfather make a chart to tell him how many square feet of wallpaper are on a certain number of rolls. How many feet of wallpaper are on 6 rolls? Explain how you found your answer.

Number of rolls	1	2	3	4	5	6
Number of square feet	56	112	168	224	280	

There are 336 square feet on 6 rolls.

I found a pattern in the table and then I added.

14. Is the answer that is given worth 4 points, using the rubric that is shown on the next page? Explain.

15. If the answer is not worth 4 points, tell how to improve the answer.

Scoring Rubric

4 points

Full credit: 4 points

The answer is correct. A full explanation is given as to how the answer is found.

3 points

Partial credit: 3 points

The answer is correct, but the explanation does not fully explain how the answer was found.

2 points

Partial credit: 2 points

The answer is correct or the explanation is correct, but not both.

1 point

Partial credit: 1 point

A solution is attempted, but the answer is incorrect. The explanation is unclear.

0 points

No credit: 0 points

The solution is completely incorrect or missing.

For more on Test-Taking Strategies, see the following Test Talk pages.

Test-Taking Strategies

Test Prep

As you use your book, look for these features that help you prepare for tests.

Test Talk before each chapter test teaches Test-Taking Strategies.

Think It Through
• I will check if the answer is complete.
• I will check if the answer makes sense.

Test Talk: Think It Through within lessons helps you do the kind of thinking you need to do when you take a test.

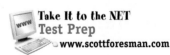
Mixed Review and Test Prep

Mixed Review and Test Prep at the end of lessons gives you practice with the kind of items on tests.

Take It to the NET
Test Prep
www.scottforesman.com

Take It to the Net: Test Prep at the end of lessons offers online test prep.

Cumulative Review and Test Prep

Cumulative Review and Test Prep at the end of chapters helps you remember content you'll need to know when you take tests.

 DIAGNOSING READINESS

A Vocabulary
(Grade 4)

Choose the best term from the box.

1. The numbers 0, 1, 2, 3, . . . are ___?___.

2. One ___?___ is the same as 1,000,000.

3. The number 65.14 is a ___?___.

Vocabulary

- **decimal** *(Grade 4)* • **thousand** *(Grade 4)*
- **million** *(Grade 4)* • **whole numbers** *(Grade 4)*

B Place Value
(Grade 4)

Write the value of the underlined digit.

4. 3,1<u>6</u>9   **5.** <u>1</u>86   **6.** 4,02<u>2</u>

7. 6<u>5</u>,403   **8.** <u>3</u>5   **9.** <u>8</u>,134

10. 17,0<u>5</u>7   **11.** 5,<u>9</u>09   **12.** <u>4</u>8,686

13. What does the zero tell you in 1,083?

Do You Know...

How much do the largest cruise ships weigh?

You will find out in Lesson 1-15.

A DORLING KINDERSLEY BOOK

LOOK INSIDE
CROSS-SECTIONS
SHIPS
SEE INSIDE 10 FASCINATING VESSELS

C ## Rounding Whole Numbers
(Grade 4)

Round each number to the underlined place.

14. <u>5</u>2   **15.** <u>8</u>41   **16.** 1,<u>9</u>77

17. 3<u>2</u>9   **18.** <u>6</u>5   **19.** 2,1<u>5</u>2

20. 4<u>3</u>0   **21.** <u>1</u>56   **22.** <u>7</u>,824

23. A school collects 659 cans of food for a charity. Round this amount to the nearest hundred.

D ## Adding Whole Numbers
(Grade 4)

24. 3 + 6   **25.** 8 + 70   **26.** 20 + 40

27. 60 + 1   **28.** 9 + 6   **29.** 100 + 20

30. 5 + 700   **31.** 30 + 60   **32.** 90 + 9

33. Find two numbers with a sum of 47.

34. Ellen read 30 pages in her book last night and 9 pages tonight. How many pages did she read in all?

Key Idea
The place and period of a digit determines its value.

Vocabulary
• standard form
• expanded form
• word form
• digits
• place value
• period

Place Value

LEARN

How can you show numbers?

The diameter of the planet Jupiter is about 88,700 miles.

At times, the planet Pluto is 4,500,000,000 miles from the sun.

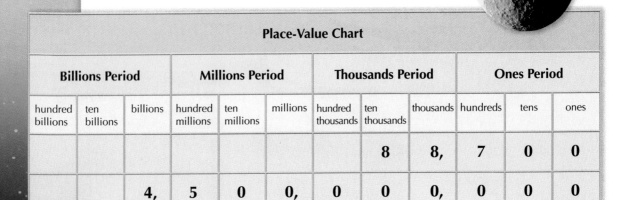

Place-Value Chart

Billions Period			Millions Period			Thousands Period			Ones Period		
hundred billions	ten billions	billions	hundred millions	ten millions	millions	hundred thousands	ten thousands	thousands	hundreds	tens	ones
							8	8,	7	0	0
	4,	5	0	0,	0	0	0,	0	0	0	0

Standard form: 88,700
4,500,000,000

Expanded form: 80,000 + 8,000 + 700
4,000,000,000 + 500,000,000

Word form: eighty-eight thousand, seven hundred
four billion, five hundred million

Numbers are written using the **digits** 0, 1, 2, 3, 4, 5, 6, 7, 8, and 9.

In 88,700, the 7 has a **place value** in the hundreds, so its **value** is 700.

Each group of three digits starting from the right is called a **period**.

✔ Talk About It

1. What is the expanded form of 84,308,065?

Write the word form for each number and tell the value of the red digit.

1. **9**,235   **2.** **1**35,100   **3.** 25,**5**03,400   **4.** **3**42,124,567,111

5. Write 67,192,000,347 in expanded form.

Write each number in standard form.

6. 50,000,000 + 8,000,000 + 600 + 9   **7.** six billion, two hundred million, twelve thousand, five

8. Number Sense What number is 100,000,000 more than 2,439,290,348?

A Skills and Understanding

Write the word form for each number and tell the value of the red digit.

9. **6**7,125   **10.** **8**,000,345   **11.** 1**2**4,000

12. **1**65,987,425   **13.** 1,2**5**7,000,000   **14.** 1**7**,983,024,000

Write each number in expanded form.

15. 7,357   **16.** 761,324   **17.** 1,230,000   **18.** 676,541,900

Write each number in standard form.

19. 90,000,000 + 5,000,000 + 300 + 7

20. thirty billion, forty-eight million

21. Number Sense What number is 10,000 less than 293,238?

B Reasoning and Problem Solving

In the 2000 U.S. Census, Texas's population was 20,851,820, and Wyoming's was 493,782. Give each population after:

22. an increase of 100,000.   **23.** a decrease of 10,000.

24. an increase of 1,000,000.   **25.** an increase of 10,000,000.

26. **Writing in Math** Explain how you would write 201,000,700,005 in words.

Mixed Review and Test Prep   **Take It to the NET**
Test Prep
www.scottforesman.com

Find each answer.

27. 999 + 1   **28.** 10,000 − 1   **29.** $10 \times 10 \times 10 \times 10$ **30.** 10,000 + 100

31. Which is shorter than 1 yard?

    A. 40 inches   **B.** 3 feet   **C.** 35 inches   **D.** 4 feet

Key Idea
You can use place value to compare and order whole numbers.

Comparing and Ordering Whole Numbers

WARM UP

Tell the value of each underlined digit.

1. <u>8</u>,876   2. 2<u>39</u>,000

3. 4,<u>1</u>29,000

LEARN

How can you compare and order whole numbers?

Example A

Which had a greater population in 2000, Dallas or Philadelphia?

STEP 1 Line up the places. Begin at the left. Compare.

1,188,580
1,517,550

STEP 2 Find the first place where the digits are different and compare.

1,**1**88,580
1,**5**17,550
5 > 1

So, 1,517,550 > 1,188,580.
Philadelphia had a greater population.

Data File

City	2000 U.S. Census Population
Chicago	2,896,016
Dallas	1,188,580
Philadelphia	1,517,550

Think It Through
• I know that > means "is greater than" and < means "is less than."

Example B

Order the cities by their populations from least to greatest.

STEP 1 Write the numbers, lining up places. Compare.

2,896,016 ← greatest
1,188,580
1,517,550

STEP 2 Write the remaining numbers, lining up places. Compare.

1,188,580
1,517,550 ← greater

STEP 3 Write the numbers from least to greatest.

1,188,580,   1,517,550   2,896,016

In order by their populations, the cities are Dallas, Philadelphia, and Chicago.

✔ Talk About It

1. How do you know that Chicago had the greatest population?

Take It to the NET
More Examples
www.scottforesman.com

For another example, see Set 1-2 on p. 56.

Copy and complete. Write >, <, or = for each ⬤.

1. 9,813 ⬤ 9,624   **2.** 200,000 ⬤ 199,999   **3.** 1,784,387 ⬤ 1,785,000

Order these numbers from least to greatest.

4. 243,839   238,502   242,398   **5.** 1,444,400   1,444,238   2,000,300

6. Number Sense If a number is greater than 900,000 and less than 901,000, what digit will be in the thousands place?

PRACTICE

For more practice, see Set 1-2 on p. 60.

Ⓐ Skills and Understanding

Copy and complete. Write >, <, or = for each ⬤.

7. 3,456 ⬤ 3,543   **8.** 19,320 ⬤ 19,212   **9.** 9,459,000 ⬤ 10,000,000

Order these numbers from least to greatest.

10. 642,019   642,010   642,300   **11.** 6,777,111   6,677,111   6,776,111

12. Number Sense What digit could be in the ten millions place of a number that is greater than 70,000,000 but less than 100,000,000?

Ⓑ Reasoning and Problem Solving

Which state has a greater area?

13. Florida or Texas   **14.** Oklahoma or Missouri

15. Write the states in order from the one with the greatest area to the one with the least.

16. **Writing in Math** Explain why 35,925 is greater than 35,790.

Data File	
State	**Area in Square Miles**
Florida	65,755
Missouri	69,704
Oklahoma	69,898
Texas	268,581

 **Mixed Review and Test Prep**

Take It to the NET
Test Prep
www.scottforesman.com

17. Three sisters each bought a $5 movie ticket and a $2 bag of popcorn. Together they had $30. How much was left?

18. What is the standard form for 3,000,000 + 500,000 + 50?

   A. 355   **C.** 3,500,050

   B. 3,500,500   **D.** 3,005,005

Vocabulary
- tenths
- hundredths
- thousandths
- equivalent decimals

Place Value Through Thousandths

LEARN

How can you represent decimals?

When Trisha went to England, she got 1.516 British pounds for each U.S. dollar.

Here are different ways to represent 1.516.

Grids:

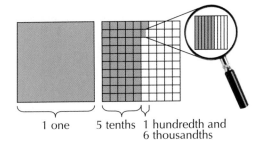

1 one   5 tenths   1 hundredth and 6 thousandths

Number line:

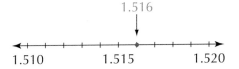

Place-value chart:

decimal point

Ones		Tenths	Hundredths	Thousandths
1	.	5	1	6

Expanded form: $1 + 0.5 + 0.01 + 0.006$

Standard form: 1.516

Word form: one and five hundred sixteen thousandths

✔ Talk About It

1. There are two 1s in 1.516. Does each 1 have the same value? Explain.

2. In word form, how do you read the decimal point?

What are equivalent decimals?

Equivalent decimals name the same amount.

Example A

Name two decimals that are equivalent to 0.8.

Eight tenths is 80 hundredths.
So 0.8 = 0.80.

Eight tenths is 800 thousandths.
So 0.8 = 0.800.

So 0.8 = 0.80 = 0.800.

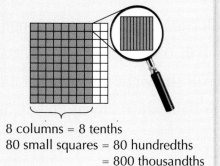

8 columns = 8 tenths
80 small squares = 80 hundredths
　　　　　　　 = 800 thousandths

Example B

If 0.37 has 3 tenths and 7 hundredths,
why is it read 37 hundredths?

One Way
Heather thought
3 tenths is the same
as 30 hundredths.

So 30 hundredths
and 7 hundredths is
37 hundredths.

Another Way
Zach drew a model.

37 small squares = 37 hundredths

3 tenths 7 hundredths = 37 hundredths

✔ Talk About It

3. In Example A, how many thousandths
would there be in the entire 10 × 10 grid?

4. Why do we read 0.375 as 375 thousandths?

5. Are 0.03 and 0.003 equivalent decimals? Explain.

**CHECK** ✓

For another example, see Set 1-3 on p. 56.

Write the word form for each number and tell the value of the red digit.

1. 5.63   **2.** 6.218   **3.** 2.349   **4.** 4.067

Write each number in standard form.

5. 8 + 0.7 + 0.01 + 0.002

6. two and four hundred twenty-two thousandths

Write two decimals that are equivalent to each number.

7. 0.4   **8.** 0.70   **9.** 0.200

10. Name two decimals shown by the model at the right.

11. Number Sense Explain why 0.78 has 78 hundredths.

PRACTICE

For more practice, see Set 1-3 on p. 60.

A Skills and Understanding

Write the word form for each number and tell the value of the red digit.

12. 1.19   **13.** 3.374   **14.** 8.952   **15.** 2.315

16. 9.919   **17.** 5.001   **18.** 4.808   **19.** 7.030

Write each number in standard form.

20. 5 + 0.06 + 0.007

21. five and sixty-seven thousandths

Write two decimals that are equivalent to each number.

22. 0.600   **23.** 0.30   **24.** 0.9

25. Name two decimals shown by the model at the right.

26. Number Sense Explain why 0.3 and 0.300 are equivalent.

B Reasoning and Problem Solving

Math and Social Studies

Write the word form for the life expectancy of

27. females in Japan.

28. males in Switzerland.

Tell the value of the 6 in the life expectancy of

29. males in Japan.

30. females in Switzerland.

Data File

Life Expectancy		
Country	Males	Females
Japan	77.62	84.15
Switzerland	76.85	82.76
United States	74.37	80.05

31. <u>Writing in Math</u> Is the explanation below correct? If not, tell why and write a correct response.

Explain how you would write the number 3.085 in words.

1. The whole number part is 3.
2. The decimal point is read "and."
3. The place value of the last digit is thousandths. That tells me there are 85 thousandths.
4. So I write three and eighty-five thousandths.

Think It Through
When several steps are involved, I need to **describe the steps in order.**

C Extensions

The place-value chart on page 8 can be extended to the right.
The next two places are the *ten-thousandths place* and the *hundred-thousandths place*.
Write the word form for each number and tell the value of the red digit.

32. 4.02**8**5   **33.** 7.1006   **34.** 0.5289**6**

Mixed Review and Test Prep

Take It to the NET
Test Prep
www.scottforesman.com

Order these numbers from least to greatest.

35. 164,793   174,812   164,973   **36.** 6,982,010   6,982,001   6,982,011

37. Which number is less than 6,230,795?

   A. 6,231,795   **B.** 6,230,796   **C.** 6,230,885   **D.** 6,230,695

Learning with Technology

Spreadsheet/Data/Grapher eTool

A spreadsheet is organized into boxes called *cells*.

The cells are named by a letter that identifies the column and a number that identifies the row. In the spreadsheet below, cell C2 is highlighted.

1. What appears in cell B1?

2. Name the cell that contains Allisha's score for Game 3.

3. Create a spreadsheet with these scores. Make up scores for Games 4–6. Add two more players.

	A	B	C	D
1	Player	Game 1	Game 2	Game 3
2	Carlos	143	127	155
3	Allisha	124	118	131

Comparing and Ordering Decimals

LEARN

How can you compare and order decimals?

Gymnast	Score
Bill	4.903
Todd	4.827
Chris	4.844

Example A

Who had a greater score, Bill or Chris?

STEP 1

Line up the places. Begin at the left. Compare.

4.903
4.844

STEP 2

Find the first place where the digits are different and compare.

4.903
4.844 9 > 8

So, 4.903 > 4.844. Bill had a greater score.

Example B

List the scores in order from greatest to least.

STEP 1

Write the numbers, lining up places. Compare.

4.903
4.827
4.844

4.903 is the greatest.

STEP 2

Write the remaining numbers, lining up places. Compare.

4.827
4.844

4.844 is greater.

STEP 3

Write the numbers from greatest to least.

4.903
4.844
4.827

In order from greatest to least, the scores are 4.903, 4.844, and 4.827.

✓ Talk About It

1. Suppose Zach's score of 3.580 is added to the three scores above. How do you know that 3.580 is the lowest or least score?

For another example, see Set 1-4 on p. 56.

Copy and complete. Write >, <, or = for each ⬡ .

1. 8.383 ⬡ 8.291

2. 5.063 ⬡ 5.072

3. 7.23 ⬡ 7.231

Order these numbers from least to greatest.

4. 3.952, 3.862, 3.96, 3.713

5. 6.032, 6.475, 5.034, 6.575

6. Number Sense A decimal is greater than 0.1 and less than 0.11. What could the decimal be?

PRACTICE

For more practice, see Set 1-4 on p. 60.

Ⓐ Skills and Understanding

Copy and complete. Write >, <, or = for each ⬡ .

7. 1.121 ⬡ 1.212

8. 0.66 ⬡ 0.659

9. 9.403 ⬡ 9.404

10. 28.430 ⬡ 28.43

11. 195.36 ⬡ 195.357

12. 7.58 ⬡ 7.582

Order these numbers from least to greatest.

13. 4.162, 4.7, 4.316, 4.361

14. 0.002, 0.202, 0.020, 0.222

15. Number Sense Name three numbers between 0.24 and 0.25.

Ⓑ Reasoning and Problem Solving

Which diver had a better score?

16. Pedro or Cal

17. Cal or Lee

18. Which diver had the greatest score?

19. **Writing in Math** Explain why it is not reasonable to say that 2.16 is less than 2.06.

Diver	Score
John	55.375
Pedro	49.272
Cal	49.3
Lee	50.17

Mixed Review and Test Prep

Take It to the NET
Test Prep
www.scottforesman.com

Write the word form for each number and tell the value of the red digit.

20. 0.5**3**1

21. 2.8**9**2

22. 4.**6**00

23. 6.07**5**

24. What is the standard form for 2 + 0.1 + 0.03 + 0.004?

25. Which is equivalent to 0.9?

A. 0.900

B. 0.09

C. 0.009

D. 9

Key Idea
There are many patterns in our system for naming numbers.

Materials
calculator

Think It Through
I can **find a pattern** in place values.

Place-Value Patterns

LEARN

Activity

How are place values related?

a. Enter 1,000 into your calculator. Divide by 10. Divide the result by 10.

Continue to divide by 10 five more times. Record your results.

b. Repeat **part a** by starting with 4,000. Record your results.

c. Place value can be used to name a number such as 5,000 in different ways.

Thousands	Hundreds	Tens	Ones
5	0	0	0
5	0	0	0
5	0	0	0
5	0	0	0

→ 5 thousands or 5 × 1,000
→ 50 hundreds or 50 × 100
→ 500 tens or 500 × 10
→ 5,000 ones or 5,000 × 1

Complete each sentence with *ones, tens, hundreds,* or *thousands.*

3,000 is 30 ___.   7,000 is 700 ___.

4,000 is 4,000 ___.   9,000 is 9 ___.

d. Use a calculator to find the products.

0.9 × 10 = ___
0.9 × 100 = ___
0.9 × 1,000 = ___

e. Use the results of **part d** to complete these sentences.

9 = 0.9 × ___
90 = 0.9 × ___
900 = 0.9 × ___

✔ **Talk About It**

Complete each sentence.

1. 8,500 is 85 ___.

2. 80 = 0.8 × ___.

✔ **WARM UP**

Identify the value of the underlined digit.

1. 4<u>4</u>,504,092

2. 46<u>3</u>,281,004,750

3. 9.5<u>8</u>0

4. 7.4<u>1</u>9

How can you name the same number in different ways?

A place-value chart can help you name a number in different ways.

Example A

Name 800,000 in three different ways using both words and numbers for place-value names.

Hundred Thousands	Ten Thousands	Thousands	Hundreds	Tens	Ones
8	0	0	0	0	0
8	0	0	0	0	0
8	0	0	0	0	0

→ 8 hundred thousands or $8 \times 100{,}000$
→ 80 ten thousands or $80 \times 10{,}000$
→ 800 thousands or $800 \times 1{,}000$

Example B

Use the digits shown in red and place value to rename each number.

$7{,}000 = 70 \times \underline{\quad}$
↳ hundreds place

70 hundreds or
70×100

$200{,}000 = 20{,}000 \times \underline{\quad}$
↳ tens place

20,000 tens or
$20{,}000 \times 10$

$8{,}000{,}000 = 800 \times \underline{\quad}$
↳ ten thousands place

800 ten thousands or
$800 \times 10{,}000$

✔ Talk About It

3. In Example B, tell some other ways you could use place value to rename each number.

4. How many thousands are in a million? How many millions are in a billion?

Take It to the NET
More Examples
www.scottforesman.com

For another example, see Set 1-5 on p. 57.

CHECK ✔

Tell how many *tens*, *hundreds*, and *thousands* are in each number.

1. 30,000
2. 7,000
3. 6,000,000
4. 400,000

What number makes each statement true?

5. $2{,}500 = 25 \times \underline{\quad}$
6. $8{,}600 = 86 \times \underline{\quad}$
7. $76{,}000 = 760 \times \underline{\quad}$
8. $300{,}000 = 30 \times \underline{\quad}$
9. $90{,}000 = 900 \times \underline{\quad}$
10. $7 = 0.7 \times \underline{\quad}$

11. **Number Sense** How many hundreds are in 10,000?

A Skills and Understanding

Tell how many *tens*, *hundreds*, and *thousands* are in each number.

12. 6,000   **13.** 14,000   **14.** 600,000   **15.** 3,000,000

What number makes each statement true?

16. $8,000 = 800 \times \underline{\hspace{0.5cm}}$ **17.** $700,000 = 70 \times \underline{\hspace{0.5cm}}$ **18.** $2 = 0.2 \times \underline{\hspace{0.5cm}}$

19. $67,000 = 670 \times \underline{\hspace{0.5cm}}$ **20.** $2,000,000 = 200 \times \underline{\hspace{0.5cm}}$ **21.** $30 = 0.3 \times \underline{\hspace{0.5cm}}$

Name each number two different ways.

22. 30,000,000   **23.** 70,000   **24.** 700,000,000   **25.** 60,000

26. Number Sense How many thousands are in 1,000,000?

B Reasoning and Problem Solving

 Math and Social Studies

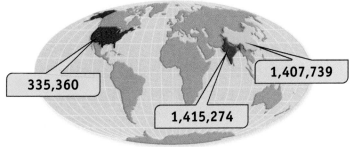

335,360   1,407,739   1,415,274

Data File

Projected Population in 2025 of the Most Populated Countries	
Country	**Population in Thousands**
China	1,407,739
India	1,415,274
United States	335,360

Write, in standard form, the projected population of:

27. India   **28.** United States

29. If China has ten times as many people in 3025 as in 2025, what will the population be?

30. <u>Writing in Math</u> Is the explanation below correct? If not, tell why and write a correct response.

What number makes the statement true? $0.05 \times \underline{\hspace{0.5cm}} = 0.5$

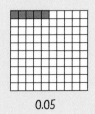

0.05   0.5 $0.05 \times 10 = 0.5$

Think It Through
I can **draw pictures** to explain my thinking.

C Extensions

What number makes each statement true?

31. 0.4 = ___ hundredths

32. 0.07 = ___ thousandths

Mixed Review and Test Prep

**Take It to the NET
Test Prep**
www.scottforesman.com

Copy and complete. Write >, <, or = for each ⬤.

33. 2.015 ⬤ 2.105   **34.** 6.159 ⬤ 5.159   **35.** 7.010 ⬤ 7.01

36. What is the standard form for 6 + 0.1 + 0.03 + 0.005?

A. 0.6135   **B.** 6.135   **C.** 61.35   **D.** 6,135

Enrichment

Powers of Ten

Numbers can be written in a shorter form with **exponents.** One thousand is a power of ten because it can be written as 10 with an exponent. The exponent is 3 because you multiply 3 factors of 10 to get 1,000.

Similarly, $100,000 = 10 \times 10 \times 10 \times 10 \times 10 = 10^5$.

$$1,000 = 10 \times 10 \times 10$$
$$= 10^3 \quad \text{exponent}$$
$$\text{base}$$

The system we use to write numbers is based on powers of ten.

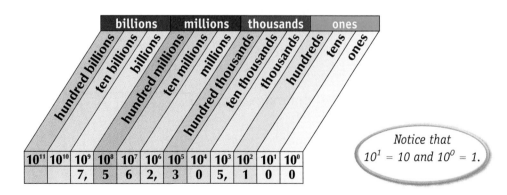

Notice that $10^1 = 10$ and $10^0 = 1$.

The following shows 7,562,305,100 in expanded notation with exponents.

$$7,562,305,100 = (7 \times 10^9) + (5 \times 10^8) + (6 \times 10^7) + (2 \times 10^6) + (3 \times 10^5) + (5 \times 10^3) + (1 \times 10^2)$$

Write each number in expanded notation with exponents.

1. 3,529

2. 854,207,340

3. 621,460,872,000

Problem-Solving Skill

Reading Helps!

Identifying steps in a process

can help you with...

the *Read and Understand* phase of the problem-solving process.

Key Idea
Read and Understand is the first phase of the problem-solving process.

Read and Understand

LEARN

What steps can be used to read and understand a problem?

Blue Angels The Blue Angels' first flight demonstration was in June, 1946. In what year did the Blue Angels celebrate their 50th anniversary?

Read and Understand

Step 1: What do you know?

- Tell the problem in your own words.

  The Blue Angels started flying in 1946.

- Identify key details and facts.

  Their first flight was June, 1946. They celebrated their 50th anniversary.

Step 2: What are you trying to find?

- Tell what the question is asking.

  The question is asking for the year they celebrated their 50th anniversary.

- Show the main idea.

?	
1946	50

1946	+	50	=	?
year started		years later		year of 50th anniversary

✔ Talk About It

1. Give the answer in a complete sentence.

2. **Reasonableness** Without finding the exact answer, how could you tell the answer had to be before the year 2000?

For another example, see Set 1-6 on p. 57.

For Problems 1–3, use the Monument Acreage problem.

1. **Step 1:** What do you know?

   a. Tell what you know about the problem in your own words.

   b. Identify key facts and details.

2. **Step 2:** What are you trying to find?

   a. Tell what the question is asking.

   b. Show the main idea.

3. Solve the problem and write your answer in a complete sentence.

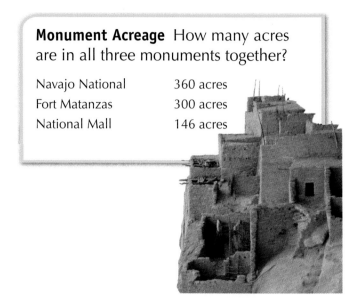

Monument Acreage How many acres are in all three monuments together?

Navajo National	360 acres
Fort Matanzas	300 acres
National Mall	146 acres

PRACTICE

For more practice, see Set 1-6 on p. 61.

For Problems 4–6, use the Flyers and Sailors problem.

4. **Step 1:** What do you know?

   a. Tell what you know about the problem in your own words.

   b. Identify key facts and details.

5. **Step 2:** What are you trying to find?

   a. Tell what the question is asking.

   b. Show the main idea.

6. Solve the problem and write your answer in a complete sentence.

7. Solve the Books problem.

8. How many more people said they get books from the library than from a friend?

9. How many people in the survey did not get their books from the library?

10. **Writing in Math** Explain how you solved the Books problem.

Flyers and Sailors Out of each 100 enlisted people, how many more women were in the Air Force than in the Navy?

Air Force: 13 women out of 100 enlisted people
Navy: 9 women out of 100 enlisted people

Books How many people said they get books in a bookstore or at the library?

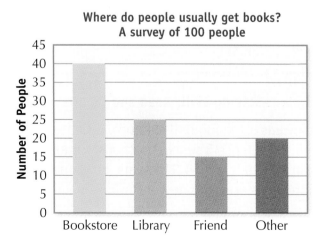

Where do people usually get books? A survey of 100 people

All text pages available online and on CD-ROM.

Do You Know How?

Do You Understand?

Place Value through Billions (1-1)
Place Value through Thousandths (1-3)

Write the word form for each number and tell the value of the red digit.

1. 21,904,352   **2.** 3.27

3. 79,652,478,010   **4.** 9.065

5. 395,013,476,998 **6.** 5.908

A Tell how you found the values of the red digits in Exercises 3 and 4.

B Describe the periods in 651,078,219,003.

Comparing and Ordering Whole Numbers (1-2)
Comparing and Ordering Decimals (1-4)

Compare. Write >, <, or = for each ●.

7. 4,865,329 ● 4,864,961

8. 3.054 ● 3.063

C Explain how you could use place value to make each comparison.

D Explain how to write 0.295, 0.32, and 0.296 in order from greatest to least.

Place-Value Patterns (1-5)

What number should replace each blank?

9. $4,000 = 40 \times$ ____

10. $50,000 = 50 \times$ ____

11. $800,000 = 8,000 \times$ ____

12. $200,000 = 20 \times$ ____

E Tell how you used place-value patterns to find the number to replace each blank.

F Explain how you could use place-value patterns to name 35,000 in three different ways.

Problem-Solving Skill: Read and Understand (1-6)

Stadiums One football stadium, built in 1982, has 64,035 seats. Another stadium, built in 1987, has 74,916 seats. How many more seats does the newer stadium have?

13. Name the key details and facts.

14. Show the main idea.

G Tell how you decided what the key details and facts were.

H Explain how to solve the problem.

Think It Through

Identify the main idea in a question by finding key words like NOT.

MULTIPLE CHOICE

1. Which word makes this statement true? (1-5)

$$50,000 = 500 \underline{\quad}$$

   A. ones   **B.** tens   **C.** hundreds   **D.** thousands

2. Which decimal below is NOT equivalent to the rest? (1-3)

   A. 0.4   **B.** 0.004   **C.** 0.400   **D.** 0.40

FREE RESPONSE

Write the word form for each number and tell the value of the red digit. (1-1 and 1-3)

3. 333,444,111,222   **4.** 1.5**5**5   **5.** 4.**8**97

Write each number in standard form. (1-1 and 1-3)

6. nine billion, five hundred seventeen thousand, one hundred four   **7.** $4 + 0.9 + 0.003$

Compare. Write >, <, or = for each ⬤. (1-2 and 1-4)

8. 36,980,800 ⬤ 36,980,793   **9.** 7.8 ⬤ 7.800   **10.** 2.699 ⬤ 2.599

Order these numbers from least to greatest. (1-2 and 1-4)

11. 23,010,623   23,100,236   23,010,326   **12.** 3.631, 3.136, 3.613, 3.316

Use the Starfish problem for 13–16. (1-6)

13. Tell what you know in your own words. Identify key facts and details.

14. Tell what the question is asking.

15. Show the main idea.

16. Solve the problem.

Starfish Marty counted 14 starfish on the beach, Megan counted 19 starfish, and Mindy counted 9 starfish. How many more starfish did Marty count than Mindy?

Writing in Math

17. Explain why the 8 in 786,009,231,432 has a value of 80,000,000,000. (1-1)

18. Explain how to write 40,000 in two different ways. (1-5)

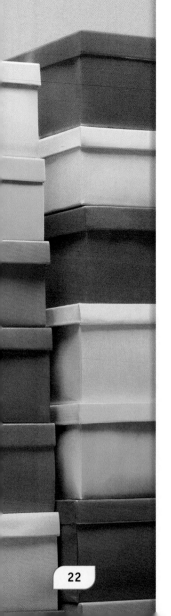

Key Idea
There is more than one way to add and subtract mentally.

Vocabulary
- Commutative Property of Addition
- Associative Property of Addition
- Identity Property of Addition
- compatible numbers
- compensation

Adding and Subtracting Mentally

✓ WARM UP

1. 2,800 + 200

2. 6,820 − 320

3. 2,000 − 500

LEARN

How can you add mentally?

When you add mentally, you can use these properties of numbers.

Commutative Property of Addition You can add two numbers in any order.	$12 + 25 = 25 + 12$
Associative Property of Addition You can change the grouping of addends.	$12 + (20 + 5) = (12 + 20) + 5$
Identity Property of Addition You can add zero to any number and the sum will be the number.	$18 + 0 = 18$ $27 + (1 − 1) = 27$

Numbers that are easy to add mentally are called **compatible numbers**. By using compatible numbers and the Commutative and Associative Properties, it is often easy to add mentally.

Example A

John works in a shipping department. One week he wanted to find how many packages he had shipped on three different days.

Wednesday   7 packages

Thursday   64 packages

Friday   93 packages

7 and 93 are compatible numbers.
$(7 + 93) + 64 = 100 + 64 = 164$

John shipped 164 packages over the three days.

Another useful method for adding mentally is **compensation**. With compensation, you adjust one number to make computation easier and compensate by changing the other.

Example B

Add 49 + 33 mentally.

49 + 33
+1   −1
↓   ↓
50 + 32 = 82

I added 1 to 49 since it is easy to add 50. Then I subtracted 1 from 33 to compensate for adding 1.

Adding 1 to a number and then subtracting 1 from the other is the same as adding 0 to 49 + 33.

✔ **Talk About It**

1. What property allows you to think of 97 + 177 + 3 as 97 + 3 + 177?

2. Kris found 58 + 37, by thinking 60 + 35. How did he use compensation?

3. Rosita found 58 + 37, by thinking 55 + 40. How did she use compensation?

How can you subtract mentally?

Which is easier to subtract mentally, 369 − 199 or 370 − 200? Both have a difference of 170. Comparing these problems suggests a useful technique for subtracting mentally. This technique is called **equal additions**.

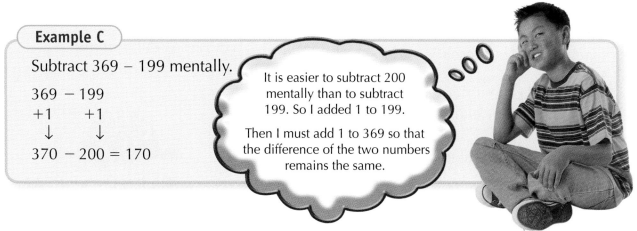

Example C

Subtract 369 − 199 mentally.

369 − 199
+1   +1
↓   ↓
370 − 200 = 170

It is easier to subtract 200 mentally than to subtract 199. So I added 1 to 199.

Then I must add 1 to 369 so that the difference of the two numbers remains the same.

✔ **Talk About It**

4. How could you use equal additions to find 246 − 97?

Use mental math to add or subtract.

1. 390 + 233   **2.** 980 – 890   **3.** 612 – 298   **4.** 93 + 87 + 7

5. Number Sense Which numbers are easier to subtract, 741 – 200 or 739 – 198? Explain.

PRACTICE   *For more practice, see Set 1-7 on p. 61.*

Ⓐ Skills and Understanding

Use mental math to add or subtract.

6. 20 + 40 + 80   **7.** 332 – 195   **8.** 291 + 337 + 9   **9.** 583 – 289

10. 1,640 – 70   **11.** 530 + 110 + 70   **12.** 1,700 – 1,275   **13.** 3,630 – 470

14. 79 + 38 + 21   **15.** 379 + 621   **16.** 468 – 190   **17.** 813 – 179

18. Number Sense Kathy and Roger are adding 480 + 260. Kathy added 500 + 240. Roger added 440 + 300. Are both correct? Explain.

Ⓑ Reasoning and Problem Solving

🎵 Math and Music

19. How many more hours of music did Haydn compose than Handel?

20. How many more hours of music did Mozart compose than Beethoven?

21. How many more hours of music did Bach compose than Schubert?

22. What is the total number of hours composed by these six composers?

23. **Writing in Math** Is the explanation below correct? If not, tell why and write a correct response.

Show how to subtract 468 – 270 mentally.

468	–	270
– 30		+ 30
to adjust		
↓		↓
438	–	300 = 138

Johann Sebastian Bach

Data File

Classical Composers	
Composer	**Number of hours of music composed**
Franz Joseph Haydn	340
George Handel	303
Wolfgang Amadeus Mozart	202
Johann Sebastian Bach	175
Franz Schubert	134
Ludwig van Beethoven	120

TEST TALK

Think It Through

I should always **check that my answer is reasonable.**

C Extensions

In Example A, John used compatible numbers. Here's why it works.

7 + 64 + 93 = 7 + 93 + 64	Commutative Property of Addition
(7 + 93) + 64	Associative Property of Addition
100 + 64	Addition
164	Addition

24. Find 260 + 190 + 40 by using compatible numbers. Show why it works.

Mixed Review and Test Prep

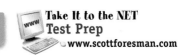
Take It to the NET
Test Prep
www.scottforesman.com

Use the Competition problem for 25–28.

25. Tell what you know in your own words. Identify key facts and details.

26. Tell what the question is asking.

27. Show the main idea.

28. Solve the problem.

29. 8,000 is the same as 80 ___.

    A. ones   **B.** tens   **C.** hundreds   **D.** thousands

> **Competition** Lars read 54 books in one school year. Kim read 49 books in one year. Lani read 55 books in one year. How many more books did Lani read than Kim?

Practice Game

Dueling Decimals

Players: 2   **Materials:** 2 number cubes, recording sheet

1. Each player records 2 zeros on any of the six blanks.

2. Players take turns tossing 2 number cubes and writing the numbers in any of the four remaining blanks. Players read their numbers aloud and compare them.

3. The player with the smaller number wins the round. The first player to win 5 rounds wins the game.

	Digit	Digit	Digit		Digit	Digit	Digit
Player A:	5	0	3	•	2	0	6
Player B:	3	6	0	•	1	5	0

Key Idea
Place value can help you round numbers.

Vocabulary
• rounding

Materials
• grid paper

Rounding Whole Numbers and Decimals

LEARN

How can you round whole numbers and decimals?

Rounding a number is replacing one number with another number that tells about how many or how much.

You can show that 63,281,025 is closer to 63,000,000 by drawing a number line. The steps below can be used to round numbers.

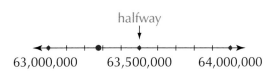

Example A

Round 63,281,025 to the nearest million.

STEP 1	Find the rounding place. Look at the digit to the right of the rounding place.	63,[2]81,025
STEP 2	If this digit is 5 or more, add 1 to the rounding digit. If the digit is less than 5, leave the rounding digit alone.	Since 2 < 5, leave 3 alone.
STEP 3	Change all the digits to the right of the rounding digit to zeros.	63,000,000

Example B

Round 3.47 to the nearest tenth.

STEP 1	Find the rounding place. Look at the digit to the right of the rounding place.	3.4[7]
STEP 2	If this digit is 5 or more, add 1 to the rounding digit. If the digit is less than 5, leave the rounding digit alone.	Since 7 > 5, add 1 to 4.
STEP 3	Drop the digits to the right of the rounding digit.	3.47 rounds to 3.5.

✔ **Talk About It**

1. Draw a number line to show that 3.47 rounds to 3.5.

For another example, see Set 1-8 on p. 57.

Round each number to the place of the underlined digit.

1. 2̲95,720   **2.** 85,5̲64,219   **3.** 17.36̲5   **4.** 4.0̲92

5. Number Sense Name two different numbers that can be rounded to 500,000 when they are rounded to the nearest hundred thousand.

TEST TALK

Think It Through
I can **draw a picture** of a number line to find the closest number.

PRACTICE

For more practice, see Set 1-8 on p. 61.

Ⓐ Skills and Understanding

Round each number to the place of the underlined digit.

6. 7̲43,963   **7.** 28̲.754   **8.** 2̲07,513,978   **9.** 9.1̲52

10. 14.9̲46   **11.** 129̲,801   **12.** 71.08̲2   **13.** 70,8̲61

14. 2̲67,139   **15.** 8̲,123,000   **16.** 3.1̲66   **17.** 0.03̲9

18. Reasoning Name two different numbers that round to 2.6 when rounded to the nearest tenth.

Ⓑ Reasoning and Problem Solving

Round the area of each country to the nearest hundred thousand square miles.

19. China   **20.** Russia

Round the area of each country to the nearest tenth of a square mile.

21. Monaco   **22.** Vatican City

23. **Writing in Math** Is Russia more than twice the area of China? Explain.

Data File

Country	Area in Square Miles
China	3,596,600
Monaco	0.75
Russia	6,592,800
Vatican City	0.17

 **Mixed Review and Test Prep**

Take It to the NET
www **Test Prep**
www.scottforesman.com

Use mental math to add or subtract.

24. 90 + 30 + 10   **25.** 260 − 180   **26.** 364 + 198   **27.** 830 − 740

28. In using mental math to find 94 + 189 + 6, Ilene thought "94 + 189 + 6 = 94 + 6 + 189. So the sum is 289." Which property of addition allows her to do this?

29. Which number is less than 0.54?

          A. 0.543   **B.** 0.55   **C.** 0.541   **D.** 0.459

Vocabulary
• front-end estimation
• rounding (p. 26)

TEST TALK

Think It Through
I only need an **estimate** because it asks about how many pounds.

Estimating Sums and Differences

LEARN

How can you estimate sums?

Students at Skyline Elementary collected aluminum cans for recycling. About how many pounds of cans did they collect in all?

Recycling Cans				
Grade	3rd	4th	5th	6th
Pounds Collected	398	257	285	318

You can estimate 398 + 257 + 285 + 318 two ways.

Jon used **rounding**.

Kylie used **front-end estimation** and adjusted the estimate.

I'll round each number to the nearest hundred.

$$
\begin{array}{rcl}
398 & \rightarrow & 400 \\
257 & \rightarrow & 300 \\
285 & \rightarrow & 300 \\
+\ 318 & \rightarrow & +\ 300 \\
\hline
& & 1{,}300
\end{array}
$$

About 1,300 pounds

I'll first add the front-end digits.

$$
\begin{array}{rcl}
398 & \rightarrow & 300 \\
257 & \rightarrow & 200 \\
285 & \rightarrow & 200 \\
+\ 318 & \rightarrow & +\ 300 \\
\hline
& & 1{,}000
\end{array}
$$

Then I'll adjust to include the remaining numbers.
98 → 100.
85 → 100.
57 + 18 → 100.
Less than 1,300 pounds

Example A

Estimate 8.3 + 10.9.

One Way
Use rounding. Round to the nearest whole number.

$$8.3 \rightarrow 8$$
$$+ 10.9 \rightarrow + 11$$
$$\overline{ 19}$$

8.3 + 10.9 is about 19.

Another Way
Use front-end estimation and adjust.

$$\begin{array}{ll} \mathbf{8.3} & \text{0.3 + 0.9 is more than 1.} \\ + \mathbf{10.9} & \\ \hline 18 & 18 + 1 = 19 \end{array}$$

8.3 + 10.9 is more than 19.

✔ Talk About It

1. Explain how Kylie adjusted her estimate on page 28.

How can you estimate differences?

Example B

Estimate 86,395 − 23,783.

One Way
Use rounding.

$$86,395 \rightarrow 90,000$$
$$- 23,783 \rightarrow - 20,000$$
$$\overline{ 70,000}$$

The difference is about 70,000.

Another Way
Use front-end estimation and adjust.

$$\mathbf{86,395}$$
$$- \mathbf{23,783}$$

$$80,000 - 20,000 = 60,000$$

Since 6,395 > 3,783, the difference is greater than 60,000.

Example C

Estimate 6.75 − 3.9.

One Way
Use rounding.

$$6.75 \rightarrow 7$$
$$- 3.9 \rightarrow - 4$$
$$\overline{ 3}$$

The difference is about 3.

Another Way
Use front-end estimation and adjust.

$$\begin{array}{ll} \mathbf{6.75} & 6 - 3 = 3 \\ - \mathbf{3.9} & \end{array}$$

Since 0.75 < 0.9, the difference is less than 3.

✔ Talk About It

2. In Example B, is 70,000 an overestimate or an underestimate of 86,395 − 23,783? Explain.

Estimate each sum or difference.

1. 20.6 − 5.4   **2.** 98 + 43 + 56   **3.** 6,598 − 2,136   **4.** 675 + 731 + 692

5. Number Sense Nora estimated 4.85 + 1.6 to be about 7.
Is this an overestimate or an underestimate? Explain.

PRACTICE

For more practice, see Set 1-9 on p. 62.

Ⓐ Skills and Understanding

Estimate each sum or difference.

6. 81 + 78 + 83   **7.** 521 + 878 + 463   **8.** 3,602 − 1,237   **9.** 9.1 + 3.5 + 5.9

10. 1,052 + 963   **11.** 3.8 + 4.2 + 4.3   **12.** 54,663 − 19,053   **13.** 78.22 − 9.18

14. 8,999 + 6,103   **15.** 3,205 − 2,812   **16.** 25.4 − 6.8   **17.** 99.9 − 37.8

18. Number Sense Todd estimated 6.39 − 4.18 to be about 2.
Is this an overestimate or an underestimate? Explain.

Ⓑ Reasoning and Problem Solving

Math and Everyday Life

About how much is the total weight of

19. one can of each?

20. two cans of corn?

21. About how much greater is the weight
of a can of corn than the weight of a can
of tomato soup?

Data File	
Weight of Cans of Food	
Food	**Ounces**
Corn	15.25
Tuna	6
Tomato Soup	10.75

22. **Writing in Math** Is the explanation below correct? If not,
tell why and write a correct response.

> Explain how to estimate 593,528 + 328,472 with
> front-end estimation and adjusting.
>
> 500,000 + 300,000 = 800,000
>
> 93,528 → 100,000
> 28,472 → 100,000
>
> 800,000 + 200,000 = 1,000,000
>
> 593,528 + 328,472 is about 1,000,000

Think It Through
I need to
**understand
vocabulary,** like
front-end
estimation.

C Extensions

You can use **clustering** to estimate a sum if all the numbers
are near the same number. In 24 + 26 + 23 + 25, all the numbers
are close to 25. So 4 × 25 or 100 is a good estimate.

Estimate each sum by using clustering.

23. 29 + 31 + 32

24. 49 + 48 + 52 + 51

25. 23 + 27 + 24 + 27 + 26

26. 49 + 51 + 48 + 52 + 51 + 50

 **Mixed Review and Test Prep**

Take It to the NET
Test Prep
www.scottforesman.com

Round each number to the place of the underlined digit.

27. 24.8<u>6</u>1

28. <u>3</u>1,700,386

29. 20.4<u>3</u>3

30. <u>6</u>3,395

31. Which number has a 4 in the hundredths place?

    A. 2.483   **B.** 2.834   **C.** 2.843   **D.** 4.832

Discovery CHANNEL SCHOOL

Discover Math in Your World

Structures: Bridges

The Golden Gate Bridge is 1.7 miles
long, with an average daily traffic
count of 125,000 vehicles.

1. Use rounding to estimate the
difference between the length of
the Golden Gate Bridge and
Brooklyn Bridge, which is 0.66
mile long.

2. About how many vehicles cross
the Golden Gate Bridge in 2 days?
In 4 days? In 8 days?

Take It to the NET
Video and Activities
www.scottforesman.com

 All text pages available online and on CD-ROM.

Problem-Solving Skill

Key Idea
Plan and Solve is the second phase of the problem-solving process.

Plan and Solve

LEARN

How can you make a plan to solve a problem?

Celebration Cake A cake was in the shape of a rectangle, 12 inches long and 6 inches wide. A rose was placed at each corner and every two inches in between corners. How many roses were on the cake?

Plan and Solve

Step 1: Choose a strategy.
Think about which strategy or strategies might work.

STRATEGIES

- **Show What You Know**
  Draw a Picture
  Make an Organized List
  Make a Table
  Make a Graph
  Act It Out or Use Objects
- **Look for a Pattern**
- **Try, Check, and Revise**
- **Write an Equation**
- **Use Logical Reasoning**
- **Solve a Simpler Problem**
- **Work Backward**

Choose a tool

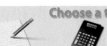 

Mental Math

Step 2: Stuck? Don't give up.
Try the tips at the right when you get stuck.

TEST TALK

Think It Through
- Reread the problem.
- Tell the problem in your own words.
- Tell what you know.
- Identify key facts and details.
- Show the main idea.
- Try a different strategy.
- Retrace your steps.

Step 3: Answer the question.

There were 18 roses on the cake.

✔ Talk About It

1. What strategy or strategies were used to solve the Celebration Cake problem?

For another example, see Set 1-10 on p. 58.

CHECK ✓

Balloons Kevin played a break-the-balloon game at a carnival. He broke 4 numbered balloons and scored 130 points. Which balloons did he break?

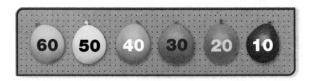

60 50 40 30 20 10

1. Name the strategy Will used to solve the Balloons problem.

2. Give the answer to the Balloons problem in a complete sentence.

Will

Try 60 + 50 + 40 + 10 = 160 too high
Try 50 + 40 + 30 + 20 = 140 too high
Try 50 + 40 + 30 + 10 = 130 That's it!

PRACTICE

For more practice, see Set 1-10 on p. 62.

Pets Use the graph at the right. How many more students like either dogs or turtles than cats?

3. Name the strategies Shelly used to solve the Pets problem.

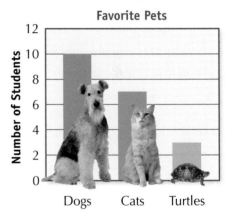

Favorite Pets

Number of Students

Dogs   Cats   Turtles

10		3
7		?

6 more

10 + 3 = 13 and 13 − 7 = 6

4. Give the answer in a complete sentence.

Coin Combinations Aimee has coins worth a total of 35¢. None of the coins are pennies. How many combinations of coins might Aimee have?

quarters	1	1	0	0	0	0
dimes	1	0	3	2	1	0
nickels	0	2	1	3	5	7
Total value	35¢	35¢	35¢	35¢	35¢	35¢

6 combinations
total 35¢

5. Name the strategy Aimee used to solve the Coin Combinations problem.

6. Give the answer in a complete sentence.

7. Refer to the steps of Read and Understand. Answer the questions in the Coin Combinations problem.

Reading and Understanding Problems

STEP 1 What do you know?

STEP 2 What are you trying to find?

Do You Know How?

Do You Understand?

Adding and Subtracting Mentally (1-7)

Use mental math to add or subtract.

1. 1,940 + 3,160   **2.** 110 + 40 + 90

3. 372 − 197   **4.** 2,360 − 2,290

Ⓐ Tell how you used mental math to find the answer for Exercise 1.

Ⓑ Explain how you could use equal additions to find the answer in Exercise 3.

Rounding Whole Numbers and Decimals (1-8)

Round each number to the place of the underlined digit.

5. 4<u>7</u>3,281,553   **6.** 981,387

7. 23.1<u>0</u>5   **8.** 46.<u>8</u>46

Ⓒ Tell how you rounded each number.

Ⓓ Explain why 47.615 is closer to 48 than 47.

Estimating Sums and Differences (1-9)

Estimate the sum or difference.

9. 769 + 372   **10.** 8,436 − 2,609

11. 14.81 − 11.14   **12.** 3.9 + 4.4

Ⓔ Explain how you found your estimate for Exercise 9.

Ⓕ Tell if your answer for Exercise 9 is an overestimate or an underestimate. Explain.

Problem-Solving Skill—Plan and Solve (1-10)

Quilt Blocks Rhonda made a square quilt for her daughter that had 8 rows and 8 columns. She wants to make a larger one for herself. What is the least number of blocks she could add and still have a square?

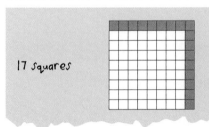

17 squares

Ⓖ Tell how you decided which strategy Rhonda used to solve the Quilt Blocks problem.

Ⓗ Give the answer to the Quilt Blocks problem in a complete sentence.

13. Name the strategy Rhonda used to solve the Quilt Block problem.

Think It Through
Be sure to determine whether you need to **find the exact answer** or **an estimate.**

MULTIPLE CHOICE

1. Which number shows 562,930,067 rounded to the nearest hundred thousand? (1-8)

   A. 560,000,000   **C.** 562,900,000

   B. 562,000,000   **D.** 563,000,000

2. Which is the best estimate for 7,834 + 7,692 + 8,374? (1-9)

   A. 20,000   **B.** 22,000   **C.** 23,000   **D.** 24,000

FREE RESPONSE

Use mental math to add or subtract. (1-7)

   3. 820 − 270   **4.** 1,396 + 238   **5.** 2,632 − 2,495   **6.** 1,800 + 400 + 200

Round each number to the place of the underlined digit. (1-8)

   7. 2<u>6</u>,059   **8.** 1,981,<u>7</u>82   **9.** 8<u>8</u>.228   **10.** 9.9<u>9</u>4

Pounds Carolyn said that she and one of her friends collected a total of 200 pounds of cans. Which friend is Carolyn talking about?

11. Solve the Pounds problem. Name the strategy you used to solve the problem. Give the answer in a complete sentence. (1-10)

12. Estimate the total pounds the five girls collected. (1-9)

13. Show how you could find how much Lisa and Keira collected together, using mental math. (1-7)

Student	Pounds Collected to be Recycled
Lisa	107
Keira	98
Carolyn	102
Carlie	93
Josie	94

Writing in Math

14. Whitney's estimate of 16.54 + 22.86 is about 39. Is this an overestimate or an underestimate? Explain how you know. (1-9)

15. Explain why 67.754 rounds to 67.8. (1-8)

Think It Through
I should always **check that my answer is reasonable.**

Adding and Subtracting Whole Numbers

LEARN

How do you add and subtract whole numbers?

Example A

Find the total area of Lake Michigan and Lake Ontario.

Estimate: 70,000 + 30,000 = 100,000

STEP 1

Write the numbers, lining up places. Add the ones and tens.

$$\begin{array}{r} 67,900 \\ + 34,850 \\ \hline 50 \end{array}$$

STEP 2

Continue adding. Regroup as needed.

$$\begin{array}{r} {\scriptstyle 1\,1} \\ 67,900 \\ + 34,850 \\ \hline 102,750 \end{array}$$

The total area is 102,750 square miles. The answer is reasonable because it is close to the estimate.

Data File

Great Lake	Area in square miles
Superior	81,000
Michigan	67,900
Huron	74,700
Erie	32,630
Ontario	34,850

You can use regrouping to subtract with zeros.

Example B

Find 4,006 − 2,748.

STEP 1

Subtract the ones. Think of 4,000 as 400 tens. Regroup.

$$\begin{array}{r} {\scriptstyle 3\ \ 99\,16} \\ 4,006 \\ - 2,748 \\ \hline 8 \end{array}$$

STEP 2

Subtract tens, hundreds, and thousands.

$$\begin{array}{r} {\scriptstyle 3\ \ 99\,16} \\ 4,006 \\ - 2,748 \\ \hline 1,258 \end{array}$$

CHECK

$$\begin{array}{r} {\scriptstyle 1\ 11} \\ 1,258 \\ + 2,748 \\ \hline 4,006 \end{array}$$

The answer checks.

✓ **Talk About It**

1. Explain the regrouping in Example B, Step 1.

Take It to the NET
More Examples
www.scottforesman.com

For another example, see Set 1-11 on p. 58.

Add or subtract.

1.   8,243
       + 7,485

2.   4,825
       − 1,937

3.   4,185
       + 58,276

4.   8,000
       − 3,146

5. Number Sense Is 44,582 a reasonable estimate for 35,843 + 28,742? Explain.

PRACTICE

For more practice, see Set 1-11 on p. 62.

Ⓐ Skills and Understanding

Add or subtract.

6.   9,006
       − 3,129

7.   7,962
       + 3,873

8.   72,900
       + 18,563

9.   50,000
       − 27,174

10. 56 + 67 + 347   **11.** 9,800 − 1,770   **12.** 10,000 − 3,547   **13.** 506 + 7,809

14. 20,000 − 267   **15.** 99 + 76 + 38   **16.** 7,900 − 2,468   **17.** 9,999 + 999

18. Number Sense Is 141 a reasonable estimate for 4,725 − 2,584? Explain.

Ⓑ Reasoning and Problem Solving

19. How many farms were in New York and Idaho together?

20. How many more farms were in Florida than Idaho?

21. How many more farms were in Texas than in Florida and New York combined?

22. **Writing in Math** Mary is adding 43,275 and 35,305. Should her answer be greater than or less than 100,000? Explain how you know.

Data File

State	Number of Farms in 2000
Florida	44,000
Idaho	24,500
New York	38,000
Texas	226,000

🦉 Mixed Review and Test Prep

Take It to the NET
Test Prep
www.scottforesman.com

23. What strategy did you use in Exercise 21?

24. Which shows 34.9_07 rounded to the nearest hundredth?

   A. 34.9   **B.** 34.90   **C.** 34.91   **D.** 35

25. A printer costs $159. A computer costs $999. If you have saved $100, which operations could you use to find how much more money you need to buy the printer?

   A. 159 + 100   **B.** 159 − 100   **C.** 159 + 100 + 999   **D.** 999 − 159

Think It Through

- I can **estimate** before I add.
- I can use the estimate to check if the answer is **reasonable.**

Adding Decimals

LEARN

✔ WARM UP
Find two decimals equivalent to each.

1. 0.8   2. 0.70

3. 0.500   4. 0.6

How can you add decimals?

Mrs. Piper combined two packages of ground beef. One had 0.25 pound of beef. The other had 0.37 pound. How much ground beef did she have in all?

Example A

Add 0.25 + 0.37.   Estimate: 0.3 + 0.4 = 0.7

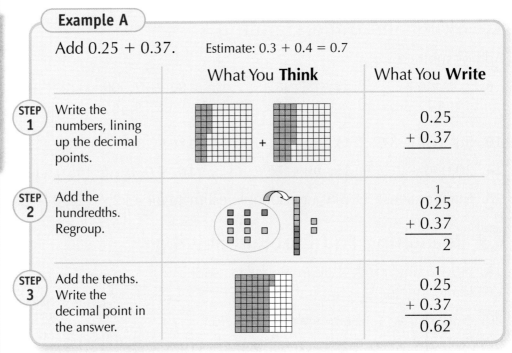

	What You **Think**	What You **Write**
STEP 1 Write the numbers, lining up the decimal points.		0.25 + 0.37
STEP 2 Add the hundredths. Regroup.		1 0.25 + 0.37 ___ 2
STEP 3 Add the tenths. Write the decimal point in the answer.		1 0.25 + 0.37 ___ 0.62

Mrs. Piper had 0.62 pound of ground beef in all.

Example B

Add 2.8 + 1.765.   Estimate: 3 + 2 = 5

STEP 1	**STEP 2**
Write the numbers. Line up the decimal points. Write zeros to show place value.	Add as you would whole numbers. Write the decimal point in the answer.
2.800 + 1.765	1 2.800 + 1.765 ___ 4.565

✔ Talk About It

1. Is the sum 0.62 reasonable in Example A? Explain.

Add.

1. 1.93
     + 0.36

2. 12.16
     + 8.568

3. 32.125
     + 17.87

4. 74.9
     + 5.651

5. 92.3
     + 99.99

6. Number Sense Is 106 a reasonable sum for 4.7 + 5.9? Tell how you know.

PRACTICE

For more practice, see Set 1-12 on p. 63.

Ⓐ Skills and Understanding

7. 4.7
     + 3.6

8. 6.1
     + 2.69

9. 21.361
     + 12.783

10. 19.2
      + 6.854

11. 28.714
      + 87.309

12. 12.11 + 0.8   **13.** 78.8 + 0.63   **14.** 19.21 + 8.59   **15.** 3.2 + 9.273

16. 3.1 + 6.8 + 9   **17.** 1.8 + 0.12 + 3.4   **18.** 0.98 + 9.8   **19.** 7.12 + 0.88

20. Number Sense Maria adds 3.6 and 2.98. Should her sum be greater or less than 5? 7? Tell how you know.

Ⓑ Reasoning and Problem Solving

21. How much precipitation fell in Miami and New Orleans combined?

22. How much precipitation fell in the three cities together?

23. Did Miami have more precipitation than New Orleans and Albany combined? Explain.

24. Which city has the greatest annual precipitation?

25. **Writing in Math** Explain how to add 3.3 and 0.7.

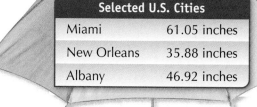

Annual Precipitation 2000	
Selected U.S. Cities	
Miami	61.05 inches
New Orleans	35.88 inches
Albany	46.92 inches

🦉 Mixed Review and Test Prep

Take It to the NET
Test Prep
www.scottforesman.com

Add or subtract.

26. 5,463 + 6,795   **27.** 8,000 − 1,299   **28.** 9,216 − 337

29. Which number is greater than 7.892?

   A. 7.891   **B.** 7.8   **C.** 7.89   **D.** 7.898

30. Which digit in the number 275,197 has a place value of ten thousand?

   A. 2   **B.** 7   **C.** 5   **D.** 1

Subtracting Decimals

LEARN

How can you subtract decimals?

Heather caught a trout weighing 3.5 pounds and a bass weighing 1.32 pounds. How much more does the trout weigh than the bass?

Example

Subtract 3.5 − 1.32.
Estimate: 3 − 1 = 2. Since 0.5 > 0.32 the difference should be more than 2.

		What You **Think**	What You **Write**
STEP 1	Write the numbers, lining up the decimal points.		3.50 − 1.32
STEP 2	Subtract the hundredths. Decide if you need to regroup.	Regroup 5 tenths as 4 tenths and 10 hundredths.	4 10 3.5̶0̶ − 1.32 8
STEP 3	Subtract the tenths and the ones. Place the decimal point in the answer.		4 10 3.5̶0̶ − 1.32 2.18

The difference 2.18 is more than 2, so it is reasonable.

Check: 2.18 + 1.32 = 3.50. The answer checks.

The trout weighs 2.18 pounds more than the bass.

✓ Talk About It

1. Explain why 5 tenths equal 4 tenths and 10 hundredths.

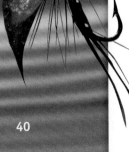

For another example, see Set 1-13 on p. 59.

CHECK ✓

1. 17.5 − 13.6 **2.** 23.8 − 12.62 **3.** 9.65 − 3.931 **4.** 71.9 − 2.57

5. Number Sense Matt subtracted 1.9 from 20.8 and got 1.8.
Explain why this is not reasonable.

PRACTICE

For more practice, see Set 1-13 on p. 63.

Ⓐ Skills and Understanding

6.   8.3
   − 5.4

7.   16.8
   − 11.58

8.   91.64
   − 12.369

9.   20.7
   − 6.925

10. 7.4 − 0.9 **11.** 29.8 − 6.93 **12.** 44.8 − 16.334 **13.** 5.5 − 3.601

14. Number Sense Explain why it is easier to find 10 − 1.9
mentally than with paper-and-pencil.

Ⓑ Reasoning and Problem Solving

On May 27, 2001, a high school student ran a mile in
3 minutes 53.43 seconds. This broke the previous
U.S. record of 3 minutes 55.3 seconds set in 1965. The
world record in 2001 was 3 minutes 43.13 seconds.

How much faster is

15. the 2001 U.S. record than the 1965 U.S. record?

16. the world record than the 1965 U.S. record?

17. the world record than the 2001 U.S. record?

18. 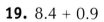 **Writing in Math** Explain how to subtract 4.6 from 13.06.

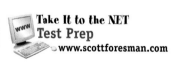

🦉 Mixed Review and Test Prep

**Take It to the NET
Test Prep**
www.scottforesman.com

19. 8.4 + 0.9 **20.** 2.9 + 8.93 **21.** 45.8 + 15.334 **22.** 0.5 + 5.505

23. Using each of the digits 3, 6, 1, and 7 only once, what is the greatest
4-digit number you can make with 3 in the hundreds place?

24. What is the difference of 589,080 and 215,808?

   A. 373,172 **B.** 373,272 **C.** 374,888 **D.** 804,888

Problem-Solving Skill

Reading Helps!

Identifying steps in a process

can help you with...

the *Look Back and Check* phase of the problem-solving process.

Key Idea
Look Back and Check is the final phase of the problem-solving process.

Look Back and Check

LEARN

What are the last steps in solving a problem?

The Redwood Tree To celebrate the 200th birthday of the United States, a class planted a 6-year-old redwood tree on July 4, 1976. How old was that tree on July 4, 2002?

> Ann
> 2000 – 1976 is 24 years.
> 2002 – 2000 = 2 years.
> 1976 to 2002 is 26 years.
> 26 + 6 = 32 years.
> The tree was 32 years old.

Look Back and Check

Step 1: Have you checked your answer?

- Check that you answered the right question.

  Ann found the total number of years.

- Use estimation and reasoning to decide if the answer makes sense.

  There are 30 years from 1970 to 2000. The answer makes sense.

Step 2: Have you checked your work?

- Look back at your work and compare it against the information in the problem.

  Ann used all the information in the problem correctly.

- Check that you used the correct operation or procedure.

  Ann subtracted to find the number of years from 1976 to 2002. Then she added the tree's age.

✔ Talk About It

1. Steve wrote the answer at the right for the Redwood Tree problem. What mistake did he make?

> Steve
> The tree was 26 years old.

CHECK ✓

For 1–4, use the Four Sisters problem.

1. Joe's work is shown below the problem. Did Joe answer the right question?

2. Does Joe's work match the information in the problem?

3. Did Joe use a correct procedure?

4. Does Joe's answer seem reasonable, that is, does it make sense?

Four Sisters Lexie is older than Lindy, but younger than Gabby. Katie is the youngest. Order the four sisters from oldest to youngest.

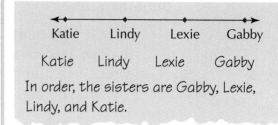

Katie   Lindy   Lexie   Gabby

In order, the sisters are Gabby, Lexie, Lindy, and Katie.

PRACTICE

For more practice, see Set 1-14 on p. 63.

Use the Shaking Hands problem for 5–8.

5. Did Pat answer the right question?

6. Does Pat's work match the information in the problem?

7. Did Pat use a correct procedure?

8. Is Pat's answer reasonable?

Shaking Hands Four students shook hands. Each person shook hands with each of the others one time. How many handshakes were there?

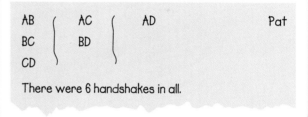

There were 6 handshakes in all.

Use the Swimmer problem for 9–11.

9. Solve the problem. Give the answer in a complete sentence.

10. Check your answer. Did you answer the right question? Is your answer reasonable?

11. Check your work. Does your work match the information in the problem? Did you use correct operations and procedures?

Swimmer Jim's time for the 50-meter races combined was how much less than his time for the 100-meter race?

100 meters: 59.4 seconds
50 meters: 27.04 seconds
50 meters: 28.58 seconds

Problem-Solving Applications

Cruise Ships Today's cruise ships are floating resorts with many activities for their passengers. The passengers can socialize on deck, cool off in a swimming pool, go dancing, or play tennis. Some ships even have ice-skating rinks and rock-climbing walls!

Trivia One of the most famous cruise ships, the *Queen Mary,* was 1,019.5 feet long and had four 35-ton propellers. The ship traveled only 13 feet for every gallon of fuel it burned.

1 The *Canberra* once had a crew of 803 people. If 194 crew members worked in the kitchen, how many crew members were NOT kitchen staff?

2 During a world cruise, more than 250,000 cakes and pastries were baked, together with 35,000 loaves of bread and 500,000 rolls. How many more rolls were baked than cakes and pastries?

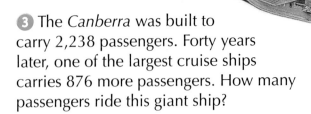

3 The *Canberra* was built to carry 2,238 passengers. Forty years later, one of the largest cruise ships carries 876 more passengers. How many passengers ride this giant ship?

4 Two propellers pushed the *Canberra* through the water at an average speed of 27.50 knots. Its highest speed was 1.77 knots faster. What was the top speed of the ship?

5 **Writing in Math** Use the information given in this lesson to write your own word problem. Solve it and write the answer in a full sentence.

Key Facts
Canberra

- Height   106 feet
- Length   818.5 feet
- Width   102 feet
- Propellers   29 tons each
- Tonnage   45,000 tons
- Operated   June 1961–Sept. 1997

Using Key Facts

6 The *Titanic* weighed about 46,000 tons. One of today's largest cruise ships weighs 5,000 tons more than the *Canberra* and two *Titanic*s combined! How much does this giant ship weigh?

7 **Decision Making** Use the table below to plan a cruise that starts in Norfolk, Virginia, goes to an island for 1 day, and from there it goes to a second island for 3 days, and then it returns to Norfolk. Name the islands you would visit. How many kilometers would your entire cruise cover? Remember that the distances in the table apply for traveling in either direction between destinations.

Traveling Between	Distance
Norfolk/Bermuda	1,200 km
Norfolk/Puerto Rico	2,200 km
Norfolk/Key Largo	1,300 km
Key Largo/Bermuda	1,600 km
Key Largo/Puerto Rico	1,600 km
Puerto Rico/Bermuda	1,500 km

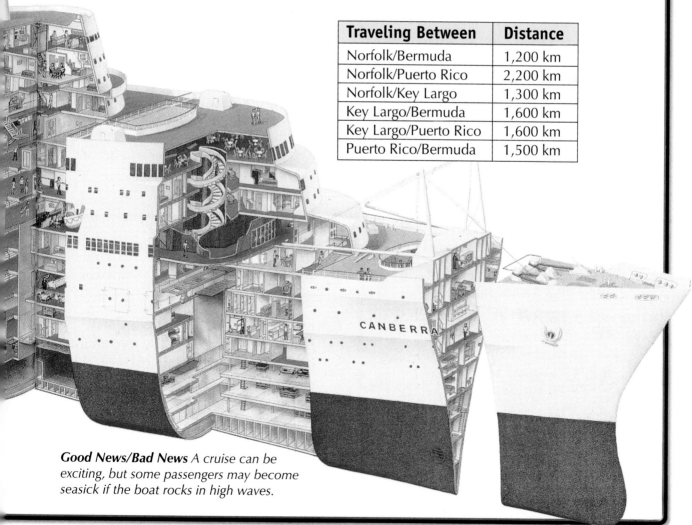

CANBERRA

Good News/Bad News *A cruise can be exciting, but some passengers may become seasick if the boat rocks in high waves.*

Do You Know How?

Do You Understand?

Adding and Subtracting Whole Numbers (1-11)

Add or subtract.

1. 9,656
       + 2,894

2. 84,062
       − 55,324

3. 416,099 + 37,983

4. 700,803 − 59,004

A Explain the steps you followed to regroup in Exercise 3.

B Explain how you can check that each answer is reasonable.

Adding Decimals (1-12)

Add.

5. 8.92
       + 3.4

6. 17.8
       + 36.284

7. 0.63 + 4.927

8. 46.9 + 3.61

C Tell how you found each sum.

D Explain why it is important to line up the decimal points when you are adding.

Subtracting Decimals (1-13)

Subtract.

9. 9.82
       − 6.15

10. 11.1
        − 8.525

11. 47.86 − 13.678

12. 0.2 − 0.173

E Tell how you found each difference.

F Explain why it is important to write zeros to show place value in Exercise 12.

Problem-Solving Skill: Look Back and Check (1-14, 1-15)

Ages Mitch is 14 years old. His sister is 6 years older than his brother. Mitch's brother is 2 years younger than Mitch. How old is Mitch's sister?

> Mitch's age - 2 = brother's age   Keith
>   14   - 2 =   12
> brother's age + 6 = sister's age
>   12   + 6 =   18
> Mitch's sister is 18 years old.

13. Did Keith answer the right question?

G Tell how you know Keith's answer is reasonable.

H Explain how to check Keith's work. Does his work match the information in the problem? Did he use correct operations and procedures?

MULTIPLE CHOICE

Think It Through
Always **check that your answer is reasonable.**

1. Find the sum of 290,063 and 59,957. (1-11)

   A. 230,106   **B.** 340,010   **C.** 349,910   **D.** 350,020

2. Find the difference of 10.6 and 7.777. (1-13)

   A. 2.223   **B.** 2.823   **C.** 2.977   **D.** 18.377

FREE RESPONSE

Add or subtract. (1-11, 1-12, 1-13)

3. $3.3 + 0.751$ 4. $12.74 - 0.359$ 5. $14.8 + 6.36$ 6. $204,305 - 32,173$

7. $43.8 - 15.327$ 8. $7,895 + 14,306$ 9. $4,000 - 346$ 10. $25.92 + 8.855$

11. How much do Marsha's and Diego's pumpkins weigh together? (1-12)

12. How much more does Marsha's pumpkin weigh than Robert's? (1-13)

13. How much more does Marsha's pumpkin weigh than the boys' pumpkins combined? (1-12, 1-13)

Pumpkin Owner	Pumpkin Weight
Robert	17.625 lb
Marsha	49.25 lb
Diego	23.5 lb

For 14–17, use the Puppies problem. (1-14, 1-15)

14. Did Bob answer the right question?

15. Does Bob's work match the information in the problem?

16. Did Bob use a correct procedure?

17. Is Bob's answer correct?

Puppies How many different ways can a black, a tan, and a white puppy sit in a row looking out a window?

BTW   TWB
BWT   TBW

There are 4 different ways for the puppies to sit.

Writing in Math

18. Shannon said that $28,765 + 41,208 = 32,973$. Explain how you could tell that this answer is not reasonable. (1-11)

19. Explain how to subtract $2.1 - 0.689$. (1-13)

CHAPTER 1
Test Talk

Test-Taking Strategies

Understand the question.

Get information for the answer.

Plan how to find the answer.

Make smart choices.

Use writing in math.

Improve written answers.

Understand the Question

Before you can answer a test question, you have to understand it. You can use the tips below to help you understand what the question is asking.

1. Mount Waialeale, Hawaii, is the rainiest place in the world. It receives an average of 460 inches of precipitation each year. Honolulu, Hawaii, receives an average 22.02 inches of precipitation each year.

Compare the average yearly precipitation on Mount Waialeale and in Honolulu. How much **more** rain falls on Mount Waialeale?

A. 249.8 inches

B. 437.98 inches

C. 448.98 inches

D. 482.02 inches

Understand the Question

• Look for important words (words that tell what the problem is about and highlighted words).

• Turn the question into a statement that begins: "I need to find ... ."

I need to find how much more rain falls on Mount Waialeale than in Honolulu.

Compare and more are in bold type. This tells me I am to find how much more one number is than the other number.

2. Pita made a list showing the times of Olympic winners in the women's 100-meter run.

Date	Winner	Time
1988	Griffith-Joyner	10.54 sec
1992	Devers	10.82 sec
1996	Devers	10.94 sec
2000	Jones	10.75 sec

Which person ran the distance in the **least** amount of time?

Think It Through

The word **least** is in bold type. I need to find the person listed in the table that ran the distance in the least amount of time.

Now it's your turn.

For each problem, identify important words. Finish the statement "I need to find ..."

3. Lorie made a table to compare the lengths of the main spans of four suspension bridges.

Bridge	Country	Length of Main Span
Golden Gate	USA	0.80 mile
Akashi Kaikyo	Japan	1.24 miles
Humber	England	0.88 mile
Jiangyin Yangtze	China	0.86 mile

Suppose Lorie had given the lengths in order from **greatest** to **least.** What is the length, in miles, of the **third** longest bridge?

4. The land area of the state of Alaska is 570,374 square miles. The inland water area is 44,856 square miles.

Which of the following gives the total land area and inland water area?

A. 1,018,934 square miles

B. 614,120 square miles

C. 525,518 square miles

D. 615,230 square miles

Self Check

Numbers can be written different ways. (Lessons 1-1, 1-2, 1-3, 1-4, 1-5)

The number 897,264,770.684 is written in standard form.

Write it in **word form** and in **expanded form**.

Describe the **value** of each digit in words. Separate each **period** with a comma.

eight hundred ninety-seven million, two hundred sixty-four thousand, seven hundred seventy *and* six hundred eighty-four thousandths.

millions period			thousands period			ones period		decimals		
hundred millions	ten millions	millions	hundred thousands	ten thousands	thousands	hundreds	tens	ones	tenths	hundredths	thousandths
8	9	7,	2	6	4,	7	7	0 .	6	8	4

Use **place value** to expand.

800,000,000 + 90,000,000 + 7,000,000 + 200,000 + 60,000 + 4,000 + 700 + 70 + 0.6 + 0.08 + 0.004

1. Write the value of the underlined digit in 58,7<u>4</u>1 and <u>6</u>38,850,247.

> *When you expand a telescope, you make it longer. The **expanded form** of a number makes it longer by writing a number as a sum of the place values as its digits. (p. 4)*

Self Check

Pay attention to place value when adding or subtracting numbers. (Lesson 1-11, 1-12, 1-13, 1-14)

Find 85,247.3 + 788.05.

Line up the decimal points.

```
  1 11
85,247.3      Add. Be sure to place
+ 788.05      the decimal point in
86,035.35     the sum.
```

Find 5.4 − 1.25.

Line up the decimal points.

```
   310
  5.40       Rewrite using equivalent
− 1.25       decimals. Regroup as
  4.15       necessary to subtract.
```

2. Add or subtract to find 57,454 − 6,735.6 and 159,624 + 598,384.

*When I broke my ankle, I compensated by using crutches to walk. In mental math, if I add a number, I must **compensate** by subtracting the same number later. (p. 22)*

Self Check ✓

There is more than one way to add or subtract mentally. (Lessons 1-7, 1-9)

Find 1,800 + 1,300 + 1,200.

Use **compatible numbers.**	Use **compensation.** Add 200 to 1,800.	**Round** to check.
1,800 + 1,300 + 1,200 =	1,800 + 1,300 + 1,200	1,800 + 1,300 + 1,200
1,800 + 1,200 + 1,300 =	↓	
3,000 + 1,300 = 4,300	2,000 + 1,300 + 1,200 = 4,500	2,000 + 1,000 + 1,000 = 4,000
	4,500 − 200 = 4,300	4,300 is reasonable.

3. Add or subtract mentally to find 50 + 40 + 80 and 3,740 − 690.

*I think French fries and ketchup are compatible because they go well together. When doing mental math, I look for **compatible numbers** because they go well together. (p. 22)*

Self Check ✓

Read and Understand and Plan and Solve to **solve problems.** (Lessons 1-6, 1-10)

To read and understand, look for key words. Tell what the question is asking.

Jason makes $6.50 per hour. How much does Jason earn after 5 hours?

"How much" asks for the total.

To plan and solve, think of a strategy that would help. Then solve.

Make a table to find the answer.

Hours	1	2	3	4	5
Pay	$6.50	$13.00	$19.50	$26.00	$32.50

Jason earns $32.50 after working for 5 hours.

4. A game is played where every red chip is worth 5 points and every blue chip is worth 8 points. Elaine has 5 red chips and 6 blue chips. How many points does she have?

1. 40 and 600,000,000; 2. 50,718.4 and 758,008; 3. 170 and 3,050; 4. 73 points

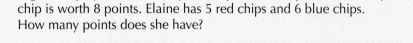
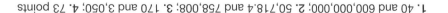

MULTIPLE CHOICE

Choose the correct letter for each answer.

1. Write *two billion, five hundred twenty-six million, three hundred thousand, eight hundred seventy* in standard form.

   A. 252,630,387

   B. 2,526,003,870

   C. 2,526,300,870

   D. 2,562,300,870

2. What is the value of the underlined digit in 3.6<u>5</u>5?

   A. five

   B. five tenths

   C. five hundreds

   D. five hundredths

3. Write 60 + 3 + 0.5 + 0.004 in standard form.

   A. 63.54   **C.** 63.054

   B. 63.504   **D.** 6.354

4. Which decimal is less than 3.251?

   A. 3.125   **C.** 3.255

   B. 3.521   **D.** 32.51

5. How many hundreds are there in 45,000?

   A. 45 hundreds

   B. 450 hundreds

   C. 4,500 hundreds

   D. 45,000 hundreds

6. Which is the best estimate for 56,904 + 8,033?

   A. 48,000   **C.** 65,000

   B. 49,000   **D.** 66,000

7. Read the problem below. Look at the solution. Name a problem-solving strategy used to solve the problem.

In Shelby's class, there are 13 girls and 17 boys. Megan's class has the same number of students, but there are 20 girls in her class. How many boys are in Megan's class?

13	17
20	?

13 + 17 = 30
30 − 20 = 10

   A. Solve a simpler problem.

   B. Use objects.

   C. Draw a picture.

   D. Try, check, and revise.

8. Find 24.5 − 18.92.

   A. 5.58   **C.** 5.63

   B. 5.6   **D.** 6.5

9. Find 337,402 + 6,679.

   A. 340,191

   B. 342,679

   C. 344,079

   D. 344,081

10. Round 8.0<u>9</u>9 to the underlined place.

   A. 7.00

   B. 8.08

   C. 8.090

   D. 8.10

Write the word form for each number and tell the value of the underlined digit.

11. 7,<u>8</u>02,440,000

12. 3.8<u>1</u>1

Order from least to greatest.

13. 577,577   575,575   755,755

14. 4.136   4.157   4.150

Write >, <, or = for each ●.

15. 625,441 ● 625,714

16. 87.3 ● 87.03

17. 2.19 ● 2.190

Round to the underlined place.

18. 56<u>4</u>,527

19. <u>3</u>,057,624

Use mental math to add or subtract.

20. 855 + 950 + 50

21. 789 − 299

Estimate.

22. 2,880 − 1,260

23. 36.4 + 3.7

Add or subtract.

24. 84,726 − 6,811

25. 133.9 − 115.28

26. 65.21 + 17.9

Writing in Math

For 27-29, use the Board Cutting problem.

> **Board Cutting** Sheldon has a board that is 6 ft long. He needs to cut off pieces that are 2.5 ft and 3.25 ft long. What is the length of the board that is left over?

27. Write what you know and what you are trying to find.

28. Solve the problem and write your answer in a complete sentence. What strategy did you use to complete the problem?

TEST TALK

Think It Through

I need to **pay attention to decimal points** when performing operations with decimals.

29. Describe how you would look back and check your answer.

Number and Operation

MULTIPLE CHOICE

1. Which does NOT have the same product as 6×4?

  A. 8×3 **C.** 12×2

  B. 5×5 **D.** 24×1

2. What fraction does the shaded portion represent?

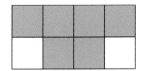

  A. $\frac{2}{8}$ **C.** $\frac{8}{6}$

  B. $\frac{2}{6}$ **D.** $\frac{6}{8}$

3. Monique earned $50 on Monday and $35 on Tuesday. Then she spent $15. Which expression would you use to find how much she had left?

  A. $50 + 35 + 15$

  B. $50 - 35 - 15$

  C. $50 - 35 + 15$

  D. $50 + 35 - 15$

FREE RESPONSE

4. List the numbers in order from greatest to least.

  25,904   24,668   25,921

5. Miss Fox needs 25 copies of the math quiz for each class. She has 5 classes. How many copies of the math quiz will she need in all?

Writing in Math

6. Estimate $156 + 93$. Explain how you made your estimate.

Geometry and Measurement

MULTIPLE CHOICE

7. How many sides does a pentagon have?

  A. 4   **C.** 6

  B. 5   **D.** 8

8. Which is the best estimate for the height of a door?

  A. 3 inches   **C.** 3 meters

  B. 3 feet   **D.** 3 kilometers

FREE RESPONSE

9. Find the perimeter of the figure below.

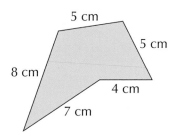

10. How many pints are in 3 quarts? Show your work.

11. List three things in your classroom that are spheres.

Writing in Math

12. Is a rectangle always a square? Is a square always a rectangle? Explain how you know.

Data Analysis and Probability

MULTIPLE CHOICE

13. Which spinner gives the best chance of spinning a 4?

A.

C.

B.

D.

14. Which type of graph uses symbols to represent data?

   A. pictograph   **C.** bar graph

   B. line graph   **D.** circle graph

FREE RESPONSE

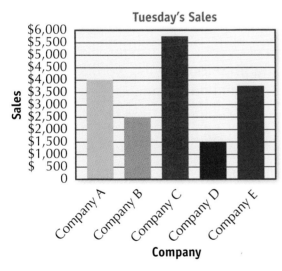

15. Which company had the greatest sales?

16. How much more did Company A make in sales than Company B?

Writing in Math

17. How would you plot the point (5, 2) on a coordinate grid?

Algebra

MULTIPLE CHOICE

18. Solve: $6 + n = 18$

   A. $n = 3$ **C.** $n = 9$

   B. $n = 6$ **D.** $n = 12$

19. Which of the following is NOT true?

   A. $4.2 > 3.5$

   B. $6.49 < 7.03$

   C. $8.8 < 8.629$

   D. $9.63 < 9.66$

Think It Through

• I need to **watch for highlighted words like NOT and EXCEPT.**

• I will **look for a pattern.**

FREE RESPONSE

20. Write four number sentences to show the fact family for 2, 5, and 10.

21. What are the next three numbers in this pattern?

   6, 15, 24, 33, . . .

22. What is the rule for this table?

In	2	4	6	8
Out	1	2	3	4

Writing in Math

23. Does $81 + 22 = 22 + 81$? Explain why or why not.

24. Look at the inequality below.

$$n < 5$$

Explain how you could use the number line below to show all whole numbers greater than 0 that n could represent to make the inequality true.

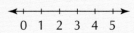

Set 1-1 (pages 4–5)

Write the word form and tell the value of the red digit for 158,392,640,736.

One hundred fifty-eight billion, three hundred ninety-two million, six hundred forty thousand, seven hundred thirty-six

The 5 is in the ten billions place. Its value is 50,000,000,000.

Remember that each group of three digits starting from the right forms a period, and periods are separated by commas.

1. 470,063,021
2. 2,800,470,309
3. 623,150
4. 18,000,636,000
5. 33,001
6. 706,539,002,400

Set 1-2 (pages 6–7)

Write >, <, or = for ● in 8,967,563 ● 8,938,256.

8,967,563   Compare the ten thousands.
8,938,256

6 ten thousands > 3 ten thousands
So, 8,967,563 > 8,938,256.

Remember to line up the place values to help you compare.

1. 32,901,461 ● 32,911,461
2. 23,856 ● 3,691
3. 47,600,963 ● 47,603,984

Set 1-3 (pages 8–11)

Write the word form and tell the value of the red digit for the number 3.068.

Ones		Tenths	Hundredths	Thousandths
3	.	0	6	8

Three and sixty-eight thousandths

The 6 is in the hundredths place. Its value is 0.06.

Remember to write the word *and* for the decimal point.

1. 8.926   2. 5.14
3. 0.363   4. 1.275
5. 2.007   6. 9.85

Set 1-4 (pages 12–13)

Write >, <, or = for ● in 6.52 ● 6.54.

6.52   Compare the hundredths.
6.54

2 hundredths < 4 hundredths
So, 6.52 < 6.54.

Remember that equivalent decimals, like 0.54 and 0.540, can help you compare.

1. 9.063 ● 9.603
2. 0.06 ● 0.04
3. 4.463 ● 4.492
4. 1.4 ● 1.40
5. 7.239 ● 7.328
6. 0.547 ● 0.54

How many hundreds are in 7,000?

Thousands	Hundreds	Tens	Ones	
7	0	0	0	→ 7 thousands
7	0	0	0	→ 70 hundreds
7	0	0	0	→ 700 tens
7	0	0	0	→ 7,000 ones

There are 70 hundreds in 7,000.

Remember that each place in our number system is 10 times the place on its right.

1. $0.9 \times$ _____ $= 90$

2. $80 \times$ _____ $= 800$

3. $700 \times$ _____ $= 7,000,000$

4. $0.05 \times$ _____ $= 50$

Tell the problem in your own words and what the question is asking.

Art Museum Westwood Elementary sent 25 fourth-grade students, 18 fifth-grade students, and 38 sixth-grade students to the art museum. The fourth- and fifth-grade students went on the first tour together. How many students went on the first tour?

There were 25 fourth-grade and 18 fifth-grade students on the first tour. I need to find how many students went on the first tour.

Remember to start a problem by asking yourself what you know and what you are trying to find.

Use the Art Museum problem.

1. Identify the key facts and details.

2. Show the main idea.

3. Solve the problem. Write your answer in a complete sentence.

Show how you could add $580 + 460$ using mental math.

Use compensation.

580   +   460
Add 20   Subtract 20 to adjust

600   +   440 $= 1,040$

So, $580 + 460 = 1,040$.

Remember that you can use compatible numbers, compensation, or equal additions to find sums and differences.

1. $1,990 + 1,360$

2. $2,940 - 1,820$

3. $5,130 + 470$

4. $670 - 280$

5. $3,560 - 1,460$

6. $60 + 120 + 140$

Set 1-8 (pages 26–27)

Round 0.6<u>4</u>8 to the underlined place.

0.6<u>4</u>8   Look at the number
following the underlined digit.

Round to the next higher number
of hundredths since $8 \geq 5$.

0.648 is about 0.65.

Remember that rounding a number means replacing it with another number that tells about how much.

1. 6.<u>9</u>15

2. 8.7<u>5</u>6

3. 3<u>3</u>3,333

4. <u>9</u>8,403

5. 0.<u>3</u>28

6. 1<u>2</u>.512

Set 1-9 (pages 28–31)

Estimate 17.9 + 21.4

$$\begin{array}{r} 17.9 \rightarrow \quad 18 \\ + 21.4 \rightarrow + 21 \\ \hline 39 \end{array}$$

Round to the nearest whole number.

17.9 + 21.4 is about 39.

Remember that you can also use front-end estimation and clustering to estimate.

1. 19.54 + 26.92

2. 17.6 − 4.4

3. 1,356 + 2,875

4. 91,540 − 32,112

5. 6.8 + 7.3 + 6.9

6. 46 + 53 + 52

Set 1-10 (pages 32–33)

Heather, Erin, and Greg are having a family picture taken. In how many different ways can they line up to have their picture taken?

Ahmet's solution:
HEG   EHG   GHE
HGE   EGH   GEH

6 different ways

Remember that you need to develop and carry out a plan to solve a problem after you read and understand it.

1. Tell what strategy Ahmet used to solve the problem.

2. Write the answer to the problem in a complete sentence.

3. Describe another way to solve the problem.

Set 1-11 (pages 36–37)

Find 51,906 − 39,874.

Estimate: 50,000 − 40,000 = 10,000

Subtract each place, starting from the right. Regroup as necessary.

$$\begin{array}{r} {}^{4\,11\ 8\,10} \\ \cancel{51,906} \\ - 39,874 \\ \hline 12,032 \end{array}$$

Check

$$\begin{array}{r} {}^{1\quad 1} \\ 12,032 \\ + 39,874 \\ \hline 51,906 \end{array}$$

The answer checks.

The answer 12,032 is reasonable because it is close to the estimate.

Remember to first estimate and then check that your answer is reasonable.

1. 13,659
 − 7,948

2. 6,542
 + 9,963

3. 70,983
 − 35,494

4. 514,819
 + 177,891

5. 331,763 − 59,757

6. 85,107 + 4,992

7. 188,856 − 98,765

Find 6.78 + 3.376.

Estimate: 7 + 3 = 10

1

Write the numbers. Line up the decimal points. Write zeros to show place value.

2

Add as you would whole numbers. Bring the decimal point straight down in the answer.

```
  6.780
+ 3.376
```

```
  1 1
  6.780
+ 3.376
 10.156
```

10.156 is reasonable since it is close to 10.

Remember to line up the decimal points when you add.

1. 9.8 + 2.563   **2.** 0.7 + 0.685

3. 14.55 + 8.92   **4.** 33.42 + 17.833

5. 1.19 + 15.86   **6.** 76.75 + 7.675

7. 0.19 + 0.999   **8.** 92.5 + 8.825

Find 6.9 − 3.876.

Estimate: 7 − 4 = 3

Line up the decimal points. Write zeros to show place value. Subtract as you would whole numbers. Bring the decimal point straight down in the answer.

Check
```
  1 1
  3.024
+ 3.876
  6.900
```

```
      9
  8 10 10
  6.900
− 3.876
  3.024
```

The answer checks.

3.024 is reasonable since it is close to 3.

Remember that you can check your answer by adding.

1. 3.8 − 2.63   **2.** 4.83 − 2.165

3. 22.31 − 8.203   **4.** 6.2 − 0.5

5. 47.51 − 33.415   **6.** 0.9 − 0.778

7. 2.78 − 0.09   **8.** 10.0 − 4.32

Art Class Trisha, Todd, and Pierre are in the same art class. Trisha said there are between 18 and 23 students in the class. Todd said there are fewer than 22. Pierre said the number of students is even. How many students are in the class?

Katie's solution:

Possible numbers:
19 20 21 22   between 18 and 23
19 20 21   fewer than 22
    20   even

There are 20 students in the class.

Remember to look back and check after you solve a problem.

1. Did Katie answer the right question?

2. Does Katie's work match the information in the problem?

3. Did Katie use a correct procedure?

Chapter 1
More Practice

Write each number in standard form.

1. 10,000,000,000 + 30,000,000 + 600,000 + 20,000 + 500 + 3

2. six hundred forty-eight billion, one hundred twelve million, thirty-three thousand, nine hundred nine

Give the value of the red digit.

3. 76,523,908   **4.** 543,600,211   **5.** 6,503,829,352

6. In the 2000 U.S. Census, the population of Texas was 20,851,820. Write this number in word form.

Copy and complete. Write >, <, or = for each ●.

1. 3,998,501 ● 3,988,921   **2.** 22,801,361 ● 22,811,361   **3.** 57,819 ● 57,918

Order these numbers from least to greatest.

4. 368,852   352,036   381,957   **5.** 5,603,487   5,630,487   5,063,487

6. In the year 2000, the population of New York City was about 14,650,000, while that of Calcutta, India was about 14,090,000. Which city had the greater population?

Write the word form for each number and give the value of the red digit.

1. 0.631   **2.** 9.205   **3.** 8.637   **4.** 5.424

5. 2.04   **6.** 3.943   **7.** 4.064   **8.** 7.008

9. In 1925, Roger Hornsby was the National League batting champion with an average of 0.403. Write this number in word form.

Copy and complete. Write >, <, or = for each ●.

1. 4.863 ● 4.868   **2.** 8.752 ● 8.849   **3.** 3.011 ● 3.001   **4.** 1.980 ● 1.98

Order these numbers from least to greatest.

5. 2.866, 2.692, 2.668, 2.868   **6.** 1.660, 1.616, 1.661, 1.166

7. Leo ran the race in 9.376 seconds. Renaldo ran the race in 9.901 seconds. Who ran the race faster?

Take It to the NET
More Practice
www.scottforesman.com

Set 1-5 (pages 14–17)

Tell how many *tens, hundreds,* and *thousands* are in each number.

1. 3,000 **2.** 40,000 **3.** 500,000 **4.** 6,000,000

What number makes each statement true?

5. 50,000 = 500 × ___?___ **6.** 7,000,000 = 7,000 × ___?___

7. 10,000 = 1,000 × ___?___ **8.** 900,000 = 90 × ___?___

9. A car costs $18,000. How many hundreds are in 18,000?

Set 1-6 (pages 18–19)

Use the Hiking problem.

1. Tell what you know. Identify key facts and details.

2. Tell what the question is asking.

3. Show the main idea.

4. Solve the problem.

> **Hiking** Kathleen hiked 12 miles, Mark hiked 8 miles, and Denise hiked 21 miles. How much farther did Denise hike than Kathleen?

Set 1-7 (pages 22–25)

Use mental math to add or subtract.

1. 80 + 79 + 20 **2.** 308 + 95 + 5 **3.** 480 + 255 + 20

4. 365 + 289 **5.** 523 − 198 **6.** 537 + 180

7. 325 + 239 + 75 **8.** 87 + 38 + 62 **9.** 4,500 − 280

10. To add 390 + 420 with mental math, Carlton added 400 + 410. Is he correct? Explain why or why not.

Set 1-8 (pages 26–27)

Round each number to the place of the underlined digit.

1. 3<u>8</u>1,574 **2.** 10.2<u>8</u>4 **3.** <u>1</u>82,601,597 **4.** 36.<u>9</u>1

5. 659,<u>0</u>14 **6.** 81.9<u>8</u>5 **7.** 7<u>8</u>4,331,562 **8.** 5.5<u>4</u>8

9. The average distance of a golfer's drives is 298.6 yards. Round this distance to the nearest 10 yards.

Set 1-9 (pages 28–31)

Estimate each sum or difference.

1. $78 + 91$
2. $2.8 + 3.3$
3. $89.1 - 27.3$
4. $8,911 - 1,332$
5. $7.9 + 8.2 + 8.1$
6. $8,742 + 5,312$
7. $97.98 - 32.86$
8. $5,012 - 1,113$
9. $31,976 + 42,126$
10. $26.91 - 13.27$
11. $581 + 562 + 630$
12. $791 + 326 + 182$

13. On Thursday Cheri addressed 217 envelopes. On Friday she addressed 198 envelopes. On each of the following two days she addressed 225 envelopes. About how many did she address in all?

Set 1-10 (pages 32–33)

For 1-3, use the Game problem.

1. Name the strategy Rob used to solve the Game problem.

2. Give the answer to the Game problem in a complete sentence.

3. Name another strategy you could use to solve the problem.

Game Misty is playing a game. She moves forward 5 spaces and then backwards 3 spaces on each turn. Once she reaches 10 spaces forward from the start, she finishes. How many turns will it take her to finish?

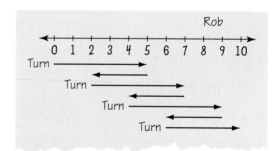

Set 1-11 (pages 36–37)

Add or subtract.

1. $\begin{array}{r} 379 \\ + 187 \\ \hline \end{array}$
2. $\begin{array}{r} 398 \\ - 139 \\ \hline \end{array}$
3. $\begin{array}{r} 2,199 \\ + 3,236 \\ \hline \end{array}$
4. $\begin{array}{r} 600 \\ - 139 \\ \hline \end{array}$
5. $\begin{array}{r} 7,000 \\ - 1,461 \\ \hline \end{array}$

6. $\begin{array}{r} 8,519 \\ + 3,212 \\ \hline \end{array}$
7. $\begin{array}{r} 4,065 \\ - 1,917 \\ \hline \end{array}$
8. $\begin{array}{r} 66,809 \\ + 17,139 \\ \hline \end{array}$
9. $\begin{array}{r} 75,006 \\ - 19,522 \\ \hline \end{array}$
10. $\begin{array}{r} 348,924 \\ + 156,056 \\ \hline \end{array}$

11. $401,883 - 51,694$
12. $874,633 + 58,297$
13. $946,067 - 355,058$

14. The state of Colorado has a total area of 104,100 square miles. The state of Washington has a total area of 68,138 square miles. How much larger is the area of Colorado than the area of Washington?

Take It to the NET
More Practice
www.scottforesman.com

Set 1-12 (pages 38–39)

Add.

1.   8.9
   + 3.4

2.   7.42
   + 6.8

3.   14.4
   + 5.93

4.   26.1
   + 9.961

5.   37.24
   + 11.859

6.   18.28
   + 16.559

7.   28.88
   + 19.375

8.   16.10
   + 3.989

9.   474.1
   + 78.9

10.   78.119
   + 88.376

11. 2.4 + 0.638   **12.** 14.99 + 5.63   **13.** 58.1 + 0.954   **14.** 99.9 + 9.99

15. Tomika has 2 cats. Fluffy weighs 9.625 pounds and Prince weighs 10.25 pounds. How much do the cats weigh together?

Set 1-13 (pages 40–41)

Subtract.

1.   6.5
   − 2.1

2.   8.4
   − 6.5

3.   15.3
   − 0.57

4.   26.32
   − 19.275

5.   98.9
   − 17.952

6.   3.15
   − 0.382

7.   0.9
   − 0.266

8.   2.03
   − 1.999

9.   3.004
   − 1.119

10.   17.339
   − 1.34

11. 0.9 − 0.889   **12.** 36.55 − 19.45   **13.** 18.21 − 7.3   **14.** 47.47 − 0.747

15. Marcus swam the race in 19.67 seconds. Mark swam the race in 21.4 seconds. Find the difference in their times.

Set 1-14 (pages 42–43)

For 1-3, use the Rain problem.

1. Solve the problem. Give the answer in a complete sentence.

2. Check your answer. Did you answer the right question? Is your answer reasonable?

3. Check your work. Does your work match the information in the problem? Did you use correct operations and procedures?

Rain It rained 0.65 inch on Monday, 1.2 inches on Tuesday, and 0.5 inch on Wednesday. How much more did it rain on Tuesday than on Monday and Wednesday combined?

CHAPTER 2

Multiplying Whole Numbers and Decimals

DIAGNOSING READINESS

A Vocabulary
(pages 22, 26, 28)

Choose the best term from the box.

1. When you do not need an exact answer, you can find an __?__.

2. __?__ is changing a number into another number that has about the same value.

3. __?__ are numbers that are easy to compute with mentally.

Vocabulary

compatible numbers *(p. 22)*   estimate *(p. 28)*
compensation *(p. 22)*   rounding *(p. 26)*

B Multiplication Facts
(Grade 4)

4. 5×2 5. 3×3 6. 8×4

7. 1×9 8. 2×7 9. 5×6

10. 7×8 11. 9×6 12. 9×9

13. How can you use the product of 2×8 to find 4×8?

14. Mandy buys 3 packages of pencils. There are 6 pencils in each package. How many pencils does she buy in all?

Do You Know...

How much does a baby humpback whale weigh?

You will find out in lesson 2-16.

RUSSELL ASH
INCREDIBLE COMPARISONS

C Rounding Whole Numbers and Decimals

(pages 26–27)

Round each number to the underlined place.

15. 1<u>2</u>5

16. <u>5</u>39

17. 3.<u>7</u>8

18. 1,<u>0</u>90

19. 2<u>1</u>.46

20. 0.9<u>3</u>6

21. <u>5</u>40.1

22. 0.8<u>0</u>2

23. 15,<u>4</u>87

24. What number is halfway between 1 and 2?

25. A dog weighs 74.5 pounds. Round this amount to the nearest ten.

D Multiplying Three Factors

(Grade 4)

26. $2 \times 5 \times 9$

27. $2 \times 4 \times 9$

28. $3 \times 2 \times 4$

29. $5 \times 6 \times 3$

30. $8 \times 4 \times 2$

31. $3 \times 5 \times 4$

32. Joel bought 3 T-shirts at $9 each and 6 pairs of socks for $2 each. How much did he spend in all?

Vocabulary
- factor
- product
- Commutative Property of Multiplication
- Associative Property of Multiplication

Materials
- calculator

Think It Through
I can **look for a pattern** to find a rule.

Multiplication Patterns

LEARN

Activity

What's the pattern?

a. Use a calculator to find each product.

3 × 5	3 × 50	3 × 500
30 × 5	30 × 50	30 × 500
300 × 5	300 × 50	300 × 500

Factors are numbers that are multiplied to get a *product*.

b. Find the following products without a calculator. Then check your answers with a calculator.

5 × 8, 50 × 8, 50 × 80, 500 × 8, 500 × 80, 500 × 800

c. Describe a rule that tells how to find each product.

How can properties help you multiply more easily?

Commutative Property of Multiplication

You can change the order of the factors.

34 × 8 = 8 × 34

Associative Property of Multiplication

You can change the grouping of factors.

(7 × 25) × 4 = 7 × (25 × 4)

Example A

Find 20 × 5 × 6.

Using the Associative Property, you can think:

(20 × 5) × 6 = 100 × 6 = 600 OR
20 × (5 × 6) = 20 × 30 = 600.

Example B

Find 2 × 70 × 50.

Use the properties to change the order and the groupings.

2 × 70 × 50 = 2 × (70 × 50)
= 2 × (50 × 70)
= (2 × 50) × 70
= 100 × 70
= 7,000

✔ Talk About It

1. How is the Associative Property used in Example B?

2. How is the Commutative Property used in Example B?

3. Can you use the Associative Property for 2 × (5 + 6)? Explain.

Find each product. Use patterns and properties to compute mentally.

1. 40×80 **2.** 60×900 **3.** $3 \times 40 \times 5$ **4.** $2 \times 30 \times 500$

5. Number Sense If you know 8×3, how can you find 80×30?

PRACTICE

For more practice, see Set 2-1 on p. 126.

Ⓐ Skills and Understanding

Find each product. Use patterns and properties to compute mentally.

6. 80×60 **7.** 70×900 **8.** $50 \times 4 \times 20$ **9.** $4 \times 40 \times 25$

10. $35 \times 2 \times 20$ **11.** $25 \times 10 \times 4$ **12.** $20 \times 57 \times 5$ **13.** $2 \times 33 \times 50$

14. $20 \times 6 \times 50$ **15.** $9 \times 200 \times 5$ **16.** $500 \times 13 \times 2$ **17.** $4 \times 7 \times 250$

18. Number Sense If you know 6×9, how can you find 600×900?

Ⓑ Reasoning and Problem Solving

19. How many desks are in each wing of the school building?

20. How many desks are in the school building?

21. Find three different solutions for
___ $\times$ ___ $\times$ ___ $= 1,200$.

22. Algebra $m \times n = 4,200$. If m and n are two-digit multiples of 10, what numbers could m and n be?

23. **Writing in Math** Explain in writing how you can easily determine the product $5 \times 75 \times 20$ using mental math.

School Building
Desks per room: 30
Rooms per wing: 8
Wings in building: 5

Mixed Review and Test Prep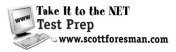

**Take It to the NET
Test Prep**
www.scottforesman.com

Find each sum or difference.

24. $6.02 + 4.18$ **25.** $23.6 - 6.8$ **26.** $6.08 + 7.09 + 8.91$

27. After solving the problem below, use the steps for Look Back and Check on page 42 to check your answer and work.

A roll of film costs $5.59 and its processing costs $12.50. If you pay for both the film and its processing with a $20 bill, how much change would you get?

A. $18.10   **B.** $17.09   **C.** $2.91   **D.** $1.91

All text pages available online and on CD-ROM.

Key Idea
There are several
appropriate
strategies for
estimating
products.

Vocabulary
• overestimate
• underestimate
• rounding (p. 26)
• compatible
  numbers (p. 22)

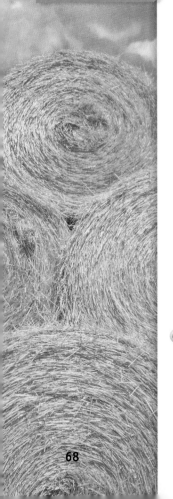

Think It Through
I only need an
estimate because I
just need to know if
there's enough.

Estimating Products

LEARN

Exact answer or estimate?

An adult zoo elephant eats about 87 pounds
of hay each day. A zookeeper needs to feed
4 elephants for 28 days in February. The
zookeeper has 12,000 pounds of hay. Is this
enough hay for the month?

You need to estimate $87 \times 28 \times 4$.

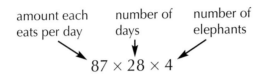

amount each   number of   number of
eats per day   days   elephants

$$87 \times 28 \times 4$$

What are some ways to estimate products?

When you only round factors to larger numbers, you get an
overestimate. When you only round factors to smaller numbers,
you get an **underestimate.**

Example

Estimate $87 \times 28 \times 4$.

One Way
Tim rounded 87 to 100
and 28 to 30.

$87 \times 28 \times 4$

$100 \times 30 \times 4 = 3,000 \times 4$
$= 12,000$

Another Way
Sally substituted
compatible numbers. She
substituted 25 for 28.

$87 \times 28 \times 4$

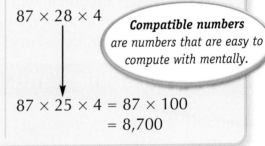

*Compatible numbers
are numbers that are easy to
compute with mentally.*

$87 \times 25 \times 4 = 87 \times 100$
$= 8,700$

Since the zookeeper has 12,000 pounds of hay,
there is enough to feed the elephants for the month.

✔ Talk About It

1. Why did Sally adjust 28 to 25?

2. Which student arrived at an overestimate? How do you know?

3. Which student arrived at an underestimate? How do you know?

✔ **WARM UP**

1. 72×10
2. 973×10
3. 38×100
4. $3 \times 10 \times 8$
5. $8 \times 100 \times 9$

Estimate each product.

1. $53 \times 4 \times 28$ **2.** $33 \times 58 \times 3$ **3.** $7 \times 63 \times 10$ **4.** $18 \times 19 \times 50$

5. Number Sense What are two different ways you could estimate $4 \times 259 \times 5$?

PRACTICE

For more practice, see Set 2-2 on p. 126.

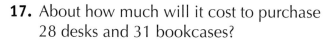

Ⓐ Skills and Understanding

Estimate each product.

6. $98 \times 14 \times 3$ **7.** $51 \times 9 \times 21$ **8.** $4 \times 79 \times 24$ **9.** $38 \times 59 \times 5$ **10.** $76 \times 22 \times 9$

11. $24 \times 39 \times 3$ **12.** $41 \times 27 \times 52$ **13.** $38 \times 12 \times 18$ **14.** $26 \times 54 \times 40$ **15.** $12 \times 72 \times 11$

16. Number Sense Give three numbers whose product is about 6,000.

Ⓑ Reasoning and Problem Solving

The table shows the cost of several items that are needed to furnish a college dormitory room.

Think It Through
I can get information from tables.

17. About how much will it cost to purchase 28 desks and 31 bookcases?

18. Estimate to decide which costs more–9 bookcases or 20 desks.

19. Reasoning To find $4 \times 27 \times 48$, Tim used rounding and wrote $4 \times 30 \times 50 = 6,000$. Sally substituted compatible numbers and wrote $4 \times 25 \times 48 = 4,800$. Which is an overestimate and which is an underestimate? Explain.

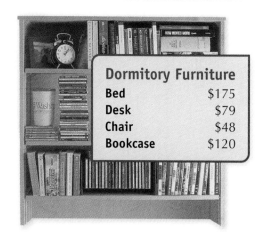

Dormitory Furniture
Bed	$175
Desk	$79
Chair	$48
Bookcase	$120

20. Writing in Math Pat needs to estimate the product of $91 \times 24 \times 4$. Explain two different ways that Pat could use to make a reasonable estimate for this product.

🦉 Mixed Review and Test Prep

Take It to the NET
Test Prep
www.scottforesman.com

Find each product. Use patterns and properties to compute using mental math.

21. 2×70 **22.** 15×40 **23.** $9 \times 4 \times 50$

24. How many hundreds are in 50,000?

A. 5   **B.** 50   **C.** 500   **D.** 5,000

All text pages available online and on CD-ROM.

Algebra

Key Idea
The distributive property helps you break numbers apart so they are easier to multiply.

Vocabulary
• Distributive Property

Mental Math: Using the Distributive Property

LEARN

How does the Distributive Property help you multiply mentally?

Al donated 28 quarts of lemonade for a charity picnic. How many cups of lemonade is this? Remember that 1 quart is 4 cups.

To find 4×28 by mental math, break apart 28 into two numbers that are easier to multiply by 4.

Distributive Property
Multiplying a sum (or difference) by a number is the same as multiplying each number in the sum (or difference) by the number and adding (or subtracting) the products.

$8 \times (40 + 5) = (8 \times 40) + (8 \times 5)$
$9 \times (20 - 3) = (9 \times 20) - (9 \times 3)$

Example A

Method 1	Method 2	Method 3
Rhonda split 28 into $20 + 8$.	Mike split 28 into $25 + 3$.	Sue split 28 into $30 - 2$.
$4 \times 28 =$ $4 \times (20 + 8) =$ $(4 \times 20) + (4 \times 8) =$ $80 + 32 =$ 112	$4 \times 28 =$ $4 \times (25 + 3) =$ $(4 \times 25) + (4 \times 3) =$ $100 + 12 =$ 112	$4 \times 28 =$ $4 \times (30 - 2) =$ $(4 \times 30) - (4 \times 2) =$ $120 - 8 =$ 112

The Distributive Property can also be used to find products involving larger numbers.

Example B

Find 5×198.

$$5 \times 198 = 5 \times (200 - 2)$$
$$= (5 \times 200) - (5 \times 2)$$
$$= 1,000 - 10$$
$$= 990$$

✔ Talk About It

1. What was the same about each method in Example A? What was different?

2. In Example B, why was 198 changed to $200 - 2$?

Use the Distributive Property to multiply using mental math.

1. 3×17 **2.** 6×31 **3.** 15×99 **4.** 498×3

5. Number Sense Give two different ways to use the Distributive Property to find 9×19.

PRACTICE

For more practice, see Set 2-3 on p. 126.

Ⓐ Skills and Understanding

Use the Distributive Property to multiply using mental math.

6. 4×509 **7.** 12×103 **8.** 6×310 **9.** 195×5 **10.** 99×50

11. 102×13 **12.** 25×110 **13.** 197×15 **14.** 20×85 **15.** 390×30

16. Number Sense How could you use the Distributive Property to find 3×999?

Ⓑ Reasoning and Problem Solving

Use the Distributive Property to find the products using mental math.

17. How many minutes are in 29 hours?

18. How many inches are in 101 feet?

19. How many feet are in 798 yards?

20. Algebra If $5 \times 206 = (5 \times n) + (5 \times 6)$, what is the value of n?

21. **Writing in Math** Would you use the Distributive Property to find 800×7? Explain why or why not.

Think It Through
I need to remember that there are:
- 60 minutes in an hour.
- 12 inches in a foot.
- 3 feet in a yard.

Mixed Review and Test Prep

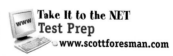

Take It to the NET
Test Prep
www.scottforesman.com

Estimate each product. Tell if your estimate is an under- or overestimate.

22. $14 \times 8 \times 53$ **23.** $21 \times 80 \times 12$ **24.** $19 \times 78 \times 5$

Copy and complete. Write $<$, $>$, or $=$ for each ●.

25. 43,304 ● 43,340 **26.** 9,999 ● 10,000 **27.** 3.8 ● 3.80

28. If $n \times 7$ is about 200, what is a reasonable estimate for n?

　　A. 45 **B.** 42 **C.** 40 **D.** 30

29. A bus departed with 28 passengers. At the first stop, 3 people got on, but no one left. At the second stop, 5 people got off the bus, but one got on. Which expression shows the number of passengers now on the bus?

　　A. $28 + 5 + 3$ **B.** $28 - 5 - 3$ **C.** $28 + 5 - 3$ **D.** $28 + 3 - 5 + 1$

Key Idea
To find products, use place value to break apart factors.

Vocabulary
• partial product

Think It Through
Estimate the answer before you begin.

Multiplying Whole Numbers

LEARN

How do you multiply by one-digit numbers?

Mr. Chen bought 4 new custom wheels for his car. Each cost $253. How much did the wheels cost?

Example A

Find 253×4.

	What You Think	What You Write
STEP 1 Multiply the ones. Regroup if necessary.	4×3 ones = 12 ones. Regroup 12 ones as 1 ten 2 ones.	$\overset{1}{253} \times 4 \over 2$
STEP 2 Multiply the tens. Regroup if necessary.	4×5 tens = 20 tens. 20 tens + 1 ten = 21 tens. Regroup as 2 hundreds 1 ten.	$\overset{2\,1}{253} \times 4 \over 12$
STEP 3 Multiply the hundreds. Regroup if necessary.	4×2 hundreds = 8 hundreds. 8 hundreds + 2 hundreds = 10 hundreds. Regroup as 1 thousand.	$\overset{2\,1}{253} \times 4 \over 1{,}012$

The 4 wheels cost $1,012.

✔ Talk About It

1. In Step 1, what does the little 1 above the tens column mean?

2. In Step 3, why were 2 hundreds added to the 8 hundreds?

How do you multiply by two-digit numbers?

Multiplying by a 2-digit number is like multiplying by a 1-digit number.

Example B

Find 689 × 15.

		What You Think	What You Write
STEP 1	Multiply by the ones. Regroup as necessary.	5 × 9 ones = 45 ones. Regroup 45 ones as 4 tens 5 ones. 5 × 8 tens = 40 tens. 40 tens + 4 tens = 44 tens. Regroup 44 tens as 4 hundreds 4 tens. 5 × 6 hundreds = 30 hundreds. 30 hundreds + 4 hundreds = 34 hundreds. Regroup as 3 thousands 4 hundreds.	4 4 689 × 15 ——— 3445
STEP 2	Multiply by the tens. Regroup as necessary.	10 × 9 ones = 90 ones or 9 tens. 10 × 8 tens = 80 tens or 8 hundreds. 10 × 6 hundreds = 60 hundreds or 6 thousands.	4 4 689 × 15 ——— 3445 6890
STEP 3	Add the **partial products.**	5 × 689 = 3,445 10 × 689 = 6,890	4 4 689 × 15 ——— partial product ⟶ 3445 partial product ⟶ 6890 ——— 10,335

Think It Through
Use your **estimate** to check your answer for reasonableness.

✔ Talk About It

3. In Step 1, what do the little 4s above the tens and hundreds columns mean?

4. In Step 3, which numbers are the partial products? Why do you add the partial products?

5. Estimate 689 × 15 to decide if the answer in Step 3 is reasonable. Is your estimate an overestimate or underestimate? Why?

Take It to the NET
More Examples
www.scottforesman.com

CHECK ✓

Find the product. Estimate to check that your answer is reasonable.

1. 349
    × 8

2. 458
    × 7

3. 225
    × 67

4. 112
    × 43

5. **Number Sense** Is 2,567 a reasonable answer for the product 835 × 32? Why or why not?

PRACTICE

For more practice, see Set 2-4 on p. 126.

Ⓐ Skills and Understanding

Find each product. Estimate to check that your answer is reasonable.

6. 552 × 7   7. 319 × 4   8. 635 × 9   9. 409 × 83   10. 138 × 28

11. 52 × 43   12. 17 × 35   13. 191 × 88   14. 102 × 24   15. 211 × 74

16. 15
     × 36

17. 315
     × 6

18. 69
     × 48

19. 73
     × 51

20. 143
     × 89

21. 211
     × 28

22. 471
     × 9

23. 737
     × 55

24. 181
     × 42

25. 409
     × 36

26. 209 × 9   27. 716 × 41   28. 36 × 79

29. 628 × 4   30. 35 × 72   31. 413 × 28

32. How could you use the Distributive Property to multiply 15 × 95?

33. **Number Sense** Max multiplied 478 by 7 and got 3,346. Use estimation to check the reasonableness of his answer.

Ⓑ Reasoning and Problem Solving

 Math and Science

The length of one Earth day is 86,400 seconds, or 24 hours.

34. How many Earth hours long is a day on Mercury? on Venus?

35. How many Earth minutes long is a Pluto day?

36. **Reasoning** If the multiplication key on your calculator were broken, explain how you could use that calculator to find 5 × 143.

Venus

Planet	Approximate Length of Day
Mercury	59 Earth days
Venus	243 Earth days
Pluto	6 Earth days

37. <u>**Writing in Math**</u> Is the explanation below correct? If not tell why and write a correct response.

> Find 3 × 729.
>
> ```
>     7 2 9
>   ×     3
>   ─────────
>   2 1 6 2 7
> ```
>
> 3 × 9 ones = 27 ones.
> 3 × 2 tens = 6 tens.
> 3 × 7 hundreds = 21 hundreds.
> So I write 27, 6, and 21 in the product.

C **Extensions**

38. Patterns Find 11 × 11 and 111 × 111. Look for a pattern and predict what you think 1,111 × 1,111 will be. Then check your answer with a calculator.

Mixed Review and Test Prep

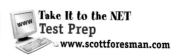
Take It to the NET
Test Prep
www.scottforesman.com

Estimate each product.

39. 48 × 42 × 2

40. 71 × 13 × 9

41. 54 × 8 × 21

42. Which illustrates the Associative Property of Multiplication?

    A. 8 × 10 = 10 × 8   **B.** 1 × 7 = 7   **C.** 8 + 0 = 8   **D.** 1 × (2 × 3) = (1 × 2) × 3

Practice Game

Home on the Range

Players: 2   **Materials:** Number cards 0–9 (4 sets)
                                Spinner (labeled 1–6)

1. Cards are shuffled and placed face down.

2. Players spin the spinner to determine their product range.

3. Each player draws 4 cards and makes two 2-digit factors that will yield a product in his or her range.

4. After factors have been made, players use a calculator to check products.

5. The player earns 1 point if the product falls within the correct range. Otherwise, the player earns no points for that round. The winner is the player with the most points after 6 rounds.

Number on Spinner	Product Range
6	7,000 or greater
5	5,000 – 6,999
4	4,000 – 4,999
3	2,000 – 3,999
2	1,000 – 1,999
1	999 or less

All text pages available online and on CD-ROM.

Key Idea
Depending on the numbers, you can find products using mental math, paper and pencil, or a calculator.

Materials
• calculator

Vocabulary
• Identity Property of Multiplication
• Zero Property of Multiplication

Think It Through
Before I do a calculation, I should **decide which method makes sense.**

Choose a Computation Method

LEARN

Which computation method should you use?

Worldwide the average usage of water is equivalent to 22 bathtubs per person per day. A standard-sized bathtub holds 33 gallons.

Example A

Find the average water usage per person in bathtubs per week.

Find 7×22.

These numbers are easy to multiply in my head, so I'll use **mental math.**

$7 \times 22 =$
$7 \times (20 + 2) =$
$(7 \times 20) + (7 \times 2) =$
$140 + 14 = 154$

The average usage of water per week is equivalent to 154 bathtubs per person.

Example B

Find the average water usage in gallons per person per day.

Find 33×22.

These numbers are not easy to multiply mentally. Use **paper and pencil.**

$$\begin{array}{r} 33 \\ \times\ 22 \\ \hline 66 \\ 660 \\ \hline 726 \end{array}$$

The average usage of water per person per day is 726 gallons.

Example C

Find the average annual water usage in gallons per person.

Find 365×726.

These numbers are large. I want the exact answer quickly, so I'll use a **calculator.**

Press:
365 ⊠ 726 ⊟

Display:

| 264990 |

Annually, the world average usage of water per person is 264,990 gallons.

✔ **Talk About It**

1. Describe how you decide when to use mental math, paper and pencil, or a calculator.

2. The following properties are useful when choosing a computation method. Give an example for each property.

Zero Property of Multiplication	**Identity Property of Multiplication**
When you multiply any number by 0, the product is 0.	When you multiply any nonzero number by 1, the product is the number.

Find each product. Tell which computation method you used.

1. 600×20 **2.** 17×40 **3.** 95×62 **4.** 146×827

5. Number Sense Kit said she used paper and pencil to find 5×32.
Explain how Kit could use mental math to find the product.

PRACTICE For more practice, see Set 2-5 on p. 127.

Ⓐ Skills and Understanding

Find each product. Tell which computation method you used.

6. 400×30 **7.** 36×5 **8.** 27×16 **9.** $9,327 \times 1$

10. 399×705 **11.** 102×0 **12.** 280×300 **13.** 700×40

14. 914×279 **15.** 42×40 **16.** 100×280 **17.** 3×197

18. 123×12 **19.** $2 \times 50 \times 3$ **20.** 50×500 **21.** $25 \times 6 \times 4$

22. 125×7 **23.** 44×11 **24.** 800×900 **25.** 787×235

26. 444×76 **27.** $300 \times 0 \times 70$ **28.** 14×75 **29.** $400 \times 5,000$

30. Number Sense Why is using a calculator not an efficient way to
find $2 \times 30 \times 50$?

Ⓑ Reasoning and Problem Solving

Solve and tell which computation method you used.

31. What is the cost of 5 mufflers?

32. How much is the cost of 30 batteries?

33. Your car needs a muffler, battery, and 2 tires.
What is the total cost?

34. Estimate 43×267. Is it closer to 8,000 or
12,000? Explain.

35. Writing in Math Explain why it is not always efficient
to find products with a calculator. Give an example.

Car Parts

Muffler	$80
Battery	$59
Tire	$60
Wiper Blade	$16
Water Pump	$150

🦉 Mixed Review and Test Prep

Take It to the NET
Test Prep
www.scottforesman.com

Use any method to find each product.

36. 27×5 **37.** 40×15 **38.** 25×36

39. Which is equivalent to 8×52?

A. $(8 \times 5) + (8 \times 2)$ **B.** $(8 \times 50) - (8 \times 2)$ **C.** $(8 \times 50) + (8 \times 2)$ **D.** 5×82

 All text pages available online and on CD-ROM.

Understand Graphic Sources: Lists

Understanding graphic sources such as lists when you read in math can help you use the **problem-solving strategy, Make an Organized List,** in the next lesson.

In reading, understanding lists can help you understand what you read. In math, understanding lists can help you solve problems.

The labels at the top of the list tell what types of items are included in each combination.

Tomas made an organized list of all possible combinations of a shirt and pants that he could wear.

Shirt	Pants
blue	black
blue	brown
red	black
red	brown
green	black
green	brown

There are 6 different possible combinations.

The number of rows tells the number of different possible combinations.

Each row describes a different combination.

1. How many different colors of pants are there?

2. How many combinations include a red shirt?

3. How could Tomas have organized his list in a different way?

For 4–7, use the problem below and the list at the right.

Elliot made an organized list to show the different combinations of snacks he could have after school.

Bread	Fruit	Drink
granola bar	apple	juice
granola bar	apple	milk
granola bar	orange	juice
granola bar	orange	milk
crackers	apple	juice
crackers	apple	milk
crackers	orange	juice
crackers	orange	milk

4. How many items are in a snack? What types are they?

5. How many different items are there in all?

6. How many of the combinations include an apple?

7. **Writing in Math** How could Elliot have organized his list in a different way?

For 8–11, use the problem below and the list at the right.

Jill has only enough money to buy 3 jars of glitter for an art project. The colors she is trying to choose from include gold, silver, red, and blue.

Jar 1	Jar 2	Jar 3
gold	silver	blue
gold	silver	red
gold	blue	red
silver	blue	red

8. From how many different colors is Jill choosing?

9. How many different combinations of 3 colors are possible?

10. How many different combinations include gold and silver?

11. **Writing in Math** Why didn't Jill add a row that shows silver, blue, gold?

For 12–14, use the problem below and the list at the right.

Lindsey has three activities planned for her first day at camp. She is trying to decide in which order she will do them.

12. What activities will Lindsey do?

13. How many different orders are possible?

14. **Writing in Math** Describe how Lindsey organized her list.

Morning	Midday	Afternoon
swimming	hiking	crafts
swimming	crafts	hiking
hiking	swimming	crafts
hiking	crafts	swimming
crafts	swimming	hiking
crafts	hiking	swimming

Problem-Solving Strategy

Key Idea
Learning how and when to make an organized list can help you solve problems.

Think It Through

Understanding **graphic sources such as lists** will help me make a list to find the possible scores.

Make an Organized List

LEARN

How can you make an organized list to solve problems?

Dart Board Three darts are thrown at a dart board. If at least one dart scores 5 points, what scores are possible? Assume every dart scores some points.

Read and Understand

What do you know?   Each of the three darts scores some points. The point values are 5, 3, and 1. At least one dart is worth 5 points.

What are you trying to find?   Find what scores are possible if at least one dart scores 5 points.

Plan and Solve

What strategy will you use?   **Strategy:** Make a List.

	Score
5, 5, 5	15
5, 5, 3	13
5, 5, 1	11
5, 3, 3	11
5, 3, 1	9
5, 1, 1	7

First find the combinations with three 5-point darts. Then find the combinations with two 5-point darts, and so on.

Answer: Possible scores are 15, 13, 11, 9, and 7.

How to Make a List

Step 1   Identify the items to be combined.

Step 2   Choose one of the items. Find combinations keeping that item fixed.

Step 3   Repeat Step 2 as often as needed.

Look Back and Check

Is your work correct?   Yes, each combination uses at least one dart worth 5 points.

✔ Talk About It

1. How many different scores are possible with three 5-point darts? two 5-point darts? one 5-point dart?

2. Why is organizing a list helpful?

For another example, see Set 2-6 on p. 123.

Complete the organized list which has been started for you. Then solve each problem.

1. Amy, Todd, and Lana are posing for a photograph for the school newspaper. How many different ways can the three children stand together in a row?

ATL, ALT, . . .

2. A game has white, blue, green, and red counters. How many 2-color counter combinations can you make?

WB, WG, WR, . . .

PRACTICE

For more practice, see Set 2-6 on p. 127.

Solve each problem. Write the answer in a complete sentence.

3. Elsa is younger than Kayla and Tom. Brian is older than Kayla and younger than Tom. Who is the second oldest?

4. You are making a call from a pay phone. The cost of the call is $0.65. You cannot use half dollars or pennies. How many different combinations of coins can you use if at least one of the coins is a quarter?

5. A woman requests a special license plate with the first initial of each of her four children's names. The children's initials are B, K, L, and H. How many possible ways could the letters be arranged?

6. Carlos is thinking of an odd number that uses each of the digits 0, 1, 2, and 3 only once. The number is greater than 3,000, but less than 4,000. There is a 2 in the tens place. What is the number?

7. Mr. Majko bought a 10-year-old house on June 1, 1990. He sold the house on July 30, 2002. How many years old was the house when he sold it?

8. <u>Writing in Math</u> Explain how you completed the list in Exercise 1.

STRATEGIES

- **Show What You Know**
  Draw a Picture
  Make an Organized List
  Make a Table
  Make a Graph
  Act It Out or Use Objects
- **Look for a Pattern**
- **Try, Check, and Revise**
- **Write an Equation**
- **Use Logical Reasoning**
- **Solve a Simpler Problem**
- **Work Backward**

Choose a tool

Mental Math

TEST TALK

Think It Through

Stuck? I won't give up. I can:
- Reread the problem.
- Tell what I know.
- Identify key facts and details.
- Tell the problem in my own words.
- Show the main idea.
- Try a different strategy.
- Retrace my steps.

 All text pages available online and on CD-ROM.

Do You Know How?

Do You Understand?

Multiplication Patterns (2-1)
Mental Math: Using the Distributive Property (2-3)

Find each product. Use patterns and properties to compute mentally.

1. 50×90 **2.** 700×300

3. 97×8 **4.** 7×406

5. $6 \times 80 \times 5$ **6.** $45 \times 2 \times 60$

A Tell what patterns and properties you used in each exercise.

B Explain how the Distributive Property can help you find the product in Exercise 4.

Estimating Products (2-2)

Estimate each product.

7. $9 \times 84 \times 20$ **8.** $22 \times 6 \times 47$

9. $37 \times 4 \times 98$ **10.** $60 \times 75 \times 11$

C Explain how you found your estimates in Exercises 7 and 8.

D Is your estimate an overestimate or underestimate for Exercise 9? Tell why.

Multiplying Whole Numbers (2-4)
Choose a Computation Method (2-5)

Find each product.

11. 51×6 **12.** 623×8

13. 800×400 **14.** 1×599

15. 367×0 **16.** 254×187

E Tell which computation method you chose for each exercise.

F Is it reasonable to use paper and pencil to find the product in Exercise 12? Explain.

Problem-Solving Strategy: Make an Organized List (2-6)

17. Chris is packing his suitcase for a trip. He packs a blue, a green, and a red shirt. He also packs one tan pair and one black pair of pants. How many different outfits can be made from these clothes?

G Identify the information given in the problem. Tell what you need to find out.

H Tell how you solved the problem. What strategy did you use?

Think It Through
For multiple-choice items, first **eliminate any unreasonable answers.**

MULTIPLE CHOICE

1. Which two numbers have a product of 24,000? (2-1)

　　A. 60 and 40 　**B.** 4 and 600 　　**C.** 60 and 400 　　**D.** 600 and 400

2. Which is the best estimate of 11 × 57 × 3? (2-2)

　　A. 1,500 　　**B.** 1,800 　　**C.** 15,000 　　**D.** 18,000

FREE RESPONSE

Find each product. Use patterns and properties to compute mentally. (2-1, 2-5)

3. 7 × 600 　　　**4.** 20 × 0 　　　**5.** 800 × 40 　　　**6.** 90 × 3 × 30

Estimate each product. (2-2)

7. 41 × 2 × 82 　　**8.** 7 × 98 × 12 　　**9.** 30 × 29 × 67 　　**10.** 17 × 83 × 54

Use the Distributive Property to multiply mentally. (2-3)

11. 52 × 4 　　　**12.** 6 × 198 　　　**13.** 8 × 302 　　　**14.** 12 × 25

Find each product. Estimate to check that your answer is reasonable. (2-4)

15. 　67　
　　　× 59

16. 　132　
　　　×　8

17. 　419　
　　　×　65

18. 　893　
　　　× 240

19. The picture at the right shows a towel with a customer's initials. However, the initials were put on in the wrong order. What are the other ways the letters could be arranged? (2-6)

Writing in Math

20. Estimate to decide if 26 × 74 × 30 is greater than or less than 72,000. Tell how you decided. (2-2)

21. Explain how to use the Distributive Property to find 805 × 6. (2-3)

22. If you had to multiply 941 × 536, what method would you use? Explain. (2-5)

Key Idea
You can use patterns to mentally multiply decimals by 10, 100, and 1,000.

Materials
• calculator

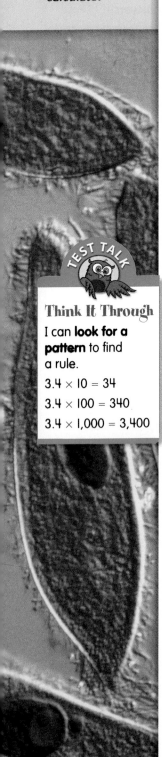

Decimal Patterns

LEARN

Activity

What's the rule?

a. Use a calculator to find each missing product.

24.3 × 10 = 243	0.57 × 10 = 5.7	6.891 × 10 = 68.91
24.3 × 100 = ?	0.57 × 100 = ?	6.891 × 100 = ?
24.3 × 1,000 = ?	0.57 × 1,000 = ?	6.891 × 1,000 = ?

b. Find each product without a calculator. Then check your answers with a calculator.

0.005 × 10	4.93 × 10	1.7 × 10
0.005 × 100	4.93 × 100	1.7 × 100
0.005 × 1,000	4.93 × 1,000	1.7 × 1,000

c. Describe the rule that tells how to find each of the products above.

Can you show how to use your rule?

Think It Through
I can **look for a pattern** to find a rule.
3.4 × 10 = 34
3.4 × 100 = 340
3.4 × 1,000 = 3,400

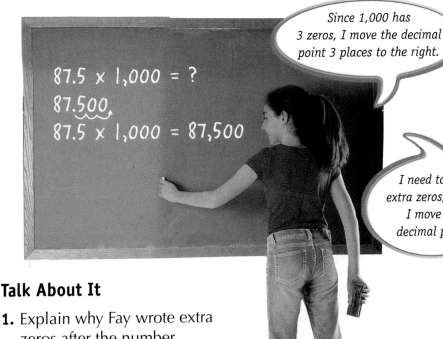

Since 1,000 has 3 zeros, I move the decimal point 3 places to the right.

$$87.5 \times 1{,}000 = ?$$
$$87.500$$
$$87.5 \times 1{,}000 = 87{,}500$$

I need to add extra zeros, before I move the decimal point.

✓ Talk About It

1. Explain why Fay wrote extra zeros after the number before moving the decimal point to find her answer.

Find each product. Use mental math.

1. 2.5×10 **2.** 5.4×100 **3.** 10×0.08 **4.** $3.061 \times 1{,}000$

5. Number Sense Tell what number goes in the blank. To find 0.42×100, move the decimal point in 0.42 ___ places to the right.

PRACTICE

For more practice, see Set 2-7 on p. 127.

Ⓐ Skills and Understanding

Find each product. Use mental math.

6. 0.22×10 **7.** 100×4.005 **8.** 1.853×10 **9.** $1{,}000 \times 6.3$

10. 71.4×100 **11.** $0.1 \times 1{,}000$ **12.** 10×506.8 **13.** 100×0.999

14. 10×4.137 **15.** 0.003×10 **16.** 692.64×100 **17.** $5.02 \times 1{,}000$

18. Number Sense Tell what numbers go in the blanks. To find $7.9 \times 1{,}000$, add ___ extra zeros at the end of 7.9 and move the decimal point ___ places to the right.

Ⓑ Reasoning and Problem Solving

19. To view a slide of an amoeba, Tad sets a microscope to enlarge objects 100 times their actual size. If the actual diameter of the amoeba is 0.25 mm, what is its diameter as seen through the microscope?

20. Algebra What is n if $98.7 \times n = 98{,}700$?

21. **Writing in Math** Explain how you would place the decimal point in the products of 6.413×10, 6.413×100, and $6.413 \times 1{,}000$.

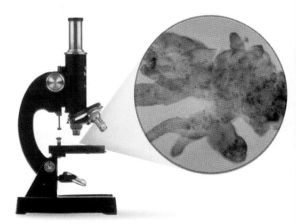

🎧 Mixed Review and Test Prep

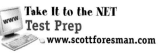

Take It to the NET
Test Prep
www.scottforesman.com

22. 20×700 **23.** 34×55 **24.** 400×63 **25.** 187×92

26. Ann received 4 posters as a gift, but she can only hang 2 of the posters in her room. How many different pairs of posters are possible?

    A. 2   **B.** 4   **C.** 6   **D.** 8

27. Which is NOT another name for 3,000?

    A. 3 thousands   **B.** 30 tens   **C.** 30 hundreds   **D.** 300 tens

 All text pages available online and on CD-ROM.

Vocabulary
• compatible numbers (p. 22)

Think It Through

• I only need an **estimate** because the question asks for about how much.

• Before I estimate, I should **decide which estimation method to use.**

Estimating Decimal Products

LEARN

What are some ways to estimate products of decimals?

George wants to buy 1.6 pounds of cheese. About how much will the cheese cost?

CHEESE
$8.99
per pound

Example

One Way

George could round both numbers.

1.6×8.99

$2 \times 9 = 18$

1.6×8.99 is about 18.

So, the cheese will cost about $18.

Another Way

George could substitute **compatible numbers** that are easy to multiply.

1.6×8.99

$1.6 \times 10 = 16$

1.6×8.99 is about 16.

So, the cheese will cost about $16.

✓ Talk About It

1. Is the first estimate in the example an overestimate or an underestimate? Tell how you know.

2. In the second part of the example, why did George adjust $8.99 to $10?

3. When shopping, is it usually better to overestimate or underestimate a cost? Explain.

4. **Number Sense** Is 7×6.12 greater than or less than 42? Tell how you know.

Take It to the NET
More Examples
www.scottforesman.com

CHECK ✓

For another example, see Set 2-8 on p. 124.

Estimate each product.

1. 2.4×7 **2.** 53×1.89 **3.** 63.2×0.78 **4.** 4.01×19.95

5. Number Sense Estimate 3.5×9 in two different ways. Tell how you found each estimate.

PRACTICE

For more practice, see Set 2-8 on p. 127.

Ⓐ Skills and Understanding

Estimate each product.

6. 82×4.1 **7.** 6.78×5 **8.** 3.15×12.4 **9.** 559×2.8

10. 0.03×95 **11.** 4.16×2.7 **12.** 1.75×6.79 **13.** 89×5.3

14. 4.8×1.32 **15.** 0.9×7.04 **16.** 629.38×12 **17.** 4.06×124.3

18. Number Sense Is 40 a reasonable estimate for 2.04×1.993? Explain.

Ⓑ Reasoning and Problem Solving

19. Marla bought 2.35 pounds of potato salad that sells for $4.29 per pound. Find an underestimate and an overestimate to establish a range for the actual cost of the potato salad.

20. Which product is greater, 5.205×7.5 or 5.215×7.5? Explain.

21. Algebra If $n \times 3.82$ is about 120, what is a reasonable estimate for n?

22. Writing in Math Explain how you know that a reasonable estimate for 42.1×5.8 is about 240.

Mixed Review and Test Prep

Take It to the NET
Test Prep
www.scottforesman.com

Compare. Write >, <, or = for each ◉.

23. 0.4 ◉ 0.400 **24.** 3.69 ◉ 3.7 **25.** 0.8 ◉ 0.08 **26.** 1.2 ◉ 1.1

Estimate each sum or difference.

27. $89 + 92$ **28.** $302 - 192$ **29.** $8.9 + 6.3$ **30.** $79.4 - 28.3$

31. Round 3,456,130 to the nearest thousand.

A. 3,456,000 **B.** 3,457,000 **C.** 3,500,000 **D.** 3,000,000

32. What is the product of 8.7 and 1,000?

A. 0.0087 **B.** 0.087 **C.** 8,700 **D.** 87,000

Think It Through

- I can **multiply decimals as though they were whole numbers.**
- I can **use estimation** to check the placement of the decimal point in the product.

Multiplying Whole Numbers and Decimals

LEARN

How do you multiply whole numbers by decimals?

The cheetah has the fastest maximum speed of any mammal. What is the maximum speed of a cheetah if it is 2.56 times as fast as the elephant?

25 mph

? mph

Example A

Find 25×2.56.

STEP 1

Estimate: $25 \times 3 = 75$
Multiply as you would with whole numbers.

```
  1 1
  2 3
  2.56
×   25
  1280
  5120
  6400
```

STEP 2

Write the decimal point in the product.

```
   2.56   2 decimal places
×    25   0 decimal places
   1280
   5120
  64.00   2 decimal places
```

> Count the decimal places in both factors. The total is the number of decimal places in the product.

Look back at your estimate to see if your answer is reasonable. 64.00 is close to 75.

The maximum speed of a cheetah is 64 mph.

✓ Talk About It

1. How does multiplying a whole number by a decimal compare to multiplying two whole numbers?

2. If you multiplied 25 by 2.6, how many decimal places would be in the product? Explain.

3. **Estimation** Suppose you wrote 6.400 instead of 64.00 as the product in Example A. How does estimation help you know your answer is wrong?

When do you insert extra zeros in the product?

Sometimes you need to insert extra zeros to be able to place the decimal point in the product.

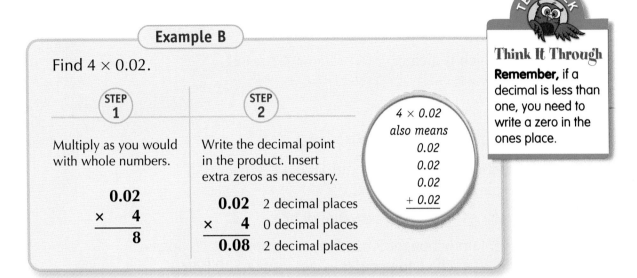

Example B

Find 4×0.02.

STEP 1

Multiply as you would with whole numbers.

$$\begin{array}{r} 0.02 \\ \times \quad 4 \\ \hline 8 \end{array}$$

STEP 2

Write the decimal point in the product. Insert extra zeros as necessary.

$$\begin{array}{r} 0.02 \quad \text{2 decimal places} \\ \times \quad 4 \quad \text{0 decimal places} \\ \hline 0.08 \quad \text{2 decimal places} \end{array}$$

4×0.02
also means
0.02
0.02
0.02
+ 0.02

Think It Through
Remember, if a decimal is less than one, you need to write a zero in the ones place.

✔ Talk About It

4. Why do you need to insert a zero in front of the 8 in the product for Example B?

5. If you multiplied 0.002 by 40, how many zeros would you need to insert between the decimal point and 8 in the product?

Take It to the NET
More Examples
www.scottforesman.com

CHECK ✔

For another example, see Set 2-9 on p. 124.

1. $\begin{array}{r} 5.1 \\ \times \quad 9 \\ \hline \end{array}$

2. $\begin{array}{r} 3.8 \\ \times \quad 6 \\ \hline \end{array}$

3. $\begin{array}{r} 0.44 \\ \times \quad 5 \\ \hline \end{array}$

4. $\begin{array}{r} 0.001 \\ \times \quad 9 \\ \hline \end{array}$

5. 27×4.9

6. 11.3×50

7. 62×0.78

8. 34×8.01

9. **Number Sense** How does the product of 6.3 and 7 compare to the product of 63 and 7?

PRACTICE

For more practice, see Set 2-9 on p. 128.

A Skills and Understanding

10. $\begin{array}{r} 8.1 \\ \times \quad 6 \\ \hline \end{array}$

11. $\begin{array}{r} 9.4 \\ \times \quad 5 \\ \hline \end{array}$

12. $\begin{array}{r} 0.03 \\ \times \quad 2 \\ \hline \end{array}$

13. $\begin{array}{r} 4.06 \\ \times \quad 7 \\ \hline \end{array}$

14. 9.5×2

15. 0.014×3

16. 61×5.7

17. 3.004×11

18. 8.08×26

19. 39.5×47

20. 18×0.26

21. 53.7×91

Copy each equation. Then insert a decimal point in each product to make the equation true.

22. $3 \times 4.1 = 123$

23. $0.61 \times 9 = 549$

24. $7.002 \times 8 = 56016$

25. $17 \times 5.4 = 918$

26. $10 \times 9.32 = 932$

27. $2.647 \times 7 = 18529$

28. Number Sense Which is greater, 2.01×82 or 2.1×82? Tell how you know.

B Reasoning and Problem Solving

29. Nelson says that the product of 6.32 and 18 is 11.376. Is he correct? Explain.

30. Algebra If $0.2 \times n = 1.4$, what is the value of n?

31. At a fair, the Piper family bought 5 hamburgers costing $2.75 apiece, including tax. How much change did they get from a $20 bill?

Math and Science

32. What is the maximum speed of a pronghorn antelope if it is 1.22 times as fast as the lion?

33. What is the maximum speed of a chicken if it is 300 times as fast as the garden snail?

34. How much faster is the lion than the human?

35. What is the maximum speed of a quarter horse if it is 32.5 miles per hour faster than the black mamba snake?

36. How much faster is the maximum speed of the three-toed sloth than the garden snail?

37. Writing in Math Is the explanation below correct? If not, tell why and write a correct response.

Find the product of 5.9 and 12.

$$\begin{array}{r} 5.9 \\ \times\ 12 \\ \hline 118 \\ 590 \\ \hline 70.8 \end{array}$$

I multiply the same way as I do with whole numbers. I count the total number of decimal places in both factors. There is a total of one decimal place. I place the decimal point so there is one decimal place in the product.

Data File

Animal Speeds	
Animal	**Maximum Speed (mph)**
Lion	50
Human	27.89
Black mamba snake	15
Three-toed sloth	0.15
Garden snail	0.03

TEST TALK

Think It Through

I can **estimate** to see if the answer is reasonable.

C Extensions

38. Number Sense If you multiply a nonzero whole number by a decimal less than one, will the product be less than or greater than the whole number? Give an example to support your answer.

39. Number Sense If you multiply a nonzero whole number by a decimal greater than one, will the product be less than or greater than the whole number? Give an example to support your answer.

Mixed Review and Test Prep

Take It to the NET
Test Prep
www.scottforesman.com

Find each difference.

40. 5.8 − 2.3 **41.** 67.3 − 0.5 **42.** 8.91 − 4.4 **43.** 77.6 − 0.53

Estimate each product.

44. 22 × 39 **45.** 8 × 578 **46.** 236 × 95 **47.** 56 × 421

48. Which is the most reasonable estimate for 3.6 × 72?

   A. about 28   **C.** about 420

   B. about 280   **D.** about 2,800

49. Which number when rounded to the nearest ten thousand is 70,000?

   A. 6,499   **C.** 64,999

   B. 7,499   **D.** 74,999

Learning with Technology

Using a Calculator to Round Numbers

The **Fix** key allows you to round numbers. To round 3.799 to hundredths

Press: [Fix] 2 then 3.799 [=]

or [Fix] [0.01] 3.799 [ENTER =], depending on your calculator.

Display: 3.80

You can turn off rounding by pressing [Fix] [·]

1. What keys would you use to round a number to the nearest tenth? thousandth?

Use your calculator to round 45,052.1675 to the nearest

2. tenth.   **3.** hundredth.

4. thousandth.

Think It Through

I can **make a model** to show multiplication of decimals.

Using Grids to Multiply Decimals by Decimals

LEARN

How can you model the multiplication of decimals?

One way is to show the product of decimals using a 10 × 10 grid. Remember that a 10 × 10 grid represents one whole. It shows both tenths and hundredths.

✓ WARM UP

Write each number in decimal form.

1. 5 tenths

2. 3 tenths

3. 6 hundredths

4. 23 hundredths

Example

Find 0.8 × 0.4. This is the same as finding 0.8 of 0.4.

0.8 = 8 tenths or 80 hundredths   0.4 = 4 tenths or 40 hundredths

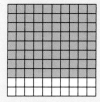   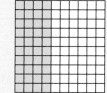

The decimals 0.8 and 0.4 are shown together on the grid below. The green squares indicate where the grid was shaded with both blue and yellow. The 32 green squares represent the product of 0.8 and 0.4.

Remember, each small square represents 1 hundredth or 0.01.

So, 0.8 × 0.4 = 32 hundredths or 0.32.

✔ Talk About It

1. What decimal names the part of the grid that was shaded both blue and yellow?

2. Why is the color green used for the squares that were shaded twice?

Write a multiplication sentence that describes the shaded areas of each grid.

1. **2.** **3.** **4.**

5. Find the product 0.6×0.3. You can use a 10×10 grid to help.

6. Number Sense Is 0.7×0.5 greater than or less than 0.7×0.4? Explain.

PRACTICE

For more practice, see Set 2-10 on p. 128.

Ⓐ Skills and Understanding

Write a multiplication sentence that describes the shaded areas of each grid.

7. **8.** **9.** **10.**

Find each product. You can use 10×10 grids to help.

11. 0.2×0.9 **12.** 0.3×0.7 **13.** 0.8×0.8 **14.** 0.6×0.1

15. 0.7×0.6 **16.** 0.5×0.2 **17.** 0.4×0.9 **18.** 0.2×0.4

19. Number Sense Ed said that $0.9 \times 0.1 = 0.9$. Is he correct? Explain.

Ⓑ Reasoning and Problem Solving

20. Paula has completed 3 tenths of a trail that is 8 tenths of a mile long. How far has she walked?

21. A can of dog food contains 0.4 pound of food. At each meal, Rich's dog Tosha gets 0.5 can of food. How much does each of Tosha's meals weigh?

22. Write two numbers whose product is 0.45.

23. <u>**Writing in Math**</u> Explain how to use a 10×10 grid to show the product of 0.4 and 0.3.

Mixed Review and Test Prep

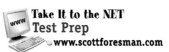
Take It to the NET
Test Prep
www.scottforesman.com

24. Estimate $3 \times 52 \times 41$.

25. What is 7×1.6?

   A. 1.12   **B.** 7.6   **C.** 11.2   **D.** 112

Think It Through

- I can **draw a picture** to show the main idea.
- I can **multiply** by finding the sum of the partial products.

Multiplying Decimals by Decimals

LEARN

How do you multiply decimals by decimals?

Royal Gala apples are on sale. What is the cost of 3.7 pounds of apples?

Find $3.7 \times \$0.89$.
Think of 3.7 as $3 + 0.7$.
Find $3 \times \$0.89$ and $0.7 \times \$0.89$.

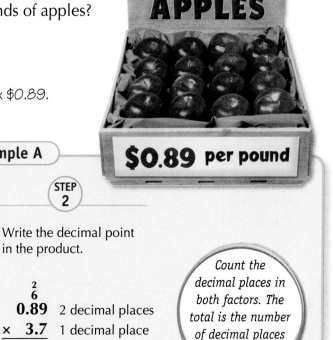

APPLES

$0.89 per pound

Example A

STEP 1	STEP 2	
Multiply as though both numbers were whole numbers.	Write the decimal point in the product.	*Count the decimal places in both factors. The total is the number of decimal places in the product.*

STEP 1:

$$\begin{array}{r} \overset{2}{\underset{6}{}} \\ 0.89 \\ \times\ \ 3.7 \\ \hline 623 \\ 2670 \\ \hline 3293 \end{array}$$

STEP 2:

$$\begin{array}{r} \overset{2}{\underset{6}{}} \\ 0.89 \\ \times\ \ 3.7 \\ \hline 623 \\ 2670 \\ \hline 3.293 \end{array}$$

0.89 2 decimal places
3.7 1 decimal place
3.293 3 decimal places

Rounded to the nearest cent, the cost of the apples is $3.29.

✓ Talk About It

1. How is multiplying a decimal by a decimal different from multiplying two whole numbers?

2. Why was the product in Example A rounded to the nearest hundredth?

3. **Estimation** How could you use estimation to check the reasonableness of the answer in Example A?

When do you insert extra zeros in the product?

Sometimes you need to insert extra zeros to be able to place the decimal point in the product.

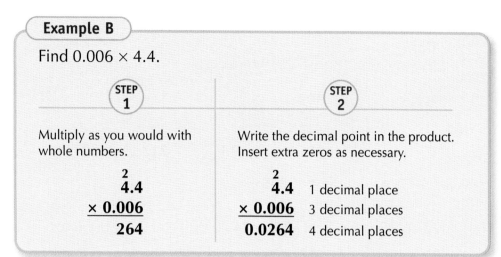

Example B

Find 0.006 × 4.4.

STEP 1

Multiply as you would with whole numbers.

$$\begin{array}{r} \overset{2}{4.4} \\ \times\ 0.006 \\ \hline 264 \end{array}$$

STEP 2

Write the decimal point in the product. Insert extra zeros as necessary.

$$\begin{array}{r} \overset{2}{4.4} \quad \text{1 decimal place} \\ \times\ 0.006 \quad \text{3 decimal places} \\ \hline 0.0264 \quad \text{4 decimal places} \end{array}$$

Example C

Find 0.05 × 0.084.

$$\begin{array}{r} \overset{2}{0.084} \quad \text{3 decimal places} \\ \times\ \ 0.05 \quad \text{2 decimal places} \\ \hline 0.00420 \quad \text{5 decimal places} \end{array}$$

Notice that the final zero in 0.00420 can be deleted since 0.00420 = 0.0042.

So, 0.05 × 0.084 = 0.00420 or 0.0042.

✔ Talk About It

4. Why do you need to insert a zero in front of the digits 264 in the product for Example B?

5. If you multiplied 0.006 by 0.44, how many decimal places would be in the product? Explain.

6. **Reasoning** Since 8 × 2 = 16, what is 0.8 × 2? 8 × 0.2? 0.8 × 0.2? 0.08 × 0.2?

CHECK ✔

For another example, see Set 2-11 on p. 124.

Find each product.

1. $\begin{array}{r} 5.6 \\ \times\ 0.7 \\ \hline \end{array}$

2. $\begin{array}{r} 3.4 \\ \times\ 2.2 \\ \hline \end{array}$

3. $\begin{array}{r} 1.95 \\ \times\ \ 0.6 \\ \hline \end{array}$

4. $\begin{array}{r} 4.2 \\ \times\ 0.03 \\ \hline \end{array}$

5. 80.3 × 0.1

6. 0.09 × 0.12

7. 6.1 × 0.008

8. 3.9 × 7.24

9. **Number Sense** Which is greater 9.4 × 0.013 or 9.4 × 0.13? Tell how you know.

A Skills and Understanding

Find each product.

10.
$$2.8 \times 0.7$$

11.
$$4.3 \times 0.1$$

12.
$$0.52 \times 8.6$$

13.
$$0.6 \times 0.9$$

14.
$$5.31 \times 1.8$$

15.
$$20.2 \times 0.5$$

16.
$$6.4 \times 0.003$$

17.
$$1.8 \times 4.9$$

18. 3.74×0.001 **19.** 0.03×0.2 **20.** 0.6×0.98 **21.** 15.4×1.2

Copy each equation and insert a decimal point in the product to make the equation true.

22. $0.6 \times 4.7 = 282$ **23.** $6.25 \times 1.9 = 11875$ **24.** $0.008 \times 0.77 = 000616$

25. Number Sense The product of 5.2 and 8.3 is 43.16. What is the product of 5.2 and 0.83? of 5.2 and 83?

B Reasoning and Problem Solving

 Math and Social Studies

The table at the right shows the cost of common items that pioneers could stock up on in Independence, Missouri, before setting out on the Oregon Trail in 1850. Remember to round your answers to the nearest cent.

26. What is the cost of 4.3 pounds of rice?

27. What is the cost of 12.75 yards of cloth?

28. What is the cost of 2.25 bushels of beans?

29. The price of lard per pound is how many times the price of salt per pound?

30. <u>Writing in Math</u> Dawn has solved the problem below. Is she correct? If not, tell why and write a correct explanation.

> Is it possible to write the product of 3.15 and 0.2 with only two places to the right of the decimal point? Explain.
>
> *No; The product must have 3 decimal places since the sum of the decimal places in the factors is 3.*

Data File

General Store	
Item	**Cost**
Beans	$1.50/bushel
Cloth	$0.25/yard
Corn Meal	$0.17/lb
Lard	$0.10/lb
Rice	$0.15/lb
Salt	$0.02/lb

TEST TALK

Think It Through
- I will **check if the answer is complete.**
- I will **check if the answer makes sense.**

C Extensions

31. Algebra If $2.5 \times n$ is between 5 and 10, what is a reasonable value for n?

32. Algebra If $0.1 \times n$ is between 0.003 and 0.004, what is a reasonable value for n?

Mixed Review and Test Prep

Take It to the NET
Test Prep
www.scottforesman.com

Write a multiplication sentence that describes the shaded areas of each grid.

33.   **34.**   **35.**   **36.**

Find each sum.

37. $2.3 + 6.7$ **38.** $13.4 + 1.09$ **39.** $8.93 + 4.52$ **40.** $0.71 + 2.5$

41. Which is the value of the underlined digit in 6,8<u>5</u>1,232?

   A. 5   **C.** 50,000

   B. 50   **D.** 500,000

42. What is the standard form for 8 hundredths?

   A. 800   **C.** 0.88

   B. 0.8   **D.** 0.08

Discovery CHANNEL SCHOOL
Discover Math in Your World

Take It to the NET
Video and Activities
www.scottforesman.com

Listening With Toenails and Trunks

Elephants may be the only large land animals that transmit and receive underground messages. They use their toenails and trunks to detect seismic signals.

1. The African elephant weighs up to 7.5 tons. Mentally calculate this weight in pounds (1 ton = 2,000 lb).

2. The sound waves of an elephant call will travel through both air and ground. Through the air, the waves may travel 6.63 miles. They will travel 1.5 times as far through the ground. Estimate the ground distance.

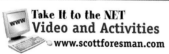

All text pages available online and on CD-ROM.

Do You Know How?

Do You Understand?

Investigating Decimal Patterns (2-7)

Find each product. Use mental math.

1. 10×3.69

2. 0.204×100

3. 0.06×10

4. $1,000 \times 17.55$

5. 100×412.3

6. $5.8 \times 1,000$

A Tell how you found each product.

B Why did you need to write extra zeros after the number before placing the decimal point in Exercise 6?

Estimating Decimal Products (2-8)

Estimate each product.

7. 4.3×6

8. 7.06×18.1

9. 3×9.17

10. 0.89×56.6

11. 107.4×65

12. 44.51×72.3

C Tell how you found the estimates in Exercises 11 and 12.

D Describe two ways to estimate the product in Exercise 9.

Multiplying Whole Numbers and Decimals (2-9)

Find each product.

13. 1.7×4

14. 3×7.8

15. 2×0.02

16. 9.54×67

17. 0.005×9

18. 6.004×53

E Tell how you found the products in Exercises 15 and 16.

F If you multiplied 0.007 by 203, how many decimal places would be in the product? Explain.

Using Grids to Multiply Decimals by Decimals (2-10)
Multiplying Decimals by Decimals (2-11)

Find each product.

19. 0.6×0.9

20. 7.8×0.56

21. 0.07×6.92

22. 0.3×0.1

G Tell how you found the products in Exercises 21 and 22.

H Does 4,094.28 seem reasonable for the product 9.18×44.6? Explain.

Think It Through

For multiple-choice items, **read the question carefully and watch for words like NOT.**

MULTIPLE CHOICE

1. Which two numbers do NOT have a product of 0.6? (2-7, 2-9)

A. 2 and 0.3   **B.** 0.2 and 3   **C.** 0.6 and 1   **D.** 10 and 0.006

2. If you multiplied 0.341 and 82.5, how many decimal places would be in the product? (2-11)

A. 3 places   **B.** 4 places   **C.** 5 places   **D.** 7 places

FREE RESPONSE

Find each product. Use mental math. (2-7)

3. 7.23 x 10   **4.** 8.1 x 100   **5.** 100 x 96.6   **6.** 1,000 x 0.4

Estimate each product. (2-8)

7. 5.7 x 4   **8.** 84.6 x 38.5   **9.** 12 x 7.3   **10.** 0.92 x 6.3

Find each product. (2-9, 2-11)

11. 8 x 0.6   **12.** 1.3 x 4.5   **13.** 0.009 x 7   **14.** 20.8 x 15.6

15. $\begin{array}{r} 7.4 \\ \times\ 0.03 \\ \hline \end{array}$ **16.** $\begin{array}{r} 66.4 \\ \times\ \ \ 9 \\ \hline \end{array}$ **17.** $\begin{array}{r} 0.33 \\ \times\ \ 0.5 \\ \hline \end{array}$ **18.** $\begin{array}{r} 12.8 \\ \times\ 4.07 \\ \hline \end{array}$

19. $\begin{array}{r} 1.8 \\ \times\ 2.3 \\ \hline \end{array}$ **20.** $\begin{array}{r} 0.05 \\ \times\ 0.06 \\ \hline \end{array}$ **21.** $\begin{array}{r} 0.27 \\ \times\ \ 2.7 \\ \hline \end{array}$ **22.** $\begin{array}{r} 0.006 \\ \times\ 0.25 \\ \hline \end{array}$

Write a multiplication sentence that describes the shaded areas of each grid. (2-10)

23.   **24.**   **25.**   **26.**

Writing in Math

27. Explain how to find 7.08 x 1,000 using mental math. (2-7)

28. Is 3,000 an overestimate or an underestimate for the product of 54.2 and 61.9? Tell how you know. (2-8)

29. Brandon says that the product of 0.2 and 0.2 is 0.4. Is he correct? If not tell why and explain how to find the correct product. (2-10)

Algebra

Key Idea
Variables can be used to write algebraic expressions that describe real-world situations.

Vocabulary
• variable
• algebraic expression

T E S T   T A L K

Think It Through
There is often more than one way that I can **write an algebraic expression.**

Variables and Expressions

⊏ LEARN ⊐

What is an algebraic expression?

Monique wants to buy tickets to a basketball game for herself and some friends. Write an algebraic expression to represent the total cost of the tickets.

In the chart below, n represents the number of tickets that Monique buys. The total cost of the tickets can be represented by $\$5.50 \times n$.

Cost per Ticket	Number of Tickets	Total Cost
$5.50	1	$5.50 × 1
$5.50	2	$5.50 × 2
$5.50	3	$5.50 × 3
.	.	.
.	.	.
$5.50	n	$5.50 × n

We call n a **variable** because it stands for a value that can change or vary. $\$5.50 \times n$ is called an **algebraic expression.** An algebraic expression is a mathematical phrase involving variables, numbers, and operations.

Other examples of algebraic expressions are shown below.

Addition	Subtraction	Multiplication	Division
$4 + a$, or $a + 4$	$b - 4$	$4 \times c$, or $4c$	$d \div 4$, or $\dfrac{d}{4}$

✔ Talk About It

1. Why was a variable used to represent the number of tickets Monique buys?

2. If each ticket cost $6.75 instead of $5.50, what expression could you use to represent the total cost of the tickets?

3. Explain the meaning of the algebraic expression $\$5.50n$.

How can you evaluate an algebraic expression?

You can evaluate an algebraic expression by replacing the variable with a number, and then performing the computation.

Example A

Evaluate $x + 4$ for $x = 6$.

Replace x with 6 in the expression.

$x + 4$
↓
$6 + 4 = 10$

Example B

Evaluate $y - 7$ for $y = 18.5$.

Replace y with 18.5 in the expression.

$y - 7$
↓
$18.5 - 7 = 11.5$

Example C

Evaluate $z \div 3$ for $z = 27$.

Replace z with 27 in the expression.

$z \div 3$
↓
$27 \div 3 = 9$

Example D

After 8 weeks, Mia's plant was h inches tall, and Fred's plant was 2 inches taller than Mia's plant. Write an expression for the height of Fred's plant and evaluate the expression for $h = 7, 8,$ and 9.

expression: $h + 2$

h	$h + 2$
7	$7 + 2 = 9$
8	$8 + 2 = 10$
9	$9 + 2 = 11$

Mia's plant   Fred's plant

✔ Talk About It

4. In Example D, what expression would express the height of Fred's plant if it were 2 inches *shorter* than Mia's plant?

CHECK ✔

For another example, see Set 2-12 on p. 125.

1. Write an algebraic expression to represent the cost of a CD for $\$k$ with a coupon for $2 off.

Evaluate each expression for $n = 7$ and $n = 8$.

2. $n - 3$ **3.** $4.3 + n$ **4.** $n \times 5$ **5.** $96 - n$ **6.** $\dfrac{56}{n}$

7. Representation What is another way to write the expression $8p$?

A Skills and Understanding

8. Write an algebraic expression to represent the cost of a coat for $h with a shipping fee of $5.98.

9. Write an algebraic expression to represent the cost of m pounds of cashew nuts if each pound costs $3.99.

Evaluate each expression for $n = 4$ and $n = 5$.

10. $0.1 \times n$ **11.** $n - 2.6$ **12.** $20 \div n$ **13.** $n + 69$ **14.** $12n$

15. $11.3 - n$ **16.** $\frac{40}{n}$ **17.** $n \times 7.5$ **18.** $6n$ **19.** $82.3 + n$

Evaluate each expression for $n = 6$ and $n = 10$.

20. $n + 9.4$ **21.** $\frac{n}{2}$ **22.** $50 - n$ **23.** n **24.** $23.9n$

Copy and complete each table.

25.

n	n + 4
3	
6	
9	
12	

26.

n	5.9 − n
0.1	
0.5	
1.2	
3.7	

27.

n	n ÷ 3
3	
9	
18	
24	

28.

n	2n
0	
1	
5	
10	

29. Representation What is another way to write the expression $\frac{34}{y}$?

B Reasoning and Problem Solving

Math and Music

A unit of time in music is called a measure. The number of beats per measure varies from song to song. In the song, "America," there are 3 beats per measure. Another patriotic song, "You're a Grand Old Flag," has 4 beats per measure. Use this information to complete the tables below.

30. "America"

Number of Measures	Number of Beats
1	
4	
6	
9	
w	

31. "You're a Grand Old Flag"

Number of Measures	Number of Beats
1	
3	
5	
8	
s	

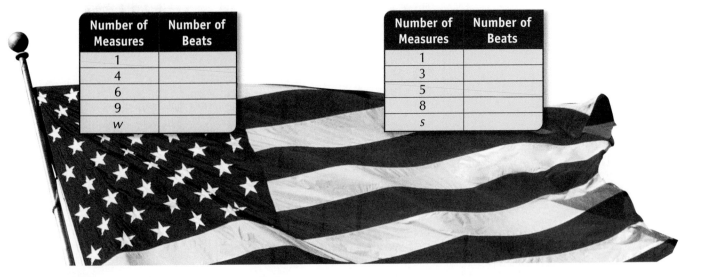

32. Writing in Math Is the explanation for the problem below correct? If not, tell why and write a correct response.

> Explain the meaning of the expression 15*t*, and then explain how to evaluate the expression for *t* = 3.
>
> *The expression 15t means 15 + t. You can evaluate the expression by replacing t with 3 and then solving: 15 + 3 = 18.*

C Extensions

33. Writing in Math Write a situation that can be represented by the algebraic expression *x* + 3.

34. Writing in Math Write a situation that can be represented by the algebraic expression *x* − 3.

Mixed Review and Test Prep

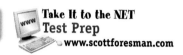

Take It to the NET
Test Prep
www.scottforesman.com

Compare. Write >, <, or = for each ⬤.

35. 30,999 ⬤ 31,000 **36.** 5,902 ⬤ 5,092 **37.** 43,470 ⬤ 38,997

Find each product.

38. 0.2×0.15 **39.** 3.4×0.6 **40.** 0.9×8.07 **41.** 6.5×4.8

42. What is 98,390 − 549?

   A. 97,841 **C.** 98,841

   B. 97,851 **D.** 98,939

43. Which number is less than 0.09?

   A. 0.9 **C.** 0.1

   B. 0.01 **D.** 0.11

Enrichment

Venn Diagrams

A **Venn diagram** uses rings or circles to show relationships among sets of data or objects. Each circle is named for the group it represents. Sometimes circles overlap, or intersect, because some data belong to more than one group.

1. Name the factors of 40 that are NOT factors of 18 and 32.

2. Which factors of 40 are also factors of 32?

3. Which factors appear in the overlap for all three circles?

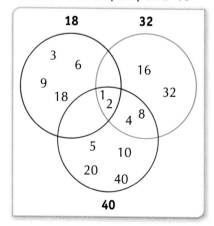

Factors of 18, 32, and 40

Problem-Solving Skill

Algebra

Key Idea
Translating words to numerical expressions can help you solve problems.

Vocabulary
• variable (p. 100)
• algebraic expression (p. 100)
• sum
• difference
• product
• quotient

Think It Through
Since the weight of the salad varies, I can **draw the conclusion** that I need to use a variable and write an expression.

Translating Words into Expressions

LEARN

How can you translate words into expressions?

Salad Bar Problem At a salad bar, the salad is weighed on plates weighing 4 ounces. What expression shows the salad weight after the weight of the plate is subtracted?

Plan and Solve

The total weight of the salad varies. Let a **variable** such as w stand for the total weight. Then $w - 4$ is the salad weight after the plate's weight is subtracted.

Often there is more than one way to translate an **algebraic expression.**

Example

Operation	Word Phrase	Algebraic Expression
Addition	A number *plus* 18; **Sum** of a number and 18; 18 *more than* a number; A number *increased by* 18	$x + 18$
Subtraction	A number *minus* 6; The **difference** between a number and 6; 6 *less than* a number; A number *decreased by* 6	$x - 6$
Multiplication	3 *times* a number; A number *multiplied by* 3; The **product** of 3 and a number	$3 \times n$ $3 \cdot n$ $3n$
Division	A number *divided by* 12; The **quotient** of a number and 12	$\dfrac{m}{12}$ $m \div 12$

✔ Talk About It

1. Why is a variable used in the Salad Bar problem?

2. Give two word phrases that could be translated as $48 - n$.

Write each word phrase as an algebraic expression.

1. 5 added to a number

2. 9 less than the height

3. the quotient of *x* and 2

4. 4 more than the age

5. the difference of *y* and 9

6. the product of *t* and 7

7. Number Sense Write two word phrases for the expression *x* + 6.

PRACTICE

For more practice, see Set 2-13 on p. 129.

Write each word phrase as an algebraic expression.

8. an age times 3

9. twice a certain cost

10. a width divided by seven

11. a weight plus 5

12. the product of *n* and 7

13. fifteen less than a speed

14. Number Sense Write two word phrases for the expression 5*w*.

15. Rhonda is 3 years younger than Jonah. Use *j* for Jonah's age. Which expression below shows Rhonda's age?

$j + 3$ $3j$ $j - 3$

16. A room is *f* feet long. Which expression below shows the length of the room in inches?

$12f$ $f + 12$ $f \div 12$

> 1 foot = 12 inches
> 1 yard = 3 feet
> 1 gallon = 4 quarts

17. A person's height is *y* feet. Which expression below shows the height in yards?

$3y$ $y + 3$ $y \div 3$

18. A century is 100 years. Which expression below shows the number of years in *x* centuries?

$100x$ $100 + x$ $x \div 100$

19. A gallon is 4 quarts. If a container holds *g* gallons, which expression below shows the number of quarts?

$g + 4$ $4g$ $g \div 4$

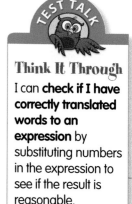

Think It Through
I can **check if I have correctly translated words to an expression** by substituting numbers in the expression to see if the result is reasonable.

20. A yard has 36 inches. Which expression below shows the number of yards in *y* inches?

$36 + y$ $36y$ $y \div 36$

21. Writing in Math Explain the difference between the expression *x* − 5 and 5 − *x*.

Algebra

Key Idea
Looking for patterns in figures and in a table of values can help you find a rule.

Vocabulary
• input/output table

Materials
• counters or
 tools

Think It Through
I can **use objects to solve a simpler problem.**

Find a Rule

LEARN

Activity

What's the rule?

a. Use counters to build the 4th figure shown below.

b. Predict how many counters are needed for the 5th figure. Build it to test your prediction.

c. How many counters are needed for the 6th figure? 7th figure? Explain how you decided.

d. How many counters would be in the 20th figure?

e. Complete the table.

f. What pattern do you see in the figures? In the table above?

g. Give a rule in words that tells how to find the total number of counters if you know the number of the figure.

Figure Number	Number of Counters
1	4
2	8
3	12
4	
5	
6	
7	
20	

How do you find a rule for a table?

A table of values is also called an **input/output table.** For Table A at the right, Mindy wrote the rule *Multiply by 5.* Juan wrote *Add 12.*

Table A

Input	Output
3	15
5	25
8	40
20	100

✔ Talk About It

1. Do both rules work for the first pair in Table A? Which rule works for the next pair in Table A?

2. Which rule works for all pairs in Table A?

3. If the input in Table A is *n,* write a rule using a variable.

Find a rule for each table. Write the rule in words.

1.

Input	Output
3	21
6	42
9	63
10	70

2.

Input	Output
8	13
11	16
12	17
20	25

3.

Input	Output
6	106
4	104
3	103
2	102

4.

Input	Output
4	400
7	700
9	900
15	1,500

5. Representation Write the rule with a variable for Exercise 4.

PRACTICE

For more practice, see Set 2-14 on p. 129.

Ⓐ Skills and Understanding

Find a rule for each table. Write the rule in words.

6.

Input	Output
0	8
1	9
5	13
9	17

7.

Input	Output
16	12
24	20
28	24
60	56

8.

Input	Output
26	36
21	31
17	27
10	20

9.

Input	Output
2	20
5	50
8	80
10	100

10. Representation Write a rule with a variable for Exercise 9.

Ⓑ Reasoning and Problem Solving

High-Speed Train The distances a high speed train can travel at maximum speed are given at the right.

Data File

High-Speed Train

Time (hr)	Distance (km)
1	300
2	600
3	900
4	1,200

11. Find a rule for the table. Write the rule in words.

12. What is the maximum distance the train could travel in 9 hours?

13. **Writing in Math** The rule for an input/output table is *Add 25*. Explain how you could make up a table for that rule.

Mixed Review and Test Prep

Take It to the NET
Test Prep
www.scottforesman.com

Evaluate each expression for $n = 10$.

14. $100 - n$ **15.** $n + 35$ **16.** $5n$ **17.** $n \div 10$

18. Which expression represents the product of a number and 100?

    A. $100 + n$ **B.** $100n$ **C.** $n \div 100$ **D.** $n - 100$

 All text pages available online and on CD-ROM.

Algebra

Key Idea
You can solve equations by mental math.

Vocabulary
• equation
• solution

Think It Through
• I can **draw a picture** to show the main idea.
• I can **think of multiplication as the addition of equal groups.**

Solving Equations

LEARN

How can you solve equations using mental math?

At the zoo, there are 18 flamingos.

If 5 of the flamingos are scarlet and the rest are pink, how many are pink?	If the flamingos are separated into 3 equal groups, how many are in each group?
Let x be the number of pink flamingos.	Let n be the number in each group.
Then $x + 5 = 18$.	Then $3n = 18$.

An **equation** is a number sentence that uses an equal sign to show that two expressions have the same value. Some equations like those above contain a variable.

You can use pictures to solve an equation using mental math. When you solve an equation, you find the value of the variable that makes the equation true. This value is called the **solution.**

Example A

Solve $x + 5 = 18$.

What number plus 5 equals 18?

$13 + 5 = 18$ Use mental math.
$18 = 18$ Check that the equation is true.

Solution: $x = 13$

Example B

Solve $3n = 18$.

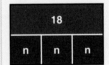

What number times 3 equals 18?

$3 \times 6 = 18$ Use mental math.
$18 = 18$ Check that the equation is true.

Solution: $n = 6$

✔ Talk About It

1. Would the equation $x - 5 = 18$ lead to the same solution as in Example A? Explain.

2. In Example B, why does the equation involve multiplication instead of addition?

Solve each equation by using mental math.

1. $g + 8 = 12$ **2.** $120 - b = 100$ **3.** $48 \div f = 6$ **4.** $5m = 35$

5. Reasoning Al says the solution of $m - 4 = 9$ is 5. Is he correct? Explain.

PRACTICE   *For more practice, see Set 2-15 on p. 129.*

Ⓐ Skills and Understanding

Solve each equation by using mental math.

6. $k - 5 = 20$ **7.** $1 + h = 10$ **8.** $8c = 64$ **9.** $15 \div e = 3$

10. $j + 0.4 = 7.4$ **11.** $12p = 0$ **12.** $37 - u = 31$ **13.** $31.5q = 315$

14. $16 - z = 9$ **15.** $v \div 2 = 6$ **16.** $15a = 45$ **17.** $n + 35 = 43$

18. Reasoning Does $7 + m = 15$ have the same solution as $m + 7 = 15$? Explain.

Ⓑ Reasoning and Problem Solving

Write and solve the equation represented by each picture.

19.

20.

21. To solve the equation $n + 25 = 33$, Susan tested values for n until she found one that would work. She tested 6, 7, and 8. Which is correct?

22. Reasoning Write an equation that has a solution of $x = 3.4$.

23. **Writing in Math** Write a problem that would require you to solve the equation $x + 10 = 25$.

🦉 Mixed Review and Test Prep

Take It to the NET
Test Prep
www.scottforesman.com

Write the value of each underlined digit.

24. 0.4<u>5</u>2   **25.** 2,015.7<u>2</u>   **26.** 0.00<u>9</u>   **27.** 15,360.<u>1</u>

28. Which of the following is the rule for the table at the right?

  A. Add 2.

  B. Subtract 2.

  C. Multiply by 3.

  D. Divide by 3.

Input	Output
1	3
4	12
7	21
9	27

Problem-Solving Applications

Weight Objects that have the same size do not always have the same weight. A golf ball is about the size of a hummingbird, but it has about 14 times the weight of a hummingbird. Why is this? An object's weight greatly depends on the types of atoms it has and their arrangements.

Trivia The Empire State Building is much taller than the Great Pyramid, but even 15 of these skyscrapers would weigh less than the ancient tomb.

1 A human infant may weigh 8 pounds. A baby humpback whale may weigh over 500 times as much. How much do baby humpback whales weigh?

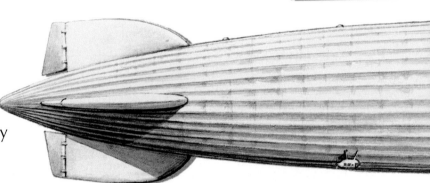

Using Key Facts

2 Even though it was lighter than an equal amount of air, the hydrogen in the Graf Zeppelin II weighed about 6.7 times as much as an African elephant. How much did the hydrogen weigh?

Key Facts

Object	Weight
• Eiffel Tower	10,100 tons
• Saturn V rocket	2,812 tons
• Statue of Liberty	225 tons
• African elephant	5.9 tons

3 The Empire State Building weighs as much as 130 Saturn V rockets. How much does the Empire State Building weigh?

4 Some pigmy shrews weigh only 0.09 oz. It takes 18 of these to equal the weight of 1 golf ball. About how much does a golf ball weigh? Write the word name for the weight of the golf ball.

Good News/Bad News Modern airships similar to the Graf Zeppelin II are lifted by helium, which is safer than hydrogen. Unfortunately, it takes more helium than hydrogen to lift an airship because helium atoms are heavier than hydrogen atoms.

6 **Decision Making** A typical blue whale weighs about the same as 26 African elephants. The heaviest blue whale weighed about 194.88 tons. Explain the best way to estimate the difference between a typical whale and the heaviest whale.

5 Which has a greater weight: 2 Eiffel Towers or 8 Saturn V rockets?

7 **Writing in Math** Using information from this lesson, write a word problem for your classmates to solve. Answer your question with a complete sentence.

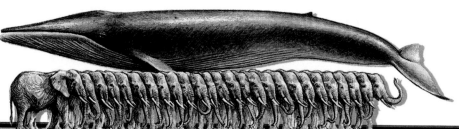

Review

| **Do You Know How?** | **Do You Understand?** |

Variables and Expressions (2-12)

Evaluate each expression for $n = 3$ and $n = 4$.

1. $0.2 \times n$ **2.** $n + 5.7$

3. $31 - n$ **4.** $24 \div n$

5. $9n$ **6.** $n - 1.8$

Ⓐ Tell how you evaluated each expression.

Ⓑ Explain the meaning of the expression $100y$.

Problem-Solving Skill: Translating Words into Expressions (2-13)

Write each word phrase an as algebraic expression.

7. 3.5 more than a number

8. A length decreased by 12

9. The quotient of a number and 6

Ⓒ Explain how you found each algebraic expression.

Ⓓ Write two word phrases for the algebraic expression $9x$.

Find a Rule (2-14)

Find a rule for each table. Write the rule in words and with a variable.

10.

Input	Output
55	49
42	36
28	22
13	7

11.

Input	Output
1	9
5	45
7	63
11	99

Ⓔ Tell how you found the rule for each table.

Ⓕ In Exercise 11, if 30 is listed as an input number, what would the output number be? Explain.

Solving Equations (2-15)

Solve by using mental math.

12. $h - 60 = 6$

13. $7m = 56$

14. $25 + t = 52$

15. $100m = 800$

16. $x + 100 = 800$

Ⓖ Explain how you solved each equation.

Ⓗ Does $t + 25 = 52$ have the same solution as Exercise 14? Explain why or why not.

MULTIPLE CHOICE

1. Which algebraic expression represents the cost of g CDs if each CD costs $15? (2-13)

   A. $g + 15$ **B.** $g - 15$ **C.** $15g$ **D.** $g \div 15$

2. Which is the solution to the equation $43 - k = 36$? (2-15)

   A. $k = 7$ **B.** $k = 8$ **C.** $k = 79$ **D.** $k = 80$

FREE RESPONSE

Evaluate each expression for $m = 7$ and $m = 9$. (2-12)

3. $4m$ 4. $29 + m$ 5. $m - 7$ 6. $\dfrac{63}{m}$

Write each word phrase as an algebraic expression. (2-13)

7. The sum of a number and 70   8. 8 multiplied by a number

Find a rule for each table. Write the rule in words and with a variable. (2-14)

9.
Input	Output
4	106
8	110
15	117
20	122

10.
Input	Output
9	1
27	3
45	5
54	6

11.
Input	Output
36	30
24	18
12	6
6	0

12.
Input	Output
2	24
5	60
6	72
10	120

Solve each equation by using mental math. (2-15)

13. $j + 11 = 20$ 14. $\dfrac{n}{4} = 4$ 15. $7.1 - y = 2.1$

16. $3s = 30$ 17. $a - 9 = 59$ 18. $5p = 55$

19. At three months, Mia weighs 6 pounds more than she did at birth. Use w for Mia's weight at birth. Which expression shows her weight at 3 months? (2-13, 2-16)

   $w + 6$ $w - 6$ $6w$

Writing in Math

20. Joan says that if you evaluate $6z$ for $z = 7$, the answer is 67. Is she correct? If not, tell why and then explain how you would evaluate the expression. (2-12)

21. Explain how to use mental math to solve the equation $2 + b = 9$. (2-15)

Test-Taking Strategies

Understand the question.

Get information for the answer.

Plan how to find the answer.

Make smart choices.

Use writing in math.

Improve written answers.

Get Information for the Answer.

After you understand a test question, you need to get information for the answer. Some test questions do not contain all the information you need in the text. You may need to look for more information in a picture, map, diagram, table, or graph.

1. Over a short period of time, a rabbit can run **three times** as fast as a squirrel.

Let *n* represent speed of a squirrel. Which **expression** could be used to find the speed of a rabbit?

A. $n + 3$

B. $3 - n$

C. $n \div 3$

D. $3 \times n$

Understand the question.

I need to find the expression that represents the speed of a rabbit.

Get information for the answer.

- Look for important information in the text.

- Look for important information in pictures, maps, diagrams, tables, or graphs.

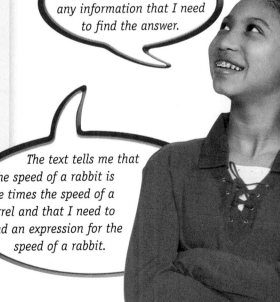

In this problem, the picture does not give me any information that I need to find the answer.

The text tells me that the speed of a rabbit is three times the speed of a squirrel and that I need to find an expression for the speed of a rabbit.

2. Most caterpillars have **twice** as many legs as spiders have.

Insect: 6 legs

Caterpillar: 16 legs

Which **expression** could be used to calculate the number of legs a spider has?

   A. 16 − 2

   B. 16 + 2

   C. 16 × 2

   D. 16 ÷ 2

Think It Through

I need to find out which expression could be used to find the number of legs a spider has. The text tells me that a caterpillar has twice as many legs as a spider. The pictures and captions tell me that a caterpillar has 16 legs.

Now it's your turn.

For each problem, tell what information is needed to solve the problem.

3. The pictograph below shows the number of pies sold each day at the school's weekend bake sale.

Weekend Pie Sales

Friday	🥧🥧🥧🥧🥧🥧🥧🥧
Saturday	🥧🥧🥧🥧🥧🥧🥧🥧🥧🥧🥧🥧
Sunday	🥧🥧🥧🥧🥧🥧🥧🥧🥧🥧🥧🥧🥧🥧🥧

Each 🥧 **stands for 1 pie sold.**

If each pie cost $3.50, which expression would be best to assess the total amount of money the school collected for pie sales on Friday?

   A. 8 × $3.50

   B. 32 + $3.50

   C. 32 × $3.50

   D. 3.50 ÷ 8

4. The picture shows the number of quarts in one gallon.

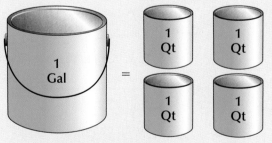

Let n represent the number of quarts. Which expression could be used to find the number of gallons?

   A. $n \div 4$

   B. $n - 4$

   C. $4 + n$

   D. $4 \times n$

The end result, or end product, of the quality of our class play is affected by factors like the number of rehearsals. **Factors** are multiplied to get a **product**. *(p. 66)*

Self Check ✓

Properties help you multiply more easily.
(Lessons 2-1, 2-2, 2-3, 2-4, 2-5)

Find 25 × 16 × 4.

Use the **Associative Property of Multiplication** to change the grouping of the factors.

25 × 16 × 4 =

(25 × 4) × 16 =

100 × 16 = 1,600

Find 12 × 99.

Use the **Distributive Property of Multiplication** to break up the factors into **compatible numbers**.

12 × 99 =

12 × (100 − 1) =

(12 × 100) − (12 × 1) =

1,200 − 12 = 1,188

1. Use properties to find 20 × 6 × 5, 6 × 89, and 33 × 21.

When I distribute invitations, I give one to each of my friends. When using the **Distributive Property of Multiplication**, I take one factor and multiply it by each number in a sum or difference. *(p. 70)*

Self Check ✓

Pay attention to decimal points when multiplying decimals.
(Lesson 2-7, 2-8, 2-9, 2-10, 2-11)

Find 12.6 × 8.2.

First multiply.

```
    12.6
 ×  8.2
    252
+ 10080
  10332
```

Then place a decimal point in the product. Count the decimal places in both factors before placing the decimal point.

```
    12.6  ←——— 1 decimal place
 ×  8.2   ←——— 1 decimal place
    252
+ 10080
  103.32  ←——— 2 decimal places
```

2. Find 0.6 × 0.8, 4.2 × 0.03, and 21.6 × 18.

*The clothes I wear to school vary, or change, depending on the weather. **Variables** in math are letters or symbols that can change value. (p. 100)*

Self Check

Variables can be used to represent unknown values.
(Lessons 2-12, 2-14, 2-15)

Find *s* if 52 + *s* = 65.

> Use **mental math.** Ask yourself:
> What number plus
> 52 equals 65?
>
> 52 + 13 = 65
> *s* = 13

Test different values.
Try *s* = 12, 13, 14

52 + *s* = 65	52 + *s* = 65
52 + 12 = 65	52 + 13 = 65
64 ≠ 65	65 = 65

The **solution** is 13.

---

3. Write an expression using the variable *n* that explains the rule in the table.

Input	Output
9	3
15	5
18	6
30	10

Self Check

*When you express yourself, you use words to describe an idea. An **algebraic expression** uses numbers and symbols to describe a math idea. (p. 100)*

You can make an organized list or translate words into expressions to **solve problems.** (Lessons 2-6, 2-13)

To make an organized list, make all the possible combinations of items.

Elyse and Jonah have an apple and an orange. How many combinations of people and fruit are there?

Elyse, apple   Elyse, orange
Jonah, apple   Jonah, orange

There are 4 different combinations.

To translate words into **algebraic expressions,** look at the key words. Think about the operations. Pick a variable.

Word phrase: a number times 3

Let *n* be the number.

Times means multiplication.

The expression is 3*n*.

---

4. Write two different word expressions for *t* + 15.

1. 600, 534, and 693; **2.** 0.48, 0.126, 388.8; **3.** $\frac{n}{3}$ or *n* ÷ 3; **4.** Sample answer: a number times 15, the sum of a number and 15.

MULTIPLE CHOICE

Choose the correct letter for each answer.

1. Find $50 \times 16 \times 2$.

   A. 116   **C.** 1,600

   B. 802   **D.** 16,000

2. Which is the most reasonable estimate for $29 \times 12 \times 6$?

   A. 6,000   **C.** 180

   B. 1,800   **D.** 47

3. Find 199×6.

   A. 644   **C.** 1,194

   B. 1,144   **D.** 1,564

4. Find 15×44.

   A. 660   **C.** 600

   B. 640   **D.** 440

5. Find 36×99.

   A. 3,334   **C.** 3,564

   B. 3,534   **D.** 3,600

6. Find 3.2×100.

   A. 32   **C.** 3,200

   B. 320   **D.** 32,000

7. Which is the most reasonable estimate for 3.29×7.8?

   A. 11   **C.** 24

   B. 21   **D.** 32

8. Find 54.5×8.

   A. 43.6   **C.** 436

   B. 402   **D.** 438

9. Find 0.7×0.2.

   A. 0.0014   **C.** 0.14

   B. 0.014   **D.** 1.4

10. Find 0.54×2.1.

   A. 0.1134   **C.** 11.34

   B. 1.134   **D.** 113.4

11. Which is an algebraic expression for 5 less than a number?

   A. $x + 5$ **C.** $5x$

   B. $5 - x$ **D.** $x - 5$

12. What is the rule for the table?

Input	Output
3	6
5	10
7	14
9	18

   A. Add 3

   B. Add 5

   C. Multiply by 2

   D. Multiply by 4

TEST TALK

Think It Through

- I need to **read the entire table before** deciding on a rule.
- I can **eliminate unreasonable answers.**

13. Elizabeth is choosing an outfit for a party. She has a black dress, a green dress, and a blue dress. She has black shoes and brown shoes. How many different combinations of dresses and shoes does Elizabeth have to choose from?

   A. 3 combinations

   B. 6 combinations

   C. 9 combinations

   D. 12 combinations

14. Which correctly uses the Distributive Property?

    A. $6 \times 98 = (6 \times 90) + (6 \times 8)$

    B. $6 \times 98 = (3 \times 2) + (90 \times 8)$

    C. $6 \times 98 = (6 \times 90) + 8$

    D. $6 \times 98 = 98 \times 6$

FREE RESPONSE

Estimate each product.

15. $31 \times 9 \times 8$

16. 63.5×5.2

Find each product using properties and mental math.

17. $20 \times 15 \times 5$

18. 47×101

19. $5.6 \times 1{,}000$

20. $18 \times 25 \times 4$

21. Rewrite the product with the decimal point in the correct place.

    $9.8 \times 15.5 = 15190$

Find each product. Tell which computation method you used.

22. 0×105

23. 48×62

24. 5.9×12

25. 0.23×10

26. 1.2×3.77

27. 0.9×0.7

Evaluate each expression for $d = 4$.

28. $5d$

29. $32 - d$

Solve each equation using mental math.

30. $k \div 5 = 20$

31. $12 + w = 19$

Write the rule for the table in words and with a variable.

32.

Input	Output
3	15
12	24
18	30
80	92

Writing in Math

33. Explain how to find 36.59×10 using mental math.

34. Make an organized list to solve this problem.

Jeffrey is taking a picture of his friends Bob, Stan, and Joseph. He wants them to stand in a line. How many different ways can the three friends stand in a line for the picture?

Think It Through
- I need to **make an organized list** that shows all the possible arrangements.
- I need to be able to **explain my thinking.**

35. A decade is 10 years. Which expression gives the number of years in d decades, $10 + d$, $10d$, or $d \div 10$. Explain your choice.

Number and Operation

MULTIPLE CHOICE

1. Which is the best estimate for 5,906 + 8,062?

   A. 13,000   **C.** 15,000

   B. 14,000   **D.** 16,000

2. Which represents two hundred thirty thousand, six hundred sixty and nine hundredths?

   A. 230.669   **C.** 230,660.9

   B. 230,660.99   **D.** 230,660.09

3. Which is the correct word form for 3,000,000,000?

   A. three thousand

   B. three million

   C. three billion

   D. three trillion

FREE RESPONSE

4.

Books for $2.24 each including tax.

How much will it cost to buy 6 books?

5. Estimate 2.6 × 15.1.

Writing in Math

6. Explain how to use the Distributive Property to find 8 × 63.

Geometry and Measurement

MULTIPLE CHOICE

7. Give the best name for a four-sided figure whose angles are all right angles and whose sides are the same length.

   A. parallelogram

   B. quadrilateral

   C. rectangle

   D. square

8. How many centimeters are in 5 meters?

   A. 500 cm

   B. 50 cm

   C. 0.5 cm

   D. 0.05 cm

FREE RESPONSE

Use the figure to answer 9–10.

9. What kind of angles are in the triangle at the right, acute or obtuse?

10. Are the lines at the right intersecting, parallel, or perpendicular?

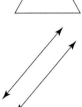

Writing in Math

11. Describe how to find the total number of cubes in the two layers.

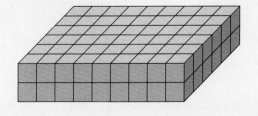

Data Analysis and Probability

MULTIPLE CHOICE

12. Which color is most likely if one square is pulled from the bowl?

   A. purple   **C.** orange

   B. blue   **D.** red

13. Which is most likely if you toss a number cube?

   A. the result is an even number

   B. the result is a number greater than 1

   C. the result is 3

   D. the result is 1

FREE RESPONSE

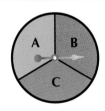

14. Imagine you spin each of the spinners above once. What are all the different combinations of numbers and letters you could spin?

Writing in Math

15. Is the spinner at the right fair? Explain why or why not.

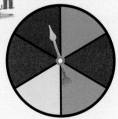

Algebra

MULTIPLE CHOICE

16. Which is an expression for "the product of a number and 8?"

   A. $8v$

   B. $8 + v$

   C. $8 \div v$

   D. $v - 8$

17. Which is a correct word phrase for $x - 2$?

   A. the sum of a number and 2

   B. two less than a number

   C. the product of a number and 2

   D. the quotient of a number and 2

18. What number is missing from the pattern?

     15, 30, 60, ___, 240

   A. 75   **C.** 120

   B. 100   **D.** 155

FREE RESPONSE

19. Solve the equation by using mental math.

$$\frac{b}{9} = 6$$

Writing in Math

20. William gave the following solution for $4x = 20$: $x = 4 \times 20$, so $x = 80$. Is his solution correct? If not, explain why not and give the correct solution.

Set 2-1 (pages 66–67)

Find $44 \times 20 \times 5$.

Use properties to help.

$(44 \times 20) \times 5 = 44 \times (20 \times 5)$ Associative Property

$= 44 \times 100$

$= 4,400$

Remember that when numbers are multiplied, the order of the factors will not change the product.

1. 70×20 **2.** 100×22

3. 25×30 **4.** 300×800

5. $4 \times 12 \times 5$ **6.** $20 \times 5 \times 8$

7. $2 \times 66 \times 50$ **8.** $25 \times 9 \times 4$

Set 2-2 (pages 68–69)

Estimate $48 \times 19 \times 5$.

$48 \times 19 \times 5$ Use rounding.

$50 \times 20 \times 5 = 1,000 \times 5$

$5 = 5,000$

So $48 \times 19 \times 5$ is about 5,000.

Remember that compatible numbers are numbers that are easy to compute in your head.

1. $97 \times 4 \times 18$ **2.** $26 \times 14 \times 6$

3. $12 \times 38 \times 11$ **4.** $7 \times 26 \times 5$

5. $16 \times 29 \times 40$ **6.** $28 \times 52 \times 10$

7. $3 \times 19 \times 78$ **8.** $62 \times 9 \times 5$

Set 2-3 (pages 70–71)

Find 5×79.

$5 \times 79 = 5 \times (80 - 1)$ Rename 79 as 80 − 1.

$= (5 \times 80) - (5 \times 1)$ Use the Distributive Property.

$= 400 - 5 = 395$

Remember that multiplying a sum or difference by a factor gives the same result as multiplying each number in the sum or difference by that factor and then finding the sum or difference.

1. 4×402 **2.** 5×230

3. 10×105 **4.** 30×48

5. 6×99 **6.** 5×28

7. 20×36 **8.** 205×9

Set 2-4 (pages 72–75)

Find 17×84.

Multiply by the ones.   Multiply by the tens.

$$\begin{array}{r} \overset{2}{8}4 \\ \times\ 17 \\ \hline 588 \end{array}$$

$$\begin{array}{r} \overset{2}{8}4 \\ \times\ 17 \\ \hline 588 \\ +\ 840 \\ \hline 1,428 \end{array}$$ Add partial products.

Remember to regroup if necessary.

1. 15×36 **2.** 14×88

3. 405×6 **4.** 3×625

5. 56×84 **6.** 51×28

7. 364×22 **8.** 45×712

Find 8 × 24. Tell which computation method you used.

8 × 24 =
8 × (20 + 4) =
(8 × 20) + (8 × 4) =
160 + 32 =
192

The numbers were easy to multiply in my head so I used **mental math.**

Remember that you can find the product of two numbers by using mental math, paper and pencil, or a calculator. Find each product. Tell what computation method you used.

1. 300 × 40

2. 195 × 0

3. 5 × 47

4. 11 × 11

5. 200 × 9

6. 50 × 55

7. 7 × 321

8. 1,221 × 1

Isabelle can pick one of 3 letters (A, B, or C) and one of 3 numbers (1, 2, or 3) to make labels consisting of one letter and one number. How many labels can she make?

Step 1 Identify the items to be combined.
Possible letters: A, B, C
Possible numbers: 1, 2, 3

Step 2 Choose one of the items. Find all the possible combinations keeping that item fixed.
A1, A2, A3

Step 3 Repeat Step 2 until all of the items have been combined.
A1, A2, A3, B1, B2, B3, C1, C2, C3

Remember to check that your answer makes sense.

1. Jennifer spins a spinner with four equal sections labeled 1, 2, 3, and 4, and tosses a penny. How many different combinations of numbers and heads or tails can she get?

2. Theresa's school serves cheese, turkey, and peanut butter sandwiches. Each sandwich comes with an apple or an orange. How many different combinations of sandwiches and fruits are there?

Find 9.25 × 100.

Use mental math.

9.25 × 100 = 9.25,   There are 2 zeros in 100.
                      Move the decimal point
9.25 × 100 = 925   2 places to the right.

Remember that when multiplying by 10, 100, or 1,000, the number of zeros tells you how far right to move the decimal point.

1. 2.25 × 10

2. 3.254 × 10

3. 41.6 × 100

4. 78.3 × 100

5. 100 × 5.95

6. 1,000 × 3.544

7. 1.9 × 1,000

8. 100 × 0.4

Set 2-8 (pages 86-87)

Estimate 6.1 × 9.8.

6.1 × 9.8   Use rounding.

↓   ↓

6 × 10 = 60, so 6.1 × 9.8 is about 60

Remember you can use rounding or compatible numbers to estimate products.

1. 8.5 × 7   **2.** 89 × 2.2

3. 1.9 × 7.3   **4.** 12.1 × 15

5. 99.6 × 1.5   **6.** 0.9 × 25

Set 2-9 (pages 88–91)

Jose bought 26 quarts of potting soil priced at $0.29 per quart. How much did he spend?

```
      26
   × 0.29 ◄────── 2 decimal places
     234
     520
    7.54 ◄────── 2 decimal places
```

José spent $7.54 on potting soil.

Remember to count the decimal places in both factors before placing the decimal point in the product.

1. 5.2 × 8   **2.** 19.5 × 2

3. 8.2 × 11   **4.** 10 × 5.411

5. 6.02 × 5   **6.** 48 × 6.3

7. 8.4 × 22   **8.** 0.15 × 17

Set 2-10 (pages 92–93)

Find 0.2 × 0.8 using a grid.

Look at where the grids overlap.

 × =

0.2 × 0.8 = 0.16

Remember that you can use a 10 × 10 grid to help you multiply.

1. 0.1 × 0.8   **2.** 0.5 × 0.5

3. 0.9 × 0.8   **4.** 0.7 × 0.4

5. 0.1 × 0.1   **6.** 0.3 × 0.5

7. 0.1 × 0.6   **8.** 0.2 × 0.2

Set 2-11 (pages 94–97)

Find 0.15 × 6.8.

```
      3
      4
   0.15 ◄─ 2 decimal places
   × 6.8 ◄─ 1 decimal place
    120
  + 900
  1.020 ◄─ 3 decimal places
```

Decimals are multiplied in the same way as whole numbers.

Remember to place the decimal point in the correct place in the product.

1. 5.6 × 0.8   **2.** 4.2 × 7.2

3. 2.5 × 0.34   **4.** 5.5 × 0.2

5. 2.1 × 8.5   **6.** 0.09 × 3.5

7. 4.02 × 1.8   **8.** 36.5 × 0.6

Find $b + 5$ for $b = 14$.

$b + 5 = 14 + 5$

Substitute the given value for the variable.

$= 19$

Remember that variables are letters that represent a number in an expression.

Evaluate for $n = 6$ and $n = 10$.

1. $15n$ **2.** $54 + n$

3. $\frac{n}{2}$ **4.** $85 - n$

5. $3.5 \times n$ **6.** $30 \div n$

Write the phrase, a number plus 55, as an algebraic expression.

A number plus 55

- Look for key words.
- Decide what operation is involved.
- Use a variable to represent the unknown number.

$y + 55$

Remember that there are several ways to describe the same expression.

1. 18 more than a number

2. a number minus 3

3. the product of 6 and a number

4. 25 less than a number

5. 45 times a number

6. the quotient of a number divided by 3

Find the rule. Write the rule in words.

Input	Output
4	12
5	15
6	18
7	21

Remember to look at all the pairs of numbers before deciding on a rule.

1.

Input	Output
8	17
11	20
65	74
180	189

2.

Input	Output
12	7
18	13
32	27
50	45

Because $4 \times 3 = 12$, $5 \times 3 = 15$, $6 \times 3 = 18$, and $7 \times 3 = 21$, the rule is "multiply by 3."

Solve $x + 8 = 17$ using mental math.

Ask: What number plus 8 equals 17?

Since $9 + 8 = 17$, x must equal 9.

Remember that you can solve many equations by using mental math.

1. $21 \div f = 7$ **2.** $5b = 5$

3. $24 - w = 12$ **4.** $r + 45 = 55$

Set 2-1 (pages 66–67)

Use patterns and properties to find each product mentally.

1. 20×40
2. 400×30
3. 600×100
4. 750×20

5. 80×70
6. 300×90
7. $4 \times 25 \times 10$
8. $3 \times 40 \times 5$

9. $2 \times 30 \times 25$
10. $25 \times 16 \times 4$
11. $20 \times 66 \times 50$
12. $20 \times 18 \times 5$

13. Josephine planted 50 tulips in each garden. How many tulips did she plant in 4 gardens?

Set 2-2 (pages 68–69)

Estimate each product.

1. $28 \times 31 \times 3$
2. $22 \times 4 \times 10$
3. $16 \times 22 \times 9$
4. $4 \times 26 \times 15$

5. $6 \times 21 \times 19$
6. $39 \times 95 \times 10$
7. $52 \times 8 \times 12$
8. $16 \times 8 \times 19$

9. $29 \times 21 \times 2$
10. $32 \times 21 \times 7$
11. $12 \times 72 \times 9$
12. $8 \times 19 \times 78$

13. Pencils come 20 to a package, 48 packages to a carton, and 12 cartons to a case. About how many pencils are in a case?

Set 2-3 (pages 70–71)

Use the Distributive Property to multiply mentally.

1. 5×66
2. 8×39
3. 9×31
4. 4×220

5. 99×16
6. 22×9
7. 30×62
8. 204×7

9. 306×8
10. 199×4
11. 398×2
12. 60×24

13. Each ticket to a concert costs $18. How much will 20 tickets cost?

Set 2-4 (pages 72–75)

Find each product.

1. 12×48
2. 26×33
3. 54×18
4. 15×35

5. 318×2
6. 6×258
7. 542×8
8. 987×2

9. 5×154
10. 614×54
11. 621×50
12. 374×14

13. Henry used 28 nails to make each bird house. How many nails did he use to make 12 bird houses?

14. Mr. Blecha drove 6 hours at an average speed of 62 miles per hour. How far did he drive?

Take It to the NET
More Practice
www.scottforesman.com

Set 2-5 (pages 76–77)

Find each product. Tell which computation method you used.

1. 20×500
2. 600×12
3. 14×14
4. 0×784
5. 321×10
6. 88×99
7. 612×19
8. 683×1
9. 111×50
10. 26×4
11. 362×50
12. 20×185

13. Sue Lin bought 5 shirts at $17 each, 2 pairs of jeans for $28 each, and a pair of sandals for $19. How much did she spend in all? Tell what computation method you used.

Set 2-6 (pages 80–81)

Make an organized list to solve. Write each answer in a complete sentence.

1. Julia has 35¢ in her wallet. There are no pennies. How many different combinations of coins are possible?

2. At a popular fast-food restaurant, each value meal comes with a main dish and a side dish. The main dishes are hamburger, cheeseburger, chicken sandwich, or veggie burger. The side dishes are french fries, baked potato, or salad. How many combinations of a main dish and a side dish are there?

Set 2-7 (pages 84–85)

Find each product.

1. 10×3.2
2. 100×82.35
3. 10×16.33
4. 10×87.4
5. 3.21×10
6. 100×6.3
7. 10×46.15
8. 54.211×10
9. 1.11×100
10. $5.6 \times 1,000$
11. 62.59×10
12. $1,000 \times 1.85$

13. A kilometer is 1,000 meters. How many meters are in 0.87 kilometer?

Set 2-8 (pages 86–87)

Estimate each product.

1. 19×5.8
2. 12.5×20
3. 3.01×14
4. 46.1×8
5. 31×3.55
6. 13.9×15
7. 99.8×19.5
8. 68.3×5.87
9. 16.2×50
10. 4.8×63.3
11. 0.99×15.5
12. 12.6×1.85

13. Maria bought 2.06 pounds of granola. The cost of granola is $3.99 per pound. About how much did Maria spend?

Set 2-9 (pages 88–91)

Find each product.

1. 16.8×6 2. 92.55×8 3. 12×6.25 4. 9×15.23

5. 4.68×5 6. 0.88×7 7. 48×1.9 8. 14.29×6

9. 76.1×15 10. 16.24×5 11. 2.8×59 12. 22×18.5

13. Yvette runs 6.62 miles per hour. How far will she travel in 4 hours?

Set 2-10 (pages 92–93)

Find each product. You can use 10×10 grids to help.

1. 0.4×0.6 2. 0.8×0.5 3. 0.1×0.5 4. 0.6×0.2

5. 0.3×0.3 6. 0.8×0.3 7. 0.7×0.5 8. 0.9×0.5

9. 0.8×0.7 10. 0.5×0.5 11. 0.1×0.9 12. 0.7×0.7

13. The track around Jeff's school is 0.5 kilometer long. Jeff has walked0.6 of the distance around it. How far has Jeff walked?

Set 2-11 (pages 94–97)

Find each product.

1. 2.3×1.8 2. 6.6×4.2 3. 0.14×0.5 4. 22.5×9.1

5. 6.3×4.8 6. 3.6×0.5 7. 17.9×0.1 8. 33.5×0.22

9. 1.48×0.2 10. 3.6×0.09 11. 5.5×1.9 12. 3.8×5.1

13. 2.9×4.6 14. 14.2×6.6 15. 1.6×0.49 16. 7.8×0.003

17. Turkey sells for $1.25 per pound. How much will a 10.6-pound turkey cost?

Set 2-12 (pages 100-103)

Evaluate each expression for $b = 5$ and $b = 8$.

1. $16 + b$ 2. $5b$ 3. $22 - b$ 4. $b + 18$

5. $40 \div b$ 6. $b \times 7$ 7. $88 + b$ 8. $b - 5$

9. $\dfrac{120}{b}$ 10. $b + 15$ 11. $100 - b$ 12. $20 \times b$

13. $0 \div b$ 14. $150 + b$ 15. $b - 0$ 16. $2b$

17. There are 16 ounces in a pound. Write an expression showing how many ounces there are in f pounds.

Take It to the NET
More Practice
www.scottforesman.com

Set 2-13 (pages 104–105)

Write each as an algebraic expression.

1. 26 more than a number

2. a number minus 2

3. the product of 5 and a number

4. the difference between a number and 8

5. 6 times a number

6. the quotient of a number divided by 3

7. 8 divided by a number

8. a number increased by 1,000

9. 15 less than a number

10. the sum of a number and 48

11. Elena is 4 years older than Juan. Use j for Juan's age.
Which expression below gives Elena's age?
$j - 4$　　　$4j$　　　$j + 4$

Set 2-14 (pages 106–107)

Write a rule for each table in words and with a variable.

1.

Input	Output
1	6
2	7
3	8
4	9

2.

Input	Output
1	3
2	6
3	9
4	12

3.

Input	Output
1	10
2	20
3	30
4	40

4.

Input	Output
4	2
7	5
10	8
30	28

5.

Input	Output
16	8
24	16
28	20
60	52

6.

Input	Output
5	50
8	80
20	200
100	1,000

7. Make an Input/Output table to represent the rule *Add 6*.

Set 2-15 (pages 108–109)

Solve each equation using mental math.

1. $16 + p = 21$

2. $9v = 45$

3. $60 - s = 40$

4. $f + 15 = 27$

5. $56 \div d = 8$

6. $11 \times b = 11$

7. $62 + w = 78$

8. $q - 14 = 30$

9. $48 - b = 2$

10. $5 \times e = 110$

11. $64 \div k = 8$

12. $9s = 72$

13. Marisa says the solution of $r - 15 = 30$ is $r = 15$. Is she correct?
If not, give the correct value of r.

CHAPTER 3

Dividing with One-Digit Divisors

DIAGNOSING READINESS

A Vocabulary
(Grade 4 and pages 66,104)

Choose the best term from the box.

1. In the number sentence $7 \times 8 = 56$, 7 is a __?__ and 56 is the __?__.

2. In the number sentence $18 \div 3 = 6$, 6 is called the __?__.

3. An arrangement of objects in rows and columns is called an __?__.

Vocabulary

- **array** *(Grade 4)*
- **product** *(p. 66)*
- **factor** *(p. 66)*
- **quotient** *(p.104)*

B Division Facts
(Grade 4)

4. $24 \div 6$ 5. $18 \div 9$ 6. $56 \div 8$

7. $72 \div 8$ 8. $35 \div 5$ 9. $20 \div 4$

10. $63 \div 7$ 11. $40 \div 8$ 12. $32 \div 4$

13. Draw an array to show 3 rows of 8 objects. Then circle groups of 4. How many groups of 4 are in the array? What division sentence is shown?

Do You Know...

How fast is the fastest steel-rail train?

You will find out in Lesson 3-16.

MACHINES *and* HOW THEY WORK

C Place Value

(pages 13–16)

Copy and complete with tens, hundreds, or thousands.

14. 1,700 is the same as 17 __?__.

15. 130 is the same as 13 __?__.

16. 350 is the same as 3 __?__ and 5 __?__.

17. 4,200 is the same as 4 __?__ and 2 __?__.

D Rounding

(pages 26–27)

Round each number to the place value of the underlined digit.

18. 6̲7   **19.** 4̲3   **20.** 1̲34

21. 7̲50   **22.** 9̲87   **23.** 1̲,323

24. 7̲,896   **25.** 1̲,500   **26.** 9̲,999

27. Write and explain how to round 378 to the hundreds place.

Key Idea
There are different kinds of division situations.

Vocabulary
• inverse operations

Think It Through
I can **draw a picture to show the problem.**

The Meaning of Division

LEARN

What are different kinds of division situations?

Division can be used to find how many are in each group when an amount is shared equally. This is called division as **sharing.**

Example A

A total of 24 students are being separated into 4 equal teams. How many students are on each team?

What You Show	What You Think	What You Write
X X X X X X X X X X X X X X X X X X X X X X X X	24 separated into 4 equal teams.	$24 \div 4 = 6$ Six students are on each team.

Another type of division situation is division as **repeated subtraction.**

Example B

Ally has 24 photos that she is putting into an album. Each page holds 4 photos. How many pages can she fill?

What You Show	What You Think	What You Write
X X X X → $24 - 4 = 20$ X X X X → $20 - 4 = 16$ X X X X → $16 - 4 = 12$ X X X X → $12 - 4 = 8$ X X X X → $8 - 4 = 4$ X X X X → $4 - 4 = 0$	How many times can I subtract 4 from 24 until nothing is left?	$\mathbf{24 \div 4 = 6}$ Ally can fill 6 pages with photos.

✔ Talk About It

1. In Example A, how many students are being split into equal groups? How many groups are there?

2. In Example A, if the students had been split into teams of 6, how many teams would there be?

3. In Example B, how many times did Ally subtract 4 photos from the 24 she had? How many were left?

How are multiplication and division related?

Multiplication and division are called **inverse operations** because division undoes multiplication, and multiplication undoes division. For example, since $2 \times 5 = 10$, you know $10 \div 2 = 5$ and $10 \div 5 = 2$. Also, since $54 \div 6 = 9$ and $54 \div 9 = 6$, then $9 \times 6 = 54$.

In some situations, you use division to find a **missing factor.**

Example C

A zoo has 24 penguins. There are 4 times as many penguins at the zoo as there are ostriches. How many ostriches are in the zoo?

Tim looks for the missing factor. He thinks "4 times what number equals 24?" or "$4 \times n = 24$."

What You Show	What You Think	What You Write
24 n | n | n | n	$4 \times n = 24$ $4 \times 6 = 24$	$24 \div 4 = 6$ There are 6 ostriches in the zoo.

✔ Talk About It

4. What is the missing factor in Example C?

5. Suppose a zoo with 24 penguins had 6 times as many penguins as ostriches. How many ostriches were in the zoo?

6. How are Examples A, B, and C alike? How are they different?

Draw a picture or use objects to show each division situation. Then find the quotient.

1. Juanita has a roll of 21 stamps. She removes 3 stamps at a time to put on envelopes that each require 3 stamps. How many envelopes can be stamped?

   Find $21 \div 3 = n$.

2. Arnold has 32 goldfish that he is putting into bowls with 8 fish in each bowl. How many bowls are needed?

   Find $32 \div 8 = n$.

3. In a pet store there are 5 times as many birds as there are dogs. If the store has 35 birds, how many dogs does the store have?

   Find $35 \div 5 = n$. HINT: Think $5 \times n = 35$.

4. **Reasoning** Which best describes division in Exercises 1–3, division as *sharing, repeated subtraction,* or *missing factor?*

PRACTICE

For more practice, see Set 3-1 on p. 196.

Ⓐ Skills and Understanding

Draw a picture or use objects to show each division situation. Then find the quotient.

5. In a hotel with 54 rooms there are 9 times as many rooms as there are floors. How many floors does the hotel have?

   Find $54 \div 9 = n$. HINT: Think $9 \times n = 54$.

6. How many teams of 4 can be formed if there are 28 students?

   Find $28 \div 4 = n$.

7. On a school bus filled with 40 students, 5 students get off at each stop. No one gets on. How many stops does the bus make until it is empty?

   Find $40 \div 5 = n$.

8. **Reasoning** Which best describes each situation in Exercises 5–7, division as *sharing, repeated subtraction,* or *missing factor?*

B Reasoning and Problem Solving

Name the operation needed to solve each problem. Then solve.

9. A sheet of stickers has 8 rows of stickers with 7 stickers in each row. How many stickers are there in all?

10. Thirty students are being placed in groups of 6. How many groups can be formed?

11. A bus has 18 passengers, but 6 passengers get off. How many passengers are left?

 Math and Social Studies

Team sports are played in countries all over the world.

12. For 50 students, which sport allows the greatest number of teams to be formed? How many complete teams could be formed?

13. If only 45 students are available, which sports would allow complete teams to be formed without any students left over?

14. <u>Writing in Math</u> Is the explanation below correct? If not, tell why and write a correct response.

> What is 15 ÷ 3?
> I know 15 - 3 = 12, 12 - 3 = 9, 9 - 3 = 6, 6 - 3 = 3, 3 - 3 = 0.
> I could subtract 3 from 15 for a total of 5 times until I have 0 left. So, 15 ÷ 3 = 5.

Sport	Team Size
baseball	9
basketball	5
football	11
cricket	11
soccer	11
rugby	15, 10, or 7

C Extensions

15. A coach wants to divide 16 players into two or more equal teams with 2 or more players. Describe each of the ways this could be done.

Mixed Review and Test Prep

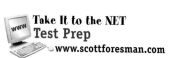
Take It to the NET
Test Prep
www.scottforesman.com

16. Algebra Solve $x + 14 = 23$ by using mental math.

17. Which rule describes the table at the right?

   A. Add 9.   **C.** Multiply by 9.

   B. Subtract 9.   **D.** Divide by 9.

Input	Output
11	2
37	28
40	31

Key Idea
Basic facts and place-value patterns can help you find quotients like 2,700 ÷ 9 easily.

Materials
• calculator

Think It Through
I can **look for a pattern** to find a rule.

Division Patterns

LEARN

Activity

What's the pattern?

a. Use a calculator to find each quotient. Look for patterns in the numbers of zeros.

$18 \div 3 = n$	$42 \div 6 = n$	$30 \div 5 = n$
$180 \div 3 = n$	$420 \div 6 = n$	$300 \div 5 = n$
$1{,}800 \div 3 = n$	$4{,}200 \div 6 = n$	$3{,}000 \div 5 = n$
$18{,}000 \div 3 = n$	$42{,}000 \div 6 = n$	$30{,}000 \div 5 = n$

b. Find each quotient without a calculator. Then check your answers with a calculator.

$81 \div 9$	$48 \div 8$	$50 \div 5$
$810 \div 9$	$480 \div 8$	$500 \div 5$
$8{,}100 \div 9$	$4{,}800 \div 8$	$5{,}000 \div 5$
$81{,}000 \div 9$	$48{,}000 \div 8$	$50{,}000 \div 5$

c. Describe the pattern that tells how to find each quotient mentally.

How can you divide mentally?

Example A

What is $2{,}800 \div 4$?

$28 \div 4 = 7$

So, $2{,}8\underline{00} \div 4 = 7\underline{00}$.

Example B

What is $40{,}000 \div 8$?

$40 \div 8 = 5$

So, $40{,}\underline{000} \div 8 = 5{,}\underline{000}$.

✔ Talk About It

1. How did patterns with zeros help you divide mentally in Examples A and B?

2. How could you have used multiplication to solve Examples A and B?

3. Find $420 \div 6$ and $63{,}000 \div 7$ mentally.

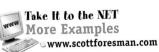

Take It to the NET
www **More Examples**
www.scottforesman.com

**CHECK** ✓

For another example, see Set 3-2 on p. 192.

Find each quotient. Use mental math.

1. $24 \div 3$ **2.** $240 \div 3$ **3.** $4{,}200 \div 7$ **4.** $49{,}000 \div 7$ **5.** $20{,}000 \div 4$

6. Number Sense How is dividing 320 by 4 similar to dividing 32 by 4?

PRACTICE

For more practice, see Set 3-2 on p. 196.

Ⓐ Skills and Understanding

Find each quotient. Use mental math.

7. $27 \div 3$ **8.** $270 \div 3$ **9.** $2{,}700 \div 3$ **10.** $27{,}000 \div 3$ **11.** $450 \div 5$

12. $54 \div 9$ **13.** $5{,}400 \div 9$ **14.** $720 \div 8$ **15.** $8{,}000 \div 8$ **16.** $2{,}500 \div 5$

17. $480 \div 6$ **18.** $2{,}100 \div 3$ **19.** $48{,}000 \div 8$ **20.** $63{,}000 \div 9$ **21.** $5{,}600 \div 7$

22. $560 \div 8$ **23.** $7{,}200 \div 9$ **24.** $32{,}000 \div 8$ **25.** $8{,}100 \div 9$ **26.** $64{,}000 \div 8$

27. Number Sense How is dividing 2,100 by 7 similar to dividing 21 by 7? How is dividing 2,100 by 7 similar to dividing 210 by 7?

Ⓑ Reasoning and Problem Solving

28. If a hiker covers 150 miles in 5 days and hikes the same distance each day, how many miles does the hiker cover each day?

Use mental math to answer the following questions. Refer to the Theater Design shown at the right.

29. How many seats are there per section?

30. How many seats are there per row?

31. Algebra If $n \times 300 = 18{,}000$, find n.

32. _Writing in Math_ Explain how you can determine mentally that $36{,}000 \div 9$ is equal to 4,000.

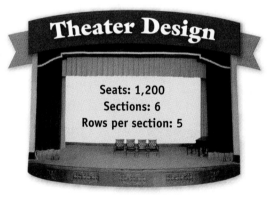

Theater Design

Seats: 1,200
Sections: 6
Rows per section: 5

🦉 Mixed Review and Test Prep

Take It to the NET
Test Prep
www.scottforesman.com

33. Algebra Solve the equation $x + 50 = 72$.

34. If 45 books are put on 9 shelves with an equal number on each shelf, how many books are on each shelf? Draw a picture or use objects to show the situation. Then solve.

35. A theater has 1,000 seats, but only 289 seats are filled. How many seats are empty?

     A. 1,289 seats   **B.** 889 seats   **C.** 811 seats   **D.** 711 seats

 All text pages available online and on CD-ROM.

Vocabulary
• compatible numbers (p. 22)
• rounding (p. 26)
• overestimate (p. 68)
• underestimate (p. 68)

TEST TALK

Think It Through
I only need an **estimate** since I need to find **about** how much.

Estimating Quotients

LEARN

Exact or Estimate?

Six friends collected a total of 262 used books for a book fair. Each collected about the same amount. About how many books did each collect?

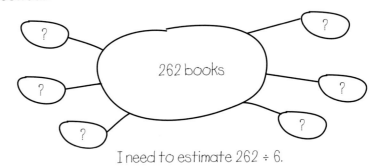

262 books

I need to estimate 262 ÷ 6.

What are some estimation techniques?

Example A

Estimate 262 ÷ 6.

Use rounding.	Use compatible numbers.	Use multiplication.
Round 262 to 300. $$300 \div 6 = 50$$ 50 books is an **overestimate** since 262 was rounded to 300.	Substitute 240 for 262 because 24 is a multiple of 6. $$240 \div 6 = 40$$ 40 books is an **underestimate** since 262 was changed to 240.	Think: 6 times what is about 262? $$6 \times 50 = 300$$ So a good estimate is a little less than 50 or about 45.

✓ **Talk About It**

1. What makes two numbers "compatible" and therefore easy to divide?

2. In the last method shown in Example A, how do you know the estimate should be less than 50?

3. If you wanted to estimate 262 ÷ 7, would it be better to use 210 ÷ 7 or 280 ÷ 7 as compatible numbers? Explain.

How can you estimate money amounts?

Example B

The cost of 8 used books is $26.95. About how much does each book cost?

Estimate $26.95 ÷ 8.

Use rounding.	Use compatible numbers.	Use multiplication.
$26.95 rounds to 30. 8 rounds to 10.	Adjust $26.95 to $24 since 24 is a multiple of 8.	8 times what is about 27?
30 ÷ 10 = 3	24 ÷ 8 = 3	8 × 3 is 24.
So a good estimate is $3 per book.	So a good estimate is $3 per book.	So a good estimate is a little more than $3 per book.

✔ Talk About It

4. How is estimating quotients with money amounts the same as estimating quotients with whole numbers? How is it different?

5. How do you know that $3 is an underestimate when you used 24 and 8 as compatible numbers?

6. Lou needs to save $289 in 4 months. She estimates by using 280 ÷ 4 = 70. If she saves $70 per month, will she have enough money? Is $70 an overestimate or an underestimate?

Example C

Is $38.95 ÷ 4 more or less than $10. How do you know?

Since $40 ÷ 4 = $10 and $38.95 < $40, you know that $38.95 ÷ 4 is less than $10.

CHECK ✔

For another example, see Set 3-3 on p. 192.

Estimate each quotient.

1. 157 ÷ 3   2. 735 ÷ 8   3. $41.90 ÷ 7   4. 20,963 ÷ 3   5. $83.72 ÷ 9

6. **Reasoning** If you estimate 269 ÷ 5 by using 300 ÷ 5 = 60, is 60 greater than or less than the exact answer? How did you decide? Is 60 an overestimate or an underestimate?

A Skills and Understanding

Estimate each quotient.

7. $638 \div 8$ **8.** $209 \div 4$ **9.** $759 \div 9$ **10.** $389 \div 6$ **11.** $539 \div 7$

12. $568 \div 6$ **13.** $460 \div 5$ **14.** $578 \div 8$ **15.** $271 \div 3$ **16.** $355 \div 5$

17. $\$19.80 \div 4$ **18.** $\$49.12 \div 8$ **19.** $\$67.50 \div 8$ **20.** $\$5.89 \div 6$

21. $\$24.95 \div 5$ **22.** $\$353.80 \div 8$ **23.** $\$309 \div 4$ **24.** $\$709.67 \div 8$

25. Reasoning If you use $\$72 \div 9$ to estimate $\$75.19 \div 9$, is $8 greater than or less than the exact answer? How did you decide?

26. Reasoning If you use $\$450 \div 5$ to estimate $\$445.99 \div 5$, is $90 greater than or less than the exact answer? How did you decide?

27. Number Sense Give two different sets of compatible numbers you can use to estimate the quotient of $375 \div 5$.

B Reasoning and Problem Solving

28. A waiter earned $4,730 in tips during 6 months. About how much did the waiter earn per month?

29. A group of seven friends plans to split a bill of $38.59. About how much does each owe? Is it better to overestimate or underestimate in this case?

Reasoning Which quotient is greater? Explain how you know.

30. $4,920 \div 4$ or $4,742 \div 4$ **31.** $2,802 \div 9$ or $2,802 \div 8$

Math and Social Studies

32. A relief agency sent the following items to a foreign country after an earthquake. Estimate the cost of each item.

Item	Number per carton	Cost per carton	Approximate cost per item
Shirts	8	$78.95	**a.**
Shorts	5	$36.75	**b.**
Socks	9	$28.50	**c.**
Sweaters	6	$52.99	**d.**

33. <u>Writing in Math</u> Is Jen's explanation below correct? If not, tell why and write a correct response.

> Explain how to estimate 634 ÷ 7.
>
> 634 ÷ 7 is between 630 ÷ 7 = 90 and 700 ÷ 7 = 100.
> I think the exact answer for 634 ÷ 7 is closer to 700 ÷ 7
> since 634 is greater than 600.

C Extensions

Number Sense In 34-36, use estimation to help you find two numbers whose quotient is between:

34. 80 and 100   **35.** 600 and 800   **36.** 2,000 and 3,000

Mixed Review and Test Prep

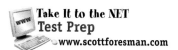

Take It to the NET
Test Prep
www.scottforesman.com

Find each quotient. Use mental math.

37. 630 ÷ 7   **38.** 28,000 ÷ 7   **39.** 60,000 ÷ 100   **40.** 4,200 ÷ 7

41. Find 0.7×0.9.

     A. 0.063   **B.** 0.63   **C.** 6.3   **D.** 63

Enrichment

Square Numbers and Triangular Numbers

Materials: 150 counters

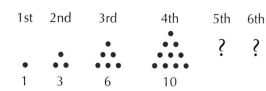

Square Numbers

1st	2nd	3rd	4th	5th	6th
1	4	9	16	?	?

Triangular Numbers

1st	2nd	3rd	4th	5th	6th
1	3	6	10	?	?

1. What are the next two square numbers and the next two triangular numbers? Use counters to help you decide.

2. Add any two adjoining triangular numbers. Is the number a square number? Try another pair and see if the same thing happens.

3. Use 150 counters. What is the largest square number you can form by using these counters? Name two triangular numbers having the same sum as the square number you formed.

Predict and Generalize

Predicting and generalizing when you read in math can help you use the **problem-solving strategy,** *Look for a Pattern,* in the next lesson.

In reading, predicting and generalizing can help you figure out what comes next in a story. In math, predicting and generalizing can help you figure out what comes next in a pattern.

First figure out how to get the second number from the first number.

Give the missing numbers. Describe the pattern.

2, 8, 32, 128, 512, ___, ___

$2 \times 4 = 8$ $8 \times 4 = 32$

Next figure out how to get the third number from the second number.

Multiply by 4 works for the first 3 numbers. Check the other numbers.

$32 \times 4 = 128$

$128 \times 4 = 512$

Generalize to describe the pattern: multiply by 4 to get the next number. Then predict the missing numbers:
$512 \times 4 = 2,048$
$2,048 \times 4 = 8,192$

1. Predict the eighth number in the pattern.

2. If the pattern stayed the same but the first number was 3, what would the fifth number be?

For 3–6, use the picture at the right.

3. Starting at the left, how can you get the number on the second flag from the number on the first flag?

4. How can you get the third flag from the second flag number?

5. **Writing in Math** Generalize by describing the pattern.

6. Predict the number that will be written on the fifth flag.

For 7–11, use the picture below.

7. Starting at the left, how can you get the second bird formation from the first?

8. How can you get the third formation from the second?

9. Generalize to describe the pattern.

10. Use dots for birds and draw the sixth bird formation.

11. **Writing in Math** Is there a pattern in the number of birds in each formation? If so, describe it.

For 12–16, use the table at the right.

12. In the top row of numbers, how can you get the third number from the first two numbers?

13. In the second row of numbers, how can you get the third number from the first two numbers?

14. Generalize to describe the pattern.

15. Predict the missing numbers.

16. **Writing in Math** How did you find the missing number in the last row?

First number	Second number	Third number
85	26	111
132	5	137
150	48	198
205	205	?
256	?	274

Problem-Solving Strategy

Key Idea
Learning how and when to look for a pattern can help you solve problems.

Think It Through
I can **predict and generalize** the pattern to find how many ties are needed for 6 steps.

Look for a Pattern

LEARN

What are the patterns?

Step Problem A landscaper is making a set of steps by using railroad ties. How many ties are needed for 6 steps?

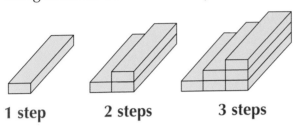

1 step   **2 steps**   **3 steps**

Read and Understand

What do you know?   There is 1 tie for 1 step, 3 ties for 2 steps, and 6 ties for 3 steps.

What are you trying to find?   Find the number of ties for 6 steps.

Plan and Solve

What strategy will you use?

Strategy: Look for a pattern

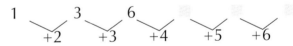

| 1 step | 2 steps | 3 steps | 4 steps | 5 steps | 6 steps |

1   3   6
   +2   +3   +4   +5   +6

For 4 steps, 10 ties are needed.
For 5 steps, 15 ties are needed.

Answer: For 6 steps, 21 ties are needed.

Look Back and Check

Is your answer reasonable?   The number of ties needed for 1, 2, 3, 4 and 5 steps was 1, 3, 6, 10, and 15 ties. So 21 ties is reasonable for 6 steps.

✔ Talk About It

1. How many ties would be needed for 7 steps?

2. What pattern do you notice in the following list: 1, 2, 4, 8, 16,...? What would the next three numbers be?

CHECK ✓

1. What are the missing numbers? Describe the pattern.

3, 103, 203, ___, ___, ___

2. What is the missing figure? What is the pattern?

1st 2nd 3rd   4th   5th

?

PRACTICE

For more practice, see Set 3-4 on p. 196.

Look for a pattern. Write the missing numbers or draw the missing figures.

3. 80, 70, 60, ___, ___, ___

4. 1, 2, 4, 7, 11, 16, ___, ___, ___

5. 1, 3, 9, 27, ___, ___, ___

6. 343, 443, 543, ___, ___, ___

7. 1st   2nd   3rd   4th   ?

8. 1st   2nd   3rd   4th   ?

9. 1st   2nd   3rd   4th   ?

10. 1st   2nd   3rd   4th   ?

11. 1st   2nd   3rd   4th   ?

12. 1st   2nd   3rd   4th

10:15   10:30   10:45   ?

Look for a pattern on each chart. Copy and write the missing numbers.

13.
4 ÷ 4 = 1
44 ÷ 4 = 11
444 ÷ 4 = 111
⋮
44,444 ÷ 4 = ?

14.
10 + 1 = 11
100 + 10 + 1 = 111
1,000 + 100 + 10 + 1 = 1,111
⋮
100,000 + 10,000 + 1,000 + 100 + 10 + 1 = ?

Each set of flash cards below has numbers that were developed by using a pattern. For each set of cards, name 3 other numbers that could be included. HINT: Think about multiplication facts.

15. (20) (16) (8)
(36) (24)

16. (27) (18) (54)
(72) (90)

17. **Writing in Math** The numbers below are called Fibonacci numbers.

1, 1, 2, 3, 5, 8, 13, 21, 34, 55,...

Explain how you could find the next two numbers in the series. HINT: Addition is useful in finding the pattern.

All text pages available online and on CD-ROM.

Do You Know How?

Do You Understand?

The Meaning of Division (3-1)

Draw picture to show each situation. Then find the quotient.

1. Eighteen people are waiting to enter a store, and only 6 people are allowed to enter at a time. How many groups will need to enter?

2. In an animal shelter, there are 4 times as many cats as dogs. If there are 36 cats, how many dogs are in the shelter?

A Show the picture you drew for each problem. How does it show the quotient?

B Is the division situation in each problem best described as *division as sharing, division as repeated subtraction,* or *division as a missing factor?*

Division Patterns (3-2)

Find each quotient mentally.

3. $800 \div 2$

4. $3{,}200 \div 4$

5. $3{,}600 \div 6$

6. $40{,}000 \div 5$

C Tell how you can find each quotient using mental math.

D How can you use $24 \div 6 = 4$ to find $2{,}400 \div 6$?

Estimating Quotients (3-3)

Estimate each quotient.

7. $368 \div 9$

8. $1{,}906 \div 4$

9. $\$50.85 \div 7$

10. $10{,}311 \div 5$

E Explain how you found each estimate.

F Tell if each estimate is an overestimate or an underestimate. Explain how you know.

Problem-Solving Strategy: Look for a Pattern (3-4)

Look for a pattern. Write the missing numbers or draw the missing figures.

11. 15, 26, 37, 48, ___, ___

12. ⇨, ⇦, ⇧, ⇩, ⇨, ___, ___

G Describe the pattern in Exercise 11.

H Describe the pattern in Exercise 12.

Think It Through
I should **reread the problem** to make sure I answered the question.

MULTIPLE CHOICE

1. A teacher separates 28 students into 4 equal groups to play a game. How many students are in each group? (3-1)

   A. 4 students **B.** 7 students **C.** 8 students **D.** 28 students

2. What are the next two numbers in the pattern? (3-4)

   $$1, 2, 4, 5, 7, 8, 10, \underline{\quad}, \underline{\quad}$$

   A. 10, 12 **B.** 11, 12 **C.** 11, 13 **D.** 12, 13

FREE RESPONSE

Find each quotient. Use mental math. (3-2)

3. $3,600 \div 4$ **4.** $250 \div 5$ **5.** $72,000 \div 9$

6. $56,000 \div 7$ **7.** $2,100 \div 3$ **8.** $54,000 \div 6$

Estimate each quotient. (3-3)

9. $38 \div 8$ **10.** $264 \div 6$ **11.** $5,000 \div 7$

12. $214 \div 4$ **13.** $\$79.25 \div 8$ **14.** $1,875 \div 5$

Use the table at the right for 15–16. (3-3)

15. About how many miles, on average, were traveled each day on the 4-day trip?

16. About how many miles, on average, were traveled each day on the 7-day trip?

Summer Trips	
Days in Trip	Miles Traveled
2	652
4	788
7	2,254
10	2,146

17. Look for a pattern in the products below. Then find the missing number. (3-4)

   $9 \times 9 = 81$ $9 \times 99 = 891$ $9 \times 999 = 8,991$ $9 \times 9,999 = 89,991$

   $9 \times 99,999 = \underline{\qquad}$

Writing in Math

18. Write and solve a word problem that could be solved using the number sentence $18 \div 3 = n$. (3-1)

19. Explain how patterns and basic facts are used to find $30,000 \div 5$. (3-2)

20. Estimate to decide if the quotient of $2,656 \div 3$ is greater than or less than 900. Tell how you decided. (3-3)

Key Idea
There is a way to record the steps in division that follows the process of sharing money.

Materials
• play money: $100, $10, and $1 bills or

 tools

TEST TALK

Think It Through
I can **use objects** or **make a model** to solve a problem.

Understanding Division

 **LEARN**

Activity

How can 4 people equally share $136?

Suppose 4 students earned $136 raking leaves and are paid with a $100 bill, three $10 bills, and six $1 bills. How can they divide the earnings so that each gets the same amount of money?

a. Use play money to represent $136. Start with one $100 bill, three $10 bills, and six $1 bills.

b. Share the money equally. Trade the $100 bill for ten $10 bills or ten $1 bills for one $10 bill as needed.

c. How much money did each get?

d. Use play money and sharing to find each amount.

- a $100 bill and six $10 bills shared by 5 people

- two $100 bills, six $10 bills, and one $1 bill shared by 3 people

- six $100 bills and three $10 bills shared by 6 people

- nine $100 bills and four $1 bills shared by 8 people

e. How could you check your answers in step **d** to be sure that the entire amount was shared equally?

How can you model and record division?

Suppose that 3 people need to share $423. Here's how you can model and record the process.

Example

What You **Show**	What You **Think**	What You **Write**
	Share the $100 bills. Each person gets one $100 bill.	$\begin{array}{r} 1 \\ 3\overline{)423} \end{array}$
	Three $100 bills have been shared.	$\longrightarrow \quad -3$
	One $100 bill is left.	$\longrightarrow \quad \overline{1}$
	Trade the $100 bill for ten $10 bills. Now there are twelve $10 bills. Share the $10 bills. Each person gets four $10 bills.	$\begin{array}{r} 14 \\ 3\overline{)423} \\ \underline{-3} \\ 12 \end{array}$
	3 x four $10 bills have been shared.	$\longrightarrow \quad -12$
	No $10 bills are left to be shared.	$\longrightarrow \quad \overline{0}$
	Share the $1 bills. Each person gets one $1 bill.	$\begin{array}{r} 141 \\ 3\overline{)423} \\ \underline{-3} \\ 12 \\ \underline{-12} \end{array}$
	Three $1 bills are left.	$\longrightarrow \quad 03$
	Three $1 bills have been shared.	$\longrightarrow \quad -3$
	No $1 bills are left.	$\longrightarrow \quad \overline{0}$

Each person gets one $100 bill, four $10 bills, and one $1 bill, or $141.

✓ Talk About It

1. Into how many equal groups did you divide the $423? Were any bills left over?

2. Why did you need to trade one of the $100 bills for ten $10 bills?

3. How could four $100 bills be shared equally by five people?

For another example, see Set 3-5 on p. 193.

1. Four people share $112 equally. The $100 bill is replaced with ten $10 bills.

    a. How many $10 bills are there after the $100 bill is replaced?
    b. How many $10 bills does each person get?
    c. How many $10 bills are left?

The remaining $10 bills are replaced by $1 bills.

    d. How many $1 bills does each person get?
    e. Is any money left?
    f. How much does each person get in all?
    g. Copy and complete the division shown at the right to show how to divide $112 by 4.

2. **Number Sense** Each of 5 servers got $38 after all the tips were shared equally. What was the total amount of tips?

For more practice, see Set 3-5 on p. 197.

Ⓐ Skills and Understanding

3. Six people share $354 equally. All $100 bills are replaced with $10 bills.

    a. How many $10 bills will there be?
    b. How many $10 bills does each person get?
    c. How many $10 bills are left?

The remaining $10 bills are replaced with $1 bills.

    d. How many $1 bills will there be?
    e. How many $1 bills does each person get?
    f. What is the total amount each gets.
    g. Copy and complete the division at the right to show how to divide $354 by 6.

$$6)\overline{3\ 5\ 4}$$

Copy and complete. You may use play money to help.

4. $4)\overline{1\ 8\ 4}$

5. $5)\overline{3\ 7\ 5}$

6. $6)\overline{7\ 8\ 6}$

7. $7)\overline{8\ 8\ 2}$

8. **Number Sense** Is it always necessary to replace one $100 bill with ten $10 bills (or a $10 bill with ten $1 bills) when you divide?

B Reasoning and Problem Solving

A treasure chest has three $100 bills, two $10 bills, and four $1 bills.

9. If two people divide the money evenly, how much will each get?

10. If three people divide the money evenly, how much will each get?

11. If four people divide the money, how much will each get?

Math and Art

Most major cities in America have an art museum. The admission prices vary. On an art tour, a group of 4 adults and 15 students visits each museum shown at the right. What is the group's total cost of admission at each museum?

12. Art Institute of Chicago

13. Los Angeles County Museum of Art

14. Miami Art Museum

15. How many adult tickets could be purchased for $280 at each museum?

16. **Writing in Math** Write a story problem involving division where the answer is $50.

Suggested Admission Prices		
	Adults	**Students**
Art Institute of Chicago	$10	$6
Los Angeles County Museum of Art	$7	$5
Miami Art Museum	$5	$2.50

C Extensions

17. Mrs. Blue has 3 children. Together she gives them one $1,000 bill, one $100 bill, and one $1 bill. She tells them they can share the money equally. How can do they do this? How much money will each get?

Mixed Review and Test Prep

Take It to the NET
Test Prep
www.scottforesman.com

18. What is the next number in the following set of numbers?

10   40   70   100   ?

19. Use mental math to find 27,000 ÷ 3.

A. 9 **B.** 90 **C.** 900 **D.** 9,000

Key Idea
To find quotients such as 768 ÷ 6, you can use a procedure involving estimation, multiplication, and subtraction.

Vocabulary
• dividend
• divisor
• quotient
• remainder
• inverse operations (p. 133)

Think It Through
• I can **draw a picture to show the main idea.**
• I can **divide to find a missing factor.**

Dividing Whole Numbers

LEARN

Why use division?

To raise money for a school trip, a fifth-grade class grew geraniums from seed. They now have a total of 768 plants that will be sold in baskets of 6 each. How many baskets are needed?

768 in all

6 plants in each basket

Don't know how many baskets. Let *n* be the number of baskets.

So 6 × n = 768. Find 768 ÷ 6.

What are the steps for dividing?

Example A

STEP 1

Estimate. Decide where to place the first digit in the quotient.

Use compatible numbers.
600 ÷ 6 = 100

The first digit goes in the hundreds place. Start by dividing hundreds.

STEP 2

Divide the hundreds. Multiply and subtract.

$$\begin{array}{r} 1 \\ 6\overline{)768} \\ -\,6 \\ \hline 1 \end{array}$$

Divide. 7 ÷ 6 = 1.

Multiply. 1 × 6 = 6
Subtract. 7 − 6 = 1
Compare. 1 < 6

STEP 3

Bring down the tens. Divide the tens. Multiply and subtract.

$$\begin{array}{r} 12 \\ 6\overline{)768} \\ -\,6\downarrow \\ \hline 16 \\ -\,12 \\ \hline 4 \end{array}$$

Divide. 16 ÷ 6 = 2
Multiply. 2 × 6 = 12
Subtract. 16 − 12 = 4
Compare. 4 < 6

STEP 4

Bring down the ones. Divide the ones. Multiply and subtract.

$$\begin{array}{r} 128 \\ 6\overline{)768} \\ -\,6| \\ \hline 16 \\ -\,12\downarrow \\ \hline 48 \\ -\,48 \\ \hline 0 \end{array}$$

Remember:
768 is the **dividend,**
6 is the **divisor,**
128 is the **quotient,**
0 is the **remainder.**

Divide. 48 ÷ 6 = 8
Multiply. 8 × 6 = 48
Subtract. 48 − 48 = 0
Compare. 0 < 6

So 128 baskets are needed for the geraniums.

Example B

Find $268 \div 7$.

STEP 1

Estimate. Decide where to place the first digit in the quotient.

Use compatible numbers.

$280 \div 7 = 40$

So the first digit is in the tens place.

STEP 2

Divide the tens. Multiply and subtract.

$$\begin{array}{r} 3 \\ 7\overline{)268} \\ -21 \\ \hline 5 \end{array}$$

Divide. $26 \div 7 = 3$

Multiply. $3 \times 7 = 21$

Subtract. $26 - 21 = 5$

Compare. $5 < 7$

STEP 3

Bring down the ones. Divide the ones. Multiply and subtract.

$$\begin{array}{r} 38 \text{ R2} \\ 7\overline{)268} \\ -21\downarrow \\ \hline 58 \\ -56 \\ \hline 2 \end{array}$$

Divide. $58 \div 7 = 8$

Multiply. $8 \times 7 = 56$

Subtract. $58 - 56 = 2$

Compare. $2 < 7$

Write the remainder in the quotient.

Example C

$$\begin{array}{r} 75 \text{ R4} \\ 5\overline{)379} \\ -35 \\ \hline 29 \\ -25 \\ \hline 4 \end{array}$$

Example D

$$\begin{array}{r} 93 \\ 9\overline{)837} \\ -81 \\ \hline 27 \\ -27 \\ \hline 0 \end{array}$$

Example E

$$\begin{array}{r} 145 \text{ R4} \\ 6\overline{)874} \\ -6 \\ \hline 27 \\ -24 \\ \hline 34 \\ -30 \\ \hline 4 \end{array}$$

✔ Talk About It

1. Why is the first digit of the quotient in the hundreds place for Example A, but in the tens place for Example B.

How can you check division?

To check division, you can use the idea that multiplication and division are **inverse operations**. Multiply the **quotient** by the **divisor**. Then add the **remainder**. The sum should equal the **dividend**.

The check for Example E is shown at the right.

$$\begin{array}{r} 145 \\ \times \quad 6 \\ \hline 870 \\ + \quad 4 \\ \hline 874 \end{array}$$

quotient
divisor

remainder
dividend

✔ Talk About It

2. Name the quotient, divisor, remainder, and dividend in Example C.

3. How could you check the answer for Example D?

CHECK ✓

For another example, see Set 3-6 on p. 193.

Divide. Check by multiplying.

1. 6)126   **2.** 5)755   **3.** 4)567   **4.** 8)278   **5.** 7)778

6. Number Sense When you divide 459 by 8, how does estimation tell you where to place the first digit in the quotient?

PRACTICE

For more practice, see Set 3-6 on p. 197.

Ⓐ Skills and Understanding

Divide. Check by multiplying.

7. 4)113   **8.** 5)724   **9.** 3)557   **10.** 8)219   **11.** 5)214

12. 5)427   **13.** 3)382   **14.** 8)341   **15.** 7)560   **16.** 9)781

17. 9)782   **18.** 6)428   **19.** 4)618   **20.** 7)321   **21.** 8)765

22. 495 ÷ 5   **23.** 353 ÷ 8   **24.** 309 ÷ 4   **25.** 709 ÷ 8

26. Number Sense How can you tell before you divide 387 by 4 that the first digit of the quotient is in the tens place?

Ⓑ Reasoning and Problem Solving

Math and Social Studies

A regular (non-leap) year has 365 days with 7 days per week. In some parts of the world, such as West Africa, a week does NOT have 7 days. It might have 3, 4, 5, 6, or 8 days and depends upon local customs. Find the number of complete weeks in 365 days for the following.

27. 3-day week   **28.** 4-day week   **29.** 5-day week   **30.** 6-day week

31. If you buy a television for $486, including tax, and are allowed to pay for it in 6 equal payments, how much will each payment be?

32. In 7 days, how many more hours does a koala sleep than a giraffe?

33. In 7 days, how many more hours does a chimpanzee sleep than a zebra?

34. Estimation In a year (365 days), about how many hours does a human sleep?

Data File

Average hours of sleep per day	
Animal	**Hours**
koala	22
chimpanzee	10
giraffe	4
human	7
zebra	3

35. <u>Writing in Math</u> **Correct or Incorrect** Is Jen's explanation below correct? If not, tell why.

> If you divide 428 by 7 and get 61 R1, how could you check your answer?
>
> I multiply the quotient by the divisor and add the remainder. The result should equal the dividend. Since 61 × 7 = 427 and 427 + 1 = 428, I know the answer is correct.

C Extensions

Complete each statement with *greater than, less than,* or *equal to.*

36. For multiplication,

    a. If both factors are greater than 1, the product is ___ either factor.

    b. If one factor is 1 and the other factor is greater than 1, the product is ___ the other factor.

37. For division,

    a. When the divisor is 1, the quotient is ___ the dividend.

    b. When the divisor is greater than 1, the quotient is ___ the dividend.

Mixed Review and Test Prep

Take It to the NET
Test Prep
www.scottforesman.com

38. Find 32,000 ÷ 4.

    A. 8   **B.** 80   **C.** 800   **D.** 8,000

39. <u>Writing in Math</u> Explain how two $100 bills, four $10 bills, and three $1 bills could be divided equally among 3 people.

Discover Math in Your World

Take It to the NET
Video and Activities
www.scottforesman.com

Steel Dragon

At its highest point, the Steel Dragon 2000 in Japan is 318 feet tall and 8,133 feet long.

1. What is the height and length of the Steel Dragon 2000 in yards?

2. A football field is about 100 yards long. About how many football fields tall and long is the Steel Dragon 2000?

Think It Through
Use these steps to divide: **divide, multiply, subtract, compare.**

Zeros in the Quotient

LEARN

When do you write a zero in the quotient?

One plane flew 919 miles in 3 hours. Another plane flew 520 miles in 4 hours. How far did each plane fly per hour?

		Example A	Example B
STEP 1	Estimate. Decide where to place the first digit in the quotient.	Find $919 \div 3$. $900 \div 3 = 300$. The first digit in the quotient is in the hundreds place.	Find $520 \div 4$. $400 \div 4 = 100$ The first digit in the quotient is in the hundreds place.
STEP 2	Divide the hundreds.	$\begin{array}{r} 3 \\ 3\overline{)919} \\ -9 \\ \hline 0 \end{array}$ $\begin{array}{l} 9 \div 3 = 3 \\ 3 \times 3 = 9 \\ 9 - 9 = 0 \\ 0 < 3 \end{array}$	$\begin{array}{r} 1 \\ 4\overline{)520} \\ -4 \\ \hline 1 \end{array}$ $\begin{array}{l} 5 \div 4 = 1 \\ 1 \times 4 = 4 \\ 5 - 4 = 1 \\ 1 < 4 \end{array}$
STEP 3	Bring down the tens. Divide the tens. Multiply and subtract.	$\begin{array}{r} 30 \\ 3\overline{)919} \\ -9\downarrow \\ \hline 01 \end{array}$ There is just 1 ten. You cannot divide tens. Write 0 in the tens place.	$\begin{array}{r} 13 \\ 4\overline{)520} \\ -4\downarrow \\ \hline 12 \\ -12 \\ \hline 0 \end{array}$ $\begin{array}{l} 12 \div 4 = 3 \\ 3 \times 4 = 12 \\ 12 - 12 = 0 \\ 0 < 4 \end{array}$
STEP 4	Bring down the ones. Divide the ones. Multiply and subtract.	$\begin{array}{r} 306 \text{ R1} \\ 3\overline{)919} \\ -9\downarrow \\ \hline 019 \\ -18 \\ \hline 1 \end{array}$ $\begin{array}{l} 19 \div 3 = 6 \\ 6 \times 3 = 18 \\ 19 - 18 = 1 \\ 1 < 3 \end{array}$	$\begin{array}{r} 130 \\ 4\overline{)520} \\ -4\downarrow \\ \hline 12 \\ -12\downarrow \\ \hline 00 \end{array}$ There are 0 ones. Write 0 in the ones place.

The first plane flew about 306 miles per hour, and the second plane flew 130 miles per hour.

✓ **Talk About It**

1. Why is the zero placed in the tens place of the quotient in Example A, but in the ones place in Example B?

2. How can you check your answers in both examples?

For another example, see Set 3-7 on p. 193.

Find each quotient. Check your answers by multiplying.

1. 520 ÷ 4   **2.** 271 ÷ 5   **3.** 808 ÷ 4   **4.** 905 ÷ 3

5. Number Sense How can you tell easily that 909 ÷ 9 could not be 11?

PRACTICE

For more practice, see Set 3-7 on p. 197.

Ⓐ Skills and Understanding

Find each quotient. Check your answers by multiplying.

6. 324 ÷ 3   **7.** 550 ÷ 5   **8.** 840 ÷ 6   **9.** 880 ÷ 4

10. 2)880   **11.** 3)323   **12.** 9)181   **13.** 3)724

14. 7)774   **15.** 5)540   **16.** 3)992   **17.** 4)839

18. Number Sense How can you tell that you have made a mistake if you find that 927 ÷ 3 = 39? What should the quotient be?

Ⓑ Reasoning and Problem Solving

19. Miguel earned $505 doing chores at $5 per hour. How many hours did Miguel work?

20. A factory sends a total of 921 cartons to 3 distribution centers. If each center receives the same number of cartons, how many cartons are sent to each center?

21. Each plane ticket for a family of 4 people costs $196. What is the cost of the 4 tickets?

22. Mackenzie won $1,000 on a quiz show. But she had to pay $280 in taxes. How much money did she have left?

23. **Writing in Math** Is 513 ÷ 5 a little less than 10, a little more than 10, a little less than 100, or a little more than 100? Explain.

Think It Through
My answer should be **brief but complete.**

👀 Mixed Review and Test Prep

Take It to the NET
Test Prep
www.scottforesman.com

Find each product.

24. 80 × 700   **25.** 34 × 9   **26.** 324 × 19

27. Give the next number in this pattern: 37, 49, 61, 73, …

     A. 83   **B.** 84   **C.** 85   **D.** 86

Key Idea
You can divide larger numbers using the same processes that you used with smaller numbers.

Dividing Larger Dividends

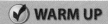
LEARN

How can you divide with larger numbers?

A town purchased 7 tons of salt for snow removal. The total cost was $4,382. What was the cost per ton?

Example A

Find 4,382 ÷ 7.

STEP 1
Estimate first.

Use compatible numbers.

4,200 ÷ 7 = 600.

The first digit will be in the hundreds place.

STEP 2
Divide the hundreds. Multiply and subtract.

$$\begin{array}{r} 6 \\ 7\overline{)4,382} \\ -4\ 2 \\ \hline 1 \end{array}$$

STEP 3
Bring down the tens. Divide the tens. Multiply and subtract.

$$\begin{array}{r} 62 \\ 7\overline{)4,382} \\ -4\ 2 \\ \hline 18 \\ -14 \\ \hline 4 \end{array}$$

STEP 4
Bring down the ones. Divide the ones. Multiply and subtract.

$$\begin{array}{r} 626 \\ 7\overline{)4,382} \\ -4\ 2 \\ \hline 18 \\ -14 \\ \hline 42 \\ -42 \\ \hline 0 \end{array}$$

STEP 5
Check by multiplying.

$$\begin{array}{r} 626 \\ \times\ \ \ 7 \\ \hline 4,382 \end{array}$$

The cost per ton was $626.

Example B

$$\begin{array}{r} 2,041\ R2 \\ 3\overline{)6,125} \\ -6 \\ \hline 0\ 12 \\ -12 \\ \hline 05 \\ -3 \\ \hline 2 \end{array}$$

Check:
$$\begin{array}{r} 2,041 \\ \times\ \ \ 3 \\ \hline 6,123 \\ +\ \ \ 2 \\ \hline 6,125 \end{array}$$

Example C

$$\begin{array}{r} 1,280\ R3 \\ 4\overline{)5,123} \\ -4 \\ \hline 1\ 1 \\ -8 \\ \hline 32 \\ -32 \\ \hline 03 \end{array}$$

Check:
$$\begin{array}{r} 1,280 \\ \times\ \ \ 4 \\ \hline 5,120 \\ +\ \ \ 3 \\ \hline 5,123 \end{array}$$

✔ Talk About It

1. Why is a zero needed in the quotients for Examples B and C, but not in Example A?

Take It to the NET
More Examples
www.scottforesman.com

For another example, see Set 3-8 on p. 193.

Divide. Check by multiplying.

1. $4\overline{)2,354}$ **2.** $6\overline{)5,765}$ **3.** $7\overline{)8,123}$ **4.** $5\overline{)8,987}$

5. Number Sense Explain how you know that the answer to $4,933 \div 5$ must be less than 1,000.

For more practice, see Set 3-8 on p. 197.

Ⓐ Skills and Understanding

6. $6\overline{)1,357}$ **7.** $9\overline{)4,576}$ **8.** $2\overline{)8,444}$ **9.** $6\overline{)5,910}$

10. $2\overline{)7,567}$ **11.** $3\overline{)8,887}$ **12.** $5\overline{)1,002}$ **13.** $6\overline{)7,025}$

14. $2,010 \div 2$ **15.** $8,401 \div 4$ **16.** $1,198 \div 8$ **17.** $3,026 \div 3$

18. Number Sense Explain how you know that the answer to $5,831 \div 5$ must be greater than 1,000.

Ⓑ Reasoning and Problem Solving

19. Delmain's dad has a collection of 1,840 CDs. If he stores them in 8 boxes and has the same number in each box, how many CDs are in each box?

20. Estimation There are 7 days in a week. About how many weeks are in 495 days? 3,040 days?

21. Estimation There are approximately 4 weeks in a month. About how many months are 284 weeks?

22. Zachary plans to buy a hang glider costing $3,475. He now has $250. How much does he need to save each month during the next 5 months to have enough money?

23. 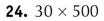 **Writing in Math** Is $1,473 \div 5$ a little less than 30, a little more than 30, a little less than 300, or a little more than 300? Explain your thinking.

🦉 Mixed Review and Test Prep

Take It to the NET
Test Prep
www.scottforesman.com

24. 30×500 **25.** 3.8×9 **26.** 0.3×0.4 **27.** 0.03×0.04

28. Find $324 \div 3$.

     A. 18   **B.** 108   **C.** 180   **D.** 1,080

Think It Through
I can choose
division when I
need to split an
amount into
equal parts.

Dividing Money

LEARN

How can you divide money?

Which is the better buy, a 9-pound package
of trail mix for $19.53, or a 7-pound
package for $15.89?

You can divide to find the price per pound of each package.
Extend the process of dividing whole numbers to dividing money.

Example

Divide $19.53 by 9.

STEP 1	STEP 2	STEP 3	STEP 4	STEP 5
Estimate.	Place the decimal point in the quotient.	Divide the ones.	Bring down the tenths. Divide the tenths. Multiply and subtract.	Bring down the hundredths. Divide the hundredths. Multiply and subtract.
Use compatible numbers.				

Step 1:
$20 ÷ 10 = $2

The first digit
in the quotient
is the ones
digit.

Step 2:
$$9\overline{)\$19.53}$$
with decimal point

Step 3:
$$\begin{array}{r} 2. \\ 9\overline{)\$19.53} \\ -18 \\ \hline 1 \end{array}$$

Step 4:
$$\begin{array}{r} 2.1 \\ 9\overline{)\$19.53} \\ -18 \\ \hline 15 \\ -9 \\ \hline 6 \end{array}$$

Step 5:
$$\begin{array}{r} \$2.17 \\ 9\overline{)\$19.53} \\ -18 \\ \hline 15 \\ -9 \\ \hline 63 \\ -63 \\ \hline 0 \end{array}$$

The cost of the 9-pound package is $2.17 per pound.

✔ Talk About It

1. How could you check your answer?

2. How could you find the price per pound of the 7-pound package?
   What is the price per pound? Which package is the better buy?

CHECK ✔

For another example, see Set 3-9 on p. 194.

Find the quotient. Check your answers by multiplying.

1. $4.92 ÷ 2   2. $36.15 ÷ 5   3. $84.12 ÷ 6

4. **Number Sense** How can you use estimation to tell that
   $29.50 ÷ 5 could not be $59?

For more practice, see Set 3-9 on p. 198.

Ⓐ Skills and Understanding

Find the quotient. Check your answers by multiplying.

5. $3.62 ÷ 2   **6.** $26.15 ÷ 5   **7.** $44.10 ÷ 3   **8.** $37.45 ÷ 7

9. 3)$9.63   **10.** 5)$65.00   **11.** 9)$16.74   **12.** 4)$30.00

13. 6)$89.52   **14.** 3)$59.58   **15.** 7)$138.81   **16.** 5)$172.55

17. Number Sense How can you use estimation to tell that $51.20 ÷ 8 could not be $64?

Ⓑ Reasoning and Problem Solving

18. Three friends attended a ballgame. Besides the ticket cost, they spent $17.85 more for food. If they split the total cost of the tickets and food equally, how much did each pay?

Admit One
$9.25

19. One brand of socks is on sale at 3 pairs for $5.97. Another brand is on sale at 5 pairs for $9.75. Which is the better buy?

20. In *Rachel Field's Hitty: Her First Hundred Years,* Hitty has an adventure in a "Shop of Dreams." There is a train with a price tag of $75. The shopkeeper had paid $5 for the train. The asking price is how many times as much as the amount the shopkeeper had paid?

21. Number Sense Is the quotient of $85.50 divided by 4 about $0.20, $2.00 or $20? Explain how you know.

22. <u>Writing in Math</u> Explain to a friend in a paragraph how you could divide $35.80 by 5.

🦉 Mixed Review and Test Prep

Take It to the NET
Test Prep
www.scottforesman.com

23. How many groups of 5 stamps could you remove from a sheet of 35 stamps? Draw a picture to show this division situation. Then find the quotient.

Find each product. Use mental math.

24. 7.89 × 100   **25.** 1,000 × 3.9   **26.** 50 × 73 × 2   **27.** 700 × 90

28. Find 306 ÷ 3.

   A. $1.20   **B.** 12   **C.** 102   **D.** 120

All text pages available online and on CD-ROM.

Think It Through
I can **use divisibility rules** to help find factors of a number quickly.

Factors and Divisibility

LEARN

How can you find all the factors of a number?

A circle has 360°, and 360 is the smallest number that can be divided by 2, 3, 4, 5, 6, 8, 9, 10, 12, 15 and 18 without a remainder!

A number is **divisible** by another when the quotient is a whole number and the remainder is 0. So 360 is divisible by 2, 3, 4, 5, 6, 8, 9, 10, 12, 15 and 18. Each of these numbers is called a **factor** of 360.

A number is divisible by

2 →	If the number is even.
3 →	If the sum of the digits of the number is divisible by 3.
4 →	If the last two digits are divisible by 4.
5 →	If the last digit is 0 or 5.
6 →	If the number is divisible by BOTH 2 and 3.
9 →	If the sum of the digits is divisible by 9.
10 →	If the last digit 0.

You can use the **divisibility rules** above to help find factors of a number. When you know one factor of a certain number, you can divide the number by the known factor to find another factor. The two factors are called a **factor pair**.

Example

Find all the factors of 72.

Try:	Is it a factor?	Factor pair
1	Yes; 1 is a factor of every whole number.	1 and 72
2	Yes; 72 is even.	2 and 36
3	Yes; 7 + 2 = 9, and 9 is divisible by 3.	3 and 24
4	Yes; 72 is divisible by 4.	4 and 18
5	No	
6	Yes; 72 is divisible by both 2 and 3.	6 and 12
7	No	
8	Yes; 72 is divisible by 8.	8 and 9

Notice that numbers greater than 8 were not tested because after 8 the factor pairs begin to repeat.

Talk About It

1. Why is it helpful to know the divisibility rules?

2. From the example above, what are all the factors of 72? How do you know that these are all the factors?

For another example, see Set 3-10 on p. 194.

1. Is 165 divisible by 5? How do you know?

Find all the factors of each number.

2. 18   **3.** 25   **4.** 20   **5.** 36   **6.** 42

7. Number Sense What factor pair does every number have?

PRACTICE

For more practice, see Set 3-10 on p. 198.

Ⓐ Skills and Understanding

8. Is 112 divisible by 4? How do you know?

Find all the factors of each number.

9. 28   **10.** 35   **11.** 29   **12.** 26   **13.** 50

14. 55   **15.** 60   **16.** 63   **17.** 56   **18.** 85

19. Number Sense Mary said that 6 is a factor of 106. Is she correct? Explain.

Ⓑ Reasoning and Problem Solving

20. A marching band in one school has 40 members. They can march single file, in rows of 2, or in any other arrangement in which all the rows have the same number of people. (This includes one row of 40.) How many different marching arrangements are possible for the band?

21. Reasoning Are all numbers that are divisible by 9 also divisible by 3? Are all numbers that are divisible by 3 also divisible by 9? How do you know?

22. **Writing in Math** Explain how to find all the factor pairs of 30.

 **Mixed Review and Test Prep**

Take It to the NET
Test Prep
www.scottforesman.com

23. Find $15.25 ÷ 5. Check your answer by multiplying.

24. A group of 8 cousins attended a movie. Their grandmother gave them $100 to spend in all. Each cousin spent $4 on refreshments and $6 on a ticket. There were 240 people at the movie. How much money was left over from the $100?

    A. $20   **B.** $48   **C.** $52   **D.** $80

25. Algebra Evaluate the expression $n + 6$ for $n = 25$.

    A. 19   **B.** 31   **C.** 150   **D.** 256

Think It Through
I can **use logical reasoning** to determine if a number is prime or composite.

Prime and Composite Numbers

LEARN

How can you tell if a number is prime or composite?

Numbers such as 2, 3, 5, 7, and 11 have a special property that many numbers do not have. Mathematicians call these numbers **prime numbers.** A prime number has exactly two different factors, itself and 1.

A whole number greater than 1 that has more than two factors is called a **composite number.**

5 is an example of a prime number. It has only two factors, 1 and 5. It has only one **rectangular array.**

$1 \times 5 = 5$

6 is an example of a composite number. Its factors are 1, 2, 3, and 6. It has more than one rectangular array.

$1 \times 6 = 6$

$2 \times 3 = 6$

To determine if a number is prime or composite, you can use divisibility rules to help you test possible factors.

Example A	Example B
Is 141 prime or composite?	Is 84 prime or composite?
141 is NOT divisible by 2 because it is odd.	84 is divisible by 2 because it is even.
141 is divisible by 3 because $1 + 4 + 1 = 6$ and 6 is divisible by 3.	So, 84 is composite.
So, 141 is composite.	

✓ **Talk About It**

1. How is a prime number such as 17 different from the numbers in Example A and B?

How can you write a number as a product of prime factors?

Every composite number can be written as a product of prime factors. This product is called the **prime factorization** of a number. You can use a "factor tree" to find a prime factorization.

TEST TALK

Think It Through
I can **use divisibility rules** to help find factors of a number.

Example C

Write 18 as a product of prime factors.

First write 18 as a product of two factors. This can be done in more than one way. Then write each factor that is not prime as a product. Continue until all branches end in prime numbers.

One Way

18
/ \
2 × 9
/ \
2 × 3 × 3

So, 18 = 2 × 3 × 3.

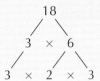

Another Way

18
/ \
3 × 6
/ \
3 × 2 × 3

Remember that by the Commutative Property,
2 × 3 × 3 = 3 × 2 × 3.

✔ Talk About It

2. In the first factor tree for 18, why was the 2 written in the last row, but the 9 was not?

3. Do the first two factors you select for a number in a factor tree, such as 2 and 9, change the final result? Explain.

4. If the last row in a factor tree is 2 × 3 × 10, how do you know the factor tree is not complete?

Take It to the NET
More Examples
www.scottforesman.com

CHECK ✓

For another example, see Set 3-11 on p. 194.

Write whether each number is prime or composite.

1. 13 **2.** 54 **3.** 23 **4.** 675 **5.** 41

Use factor trees to find the prime factorization of each number.

6. 15 **7.** 22 **8.** 28 **9.** 36 **10.** 40

11. Number Sense It is not always easy to tell if a number is prime. But some numbers are easily seen to be composite. How do you immediately know that 12,345,755 is composite?

Ⓐ Skills and Understanding

Write whether each number is prime or composite.

12. 19 **13.** 75 **14.** 26 **15.** 57 **16.** 83

17. 31 **18.** 51 **19.** 70 **20.** 603 **21.** 1,024

Use factor trees to find the prime factorization of each number.

22. 21 **23.** 42 **24.** 66 **25.** 45 **26.** 32

27. Number Sense The prime factorization of a number is $2 \times 3 \times 5$. What is the number?

Ⓑ Reasoning and Problem Solving

Math and Social Studies

Eratosthenes was born in Cyrene (in what is now Libya) about 230 B.C. He developed the following method for determining if a number is prime. It is called the Sieve of Eratosthenes because it "strains out" prime numbers from other numbers.

28. Use a hundred chart. Find all the prime numbers between 1 and 100.

    a. Cross out 1. It has only 1 factor.

    b. Circle 2, the least prime number. Cross out every *second* number after 2.

    c. Circle 3, the next prime number. Cross out every *third* number after 3 (even if it has already been crossed out).

    d. Circle 5, and repeat the process.

    e. Circle 7, and repeat the process.

    f. List all the circled numbers. There should be 25.

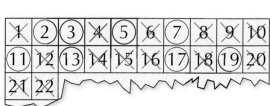

29. <u>**Writing in Math**</u> Joe has solved the problem below. Is he correct? If not, tell why and write a correct explanation.

> Is every even number greater than 2 a composite number? Explain.
>
> *Yes; Any even number greater than 2 will have 2 as a factor. So the number will be composite.*

C Extensions

An exponent shows repeated multiplication of the same factor.

$$5 \times 5 \times 5 = 5^3$$ The 3 means 5 is used as a factor 3 times.

Exponents are useful in expressing the prime factorization of a number.

$$24 = 2 \times 2 \times 2 \times 3 = 2^3 \times 3 \qquad\qquad 100 = 2 \times 2 \times 5 \times 5 = 2^2 \times 5^2$$

Write the prime factorization of each number. Use exponents when possible.

30. 45   **31.** 28   **32.** 200   **33.** 162   **34.** 250

Mixed Review and Test Prep

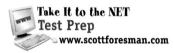

Take It to the NET
Test Prep
www.scottforesman.com

Compare. Write >, <, or = for each ●.

35. 0.3 ● 0.4   **36.** 1.9 ● 1.09   **37.** 2.5 ● 2.50

Find all the factors of each number.

38. 25   **39.** 11   **40.** 34   **41.** 50   **42.** 62

43. What is the product of 0.4 and 0.12?

   A. 0.048   **B.** 0.16   **C.** 0.48   **D.** 0.52

Learning with Technology

What is a square root?

To find the area of a square, you *square* the length of the side. That is, you multiply the length by itself. If the side is *s*, the area is $s \times s$ or s^2.

To find the length of the side of a square when you know the area, you find the **square root** of the area. Finding a **square root** is the inverse operation of squaring. The symbol used for square root is $\sqrt{}$.

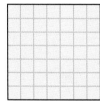

Area $= 5 \times 5 = 5^2 = 25$
So, $\sqrt{25} = 5$.

Area $= 7 \times 7 = 7^2 = 49$.
So, $\sqrt{49} = 7$

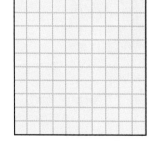

Area $= 10 \times 10 = 10^2 = 100$
So, $\sqrt{100} = 10$

Most calculators have a square root key such as ▨ . To find a square root, press the number followed by ▨ . Use a calculator to find each square root.

   1. $\sqrt{81}$ **2.** $\sqrt{121}$ **3.** $\sqrt{64}$ **4.** $\sqrt{144}$ **5.** $\sqrt{256}$ **6.** $\sqrt{400}$

Problem-Solving Skill

Reading Helps!

Creating graphic organizers **can help you with...** interpreting remainders.

Key Idea
The real-world situation tells how to interpret the remainder.

Interpreting Remainders

LEARN

How do you interpret a remainder in a division problem?

TEST TALK

Think It Through
Once I **identify the main idea** in each question, I can interpret the remainder in order to answer each question.

When you solve a story problem using division, the real-world situation tells how to make sense of the remainder.

Lunchroom Problem There are 135 fifth-grade students in a certain school. Each table in the lunchroom seats six students.

Question 1	Question 2	Question 3
Read and Understand		
How many tables are needed to seat all fifth graders?	How many tables will be filled?	How many students will be at the table that is not filled?
Plan and Solve		
$135 \div 6 = 22$ R3 23 tables are needed.	$135 \div 6 = 22$ R3 22 tables will be filled.	$135 \div 6 = 22$ R3 Three students will be at a table that is not filled.
Look Back and Check		
One more table is needed for the 3 extra students So, $22 + 1 = 23$ tables are needed.	22 tables will have six students. One will have less than six.	The remainder of 3 tells us there are 3 extra students.

✔ **Talk About It**

1. What is the answer to each of the three questions above?

2. **Reasoning** How many students will be seated in all at the full tables? Tell how you know.

CHECK ✓

For another example, see Set 3-12 on p. 194.

1. A wood carver has made 179 carved animals that will be shipped in boxes that hold 8 animals.
   a. How many boxes can be completely filled?
   b. How many animals are left over?

PRACTICE

For more practice, see Set 3-12 on p. 198.

2. Sarah's video collection is stored in a cabinet that holds 6 videos on each shelf. She has 89 videos in her collection.
   a. How many shelves can be completely filled?
   b. How many shelves are needed in all?

For a school play, tickets are sold for three different prices as shown in the sign at the right.

Ticket Costs	
Students (12 or under)	$4
Students (13 through 21)	$6
Adults (over 21)	$8

3. A group of 11-year-old friends have pooled their money to buy tickets to the play. They have $50.
   a. How many tickets can they buy?
   b. How much money is left over?

4. A group of 86 adults and students plan to travel to the play in vans that hold 8 people.
   a. How many vans could be completely filled?
   b. How many vans are needed in all? How many empty seats will there be in the van that is not filled?

5. **Reasonableness** Suppose a total of $784 was collected for tickets. Is 300 a reasonable estimate for the number of tickets sold? Explain.

6. What is the maximum number of tickets that could have been sold? What is the minimum number of tickets that could have been sold? Explain.

7. At the play, a total of $568 is collected from adults. How many adult tickets were sold?

8. A total of $494 was collected from student tickets. A total of 57 tickets were sold to students ages 13 through 21. How many tickets were sold to students 12 or under?

9. **Writing in Math** Suppose three friends want to share equally the cost of a large pizza and large bottle of soda. How much would each pay? Explain.

	Pizza	Soda
Small	$8.25	$1.25
Medium	$10.50	$2.25
Large	$14.75	$3.50

Do You Know How?

Do You Understand?

Understanding Division (3-5)

Tell how much each person will get.

1. 3 people share $372 equally

2. 4 people share $324 equally

Ⓐ For each exercise, tell what bills each person will get.

Ⓑ Explain how you could regroup the bills in Exercise 1, if you began with three $100 bills, seven $10 bills, and two $1.

Dividing Whole Numbers (3-6)
Problem-Solving Skill: Interpreting Remainders (3-12)

3. 4)564   **4.** 7)481

5. In the cafeteria, each table seats 6 people. There are 87 people that need to be seated. How many tables must be set up?

Ⓒ Tell how you found each quotient in Exercises 3 and 4.

Ⓓ In Exercise 5, how does the remainder affect your answer?

Zeros in the Quotient (3-7)
Dividing Larger Dividends (3-8)
Dividing Money (3-9)

Find each quotient. Check your answers by multiplying.

6. 621 ÷ 3   **7.** $7.08 ÷ 6

8. 1,239 ÷ 4   **9.** 5,659 ÷ 2

10. 5)4,720   **11.** 7)$59.99

Ⓔ In Exercise 9, identify the quotient, dividend, divisor, and remainder.

Ⓕ Explain how you checked each quotient.

Factors and Divisibility (3-10)
Prime and Composite Numbers (3-11)

List all the factors of each number. Tell if it is prime or composite.

12. 45   **13.** 64   **14.** 19

Ⓖ Can a whole number be prime if it has a ones digit of 0? Tell why or why not.

MULTIPLE CHOICE

1. What is the quotient of 232 ÷ 8? (3-6)

    A. 2 R9   **B.** 19   **C.** 28   **D.** 29

2. What is the quotient of 3,048 ÷ 6? (3-7)

    A. 58   **B.** 507 R5   **C.** 508   **D.** 509

FREE RESPONSE

Find each quotient. Check your answers by multiplying.
(3-6, 3-7, 3-8, 3-9)

3. 783 ÷ 9   **4.** 392 ÷ 7   **5.** $5.60 ÷ 2

6. $8\overline{)5,656}$ **7.** $4\overline{)1,992}$ **8.** $5\overline{)3,533}$

9. $6\overline{)290}$ **10.** $9\overline{)\$3.06}$ **11.** $8\overline{)\$91.36}$

Find all the factors of each number. Tell whether each number is prime or composite. (3-10, 3-11)

12. 10   **13.** 48   **14.** 17   **15.** 40   **16.** 53

For 17–18, use the information at the right. (3-12)

17. How many vans are needed to transport everyone to the train at the same time? Explain your answer.

18. If one adult is willing to drive 4 students, will the number of vans needed change? Explain.

> **Getting to the Train**
> Ten adults and 100 students plan to take the train to a nearby city. To transport everyone to the train, the school will use vans that carry 8 passengers each.

Writing in Math

19. Money is used to model $648 ÷ 4. If there are six $100 bills, four $10 bills, and eight $1 bills to start, explain how the money can be divided equally. (3-5)

20. Without dividing, how would you determine if a number is divisible by 2, 3, 4, 5 and 6? (3-10)

21. Write a problem in which the remainder is the answer. (3-11)

Algebra

Key Idea
When more than one operation is involved, you must follow the rules for order of operations

Vocabulary
• order of operations

$36 + 9 \div 3 \times 5$

$36 + 3 \times 5$

$36 + 15$

51

Order of Operations

How do you evaluate expressions with more than one operation?

Two students evaluated $36 + 9 \div 3 \times 5$ and got different answers.

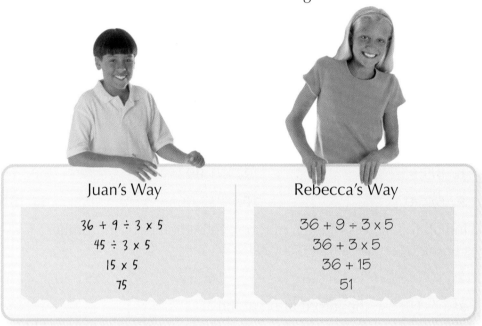

Juan's Way	Rebecca's Way
$36 + 9 \div 3 \times 5$	$36 + 9 \div 3 \times 5$
$45 \div 3 \times 5$	$36 + 3 \times 5$
15×5	$36 + 15$
75	51

To avoid getting more than one answer, mathematicians use the **order of operations** given below. Rebecca used the correct order. The value of the expression is 51.

Order of Operations

1. First do the operations inside parentheses.

2. Then, multiply and divide in order from left to right.

3. Finally, add and subtract in order from left to right.

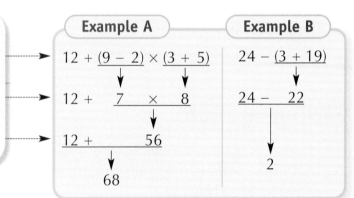

Example A

$12 + \underline{(9 - 2)} \times \underline{(3 + 5)}$

$12 + \quad 7 \quad \times \quad 8$

$12 + \qquad 56$

68

Example B

$24 - \underline{(3 + 19)}$

$24 - \quad 22$

2

✓ Talk About It

1. Why didn't Juan get 51 for an answer? How did his method differ from the rules listed above?

2. Follow the order of operations to evaluate $15 + (8 - 2) \times 4$.

Use the order of operations to evaluate each expression.

1. $14 - 6 \div 2$

2. $63 \div (3 \times 3) - 4$

3. $6 \times (11 - 7) - (8 \div 4)$

4. Number Sense Would the value of $(12 - 4) \div 2 + 7$ change if the parentheses were removed? Explain your thinking.

PRACTICE

For more practice, see Set 3-13 on p. 199.

A Skills and Understanding

Use the order of operations to evaluate each expression.

5. $4 + 2 \times 6$

6. $5 \times 2 + 10 \div 2$

7. $16 - (4 + 9)$

8. $(30 + 6) \div 4$

9. $4 \times (6 - 1.5)$

10. $5 + 7 \times 6 - 4$

11. $(15 - 8) \times (2 + 6)$

12. $72 \div 8 \div 3 \div 3$

13. $0.25 \times 8 + (15 \div 5)$

14. $34 - 9 - 80 \div 4 + 7$

15. $12 \times (10 - 3) + (1.8 \div 3)$

16. $(5 + 63) - 4 \times (78 \div 6)$

17. $(25 + 5) \div (6 - 1)$

18. $80 \times 2 + 3 \times (7 + 4)$

19. $(10 - 7) \times 5 - 2 \times 3$

Insert parentheses to make each statement true.

20. $11 - 6 - 1 = 6$

21. $30 - 4 \times 2 + 5 = 2$

22. $64 \div 2 \times 4 \div 2 = 4$

23. Number Sense Which is greater, $1 \times 7 + 4$ or $1 + 4 \times 7$?

B Reasoning and Problem Solving

For 24–25, insert parentheses in the expression $4 \times 10 - 3$ so that the new expression has:

24. the same value as $4 \times 10 - 3$.

25. a different value than $4 \times 10 - 3$.

26. <u>Writing in Math</u> Explain why $2 \times 5 + 9$ has a different value than $2 \times (5 + 9)$.

Mixed Review and Test Prep

Take It to the NET
Test Prep
www.scottforesman.com

27. At a ski lift, 41 people are waiting to board cars that hold 6 people each. How many cars can be completely filled? How many people are left over to board the last car?

Find each quotient.

28. $53 \div 7$

29. $656 \div 8$

30. $152 \div 5$

31. $2,709 \div 6$

32. Round 542.078 to the nearest ten.

A. 543

B. 542.10

C. 542.088

D. 540

Algebra

Key Idea
An ordered pair of numbers is used to locate a point on a coordinate grid.

Vocabulary
• coordinates
• ordered pair

Materials
• grid paper or

⚙ **tools**

Graphing Ordered Pairs

LEARN

How do you locate a point on a grid?

Tia made a star chart of the Big Dipper on a coordinate grid. The **coordinates** of point *A* are 13 and 9. Tia used the **ordered pair** of numbers, (13, 9), to describe the location of point *A*.

(13, 9)

The first number tells how far to move to the right from zero.

The second number tells how far to move up.

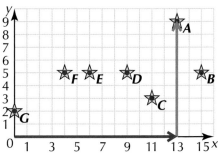

✔ **Talk About It**

1. What is the ordered pair for point *B*? for point *G*? How do you know?

How do you graph a point?

Example

Graph point *R* at (4, 5).

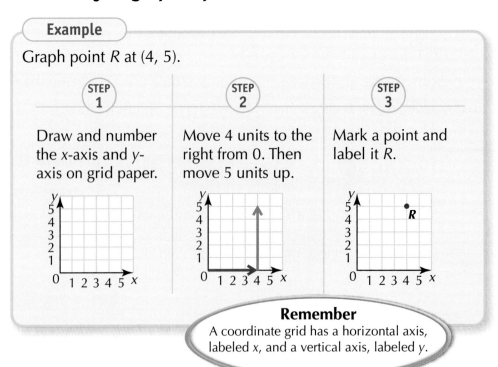

STEP 1	STEP 2	STEP 3
Draw and number the *x*-axis and *y*-axis on grid paper.	Move 4 units to the right from 0. Then move 5 units up.	Mark a point and label it *R*.

Remember
A coordinate grid has a horizontal axis, labeled *x*, and a vertical axis, labeled *y*.

✔ **Talk About It**

2. Why do you need two coordinates to locate a point?

Use the grid at the right for Exercises 1–8.
Name the point that is located by each ordered pair.

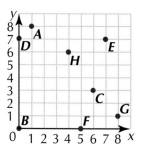

1. (8, 1) **2.** (5, 0) **3.** (0, 0) **4.** (1, 8)

Write the ordered pair for each point.

5. *C* **6.** *H* **7.** *D* **8.** *E*

9. Reasoning Write the ordered pair for a point 3 units to the right of the *y*-axis and 6 units above the *x*-axis.

PRACTICE

For more practice, see Set 3-14 on p. 199.

Ⓐ Skills and Understanding

Use the grid at the right for Exercises 10–15.
Name the point that is located by each ordered pair.

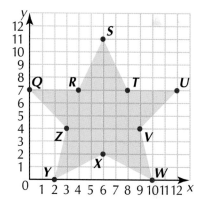

10. (9, 4) **11.** (4, 7) **12.** (0, 7)

Write the ordered pair for each point.

13. *W* **14.** *S* **15.** *Z*

Graph each point on the same grid. Label each point.

16. *J*(1, 8) **17.** *M*(0, 4) **18.** *F*(0, 0)

19. *D*(2, 2) **20.** *H*(5, 10) **21.** *B*(7, 0)

Ⓑ Reasoning and Problem Solving

22. Refer to the 12-by-12 grid above. What point is 2 units to the right and 5 units up from the point at (6, 2)?

23. Reasoning Do (3, 5) and (5, 3) represent the same point? Explain.

24. **Writing in Math** What do you think it means if two points have the same first coordinates or the same second coordinates? Give examples.

🦉 Mixed Review and Test Prep

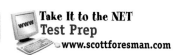
Take It to the NET
Test Prep
www.scottforesman.com

Find each missing number. Use mental math.

25. $200 \div n = 2$ **26.** $n + 30 = 60$ **27.** $900 \times n = 6{,}300$ **28.** $450 - n = 300$

29. If there are 8 pens in a package, how many pens are in 24 packages?

  A. 3 pens **B.** 162 pens **C.** 192 pens **D.** 196 pens

Algebra

Key Idea
Rules, tables, and graphs can be used to show how one quantity is related to another.

Vocabulary
• variable (p. 100)
• table of values

Materials
• grid paper or
 tools

Think It Through
I know that a variable is any symbol or letter that is used to represent a number.

Rules, Tables, and Graphs

LEARN

How do you use a rule to make a table?

Tickets to the county fair are $3 per person plus $1 for parking. A rule can be written to show that the total cost is $3 times the number of people, plus $1.

Rule in words: **Multiply by 3, then add 1.**

Rule using a variable: $3x + 1$.

Example A

Make a **table of values** for the rule.

Multiply by 3, then add 1: $3x + 1$

Evaluate the expression $3x + 1$ using 1, 2, 3, 4, and 5 for x.

x	$3x + 1$
1	4
2	7
3	10
4	13
5	16

⟵ For $x = 1$, $3x + 1 = 3 \times 1 + 1 = 4$.
⟵ For $x = 2$, $3x + 1 = 3 \times 2 + 1 = 7$.
⟵ For $x = 3$, $3x + 1 = 3 \times 3 + 1 = 10$.
⟵ For $x = 4$, $3x + 1 = 3 \times 4 + 1 = 13$.
⟵ For $x = 5$, $3x + 1 = 3 \times 5 + 1 = 16$.

Example B

Make a table of values for the rule.

Divide by 5: $\frac{x}{5}$

x	$\frac{x}{5}$
0	0
5	1
10	2
15	3
20	4

⟵ Remember that 0 divided by any nonzero number is 0. However, you can never divide by 0.

HINT: Select values for x that are easy to work with mentally.

The numbers in each row of a table of values is an ordered pair. For example, in Example B, the ordered pairs for the table are (0, 0), (5, 1), (10, 2), (15, 3), and (20, 4).

✔ Talk About It

1. How much will Anjali and her parents pay to attend the fair and park their car? Which ordered pair in the table represents this?

2. What are some other ordered pairs that might be in the table in Example A?

3. **Number Sense** In Example B, would 14 be a good choice as a value for *x*? Why or why not?

How do you make a graph for a table of values?

Example C

Make a graph for the table of values in Example A.

Graph each of the ordered pairs in the table:
(1, 4), (2, 7), (3, 10), (4, 13), (5, 16).

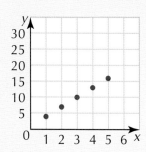

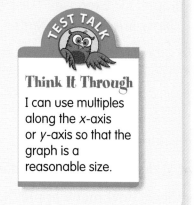

Think It Through

I can use multiples along the *x*-axis or *y*-axis so that the graph is a reasonable size.

✔ Talk About It

4. What do you notice about the points in the graph?

5. **Reasoning** How could you use the graph to find another ordered pair that fits the rule in Example A?

6. Do you think (6, 10) fits the rule? How can you tell without doing any computation?

CHECK ✓

For another example, see Set 3-15 on p. 195.

Create a table of values and make a graph for each rule.

1. *Subtract 7: x − 7*

2. *Divide by 2, then add 3: $\frac{x}{2} + 3$*

3. **Reasoning** Does the ordered pair (10,8) fit the rule in exercise 2? What are two different ways you can tell?

A Skills and Understanding

Create a table of values for each rule. Use at least four values for _x_.

4. _Add 3: x + 3_

5. _Multiply by 4: 4x_

6. _Multiply by 2, then add 5: 2x + 5_

7. _Subtract 8: x − 8_

8. _Divide by 3: $\frac{x}{3}$_

9. _Divide by 2, then subtract 1: $\frac{x}{2} − 1$_

10–15. On separate grids, make a graph for each table in Exercises 4–9.

16. Reasoning Does (6,11) fit the rule in Exercise 6? Explain.

B Reasoning and Problem Solving

17. Look over your graphs for Exercises 10–15. How are they similar? How are they different?

Luis is making a fruit salad. He uses twice as many apples as oranges. A rule can be written to show that the number of apples is 2 times the number of oranges.
Multiply by 2: 2x

18. Make a table of values for this rule.

19. In your table, what does _x_ represent? What does _2x_ represent?

20. If Luis uses 8 oranges, how many apples would he use?

21. Make a graph for your table of values.

Math and Science

If a temperature is given in degrees Celsius (°C), you can use the following rule for changing the temperature to a Fahrenheit temperature:

> _Rule in words: Multiply the Celsius temperature by 1.8. Then add 32._
>
> _Rule using a variable: 1.8C + 32_

Change each Celsius temperature to a Fahrenheit temperature.

22. 0°C

23. 10°C

24. 20°C

25. Mr. Kaster's cousin from Greece called him and said the temperature was 30°C. What was the Fahrenheit temperature?

26. **Writing in Math** Tell how you would make a table of values for the following rule: _Multiply by 4, then subtract 2: 4x − 2._

C Extensions

For each exercise, create a table of values for each rule. Then use three different colors to make graphs for the three tables of values all on the same grid.

27. *Add 2: x + 2*   *Add 4: x + 4*   *Add 7: x + 7*

28. *Multiply by 1: 1x*   *Multiply by 3: 3x*   *Multiply by 6: 6x*

29. What patterns do you notice in the graphs for Exercise 27? in the graphs for Exercise 28?

Mixed Review and Test Prep

Take It to the NET
Test Prep
www.scottforesman.com

Find each answer.

30.
$$128 \times 5$$

31.
$$60.9 + 41.47$$

32.
$$4{,}726 - 3{,}718$$

33.
$$23.15 \times 8$$

34.
$$734 \times 23$$

35. The park district paid $145.80 for 6 volleyballs. What was the price for each one?

   A. $2.43   **C.** $24.30

   B. $20.43   **D.** $243.00

36. Which of the following is equal to 17 thousandths?

   A. 17,000   **C.** 0.17

   B. 1,700   **D.** 0.017

Practice Game

Racking up Remainders

Players: 2–4

Materials: 4 number cubes (numbered 1–6)
              Spinner (labeled 1–9)

1. Players toss 4 number cubes and spin the spinner.

2. Players make a 4-digit number from the tossed numbers (digits on the number cubes may be used in any order) and divide this number by the number on the spinner.

3. Players earn points equivalent to their quotients' remainder. For example, a remainder of 8 earns 8 points.

4. The player with the lowest total score after 5 rounds wins the game.

Problem-Solving Applications

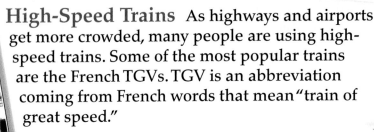

High-Speed Trains As highways and airports get more crowded, many people are using high-speed trains. Some of the most popular trains are the French TGVs. TGV is an abbreviation coming from French words that mean "train of great speed."

Trivia A TGV currently holds the speed record for a steel-rail train. It has been clocked at a blazing 320 mph!

1 One type of TGV has a weight of 848,540 pounds. Write the word name for this weight.

Using Key Facts

2 Suppose 354 of 450 total passengers were traveling second class. If passengers traveling first class or second class were distributed equally among the available cars, how many passengers were on each second-class car? On each first-class car?

Key Facts
Typical TGV

- Length   781 feet
- First class   3 cars
- Second class   6 cars
- Dining   1 car
- Motors   8
- Electric supply 25,000 volts

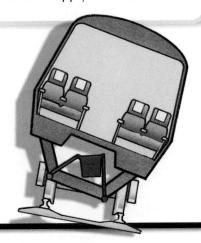

3 An experimental TGV could tilt. This allowed passengers to be more comfortable during fast turns. It was calculated that if a regular train would take a turn at 86 miles per hour, then a tilting train would take the turn at up to 120 miles per hour. How much faster would the tilting train take the turn?

4 Read the trivia. You can convert miles per hour to kilometers per hour by multiplying by 1.61. In kilometers per hour, how fast is the fastest steel-rail train?

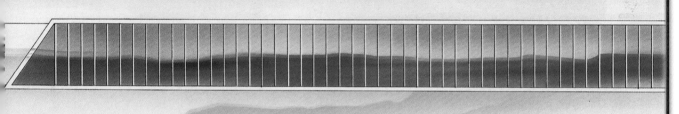

Good News/Bad News The French TGV typically travels with speeds up to 186 mph, but at these speeds, it takes almost 2 miles to stop safely!

5 Five adults paid a total of $520 to ride from Paris to Lyon. How much was each ticket?

6 Writing in Math Suppose one TGV has 485 seats and a smaller TGV has 377 seats. Explain how you would estimate the difference between the capacities of the two trains.

Car	Seats
1st class	36
2nd class	60
Cafe	16
Double deck	84

7 Decision Making Suppose you are to select the types of cars of a train. You can have any combination of 9 cars. What types of cars would you have? How many people could ride your train?

Do You Know How?

Do You Understand?

Order of Operations (3-13)

Use the order of operations to evaluate each expression.

1. $9 - 4 \div 2$

2. $31 - (7 + 2) \times 3$

3. $8 + 10 \times 4$

4. $10 \times 8 - 3 \times 2$

5. $(8 + 6) \div 7$

6. $(9 + 1) \div (8 - 3)$

7. $7 \times 3 - 6 \times 1 + 2 \times 5$

Ⓐ Explain how you used the order of operations to evaluate each expression in Exercises 1 and 2.

Ⓑ In Exercise 3, rewrite the expression with parentheses that do not change the answer.

Graphing Ordered Pairs (3-14)

Use the grid below. Write the ordered pair for each point.

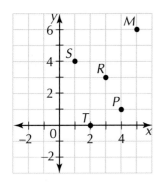

8. *R*   **9.** *S*   **10.** *T*

Ⓒ Tell how you found each ordered pair.

Ⓓ Does it matter which coordinate is written first in an ordered pair? Tell why or why not.

Ⓔ Which point is located at (5, 6)?

Rules, Tables, and Graphs (3-15)

Create a table for each rule. Use at least four values for *x*.

11. Add 7: $x + 7$

12. Multiply by 2 and then add 2: $2x + 2$

Ⓕ Theresa is given the rule *subtract 4*. How can she find an ordered pair for this rule?

Ⓖ Theresa's friend says (3,7) will be on the graph for the rule *subtract 4*. Is her friend correct? Explain.

TEST TALK

Think It Through
I should **read the problem carefully** and **watch for words like NOT.**

MULTIPLE CHOICE

1. What is the value of this expression? (3-13)

$3 + 5 \times 8 + 0$

A. 64   **B.** 43   **C.** 8   **D.** 0

2. For the rule *add 10,* which ordered pair does NOT fit? (3-15)

A. (0, 10)   **B.** (10, 0)   **C.** (5, 15)   **D.** (90, 100)

3. Which ordered pair is shown by point X?

A. (2, 5)

B. (5, 2)

C. (1, 5)

D. (5, 1)

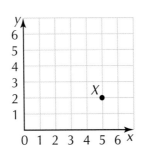

FREE RESPONSE

Use the order of operations to evaluate each expression. (3-13)

4. $1 \times 8 + 26 \div 2$

5. $25 \times 4 + 8 - 7 \div 7$

6. $13 - 2 + (8 \div 2) \times 4$

7. $18 \times (6 - 3) + 4$

8. $(12 - 6) \div 2 \times 3$

9. $(16 + 2) \div (6 \times 3)$

Use the graph at the right to write the ordered pair for each point. (3-14)

10. A **11.** E

12. C **13.** D

Which point is at each location?

14. (4, 2)   **15.** (5, 2)

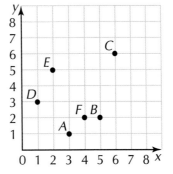

16. Create a table of values for the rule *subtract 4: x − 4.* Use at least four values for x. Then make a graph for your table. (3-15, 3-16)

Writing in Math

17. Explain how graphing (3, 5) is different from graphing (5, 3). (3-14)

18. Explain how you know that $3 + 5 \times 7$ and $3 \times 5 + 7$ do not have the same value. (3-13)

Test-Taking Strategies

Understand the question.

Get information for the answer.

Plan how to find the answer.

Make smart choices.

Use writing in math.

Improve written answers.

Plan How to Find the Answer

After you understand a test question and get needed information, you need to plan how to find the answer. Think about problem-solving skills and strategies and computation methods you know.

1. Mrs. Davies wants to buy a package of colored paper for a craft project her 3 children are working on.

Red Paper
65 sheets

Yellow Paper
50 sheets

Green Paper
40 sheets

Blue Paper
75 sheets

Which package of paper should Mrs. Davies buy so that each child gets the same number of sheets of paper with none left over?

A. Red paper **C.** Yellow paper

B. Green paper **D.** Blue paper

Understand the question.

I need to find the package of paper that the children can share equally with no sheets left over.

Get information for the answer.

*The number of children is given in the text. The **picture** gives me the number of sheets in each package of paper.*

Plan how to find the answer.

• Think about problem-solving skills and strategies.

  *I can **draw a picture** to show the main idea.*

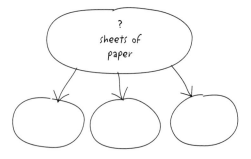

? sheets of paper

My picture shows that equal groups are being made, so I should think about division. Since the remainder must be 0, I can use divisibility rules.

• Choose computation methods.

  *I can **use mental math** to apply the divisibility rule for 3.*

2. Mark plotted the points *A* and *B* on the coordinate grid below.

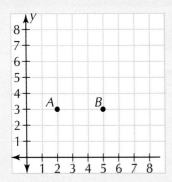

Think It Through

I need to find the coordinates of the corners of a square. The graph shows me two of the corners. I can draw the square on a grid starting by connecting A and B for the first side. I don't need to do any computations. I just need to count units to make sure all the sides of the square are the same length. Then I can find the coordinates of the other two corners of the square.

Which of these pairs of coordinates should Mark plot to make a square?

A. (5, 3) and (8, 3)

B. (2, 6) and (5, 6)

C. (6, 2) and (6, 5)

D. (2, 5) and (5, 5)

Now it's your turn.

For each problem, describe a plan for finding the answer.

3. Harriet is putting 6 cookies on a plate for a bake sale. Which of these batches of cookies could Harriet place on plates with none left over?

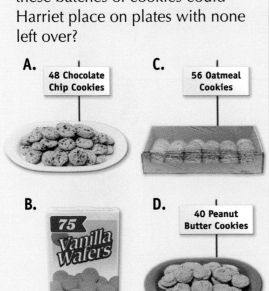

A. 48 Chocolate Chip Cookies

C. 56 Oatmeal Cookies

B. 75 Vanilla Wafers

D. 40 Peanut Butter Cookies

4. Olivia plotted the points *G* and *H* on the coordinate grid below.

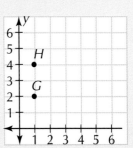

Which of these pairs of coordinates should Olivia plot to make a square?

A. (2, 3) and (4, 3)

B. (2, 2) and (2, 4)

C. (3, 3) and (4, 4)

D. (3, 2) and (3, 4)

When my teacher repeats the directions, he says them more than once. When I divide numbers using **repeated subtraction** I subtract more than once. *(p. 132)*

Self Check

There are different ways to divide numbers. (Lessons 3-1, 3-2, 3-3)

Find 35 ÷ 5.
Use **sharing**.

Break 35 up into equal groups of 5 each.

There are 7 groups.

35 ÷ 5 = 7

Use **repeated subtraction.**

35 − 5 = 30
30 − 5 = 25
25 − 5 = 20
20 − 5 = 15
15 − 5 = 10
10 − 5 = 5
5 − 5 = 0

5 was subtracted 7 times.

35 ÷ 5 = 7

Look for the **missing factor** using the **inverse operation.**

Think: "5 times what number is 35?"

$5 \times n = 35$
$5 \times 7 = 35$
$n = 7$

Write: 35 ÷ 5 = 7

1. Find 64 ÷ 8 and 18 ÷ 2.

Self Check

The inverse of something is its opposite. In math, the **inverse operation** of division is multiplication. *(p. 133)*

Division involves the process of making equal groups.
(Lesson 3-5, 3-6, 3-7 3-8, 3-9, 3-10, 3-11)

Find 196 ÷ 5.

196 is not **divisible** by 5 because 5 is not a **factor** of the **dividend.**

$$
\begin{array}{r}
39\ R1 \\
5\overline{)196} \\
-15\downarrow \\
\hline
46 \\
-45 \\
\hline
1
\end{array}
$$

There are 39 equal groups of 5 in 196, but there is one left over. The amount left over is called a **remainder.**

2. Find 414 ÷ 6 and 3,648 ÷ 9.

It takes coordination to juggle; your eyes and hands must work together. In a **coordinate pair,** two numbers work together to describe a location on a grid.

Expressions with more than one operation must be evaluated using the **Order of Operations.** (Lessons 3-13, 3-14, 3-15)

Create a table of values and make a graph for the rule: subtract 1, then multiply by 2: $(x - 1) \times 2$.

Substitute for x and follow the order of operations. Each value for x and the corresponding value for $(x - 1) \times 2$ in the table is a coordinate pair that may be plotted.

x	$(x - 1) \times 2$
1	
2	
3	
4	

$(1 - 1) \times 2$ First simplify inside parentheses.

0×2 Next multiply and divide from left to right.

0 Then add and subtract from left to right (not necessary here).

3. Complete the table of values and give three ordered pairs for the rule: multiply by 3, then subtract 2: $3x - 2$.

x	$3x - 2$
1	
2	
3	
4	
5	

You can look for a pattern or interpret remainders to **solve problems.** (Lessons 3-4, 3-12)

To find a pattern, look for how the number or geometric figure changes from one term to the next.

What are the next two numbers? Describe the pattern.

16, 46, 76, 106, ____, ____

The missing numbers are 136 and 166.

The pattern is add 30.

To interpret remainders, understand what the problem is asking.

Each sedan holds 5 people. How many sedans are needed for a group of 33 people?

$$\begin{array}{r} 6 \text{ R3} \\ 5\overline{)33} \\ -\ 30 \\ \hline 3 \end{array}$$

7 sedans are needed, because 6 sedans would leave the remaining 3 people without a seat.

4. A total of 8 baseball cards can be mounted in one case. If Robert has 78 baseball cards to be mounted, how many cases can he fill?

1. 8 and 9; 2. 69 and 405 R3; 3. 1, 4, 7, 10, 13; (1, 1), (2, 4), (3, 7), (4, 10), (5, 13); 4. 9 cases

MULTIPLE CHOICE

Choose the correct letter for each answer.

1. Find $565 \div 6$.

   A. 94 R 1   **C.** 96

   B. 94 R 2   **D.** 96 R 2

2. Which is the most reasonable estimate for $5,844 \div 3$?

   A. 1,500   **C.** 2,400

   B. 2,000   **D.** 3,000

3. Find $2,008 \div 8$.

   A. 26   **C.** 251 R 3

   B. 251   **D.** 260 R 2

4. Find $9,481 \div 5$.

   A. 1,320 R 4   **C.** 1,540 R 3

   B. 1,366 R 3   **D.** 1,896 R 1

5. Describe the pattern: 448, 112, 28, 7

   A. Subtract 336.   **C.** Divide by 7.

   B. Subtract 84.   **D.** Divide by 4.

6. Which list shows ALL the factors of 20?

   A. 1, 2, 4   **C.** 1, 2, 4, 5, 10

   B. 1, 2, 4, 5   **D.** 1, 2, 4, 5, 10, 20

7. Which is NOT a composite number?

   A. 31   **C.** 68

   B. 39   **D.** 81

8. Evaluate $6 + 9 \div (5 - 2) \times 6$.

   A. 6   **C.** 24

   B. 18   **D.** 30

9. Find $\$32.82 \div 3$.

   A. $19.40   **C.** $10.00

   B. $10.94   **D.** $1.94

10. Which number is NOT divisible by 3?

   A. 72   **C.** 145

   B. 108   **D.** 270

11. Which is the first step in evaluating $18 - 15 + 3 \times 8 - 2$?

   A. $18 - 15$ **C.** 3×8

   B. $15 + 3$ **D.** $8 - 2$

12. Name the point located at (8,7).

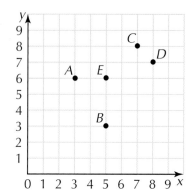

   A. point *A*

   B. point *B*

   C. point *C*

   D. point *D*

13. Which number belongs in the empty cell of the table?

x	x + 1
1	2
3	4
5	
7	8
9	10

Think It Through

- I should **watch for words like NOT** in the problem.
- I should **eliminate unreasonable answers.**

   A. 4   **C.** 6

   B. 5   **D.** 7

FREE RESPONSE

Find each quotient. Use mental math.

14. $420 \div 7$

15. $1,500 \div 3$

Estimate each quotient.

16. $295 \div 6$

17. $6,045 \div 3$

Find each quotient.

18. $157 \div 3$

19. $523 \div 5$

20. $7)\overline{4,783}$

21. $5)\overline{\$25.15}$

Use factor trees to find the prime factorization of each number.

22. 16

23. 56

Use the order of operations to evaluate each expression.

24. $6 + 5 \times (5 - 3)$

25. $16 \div 4 - 2 + 5 \times 5$

26. Tell if the division situation in the problem below is best described as *sharing, repeated subtraction,* or *missing factor.* Then solve.

Julita has a bolt of fabric that is 18 yards long. She is cutting fabric from the bolt in 3-yard strips. How many strips of fabric will she have?

Writing in Math

27. If you have three $100 bills, four $10 bills, and four $1 bills, explain how you could exchange these bills with other bills of the same value so that each of four people would get the same amount of money.

28. Explain what the remainder means when you use division to solve the following problem.

Potato salad is sold in 1-pound containers. Each container serves 5 people. How many containers must be purchased to serve 48 people?

Think It Through
Identifying the main idea can help me **interpret the remainder.**

29. Describe the pattern. Draw the missing figure.

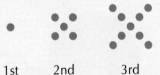

1st   2nd   3rd

Number and Operation

MULTIPLE CHOICE

1. Find $164 \div 6$.

A. 25 R 2   **C.** 27 R 2

B. 26 R 4   **D.** 29

2. What is $50,000 + 400 + 60 + 3 + 0.1 + 0.05$ in standard form?

A. 50,463.105   **C.** 50,463.51

B. 50,463.15   **D.** 54,631.5

3. Which shows expanded notation for 3,003,030?

A. $300,000,000 + 30$

B. $3,000,000 + 3,000 + 3$

C. $3,000,000 + 3,000 + 30$

D. $30,000,000 + 30$

FREE RESPONSE

4. List all prime numbers less than 20.

5. Andre is coaching a basketball team in his neighborhood. He needs to purchase basketballs. If the price of the basketball shown below includes tax and Andre has $65, how many basketballs can he afford?

$9.

Writing in Math

6. Explain how to estimate 19×53.

7. Explain how to draw a model for the fraction $\frac{3}{4}$. Then draw that model.

Geometry and Measurement

MULTIPLE CHOICE

8. The bus leaves Centerville at 4:15 P.M. and arrives in Mattstown at 5:38 P.M. How long was the bus trip?

A. 23 minutes

B. 33 minutes

C. 1 hour 23 minutes

D. 1 hour 33 minutes

9. Which figure has only one line of symmetry?

A.   **C.**

B.   **D.**

FREE RESPONSE

10. What is the perimeter of the rectangle?

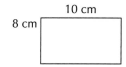

8 cm   10 cm

11. How many quarts are in two gallons?

Writing in Math

12. Describe the similarities and differences in the two figures below.

Data Analysis and Probability

MULTIPLE CHOICE

13. What color is impossible if you spin the spinner below?

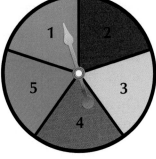

A. red

B. green

C. blue

D. white

14. Which graph best shows change over time?

A. line graph

B. bar graph

C. pictograph

D. circle graph

FREE RESPONSE

Use the graph for 15 and 16.

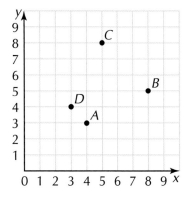

15. Which point is located at (3, 4).

16. What is the ordered pair at point B?

Writing in Math

17. Give an example of an impossible event, a certain event, and an unlikely event.

Algebra

MULTIPLE CHOICE

18. Which number belongs in the empty cell of the table?

x	x − 2
5	3
10	8
15	13
20	
25	23

A. 15

B. 18

C. 20

D. 22

FREE RESPONSE

19. Kelly planted 1 rose bush on Monday, 2 rose bushes on Tuesday, 4 rose bushes on Wednesday, and 8 rose bushes on Thursday. If she continues this pattern, how many rose bushes will she plant on Saturday?

20. Each ticket costs $3.50. A discount pack of five tickets costs $15.00. How much money does the discount pack save a group of five people?

Writing in Math

21. Describe how to use mental math to solve the equation below.

$$3b = 27$$

Set 3-1 (pages 132–135)

28 students are separated into teams of 4. How many teams are formed?

Draw a picture to show the division situation. Then find the quotient.

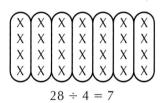

$$28 \div 4 = 7$$

So 7 teams are formed.

Remember that you can draw a picture to show a division situation. Division can mean *sharing, repeated subtraction,* or *finding a missing factor.*

1. If a class has 3 times as many girls as boys and there are 24 girls in the class, how many boys are there?

2. On a shelf with 32 books, 4 books are removed at a time until none are left. How many groups of 4 books are removed?

Set 3-2 (pages 136–137)

Find $1,400 \div 7$.

Use a basic fact and look for patterns in the number of zeros.

$$14 \div 7 = 2$$
$$140 \div 7 = 20$$
$$1,400 \div 7 = 200$$

Remember to use basic facts and patterns to help you divide.

1. $600 \div 3$ 2. $200 \div 4$

3. $2,500 \div 5$ 4. $5,400 \div 6$

5. $28,000 \div 7$ 6. $72,000 \div 9$

Set 3-3 (pages 138–141)

Estimate $551 \div 7$.

Think of a number close to 551 that is a multiple of 7. Then divide.

Think: $560 \div 7 = 80$.

So, $551 \div 7$ is about 80.

Remember that you can use rounding, compatible numbers, or multiplication to help you estimate quotients.

Estimate each quotient.

1. $731 \div 8$ 2. $1,548 \div 3$

3. $\$52.99 \div 6$ 4. $34,892 \div 5$

Set 3-4 (pages 144–145)

The table below shows the number of new members each month for a club. If the pattern continues, how many new members will there be in June?

Jan.	Feb.	Mar.	Apr.	May	June
15	30	60	120	?	?

The number doubles each month.

May: $120 \times 2 = 240$ June: $240 \times 2 = 480$

In June there will be 480 new members.

Remember to look for a pattern.

1. On the chalkboard, Karen's teacher wrote the pattern below. Find the next three numbers in the pattern.

$$1, 3, 6, 10, 15, \underline{\quad}, \underline{\quad}, \underline{\quad}$$

2. Jamel bought a rare coin for $25. He was told that it would increase in value by $9 each year. What will the coin's value be after 5 years?

Set 3-5 (pages 148–151)

Tell how much each person will get if 3 people share $561 equally.

Use play money to help you divide. How to record your work is shown at the right.

$$\begin{array}{r} 187 \\ 3\overline{)561} \\ -3 \\ \hline 26 \\ -24 \\ \hline 21 \\ -21 \\ \hline 0 \end{array}$$

Each person gets $187.
So, $561 ÷ 3 = $187.

Remember to regroup when necessary.

Use play money to divide. Tell how much each person will get.

1. 4 people share $264 equally
2. 6 people share $738 equally
3. 9 people share $387 equally

Set 3-6 (pages 152–155)

Find 645 ÷ 7.

Estimate first:
630 ÷ 7 = 90

Check:
7 × 92 + 1 = 645

So, 645 ÷ 7 = 92 R1.

$$\begin{array}{r} 92 \text{ R1} \\ 7\overline{)645} \\ -63 \\ \hline 15 \\ -14 \\ \hline 1 \end{array}$$

Remember that you can check your answer by multiplying the quotient and the divisor and then adding the remainder.

1. 89 ÷ 9	**2.** 77 ÷ 3
3. 168 ÷ 8	**4.** 455 ÷ 5
5. $2\overline{)458}$	**6.** $4\overline{)617}$

Set 3-7 (pages 156–157)

Find 839 ÷ 4.

Estimate first:
800 ÷ 4 = 200

Check:
4 × 209 + 3 = 839

So, 839 ÷ 4 = 209 R3.

$$\begin{array}{r} 209 \text{ R3} \\ 4\overline{)839} \\ -8 \\ \hline 03 \\ -0 \\ \hline 39 \\ -36 \\ \hline 3 \end{array}$$

Remember that sometimes you need to write a zero in the quotient when you divide.

1. 720 ÷ 6	**2.** 661 ÷ 3
3. 424 ÷ 4	**4.** 914 ÷ 3
5. $7\overline{)2{,}940}$	**6.** $5\overline{)1{,}532}$

Set 3-8 (pages 158–159)

Find 2,157 ÷ 5.

Estimate first:
2,000 ÷ 5 = 400

Check:
5 × 431 + 2 = 2,157

So, 2,157 ÷ 5 = 431 R2.

$$\begin{array}{r} 431 \text{ R2} \\ 5\overline{)2157} \\ -20 \\ \hline 15 \\ -15 \\ \hline 07 \\ -5 \\ \hline 2 \end{array}$$

Remember that estimating can help you place the first digit in the quotient.

1. 1,546 ÷ 2	**2.** 3,454 ÷ 3
3. $8\overline{)3{,}512}$	**4.** $4\overline{)2{,}563}$
5. $7\overline{)8{,}309}$	**6.** $9\overline{)3{,}462}$

Set 3-9 (pages 160–161)

Find $14.28 ÷ 6.

Estimate first:
$12.00 ÷ 6 = $2.00

Check:
6 × $2.38 = $14.28

So, $14.28 ÷ 6 = $2.38.

$$\begin{array}{r} \$\,2.38 \\ 6\overline{)\$14.28} \\ -12 \\ \hline 22 \\ -18 \\ \hline 48 \\ -48 \\ \hline 0 \end{array}$$

Remember to show dollars and cents in the quotient when dividing money.

1. $8.84 ÷ 4
2. $6.60 ÷ 5
3. $3.28 ÷ 4
4. $26.10 ÷ 3
5. 7)$72.38
6. 8)$92.72

Set 3-10 (pages 162–163)

Is 128 divisible by 4?

The number formed by the last 2 digits is 28. Since 28 is divisible by 4 (28 ÷ 4 = 7), 128 is divisible by 4.

Remember to use divisibility rules to help you find factors of a number.

1. Tell if 78 is divisible by 2, 3, 4, 5, 6, or 10.

List all the factors of each number.

2. 75
3. 41
4. 42

Set 3-11 (pages 164–167)

Is 575 prime or composite?

Because the last digit is 5, you know that 575 is divisible by 5. Because 575 has more factors than 1 and itself, it is composite.

Remember that a prime number is a whole number greater than 1 that has exactly two factors, 1 and itself.

Write whether each number is prime or composite.

1. 28
2. 11
3. 112
4. Use a factor tree to find the prime factorization of 27.

Set 3-12 (pages 168–169)

There are 52 students going on a school trip. If a van holds 7 students, what is the least number of vans needed?

52 ÷ 7 = 7 R3

You need to consider the remainder of 3 students. Because an extra van would be needed for these students, increase the quotient to the next whole number.

So, at least 8 vans are needed.

Remember that when you divide, you sometimes need to interpret a remainder to find a solution.

1. A train must have at least one conductor for every 5 cars. If the train is 34 cars long, how many conductors are needed?

2. Four yards of cloth are needed for each costume. What is the greatest number of costumes that can be made from 25 yards of fabric?

Use the order of operations to evaluate
$24 - (3 + 7) \div 2$.

$24 - (3 + 7) \div 2$

$24 - \quad 10 \quad \div 2 \qquad$ Parentheses first.

$24 - \qquad 5 \qquad$ Then divide.

$\qquad 19 \qquad$ Finally subtract.

$24 - (3 + 7) \div 2 = 19$

Remember that multiplication and division are done from left to right. Then, addition and subtraction are done from left to right.

Use the order of operations to evaluate each expression.

1. $5 + 3 \times 6$

2. $8 + (7 - 5) \times 9$

3. $(4 + 3) + 24 \div 6$

Use the grid below. Write the ordered pair for point G.

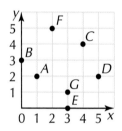

Start at the origin (0,0).
Point G is 3 units to the right and 1 unit up.
So, the ordered pair for point G is (3, 1).

Use the grid at the left. Write the ordered pair for each point.

1. Point A

2. Point B

3. Point F

Name the point located by each ordered pair.

4. (3, 0)

5. (4, 4)

6. (5, 2)

7. (3, 1)

Make a table of values for the rule *multiply by 2, then add 1*: $2x + 1$

Evaluate the expression $2x + 1$ using 1, 2, 3, 4, and 5 for x.

x	$2x + 1$	
1	3	$2 \times 1 + 1 = 3$
2	5	$2 \times 2 + 1 = 5$
3	7	$2 \times 3 + 1 = 7$
4	9	$2 \times 4 + 1 = 9$
5	11	$2 \times 5 + 1 = 11$

Remember to use values of x that are easy to work with mentally.

Make a table of values for each rule. Use at least four values for x.

1. *Subtract 2:* $x - 2$

2. *Add 10:* $x + 10$

3. *Subtract 8:* $x - 8$

4. *Add 6:* $x + 6$

5. *Multiply by 3, then add 4:* $3x + 4$

6. *Divide by 2, then add 3:* $\frac{x}{2} + 3$

Set 3-1 (pages 132–135)

Draw a picture or use objects to show
each division situation. Then find the quotient.

1. A group of 21 students are being separated into
   teams of 3. How many teams will there be?

2. Sheila is cutting 4 roses at a time from her rose bushes
   to put into vases for a party. How many vases does
   she need if she cuts 20 roses?

3. In a restaurant there are 8 times as many
   chairs as tables. If the restaurant has 72 chairs,
   how many tables are in the restaurant?

4. Which best describes each division situation in
   Exercises 1, 2, and 3—division as *sharing, repeated
   subtraction,* or *missing factor?*

Set 3-2 (pages 136–137)

Find each quotient. Use mental math.

1. $210 \div 7$	**2.** $900 \div 3$	**3.** $350 \div 5$	**4.** $560 \div 8$
5. $8,100 \div 9$	**6.** $4,800 \div 6$	**7.** $14,000 \div 2$	**8.** $36,000 \div 6$
9. $7,200 \div 8$	**10.** $630 \div 7$	**11.** $540 \div 6$	**12.** $21,000 \div 7$

13. Mike needs 240 cans of juice for a picnic. How many six-packs of
    juice should he buy?

Set 3-3 (pages 138–141)

Estimate each quotient.

1. $402 \div 5$	**2.** $821 \div 9$	**3.** $741 \div 8$	**4.** $1,791 \div 2$
5. $2,309 \div 4$	**6.** $\$11.25 \div 6$	**7.** $\$72.15 \div 9$	**8.** $48,569 \div 7$
9. $455 \div 9$	**10.** $6,411 \div 7$	**11.** $35,113 \div 7$	**12.** $5,985 \div 6$

13. Elena is reading a book with 170 pages. If she reads 9 pages
    a day, about how long will it take her to finish the book?

Set 3-4 (pages 144–145)

Look for a pattern. Write the missing numbers or draw the missing figures.

1. 1, 4, 8, 13, 19, ____, ____, ____

2. 1, 4, 16, ____, ____, ____

3. ∧, ⟩, ∨, ⟩, ∧, ____, ____,

4.

Take It to the NET
More Practice
www.scottforesman.com

Set 3-5 (pages 148–151)

Use play money to divide. Tell how much each person will get.

1. Four people share $416 equally.

2. Five people share $725 equally.

3. Suppose that three sisters buy their mother a birthday present that costs $126. If each sister pays the same amount for the present, how much does each sister spend?

Set 3-6 (pages 152–155)

Find each quotient. Check your answers by multiplying.

1. 7)95   **2.** 4)92   **3.** 6)418   **4.** 3)224

5. 980 ÷ 5   **6.** 735 ÷ 4   **7.** 225 ÷ 9   **8.** 857 ÷ 7

9. A class wants to plant 150 flowers for Earth Day. If they plan to put 8 flowers in each row, how many rows can they fill? How many flowers will be left over?

Set 3-7 (pages 156–157)

Find each quotient. Check your answers by multiplying.

1. 402 ÷ 8   **2.** 630 ÷ 9   **3.** 3)810   **4.** 5)505

5. 4)762   **6.** 3)926   **7.** 814 ÷ 2   **8.** 643 ÷ 6

9. At Thomas School, the fifth grade collected 545 cans during a can drive. Each student collected 5 cans. How many students collected cans?

Set 3-8 (pages 158–159)

Find each quotient. Check your answers by multiplying.

1. 5)3,770   **2.** 2)4,359   **3.** 8)1,245   **4.** 7)1,624

5. 5,613 ÷ 4   **6.** 1,205 ÷ 3   **7.** 1,380 ÷ 6   **8.** 9,121 ÷ 9

9. There are 2,769 seats in an auditorium. Each of the 3 sections has the same number of seats. How many seats are in each section?

10. Mrs. Hicks collects antiques. She bought 8 antique chairs for which she paid a total of $1,200. If each chair cost the same amount, how much did each chair cost?

Set 3-9 (pages 160–161)

Find each quotient. Check your answers by multiplying.

1. $6)\overline{\$7.80}$ **2.** $9)\overline{\$8.28}$ **3.** $3)\overline{\$5.85}$ **4.** $8)\overline{\$3.68}$

5. $\$69.70 \div 2$ **6.** $\$34.45 \div 5$ **7.** $\$12.16 \div 4$ **8.** $\$78.61 \div 7$

9. Maria bought 8 pounds of salmon for $63.92. What was the cost of the salmon per pound?

Set 3-10 (pages 162–163)

Find all the factors of each number.

1. 10   **2.** 6   **3.** 8   **4.** 11

5. 15   **6.** 30   **7.** 17   **8.** 45

9. 88   **10.** 93   **11.** 33   **12.** 28

13. Lucas needs to set up 50 chairs in equal rows. List all the ways that he could do this.

Set 3-11 (pages 164–167)

Write whether each number is prime or composite.

1. 13   **2.** 20   **3.** 48   **4.** 53

5. 195   **6.** 100   **7.** 23   **8.** 999

9. 8,498   **10.** 17   **11.** 9,990   **12.** 255

Use factor trees to find the prime factorization of each number.

13. 32   **14.** 45   **15.** 56   **16.** 70

17. How do you know that 199,555 is NOT a prime number?

Set 3-12 (pages 168–169)

1. Posters cost $6 each. Jared has $56. He wants to buy as many posters as possible. How many posters can he buy?

2. A group of 63 students is taking a field trip. If each car can take 4 students, what is the least number of cars they will need?

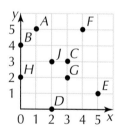
Take It to the NET
More Practice
www.scottforesman.com

Set 3-13 (pages 172–173)

Use the order of operations to evaluate each expression.

1. $(4 + 5) \times 3$

2. $9 - 1 + 2 \div 2$

3. $12 \div 6 \times 3 - 5$

4. $2 + (8 - 5) \times 6$

5. $10 \div (11 - 9) + 9$

6. $3 \times (1 + 3) + 8 \div 4$

7. $50 - 10 - 50 \div 10 + 5$

8. $8 \times (5 - 1) \div (6 - 2)$

9. $12 + 8 \times 2 + 6$

10. $(40 + 10) + 10 \div 2$

11. $100 + 2 \times 50 + 100$

12. $50 + 50 \times 2 - 50 \div 50$

13. Elena bought 3 boxes of pencils that contained 20 pencils each and 4 boxes of pens that contained 10 pens each. Write an expression to represent the total number of pencils and pens Elena bought.

Set 3-14 (pages 174–175)

Use the grid below. Write the ordered pair for each point or name the point for each ordered pair.

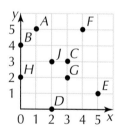

1. Point B

2. Point G

3. Point C

4. $(5, 1)$

5. $(2, 3)$

6. Point F

7. Which point is 2 units right of the origin?

Set 3-15 (pages 176–179)

Make a table of values for each rule. Use at least four values for x.

1. *Add 1: $x + 1$*

2. *Multiply by 2, then subtract 3: $2x - 3$*

3–4. Make a graph for each table in Exercises 1 and 2.

DIAGNOSING READINESS

A Vocabulary

(pages 152–153)

Choose the best term from the box.

1. In 356 ÷ 4 = 89, 89 is the __?__.

2. The number by which you divide the dividend is called the __?__.

3. The __?__ is the number that is left over after the division is complete.

Vocabulary

- **dividend** *(p.152)*
- **quotient** *(p. 152)*
- **divisor** *(p. 152)*
- **remainder** *(p. 152)*

B Division Facts

(Grade 4)

4. 12 ÷ 4   **5.** 28 ÷ 7   **6.** 63 ÷ 9

7. 54 ÷ 6   **8.** 40 ÷ 8   **9.** 25 ÷ 5

10. 18 ÷ 3   **11.** 48 ÷ 6   **12.** 72 ÷ 8

13. Write two related multiplication facts for the division fact 585 ÷ 9 = 65.

14. In one week, Pete jogged a total of 35 miles. If he jogged the same number of miles each day, how many miles did he jog each day?

Do You Know...

How many yards can a cheetah run in one second?

You will find out in lesson 4-12.

RUSSELL ASH
INCREDIBLE COMPARISONS

C **Division Patterns**

(pages 136–137)

Use patterns and basic facts to divide mentally.

15. 42 ÷ 7 =
420 ÷ 7 =
4,200 ÷ 7 =

16. 24 ÷ 6 =
240 ÷ 6 =
2,400 ÷ 6 =

17. 360 ÷ 9

18. 2,100 ÷ 3

19. How is the number of zeros in the quotient of 4,500 ÷ 9 related to the number of zeros in the dividend?

D **Compatible Numbers**

(pages 138–141)

Find compatible numbers for dividing the first number by the second number.

20. 563 and 7

21. 251 and 3

22. 4,524 and 5

23. 333 and 4

24. 7,168 and 9

25. 4,816 and 7

26. Anna earned $248 babysitting last month. If she earned $4 per hour, about how many hours did she work?

Key Idea
Basic facts and
patterns can help
you find quotients
like 2,400 ÷ 60
using mental math.

Vocabulary
• quotient (p. 104)
• multiple of 10

Materials
• calculator

TEST TALK

Think It Through
I can **look for
patterns** to see
how to divide by
multiples of 10.

Dividing by Multiples of 10

LEARN

Activity

What is the pattern?

a. Use a calculator to find each **quotient.**

$240 \div 30 = n$	$400 \div 50 = n$	$4,200 \div 70 = n$
$2,400 \div 30 = n$	$4,000 \div 50 = n$	$42,000 \div 70 = n$
$24,000 \div 30 = n$	$40,000 \div 50 = n$	$420,000 \div 70 = n$
$240,000 \div 30 = n$	$400,000 \div 50 = n$	$4,200,000 \div 70 = n$

b. Write a rule that tells how to find the quotient if the divisor
is a **multiple of 10** such as 10, 20, 30, and so on.

How can you divide mentally by multiples of 10?

Example A	Example B
What is $280 \div 40$?	What is $4,500 \div 90$?
$28 \div 4 = 7$ Use a basic fact.	$45 \div 9 = 5$ *Think:* $4,500 \div 90$ is the same as 450 tens ÷ 9 tens.
So, $28\underline{0} \div 4\underline{0} = 7$.	So, $4,50\underline{0} \div 9\underline{0} = 50$.

✔ Talk About It

1. In Example B, why is $4,500 \div 90$ the same as
450 tens ÷ 9 tens?

2. What basic fact helps you find $7,200 \div 90$?
What is $7,200 \div 90$?

CHECK ✓

For another example, see Set 4-1 on p. 250.

Find each quotient. Use mental math.

1. $270 \div 30$ **2.** $360 \div 60$ **3.** $6,300 \div 70$ **4.** $8,000 \div 40$

5. Number Sense How is dividing 320 by 40 similar to
dividing 32 by 4?

A Skills and Understanding

Find each quotient. Use mental math.

6. $560 \div 80$ **7.** $490 \div 70$ **8.** $3,600 \div 40$ **9.** $7,200 \div 90$

10. $2,000 \div 20$ **11.** $6,000 \div 50$ **12.** $3,600 \div 10$ **13.** $4,200 \div 60$

14. $54,000 \div 60$ **15.** $16,000 \div 80$ **16.** $63,000 \div 90$ **17.** $28,000 \div 40$

Solve for *n*.

18. $250 \div n = 5$ **19.** $n \div 40 = 80$ **20.** $(700 \div 70) + n = 15$

21. Number Sense How is dividing 420 by 6 like dividing 4,200 by 60?

B Reasoning and Problem Solving

For 22 and 23, use the Stadium Seating Plan at the right.

22. How many seats will be in each section?

23. How many seats will be in each row?

24. Number Sense For each pair, determine if the quotient is the same or different. Explain.

a. $360 \div 6$ and $360 \div 60$

b. $4,500 \div 50$ and $450 \div 5$

25. Algebra The number *p* is a 4-digit number and *q* is a multiple of 10 from 10 to 90. If $p \div q = 70$, what are possible values for *p* and *q*?

26. **Writing in Math** Explain how you can mentally determine that $27,000 \div 90 = 300$.

Stadium Seating Plan

Seats: 36,000
Sections: 40
Rows in each
section: 30

Mixed Review and Test Prep

Take It to the NET
www Test Prep
www.scottforesman.com

Find each quotient.

27. $352 \div 8$ **28.** $768 \div 9$ **29.** $6\overline{)492}$ **30.** $5\overline{)6,438}$

31. Create a table of values for the rule: **Multiply by 3, then subtract 2.** Use at least 4 values for *x*. Then make a graph for the table.

32. One bleacher section in a gym has 20 bleachers. Each bleacher can seat 10 spectators. What is the greatest number of spectators that can sit in that section?

A. 2 **B.** 10 **C.** 30 **D.** 200

All text pages available online and on CD-ROM.

Key Idea
There are different ways to estimate quotients.

Vocabulary
• compatible numbers (p. 22)
• estimate
• round (p. 26)

Think It Through
• I can **draw a picture** to show the main idea.
• I can use an **estimate** to find about how many.

Estimating with Two-Digit Divisors

LEARN

Exact answer or estimate?

On the average, a certain ticket collector admits 28 people per minute. About how many minutes will it take the collector to admit 1,250 people?

1,250					
28	28	28	28	28	...

I can divide to find how many 28s are in 1,250.

Estimate 1,250 ÷ 28.

✓ WARM UP

Name compatible numbers for dividing the first number by the second.

1. **3,457 and 87**

2. **28,562 and 65**

3. **48 and 23.83**

4. **$187.62 and 27**

What are some ways to estimate?

Example A

Estimate 1,250 ÷ 28.

One Way
Use **compatible numbers.**

Substitute 1,200 for 1,250 and 30 for 28.

1,200 ÷ 30 = 40

So a good estimate is about 40 minutes.

Another Way
Think multiplication.

28 × **?** is about 1,250. Round 28 to 30.

30 × 40 = 1,200

So a good **estimate** is a little more than 40 minutes or about 45 minutes.

> 28 < 30 and 1,200 < 1,250. So, the actual answer will be greater than the estimate.

✓ Talk About It

1. How does rounding 28 to 30 help when estimating using multiplication?

2. **Number Sense** What other compatible numbers could you use for 1,250 and 28? Explain.

How do you estimate with decimals and money?

Example B

Estimate: 57.4 ÷ 28

Use compatible whole numbers.

57.4 ÷ 28
↓   ↓
60 ÷ 30 = 2

A good estimate is about 2.

Example C

Estimate: 832.86 ÷ 27

First round 27 to 30 and then use multiplication.

30 × ? = 832.86
↓   ↓
30 × 30 = 900

900 is close to 832.86, so 30 is a good estimate.

Example D

If Sherry saves $12 a week, about how many weeks will it take her to save enough money to buy the CD player?

$89.95 ÷ $12 = ?
↓   ↓
$90 ÷ $10 = 9

When estimating with money, it is good to find an overestimate. Adjust the dividend up and the divisor down.

A good estimate is 9 weeks.

CD **Players**
$89.95

✔ Talk About It

3. In Example B, what other compatible numbers could be used?

4. In Example D, adjusting the dividend up and the divisor down provides an overestimate. Why?

5. Suppose Sherry decides to save $25 a week instead of $12 a week. Estimate the number of weeks it will take her to save enough for the CD player.

CHECK ✔

For another example, see Set 4-2 on p. 250.

Estimate each quotient. Tell which method you used.

1. 267 ÷ 32   **2.** 790 ÷ 78   **3.** 4,390 ÷ 68   **4.** 20,963 ÷ 72

5. $36.75 ÷ 12   **6.** $59.05 ÷ 58   **7.** 478.3 ÷ 83   **8.** $207.98 ÷ 72

9. Reasoning You estimate 4,836 ÷ 56 is about 80. Is your estimate 80 greater than or less than the exact quotient? How did you decide?

For more practice, see Set 4-2 on p. 254.

PRACTICE

A Skills and Understanding

Estimate each quotient.

10. 452 ÷ 84

11. 258 ÷ 37

12. 2,964 ÷ 71

13. 5,786 ÷ 89

14. 2,005 ÷ 65

15. 9,864 ÷ 51

16. 32.8 ÷ 17

17. 625.9 ÷ 28

18. 589.7 ÷ 62

19. 78.18 ÷ 43

20. $23.80 ÷ 12

21. $365.10 ÷ 28

22. Reasoning Max needs to estimate the quotient 975 ÷ 26. Tell two different ways that Max could make a reasonable estimate and find each estimate.

B Reasoning and Problem Solving

 Math and Science

For 23–25, use the information in the table at the right.

23. The reticulated python is about how many times as long as the bushmaster?

24. The king cobra is how much longer than the diamondback rattlesnake?

25. If you had four boa constrictors that were placed end-to-end and four diamond pythons placed end-to-end, what would be the difference in length of the two sets of snakes?

Longest Snakes	
Snake	**Maximum Length (ft)**
Reticulated python	32
Anaconda	32
Indian python	25
King cobra	18
Boa constrictor	18
Diamond python	13
Bushmaster	12
Giant brown snake	11
Indigo or gopher snake	9
Diamondback rattlesnake	8

Reasoning Which quotient is greater? Explain how you know.

26. 59.40 ÷ 92 or 57.40 ÷ 92

27. $83.59 ÷ 25 or $83.59 ÷ 28

28. **Writing in Math** Is the explanation below correct? If not, tell why and write a correct response.

> Explain why $700 is a reasonable estimate for $13,380.50 ÷ 18.
>
> I can use compatible numbers that are easy to divide.
> I substitute $14,000 for $13,380.50
> and I substitute 20 for 18.
>
> Since $14,000 ÷ 20 = $700, a good estimate is $700.

C Extensions

Algebra In 29 and 30, state a reasonable value for *n*.

29. $n \div 18$ is about 200.

30. $8{,}138 \div n$ is between 200 and 300.

Mixed Review and Test Prep

Take It to the NET
Test Prep
www.scottforesman.com

Estimate each quotient.

31. $348 \div 7$

32. $259 \div 9$

33. $6{,}593 \div 8$

34. $4{,}056 \div 6$

35. Which is the most reasonable estimate for 466×8.5?

A. 2,500 **B.** 3,000 **C.** 4,500 **D.** 5,000

Enrichment

Other Bases

In the decimal system, the **base** is 10. When you count by using base 10, each group of 10 forms the next *power of ten*.

Powers of Ten		
1 one	$\longrightarrow$	$1 = 10^0$
10 ones = 1 ten	$\longrightarrow$	$10 \times 1 = 10^1$
10 tens = 1 hundred	$\longrightarrow$	$10 \times 10 = 10^2$
10 hundreds = 1 thousand	$\longrightarrow$	$10 \times 10 \times 10 = 10^3$

There are other number systems that use different bases. For example, the *binary number system* uses base two. The binary system is used in computer programming. When you count by using base 2, each group of 2 forms another *power of two*.

Powers of Two		
1 one	$\longrightarrow$	$1 = 2^0$
2 ones = 1 two	$\longrightarrow$	$2 \times 1 = 2^1$
2 twos = 1 four	$\longrightarrow$	$2 \times 2 = 2^2$
2 fours = 1 eight	$\longrightarrow$	$2 \times 2 \times 2 = 2^3$

The position of a digit in a number determines its place value. For example, in base 10, the 1 in 1,000 means 1 thousand (10^3), but in base 2, the 1 in 1,000 means 1 eight (2^3).

1. Copy the two tables above and extend them for three more rows.

2. Make a table similar to those above, but use powers of three.

Predict and Verify

Predicting and verifying when you read in math can help you use the **problem-solving strategy**, *Try, Check, and Revise,* in the next lesson.

In reading, predicting and verifying help you think about what comes next in a story. In math, predicting and verifying help you try different answers and check if they are correct.

Abby is 8 years older than Brian. The sum of their ages is 20 years. How old is Brian?

Predict a reasonable answer to try out.

To verify it, use information in the problem and check if it works.

Predict	Verify		
Predict Brian's age.	Add to find Abby's age.	Find the sum of their ages.	Compare the sum to 20.
10	10 + 8 = 18	10 + 18 = 28	too high
5	5 + 8 = 13	5 + 13 = 18	too low
7	7 + 8 = 15	7 + 15 = 22	too high
6	6 + 8 = 14	6 + 14 = 20	correct

Use the results of your first prediction to revise your prediction. Continue predicting and verifying until you find an answer that works.

1. Which statement in the problem tells you the first prediction should be a number less than 20?

2. Why was the prediction of 5 for Brian's age too low?

For 3–6, use the problem below and the picture at the right.

Skye weighs 6 pounds more than Amy. How much does each girl weigh?

3. Make a prediction about Skye's weight.

4. **Writing in Math** Explain how you can verify your prediction.

5. If your prediction was not the correct solution, make a second prediction and check if it works.

6. How much does each girl weigh?

98 pounds

For 7–10, use the problem and the picture at the right.

The golf coach spent $115 on balls and tees. If she bought at least 3 boxes of balls, how many boxes of balls and how many bags of tees did she buy?

7. Make a prediction about how many boxes of balls the golf coach bought.

8. **Writing in Math** Verify your prediction. Was it correct? Explain.

9. If your prediction was not the correct solution, make a second prediction and check if it works.

10. How many boxes of balls and how many bags of tees did the golf coach buy?

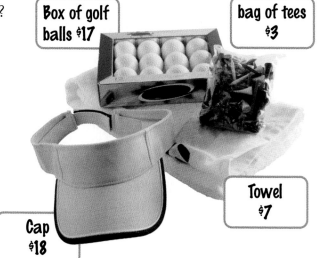

Box of golf balls $17

bag of tees $3

Towel $7

Cap $18

For 11–14, use the problem below.

The difference between the prices of two bikes is $18. The sum of the prices is $258. How much does each bike cost?

11. **Writing in Math** Phil thinks the bikes cost $118 and $100. Is he right? Explain.

12. Predict the cost of one bike. Verify your prediction.

13. If necessary, make and verify another prediction.

14. How much does each bike cost?

Problem-Solving Strategy

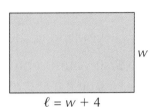

Try, Check, and Revise

Key Idea
Learning how and when to try, check, and revise can help you solve problems.

LEARN

How do you use the try, check, and revise strategy to solve a problem?

Dog Run A family plans to build a rectangular dog run for their dog Shamrock. The run will be 4 feet longer than it is wide. If 60 feet of fencing is used, what will be the length and width?

w

$\ell = w + 4$

Read and Understand

What do you know?

The dog run will be rectangular with a perimeter of 60 feet. The length is 4 ft longer than the width.

What are you trying to find?

Find the length and width of the dog run if all the fencing is used.

Plan and Solve

What strategy will you use?

Strategy: Try, Check, and Revise

Try:

15

11 [   ] 11

15

Think: 15 is 4 more than 11.

Check: $15 + 15 + 11 + 11 = 52$

Revise: 52 is too low a number. Since 52 is 8 less than 60, try adding 2 to each side.

Try:

17

13 [   ] 13

17

Check: $17 + 17 + 13 + 13 = 60$

Answer: ℓ = 17 ft and w = 13 ft

How to use Try, Check, and Revise

Step 1 Think to make a reasonable first try.

Step 2 Check by using information given in the problem.

Step 3 Revise by using your first try to make a reasonable second try. Check.

Step 4 Use previous tries to continue trying and checking until you find the answer.

Look Back and Check

Is your answer reasonable?

Yes, the length is 4 ft longer than the width and the distance around is 60 ft.

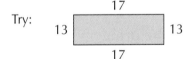 **Talk About It**

1. In Step 1, how do you know that ℓ = 15 ft and w = 11 ft are too low?

Try, check, and revise to solve. Write your answer in a sentence.

1. Suppose there is 100 ft of fencing for the dog run. If the length will still be 4 ft longer than the width, what will be the length and width?

2. The area of a rectangle is 36 square feet. The length is four times the width. What are the length and width? (Hint: The area of a rectangle is $\ell \times w$.)

PRACTICE

For more practice, see Set 4-3 on p. 254.

Solve. Write your answer in a sentence.

3. Shamrock weighs 5 pounds more than the neighbor's dog. Together they weigh 65 pounds. How much does Shamrock weigh?

4. Ed decides to build a square dog run with an area of 64 square feet (ft^2). How much fencing will he need to enclose the entire area? (Hint: The area of a square with sides of length s is $s \times s$.)

64 ft^2

5. Plans for dog runs with perimeters of 20 ft, 24 ft, 28 ft, and 32 ft are available at the local pet store. Plans for bigger runs may be ordered. If the perimeters increase in the same pattern, what will be the perimeters of the next three bigger dog runs?

6. A group of 160 students are going to a ballgame. They will travel on buses that hold 36 students. How many buses could be completely filled? How many buses will be needed? How many seats are left on the bus that is not filled?

7. **Algebra** Write an algebraic expression for each phrase given.

  a. The sum of some number x and the quotient of 376 divided by 28

  b. The product of 8 and the difference between 16 and some number n

8. **Writing in Math** Suppose the length of the dog run is twice the width, and the perimeter is 60 feet. What are the length and width? Show your work and explain how you found your solution.

STRATEGIES

- **Show What You Know**
  Draw a Picture
  Make an Organized List
  Make a Table
  Make a Graph
  Act It Out or Use Objects
- **Look for a Pattern**
- **Try, Check, and Revise**
- **Write an Equation**
- **Use Logical Reasoning**
- **Solve a Simpler Problem**
- **Work Backward**

Choose a tool
Mental Math

TEST TALK

Think It Through

Stuck? I won't give up. I can:

- Reread the problem.
- Tell what I know.
- Identify key facts and details.
- Tell the problem in my own words.
- Show the main idea.
- Try a different strategy.
- Retrace my steps.

Do You Know How?

Do You Understand?

Dividing by Multiples of 10 (4-1)

Find each quotient. Use mental math.

1. 240 ÷ 10

2. 810 ÷ 90

3. 20,000 ÷ 400

4. 28,000 ÷ 70

5. 4,800 ÷ 60

6. 56,000 ÷ 80

A Explain how you found the quotients in Exercises 1–4.

B How is dividing 3,200 by 80 the same as dividing 320 by 8?

Estimating with Two-Digit Divisors (4-2)

Estimate each quotient.

7. 424 ÷ 73

8. 8,222 ÷ 91

9. $49.24 ÷ 12

10. 452.7 ÷ 89

11. 3,461 ÷ 47

12. $72.19 ÷ 68

C Explain how you found your estimate for Exercises 7 and 8.

D Is your estimate for Exercise 9 an underestimate or an overestimate? Why?

Problem-Solving Strategy: Try, Check, and Revise (4-3)

Solve. Write your answer in a sentence.

13. Koko the poodle weighs fifteen more pounds than his owner's cat Fluffy. Together, they weigh 55 pounds. How much does each pet weigh?

14. There is 100 feet of fencing for a flower garden. If the length is to be 10 feet longer than the width, what will be the length and width?

E What strategy did you use to solve Exercise 13?

F Describe the steps you used to solve this problem.

G What are two strategies you could have used to solve Exercise 14?

MULTIPLE CHOICE

1. Use mental math to find the quotient of 6,300 ÷ 90. (4-1)

    A. 7   **B.** 70   **C.** 700   **D.** 7,000

2. Which is the best estimate of 812 ÷ 39? (4-2)

    A. 2   **B.** 20   **C.** 200   **D.** 2000

FREE RESPONSE

Find each quotient. Use mental math. (4-1)

3. 1,200 ÷ 30   **4.** 9,000 ÷ 30   **5.** 24,000 ÷ 600

6. 3,600 ÷ 300   **7.** 16,000 ÷ 40   **8.** 72,000 ÷ 90

Estimate each quotient. (4-2)

9. 492 ÷ 52   **10.** $78.17 ÷ 21   **11.** 989 ÷ 521

12. 388 ÷ 22   **13.** $94.93 ÷ 11   **14.** 5,378 ÷ 57

Solve. Write your answer in a sentence. (4-3)

15. The family decides to put a fence around a square garden that has an area of 400 square feet. How much fencing will we need to enclose this garden on all four sides? (Hint: the area of a square with sides of length s is $s \times s$.)

s

s $s \times s = 400$

16. Our high school's football team is going to the state championship tournament. 788 people signed up to take school buses to the tournament. If each bus can carry 42 people comfortably, how many buses are needed to take everyone to the tournament?

Writing in Math

17. Without dividing, how can you tell the number of zeros in the quotient of 6,300 ÷ 70? (4-1)

18. Explain why using 800 ÷ 20 gives an overestimate to the quotient of 782 ÷ 21? (4-2)

19. Explain how you would find the length of a rectangle that has an area of 6,000 square ft if you know that its width is 30 ft. (Hint: the area of a rectangle = length × width.) (4-3)

Think It Through
I can **choose division** when an amount is shared equally.

Dividing Whole Numbers by Two-Digit Divisors

✓ **WARM UP**
1. 45 ÷ 9   2. 63 ÷ 7
3. 56 ÷ 8   4. 54 ÷ 6
Estimate.
5. 128 ÷ 21 6. 353 ÷ 38

LEARN

Why use division?

The 157 fifth graders plan to take a walking trip of the municipal buildings in their town. An adult is required for every group of 18 students. How many adults must accompany the students?

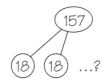

How many 18's are in 157? Find 157 ÷ 18.

What are the steps for dividing?

Example A

		What You **Think**	What You **Write**
STEP 1	Estimate. Decide where to place the first digit in the quotient.	**157 ÷ 18 is about 160 ÷ 20 or 8.** Start dividing ones.	$\dfrac{8}{18\overline{)157}}$
STEP 2	Divide the ones. Multiply and subtract.	8 groups of 18 or 8 × 18 = 144. This leaves 13 left over.	$\begin{array}{r} 8 \\ 18\overline{)157} \\ -144 \\ \hline 13 \end{array}$
STEP 3	Compare and write the answer.	Since 13 < 18, I do not have to divide again.	**157 ÷ 18 = 8 R13**
STEP 4	Check your work.	I check by multiplying and then adding.	**18 × 8 = 144** **144 + 13 = 157**

Because there is a remainder of 13, this means that 9 adults must accompany the students.

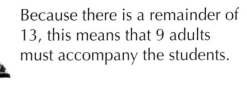

✔ Talk About It

1. Why was the 8 in the quotient for Step 2 placed above the 7 in the dividend?

2. What effect on the answer to the question does the **remainder** of 13 have in this problem?

What if your first estimate doesn't work?

Example B

	What You **Think**	What You **Write**
STEP 1 Find 260 ÷ 46. Estimate first.	**260 ÷ 46 is about 240 ÷ 40 or 6.** Start dividing ones.	
STEP 2 Divide the ones. Multiply and subtract.	**6 groups of 46 or 6 × 46 = 276** Since 276 > 260, my estimate is too high.	$$\begin{array}{r} 6 \\ 46\overline{)260} \\ -276 \\ \hline \end{array}$$ **Oops!**
STEP 3 Revise your estimate. Since 6 was too high, try 5 and divide. Then check your work.	**5 groups of 46 or 5 × 46 = 230** **260 − 230 = 30** 30 < 46 so I do not have to divide again.	$$\begin{array}{r} 5 \\ 46\overline{)260} \\ -230 \\ \hline 30 \end{array}$$ Answer: 5 R30 Check: 5 × 46 = 230 230 + 30 = 260

✔ Talk About It

3. In Example B, how do you know the estimate of 6 is too high?

4. What would you do if your estimate were too low?

Take It to the NET
More Examples
www.scottforesman.com

CHECK ✔

For another example, see Set 4-4 on p. 251.

Copy and complete.

1. $\dfrac{3\ \text{R}\ \rule{1em}{0.4pt}}{75\overline{)255}}$

2. $\dfrac{4\ \text{R}\ \rule{1em}{0.4pt}}{38\overline{)156}}$

3. $\dfrac{\rule{1em}{0.4pt}\ \text{R35}}{62\overline{)593}}$

4. $\dfrac{\rule{1em}{0.4pt}\ \text{R24}}{56\overline{)528}}$

Find each quotient. Check by multiplying.

5. $16\overline{)152}$

6. $47\overline{)389}$

7. 383 ÷ 76

8. 768 ÷ 88

9. **Number Sense** In 5–8, how could you tell that all the quotients would be less than 10?

A Skills and Understanding

Copy and complete.

10.
$$\begin{array}{r} 5 \text{ R} \\ 38\overline{)200} \end{array}$$

11.
$$\begin{array}{r} 9 \text{ R} \\ 23\overline{)208} \end{array}$$

12.
$$\begin{array}{r} \text{R}18 \\ 49\overline{)312} \end{array}$$

13.
$$\begin{array}{r} \text{R}5 \\ 56\overline{)341} \end{array}$$

Find each quotient. Check by multiplying.

14. $55\overline{)385}$

15. $57\overline{)434}$

16. $89\overline{)712}$

17. $46\overline{)163}$

18. $257 \div 43$

19. $295 \div 31$

20. $889 \div 94$

21. $618 \div 76$

22. $285 \div 87$

23. $379 \div 59$

24. $345 \div 85$

25. $276 \div 32$

26. **Number Sense** When you divide, can a remainder be greater than the divisor? Why or why not?

B Reasoning and Problem Solving

 Math and Social Studies

Use the data at the right for 27–29.

27. Juan's family drove from San Antonio to El Paso averaging 62 miles each hour. How many hours to the nearest whole hour did it take them?

28. It took Kay over 10 hours to drive from El Paso to Dallas. She drove about the same number of miles each hour. About how many miles did she drive each hour?

From	To	Distance
Houston	San Antonio	198 mi
San Antonio	El Paso	551 mi
El Paso	Dallas	648 mi
Dallas	Houston	241 mi

29. Ty drove from Dallas to Houston and then to San Antonio. He drove about the same number of miles each day. To the nearest mile, how many miles a day did he drive to arrive in San Antonio in 3 days?

30. **Writing in Math** Is the explanation below correct? If not, tell why and write a correct answer.

Find $122 \div 24$ and check by multiplying.

$$\begin{array}{r} 4 \text{ R}26 \\ 24\overline{)122} \\ \underline{96} \\ 26 \end{array} \qquad \begin{array}{r} 24 \\ \times 4 \\ \hline 96 \\ + 26 \\ \hline 112 \end{array}$$

C Extensions

Extend the method for dividing by 2-digit divisors to 3-digit divisors.
Find each quotient in 31–34.

Example C

Find 838 ÷ 212.

STEP 1

Estimate first. Decide where to place the first digit in the quotient.

838 ÷ 212 is about 800 ÷ 200 or 4.

STEP 2

Start dividing ones. Multiply and subtract.

$$
\begin{array}{r}
4 \\
212\overline{)838} \\
-848 \\
\hline
\text{Oops!}
\end{array}
$$

848 > 838
Estimate is too high.

STEP 3

Revise your estimate. Try 3.

$$
\begin{array}{r}
3 \text{ R}202 \\
212\overline{)838} \\
-636 \\
\hline
202
\end{array}
$$

Check:
$$
\begin{array}{r}
212 \\
\times\ \ 3 \\
\hline
636 \\
+ 202 \\
\hline
838
\end{array}
$$

31. 918 ÷ 112   **32.** 854 ÷ 253   **33.** 767 ÷ 321   **34.** 670 ÷ 125

Mixed Review and Test Prep

Take It to the NET
Test Prep
www.scottforesman.com

35. 2,700 ÷ 30   **36.** 90 ÷ 30   **37.** 9,000 ÷ 30   **38.** $80 ÷ 20

39. Al spent $100 on 2 items. One cost $10 more than the other. Using
Try, Check, and Revise, which would give you the correct costs?

   A. $50, $50   **B.** $40, $50   **C.** $50, $60   **D.** $45, $55

Practice Game

Some Quotients

Players: 2–4 **Materials:** 4 sets of number cards (0–9), number cube

a. Mix and then place the 4 sets of cards face down. The first player draws 3 cards and arranges them in any order to form a 3-digit dividend. Then the player tosses the number cube twice to form a 2-digit divisor. The player divides the dividend by the divisor to find the quotient (dropping the remainder). The next player repeats the process.

b. The player with the greatest quotient collects all the cards for that round. For a tie, the cards are divided between the players who tied. Play continues until there are not enough cards to complete a round. The player with the most cards wins.

Key Idea
The steps for dividing smaller numbers can be extended to larger numbers.

Dividing Larger Numbers

LEARN

Exact answer or estimate?

A candle maker has 638 candles to pack in boxes that hold 18 candles. How many boxes can be completely filled?

638 candles						
18	18	18	18	? boxes	18	18

How many 18s are in 638?

Find $638 ÷ 18$.

WARM UP

1. $359 ÷ 6$ 2. $840 ÷ 9$

3. $247 ÷ 5$ 4. $731 ÷ 8$

5. Estimate the quotient $657 ÷ 8$.

Think It Through

- I can **draw a picture to show the main idea.**

- I need to find an **exact answer** because the question asks how many boxes.

How do you divide larger numbers?

To find quotients involving larger numbers, you still estimate, multiply, and subtract.

Example A

STEP 1

Estimate. Decide where to place the first digit in the quotient.

$638 ÷ 18$ is about
$600 ÷ 20 = 30$ or 3 tens.

Start dividing tens.

STEP 2

Divide the tens. Multiply and subtract.

$$\begin{array}{r} 3 \\ 18\overline{)638} \\ \underline{54} \\ 9 \end{array}$$

Divide: $60 ÷ 20 = 3$
Multiply: $3 × 18 = 54$
Subtract: $63 − 54 = 9$
Compare: $9 < 18$

STEP 3

Bring down the ones. Divide the ones. Multiply and subtract.

$$\begin{array}{r} 35 \\ 18\overline{)638} \\ \underline{54}\downarrow \\ 98 \\ \underline{90} \\ 8 \end{array}$$

Divide: $100 ÷ 20 = 5$
Multiply: $5 × 18 = 90$
Subtract: $98 − 90 = 8$
Compare: $8 < 18$

So, 35 boxes can be completely filled.

STEP 4

Check:

$$\begin{array}{r} 35 \\ × 18 \\ \hline 280 \\ 350 \\ \hline 630 \\ + \quad 8 \\ \hline 638 \end{array}$$

When dividing larger numbers, the first digit in the quotient may be in the hundreds or thousands place.

Example B

Find 2,731 ÷ 23.

STEP 1	STEP 2	STEP 3
Estimate. Decide where to place the first digit.	Divide the hundreds. Multiply and subtract. Continue the process.	Check:

STEP 1

Estimate. Decide where to place the first digit.

Use compatible numbers.

2,700 ÷ 27 = 100

Start dividing hundreds.

STEP 2

Divide the hundreds. Multiply and subtract. Continue the process.

```
        118 R17
   23)2,731
      - 2 3
        43
      - 23
        201
        184
         17
```

STEP 3

Check:

```
      118
   ×   23
      354
     2360
     2714
   +   17
    2,731
```

✔ **Talk About It**

1. In Example A, why was the answer given as 35, not 35 R8?

2. In Example B above, why do you start by dividing hundreds?

3. **Number Sense** If you are asked to find 6,319 ÷ 59, how do you know the quotient is greater than 100 before you actually divide?

CHECK ✔

For another example, see Set 4-5 on p. 251.

Copy and complete.

1.
```
      2 1 R ▪ ▪
   45)9 8 0
    - 9 0
     ▪ 0
    - 4 5
      3 5
```

2.
```
      2 ▪ R ▪
   27)6 7 8
    - 5 4
     ▪ ▪ 8
    - 1 3 5
        3
```

3.
```
        3 ▪
   97)3,2 9 8
     ▪ ▪ 1
      3 8 ▪
    - ▪ ▪ 8
        0
```

4.
```
        4 ▪ R ▪
   72)3,3 9 0
      2 8 ▪
      5 1 ▪
    - ▪ ▪ 4
        ▪
```

Find each quotient. Check your answers by multiplying.

5. 36)5,844

6. 45)9,812

7. 56)5,674

8. 76)8,642

9. **Number Sense** How could you tell that all the quotients in Exercises 5–8 would be greater than 100?

Section B Lesson 4-5   219

A Skills and Understanding

Find each quotient. Check your answers by multiplying.

10. $27\overline{)6,732}$ **11.** $35\overline{)7,655}$ **12.** $29\overline{)5,728}$ **13.** $19\overline{)5,867}$

14. $38\overline{)5,765}$ **15.** $72\overline{)7,289}$ **16.** $87\overline{)1,198}$ **17.** $64\overline{)9,647}$

18. $7,856 \div 36$ **19.** $9,152 \div 91$ **20.** $6,388 \div 48$ **21.** $7,615 \div 55$

22. $5,486 \div 46$ **23.** $3,117 \div 23$ **24.** $4,328 \div 93$ **25.** $2,532 \div 72$

Number Sense Choose the most reasonable estimate.

26. $7,400 \div 90$ is   A. greater than 80   B. less than 80   C. exactly 80

27. $4,380 \div 60$ is   A. greater than 70   B. less than 70   C. exactly 70

28. $8,125 \div 80$ is   A. greater than 100   B. less than 100   C. exactly 100

B Reasoning and Problem Solving

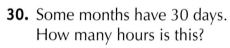
Math and Science

Use the data at the right for 29–30.

29. Earth makes one full rotation around its axis in 1 day. If 168 hours pass, how many rotations has Earth made?

30. Some months have 30 days. How many hours is this?

31.  Write a problem that would require you to divide 450 by 12 to find the answer.

Data File

Time and Measurement

60 seconds = 1 minute

60 minutes = 1 hour

24 hours = 1 day

365 days = 1 year

12 months in 1 year

C Extensions

Study the examples below. Look for a pattern. Then use the pattern to find the quotients in 32–40.

$3,600 \div 400 = 9$	$70,000 \div 700 = 100$	$3,000 \div 500 = 6$
$36,000 \div 400 = 90$	$70,000 \div 7,000 = 10$	$30,000 \div 5,000 = 6$
$360,000 \div 400 = 900$	$70,000 \div 70,000 = 1$	$300,000 \div 50,000 = 6$

32. $6,300 \div 700$ **33.** $54,000 \div 900$ **34.** $250,000 \div 5,000$

35. $50,000 \div 10,000$ **36.** $720,000 \div 9,000$ **37.** $20,000 \div 20,000$

38. $16,000 \div 2,000$ **39.** $27,000 \div 300$ **40.** $480,000 \div 6,000$

Mixed Review and Test Prep

Take It to the NET
Test Prep
www.scottforesman.com

41. $32\overline{)4{,}618}$ **42.** $65\overline{)7{,}548}$ **43.** $4{,}977 \div 72$

44. Earth completes one rotation every 24 hours. How many hours will pass with eight rotations?

   A. Fewer than 160 h   **C.** More than 240 h

   B. Between 160 h and 240 h   **D.** Exactly 240 h

Learning with Technology

The Place-Value Blocks eTool

Estimate each quotient. Then make an array with dimensions of your estimated quotient and the given divisor. Compare the size of your array to the given dividend. How close was your estimated quotient? Try different strategies to get your estimates and the actual dimensions as close to each other as you can.

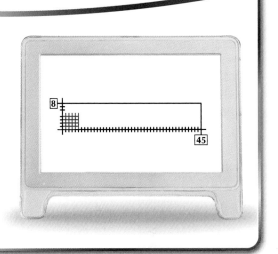

   1. $360 \div 45$ **2.** $189 \div 21$ **3.** $372 \div 62$

Discovery CHANNEL SCHOOL

Discover Math in Your World

Sizeable and Speedy

Among Africa's big cats, the lion is the largest. From tip to tail, a lion can measure over 10 feet in length and can weigh more than 500 pounds. Despite its size, a lion can reach speeds of up to 36 miles an hour.

1. A kilogram is approximately 2.2 pounds. Is a 500-pound lion more or less than 250 kilograms? Explain.

2. A lion can travel 38,016 inches per minute. Convert this speed to yards per minute (1 yard = 36 inches).

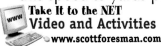
Take It to the NET
Video and Activities
www.scottforesman.com

Key Idea
You can divide using mental math, paper and pencil, or a calculator.

Materials
• calculator

TEST TALK

Think It Through
Sometimes using **mental math** or **paper and pencil** is faster than using a **calculator**.

Dividing: Choose a Computation Method

LEARN

Which computation method should you use?

When you compute, first look at the numbers and decide which method to use: mental math, paper and pencil, or a calculator.

	Example A	Example B	Example C
What You Think	Find 35,000 ÷ 70. This is easy to do in my head, so I will use **mental math.**	Find 32,340 ÷ 70. Both numbers are multiples of 10, so 32,340 ÷ 70 is the same as 3,234 ÷ 7. One-digit divisors are easy to do with **paper and pencil.**	Find 35,678 ÷ 74. There are no basic facts or zeros so using a **calculator** is the easiest way to find the quotient.
What You Do	**35,000 ÷ 70 is the same as 3,500 ÷ 7.** Since 35 ÷ 7 = 5, 35 *hundreds* ÷ 7 must be 5 *hundreds*. **So, 35,000 ÷ 70 = 500.**	$$\begin{array}{r} 462 \\ 7\overline{)3,234} \\ -28 \\ \hline 43 \\ -42 \\ \hline 14 \\ -14 \\ \hline 0 \end{array}$$ **So, 32,340 ÷ 70 = 462.**	3 5 6 7 8 ÷ ☐ 7 4 ☐ = 482.13514 **So, 35,678 ÷ 74 is a little greater than 482.**

✔ Talk About It

1. Give two numbers that are appropriate for you to divide using:

    a. Mental math   **b.** Paper and pencil   **c.** A calculator

2. **Reasoning** Give a reason why you would choose to use mental math, paper and pencil, or a calculator to find 4,500 ÷ 90.

3. In Example A, how do you know that 35,000 ÷ 70 is the same as 3,500 ÷ 7?

Divide and check. Tell what computation method you used.

1. 620 ÷ 20   **2.** 600 ÷ 30   **3.** 607 ÷ 40   **4.** 100,000 ÷ 50

5. Number Sense Beth used a calculator to find 4,200 ÷ 60. Do you think she could have found the quotient faster using a different calculation method? Explain.

PRACTICE

For more practice, see Set 4-6 on p. 255.

Ⓐ Skills and Understanding

Divide and check. Tell what computation method you used.

6. $20\overline{)600}$ **7.** $80\overline{)2,400}$ **8.** $25\overline{)3,679}$ **9.** $47\overline{)329}$

10. $70\overline{)3,570}$ **11.** $16\overline{)5,680}$ **12.** $44\overline{)44,000}$ **13.** $85\overline{)8,500}$

14. 477 ÷ 9   **15.** 3,600 ÷ 400   **16.** 56,000 ÷ 8,000   **17.** 5,649 ÷ 24

18. 34,760 ÷ 79   **19.** 81,000 ÷ 90   **20.** 22,000 ÷ 16   **21.** 240,000 ÷ 24

22. Number Sense Why is using a calculator not a good way to find 8,000 ÷ 20?

Ⓑ Reasoning and Problem Solving

Use the data at the right for 23–25.

23. Airline D carried how many times as many passengers than Airline E?

24. Airline B carried how many more passengers than Airline C?

25. **Writing in Math** Which airline carried about four times as many passengers as Airline A? Explain how you decided.

Yearly Airline Passengers

Airline	Passengers
Airline A	20,000,000
Airline B	80,000,000
Airline C	30,000,000
Airline D	87,000,000
Airline E	3,000,000

Mixed Review and Test Prep

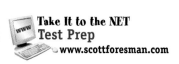

Take It to the NET
Test Prep
www.scottforesman.com

Find each quotient. Check by multiplying.

26. 3,147 ÷ 67   **27.** 3,648 ÷ 38

28. 3,500 ÷ 35   **29.** 4,675 ÷ 24

30. Algebra These ordered pairs all use the same rule: (650, 130), (40, 8), (200, 40) (55, 11). Which ordered pair uses the same rule?

     A. (50, 10)   **B.** (20, 5)   **C.** (450, 50)   **D.** (9, 45)

TEST TALK

Think It Through
I need to decide **what rule is used** for the ordered pairs.

Key Idea
You need to be careful about placing zeros in the quotient.

Vocabulary
• quotient (p. 152)
• dividend (p. 152)
• divisor (p. 152)
• remainder (p. 152)

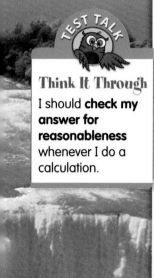

Think It Through
I should **check my answer for reasonableness** whenever I do a calculation.

Dividing with Zeros in the Quotient

LEARN

WARM UP
1. 248 ÷ 13
2. 383 ÷ 28
3. 492 ÷ 25
4. 319 ÷ 81
5. 6,122 ÷ 38
6. 6,428 ÷ 72

When is a zero placed in the quotient?

Sometimes when you bring down the next digit in dividing, you get a number less than the divisor. You need to place a zero in the quotient and bring down the next digit.

Example A

STEP 1

$74\overline{)7,854}$

Estimate. Decide where to place the first digit in the quotient.

Think:
$8,000 ÷ 80 = 100$

Start dividing hundreds.

STEP 2

Divide hundreds. Multiply, subtract, and bring down.

$$\begin{array}{r} 10 \\ 74\overline{)7,854} \\ -74 \\ \hline 45 \end{array}$$

Since 45 < 74, you cannot divide. Write a 0 in the quotient. Bring down the next digit.

STEP 3

Continue to divide.

$$\begin{array}{r} 106 \text{ R10} \\ 74\overline{)7,854} \\ -74 \\ \hline 45 \\ -0 \\ \hline 454 \\ -444 \\ \hline 10 \end{array}$$

Example B

$$\begin{array}{r} 4 \\ 22\overline{)9,020} \end{array}$$

Estimate.

Think:
$8,000 ÷ 20 = 400$

Divide.

$$\begin{array}{r} 41 \\ 22\overline{)9,020} \\ -88 \\ \hline 22 \\ -22 \\ \hline 00 \end{array}$$

Since 0 < 22, you cannot divide. You still need to bring down the last digit in the dividend.

Continue dividing.

$$\begin{array}{r} 410 \\ 22\overline{)9,020} \\ -88 \\ \hline 22 \\ -22 \\ \hline 00 \\ -0 \\ \hline 0 \end{array}$$

✔ Talk About It

1. Why are zeros needed in the quotients for Examples A and B?

Find each quotient. Check your answers by multiplying.

1. 4,320 ÷ 36   **2.** 8,262 ÷ 27   **3.** 7,795 ÷ 38

4. Number Sense How could you easily tell that the quotient 6,622 ÷ 22 could not be 31?

Think It Through
I should **estimate first.**

PRACTICE   For more practice, see Set 4-7 on p. 256.

Ⓐ Skills and Understanding

Find each quotient. Check your answers by multiplying.

5. 47)$\overline{487}$ **6.** 25)$\overline{2,575}$ **7.** 78)$\overline{3,918}$ **8.** 46)$\overline{37,036}$

9. 48)$\overline{9,851}$ **10.** 49)$\overline{10,058}$ **11.** 89)$\overline{9,889}$ **12.** 74)$\overline{33,364}$

13. 1,168 ÷ 29   **14.** 3,009 ÷ 30   **15.** 32,889 ÷ 16   **16.** 17,024 ÷ 56

17. 9,020 ÷ 22   **18.** 26,850 ÷ 66   **19.** 8,413 ÷ 40   **20.** 14,230 ÷ 75

21. Number Sense How can you tell that you have made a mistake when you find that 8,262 ÷ 27 = 36? What should the quotient be?

Ⓑ Reasoning and Problem Solving

22. Use the information at the right. How many cu yd of water flow over Paulo Afonso Falls in 1 second?

23. How many cu yd of water flow over Paulo Afonso Falls in 1 hour?

24. In 1 sec, 7,625 cubic yards of water flow over Niagara Falls. How much water flows over the falls in 1 min?

25. <u>**Writing in Math**</u> Is 4,273 ÷ 25 greater than 20, less than 20, greater than 200, or less than 200? Explain.

Every minute, 226,800 cu yd of water flow over the Paulo Afonso Falls, located in Brazil.

🦉 Mixed Review and Test Prep

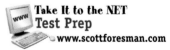
Take It to the NET
Test Prep
www.scottforesman.com

Divide. Tell whether you used mental math, paper and pencil, or a calculator.

26. 5,640 ÷ 40   **27.** 6,000 ÷ 30   **28.** 4,698 ÷ 72   **29.** 800,000 ÷ 200

30. Which is the best estimate for $68.95 ÷ 35?

    A. $200   **B.** $20   **C.** $2   **D.** $0.20

Problem-Solving Skill

Key Idea
Identifying hidden questions helps you solve multiple-step problems.

Multiple-Step Problems

LEARN

How do you find hidden questions in multiple-step problems?

Some story problems have a hidden question or questions. To solve the problem, you must first find and **answer the hidden question** or questions.

Fundraiser A school raised money for 1 year to help flood victim families. Students, staff, and parents raised $50,000 but had to pay the expenses as shown at the right. The money left was divided equally among the 25 families. How much did each family receive?

Total amount received:	$50,000
Expenses:	
Advertising	$5,000
Record keeping	$2,000

Read and Understand

Identify key facts and details and tell what the problem is asking.

$50,000 was raised.
Expenses to be deducted include $5,000 and $2,000.
The problem asks for the amount of money each of the 25 families received.

Plan and Solve

To solve problems that involve multiple steps, ask yourself what hidden questions are in the problem.

Hidden question 1: What were the total expenses for the fundraiser?

$5,000 + $2,000 = $7,000

Hidden question 2: How much money was left after expenses?

$50,000 − $7,000 = $43,000

✔ **Talk About It**

1. What are the hidden questions and why is it necessary to find the answers to these questions?

2. Give the answer to the **Fundraiser** problem in a sentence.

Write and answer the hidden question or questions in each problem and then solve the problem. Write your answer in a complete sentence. Use the information at the right for Problem 1.

1. Nancy bought 2 DVDs on sale. She gave the salesperson a $2 discount coupon and a $50 bill. The tax was $3.08. How much change should she receive?

2. **Number Sense** Could you have subtracted $2 from $50 as a first step to solve Problem 1? Explain.

PRACTICE

For more practice, see Set 4-8 on p. 256.

Write and answer the hidden question or questions in each problem and then solve the problem. Write your answer in a complete sentence. Use the information at the right for 4 and 5.

3. Ms. Jones spent $95.08, including $5.38 tax for 5 toys for her grandchildren. The price of each toy was the same. What was the price for one toy?

4. Carlos wants to buy 2 CDs on sale and a book that costs $4.95. The tax on the items will be $1.42. Carlos has only $14. How much more does he need to buy the CDs and the book?

5. A customer purchased 6 CDs and 4 cassettes for a local charitable organization. The organization does not have to pay sales tax. The customer pays with three $20 bills and one $10 bill. How much change does the customer receive?

6. Twenty copies of the same paperback book were donated to the school library. The cost, including the tax of $6.95, was $145.95. What was the cost of one paperback book?

7. **Writing in Math** Write a two-step problem about going to the movies that has a hidden question. Tell what the hidden question is and solve your problem. Write your answer in a complete sentence.

Data File

Metro-Cineplex 22 Ticket Prices		
	Before 3 PM	**Evening**
Children under 12	$5.00	$6.00
Adults	$5.00	$8.50
Seniors	$5.00	$6.00

All text pages available online and on CD-ROM.

Do You Know How?

Do You Understand?

Dividing Whole Numbers by Two-Digit Divisors (4-4)
Dividing Larger Numbers (4-5)

Find each quotient. Check by multiplying.

1. 324 ÷ 81

2. 286 ÷ 68

3. 416 ÷ 52

4. 484 ÷ 24

5. 812 ÷ 19

6. 596 ÷ 32

A Explain how you found the quotient in Exercise 2.

B How could you tell that the quotient for Exercise 6 is less than 20?

Dividing: Choose a Computation Method (4-6)
Dividing with Zeros in the Quotient (4-7)

Calculate each quotient.

7. 4,500 ÷ 900

8. 2,840 ÷ 40

9. 3,700 ÷ 37

10. 1,350 ÷ 90

11. 5,796 ÷ 28

12. 6,776 ÷ 22

C Tell what method you used for Exercise 7 and why.

D Why is a zero needed in each quotient for Exercises 11–12?

Problem-Solving Skill: Multiple-Step Problems (4-8)

Write and answer the hidden question or questions in the problem and then solve the problem. Write your answer in a complete sentence.

13. For his birthday, Pat received the same amount of money from each of his 12 friends, plus $20.00 from his older brother and $20.00 from his sister. If Pat received a total of $220.00, how much did each friend give him?

E Explain why you cannot just divide $220.00 by 12 to find how much each of Pat's friends gave him for his birthday?

F Write a two-step problem about Tina that has a hidden question. Then solve the problem.

Tina walks 4 blocks from home to school each morning. She walks 6 blocks from school to her grandmother's house everyday after school.

Think It Through
For multiple-choice items, first **eliminate any unreasonable answers.**

MULTIPLE CHOICE

1. What is the quotient of 412 ÷ 54? (4-4)

    A. 7   **B.** 7 R14   **C.** 7 R34   **D.** 8 R20

2. What is the quotient of 972 ÷ 27? (4-5)

    A. 30   **B.** 36   **C.** 40   **D.** 46

FREE RESPONSE

Find each quotient. (4-4)

3. 608 ÷ 19   **4.** 416 ÷ 53   **5.** 628 ÷ 32   **6.** 236 ÷ 42

Find each quotient. (4-5)

7. 822 ÷ 38   **8.** 4,515 ÷ 21   **9.** 7,918 ÷ 37   **10.** 9,072 ÷ 28

Use the most appropriate method to find each quotient. (4-6)

11. 7,200 ÷ 60   **12.** 42,000 ÷ 700   **13.** 43,680 ÷ 60   **14.** 21,714 ÷ 47

Find each quotient. (Hint: each quotient should contain a zero.) (4-7)

15. 4,428 ÷ 41   **16.** 8,526 ÷ 42   **17.** 8,829 ÷ 84   **18.** 7,750 ÷ 25

19. Write and answer the hidden question or questions in the problem and then solve the problem. Write your answer in a complete sentence.

Billy Bob wins $500 in a school raffle. He decides to keep $120 for himself, give $60 to charity, and divide the rest equally among his 5 brothers and sisters. How much will each brother or sister receive from Billy Bob?

Total amount Billy Bob won:	$500
Amount Billy Bob keeps:	$120
Amount Billy Bob gives to charity:	$60

Writing in Math

20. Without dividing, tell whether 8,422 ÷ 38 is more or less than 200? How did you decide on your answer? (4-4)

21. Explain how you can decide when a quotient must contain a zero? (4-7)

22. Why did you need to find and answer the hidden questions in Exercise 19 above? (4-8)

Think It Through
• I can **look for patterns** to see how to divide by 10, 100, and 1,000.
• I can **write a rule** using the patterns I find.

Dividing Decimals by 10, 100, and 1,000

LEARN

Activity

What is the pattern?

a. Use a calculator to find each quotient. Look for patterns of zeros.

$245 \div 1 = n$	$61.5 \div 1 = n$	$2.98 \div 1 = n$
$245 \div 10 = n$	$61.5 \div 10 = n$	$2.98 \div 10 = n$
$245 \div 100 = n$	$61.5 \div 100 = n$	$2.98 \div 100 = n$
$245 \div 1,000 = n$	$61.5 \div 1,000 = n$	$2.98 \div 1,000 = n$

b. Write a rule that tells how to find a quotient if the divisor is 10, 100, or 1,000.

How can you divide by 10, 100, and 1,000?

Example A

What is $12.8 \div 10$?

Dividing a number by 10 makes it smaller, so move the decimal point to the left. Place-value patterns tell you that dividing by 10 means moving the decimal point only one place.

So, $12.8 \div \underline{10} = 1.28$.

Example B

What is $44.5 \div 1,000$?

Place-value patterns tell you that dividing by 1,000 or 10^3 means moving the decimal point three places to the left.

So, $44.5 \div \underline{1,000} = 0.0445$.

You need to use a zero as a placeholder.

Remember that decimals such as 0.45 and 0.450 are equivalent. But 0.45 and 0.045 are not equivalent.

✔ Talk About It

1. In Example A, how did place-value patterns help you divide by 10 mentally?

2. In the quotient in Example B, why was it necessary to place a zero in the tenths place?

3. How is dividing 615 by 100 like dividing 6.15 by 100? How is it different?

For another example, see Set 4-9 on p. 253.

Find each quotient. Use mental math.

1. 49.1 ÷ 10   **2.** 38.3 ÷ 100   **3.** 4.8 ÷ 100   **4.** 23.92 ÷ 1,000

5. Reasoning Complete. To find 45.3 ÷ 100, move the decimal point __?__.

PRACTICE

For more practice, see Set 4-9 on p. 257.

A Skills and Understanding

Find each quotient. Use mental math.

6. 72.1 ÷ 10   **7.** 34.1 ÷ 100   **8.** 21.64 ÷ 1,000   **9.** 3.52 ÷ 100

10. 346.9 ÷ 100   **11.** 568.9 ÷ 10   **12.** 84.43 ÷ 100   **13.** 215.67 ÷ 1,000

14. 0.65 ÷ 10   **15.** 1.46 ÷ 100   **16.** 295.7 ÷ 100   **17.** 16.72 ÷ 1,000

Algebra Write 10, 100, or 1,000 for each n.

18. $3.5 ÷ n = 0.0035$ **19.** $12.5 ÷ n = 0.125$ **20.** $(26.4 + 3.2) ÷ n = 2.96$

21. Number Sense Dividing 1.28 by 10 gives the same result as dividing 12.8 by what number?

B Reasoning and Problem Solving

22. A class of 168 students plan to take a nature hike in a nearby state park. The park requires that for every 10 students one adult also be present. How many adults are needed?

23. The trail is 12 miles long. The park information recommends planning on 3 hours to hike 9 miles. At that rate, how many hours will it take the students to complete the hike?

24. **Writing in Math** 23.6 ÷ 10 is the same as 23.6 times what decimal? Explain how you found your answer.

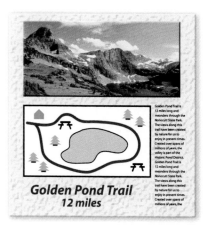

Golden Pond Trail
12 miles

Mixed Review and Test Prep

Take It to the NET
Test Prep
www.scottforesman.com

Find each n.

25. $32 × (8 − 7) = n$ **26.** $26 × n = 12 − 12$ **27.** $(48 + 22) + 5 = 48 + (22 + n)$

28. A fifth grade class earned $2,440 at a fundraiser for their class trip. However, they had to pay expenses of $690. The remaining money was split equally among the 35 students. How much did each get?

A. $5   **B.** $50   **C.** $1,750   **D.** $3,130

Dividing Money by Two-Digit Divisors

LEARN

How can you divide money?

You buy one 16-ounce bottle of cranberry juice costing $2.40. How much do you pay for each ounce of juice?

Example A

Find $2.40 ÷ 16.

STEP 1

Write the decimal point in the quotient directly above the decimal point in the dividend.

$$16\overline{)\$2.\overset{\cdot}{4}0}$$

STEP 2

16 > 2 so place a 0 above the 2.

Estimate.

$$\overset{\$0.10}{20\overline{)\$2.00}}$$

Start dividing tenths.

$$\begin{array}{r} 0.1 \\ 16\overline{)\$2.40} \\ -16 \end{array}$$

STEP 3

Bring down hundredths. Continue dividing.

$$\begin{array}{r} \$0.15 \\ 16\overline{)\$2.40} \\ -16 \\ \hline 80 \\ -80 \\ \hline 0 \end{array}$$

You pay $0.15 for 1 ounce of juice.

Example B

Find $13.59 ÷ 60.

Sometimes when you divide money, there is a remainder after you divide the cents (hundredths). You can attach a zero and continue dividing to determine the thousandths. Then you can round to the nearest cent.

So, $13.59 ÷ 60 is about $0.23.

$$\begin{array}{r} \$0.226 \\ 60\overline{)\$13.590} \\ 12\ 0 \\ \hline 1\ 59 \\ 1\ 20 \\ \hline 390 \\ 360 \\ \hline 30 \end{array}$$

← Attach a zero.

✔ Talk About It

1. In Example A, why do you place a 0 above the 2 in the dividend?

2. In Example B, why is a 0 placed after $13.59?

Take It to the NET
More Examples
www.scottforesman.com

Find each quotient. Check your answers by multiplying. (Round to the nearest cent, if necessary.)

1. $12\overline{)\$4.92}$ **2.** $35\overline{)\$26.60}$ **3.** $\$131.79 \div 46$ **4.** $\$0.86 \div 43$

5. Estimation Use estimation to explain why $\$37.50 \div 25$ could NOT be $16.

PRACTICE

For more practice, see Set 4-10 on p. 257.

Ⓐ Skills and Understanding

Find each quotient. Check your answers by multiplying. (Round to the nearest cent, if necessary.)

6. $50\overline{)\$75.00}$ **7.** $23\overline{)\$2.53}$ **8.** $76\overline{)\$182.76}$ **9.** $19\overline{)\$32.85}$

10. $\$5.00 \div 40$ **11.** $\$29.16 \div 12$ **12.** $\$82.98 \div 36$ **13.** $\$49.56 \div 84$

Number Sense Decide if each quotient is greater than or less than $1.00.

14. $28\overline{)\$65.00}$ **15.** $67\overline{)\$58.68}$ **16.** $8\overline{)\$8.08}$ **17.** $20\overline{)\$18.99}$

18. Estimation Is the quotient you get when you divide $85.50 by 20 about $0.40, $4.00, or $40? Explain.

Ⓑ Reasoning and Problem Solving

Use the data at the right for 19–21.

19. To the nearest cent, what is the cost of 1 oz of Swiss cheese?

20. Maria buys 4 oz of Swiss cheese and 11 oz of cheddar. How much does she spend?

21. Number Sense Which costs more per ounce, cheddar or provolone? How did you decide?

22. **Writing in Math** Fifteen pounds of meat cost $26.98. Is it reasonable that the price per pound is $16? Why or why not?

Data File

Cheese	Number of oz	Cost
Swiss	8	$2.56
Gouda	14	$3.79
Cheddar	22	$4.84
Provolone	15	$5.29

Mixed Review and Test Prep

Take It to the NET
Test Prep
www.scottforesman.com

Find each quotient.

23. $39 \div 100$ **24.** $5.8 \div 1,000$ **25.** $91.3 \div 10$ **26.** $4.62 \div 100$

27. If 5 people share the cost of a $12.95 pizza, how much will each person pay?

 A. $4.32 **B.** $2.59 **C.** $2.57 **D.** $2.00

Think It Through
• I need to **decide what operation to use.**

 All text pages available online and on CD-ROM.

Think It Through

- To divide **I can think about equal parts.**
- I need to **use what I already know.**

Dividing Decimals by Whole Numbers

LEARN

How can you extend what you know about dividing whole numbers to dividing decimals?

Think about what you know about dividing whole numbers and dividing money.

✔ **WARM UP**

Round to the nearest whole number.

1. 35.2   2. 1.79

Round to the nearest tenth.

3. 1.74   4. 42.88

Example A

Find 1.5 ÷ 3.

What You **Think**	What You **Write**
You can use the same process here as you use to divide money. 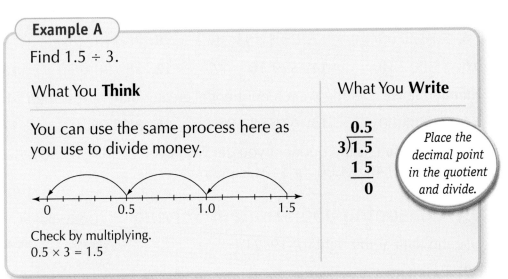 Check by multiplying. 0.5 × 3 = 1.5	$$\begin{array}{r} 0.5 \\ 3\overline{)1.5} \\ \underline{1\ 5} \\ 0 \end{array}$$ *Place the decimal point in the quotient and divide.*

Example B

Find 1.5 ÷ 30.

What You **Think**	What You **Write**
You can extend what you have learned to divide 1.5 by 30. Since 30 > 3, 1.5 ÷ 30 < 1.5 ÷ 3. Check by multiplying. 0.05 × 30 = 1.50 or 1.5.	$$\begin{array}{r} 0.05 \\ 30\overline{)1.50} \\ \underline{-\quad 0} \\ 1\ 50 \\ \underline{-\ 1\ 50} \\ 0 \end{array}$$ *Place a 0 in the dividend.*

✔ **Talk About It**

1. Why do you need to insert a zero to the right of the decimal point in the quotient of Example B?

2. How is dividing decimals like and unlike dividing whole numbers?

3. **Number Sense** Describe the pattern in the two examples.

How do you divide decimals by whole numbers?

Remember to place the decimal point in the quotient above the decimal point in the dividend. Then divide the same way you would divide whole numbers.

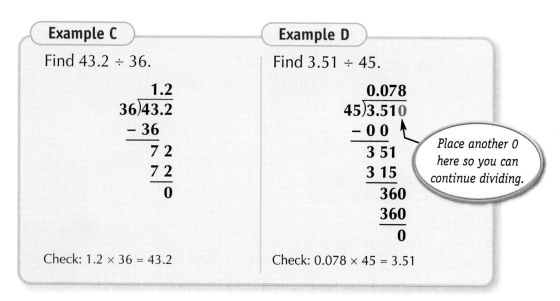

Example C

Find 43.2 ÷ 36.

```
        1.2
   36)43.2
     - 36
       7 2
       7 2
         0
```

Check: 1.2 × 36 = 43.2

Example D

Find 3.51 ÷ 45.

```
       0.078
   45)3.510
     - 0 0
       3 51
       3 15
         360
         360
           0
```

Place another 0 here so you can continue dividing.

Check: 0.078 × 45 = 3.51

✔ Talk About It

4. In Example D, why is it necessary to place a zero to the right of the decimal point in the quotient?

5. Reasoning Is 0.078 the same as .078? Explain your answer.

Take It to the NET
More Examples
www.scottforesman.com

CHECK ✔

For another example, see Set 4-11 on p. 253.

Find each quotient. Check by multiplying.

1. 12)51   **2.** 23)1.15   **3.** 24.8 ÷ 80   **4.** 2.328 ÷ 97

5. Number Sense Without doing the division, how do you know that 117.8 ÷ 38 could not be 31?

PRACTICE

For more practice, see Set 4-11 on p. 257.

Ⓐ Skills and Understanding

Find each quotient. Check by multiplying.

6. 16)19.2   **7.** 32)4.48   **8.** 45)362.7   **9.** 70)7.7

10. 87)0.87   **11.** 28)14   **12.** 93)729.12   **13.** 37)214.6

14. 656.0 ÷ 40   **15.** 68.88 ÷ 21   **16.** 67.2 ÷ 64   **17.** 3.0 ÷ 60

18. 0.76 ÷ 38   **19.** 102.8 ÷ 20   **20.** 0.44 ÷ 55   **21.** 100.62 ÷ 78

Number Sense Choose the best estimate for each.

22. $47.52 \div 83$ **A.** 60   **B.** 6   **C.** 0.6

23. $18.9 \div 21$ **A.** 0.01   **B.** 0.1   **C.** 1

24. $36.6 \div 40$ **A.** 0.09   **B.** 0.9   **C.** 9

25. Number Sense Explain how you know an error was made when you find that the quotient for $103.53 \div 51$ is 23.

B Reasoning and Problem Solving

Math and Social Studies

Unit pricing is a way in which consumers can compare the cost of items they purchase. To find the unit price, divide the total cost by the number of items. Use the information at the right for 26–28.

Item	Cans In pack	Cost
Apple juice	12	$1.09
Tomato juice	24	$2.39
Grape juice	24	$2.56

26. Find the unit price to the nearest cent of one can of each kind of juice.

27. Excluding tax, what is the total cost of three packs of each kind of juice?

28. How much more would you pay for 24 cans of grape juice than for 24 cans of apple juice?

29. A sheet of paper is 27.5 in. wide. If it is cut into 11 strips of equal width, how wide will each strip be?

30. A family of five people attends a theme park. They purchase 2 adult tickets for $27.50 each and 3 student tickets for $12.50 each. If the 5 tickets are purchased with a $100 bill, how much money is left?

31. Reasonableness Is $52.3 \div 25$ a little less than 2, a little greater than 2, a little less than 20, or a little greater than 20? Explain your thinking.

32. Writing in Math Sue's work is shown below. Find the quotient that is not correct. Write it correctly and explain the error.

> A. $35.28 \div 28 = 1.26$
> B. $1.728 \div 64 = 0.27$
> C. $725.4 \div 93 = 7.8$

C Extensions

Study the examples below. Look for a pattern.

$32 \div 80 = 0.4$	$90 \div 900 = 0.1$	$20 \div 4{,}000 = 0.005$
$3.2 \div 80 = 0.04$	$9 \div 900 = 0.01$	$2 \div 4{,}000 = 0.0005$
$0.32 \div 80 = 0.004$	$0.9 \div 900 = 0.001$	$0.2 \div 4{,}000 = 0.00005$

Find each quotient. Use mental math.

33. $4 \div 40$ **34.** $2.5 \div 50$ **35.** $0.56 \div 800$

36. $0.028 \div 700$ **37.** $8.1 \div 900$ **38.** $5.4 \div 6{,}000$

Mixed Review and Test Prep

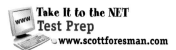

Take It to the NET
Test Prep
www.scottforesman.com

39. $\$3.12 \div 39$ **40.** $\$18.24 \div 38$ **41.** $\$191.52 \div 38$

42. Jill, Ansley, Noah, and Otto each walked 6 miles to raise money for a charity. Jill and Ansley each raised $3 for each mile walked, Noah raised $2.50 for each mile, and Otto raised $20 in all. Who raised the most money?

A. Jill   **B.** Ansley   **C.** Noah   **D.** Otto

Think It Through
• I need to **decide what operations to use.**

Enrichment

Comparing Decimals

Decimals such as 0.0005 and 0.0031 can be compared easily by extending the decimal place-value chart to the right of the thousandths place. The place-value chart below shows that $0.0005 < 0.0031$.

Compare. Write $<$, $>$, or $=$ for each ●.

1. 0.0079 ● 0.0431

2. 0.0070 ● 0.0007

3. 0.0100 ● 0.01

4. 1.2390 ● 1.0239

5. 0.0670 ● 0.067

6. 0.0100 ● 0.0099

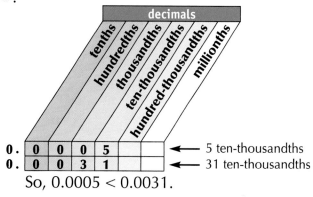

So, $0.0005 < 0.0031$.

Problem-Solving Applications

Animal Speeds
Measuring the fastest speed that an animal can swim, run, or fly can be tricky. It is difficult to determine if an animal is really moving at its top speed at a particular time. Even so, many impressive speeds have been recorded in the animal kingdom.

Trivia A cockroach can run 50 body lengths a second. If a racehorse could do this, it would be able to run at almost 300 miles per hour!

Key Facts

Animal	Speed
• Peregrine falcon	217 mph
• Sailfish	68 mph
• Greyhound	39 mph
• Elephant	25 mph
• Squirrel	12 mph
• Snail	0.03 mph
• Sea horse	0.01 mph

Using Key Facts

2 How much faster can a peregrine falcon travel than an African elephant?

1 A human sprinter can run about 929 times as fast as a snail. If a snail can move at 0.03 mile per hour, how fast can a person run?

3 Dolphins can swim about 8 miles per hour faster than a leatherback turtle. This turtle can swim about 4.4 times as fast as an Olympic swimmer. If the top speed of a swimmer is about 5 miles per hour, how fast can a dolphin swim?

4 A sloth moves extremely slowly. Even if it moved continuously for 10 hours, it would only travel 1.5 miles. Divide this distance by the time to find the sloth's speed in miles per hour. Which is faster: a snail or a sloth?

5 During migration, snow geese may fly 3,000 miles at an average speed of 50 miles per hour. Divide to find how many hours snow geese may spend in the air during migration.

6 **Writing in Math** Write a word problem involving animal speeds that can be solved using division. Write the answer to your problem in a complete sentence.

7 **Decision Making** People have raced on horses, camels, elephants, and ostriches. In the table below are approximate distances and times that animals have been known to race. Which two animals would you like to ride in races? What is the difference between the speeds of your two animals? (Remember that you find an animal's speed by dividing the distance by the time.)

Animal	Distance (yards)	Time (seconds)
Camel	440	40
Horse	1,330	70
Elephant	300	60
Ostrich	140	20

Good News/Bad News *Cats can sprint at 30 miles per hour, which is faster than many dogs. This is bad news for rats, who have a top speed of about 6 miles per hour.*

8 A cheetah was once clocked at running almost 224 yards in 7 seconds. How many yards per second is that?

Do You Know How?

Do You Understand?

Dividing Decimals by 10, 100, and 1,000 (4-9)

Find each quotient. Use mental math.

1. 18 ÷ 10

2. 18.4 ÷ 100

3. 0.037 ÷ 10

4. 456.3 ÷ 100

5. 285.73 ÷ 1,000

6. 4,238 ÷ 1,000

Ⓐ State the rule that you used to find each quotient using mental math.

Ⓑ In Exercise 1, what symbol did you put at the end of 18 and why was it needed before you could do mental math?

Dividing Money by Two-Digit Divisors (4-10)

Find each quotient.
Check your answers by multiplying.

7. $656.64 ÷ 36

8. $247.35 ÷ 17

9. 40)$650

10. 36)$61.80

11. 50)$122

12. 15)$36.45

Ⓒ In Exercise 9, why did you need to place a decimal point and two zeros in the dividend?

Ⓓ In Exercise 10, why should you round your quotient to the nearest hundredth?

Dividing Decimals by Whole Numbers (4-11)

Find each quotient.
Check your answers by multiplying.

13. 25.2 ÷ 18

14. 0.88 ÷ 55

15. 42)4.284

16. 39)100.62

17. 1.5 ÷ 60

18. 21 ÷ 60

Ⓔ Without doing the division, how do you know that the quotient in Exercise 13 must be between the numbers 1 and 2?

Ⓕ In Exercises 14, 15, 17, and 18, without doing the division, how do you know that the quotients will be less than 1?

Think It Through
For multiple-choice items, first **eliminate any unreasonable answers.**

MULTIPLE CHOICE

1. Use mental math to find the quotient of 275.42 ÷ 100. (4-9)

   A. 0.027542   **B.** 0.27542   **C.** 2.7542   **D.** 27.542

2. Find $275.42 ÷ 24 rounded to the nearest cent. (4-10)

   A. $11.4   **B.** $11.48   **C.** $11.476   **D.** $11.4758

FREE RESPONSE

Use mental math to find each quotient. (4-9)

3. 700 ÷ 10   4. 245.3 ÷ 100   5. 47.2 ÷ 1,000   6. 253 ÷ 100

Find each quotient. Check your answers by multiplying. (Round to the nearest cent, if necessary.) (4-10)

7. $605.92 ÷ 14   8. $397.95 ÷ 21   9. $730 ÷ 40   10. $249.36 ÷ 20

Find each quotient. Check by multiplying. (4-11)

11. 688.8 ÷ 42   12. 73.2 ÷ 40   13. 0.4248 ÷ 18   14. 47.52 ÷ 18

Solve. Write your answer as a sentence.

15. The local supermarket sells a 12-ounce bag of peanuts for $9.36. How much would you pay for just one ounce of peanuts? (4-10)

16. To make banners for the Fourth of July Parade, Mitchell needs to cut a long strip of cloth into four pieces of equal length. If the banner is 50.6 feet long, how long will each piece be? (4-11, 4-12)

50.6 ft

Writing in Math

17. Our school's fifth grade Math Club is having a Pizza Party Practice to prepare for the State Math Contest. The pizza delivery person presents a bill for $64.36. The team coach volunteers to contribute $10 to help pay for the cost of the pizza. If twelve students are at the practice and decide to split the remaining cost equally, how much must each pay? Explain your work and write your answer in a sentence. (4-10)

18. In Lesson 4-9, you discovered a rule for dividing any number by 10, 100, or 1,000. Use your calculator to help you discover a rule for dividing any number by 20, 200, and 2,000. Use 46, 24.8, and 4.28 as your dividends. State your rule in a sentence. (4-9)

Test-Taking Strategies

Understand the question.

Get information for the answer.

Plan how to find the answer.

Make smart choices.

Use writing in math.

Improve written answers.

Make Smart Choices

To answer a multiple-choice test question, you need to choose an answer from answer choices. The steps below will help you make a smart choice.

1. Jolene bought a pack of 12 cans of juice. How much did each can cost?

$4.20

A. $0.35 **C.** $3.50

B. $0.36 **D.** $50.40

Understand the question.

• Look for important words. Finish the statement "I need to find out..."

I need to find out how much each can cost.

Get information for the answer.

*The **text** says Jolene bought 12 cans. The **picture** shows the 12 cans cost $4.20.*

Plan how to find the answer.

The total cost must be split into equal groups, so this is a division problem.

Make smart choices.

• Eliminate wrong answer choices.

Each can could not cost more than all 12 cans, $4.20. Answer choice D, $50.40, is wrong.

Each can would have to cost less than half the total price. Half of $4.20 is about $2, so each can would have to cost less than $2. Answer choice C, $3.50, is wrong.

The correct answer is either A or B. I'll divide to make the right choice.

$4.20 ÷ 12 = $0.35

The correct answer is A, $0.35.

• Check answers for reasonableness.

If each can cost $0.35, then 12 cans should cost 12 × $0.35.

12 × $0.35 = $4.20

Since $4.20 is the price of the 12 cans given in the problem, the answer checks.

2. Mitch is making designs with pennies. Each design is shaped like a Y.

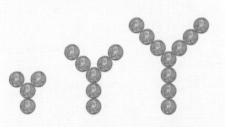

How many pennies will Mitch need for the next Y?

A. 3

B. 11

C. 13

D. 20

Think It Through

I need to find out how many pennies Mitch will need for the next Y.

The number of pennies is increasing, so he'll need more than he used in the last design, which is 10. So answer choice A, 3, is wrong. The number of pennies is not doubling each time, so answer choice D, 20, is wrong.

The correct answer is either B or C. Since the Ys used 4, 7, and 10 pennies, the pattern is Add 3. So answer choice D, 13, is correct.

I can draw the next Y to check for reasonableness.

Now it's your turn.

For each problem, give the answer and explain how you made your choice.

3. If Amanda drives 50 miles per hour from Jacksonville to Miami, about how long will the trip take?

Jacksonville

347 miles

Miami

A. 397 hours

B. 7 hours

C. 5 hours

D. 2 hours

4. Tanya is making designs with toothpicks. Each design is shaped like an X.

How many toothpicks will Tanya need for the next X?

A. 4

B. 16

C. 18

D. 24

Multiple of 10 sounds like "multiply by 10."

The multiples of 10 *are easy. They always end in 0.* (p. 202)

Use mental math to divide and to estimate quotients. (Lessons 4-1, 4-2)

Find 4,800 ÷ 80.

Think of a basic fact: 48 ÷ 8 = 6. Think about **multiples of 10:** 4,800 ÷ 80 is the same as 480 tens ÷ 8 tens, which is 6 tens.

So, 4,800 ÷ 80 = 60

Estimate 1,423 ÷ 18.

Use compatible numbers. Substitute 1,400 for 1,423 and 20 for 18.
1,400 ÷ 20 = 70

So, 1,423 ÷ 18 is about 70.

1. Find 27,000 ÷ 90 and give an estimate for 7,137 ÷ 87.

After dinner, my mom saves the leftovers, or the remainder of food, for tomorrow's lunch.

Remember, the **remainder** *of a quotient is the number that is left over after dividing.* (p. 214)

Choose a computation method and follow steps in order when your divide. (Lessons 4-4, 4-5, 4-6, 4-7)

Find 4,359 ÷ 62.

Estimate to decide where to start dividing.
4,359 ÷ 62
↓ ↓
4,200 ÷ 60 = 70

Start dividing tens.

Divide the tens. Multiply, subtract, and compare. Continue the process.

$$
\begin{array}{r}
70 \text{ R}19 \\
62\overline{)4,359} \\
-4\ 34 \\
\hline
19 \\
-0 \\
\hline
19
\end{array}
$$

19 < 62
Write a zero in the quotient. The **remainder** is 19.

Multiply and add the remainder to check the quotient.

$$
\begin{array}{r}
70 \\
\times\ 62 \\
\hline
140 \\
4\ 200 \\
\hline
4,340 \\
+\ \ 19 \\
\hline
4,359
\end{array}
$$

2. Find 234 ÷ 31 and 5,805 ÷ 72.

Pay attention to decimal points when dividing decimals. (Lessons 4-9, 4-10, 4-11)

Find $91.8 \div 27$.

Write the decimal point in the quotient directly above the decimal point in the dividend.	Divide as with whole numbers.	Divide money like decimals.
$$27\overline{)91.8}$$	$$\begin{array}{r} 3.4 \\ 27\overline{)91.8} \\ -\ 81 \\ \hline 10\ 8 \\ -\ 10\ 8 \\ \hline 0 \end{array}$$	$$\begin{array}{r} \$0.75 \\ 43\overline{)\$32.25} \\ -\ 30\ 1 \\ \hline 2\ 15 \\ -\ 2\ 15 \\ \hline 0 \end{array}$$

3. Find $42.12 \div 39$ and $\$5.32 \div 14$.

Try, check, and revise or complete multiple steps to solve problems. (Lessons 4-3, 4-8)

Use the given facts to **try** and **check** one answer. Then **revise** and try again until you solve the problem.

Tim is twice as old as Beth. The sum of their ages is 21. How old is Tim?

	Check
Try : Tim is 10.	$10 \div 2 = 5$; $10 + 5 = 15$ too low
Revise: Tim is 15.	$15 \div 2 = 7.5$; $15 + 7.5 = 22.5$ too high
Revise: Tim is 14.	$14 \div 2 = 7$; $14 + 7 = 21$ correct

Tim is 14 years old.

To solve multiple-step problems, identify the hidden questions in the problem.

Anita paid $10.21 for 18 beads, including $0.49 tax. How much did each bead cost?

What was the total price before tax? $10.21 - 0.49 = \$9.72$.

Now divide to find the cost per bead. $\$9.72 \div 18 = \$0.54$

Each bead cost $0.54.

4. The area of a rectangle is 24 ft^2. It is 5 feet longer than it is wide. Find its width.

Answers: 1. 300; possible estimate: 80; 2. 7 R17; 80 R45; 3. 1.08 and $0.38; 4. 3 feet

Chapter Test

MULTIPLE CHOICE

Choose the correct letter for each answer.

1. Find 72,000 ÷ 90.

   A. 8,000   **C.** 80

   B. 800   **D.** 8

2. Which is the most reasonable estimate for 439 ÷ 62?

   A. 7   **C.** 70

   B. 8   **D.** 80

3. Find 317 ÷ 35.

   A. 8 R37   **C.** 9 R2

   B. 9   **D.** 9 R12

4. What is 4,298 divided by 74?

   A. 57 R80   **C.** 58 R16

   B. 58 R6   **D.** 59 R68

5. Find 3,470 ÷ 17.

   A. 2,042   **C.** 204 R2

   B. 205 R15   **D.** 24 R2

6. What is 42.9 divided by 1,000?

   A. 0.0429   **C.** 4.29

   B. 0.429   **D.** 429

7. Find $86.24 ÷ 56.

   A. $0.54   **C.** $15.40

   B. $1.54   **D.** $154.00

8. Find 120.9 ÷ 93.

   A. 0.13   **C.** 1.3

   B. 1.03   **D.** 13

9. Which quotient does NOT have a remainder?

   A. 670 ÷ 36

   B. 973 ÷ 81

   C. 532 ÷ 28

   D. 2,214 ÷ 47

> **TEST TALK**
>
> **Think It Through**
> - I should **look for words like NOT or EXCEPT.**
> - I need to **read each answer choice carefully.**

10. Kwan used 24 feet of ribbon for the border of a rectangular quilt. The quilt is twice as long as it is wide. What are the length and width of the quilt?

   A. ℓ = 6 ft and w = 3 ft

   B. ℓ = 8 ft and w = 4 ft

   C. ℓ = 10 ft and w = 5 ft

   D. ℓ = 12 ft and w = 6 ft

11. Mr. Patterson spent $107.52, including $5.16 tax, for 12 CDs each at the same price. How much did each CD cost?

   A. $5.12

   B. $8.53

   C. $8.96

   D. $9.38

12. Which computation method would be best for finding 28,000 ÷ 40?

   A. calculator

   B. paper and pencil

   C. counting back

   D. mental math

Estimate each quotient.

13. $534 \div 87$

14. $\$2{,}596 \div 43$

Find each quotient using mental math.

15. $8{,}100 \div 90$

16. $24{,}000 \div 60$

17. $7.25 \div 10$

18. $85.2 \div 1{,}000$

Find each quotient.

19. $75\overline{)5{,}024}$

20. $57\overline{)\$2.85}$

21. $702 \div 39$

22. $11{,}453 \div 28$

23. Tom plans to drive the 2,496 miles from Atlanta, Georgia, to San Francisco, California. If he drives 65 miles per hour for most of the trip, estimate how many hours he will drive in all.

24. What is the combined cost of 1 oz of turkey and 1 oz of ham?

Corner Deli Prices		
Meat	**Number of oz**	**Cost**
Salami	8	$1.84
Turkey	16	$5.92
Ham	20	$7.00

25. Try, check, and revise to solve this problem.

Bill is 5 years younger than his sister Chantall. The sum of their ages is 29. How old are Bill and Chantall?

Writing in Math

26. Explain two different ways to estimate $4{,}889 \div 66$.

27. Which computation method would you use to find $72{,}000 \div 80$? Explain your choice and find the quotient.

28. Describe the steps needed to solve this problem. Then solve the problem.

A clothing manufacturer can make 6 dresses with 24 yards of material. How many dresses can be made with 450 yards of material? Will there be any material left over? Explain.

TEST TALK

Think It Through
I can solve multiple-step problems by **finding and answering hidden questions.**

Number and Operation

MULTIPLE CHOICE

1. What is the value of the underlined digit in 7,4<u>6</u>8,914,025?

   A. 6 billion

   B. 600 million

   C. 60 million

   D. 6 million

2. What is the quotient of 2.52 and 18?

   A. 15.48

   B. 14

   C. 1.4

   D. 0.14

3. Which of the following is a composite number?

   A. 7

   B. 13

   C. 21

   D. 31

FREE RESPONSE

4. Write these decimals in order from greatest to least.

   3.79   0.379   3.97   0.739

5. Samuel's paycheck was $314.79. He used $205.75 of that money to pay bills. Then he spent $58 on groceries. How much money did Samuel have left?

Writing in Math

6. Explain how to estimate 3,715 ÷ 42. Then find the actual quotient and explain how to check your answer.

Geometry and Measurement

MULTIPLE CHOICE

7. These two clocks show the start and end times for an evening concert. How long did the concert last?

   A. 1 hour 25 minutes

   B. 1 hour 35 minutes

   C. 2 hours 25 minutes

   D. 2 hours 35 minutes

8. Which of the following does NOT equal 6 feet?

   A. 2 yards

   B. 4 feet 24 inches

   C. 72 inches

   D. 18 yards

FREE RESPONSE

9. The area of a rectangle is 168 square feet. If its width is 12 feet, what is its length?

Think It Through
I can **draw pictures** to model problems.

10. Describe the similarities and differences between these two solid figures.

Writing in Math

11. Explain why a square also can be called a rectangle and a quadrilateral.

Data Analysis and Probability

MULTIPLE CHOICE

12. If you spin the spinner below 10 times, which color would you probably land on least often?

A. green

B. yellow

C. red

D. blue

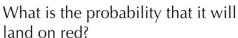

13. You spin the spinner above once. What is the probability that it will land on red?

A. $\frac{1}{4}$ **B.** $\frac{3}{8}$ **C.** $\frac{1}{2}$ **D.** 4

FREE RESPONSE

Use the line graph for Exercises 14–16.

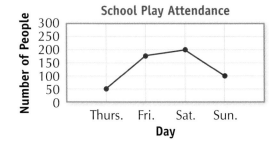

School Play Attendance

14. On which day did the most people attend the school play? The fewest people?

15. How many more people attended the play on Sunday than on Thursday?

Writing in Math

16. Between which two consecutive days did the greatest change in attendance occur? Explain how you used the graph to find your answer.

Algebra

MULTIPLE CHOICE

17. Which is an expression for "a number divided by 7"?

A. $7v$ **C.** $v - 7$

B. $7 \div v$ **D.** $v \div 7$

18. Solve $45 \div n = 5$.

A. $n = 8$ **C.** $n = 50$

B. $n = 9$ **D.** $n = 225$

19. A small pizza costs $9.00, a medium pizza costs $10.50, and a large pizza costs $12.00. If the prices continue in this pattern, how much will an extra-large pizza cost?

Think It Through
I need to **read the problem carefully** and **look for patterns.**

A. $12.50   **C.** $13.50

B. $13.00   **D.** $14.00

FREE RESPONSE

20. What is the rule for this table?

Input	12	13	14	15
Output	36	39	42	45

21. A set of 8 yard chairs costs $120. How much does each chair cost?

Writing in Math

22. Evaluate this expression and explain how you used the order of operations.

$$150 + 28 \div 7 - (6 \times 3)$$

Set 4-1 (pages 202–203)

Find 40,000 ÷ 80 with mental math.

Use basic facts and patterns to help.

40 ÷ 8 = 5 ◄── **basic fact**

400 ÷ 80 = 5

4,000 ÷ 80 = 50

40,000 ÷ 80 = 500

Think: 40,000 ÷ 80 is the same as 4,000 tens ÷ 8 tens.

Remember that if the basic fact has a zero in the dividend, it should NOT be used to find the number of zeros in the quotient.

1. 480 ÷ 60

2. 2,700 ÷ 90

3. 15,000 ÷ 30

4. 32,000 ÷ 40

5. 4,200 ÷ 70

6. 240 ÷ 80

7. 30,000 ÷ 50

8. 60,000 ÷ 20

Set 4-2 (pages 204–207)

Estimate 467 ÷ 52.

One Way: Compatible Numbers

467 ÷ 52
 ↓   ↓
450 ÷ 50 = 9

Another Way: Rounding and Multiplication

Round 52 to 50 and then use multiplication.

50 × ? = 467
 ↓   ↓
50 × 9 = 450

So, 467 ÷ 52 is about 9.

Remember that compatible numbers are numbers that are easy to compute in your head.

1. 171 ÷ 43

2. 5,386 ÷ 64

3. 2,265 ÷ 69

4. 8,106 ÷ 87

5. 94.8 ÷ 52

6. 148.3 ÷ 21

7. $613.10 ÷ 93

8. $435.29 ÷ 74

Set 4-3 (pages 210–211)

When you *try, check, and revise* to solve a problem, follow these steps.

Step 1: Think to make a reasonable first try.

Step 2: Check by using information given in the problem.

Step 3: Revise by using your first try to make a reasonable second try. Check.

Step 4: Use previous tries to continue trying and checking until you find the answer.

Remember *try, check, and revise* can help when there is no clear way to solve a problem.

1. Bryant has four more dimes than nickels. Together, the coins have a total value of $1.45. How many of each coin does Bryant have?

2. Kenya is 6 years younger than Paul. The sum of their ages is 28. How old is Kenya? How old is Paul?

Find 337 ÷ 42.

1

Estimate to decide where to place the first digit in the quotient.

$$337 ÷ 42$$
$$\downarrow \qquad \downarrow$$
$$320 ÷ 40 = 8$$
Start dividing ones.

2

Divide the ones. Multiply and subtract.

$$\begin{array}{r} 8 \\ 42\overline{)337} \\ -336 \\ \hline 1 \end{array}$$

3

Compare and write the answer.

1 < 42, so I do not have to divide again.

So, 337 ÷ 42 = 8 R1

Remember that if the product of your first quotient and the divisor is larger than the dividend, your estimate is too high. Try dividing again with the next lower number.

1. $61\overline{)587}$

2. $37\overline{)368}$

3. $29\overline{)165}$

4. $17\overline{)145}$

5. 439 ÷ 71

6. 387 ÷ 92

7. 829 ÷ 87

8. 476 ÷ 54

Find 4,782 ÷ 93.

1

Estimate to decide where to place the first digit in the quotient.

$$4,782 ÷ 93$$
$$\downarrow \qquad \downarrow$$
$$4,500 ÷ 90 = 50$$
Start dividing tens.

2

Divide the tens. Multiply, subtract, and compare.

$$\begin{array}{r} 5 \\ 93\overline{)4,782} \\ -4\,65 \\ \hline 13 \end{array}$$

3

Bring down the ones. Divide the ones. Multiply, subtract, and compare.

$$\begin{array}{r} 51\ \text{R39} \\ 93\overline{)4,782} \\ -4\,65 \\ \hline 132 \\ -93 \\ \hline 39 \end{array}$$

So, 4,782 ÷ 93 = 51 R39

Remember that you can check your answer by multiplying the quotient by the divisor, then adding the remainder to that product. The sum should be your dividend.

1. $26\overline{)7,581}$

2. $54\overline{)29,134}$

3. $48\overline{)2,163}$

4. $74\overline{)52,675}$

5. 7,654 ÷ 81

6. 3,855 ÷ 62

7. 22,639 ÷ 34

8. 46,218 ÷ 87

Set 4-6 (pages 222–223)

Find each quotient.

42,000 ÷ 70
Use mental math.
So, 42,000 ÷ 70 = 600.

44,380 ÷ 70
Use paper and pencil.
Both numbers are
multiples of 10.
So, 44,380 ÷ 70 = 634.

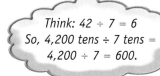
Think: 42 ÷ 7 = 6
So, 4,200 tens ÷ 7 tens =
4,200 ÷ 7 = 600.

```
        634
70)44,380
  − 42 0
     2 38
   − 2 10
       280
     − 280
         0
```

41,265 ÷ 73
Use a calculator. There are no
basic facts or zeros.

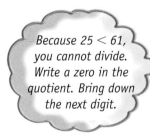

So, 41,265 ÷ 73 is a
little greater than 565.27.

Remember to first look at the numbers
in the problem to decide which method
would work best to solve it.

1. 70)49,000

2. 23)16,837

3. 40)21,840

4. 90)36,000

5. 8,517 ÷ 35

6. 7,200 ÷ 80

7. 56,640 ÷ 40

8. 6,239 ÷ 74

Set 4-7 (pages 224–225)

Find 6,350 ÷ 61.

Estimate: 6,000 ÷ 60 = 100

Start dividing hundreds.

Divide.

Because 25 < 61,
you cannot divide.
Write a zero in the
quotient. Bring down
the next digit.

```
        104 R6
61)6,350
  − 6 1
     25
    − 0
     250
   − 244
       6
```

So, 6,350 ÷ 61 = 104 R6.

Remember that when you bring down
the next digit in dividing, and you get a
number less than the divisor, you need to
place a zero in the quotient.

1. 74)7,844

2. 28)8,422

3. 66)26,850

4. 90)36,000

5. 423 ÷ 41

6. 15,890 ÷ 39

7. 8,999 ÷ 89

8. 52,135 ÷ 62

The football coach spent a total of $890.40, including $50.40 tax, for 35 shirts for the team. The price of each shirt was the same. What was the price of one football shirt?

Identify the hidden question or questions.

How much did all the shirts cost without tax?

$890.40 − $50.40 = $840.00

Solve the problem.

840 ÷ 35 = 24   So, each shirt cost $24.00.

Remember that identifying the sequence of events in a problem will help you find the hidden questions you must first answer to solve the problem.

1. Andy wants to buy 2 DVDs for $11.50 each and a book for $6.35. The tax on all the items is $1.46. Andy has $30. How much more does he need to buy all the items?

2. The cost for 20 pizzas, including $14.50 tax, is $294.50. Each pizza has the same price. What is the cost of one pizza?

Find 16.32 ÷ 100.

Dividing by 100 means moving the decimal point two places to the left.

16.32 ÷ 100 = 0.1632

Remember when dividing decimals by 10, 100, or 1,000, you may need to use a zero as a placeholder: 24.3 ÷ 1,000 = 0.**0**243.

1. 73.5 ÷ 10
2. 54.89 ÷ 100
3. 148.65 ÷ 1,000
4. 0.28 ÷ 100
5. 12.3 ÷ 100
6. 677.34 ÷ 1,000

Find $3.90 ÷ 15.

Place the decimal point in the quotient directly above the decimal point in the dividend. Divide.

So, $3.90 ÷ 15 = $0.26.

```
        $0.26
15)$3.90
     − 3 0
        90
      − 90
         0
```

Remember that when dividing money, you do not write remainders. You must place zeros at the end of the dividend and continue dividing. Round to the nearest hundredth.

1. 52)$7.28
2. 78)$32.76
3. $74.52 ÷ 36
4. $199.92 ÷ 84

Find 9.52 ÷ 28.

Place the decimal point in the quotient directly above the decimal point in the dividend. Divide.

So, 9.52 ÷ 28 = 0.34.

```
        0.34
28)9.52
    − 8 4
      1 12
    − 1 12
         0
```

Remember that when you cannot divide a place value in the dividend, you must write a zero placeholder in the quotient.

1. 85)106.25
2. 31)17.05
3. 51.6 ÷ 43
4. 199.68 ÷ 64
5. 30.74 ÷ 29
6. 68.2 ÷ 55

Chapter 4 Reteaching   253

Set 4-1 (pages 202–203)

Find each quotient. Use mental math.

1. $720 \div 90$ **2.** $4,900 \div 70$ **3.** $320 \div 40$

4. $3,500 \div 50$ **5.** $4,000 \div 80$ **6.** $240 \div 60$

7. $2,700 \div 30$ **8.** $18,000 \div 20$ **9.** $28,000 \div 40$

10. $54,000 \div 90$ **11.** $12,000 \div 60$ **12.** $42,000 \div 70$

13. There are 3,000 seats in the theater. If they are divided into 60 equal sections, how many seats are in each section?

14. If a person saves $50 a week, how long will it take to save $10,000?

Set 4-2 (pages 204–207)

Estimate each quotient.

1. $258 \div 64$ **2.** $3,714 \div 43$ **3.** $119 \div 19$

4. $6,388 \div 72$ **5.** $7,075 \div 84$ **6.** $27,406 \div 68$

7. $\$80.99 \div 87$ **8.** $5,312 \div 51$ **9.** $\$317.25 \div 41$

10. $632.9 \div 78$ **11.** $14,584 \div 33$ **12.** $\$451.35 \div 74$

13. Anita earned $475.54 in two weeks. She earned the same amount of money for each hour that she worked. If Anita worked a total of 62 hours during those 2 weeks, about how much did she earn each hour?

Set 4-3 (pages 210–211)

Try, check, and revise to solve. Write each answer in a complete sentence.

1. The Colemans used 50 feet of rope to surround their rectangular garden. The length of the garden is 4 times as much as its width. What are the length and width of the Coleman's garden in feet?

2. Madeline is 6 years older than her brother, Sam. The sum of their ages is 20 years. How old is Madeline? How old is Sam?

Take It to the NET
www More Practice
www.scottforesman.com

Set 4-4 (pages 214–217)

Find each quotient. Check by multiplying.

1. 32$\overline{)257}$ **2.** 86$\overline{)734}$ **3.** 16$\overline{)194}$

4. 54$\overline{)271}$ **5.** 27$\overline{)369}$ **6.** 41$\overline{)290}$

7. 78$\overline{)639}$ **8.** 52$\overline{)418}$ **9.** 345 ÷ 81

10. 211 ÷ 63   **11.** 575 ÷ 84   **12.** 362 ÷ 39

13. Peter's family drove 745 miles from Atlanta, Georgia, to Chicago, Illinois. They drove at an average speed of 62 miles per hour. How many hours to the nearest whole hour did it take them to drive to Chicago?

Set 4-5 (pages 218–221)

Find each quotient. Check your answers by multiplying.

1. 27$\overline{)8,415}$ **2.** 42$\overline{)2,926}$ **3.** 18$\overline{)1,423}$

4. 36$\overline{)3,184}$ **5.** 51$\overline{)4,765}$ **6.** 74$\overline{)5,142}$

7. 62$\overline{)4,319}$ **8.** 89$\overline{)5,679}$ **9.** 2,541 ÷ 27

10. 4,664 ÷ 82   **11.** 2,215 ÷ 33   **12.** 3,428 ÷ 65

13. 1,690 ÷ 32   **14.** 7,925 ÷ 53   **15.** 6,411 ÷ 26

16. A chicken farm produces an average of 1,848 eggs a week. There are 12 eggs in a dozen. How many dozen eggs does the chicken farm produce in an average week?

Set 4-6 (pages 222–223)

Divide and check. Tell what computation method you used.

1. 30$\overline{)900}$ **2.** 60$\overline{)34,560}$ **3.** 57$\overline{)81,624}$

4. 80$\overline{)64,000}$ **5.** 29$\overline{)7,598}$ **6.** 70$\overline{)49,000}$

7. 20$\overline{)17,580}$ **8.** 58$\overline{)3,712}$ **9.** 54,000 ÷ 90

10. 17,236 ÷ 31   **11.** 32,650 ÷ 50   **12.** 80,000 ÷ 40

13. 9,460 ÷ 22   **14.** 40,000 ÷ 50   **15.** 17,918 ÷ 62

16. Using the divisor 20, write and solve three different division problems using:

     a. Mental math   **b.** Paper and pencil   **c.** A calculator

Set 4-7 (pages 224–225)

Find each quotient. Check your answers by multiplying.

1. $42\overline{)430}$

2. $21\overline{)4,389}$

3. $81\overline{)41,067}$

4. $97\overline{)58,394}$

5. $28\overline{)14,080}$

6. $52\overline{)36,452}$

7. $71\overline{)5,682}$

8. $17\overline{)1,790}$

9. $67,795 \div 84$

10. $9,023 \div 36$

11. $32,895 \div 54$

12. $11,217 \div 62$

13. $13,740 \div 67$

14. $15,120 \div 42$

15. $7,531 \div 25$

16. Mr. Allen earns a yearly salary of $53,300. Because there are 52 weeks in one year, how much does Mr. Allen earn each week? Because Mr. Allen works 5 days a week, how much money does he earn each day?

Set 4-8 (pages 226–227)

Write and answer the hidden question or questions in each problem and then solve the problem. Write your answers in complete sentences.

1. The students at Washington Elementary School held three fundraisers this year to raise money for charity. At the end of the school year, the students combined all the money raised during the three fundraisers. They evenly divided the total among 12 different charities in their community. How much did the students donate to each charity?

Data File

This Year's Fundraisers

Event	Money Raised
Bake sale	$3,215
Read-a-thon	$7,465
Car wash	$5,496

2. Juan's family drove across the United States this summer. From Newark, New Jersey, they first drove to Cleveland, Ohio. Then from Cleveland, they drove to Omaha, Nebraska. From Omaha, they drove to Salt Lake City, Utah. From Salt Lake City, they drove to San Francisco, California. On average, they traveled 60 miles per hour during their trip. How many hours did Juan's family spend driving from Newark to San Francisco?

Road Mileage Between U.S. Cities		
Depart	**Arrive**	**Miles**
Newark, NJ	Cleveland, OH	473
Cleveland, OH	Omaha, NE	784
Omaha, NE	Salt Lake City, UT	931
Salt Lake City, UT	San Francisco, CA	752

Take It to the NET
www More Practice
www.scottforesman.com

Set 4-9 (pages 230–231)

Find each quotient. Use mental math.

1. $601.4 \div 10$
2. $53.71 \div 100$
3. $14.9 \div 100$
4. $937.4 \div 1,000$
5. $11.9 \div 100$
6. $1.67 \div 1,000$
7. $138.2 \div 1,000$
8. $4.78 \div 100$
9. $83.2 \div 1,000$
10. $19.9 \div 100$
11. $423.7 \div 100$
12. $8.5 \div 1,000$
13. $60.7 \div 10$
14. $2.814 \div 100$
15. $7.56 \div 1,000$

16. A microscope has settings that increase the size of a viewed object 10 times and 100 times. When viewed under the microscope at each of those settings, a fish bone appears 1.5 mm and 15 mm thick. What is the actual width of the fish bone?

Set 4-10 (pages 232–233)

Find each quotient. Check your answers by multiplying. (Round to the nearest cent if necessary.)

1. $13)\overline{\$5.72}$
2. $24)\overline{\$8.72}$
3. $78)\overline{\$4.26}$
4. $55)\overline{\$9.80}$
5. $11)\overline{\$16.39}$
6. $78)\overline{\$97.50}$
7. $26)\overline{\$88.92}$
8. $43)\overline{\$102.77}$
9. $\$6.00 \div 40$
10. $\$2.97 \div 38$
11. $\$412.25 \div 50$
12. $\$40.14 \div 30$
13. $\$37.28 \div 16$
14. $\$110.08 \div 43$
15. $\$19.70 \div 36$

16. Sara has been offered two part-time jobs this summer. The first job, at a garden center, pays $136.00 for every 16 hours worked. The second job, at the community swimming pool, pays $199.50 for every 21 hours worked. Which job would pay Sara more per hour?

Set 4-11 (pages 234–237)

Find each quotient. Check by multiplying.

1. $12)\overline{35.4}$
2. $11)\overline{4.73}$
3. $23)\overline{96.6}$
4. $40)\overline{2.84}$
5. $43)\overline{24.94}$
6. $65)\overline{54.6}$
7. $57)\overline{40.47}$
8. $13)\overline{3.003}$
9. $8.67 \div 17$
10. $2.37 \div 30$
11. $12.6 \div 63$
12. $6.842 \div 22$
13. $6.12 \div 18$
14. $22.95 \div 27$
15. $83.58 \div 42$

16. Dog food is on sale for $2.76 for 4 cans. Cat food is on sale for $4.24 for 8 cans. Thomas only wants to buy one can of dog food and one can of cat food. How much will each can cost?

DIAGNOSING READINESS

A Vocabulary
(pages 100–103, 108–109)

Choose the best term from the box.

Consider $3n = 15$.

1. n is the __?__. **2.** $3n$ is an __?__.

3. $3n = 15$ is an __?__. **4.** 5 is the __?__.

Vocabulary
- **solution** *(p. 108)* • **equation** *(p. 108)*
- **variable** *(p. 100)* • **algebraic expression** *(p. 100)*

B Graphing Ordered Pairs
(pages 174–175)

Give the ordered pair for each point.

5. G **6.** M

7. P **8.** X

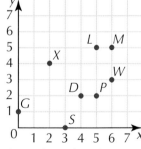

Name the point for each ordered pair.

9. (5, 5) **10.** (4, 2) **11.** (3, 0) **12.** (6, 3)

13. How are (2, 6) and (6, 2) different?

Do You Know...

How much room would be needed for all the people in the world to stand together?

You will find out in Lesson 5-13.

THE WORLD IN ONE DAY

Every day...7 million pizzas are eaten in America...one human heart pumps enough blood to fill 170 bathtubs...lightning strikes Earth 8 million times...
by RUSSELL ASH, author of INCREDIBLE COMPARISONS

C Writing Fractions

(Grade 4)

14. If 1 out of 4 marbles is green, what fraction names the green part of the marbles?

15. If 3 out of 5 pieces of fruit are bananas, what fraction names the part of the fruit containing bananas?

16. If 5 out of 6 pieces of a pizza have been eaten, what fraction of the pizza has NOT been eaten?

17. How do you know that $\frac{2}{3}$ is in simplest form?

D Rules and Tables

(pages 106–107, 176–179)

Find a rule for each table. Give the rule using words and a variable.

18.

Input	Output
21	3
28	4
42	6
49	7
56	8

19.

Input	Output
5	11
10	16
15	21
20	26
25	31

20. Create a table of values for the rule $4m$. Use at least four values for m.

Key Idea
A survey is a way of collecting data to answer a question.

Vocabulary
- survey
- data
- line plot
- frequency table
- sample

Collecting Data from a Survey

✓ **WARM UP**

1. Give a possible response to the question "What is your favorite TV show?"

LEARN

What is a survey?

Asking questions in a **survey** is a way to gather information called **data.** Data can be **facts** or **opinions.** A fact is actual information such as age, while an opinion involves what a person likes or dislikes.

Example A

Survey Question
Do you own a cat, dog, another type of pet, or have no pet?

Pets Owned

```
              X
    X         X
    X         X           X
    X         X     X     X
  <-+-----+-----+-----+->
    Cat   Dog  Other  None
```

Example B

Survey Question
What is your favorite snack?

Favorite Snacks

Snack	Number
Fruit	3
Popcorn	4
Pretzels	2
Peanuts	5

The survey results are shown by a **line plot** in Example A and by a **frequency table** in Example B. In a line plot, a horizontal line lists various responses. Each time a response occurs, an X is recorded above that response. In a frequency table, numbers are used to show how many times each response has occurred.

When people surveyed represent a larger group, the people are a **sample** of the larger group. The sample should be selected randomly. Otherwise, it does not represent the larger group well.

✓ Talk About It

1. In Examples A and B, which survey question gathers facts and which gathers opinions? In which question are the choices limited to only 4 possible responses?

2. Suppose the survey question in Example A had been asked to 50 people at a dog show. Would the sample represent the entire population well? Explain.

3. Could the results of the survey question in Example B also be shown by a line plot? Explain.

Identify each statement as either a fact or an opinion.

1. The song lasted 12 minutes.

2. Yellow is the best car color.

3. Reasoning A group of 50 fifth-grade students are asked to name their favorite type of music. Is this sample representative of the entire population of our country? Explain.

PRACTICE

For more practice, see Set 5-1 on p. 322.

Ⓐ Skills and Understanding

Identify each statement as either a fact or an opinion.

4. Blue is the best color for sweaters.

5. Six people ate spinach last week.

6. Twelve students have sisters.

7. Carol would make a good class president.

8. Representations A frequency table shows that 12 students prefer blue balloons and 16 prefer red balloons. If a line plot shows the same data, how many Xs would be above each color?

Ⓑ Reasoning and Problem Solving

Write a survey question that might gather the following information.

9. In one class, 5 students walk to school, 8 take the bus, and 20 are driven.

10. The favorite dessert of 4 people is ice cream.

Use the line plot for 11 and 12.

11. How many people responded to the survey?

12. What information was collected about families?

Number of Family Members

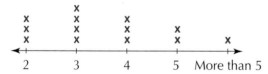

13. Make a frequency table that shows the same results as the line plot in Example A.

14. **Writing in Math** Describe how you might pick a sample of 25 people that represents all the students in your entire school.

🦉 Mixed Review and Test Prep

Take It to the NET
Test Prep
www.scottforesman.com

15. $455 \div 45$

16. $3,678 \div 29$

17. $\$28.88 \div 38$

18. $378.48 \div 76$

19. If 36 ounces of birdseed cost $3.24, what is the cost per ounce?

A. $0.09

B. $0.90

C. $9

D. $90

 All text pages available online and on CD-ROM.

Bar Graphs

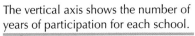 **LEARN**

How do you read a bar graph?

A **bar graph** uses bars to show data that can be counted. A **double bar graph** uses two different-colored or shaded bars to compare two similar sets of data that can be counted.

The graph below shows years of participation for four different schools in a local tennis tournament.

The vertical axis shows the number of years of participation for each school.

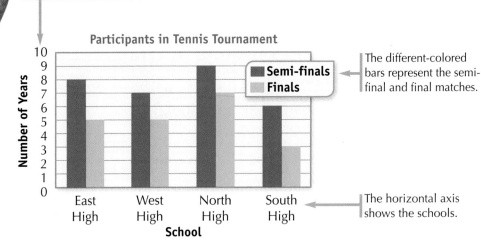

Participants in Tennis Tournament

The different-colored bars represent the semi-final and final matches.

The horizontal axis shows the schools.

✓ Talk About It

1. Of the schools represented on the graph, which school played in the most semi-final matches? Which colored bar did you look at to decide your answer? Why?

2. Which school played in the most final matches? How many more final matches did that school play in than the school which played in the least final matches?

3. **Representations** Is it possible to show the same information on a single bar graph? Why or why not?

How do you make a bar graph?

Activity

The **scale** on a bar graph is a series of numbers at equal distances along an **axis** (plural: axes).

The scale must include numbers that span from the least to the greatest numbers. The **interval** is the difference between adjoining numbers on an axis.

a. Compare the data in the Data File to the scale on the graph below. Why does it make sense to use the interval that is shown?

b. If the data being graphed involved much larger numbers, would it still make sense to use an interval of 1 on the scale? Explain.

c. In the double bar graph below, the data for Sandy and Roger have been graphed. Why are there two bars showing for Sandy, but only one bar for Roger?

d. Copy and complete the bar graph below. Then describe what your graph shows.

Data File

Men's Titles Won

Player	West Conference	East Conference
Sandy	2	4
Roger	0	5
Bob	4	3
Andy	3	2

Think It Through

I can **make a graph** to compare sets of data.

How to Make a Bar Graph

Step 1 Decide on a scale and its intervals. Draw the graph. Label the axes.

Step 2 Write a key for the two bars.

Step 3 Graph the data by drawing bars of the correct length or height.

Step 4 Title your graph.

Notice that two bars are drawn. The key indicates what each colored bar represents.

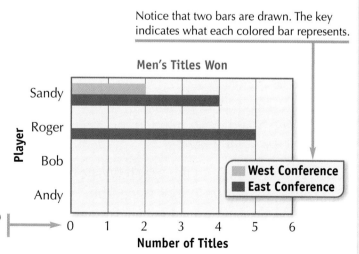

This axis has a scale from 0 to 6. The interval is 1.

For another example, see Set 5-2 on p. 318.

The Data File at the right shows the annual attendance for two different years at four different national parks. The numbers have been rounded to the nearest tenth of a million. Use the data for 1–5. Part of a double bar graph for the data is shown below.

Data File

Annual Attendance (in millions)		
National Park	**1990**	**2000**
Grand Canyon	3.8	4.5
Grand Tetons	1.6	2.6
Olympic	2.8	3.3
Yellowstone	2.8	2.8

1. Which park for which year will have the longest bar? the shortest?

2. Would a scale from 0 to 3 million be appropriate for the attendance? Explain.

3. Would an interval of 0.2 (million) for the scale be appropriate? Explain.

4. Copy and complete the graph at the right.

5. **Representations** Explain why you need to use a double bar graph and not a single bar graph to represent the data.

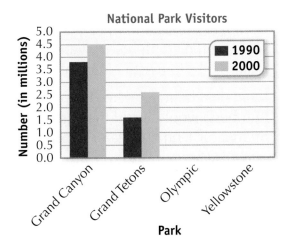

PRACTICE

For more practice, see Set 5-2 on p. 322.

A Skills and Understanding

The Data File at the right shows the population of three states for two years. The data has been rounded to the nearest tenth of a million. Use the data for 6–9.

Data File

Population (in millions)		
State	**1990**	**2000**
New Jersey	7.7	8.4
North Carolina	6.6	8.0
Virginia	6.2	7.1

6. Which state in which year will have the longest bar?

7. If a scale from 0 to 10 with an interval of 2 were used, how many intervals would the scale have?

8. Copy and complete the graph. Write a sentence that describes the graph.

9. **Representations** Can you accurately read the change in population growth for New Jersey from the graph? Explain your answer.

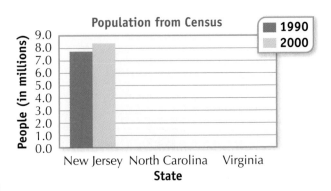

B Reasoning and Problem Solving

Math and Social Studies

Use the graph at the right for 10–12.

10. To the nearest million, about how many commercial vehicles were produced by all three countries?

11. For the year shown, about how many more cars did Germany and the United States together produce than Japan produced?

12. <u>Writing in Math</u> Rank the countries in order from the largest number of vehicles produced to the least number of vehicles produced. Explain how you determined the ranking.

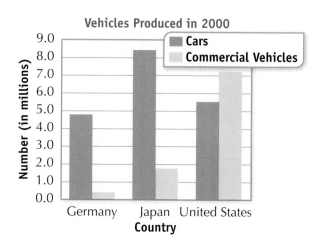

Vehicles Produced in 2000

Cars
Commercial Vehicles

Number (in millions)

Germany   Japan   United States
Country

C Extensions

A **histogram** is a type of bar graph that shows frequency of data within equal intervals. On a histogram the bars touch.

13. How many people ages 0–18 and 39–58 combined attended the tournament?

14. What is the total number of people who attended the tournament?

15. Does the histogram tell you how many 10-year-olds attended the tournament? Explain.

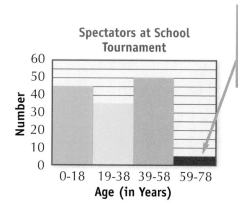

Spectators at School Tournament

Number

0-18   19-38   39-58   59-78
Age (in Years)

This bar shows that there were 5 spectators aged 59-78.

Mixed Review and Test Prep

Take It to the NET
Test Prep
www.scottforesman.com

16. <u>Writing in Math</u> Write a survey question that will gather facts, not opinions.

17. What is 87.9 ÷ 1,000?

    A. 0.0879   **B.** 0.879   **C.** 87,900   **D.** 879,000

18. Which is another name for 30,000?

    A. 300 tens   **C.** 30 hundreds

    B. 300 hundreds   **D.** 300 thousands

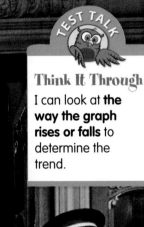
Line Graphs

LEARN

How do you read a line graph?

A **line graph** uses data points connected with line segments to represent data collected over time.

A line graph is often used to show a **trend** or general direction in data. The appearance of the graph indicates if the data numbers are increasing or decreasing.

The graph below shows how many calories are burned over a period of 4 hours. To read the graph, locate a point and read the numbers on both **axes.**

To Determine a Trend
• If the part of a line between two points is rising from left to right, the data numbers are increasing.
• Similarly, if the part of the line between the two points is falling from left to the right, the data numbers are decreasing.

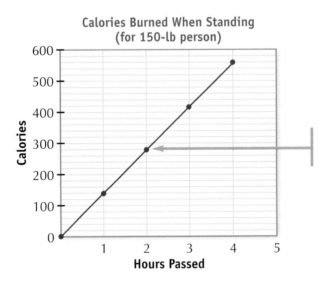

Calories Burned When Standing (for 150-lb person)

This point shows that 280 calories are burned in a 2-hour period.

✔ Talk About It

1. About how many calories are burned by a 150-lb person who stands for 3 hours?

2. Is the graph rising or falling from left to right? Describe the trend that is shown.

3. **Representations** A 150-lb person burns 100 calories each hour when sitting. If after 2 hours of standing up, a person of this weight were to then sit for 2 hours, how would the graph change?

Take It to the NET
www **More Examples**
www.scottforesman.com

How do you make a line graph?

Activity

The data below shows how many miles Ansley walked over a 3-hour period to raise money for cancer research.

Data File

Walk-a-Thon for Cancer Research				
Time Passed	0 h	1 h	2 h	3 h
Distance	0 mi	3 mi	5 mi	6 mi

Think It Through
I can **make a graph** to look for trends in data.

a. Compare the data in the Data File to the graph below. Which data is represented on the horizontal axis? Which data is represented on the vertical axis?

b. The graph shows that some of the data has been graphed. Which data still needs to be graphed?

c. Copy and complete the graph.

How to Make a Line Graph

Step 1 Copy the graph. Label the axes. Be sure to include the scale on each axis.

Step 2 Continue graphing the data by plotting points for the missing data.

Step 3 Connect the points for each set of data.

Step 4 Title your graph.

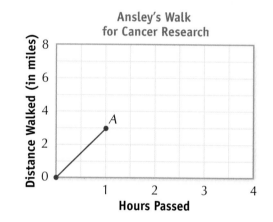

d. Why does the line of the graph start at (0, 0)?

e. What does the point labeled *A* represent?

f. How far had Ansley walked in 2 hours?

g. How far had Ansley walked after 2.5 hours? Explain how you found your answer.

h. Analyze the data on the graph. Write a summary statement describing the trend shown by the graph.

i. Number Sense If Ansley raised $24 for the cancer research fund, how much did she raise for each hour she walked?

CHECK ✓

The populations in the Data File at the right have been rounded to the nearest thousand. Use the data for 1–2.

1. Make a line graph of the data. Use a scale from 0 to 600 and an interval of 100 for the population. Write a sentence about the trend shown on the graph.

2. **Representations** Can you tell exactly how many people were in the city for each year shown? Why or why not?

Data File

Population (in thousands)	
Year	Charlotte, NC
1970	241
1980	315
1990	396
2000	541

PRACTICE

For more practice, see Set 5-3 on p. 322.

A Skills and Understanding

The Data File at the right shows how far a group of hikers hiked over a period of 4 days. Use the data for 3–4.

3. Make a line graph of the data. Use a scale from 0 to 12 and an interval of 2 for the miles hiked. Write a sentence about the trends represented on the graph.

4. During which day did the hikers hike the greatest distance?

Four-day Hike	
By End of Day	Total Miles Hiked
1	2
2	6
3	8
4	11

B Reasoning and Problem Solving

Math and Science

For their science project, Manuel and Mark decided to test whether using fertilizer on plants would really help the growth of the plants. Fertilizer was applied only at the end of Week 2. The graph at the right shows their results. Use the graph for 5–8.

5. How many inches did the plant grow from the end of Week 3 to the end of Week 4?

6. How many more inches did the plant grow from Week 3 to Week 4 than it did during the first week?

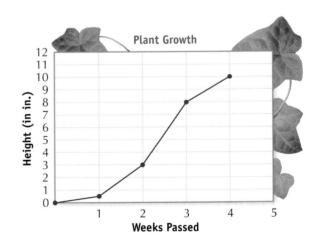

7. Reasoning If fertilizer had been added when the seeds were first planted, do you think the data point at Week 1 would be the same? Explain.

8. **Writing in Math** Is the explanation below correct? If not, tell why and write a correct response.

> Fertilizer was added again at the end of week 4. What do you think the height of the plant will be at the end of week 6?
>
> I think the height of the plant will increase at about the same rate as in weeks 3 and 4. So the height of the plant at the end of Week 6 will be 17 inches.

C Extensions

9. Reasoning Two line graphs with the same scale and intervals show the results of two boats competing in a boat race. Time is shown on the horizontal axis and distance is shown on the vertical axis. The graphs show that each boat had the same finishing time. What do you know about the last point on each line graph? Explain your answer.

 **Mixed Review and Test Prep**

Take It to the NET
Test Prep
www.scottforesman.com

10. 3.5×58 **11.** $1,000 - 46$ **12.** 3.5×100

13. For data from 200 to 950, Sally chose a scale from 0 to 1,000 to make a bar graph. Which interval would be most convenient in making the graph?

   A. 1   **B.** 10   **C.** 100   **D.** 1,000

Enrichment

Class Project

Suppose your fifth-grade class has been given the job of providing refreshments at a party honoring a teacher who is leaving. Students and teachers from the whole school will attend.

- Design a survey that will help you decide what refreshments to serve. List the survey questions that you would ask.

- Without actually surveying every person in the school, discuss how you could pick a sample that would represent all the people who will be attending.

- Discuss how you could display the data you gather.

Vocabulary
• stem-and-leaf plot
• stem
• leaf
• range

Think It Through
I can **order the data** to make it easier to read.

Stem-and-Leaf Plots

LEARN

How do you read a stem-and-leaf plot?

Julita and Aimee started a dog-walking business in which they walk dogs for people. The number of dogs they walk varies from month to month. In 8 months, they recorded the number of dogs they walked each month. These numbers are shown at the right.

Number of Dogs Walked Each Month

20, 29, 14, 52,
34, 45, 30, 48

The numbers in order from least to greatest are 14, 20, 29, 30, 34, 45, 48, and 52. The numbers can be organized using a **stem-and-leaf plot.**

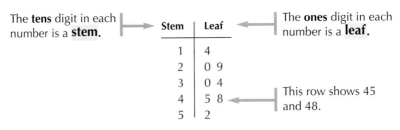

The **tens** digit in each number is a **stem**.

The **ones** digit in each number is a **leaf**.

Stem	Leaf
1	4
2	0 9
3	0 4
4	5 8
5	2

This row shows 45 and 48.

KEY: 3|0 = 30

Notice that the stems and leaves are arranged in order from least to greatest.

✔ Talk About It

1. For the number 20, what number is written in the stem? Why is it called the stem? What number is the leaf?

2. What is the least number of dogs Julita and Aimee walked in a month? How does the stem-and-leaf plot help you find the smallest number?

3. **Number Sense** For the number 45, what is the stem? What is the leaf?

Take It to the NET
More Examples
www.scottforesman.com

Activity

How do you make a stem-and-leaf plot?

The data at the right shows the ages of the first
20 people to enter a new store at the grand opening.
To arrange the data, you can use a stem-and-leaf plot.

Data File

21, 12, 31, 23, 20, 14, 58,
35, 78, 34, 50, 24, 28, 10,
44, 25, 29, 39, 58, 36

a. First rewrite the data in order from least to greatest.
Then copy and complete the plot below using the
data. Be sure to include all of the numbers, write a
key, and label the columns Stem and Leaf.

b. What is the greatest age and the least age?

c. The difference between the least and greatest numbers
in a set of data is called the **range.** What is the range
in this set of data?

TEST TALK

Think It Through
I need to **make a
graph** of the data
to organize it.

d. What leaves did you
write for the stem 5?
Why are there two
8s as leaves?

e. Which stem has the
most leaves? Which
age group does the
store seem to attract?

f. Why do you think the
plot has a 6 as a stem?

Stems are
arranged in order
vertically from
least to greatest.
Since there are no
numbers less than
10 or greater than
80, it is not
necessary to
include 0 or 8 in
the stem column.

Stem	Leaf
1	0 2 4
2	
3	
4	
5	
6	
7	

KEY: 1|2 = 12

Leaves (ones
digits) are
arranged in
numerical order
from left to right.
Leaves for each
stem have the
same tens digit.
Be sure to include
all the leaves for
each stem.

CHECK ✓

For another example, see Set 5-4 on p. 319.

Copy and complete the stem-and-leaf plot at the right
using the data below. Be sure to write the data in order
first. Then use the plot for 1–5.

21, 18, 67, 45, 58, 18, 22, 21, 32,
67, 67, 19, 20, 42, 43, 65, 45

Stem	Leaf
1	8
2	

KEY: 1|8 = 18

1. What is the range of the data? How do you know?

2. How many numbers are greater than 25?

3. How many numbers are less than 45?

4. For the number 20, what is the stem? The leaf?

5. Number Sense Which number occurs most often?
How do you know?

A Skills and Understanding

Data File

The 26 Checkpoint Distances (in miles)

20, 29, 14, 52, 34, 45, 30, 48, 93, 48, 23, 38, 90, 65, 25, 18, 60, 70, 90, 40, 58, 48, 28, 18, 55, 22

6. The Data File at the right shows the 26 distances between checkpoints in a road rally. Make a stem-and-leaf plot of the data. Title the plot "The 26 Checkpoint Distances."

7. What is the shortest distance between checkpoints? What is the longest distance? What is the range of distances?

8. How many checkpoints are more than 50 miles apart?

9. How many checkpoints are less than 30 miles apart?

10. How many checkpoints have 48 miles between them?

11. Reasoning Why is there no leaf after the stem of 8?

12. Number Sense How would you write a distance of 8 miles in the stem-and-leaf plot?

B Reasoning and Problem Solving

Math and Everyday Life

The chart at the right shows the 10 most popular breeds of dogs in a recent year based on the number of registrations in a national kennel association. Note that some breeds include more than one size category. The average weight for each type of dog is shown.

Make a stem-and-leaf plot using the Data File to help answer 13–15. HINT: Include a stem labeled 0.

13. Which stem (or stems) in the stem-and-leaf plot has the most leaves?

14. Reasoning Which stems have no leaves? Which types of dogs seem to be more popular, large or small? Explain.

15. Writing in Math How does a stem-and-leaf plot make it easier to tell which values occur most?

Data File

| \multicolumn{3}{l}{Average Weights of the Top 10 Breeds of Dogs} |
Rank	Breed	Weight (lb)
1	Labrador Retrievers	67
2	Golden Retrievers	75
3	German Shepherds	81
4	Dachshunds	
	Standard	27
	Miniature	20
5	Beagles	20
6	Yorkshire Terriers	7
7	Poodles	
	Standard	75
	Miniature	13
	Toy	10
8	Boxers	71
9	Chihuahuas	7
10	Shih Tzu	17

C Extensions

Number Sense Create a list of data for each stem-and-leaf plot as described.

16. The stem-and-leaf plot should have stems of 1, 2, 4, 6, and 9. At least two numbers in the data set should be the same.

17. Write a list of 12 numbers with a range of 36 that will form a plot with stems of 12, 13, 14, and 15. Two numbers in the data set should be repeated three times.

Mixed Review and Test Prep

Take It to the NET
Test Prep
www.scottforesman.com

18. 0.3×0.4

19. 5×5.7

20. 100×8.9

21. $176 \div 4$

22. $1,224 \div 3$

23. $132 \div 12$

24. Which number is prime?

    A. 8   **C.** 13

    B. 10   **D.** 25

25. Which number is NOT divisible by 5?

    A. 25   **C.** 100

    B. 122   **D.** 585

Learning with Technology

The Spreadsheet/Data/Grapher eTool

The frequency table below shows the number of prime-time viewers (in millions) for each day of the week. Enter the data below into a spreadsheet.

Day of the Week	Viewers (in millions)
Monday	94
Tuesday	93
Wednesday	95
Thursday	91
Friday	81
Saturday	79
Sunday	88

	A	B
1	Day of the Week	Viewers (in millions)
2	Monday	94
3	Tuesday	93
4	Wednesday	95
5	Thursday	91
6	Friday	81
7	Saturday	79
8	Sunday	88

Use the graphing feature to generate a bar graph and a line graph of the data. Scale each graph from 0–100 with an interval of 10. Print out your graphs if possible.

1. Which graph works best for comparing the data?

2. Which graph best shows how the number of viewers changes as the week progresses?

Understand Graphic Sources: Graphs

Understanding graphic sources such as graphs when you read in math can help you use the **problem-solving strategy, *Make a Graph,*** in the next lesson.

In reading, understanding graphs can help you understand what you read. In math, understanding graphs can help you solve problems.

From the scale and the length of this orange bar, you can see that North Dakota produced nearly 300 million bushels of wheat in 2001.

The key tells you that blue bars represent corn crops, and orange bars represent wheat crops.

The labels along the axes of the <u>graph</u> describe the different types of data that are in the graph.

The key tells what data set each colored bar represents.

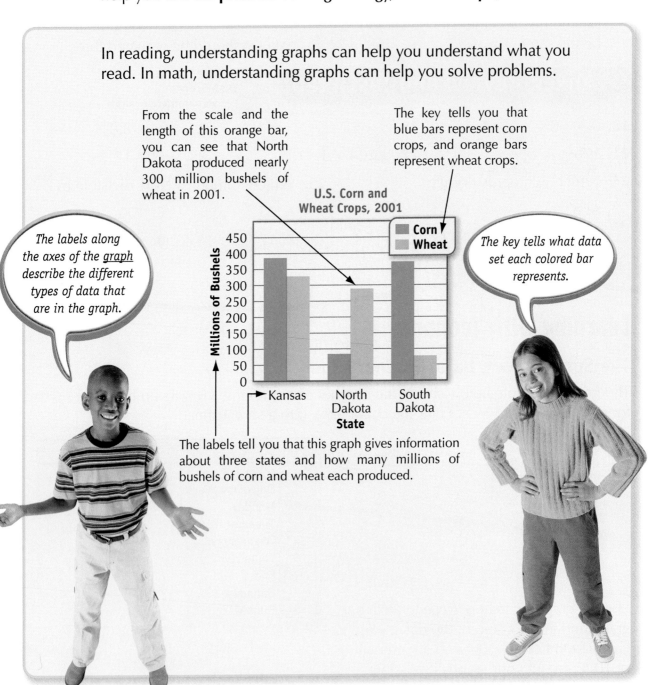

U.S. Corn and Wheat Crops, 2001

The labels tell you that this graph gives information about three states and how many millions of bushels of corn and wheat each produced.

1. How many bushels of corn did North Dakota produce in 2001?

2. Which of these states produced the most wheat in 2001?

For 3–5, use the stem-and-leaf plot below.

Ages of U.S. Presidents at Inauguration

Stem	Leaf
4	2 3 6 6 7 8 9 9
5	0 0 1 1 1 1 2 2 4 4 4 4 5 5 5 5 6 6 6 7 7 7 7 8
6	0 1 1 1 2 4 4 5 8 9

3. Theodore Roosevelt was the youngest U.S. President. How old was he when he took office?

4. Ronald Reagan was the oldest U.S. President. How old was he when he took office?

5. **Writing in Math** How many U.S. Presidents were 55 years old when they took office? Explain how you found your answer.

For 6–8, use the pictograph at the right.

6. In which city were the most houses sold?

7. **Writing in Math** What does half a house represent? Explain how you know.

8. In which two cities were the same number of houses sold?

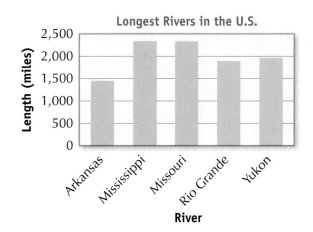

For 9–11, use the bar graph at the right.

9. Estimate the length of the Mississippi River.

10. Describe the graph's scale.

11. **Writing in Math** Which two rivers are closest in length? How can you tell from the bar graph?

Problem-Solving Strategy

Understanding graphic sources such as graphs **can help you with...**

the problem-solving strategy, *Make a Graph.*

Key Idea
Learning how and when to **make a graph** can help you solve problems.

Materials
• grid paper

Make a Graph

LEARN

How do you make a graph?

Fund Raising Two classrooms sold boxes of popcorn to raise money for a new computer. Which class was more successful selling popcorn?

Ms. Clark's Class

Boxes	7	8	9	10	11	12	13	14	15
Students	3	0	1	2	2	5	5	6	1

Mr. Arnoff's Class

Boxes	7	8	9	10	11	12	13	14	15
Students	2	3	4	5	4	4	3	0	0

Read and Understand

What do you know? You know how many students sold each number of boxes.

What are you trying to find? Find which class was more successful.

Plan and Solve

What strategy will you use?

How to Make a Graph

Step 1 Set up the graphs.
Step 2 Enter known data.
Step 3 Analyze the graphs.

Strategy: **Make a Graph.**

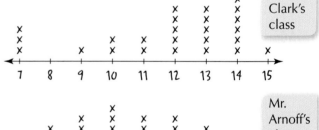

Ms. Clark's class

Mr. Arnoff's class

Answer: Ms. Clark's class was more successful. More Xs are at the right end of the plot.

Look Back and Check

Is your answer reasonable? Yes, the numbers in the table show the same trend.

✔ Talk About It

1. Do the box numbers for one of the graphs look more evenly spread out than for the other graph? Explain.

2. **Reasoning** What was the most typical number of boxes sold in each of the classes? Tell how you decided.

When might you make a graph?

Class Representatives There were elections in 3 grades for class representatives. Draw a graph to show which student won by the greatest margin.

Grade 4		Grade 5		Grade 6	
Name	Votes	Name	Votes	Name	Votes
Wilson	75	Steding	42	Cook	58
Arnoff	60	Innerst	64	Jimenez	68

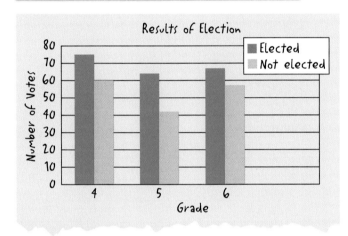

Results of Election
■ Elected
■ Not elected
Number of Votes / Grade

When to Make a Graph

Think about making a graph when:
data for an event are given.
• boxes sold
• number of votes
the question in the problem can be answered by visualizing the data in the graph.

Compare the height of each pair of bars to answer the problem.

The bar graph shows the fifth-grade student won by the greatest margin.

✔ Talk About It

3. For which grade did the most students vote? How did you decide?

CHECK ✓

For another example, see Set 5-5 on p. 319.

Copy and finish the graph to solve the problem.

1. **Membership Increase** The tables show the number of new members for two clubs during the school year. Which club's membership increased more?

Use a different line plot for each set of data.

New Computer Club Members

Month	1	2	3	4	5	6	7	8
Students	1	3	4	2	5	0	4	3

New Chess Club Members

Month	1	2	3	4	5	6	7	8
Students	1	5	2	0	6	5	2	0

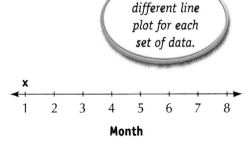

x

1 2 3 4 5 6 7 8

Month

A Using the Strategy

Completing a Graph to Solve a Problem Copy and complete the graph to solve the problem.

2. Favorite Music Store The table below shows the results of a poll that was taken of people shopping at a mall. Which store did shoppers who were polled appear to prefer?

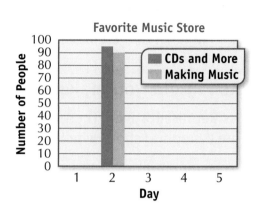

Store	Day 1	Day 2	Day 3	Day 4	Day 5
CDs and More	39	95	20	45	40
Making Music	20	90	30	5	40

Making a Graph to Solve a Problem Make a bar graph to solve the problems.

3. Which continent would you visit to reach the highest point in the world?

4. Which two continents have the greatest range between their highest points?

5. Which two continents have the least difference between their highest points?

Data File

The Seven Continents	
Continent	**Highest Point**
Africa	5,895 m
Antarctica	4,897 m
Asia (includes Middle East)	8,850 m
Australia (includes Oceania)	5,030 m
Europe	5,642 m
North America	6,194 m
South/Central America (includes the Caribbean)	6,960 m

Math and Social Studies

The U.S. Department of Labor maintains statistics for part-time and full-time workers.

6. Complete the graph to include the following data:
   For employed workers (ages 16 and older):
   19 percent part-time, 81 percent full-time.
   For employed men (ages 20 and older):
   9 percent part-time and 91 percent full-time.

7. Which group has the greatest difference between part-time and full-time employees? The least difference?

B Mixed Strategy Practice

Solve each problem. Write the answer in a complete statement.

8. A store kept track of the number of CDs purchased by customers in one hour. The numbers were 3, 2, 5, 3, 4, 1, 0, 7, 4, 2, 1, 2, 2, 6, 10, 2, 1, and 4. What was the most frequent number of CDs purchased?

9. How many different outfits consisting of a pair of jeans, a T-shirt and a jacket can you make with three pairs of jeans, four T-shirts, and two jackets?

10. CDs cost $16 and cassettes cost $10. Brian spent $94 on a total of seven items. If he bought at least one CD and one cassette, how many of each item did he buy?

11. **Writing in Math** Ms. Anderson's class has 26 students. She decides to arrange five tables like the first one shown end to end. Will all the students have seats? Explain your answer.

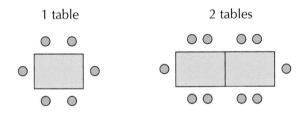

1 table   2 tables

STRATEGIES

- **Show What You Know**
  Draw a Picture
  Make an Organized List
  Make a Table
  Make a Graph
  Act It Out or Use Objects
- **Look for a Pattern**
- **Try, Check, and Revise**
- **Write an Equation**
- **Use Logical Reasoning**
- **Solve a Simpler Problem**
- **Work Backward**

Choose a tool

Mental Math

Think It Through

Stuck? I won't give up. I can:
- Reread the problem.
- Tell what I know.
- Identify key facts and details.
- Tell the problem in my own words.
- Show the main idea.
- Try a different strategy.
- Retrace my steps.

Mixed Review and Test Prep

Take It to the NET
Test Prep
www.scottforesman.com

Estimate.

12. $899 + 124$

13. 34×59

14. $567 \div 9$

15. What is 9.835 rounded to the nearest tenth?

   A. 9   **B.** 9.8   **C.** 9.84   **D.** 9.9

16. In the stem-and-leaf plot, what is the range of the data?

   A. 13   **C.** 43

   B. 36   **D.** 56

Stem	Leaf
1	3 5
2	4 6 8
3	1 3 3 6
4	1 5 7 9
5	2 6 6 6

Review

Do You Know How?

Do You Understand?

Collecting Data from a Survey (5-1)

Identify each statement as either a fact or an opinion.

1. Football is the best high school sport.

2. In a class, 5 students have no siblings.

A Explain how you determined whether Exercise 1 was a fact or opinion.

B Write a survey question that might gather the information in Exercise 2.

Bar Graphs (5-2); Make a Graph (5-5)

Quarter 1 Honor Roll

3. If 41 grade 7 girls, 39 grade 8 girls, and 45 grade 8 boys made the honor roll, copy and complete the bar graph.

C Explain what the different colored bars represent in the graph.

D Is it possible to show the same information on a single bar graph? Explain why or why not.

Line Graphs (5-3); Make a Graph (5-5)

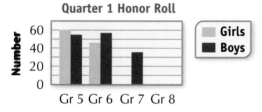

4. If the salary for working 8 hours is $40 and the salary for working 10 hours is $50, copy and complete the graph.

E Describe the trend in the data.

F Explain how you completed the graph in Exercise 4.

Stem-and-Leaf Plots (5-4)

Test scores on a fifth-grade math test were 77, 92, 76, 98, 82, 86, 88.

5. Make a stem-and-leaf plot for the scores.

G Explain how you made the stem-and-leaf plot in Exercise 5.

MULTIPLE CHOICE

1. Which statement is an opinion? (5-1)

    A. José scored an 88% on the test.   **C.** Susannah has 3 uncles.

    B. Rock music is the best type of music.   **D.** The price of the ticket is $25.

2. For the data 54, 43, 51, 24, 31, 23, and 4, how many different stems are there? (5-4)

    A. 3   **B.** 5   **C.** 7   **D.** 13

FREE RESPONSE

Use the graph and table at the right. (5-2, 5-5)

3. Copy and complete the bar graph.

4. Use the bar graph to copy and complete the table.

Railroad Tunnel	Length in Miles
Channel	
Apennine	
St. Gothard	9.3
Seikan	33.5

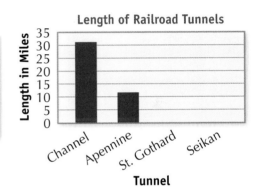

Length of Railroad Tunnels

Use the line graph at the right. (5-3, 5-5)

5. Lorna's family is planning a trip to Chicago. The line graph shows the average high temperatures in degrees Fahrenheit. Copy and complete the graph using the following data:
September, 76°F   October, 65°F
November, 50°F   December, 36°F

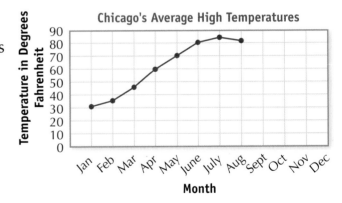

Chicago's Average High Temperatures

6. During which month should Lorna's family visit Chicago, if they want to have the warmest weather possible?

7. The number of students in the 5th grade and 6th grade homerooms are 21, 30, 15, 33, 40, 26, 27, 35, 34, 28, and 19. Arrange the data in a stem-and-leaf plot. (5-4)

8. How many of the homerooms have over 25 students? (5-4)

Writing in Math

9. Give an example of when you would use a double bar graph. (5-2, 5-5)

10. Write a survey question that requires a fact. (5-1)

Vocabulary
- average
- range (p. 271)
- median
- mean
- mode

Materials
- calculator

Mean, Median, and Mode

How can data be described by a single number?

For 7 days in a row Geneva recorded the following number of visits to the school website:

$$4, 2, 8, 9, 4, 10, 5$$

She used tiles to help find a single number to describe the typical or **average** number of visits per day.

I can find the average by making the bars even. The typical number is 6.

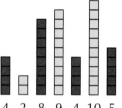

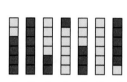

4 2 8 9 4 10 5   6 6 6 6 6 6 6

The **mean** is often called the average. To find the mean, add all the data and divide by the number of data.	The **median** is the middle number. To find the median, arrange the data in order from least to greatest.	The **mode** is the data value that occurs most often.
4 + 2 + 8 + 9 + 4 + 10 + 5 = 42 42 ÷ 7 = 6 The mean is 6.	2, 4, 4, **5**, 8, 9, 10 ↑ middle The median is 5.	2, **4**, **4**, 5, 8, 9, 10 The mode is 4.

Example

Sometimes the median does not appear in the set of values because there is an even number of values. Find the median for the following data: 3, 1, 9, 6, 4, 1.

Arrange the values in order from least to greatest.

$$1, 1, \underline{3, 4}, 6, 9$$
↑
middle

Find a number halfway between 3 and 4. Add the two middle numbers and divide by 2. Since 3 + 4 = 7 and 7 ÷ 2 = 3.5, the median is 3.5.

✔ Talk About It

1. In finding the mean, median, and mode of a set of data, in which case do you need to add all the data in the set? In which case do you need to order the data from least to greatest?

2. If there are 9 values listed in order, which value will be in the middle? If 8 values are listed in order, how do you find the middle value?

3. Can a set of values have more than one mode? No mode? Explain.

Does the mean, median, or mode best describe the data?

Activity

The technology store has 10 employees. The yearly salaries are shown in the data file.

a. Use a calculator to find the mean and median salaries.

b. How many salaries are above the mean? Below the mean? Does any one employee earn the mean salary?

c. How many salaries are above the median? Below the median?

d. What is the range of salaries? The mode?

e. If the store owner wanted to impress people that the salaries are generous, would the owner list the mean, median, mode, or range? Explain.

f. If several employees want to ask for a raise, should they use the mean, median, or mode to convince the owner that the salaries are low? Explain.

g. Do you think the mean, median, or mode is the most typical value for these salaries? Explain.

Data File

Salaries at The Technology Store

$9,950	$16,500
$10,000	$20,000
$10,000	$25,000
$10,000	$60,050
$14,500	$75,000

Remember: **Range** is the difference between the greatest and least number.

CHECK ✔

For another example, see Set 5-6 on p. 319.

Use this list of numbers for 1–4.

1. Find the mode.

2. Find the median.

3. Find the mean.

4. **Reasoning** How do the mode, median, and mean change when 14 and 32 are added to the list?

Data File

14	20	58	14	22
7	18	46	28	3

A Skills and Understanding

5. Find the mean of this data set: 1,236 855 645 764

6. Find the median of this data set: 25.4 26.8 28.6 31.5

7. Find the mode of this data set: 12 45 12 6 12 7 12 8 12

8. Number Sense Create a data set that has five numbers with a range of 10, a mode of 6, and a median of 12. What is the mean?

Find the mean, median, and mode for each set of data.

 9. 8, 6, 4, 4, 3

10. 5, 7, 13, 9, 9, 11

11. 64, 59, 58, 58, 61

12. 99, 98, 90, 79, 60, 40, 90, 80

B Reasoning and Problem Solving

13. Six cassette tapes have playing-time lengths of 23 min, 16 min, 16 min, 25 min, 27 min, and 19 min. What is the mean playing time for the tapes?

14. Reasoning A data set consisting of 3 numbers has mean of 12. The median is also 12. The least number is 5. What is the greatest number?

Math and Everyday Life

Managers in sales often keep statistics on their inventory so that ordering replacement stock is easy to do.

15. Find the mean, median, and mode of the data. Which of the three is typical of the shoe sizes sold for the week?

16. Reasoning If you were the manager, what shoe sizes would you order based on the week's sales? Explain your thinking.

17. Writing in Math Is the explanation below correct? If not, tell why and write a correct response.

Data File

Sales at a shoe store in 1 week

4 of size 5
3 of size 6
8 of size 7
2 of size 8
8 of size 9
3 of size 10
4 of size 11

Are the mean, median, and mode always numbers from a list of data?

No, the mean and median may or may not appear in the list. The mode does appear if the data has a mode. But data may not have a mode.

C Extensions

The following data was put into a stem-and-leaf plot: 5, 45, 45, 46, 48, 49, 50, 50, 57, 60. Sometimes data have a number that is not typical of the set. The number 5 in the set of data is such a number. It is called an **outlier.**

Stem	Leaf
0	5
1	
2	
3	
4	5 5 6 8 9
5	0 0 7
6	0

18. Find the range, mode, median, and mean of the data with and without the outlier. How does the outlier affect the mode, mean, and median of the set of data?

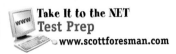

Mixed Review and Test Prep

Take It to the NET
Test Prep
www.scottforesman.com

19. George and Ann recorded the number of minutes they practiced the piano for 5 days in a row. Copy and complete the graph to determine who practiced more consistently.

	Day 1	Day 2	Day 3	Day 4	Day 5
George	40	60	50	50	60
Ann	10	90	20	60	10

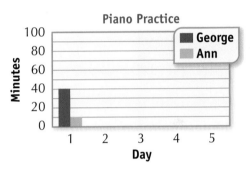

Piano Practice

20. If 16 ounces of juice cost $1.44, what is the cost for 1 ounce?

A. $0.09   **B.** $0.90   **C.** $9   **D.** $23.04

Discover Math in Your World

Take It to the NET
Video and Activities
www.scottforesman.com

In the Redds

Adult female salmon lay their eggs in underwater gravel nests called redds. The number of redds in the Hanford Reach area of the Columbia River has varied greatly.

Year	Number of Redds	Year	Number of Redds
1989	8,834	1995	3,489
1990	6,506	1996	7,620
1991	4,939	1997	7,600
1992	4,930	1998	5,638
1993	2,873	1999	6,086
1994	5,619	2000	5,507

1. What is the median for the number of redds?

Key Idea
A circle graph shows data and how parts of data relate to the total.

Vocabulary
• circle graph

Materials
• blank circles
  or  tools

Circle Graphs

LEARN

WARM UP

1. What part of a whole pizza is 6 out of 12 equal pieces?

2. What part of a whole pizza is 3 out of 12 equal pieces?

How do you read a circle graph?

The graph below is a **circle graph.** It represents all (100%) of a set of data. The sections, or wedges, show what part of the whole each portion of the data represents.

The graph shows that more cheese pizzas were made than any other kind because the section for cheese is greater than any of the other sections.

If 100 pizzas were made, then you could say that 50 pizzas with either pepperoni or cheese topping were made.

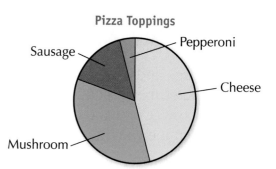

Pizza Toppings

✔ Talk About It

1. Which topping was used the least?

2. **Number Sense** Suppose 100 pizzas were made, and 45 were cheese and 35 were mushrooms. How many of the 100 pizzas were either sausage or pepperoni?

Activity

How do you label a circle graph?

The circle graph shows how Sarah spent one 24-hour period of time from midnight to midnight. She spent 2 hours eating, 10 hours sleeping, 6 hours at school, 2 hours doing homework, and 4 hours on other activities.

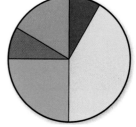

One Day of Sarah's Activities

a. Copy and label the graph. (Hint: Think about which activity took the most time and which two activities took the same amount of time.)

b. How did you know which section of the graph should be labeled School and which should be labeled Sleeping?

Think It Through
I can **use logical reasoning** to label the sections of the graph.

For another example, see Set 5-7 on p. 320.

1. Copy and complete the graph at the right using the fact that Kent spends more on school lunches than on charities.

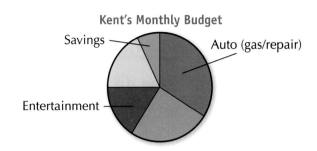

Kent's Monthly Budget

Savings | Auto (gas/repair)
Entertainment

2. Which category receives the greatest part of Kent's income?

3. Which categories are about equal?

4. **Estimation** Kent's income is $360 a month. About how much does Kent spend on lunches?

PRACTICE
For more practice, see Set 5-7 on p. 324.

A Skills and Understanding

International Translators Inc. employs 480 translators who translate Chinese, Japanese, French, or Spanish. Use this information for Exercise 6.

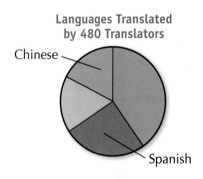

Languages Translated by 480 Translators

Chinese

Spanish

5. Copy and complete the graph at the right by labeling the missing categories. There are more Japanese translators than any other language.

6. **Estimation** About how many Spanish translators are employed?

B Reasoning and Problem Solving

Use the graph at the right for 7–8.

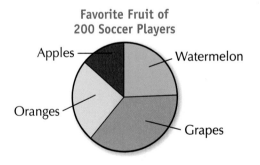

Favorite Fruit of 200 Soccer Players

Apples | Watermelon
Oranges | Grapes

7. Jeff surveyed soccer players at the local park to find out which fruit was their favorite. Estimate the number that named grapes as their favorite.

8. **Writing in Math** The number of responses for watermelon and oranges is the same. Tell how you could estimate the number of responses for apples.

Mixed Review and Test Prep

Take It to the NET
Test Prep
www.scottforesman.com

9. 4,500 ÷ 50   10. 750 ÷ 36   11. 5.67 ÷ 100

12. A waiter earned $40, $50, $60, $30, and $50 in tips on five different days. What was the mean earned per day?

   A. $40   **B.** $46   **C.** $50   **D.** $230

 All text pages available online and on CD-ROM.

Key Idea
Choosing the appropriate graph to display data helps analyze the data.

Vocabulary
- pictograph
- line plot (p. 260)
- stem-and-leaf plot (p. 270)
- line graph (p. 266)
- bar graph (p. 262)
- circle graph (p. 286)

Think It Through
- I can **use a line graph** to show trends and how data changes over time.
- I can **use a bar graph** to compare data that can be counted.

Choosing an Appropriate Graph

LEARN

How do you choose the best graph to display data?

Lien surveyed people to ask them their favorite color. She recorded the results in a spreadsheet. With her computer she used the same data to make a line graph and a bar graph.

	A	B
1	Color	Responses
2	Red	7
3	Blue	9
4	Green	10
5	Purple	7
6	Orange	6

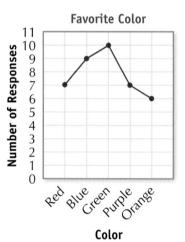

Notice that the line graph implies that data exist between colors.

The bars represent the number of responses counted for each color.

✔ Talk About It

1. Describe the data being graphed above. Do the graphs show data collected over a period of time?

2. Is the bar graph the correct graph to use to show the data collected? Why or why not?

3. **Representations** A **pictograph** compares data that can be counted. It shows the data in multiples. Part of Lien's survey data is shown in the pictograph. How many symbols should be shown for the other colors?

Favorite Color

Red	🖌🖌🖌🖌
Blue	
Green	
Purple	
Orange	

🖌 = 2

For another example, see Set 5-8 on p. 320.

The graphs below show the ages of the last ten Presidents at inauguration. Use the graphs for 1–3.

A **line plot** compares data by showing clusters of information.

```
        x         x                   x     x  x  x              x  x     x               x
    ←——+——+——+——+——+——+——+——+——+——+——+——+——+——+——+→
       42  44  46  48  50  52  54  56  58  60  62  64  66  68  70
```

1. Which plot makes it easier to find the median age of the presidents when they were inaugurated? Explain your reasoning.

2. For this data, there is no mode. How does the line plot show this? How does the stem-and-leaf plot show this?

3. For either plot, how would you determine the mean of the data?

4. **Reasoning** An **outlier** is a number that is much greater than or much less than any of the other data in a data set. Which type of plot might show this more clearly? Explain your thinking.

*A **stem-and-leaf plot** organizes data in numerical order.*

Stem	Leaf
4	3 6
5	2 4 5 6
6	1 2 4 9

PRACTICE

For more practice, see Set 5-8 on p. 324.

A Skills and Understanding

Use the graphs at the right for 5–7.

5. Which graph is easier to use to answer the question "What part of the total amount collected was given to the Homeless Fund?" Explain your reasoning.

6. From which graph can you determine how much money was collected? Why? Why can you not tell that from the other graph?

7. If the total collected had been $248, how much would have been given to the Homeless Fund? Which graph did you use?

Where Money Was Donated

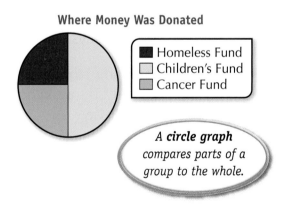

- ■ Homeless Fund
- □ Children's Fund
- ▨ Cancer Fund

*A **circle graph** compares parts of a group to the whole.*

Where Money Was Donated

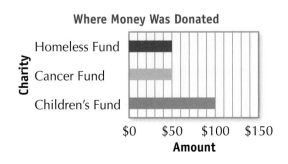

For 8–9, tell what type of graph would be most appropriate to represent the data listed.

8. How you spent your time yesterday

9. The fastest animals in miles per hour

10. Reasoning A set of data has a list of 35 numbers ranging from 11 to 89. What would be the best type of graph to use? Why?

B Reasoning and Problem Solving

11. The median number in a set of 9 numbers is 16. The range is 18 and the greatest number is 32. How many numbers are less than the median 16? What are the possible numbers?

12. Algebra An elephant lives an average of 35 years and a pig lives an average of 10 years. A graph shows that a horse's life expectancy is halfway between that of the elephant and the pig. Write an expression to show the average life expectancy of the horse.

 Math and Science

For a science project, Carol Ann graphed the noon temperatures in Orlando for five days in July. Use the graph for 13–14.

13. Describe the trend in the temperature for the five days. What was the range in the temperatures?

14. Estimation Estimate the mean temperature for the five days.

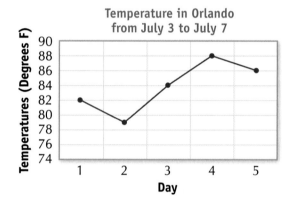

15. <u>Writing in Math</u> Dan and Beth made graphs to show the size of each park in Carroll County. Who chose the more appropriate graph and why?

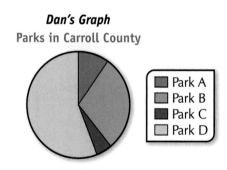

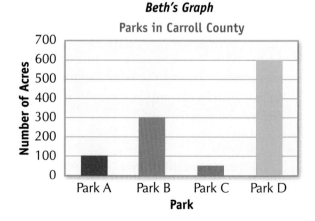

C Extensions

A double line graph compares similar data.
Use the graph at the right for 16–17.

16. Estimation About how many calories
would be burned if a 150-lb person
bicycled for 4 hours and then sat for
4 hours?

17. Reasoning Describe how the line would
look and where it would fall on the graph
if a 150-pound person were to sit for
1 hour, bike for 2 hours, and then sit
for 1 hour.

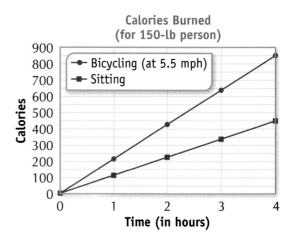

**Calories Burned
(for 150-lb person)**

Bicycling (at 5.5 mph)
Sitting

Calories
Time (in hours)

Mixed Review and Test Prep

**Take It to the NET
Test Prep**
www.scottforesman.com

Estimate.

18. $183 \div 3$ **19.** $429 \div 61$ **20.** $5{,}675 \div 78$ **21.** $\$61.25 \div 25$

22. The circle graph shows the results
of a survey of 100 people. About
how many chose red?

    A. 25   **C.** 75

    B. 50   **D.** 100

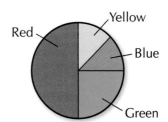

Red   Yellow   Blue   Green

Practice Game

Your Average Game

Players: 2–4
Materials: Number cards 1–20 (2 sets)

Players begin each turn with 3 points and 1 minute
on the clock. To start a turn, a player draws 5 cards
from the deck and determines the mean for that
set of numbers. When 1 minute is up, another
player uses a calculator to check the mean.
One point is deducted for each missing or
incorrect mean. The winner is the player
with the most points at the end of 3 rounds.

Problem-Solving Skill

Key Idea
There are specific things you can do to write a good comparison in math.

Think It Through
I can use the graphs to find how the data about bicycle and skateboard sales are **alike and different.**

Writing to Compare

LEARN

How do you write a good comparison?

When you **write to compare,** you need to analyze the data and tell how they are alike and different.

Bicycle and Skateboard Sales Data for 10-speed bicycle and skateboard sales for a particular company are shown in the line graphs below. Using the information from the two graphs, write two statements that compare the data about the bicycle and skateboard sales.

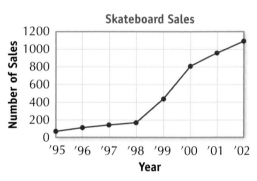

Writing a Math Comparison

- Analyze the data. Try to find trends that are similar and trends that are different.

- Use changing words like "increasing" and "decreasing" to describe trends in the graphs.

- Use words like "faster," "steeper," and "more," to compare graphs.

- *The sales for both have been increasing over the years.*

- *The difference between the number of bicycle sales and the number of skateboard sales is becoming smaller.*

✔ Talk About It

1. What other comparisons can you make about bicycle and skateboard sales?

2. If the trend continues, what can you say about the sales of both bicycles and skateboards in 2003?

Analyze the graphs below. Then answer 1–2.

Ann's Savings

Jill's Savings

1. Describe any trends you see. Write two statements that compare Ann's and Jill's saving habits for the 6 months shown.

2. Suppose the trend shown on the graphs continues. Write a statement telling what will happen to the amount the girls save over the next few months.

PRACTICE

For more practice, see Set 5-9 on p. 324.

An elementary school decided to collect cans of food for a food pantry. Analyze the graph at the right. Then answer 3–4.

3. Write two statements to describe any trends you see.

4. Suppose the school decided to collect cans of food for another week and the trend continued. Tell how the graph for the third week might look.

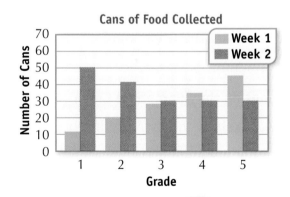

Cans of Food Collected

5. Explain how you could estimate 203 × 32. Tell whether your estimate is greater than or less than the exact answer and how you made the comparison without finding the exact answer.

6. There is a total of 12 chickens and pigs playing in a barnyard. Altogether there are 34 legs. How many chickens and how many pigs are there. Explain how you found your answer.

Do You Know How?

Do You Understand?

Mean, Median, and Mode (5-6)

Tamara's test scores: 93, 82, 85, 90, 85

1. Find the mean, median, and mode of the data set.

A Explain how you found the mean in Exercise 1.

B Tell how to find the median when there is an even number of values.

Circle Graphs (5-7)

2. If gold and green are the last two colors and more schools have gold as their school color, copy and label the remaining sections.

School Colors of 100 Schools

Blue Red

3. What is the most popular school color? The least popular?

C Tell how you determined which section to label gold in Exercise 2.

D Explain how you could estimate about how many schools have red as their school color in Exercise 3.

Choosing the Appropriate Graph (5-8)

4. To show the increase in population in a city over 5 years, which type of graph would you choose?

E Tell how you determined which graph to use in Exercise 4.

Problem-Solving Skill: Writing to Compare (5-9)

5. Write two statements that compare the trends in enrollments between Elm School and Maple School.

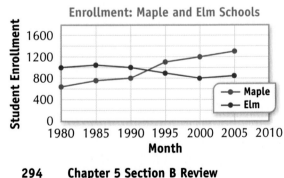

F Explain how to use the graph to answer Exercise 5.

G What do you think a good estimate would be for the enrollment in each school in 2010?

MULTIPLE CHOICE

1. Which is the mode of the data listed below? (5-6)

  23, 22, 18, 20, 31, 22, 26, 22, 20, 19, 20

  A. 22   **B.** 20 and 22   **C.** 20   **D.** 22.09

2. Which graph best describes how data changes over time? (5-8)

  F. Bar graph   **G.** Line graph   **H.** Circle graph   **J.** Stem-and-leaf plot

FREE RESPONSE

Use the table at the right. (5-6, 5-9)

3. Find the mean, median, and mode of the data.

4. How many games were above the median? Below the median?

5. If you wanted to graph the data at the right, what type of graph would you choose?

Grant Middle School 2002 Season

Game	Points Scored
Game 1	6
Game 2	6
Game 3	10
Game 4	17
Game 5	21

Use the data at the right. (5-7, 5-8, 5-9)

6. 600 Adams Middle School students were surveyed. Copy and complete the table and label the remaining sections of the circle graph.

7. What other type of graph could be used to display the data?

Adams Middle School Lunch Preferences

Lunch	Number of Students
Pizza	212
Hot Dogs	83
Fish	48
Chicken	63
Taco Salad	95
Hamburgers	

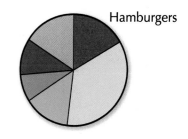

Hamburgers

Writing in Math

8. Explain the difference between a circle graph and a bar graph. Give an example of when you would use each type of graph. (5-7)

9. The double bar graph shows the requirements for pushups in order to receive a physical fitness award. Compare the boys and girls and describe any trends you see. (5-9)

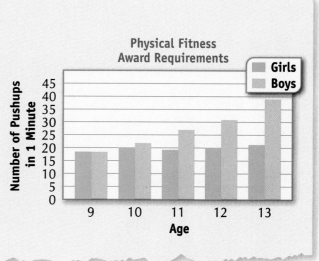

Physical Fitness Award Requirements

Key Idea
You can use an experiment to predict outcomes.

Vocabulary
• outcomes
• equally likely
• event
• impossible event
• certain event

Materials
• number cubes
  or tools

Predicting Outcomes

LEARN

What outcomes are likely?

If you toss a number cube, the possible **outcomes** are 1, 2, 3, 4, 5, and 6. Each outcome is **equally likely.** An **event** is a collection of one or more outcomes.

✔ **WARM UP**

List the possible outcomes when you

1. toss a paper cup.

2. toss a paper cone.

Example A

Compare the chances of tossing an even number and tossing an odd number.

Event: Tossing an even number	**Event:** Tossing an odd number
Favorable outcomes: 2, 4, 6	**Favorable outcomes:** 1, 3, 5
3 of 6 possible outcomes are favorable, so in 3 out of 6 tosses you can expect an even number.	3 of 6 possible outcomes are favorable, so in 3 out of 6 tosses you can expect an odd number.

Tossing an even number and tossing an odd number are equally likely events.

Example B

Compare the chances of tossing the number 6 or tossing a number less than 6.

Event: Tossing the number 6	**Event:** Tossing a number less than 6
Favorable outcome: 6	**Favorable outcomes:** 1, 2, 3, 4, 5
1 of the 6 possible outcomes is favorable, so in 1 out of 6 tosses you can expect the number 6.	5 out of 6 possible outcomes are favorable, so in 5 out of 6 tosses you can expect 1, 2, 3, 4, or 5.

Tossing a 6 is **less likely** than tossing a number less than 6.
Tossing a number less than 6 is **more likely** than tossing a 6.

✔ **Talk About It**

1. Compare the chances of tossing a 2 or tossing a 6. Is one event more likely to occur than the other? Explain.

2. **Reasoning** In 10 tosses, how many times would you expect an even number?

What other kinds of events are there?

Example C

Give an example of an event that can never happen and an example of an event that will always happen.

Event: Tossing a 7 **Favorable outcomes:** None	**Event:** Tossing a number less than 7 **Favorable outcomes:** 1, 2, 3, 4, 5, 6
7 is not one of the possible outcomes.	The favorable outcomes and the possible outcomes are the same.
So tossing a 7 is an **impossible event.**	So tossing a number less than 7 is a **certain event.**

✔ Talk About It

3. Reasoning Describe another impossible event that involves tossing a number cube.

Take It to the NET
More Examples
www.scottforesman.com

Activity

What actually happens when you toss a number cube?

When you toss a number cube, each of the 6 possible outcomes has an equal chance of occurring. In 24 tosses you would expect to toss each number 4 times. Now toss a number cube to see what actually happens.

a. Copy the table. Toss a number cube 24 times and record each outcome. Are your outcomes close to the expected outcome?

Outcome	1	2	3	4	5	6
Your outcomes						
Class outcomes						

b. Combine the results for the class. Did each number occur about the same number of times?

c. If you tossed the number cube 1,000 times, do you think the outcomes would be closer to the expected outcomes? Explain.

d. Look at the combined results of the class. Did an even number occur about the same number of times as an odd number?

e. Describe two events, A and B, in which event A is more likely to occur than event B.

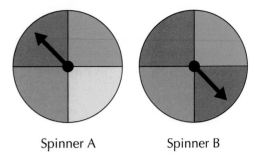

Think about spinning Spinner A.

1. What are the possible outcome colors? Are the colors equally likely? Why or why not?

2. In 100 spins, how many times would you expect Spinner A to land on red?

Now think about spinning Spinner B.

3. How many different outcome colors are possible? Are the colors equally likely to occur? Why or why not?

4. What color would you expect to occur most often?

5. **Reasoning** In 100 spins, how many times would you expect Spinner B to land on red? Explain.

Spinner A   Spinner B

PRACTICE

For more practice, see Set 5-10 on p. 325.

Ⓐ Skills and Understanding

Think of putting 5 red counters, 2 blue counters, and 1 yellow counter in a bag. Then think of drawing one counter at a time and then replacing it after each draw.

6. Consider the events "draw red," "draw blue," and "draw yellow." Are the events equally likely?

7. Which event is most likely? Least likely?

8. If you drew a counter 80 times, how many times would you expect to draw a red counter? A blue counter? A yellow counter? HINT: Think how many would be expected for each color if only 8 counters were drawn, then multiply each number by 10.

9. If you actually performed an experiment with the counters described above, do you think the results of your experiment would be the same as the expected results in question 8? Explain.

10. Describe an event about drawing a counter that is impossible.

11. Describe an event about drawing a counter that is certain.

12. Explain why some events are more likely than others.

13. **Reasoning** How might you change the number of counters of each color in the bag so that two colors would be equally likely? So that all three colors would be equally likely?

B Reasoning and Problem Solving

Math and Social Studies

Data File

AK	HI	ME	NJ	SD
AL	IA	MI	NM	TN
AR	ID	MN	NV	TX
AZ	IL	MO	NY	UT
CA	IN	MS	OH	VA
CO	KS	MT	OK	VT
CT	KY	NC	OR	WA
DE	LA	ND	PA	WI
FL	MA	NE	RI	WV
GA	MD	NH	SC	WY

Suppose you wrote each state abbreviation on a slip of paper and put the slips in a box. Then, without looking, you drew one of the slips.

14. How many different outcomes are there? Is each outcome equally likely?

What are the chances of drawing a name beginning with:

15. W?   **16.** B?   **17.** M?   **18.** D?

19. What event has the same chance of occurring as drawing a name beginning with M?

20. **Writing in Math** What do you think the expression, "Heads you win; tails you lose" means? Are the events equally likely?

C Extensions

Professional code breakers can often solve coded messages by tallying the frequency of the letters in the code.

21. Choose the first 50 letters of a paragraph in a book, newspaper or magazine. Which letter appears most frequently? Second most frequently.

22. Predict the most common letter in a 200-letter sample. Check your prediction using a 200-letter sample.

23. In a coded message, W and P occur most often. The word that appears most frequently is PZW. What do you think this PZW means?

Mixed Review and Test Prep

Take It to the NET
Test Prep
www.scottforesman.com

24. Which type of graph is best for displaying data that change over time?

A. bar graph   **B.** line graph   **C.** circle graph   **D.** line plot

25. The graphs show the number of hours worked after school by two workers. Write two different sentences to compare the number of hours worked.

Hours worked by Rich

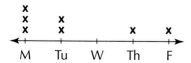

Hours worked by Mary Ann

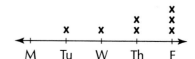

Vocabulary
- sample space
- tree diagram

Think It Through

I can solve many kinds of problems by **making an organized list.**

Listing Outcomes

LEARN

WARM UP
1. 72 + 3,619
2. 2,001 + 459
3. 7,142 − 68
4. 5,600 − 3,824

How do tree diagrams help list outcomes?

Shawn, Larry, and Ken are eligible to be captain of the football team. Juan, Andy, Ricky, and Mark are eligible to be co-captain. Each boy has an equal chance of being selected.

Example

How many possible outcomes are there for choosing a captain and a co-captain?

The set of all possible outcomes is called the **sample space.** You can make a **tree diagram** to find the sample space.

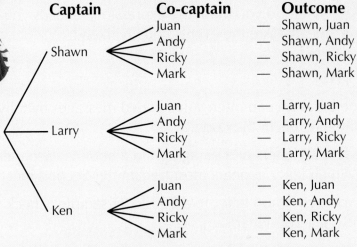

Captain	Co-captain	Outcome
Shawn	Juan	Shawn, Juan
	Andy	Shawn, Andy
	Ricky	Shawn, Ricky
	Mark	Shawn, Mark
Larry	Juan	Larry, Juan
	Andy	Larry, Andy
	Ricky	Larry, Ricky
	Mark	Larry, Mark
Ken	Juan	Ken, Juan
	Andy	Ken, Andy
	Ricky	Ken, Ricky
	Mark	Ken, Mark

There are 12 possible outcomes in the sample space.

You can also find the number of outcomes by multiplying.

Number of choices for captain		Number of choices for co-captain		Number of possible outcomes
↓		↓		↓
3	×	4	=	12

✔ Talk About It

1. Out of 12 possible outcomes, how many chances include Ken and Andy as captain and co-captain?

2. **Reasoning** What would the number of outcomes be if only 3 boys were eligible for co-captain?

1. What are the possible outcomes if you toss the number cube? Spin the spinner?

2. Make a tree diagram to show the sample space for tossing the number cube and then spinning the spinner.

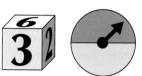

3. **Number Sense** Your chance of tossing an even number and the spinner landing on yellow is ▇ out of ▇.

PRACTICE

For more practice, see Set 5-11 on p. 325.

Ⓐ Skills and Understanding

4. Copy and complete the tree diagram to show the possible sums when two number cubes are tossed.

5. How many times does each sum occur in the tree diagram?

6. **Reasoning** When tossing two number cubes, describe an event that is likely. That is certain. That is impossible.

First Number	Second Number	Sum
1	1	— 2
	2	— 3
	3	— 4
	4	— 5
	5	— 6
	6	— 7
2	1	— 3
	2	— 4
	3	— 5
	4	— 6

Ⓑ Reasoning and Problem Solving

7. One candidate listed from each of Grades 4, 5, and 6 will be elected to the student council. Make a tree diagram to show the sample space. What is the chance Walt, Gayle, and Zoë will be elected?

8. **Writing in Math** Explain how you could multiply to find the number of possible outcomes in Exercise 7.

Candidates for Student Council		
Grade 4	**Grade 5**	**Grade 6**
Claire	Nancy	Jason
Vernon	Gayle	Zoë
Walt		

Ⓒ Extensions

9. Toss two number cubes 100 times and record each sum. Are your outcomes similar to those in Exercise 5?

10. Combine your results with that of classmates. Now are the outcomes closer to those in Exercise 5?

Think It Through
The more times I toss the number cubes, the closer I will come to the expected results.

Mixed Review and Test Prep

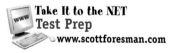

Take It to the NET
Test Prep
www.scottforesman.com

11. Evaluate $2 \times 8 + 10 \times 7$ by using the order of operations.

12. A bag contains 4 red marbles, 1 green marble, and 1 yellow marble. If you draw one marble, describe the chance of drawing a red marble.

   A. Certain   **B.** Unlikely   **C.** Impossible   **D.** Likely

 All text pages available online and on CD-ROM.

Key Idea
Probability can
be expressed as
a fraction.

Vocabulary
• probability

Materials
• spinner or
 tools

Expressing Probability as a Fraction

 **LEARN**

What is the probability of an event?

The **probability** of an event is a number that describes the chance that an event will occur.

$$\text{Probability of an event} = \frac{\text{number of favorable outcomes}}{\text{number of possible outcomes}}$$

The probability of an event ranges from 0 for an event that is impossible to 1 for an event that is certain.

Impossible   Equally likely   Certain

0   less likely $\frac{1}{2}$ more likely   1

Example A

Beatrice wrote each letter of her name on a slip of paper and put the slips in a bag. If she draws one slip of paper from the bag, what is the probability of drawing a vowel?

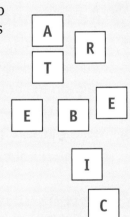

There are 8 possible outcomes (letters) and 4 favorable outcome (vowels).

$$\text{Probability of drawing a vowel} = \frac{\text{number of vowels}}{\text{number of letters}} = \frac{4}{8}$$

The probability of drawing a vowel is $\frac{4}{8}$, or $\frac{1}{2}$.

The probability of drawing a vowel can be written as $P(\text{vowel}) = \frac{1}{2}$.

✓ **Talk About It**

Use the letters in BEATRICE. Find the probability of choosing each letter or letters out of a bag.

1. a consonant   **2.** the letter E   **3.** not E

4. Reasoning If you put the letters of your name in a bag and draw one letter, what is $P(\text{vowel})$?

How can you decide if a game is fair?

A fair game is one in which all players have an equal chance of winning.
An unfair game is one in which players do not have an equal chance.
You can use probability to decide if a game is fair or is not fair.

Example B

Is One-Penny Toss a fair game?

Possible outcomes: heads, tails

$P(\text{heads}) = \frac{1}{2}$ and $P(\text{tails}) = \frac{1}{2}$,
so both players have an equally
likely chance of winning.
The game is fair.

> **One-Penny Toss**
>
> **How to play:** Toss one penny.
> If the penny lands heads up,
> Player A wins. If the penny
> lands tails up, Player B wins.

Example C

Is Two-Penny Toss a fair game?

Make a tree diagram to find the
possible outcomes:

First penny   H   T

Second penny   H   T   H   T

Outcomes   HH   HT   TH   TT

$P(\text{both heads}) = \frac{1}{4}$

$P(\text{one head and one tail}) = \frac{2}{4}$

$P(\text{both tails}) = \frac{1}{4}$

Player A is less likely to win than Player B, so the game is unfair.

> **Two-Penny Toss**
>
> **How to play:** Toss two pennies
> at the same time. If both
> pennies land heads up, Player
> A wins. If one penny lands
> heads up and the other tails
> up, Player B wins. If both
> pennies land tails up, no
> one wins.

✔ Talk About It

5. **Reasoning** How could the rules for Two-Penny Toss
be changed to make the game fair?

CHECK ✔

For another example, see Set 5-12 on p. 321.

Suppose you toss a penny and a nickel.

1. Make a tree diagram to show the possible outcomes.

2. Find $P(\text{two heads})$

3. Find $P(\text{no heads})$

4. Find $P(1 \text{ head}, 1 \text{ tail})$

5. Find $P(\text{nickel heads, penny tails})$

6. **Reasoning** Design a fair game using tossing a nickel and a penny.

Think It Through
I know that a coin is
equally likely to land
heads or tails.

A Skills and Understanding

7. In the last lesson you found the possible sums when tossing two number cubes. Copy the table and give the probability of each sum.

Sum	2	3	4	5	6	7	8	9	10	11	12
Number of Occurrences	1	2	3	4	5	6	5	4	3	2	1
Probability											

8. Which sum (or sums) has the greatest probability of occurring? Which sum (or sums) has the least probability of occurring?

9. Name two sums that have an equal chance of occurring.

For 10–14, use the spinner at the right.

10. Find P(blue)

11. Find P(yellow)

12. Find P(white)

13. Helen used this spinner for a game for 3 players. Player A was given red, player B was given green, and player C was given yellow. A player landing on his or her color scored a point. Is the game fair? If not, change the rules to make the game fair.

14. Reasoning How will the probabilities change if the yellow section is changed to red?

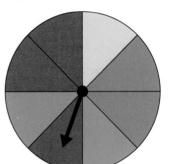

B Reasoning and Problem Solving

Math and Art

Make 2 copies of the spinner at the right.

15. On the first spinner, use blue and yellow markers to color the spinner so that blue is more likely than yellow. Then use blue and yellow to color the second spinner so that blue and yellow are equally likely results.

16. Writing in Math Explain why the first spinner you made in Exercise 15 is more likely to land on blue than yellow.

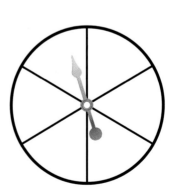

C Extensions

In 17–20, suppose each of the letters A, H, M, and T is put on a separate slip of paper and put into a bag.

17. Make a list of the ways that the letters could be drawn from the bag without replacing the letters after they are drawn, for example, AHMT. A tree diagram is a useful way to find all the possible **arrangements** (sometimes called *permutations*). Note that the order in which the letters are drawn is important.

18. Make another list showing how many 2-letter **combinations** could be drawn without replacing the letters after they are drawn. For a combination of objects, the order does NOT matter. For example, A and H is the same combination as H and A.

19. How many 3-letter combinations could be formed?

20. What is the probability that the four letters will spell MATH when they are drawn without replacement?

 Mixed Review and Test Prep

Take It to the NET
Test Prep
www.scottforesman.com

21. Sue, Ryan and Bob can be elected president. Duke and Holly can be elected vice-president. How many possibilities are there for electing a president and a vice-president?

22. 297×35 **23.** 14×0.08 **24.** $539 \div 5$ **25.** $24.992 \div 4$

26. Which number is prime?

    A. 24   **B.** 8   **C.** 17   **D.** 15

Learning with Technology

Probability eTool

You can use the Probability eTool to do probability experiments. Pick the Three Marble Tool and set the following properties: 4 red balls, 4 blue balls, 4 yellow balls. Also choose *replace*.

1. If you draw 12 times, how many times would you expect to get a red marble?

2. Draw 12 times. Do the results match your prediction?

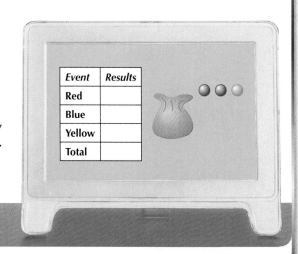

Event	Results
Red	
Blue	
Yellow	
Total	

Problem-Solving Applications

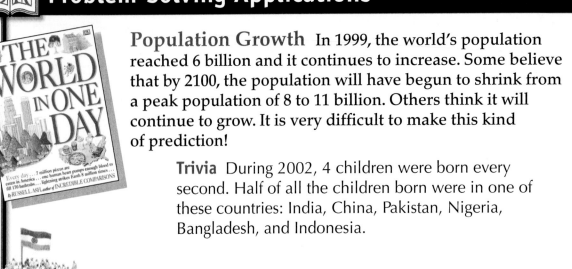

Population Growth
In 1999, the world's population reached 6 billion and it continues to increase. Some believe that by 2100, the population will have begun to shrink from a peak population of 8 to 11 billion. Others think it will continue to grow. It is very difficult to make this kind of prediction!

Trivia During 2002, 4 children were born every second. Half of all the children born were in one of these countries: India, China, Pakistan, Nigeria, Bangladesh, and Indonesia.

① It was estimated that the population of the world in the middle of 2002 was 6,228,394,430. Write the word name for this number.

② It has been projected that from 2003 to 2050 the United States' population will grow by 120,889,598 people. Estimate the 2050 population if the population in 2003 was about 283,054,745.

③ **Decision Making** In a typical group of 100 Americans, 29 are children, 21 are young adults, 38 are older adults, and 12 are senior citizens. Create the graph that best displays this data. How did you decide which type of graph to use?

4 It has been estimated that if all the people in the world were to stand together, they would take up a space that is about 13.1 times the area of Washington D.C. If this city has an area of about 69 square miles, how much room would be needed for all the people of the world to stand together?

Using Key Facts

5 For the population growths shown in the Key Facts chart, what is the range? What is the median?

Key Facts Population Growth	
Country	**Estimated Growth Per Day**
• India	44,473
• China	32,992
• Indonesia	10,145
• United States	8,889
• Nigeria	8,864
• Pakistan	8,073
• Brazil	6,775
• Bangladesh	5,825
• Mexico	4,349
• Ethiopia	3,748
• Vietnam	3,030

6 <u>**Writing in Math**</u> Write your own word problem that uses information from this lesson. Solve it and write the answer in a complete sentence.

Good News/Bad News When a country achieves a low population growth rate, it often means that unemployment is reduced. Unfortunately, it also means that businesses have a harder time finding the workers they need.

Do You Know How?

Do You Understand?

Predicting Outcomes (5-10)

There are 6 blue marbles, 5 red marbles, and 4 green marbles in a bag. You draw one marble out of the bag.

1. Which color marble are you most likely to draw out of the bag?

2. Is drawing a red marble more or less likely than drawing a green marble?

3. Are any of the colors equally likely?

(A) Describe an event about drawing a marble that is impossible.

(B) Tell how you determined the answer to Exercise 3.

Listing Outcomes (5-11)

A concession stand offers hamburgers, hot dogs, or chicken as main dishes; french fries or fruit as side dishes; and water, soda, or juice as beverages.

4. Draw a tree diagram to determine how many different lunches there are.

5. How many lunches include soda?

6. How many lunches include a hot dog and french fries?

(C) Explain how you could have found the answer to Exercise 4, without using a tree diagram.

(D) Explain how the number of outcomes would change if chicken was not offered as a main dish.

Expressing Probability as a Fraction (5-12)

Use the spinner.

7. Find *P*(green)

8. Find *P*(red)

9. Find *P*(blue)

10. Find *P*(not blue)

11. Name two colors that have an equal chance of occurring.

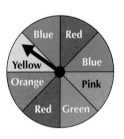

(E) Tell how you found the probability in Exercise 10.

(F) Explain how to determine which colors have an equal chance of occurring.

(G) Does any one color have the greatest chance of occurring? Explain why or why not.

MULTIPLE CHOICE

1. Which is the probability of tossing a number greater than 3 on a number cube? (5-12)

    A. $\frac{1}{6}$ **B.** 1   **C.** $\frac{1}{2}$ **D.** 0

2. Which event does not have equally likely outcomes? (5-10)

    A. Tossing a coin

    B. Spinning a spinner with two sections of equal size

    C. Tossing a number cube

    D. Choosing a vowel from the word MATH

FREE RESPONSE

Use the letters in the word RABBIT. (5-10)

3. What are two letters that are equally likely to be picked?

4. Which is more likely, picking a vowel or picking a consonant?

5. What is an impossible event, involving picking a letter in the word RABBIT?

Use the data in the table at the right. (5-11)

6. Draw a tree diagram to determine how many different outfits Hillary has packed that consist of pants and a top.

7. How many outfits include khaki pants?

8. How many outfits include jeans and a sweatshirt?

Hillary's Suitcase for Camping

Pants	Tops
Jeans	T-Shirt
Khaki pants	Sweatshirt
Sweat pants	

Using the letters in the word MATHEMATICS, find the probability of choosing each letter or letters randomly out of a bag. (5-12)

9. a vowel   10. the letter M   11. not T   12. the letter S

Suppose you toss a nickel and a quarter. (5-12)

13. Find P(two heads)   14. Find P(no tails)   15. Find P(1 head, 1 tail)

Writing in Math

16. Explain how to construct a spinner so that all outcomes are equally likely. (5-10)

17. Explain how to determine which event is most likely to occur when spinning a spinner with unequal sections. (5-10)

18. Suppose you wrote each of the letters of the word MISSISSIPPI on a slip of paper and put the slips in a bag. Describe an event that is likely. Describe an event that is unlikely. (5-11)

Test-Taking Strategies

Understand the question.

Get information for the answer.

Plan how to find the answer.

Make smart choices.

→ **Use writing in math.**

Improve written answers.

Use Writing in Math

Sometimes a test question asks for a written answer, such as an explanation, a description, or a comparison. See how one student followed the steps below to answer this test item by writing in math.

1. Tony is making a peanut butter and jelly sandwich. He will use one type of peanut butter and one flavor of jelly.

In the space below, list all the ways Tony can choose one type of peanut butter and one flavor of jelly. You may use the first letter of each peanut butter and jelly in your list (for example, S, G.)

On the lines below, explain how you made your list.

_____

Understand the question.

I need to make a list showing all the ways Tony can choose one type of peanut butter and one flavor of jelly.

Get information for the answer.

I'll need to get information from the picture.

Plan how to find the answer.

I can make a tree diagram to find all the ways and then explain what I did.

Use writing in math.

• Make your answer brief but complete.

• Use words from the problem and use math terms accurately.

• Describe steps in order.

• Draw pictures if they help to explain your thinking.

SG	CG
SR	CR
SA	CA

On the lines below, explain how you made your list.

I made a tree

diagram.

First I matched up

smooth with all the

different jellies.

Then I matched up crunchy

with all the different jellies.

```
        G — SG
   S  — R — SR
        A — SA
        G — CG
   C  — R — CR
        A — CA
```

2. Gina counted and recorded the number of letters and magazines delivered to her house each day.

Mail Delivered to My House

Day	Number of Letters	Number of Magazines
1	12	3
2	7	2
3	11	4
4		

Think It Through

*I need to predict how many letters and magazines might be delivered to Gina's house on the fourth day and explain how I made my predictions. The **mean** gives a typical amount. So I'll find the mean of the number of letters and the mean of the number of magazines and then explain what I did.*

Based on Gina's data, predict the number of letters and magazines that may be delivered on the fourth day.

___10,___ letters   ___3.___ magazines

On the lines below, explain how you made your predictions.

First, I found the mean of the

number of letters. 12 + 7 + 11 = 30,

and 30 ÷ 3 = 10. Then I found the

mean of the number of magazines.

3 + 2 + 4 = 9, and 9 ÷ 3 = 3.

Now it's your turn.

For each problem, give a complete response.

3. Tim counted and recorded the number of cats and dogs brought into his aunt's animal clinic.

Day	Number of Cats	Number of Dogs
1	6	9
2	4	13
3	8	14
4		

Predict the number of cats and dogs that might be brought in on the fourth day. Explain how you made your predictions.

4. Jen is ordering pie a la mode. She can pick apple, blueberry, cherry, or peach pie with a scoop of either vanilla or toffee ice cream.

Make a list showing all the ways Jen can choose one kind of pie and one flavor of ice cream. Then explain how you made your list.

I can't eat the whole tin of cookies, so I just take a sample.

*A **sample** is part of a larger group.* (p. 260)

Self Check

Display and describe data. (Lessons 5-1, 5-4, 5-6)

A **survey** of a **sample** of shoppers revealed that the ages of the shoppers were 25, 12, 21, 12, 16, 13, and 13. This survey gathered **facts,** not **opinions.**

Line Plot

```
    x  x
    x  x        x              x              x
  +--+--+--+--+--+--+--+--+--+--+--+--+--+--+-->
  12 13 14 15 16 17 18 19 20 21 22 23 24 25
```

Stem-and-Leaf Plot

Stem	Leaf
1	2 2 3 3 6
2	1 5

Range:

25 − 12 = 13

Mean (average):

25 + 12 + 21 + 12 + 16 + 13 + 13 = 112

112 ÷ 7 = **16**

Median: 13

12, 12, 13, 13, 16, 21, 25

Modes: 12 and **13**

1. How many of the shoppers were 20 or older?
2. What is the range, mean, median, and mode of the following set of data? 70, 50, 90, 70, 60

Many of my friends follow the latest fashion trend.

*A **trend** in data tells the direction the data is following.* (p. 266)

Self Check

Graphs are often used to display data. (Lessons 5-2, 5-3, 5-7, 5-8)

A **double-bar** graph and a **pictograph** can be used to compare sets of data that can be counted. A **line graph** shows data collected over time and sometimes reveals a **trend.** A **circle graph** shows how parts of the data relate to the whole set of data.

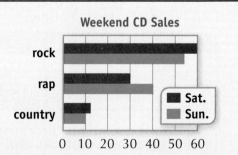

Weekend CD Sales

rock

rap

country

0 10 20 30 40 50 60

■ Sat.
■ Sun.

3. What information about rap music is displayed in the graph?.

Self Check

Find the probability of events. (Lessons 5-10, 5-11, 5-12)

You spin each spinner once.

The **sample space** is shown in the **tree diagram** at the right.

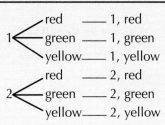

$$1 \Big< \begin{matrix} \text{red} &\text{—— 1, red} \\ \text{green} &\text{—— 1, green} \\ \text{yellow} &\text{—— 1, yellow} \end{matrix}$$

$$2 \Big< \begin{matrix} \text{red} &\text{—— 2, red} \\ \text{green} &\text{—— 2, green} \\ \text{yellow} &\text{—— 2, yellow} \end{matrix}$$

There are 6 possible outcomes. You can multiply to find the total number of outcomes: $2 \times 3 = 6$.

The **probability** of an **event** ranges from 0 to 1.

Impossible   Equally likely   Certain

$$0 \quad \boxed{\text{less likely}} \quad \tfrac{1}{2} \quad \boxed{\text{more likely}} \quad 1$$

Probability of an event $= \dfrac{\text{number of favorable outcomes}}{\text{number of possible outcomes}}$

$P(2, \text{green}) = \dfrac{1}{6}$

4. You spin the second spinner once. Find P(green).

The tree in my yard has many branches.

The branches of a tree diagram show possible outcomes.
(p. 300)

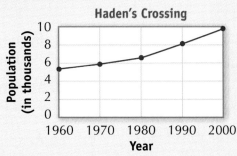

Self Check

Make graphs or write to compare when solving problems. (Lessons 5-5, 5-9)

Make a graph when data for an event are given.
Then use the graph to compare the data.

Haden's Crossing	
Year	**Population (in thousands)**
1960	5.3
1970	5.8
1980	6.6
1990	8.1
2000	9.8

5. Compare the population trend from 1960 to 1980 with the population trend from 1980 to 2000.

Answers: 1. 2; 2. 40; 68; 70; 70; 3. 30 rap CDs were sold on Saturday, and 40 were sold on Sunday. 4. $\frac{1}{3}$; 5. The population during each time period grew, but the growth was faster from 1980 to 2000.

MULTIPLE CHOICE

Choose the correct letter for each answer.

1. Which of these statements is an opinion?

   A. The sum of 8 and 10 is 18.

   B. George Washington was the first President of the United States.

   C. Chocolate is the best flavor of ice cream.

   D. A week has 7 days.

2. The difference between the largest and smallest numbers in a set of data is called the

   A. range.

   B. mean.

   C. median.

   D. mode.

3. Which type of graph uses data points connected by line segments to represent data collected over time?

   A. bar graph

   B. circle graph

   C. stem-and-leaf plot

   D. line graph

4. To show the number 45 on a stem-and-leaf plot, 4 would be the

   A. stem.

   B. leaf.

   C. range.

   D. bar.

Think It Through
I need to **identify and understand math vocabulary** in the question.

5. Find the mean of this data set: 15, 18, 20, 19, 11, 15, 21

   A. 10

   B. 15

   C. 17

   D. 18

6. In which activity does Tim spend the greatest part of his day?

   A. sleeping

   B. working

   C. eating

   D. studying

   Tim's Average Day

   Sleeping | Working
   Eating
   Studying   Other

7. What type of graph would be most appropriate to represent data about the tallest mountains in the world?

   A. line graph

   C. circle graph

   B. line plot

   D. bar graph

8. You toss a penny. Which of the following best describes the chances that the penny will land heads up?

   A. certain

   C. equally likely as tails up

   B. more likely than tails up

   D. impossible

9. You spin the spinner once. Find P(blue).

   A. $\frac{1}{5}$

   B. $\frac{2}{5}$

   C. $\frac{1}{2}$

   D. $\frac{3}{5}$

Identify each statement as a fact or an opinion.

10. A line graph shows changes over time.

11. Making a graph is the best way to solve problems.

12. A circle graph represents 100% of a data set.

Find the range, mean, median, and mode of each data set.

13. 4, 6, 3, 12, 3, 8

14. 12, 34, 44, 6, 34

For Items 15–18, use the double-bar graph.

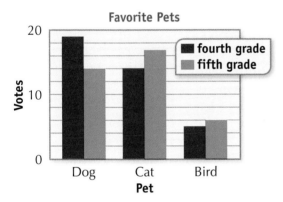

15. How many students voted in the favorite pet survey?

16. Did this survey collect facts or opinions?

17. Which pet got the most votes in all?

18. Write a statement comparing how many fourth and fifth graders voted for cats.

19. You toss a standard number cube. Find the probability of tossing a number greater than 4. Express the probability as a fraction.

Writing in Math

Average Temperatures in June

20. Look at the graph above. Describe the trend in the data. Explain.

21. You toss a penny and a nickel. Describe how you would draw a tree diagram to find the sample space of this experiment.

22. Make a line plot to solve this problem. Here is the mileage Sylvester rode each day of his bike trip: 20, 22, 21, 21, 20, 15, 21, 20, 21, 19. What is the mode of distances he traveled during the course of his trip? Explain why a line plot is helpful in finding the mode.

TEST TALK

Think It Through
- I will **write my conclusions clearly and accurately.**
- I will **use words from the problem** and **use math terms correctly.**

Number and Operation

MULTIPLE CHOICE

1. What is four hundred five and four hundredths written in standard form?

   A. 450.4

   B. 450.04

   C. 405.4

   D. 405.04

2. Estimate 29,468 + 11,054.

   A. 20,000   **C.** 40,000

   B. 30,000   **D.** 50,000

3. Find 650 ÷ 24.

   A. 27   **C.** 626

   B. 27 R2   **D.** 15,360

FREE RESPONSE

4. List all the factors of 32.

5. Cole bought four T-shirts. Each T-shirt cost $15.79. Not including tax, how much did Cole pay in all?

6. Write the following numbers in order from least to greatest.

   65,478   56,478   65,748   56,784

Writing in Math

7. Explain how you can use compatible numbers to subtract 6,430 − 580 mentally.

Think It Through

- I will **write my steps in order.**
- I will **make my answer brief but complete.**

Geometry and Measurement

MULTIPLE CHOICE

8. What is the area of this rectangle?

   A. 12 ft²

   B. 24 ft

   C. 35 ft

   D. 35 ft²

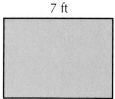

7 ft / 5 ft

9. How many weeks are in one year?

   A. 7

   B. 12

   C. 52

   D. 365

FREE RESPONSE

10. Name 3 rays and 1 line in the figure below.

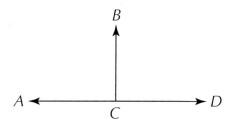

11. Write the time shown on this clock using words in two different ways.

Writing in Math

12. Maria's piano lesson started at 11:30 A.M. and ended at 12:55 P.M. How long did the lesson last? Explain how you found your answer.

Data Analysis and Probability

MULTIPLE CHOICE

13. You toss a nickel and then spin the spinner below. How many possible outcomes are there?

A. 2

B. 7

C. 9

D. 14

14. Use the spinner above to find $P(\text{odd number})$.

A. $\frac{1}{4}$

B. $\frac{3}{8}$

C. $\frac{1}{2}$

D. $\frac{4}{7}$

FREE RESPONSE

Use the bar graph for 15–17.

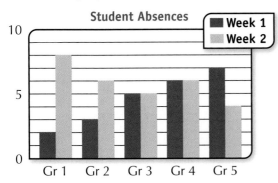

15. Which grade had the highest total absences for both weeks? the lowest?

16. For Week 1, what was the range, of all the absences?

Writing in Math

17. Describe a trend you see. Compare the 2 weeks and explain your answer.

Algebra

MULTIPLE CHOICE

18. To find the mean of a data set, Dawn used the following equation: $(24 + 14 + 16 + 16 + 15) \div n = 17$ What is the value of n?

A. $n = 5$

B. $n = 16$

C. $n = 17$

D. $n = 24$

19. Evaluate $(15 \times m) + 2$ for $m = 9$.

A. 9

B. 26

C. 135

D. 137

20. Fifty-four chairs are arranged in n rows. Which expression models the number of chairs in each row?

A. $54 \times n$

B. $54 - n$

C. $54 \div n$

D. $54 + n$

TEST TALK

Think It Through
I need to read the problem carefully to **choose an operation.**

FREE RESPONSE

21. What is the rule for this table?

In	7	8	9	10
Out	49	56	63	70

22. What is the next term in this pattern?

5.8, 6.1, 6.4, 6.7, . . .

Writing in Math

23. Explain how you can use the Distributive property to help you multiply 6×37 mentally.

Set 5-1 (pages 260–261)

How many people responded to each survey?

Survey A	
Vehicles Owned	
Car	5
Truck	3
Van	4
None	2

Survey B	
Favorite Sports	
Baseball	5
Basketball	8
Football	7
Soccer	4

Add the total number of responses.
14 people responded to Survey A.
24 people responded to Survey B.

Remember that data can be facts (actual information), or opinions (what a person likes or dislikes).

1. Which survey gathered facts, and which gathered opinions?

2. What question do you think was asked in each survey?

3. Show each data set on a line plot.

Set 5-2 (pages 262–265)

What does the length of the tallest bar on the graph represent?

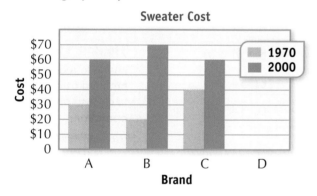

The longest bar shows that Brand B cost $70 in 2000.

Remember that a double bar graph uses two different shaded or colored bars to compare two sets of data.

1. Copy and complete the bar graph to show that Brand D cost $40 in 1970 and $30 in 2000.

2. For which brand did the price increase most from 1970 to 2000?

Set 5-3 (pages 266–269)

In which month did the most rain fall?

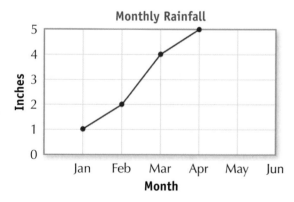

The graph shows that 5 inches of rain fell in April.

Remember that a line graph may be used to show data that changes over time.

1. What is total amount of rain that fell in January, February, March, and April?

2. Copy and complete the graph to show that 4 inches of rain fell in May and 3 inches fell in June.

Brian's math quiz scores are as follows: 75, 86, 92, 90, 88, 79, 95, 98, and 85. Organize the quiz score data using a stem-and-leaf plot.

Stem	Leaf
7	5 9
8	5 6 8
9	0 2 5 8

Remember to write the data in order from least to greatest before making your stem-and-leaf plot.

1. What digit for each quiz score is used for the stem? the leaf?

2. What is the range of the data? How do you know?

3. How many scores were greater than 90? How did the stem-and-leaf plot help you find your answer?

When you make a graph to solve a problem, follow these steps.

Step 1: Use the given information to set up the graph.

Step 2: Enter known data.

Step 3: Analyze the graph.

Remember it can help to make a graph when the answer to a question can be found by visualizing the data.

Make a graph to solve the problem.

1. The table below shows the results of a poll that was taken of people visiting an amusement park. Which roller coaster did people appear to prefer?

Ride	Day 1	Day 2	Day 3	Day 4
The Cobra	59	72	30	55
The Wolf	40	80	40	14

Find the mean, median, and mode of the data set: 16, 12, 20, 15, 12

To find the mean, add all the data and divide by the number of data.

16 + 12 + 20 + 15 + 12 = 75

75 ÷ 5 = 15   So, the mean is 15.

To find the median, list the data in order from least to greatest, and find the middle value. The mode is the value that occurs most often.

12, 12, 15, 16, 20

So, the median is 15. The mode is 12.

Remember that if there is an even number of data, you must add the two middle numbers when the data is ordered from least to greatest and divide by 2 to find the median.

1. Find the mean of this data set:
    483   642   508   724

2. Find the median of this data set:
    27.5   24.8   32.6   30.4

3. Find the mode of this data set:
    7, 9, 12, 10, 7, 11, 9, 13, 7, 15, 8

Set 5-7 (pages 286–287)

This circle graph shows a bakery's pie sales for one day. Which kind of pie was sold most?

Monday's Pie Sales

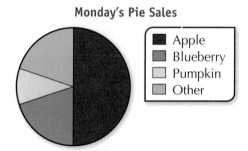

- ■ Apple
- ■ Blueberry
- □ Pumpkin
- ▨ Other

The section for apple pies is the largest, so apple pies were sold the most.

Remember that a circle graph represents 100% of a data set.

1. This circle graph shows how Ben spent one day: working—8 hours; sleeping—9 hours; eating—2 hours, other activities—5 hours. Copy and label the graph and its key.

Ben's Day

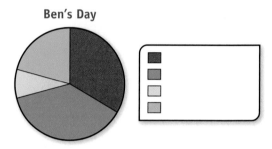

Set 5-8 (pages 288–291)

What type of graph would be most appropriate to represent the data below?

The average temperatures in Miami for four months: April: 75°F; May: 79°F; June: 81°F; July: 83°F

Because the data changes over time, a line graph would be most appropriate.

Remember that you can display data on line graphs, bar graphs, circle graphs, pictographs, line plots, and stem-and-leaf plots.

1. What type of graph should be used to represent the longest rivers in the world?

Set 5-9 (pages 292–293)

Which grade collected more cans on Day 4?

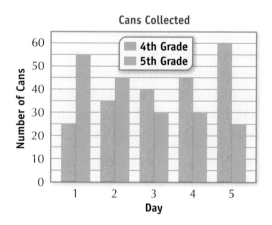

The bar for the 4th grade is taller for Day 4, so the 4th graders collected more cans.

Remember to use words such as *increasing* and *decreasing* to describe trends.

1. Use the word *fewer* to compare data shown on the graph.

2. Use the word *more* to compare data shown on the graph.

3. Compare the 2 grades to describe any trends in the graph.

You toss a number cube once. What are the chances of tossing a number less than 4?

Event: Tossing a number less than 4
Possible Outcomes: 1, 2, 3, 4, 5, 6
Favorable Outcomes: 1, 2, 3

3 out of 6 possible outcomes are favorable, so in 3 out of 6 tosses, you can expect a number less than 4.

Remember that a certain event will always happen, and an impossible event can never happen.

1. You toss the number cube once. Which outcomes are equally likely?

2. Name an impossible outcome.

3. Name a certain outcome.

Sara packed jeans, brown pants, and three shirts—red, blue, and white. How many different pant-shirt outfits can she wear?

One Way:
Draw a
tree diagram

jeans —red shirt
—blue shirt
—white shirt

brown pants —red shirt
—blue shirt
—white shirt

There are 6 possible combinations of pants and shirts, so Sara can wear 6 different outfits.

Another Way: Multiply

2 pants × 3 shirts = 6 different outfits

Remember that when you make a tree diagram, start with 1 item and list all the possible combinations with it. Continue.

1. Make a tree diagram to show the sample space for tossing a number cube and then tossing a penny.

2. The café sells chicken, tuna, and shrimp salad sandwiches. You can have wheat, white, or rye bread. How many different sandwiches can you choose?

3. If you roll a number cube and then toss a nickel, how many possible outcomes are there?

You spin the spinner once. Find P(red).

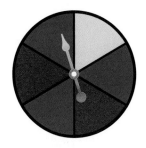

$$\text{Probability of an event} = \frac{\text{number of favorable outcomes}}{\text{number of possible outcomes}}$$

So P(red) $= \frac{2}{6} = \frac{1}{3}$

Remember that when you express a probability as a fraction, always write the fraction in simplest form.

1. Find P(yellow)   **2.** Find P(blue)

You toss a penny and a dime.

3. Find P(two heads)

4. Find P(two tails)

5. Find P(1 tail, 1 head)

6. Find P(penny heads, dime tails)

Set 5-1 (pages 260–261)

Identify each statement as a fact or opinion.

1. Fifth grade is the best grade.

2. Twelve students are on the debate team.

3. The play was too long.

4. The play lasted 1 hour and 45 minutes.

Use the line plot for 5 and 6.

5. How many students responded to the survey?

6. Which colors got the same number of votes?

```
                          x
                          x
              x     x     x
              x     x     x     x
             _____
             Red  Blue  Green Yellow
```
Class Favorite Color Survey

Set 5-2 (pages 262–265)

The Data File at the right shows the population for three states in two years. The data has been rounded to the nearest tenth of a million. Use the data for 1–5.

1. If shown on a double-bar graph, which state in which year data set would have the longest bar?

2. Would a scale from 0 to 5 million be appropriate for the graph? Explain.

3. Would an interval of 0.1 (million) for the scale be appropriate? Explain.

4. Make a double-bar graph of the information in the Data File.

5. Write a sentence about the data represented in the graph.

Data File

	Population (in millions)	
State	1990	2000
Indiana	5.5	6.1
Missouri	5.1	5.6
Iowa	2.8	2.9

Set 5-3 (pages 266–269)

The data in the Data File at right have been rounded to the nearest thousand. Use the data to answer 1–4.

1. Make a line graph of the data. Use a scale from 0 to 500 and an interval of 100 for the population.

2. Write a sentence about the trend shown on the graph.

3. During which year was Tampa's population the highest?

4. Between which two consecutive decades did Tampa's population change the most?

Data File

Population (in thousands)	
Year	Tampa, FL
1970	280
1980	274
1990	280
2000	303

Take It to the NET
More Practice
www.scottforesman.com

Set 5-4 (pages 270–273)

The Data File at right shows the class scores on last week's math test. Use the Data File for 1–4.

1. Make a stem-and-leaf plot of the data. Title the plot "Class Math-Test Scores."

2. What was the highest score on the test? the lowest score? What was the range of scores?

3. How many students scored higher than an 80?

4. How would you write a score of 85 on the stem-and-leaf plot?

Data File
Class Math-Test Scores
82, 75, 94, 69, 73, 74, 86, 92, 87, 93, 81, 70, 76, 80, 94, 97, 84, 76, 71, 83, 88, 92, 73, 91

Set 5-5 (pages 276–279)

Make a graph to solve each problem.

1. The table below shows the heights of two plants in inches as they were measured each month for 5 months. Which plant grew the fastest? Use two different line graphs for each data set.

Plant	Jan	Feb	March	Apr	May
Plant A	1.5	2.1	2.8	3.4	4.2
Plant B	2.3	2.8	3.2	4.6	5.0

2. The table below shows the results of a poll. Which baseball team did people polled appear to prefer? Make a double-bar graph to display the data.

Team	Day 1	Day 2	Day 3	Day 4	Day 5
Lions	47	76	32	81	50
Tigers	25	90	40	6	50

Set 5-6 (pages 282–285)

Use the Data File at right to answer 1–4.

1. Find the mode(s) of the data set.

2. Find the median of the data set.

3. Find the mean of the data set.

4. How do the mode, median, and mean change when 12 and 18 are included in the data set?

Data File
Ages of Swim-Team Members
9, 15, 13, 17, 16, 12, 15, 13, 10, 8, 11, 14

Set 5-7 (pages 286–287)

Use the circle graph at right for 1–4.

Mary's Monthly Budget

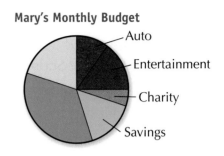

1. Mary spends more money each month on rent than on groceries. Copy and complete the circle graph at right.

2. Which category receives the greatest part of Mary's monthly budget?

3. Write two categories that Mary spends about the same amount on each month.

4. Mary's income is $1,200 a month. About how much does Mary spend on her car each month?

Set 5-8 (pages 288–291)

Tell what type of graph would be most appropriate to display the data described.

1. How you spend your time each week

2. The tallest trees in the United States

3. The populations of two states recorded every 10 years from 1950 to 2000.

4. The sales figures for 7 months at Super Groceries

5. Bill wants to show in a class report the ages of all United States senators. He decides to display the data on a line graph. Is this the best choice? Explain.

Set 5-9 (pages 292–293)

The box office recorded ticket sales for two plays and displayed the data on the graph at right. Analyze the graph. Then answer 1–4.

1. Describe any trends you see in the graph's data.

2. How did ticket sales for the two plays compare on Friday?

3. How are the data for the two plays similar? How are the data different?

4. If the graph's trend continued, how might the graph look for Saturday?

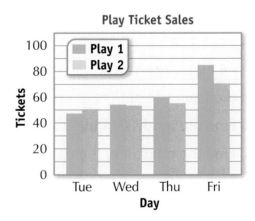

Play Ticket Sales

Take It to the NET
More Practice
www.scottforesman.com

Set 5-10 (pages 296–299)

Think about spinning Spinner A.

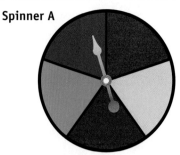
Spinner A

1. What are the possible outcome colors? Are the outcomes equally likely? Why or why not?

2. In 100 spins, how many times would you expect Spinner A to land on blue?

Now think about spinning Spinner B.

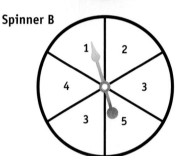
Spinner B

3. What are the possible outcome numbers? Are the outcomes equally likely to occur? Why or why not?

4. In 100 spins, how many times would you expect Spinner B to land on 3?

Set 5-11 (pages 300–301)

For 1–3, use spinners C and D below.

1. What are the possible outcomes if you spin Spinner C? Spinner D?

2. Make a tree diagram to show the sample space for spinning both spinners at the same time.

3. Your chances of spinning a 1 on Spinner C, and a 2 on Spinner D is ___ out of ___.

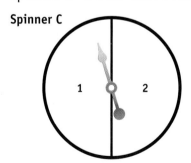
Spinner C

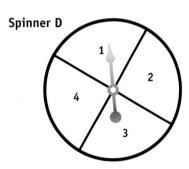
Spinner D

Set 5-12 (pages 302–305)

Suppose you toss a quarter and a dime.

1. Make a tree diagram to show the possible outcomes.

2. Find P(two heads)   3. Find P(two tails)

4. Find P(1 tail, 1 head)   5. Find P(dime heads, quarter tails)

6. Which of the events above is most likely to occur? Which events are equally likely to occur?

DIAGNOSING READINESS

A Vocabulary
(Grade 4)

Choose the best term from the box.

1. A __?__ has 5 sides.

2. A __?__ has 4 sides.

3. A __?__ has 3 sides.

4. A __?__ has 6 sides.

5. An __?__ has 8 sides.

Vocabulary

- **triangle** *(Grade 4)*
- **pentagon** *(Grade 4)*
- **octagon** *(Grade 4)*
- **hexagon** *(Grade 4)*
- **quadrilateral** *(Grade 4)*

B Geometric Ideas
(Grade 4)

Draw an example of

6. a right angle.

7. a parallelogram.

8. a ray.

9. a right triangle.

10. a rectangle.

11. a line.

12. Is a square always a rectangle? Explain why or why not.

C Congruence and Similarity (Grade 4)

Do the figures in each pair seem to be similar? If so, are they also congruent?

13.

14.

15.

16.

17.

18.

19. Explain the difference between similar figures and congruent figures.

D Symmetry (Grade 4)

For each figure, give the number of lines of symmetry.

20.   **21.**

22.  **23.**

24. Half of the figure at the right is shaded. To get the half that is not shaded, which would NOT work: a flip, a turn, or a slide?

327

Vocabulary
• point
• line
• line segment
• midpoint
• plane
• ray
• parallel lines
• intersecting lines
• perpendicular lines

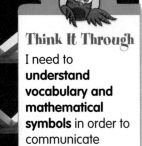

Think It Through
I need to **understand vocabulary and mathematical symbols** in order to communicate geometric ideas.

Geometric Ideas

LEARN

How do you represent basic geometric ideas?

Points, lines, line segments, and rays are basic geometric concepts. Artists, engineers, and architects use these concepts in the development of buildings and structures.

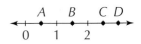
	What You **Draw**	What You **Say**	What You **Write**
A **point** is an exact location in space.	•G	"point G"	G or Point G
A **line** is a straight path of points that goes on forever in two directions.	B C	"line BC"	$\overleftrightarrow{BC}$ (or $\overleftrightarrow{CB}$)
A **line segment** is part of a line. It has two endpoints. Its **midpoint** is halfway between the endpoints.	F, T, N, midpoint	"line segment TN"	$\overline{TN}$ (or $\overline{NT}$)
A **ray** is part of a line. It has one endpoint and extends forever in only one direction.	J K	"ray JK"	$\overrightarrow{JK}$
A **plane** is an endless flat surface.	•M N• •L	"plane LMN"	▱ LMN

✔ Talk About It

1. Do you think that $\overrightarrow{KJ}$ names the same ray as $\overrightarrow{JK}$? Explain.

2. Look at the photo of the bridge on page 328. What geometric figures are suggested by the straight parts of the framework? What geometric figure is somewhat like the flat surface of the water?

What are some special lines?

Some lines are given special names depending on their relationship with other lines. These terms can also be applied to line segments and rays.

	What You **Draw**	What You **Say**	What You **Write**
Parallel lines never cross and stay the same distance apart.		"Line *AD* is parallel to line *VW*."	$\overleftrightarrow{AD} \parallel \overleftrightarrow{VW}$
Intersecting lines pass through the same point.		"Line *PE* intersects line *QC*."	$\overleftrightarrow{PE}$ intersects $\overleftrightarrow{QC}$.
Perpendicular lines are intersecting lines that form square corners.		"Line *RS* is perpendicular to line *FH*."	$\overleftrightarrow{RS} \perp \overleftrightarrow{FH}$

This symbol tells you that this is a square corner, or right angle.

Example

In the diagram at the right, identify a pair of parallel lines, a pair of intersecting line segments, and a pair of perpendicular rays.

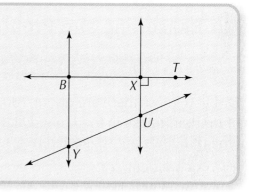

parallel lines	$\overleftrightarrow{BY} \parallel \overleftrightarrow{XU}$
intersecting line segments	$\overline{BY}$ intersects $\overline{YU}$.
perpendicular rays	$\overrightarrow{XU} \perp \overrightarrow{XT}$

✔ Talk About It

3. In the example, name a pair of intersecting rays. Name a pair of parallel line segments. Name a pair of perpendicular lines.

4. **Reasoning** Are $\overleftrightarrow{BX}$ and $\overleftrightarrow{YU}$ parallel or intersecting? Explain.

5. **Reasoning** Are all perpendicular lines also intersecting? Are all intersecting lines also perpendicular? Explain.

Take It to the NET
More Examples
www.scottforesman.com

Use the diagram at the right. Name the following.

1. three points

2. two line segments

3. two rays

4. a line

5. two parallel rays

6. two perpendicular lines

7. two intersecting, but not perpendicular, line segments

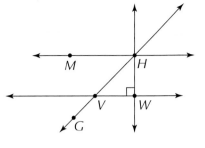

8. Reasoning Points *D, E,* and *F* lie in plane *DEF.* How many lines in plane *DEF* can you draw that contain both points *D* and *E?*

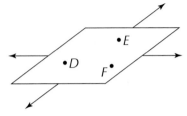

PRACTICE

For more practice, see Set 6-1 on p. 388.

A Skills and Understanding

Use the diagram at the right. Name the following.

9. two lines

10. two points

11. a ray

12. three line segments

13. two perpendicular rays

14. two parallel line segments

15. two intersecting, but not perpendicular, lines

16. Reasoning How many midpoints does $\overline{JH}$ have?

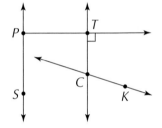

B Reasoning and Problem Solving

Math and Social Studies

Did you know there are about 200,000 miles of railroad tracks in the United States? What type of figures are suggested by

17. the green lines?

18. the red line segments?

19. the yellow lines?

20. **Writing in Math** Draw and label two lines, $\overleftrightarrow{AB}$ and $\overleftrightarrow{FG}$. Are your lines parallel, intersecting, or perpendicular? Explain why.

C Extensions

Here are some other special lines.

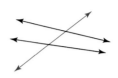
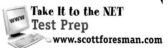

A **horizontal** line runs from left to right (like the horizon).

A **vertical** line runs up and down.

A **transversal** is a line that intersects two or more other lines.

In 21–23, use the diagram at the right.

21. Name a horizontal line.   **22.** Name a vertical line.

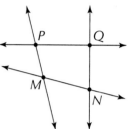

23. Name a transversal that intersects $\overleftrightarrow{PQ}$ and $\overleftrightarrow{MN}$.

24. Reasoning Are a horizontal line and a vertical line in the same plane parallel, perpendicular, or neither? Explain.

Mixed Review and Test Prep

Take It to the NET
Test Prep
www.scottforesman.com

25. A number cube is numbered from 1 to 6. What is the probability of rolling a number less than 3?

26. Algebra Which operations can be used in the boxes below to get the greatest possible result?

$$1 \ \square \ 8 \ \square \ 1$$

A. + and −   **B.** + and ÷   **C.** × and −   **D.** × and ÷

Enrichment

Optical Illusions

Look at the drawings below. In each drawing, do segments AB and CD appear to be parallel? In each case, they are parallel.

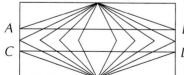
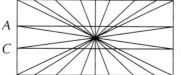
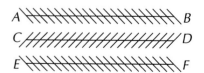

See if you can find other examples of **optical illusions.** There are many examples such as those above where what we think we see is not what we really see!

Key Idea
A number can be used to describe the size of an angle's opening.

Vocabulary
• angle
• vertex
• sides
• interior
• exterior
• degrees
• protractor
• acute angle
• right angle
• obtuse angle
• straight angle

Materials
• ruler or straightedge
• protractor

Measuring and Classifying Angles

LEARN

WARM UP

Draw an example of each figure.

1. $\overline{EK}$ 2. $\overleftrightarrow{SF}$

3. $\overrightarrow{DM}$ 4. $\overrightarrow{MD}$

5. perpendicular lines $\overleftrightarrow{AB}$ and $\overleftrightarrow{VW}$

How can you measure angles?

An **angle** is formed by two rays that have the same endpoint. The common endpoint is called the **vertex** (plural: vertices). The rays are the **sides** of the angle.

Angle RST is shown at the right. We write this as ∠RST. It can also be named ∠TSR or just ∠S. When three letters are used, the middle letter names the vertex. The **interior** and **exterior** of the angle are also shown.

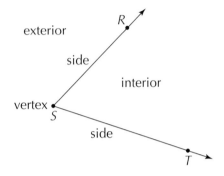

There are various ways to measure an angle's opening. For example, if we measure it in "wedges," we could say that the measure of ∠FGH is 4 wedges.

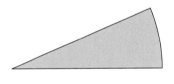

1 "wedge"

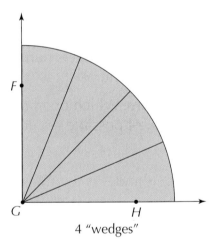

4 "wedges"

In math, we usually measure angles in **degrees** (°). One degree is a very skinny wedge. It takes 90 degrees, written 90°, to fill a square corner. The measure of ∠XYZ is 90°.

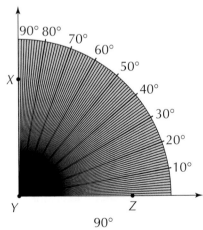

1°

90°

Activity

How do you use a protractor?

You can use a **protractor** to measure and draw angles.

a. Trace each angle and extend its sides. Follow the directions at the right to measure each angle.

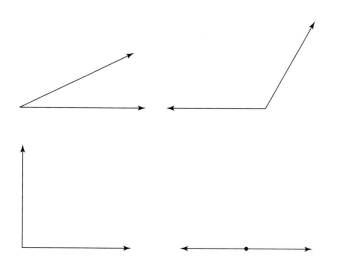

b. There are two scales of numbers on a protractor. How did you decide which one to use?

c. Follow the directions at the right to draw an angle with each measure.

160°   90°

35°   180°

To Measure an Angle

Place the protractor's center on the angle's vertex. Place the 0° mark on one side of the angle. Read the measure where the other side of the angle crosses the protractor.

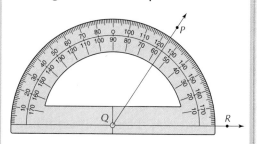

The measure of ∠PQR is 56°.

To Draw an Angle of 140°

Draw $\overrightarrow{TU}$. Be sure to label the endpoint T. Place the protractor's center on T. Line up $\overrightarrow{TU}$ with the 0° mark. Place a point at 140°. Label it W. Draw $\overrightarrow{TW}$.

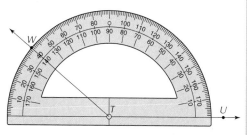

The measure of ∠WTU is 140°.

How can you classify angles?

An **acute angle** has a measure between 0° and 90°.

A **right angle** has a measure of 90°.

An **obtuse angle** has a measure between 90° and 180°.

A **straight angle** has a measure of 180°.

✔ Talk About It

1. Find an example of each of the four types of angles in your classroom.

Classify each angle as acute, right, obtuse, or straight. Then measure each angle. (Hint: Trace each angle and draw longer sides if necessary.)

1.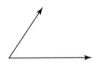
2.
3.
4.

Draw an angle with each measure.

5. 115°   **6.** 45°   **7.** 165°   **8.** 70°

9. Reasoning Give three different names for this angle. Identify the vertex and sides. Then name a point in the interior and a point in the exterior.

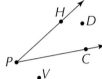

PRACTICE

For more practice, see Set 6-2 on p. 388.

A **Skills and Understanding**

Classify each angle as acute, right, obtuse, or straight. Then measure each angle. (Hint: Trace each angle and draw longer sides if necessary.)

10.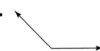
11.
12.
13.

Draw an angle with each measure.

14. 60°   **15.** 140°   **16.** 95°   **17.** 20°

18. Reasoning Draw and label ∠*FND*. Also draw and label a point in the interior and a point in the exterior. What are the vertex and sides of your angle? Which point is in the interior? the exterior?

B **Reasoning and Problem Solving**

 Math and Science

The angle formed by the sun's rays and the surface of the earth changes depending on your location, the date, and the time of day. In any location, the sun reaches its highest point at noon. (The noon sun actually occurs at 1:00 P.M. during daylight savings time.)

19. Measure the angle of the noon sun in Tampa, Florida, for each date.

June 21   September 21
Angle of the Noon Sun
Tampa, Florida

20. **Writing in Math** Britt says that twice an acute angle is always an obtuse angle. Is she right? Give examples to support your answer.

C Extensions

Estimation Estimate whether each angle is closest to 15°, 30°, 45°, 60°, or 90°. Measure each angle to check your estimate.

21. **22.** **23.** **24.** **25.**

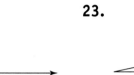

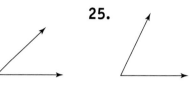 

Mixed Review and Test Prep

Take It to the NET
Test Prep
www.scottforesman.com

26. Describe an example of parallel lines in your classroom.

27. What is the mode of the following set of data?

18 23 45 44 23 41 30

A. 23 **B.** 27 **C.** 30 **D.** 32

Practice Game

What's Your Angle?

Players: 2
Materials: Circle Game Board, ruler, Degree Cards

Mix the cards and place them face down. Draw a line segment from the center of the circle to the 0° mark. The first player turns the top card over. The player uses the original segment as one side of the angle and draws the second side to form an angle with the number of degrees shown on the card, going clockwise.

The second player draws a card and draws an angle of the indicated size next to and touching the previous angle. Play continues until a player reaches exactly 360°. If a player can only construct an angle by passing 360°, the turn is lost.

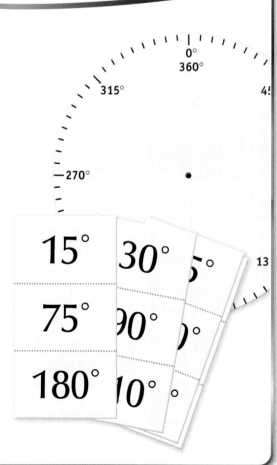

All text pages available online and on CD-ROM.

Vocabulary
- circle
- center
- radius
- diameter
- chord
- central angle

Materials
- compass
- ruler or straightedge
- protractor

Think It Through
- I can **look for a pattern** to find relationships in a circle.
- I should try to **be accurate** with my measurements.

Segments and Angles Related to Circles

LEARN

What are the names of segments and angles related to a circle?

A **circle** is a closed plane figure made up of all the points the same distance from the center. A circle is named by its **center**. Circle *O* is shown at the right.

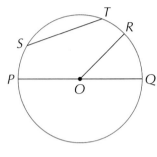

A **radius** (plural: radii) is any line segment that connects the center to a point on the circle. $\overline{OR}$ is a radius.

A **diameter** is any line segment through the center that connects two points on the circle. $\overline{PQ}$ is a diameter.

A **chord** is any line segment that connects two points on the circle. $\overline{ST}$ is a chord.

A **central angle** is an angle whose vertex is the center. ∠*ROQ* is a central angle.

Activity

What are some special relationships?

a. Follow the directions at the right to construct a circle with a radius equal in length to the length of $\overline{AB}$.

A _____ *B*

b. Use a ruler to draw a diameter. Compare its length to that of the radius.

c. Draw another diameter. Measure the four central angles. What is the sum of the measures?

d. Draw a third diameter. Measure the six central angles. What is the sum of the measures?

e. Repeat steps **a**–**d** using a different radius.

To Construct a Circle with a Given Radius

Mark and label a point, the center of the circle, on your paper.

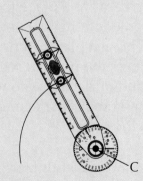

Set the compass opening to the length of $\overline{AB}$. Then place the compass point on the center and draw the circle.

Use circle A to identify the following.

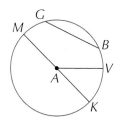

1. the center
2. two radii
3. a diameter
4. a chord
5. three central angles
6. **Reasoning** What is the sum of the measures of ∠MAK, ∠MAV, and ∠VAK?

PRACTICE

For more practice, see Set 6-3 on p. 388.

(A) Skills and Understanding

Use the terms on page 336 to identify each figure in circle H.

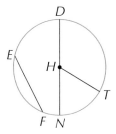

7. point H
8. $\overline{DN}$
9. $\overline{HT}$
10. ∠DHT
11. $\overline{EF}$
12. $\overline{HN}$

13. **Reasoning** Is a diameter also a chord? Explain.

(B) Reasoning and Problem Solving

14. A circular tabletop has a radius of 15 inches. How long is its diameter?

15. Find the missing angle measure in circle P.

16. Construct a circle having a radius equal in length to the given line segment.

17. In each wheel, the spokes are evenly spaced. Without measuring, find the measure of ∠A, ∠B, and ∠C.

18. **Writing in Math** Koyi thinks that all radii of a given circle are equal in length. Is he right? Explain your thinking.

Mixed Review and Test Prep

Take It to the NET
Test Prep
www.scottforesman.com

19. If an angle has a measure of 100°, is the angle acute, right, or obtuse?

20. **Algebra** What is the solution to the equation $6m = 48$?

   A. $m = 7$ **B.** $m = 8$ **C.** $m = 42$ **D.** $m = 54$

21. Which of the following decimals is equivalent to 0.3?

   A. 0.003   **B.** 0.03   **C.** 0.30   **D.** 3.0

All text pages available online and on CD-ROM.

Do You Know How?

Do You Understand?

Geometric Ideas (6-1)

Use the diagram to name the following.

1. three points

2. a line

3. two parallel rays

4. two perpendicular line segments

5. two intersecting, but not perpendicular lines

A Explain how you can tell if two intersecting lines are perpendicular.

B Describe $\overline{LN} \parallel \overline{MO}$ in words.

C Explain why points in the same plane are not necessarily on the same line.

Measuring and Classifying Angles (6–2)

Classify each angle as right, straight, acute, or obtuse. Then measure it.

6.    7.

Draw an angle with each measure.

8. 30°   9. 90°   10. 180°

D Draw an angle that is not straight. Label it $\angle RST$. What is the vertex of $\angle RST$? What are the sides of $\angle RST$?

E Using $\angle RST$ from Exercise D, label an interior point P and an exterior point Q.

F Explain how to tell if an angle is obtuse without measuring it.

Segments and Angles Related to Circles (6-3)

Use circle A to identify the following.

11. two radii

12. the center

13. a chord

14. a diameter

15. two central angles

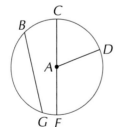

G In the circle at the left, how do you know that $\overline{CF}$ is a diameter?

H Explain how to use a compass to draw a circle with a diameter of 4 inches.

I The sum of the measures of $\angle CAD$ and what angle equals 180°? Explain how you know.

MULTIPLE CHOICE

Use the figure at the right.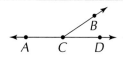

1. Which is the best description of ∠ACB? (6-2)

    A. right angle   **B.** straight angle   **C.** acute angle   **D.** obtuse angle

2. Which is the best estimate of the measure of ∠BCD? (6-2)

    A. 150°   **B.** 30°   **C.** 90°   **D.** 180°

FREE RESPONSE

Measure each angle. (6-2)

3.    4.    5.

Draw each of the following. (6-1, 6-2, 6-3)

6. $\overleftrightarrow{CD} \parallel \overleftrightarrow{VW}$

7. $\overline{MN} \perp \overline{QR}$

8. Circle K with diameter $\overline{XY}$

9. ∠DFG with a measure of 75°

10. If the radius of a circle is 5 cm long, how long is the diameter? (6-3)

11. The clock face at the right has been separated into equal central angles. What is the measure of each angle? (6-3)

Think It Through
- Be sure your protractor is **placed correctly on the angle.**
- Be sure you **read the correct scale** on the protractor.

Writing in Math

12. $\overleftrightarrow{AB}$ and $\overleftrightarrow{FG}$ are parallel and $\overleftrightarrow{RS}$ is perpendicular to $\overleftrightarrow{AB}$. Draw a picture. Are $\overleftrightarrow{RS}$ and $\overleftrightarrow{FG}$ parallel, intersecting, or perpendicular? Explain why. (6-1)

13. $\overleftrightarrow{PQ}$ and $\overleftrightarrow{ST}$ intersect at point W, but they are not perpendicular. Draw a picture. Name two sets of angles whose sum is 180°. Explain how you could tell, without measuring the angles. (6-1, 6-2)

Vocabulary
- polygon
- triangle
- quadrilateral
- pentagon
- hexagon
- octagon
- regular polygon

Materials
- geoboard or dot paper or

 tools

Think It Through
I can **use objects** or **draw a picture** to understand the main idea.

Polygons

LEARN

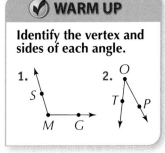

What are the names of polygons?

A **polygon** is a closed plane figure made up of line segments. The names of common polygons tell how many sides the polygon has.

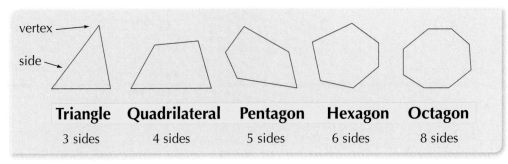

Triangle	**Quadrilateral**	**Pentagon**	**Hexagon**	**Octagon**
3 sides	4 sides	5 sides	6 sides	8 sides

A **regular polygon** has sides of equal length and angles of equal measure.

regular polygon

✔ Talk About It

1. Is each figure at the right a polygon? Explain why or why not.

Activity

What are some examples of polygons?

a. Work with a partner. On a geoboard or dot paper, create examples of polygons with 3 through 12 sides. Have your partner tell how many sides the polygon has and, if possible, name it.

b. How many angles are there in a triangle? An octagon? A 12-sided polygon? An *n*-sided polygon?

c. Tell if each road sign suggests a polygon. If so, what is its name? Does it appear to be a regular polygon?

Name each polygon. Then tell if it appears to be a regular polygon.

1.

2.

3.

4.

5. **Reasoning** How are the figures at the right alike? How are they different?

A **Skills and Understanding**

Name each polygon. Then tell if it appears to be a regular polygon.

6.

7.

8.

9.

10. **Reasoning** How are the figures at the right alike? How are they different?

B **Reasoning and Problem Solving**

11. Name the sides of the polygon at the right. Name the vertices.

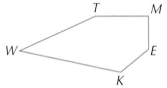

12. Miles used 26 pieces of straws to make quadrilaterals and hexagons. He made 2 quadrilaterals. How many hexagons did he make?

13. **Writing in Math** Danielle sorted some polygons into two groups. Use geometric terms to describe a characteristic of each group.

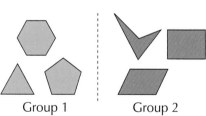

Group 1   Group 2

Mixed Review and Test Prep

Take It to the NET
Test Prep
www.scottforesman.com

14. What is the name for a segment that connects the center of a circle to a point on the circle?

15. If each carton holds 12 books, how many cartons can be completely filled if there are 125 books to be packed?

16. Which of these angle measures could NOT be that of an obtuse angle?

   A. 141°   **B.** 93°   **C.** 58°   **D.** 100°

Classifying Triangles

LEARN

How do you classify triangles?

Artists and architects often use triangular elements in their designs. Classifying triangles makes it easier to describe them.

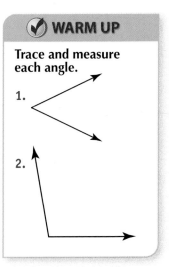
Triangles can be classified by the lengths of their sides.

  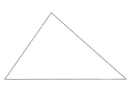

Equilateral triangle	**Isosceles triangle**	**Scalene triangle**
All sides are the same length.	At least two sides are the same length.	No sides are the same length.

You can also classify triangles by the measures of their angles.

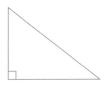  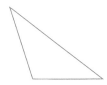

Right triangle	**Acute triangle**	**Obtuse triangle**
One angle is a right angle.	All three angles are acute angles.	One angle is an obtuse angle.

✔ Talk About It

1. Can a right triangle also be isosceles? Explain.

2. Which triangle appears to be a regular polygon? Explain.

3. Classify all the angles in a right triangle and in an obtuse triangle.

Activity

What is the sum of the measures of the angles of a triangle?

a. Use a ruler and protractor to draw a large right triangle on a sheet of paper. (Hint: Start by drawing the right angle.)

b. Cut out two identical copies of the triangle.

c. Tear off each angle of one triangle. Place the pieces next to each other with the vertices meeting at one point.

d. What appears to be true about the sum of the measures of the three angles? (Hint: What type of angle do these three pieces fill?)

e. Check your prediction by using a protractor to measure each of the angles in the other triangle. What is the sum of the measures?

f. Use your ruler and protractor to draw a large acute triangle and a large obtuse triangle. In each triangle, measure the angles. What is the sum of the measures?

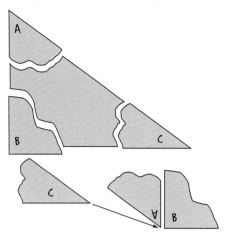

TEST TALK

Think It Through

I can measure the angles in various triangles to **try, check, and revise** my prediction.

How can you find a missing angle measure in a triangle?

Example

Find the missing angle measure.

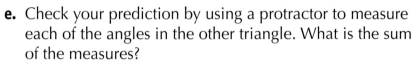

The sum of the measures of the angles of a triangle is 180°.

Add the two known angle measures. Then subtract the sum from 180 to find the measure of the third angle.

65 + 20 = 85   180 − 85 = 95

The missing angle measure is 95°.

✔ Talk About It

4. If two angles of a triangle have measures of 30° and 40°, how would you find the measure of the third angle?

For another example, see Set 6-5 on p. 385.

Classify each triangle by its sides and then by its angles.

1.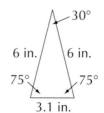

2.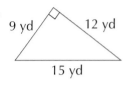

3.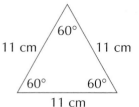

4.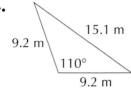

The measures of two angles of a triangle are given. Find the measure of the third angle.

5. 84°, 22°   **6.** 90°, 45°   **7.** 125°, 35°   **8.** 72°, 72°

9. Reasoning Can a triangle have two right angles? Explain.

PRACTICE

For more practice, see Set 6-5 on p. 389.

Ⓐ Skills and Understanding

Classify each triangle by its sides and then by its angles.

10.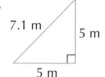

11.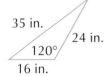

12.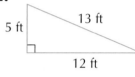

13.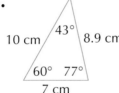

The measures of two angles of a triangle are given. Find the measure of the third angle.

14. 130°, 24°   **15.** 70°, 55°   **16.** 60°, 60°   **17.** 12°, 90°

18. Reasoning Can a triangle have two obtuse angles? Explain.

Ⓑ Reasoning and Problem Solving

Math and Social Studies

The Federal Triangle is a region of Washington, D.C. between the White House and the Capitol building. Many important federal buildings are located there including the Department of Justice building and the Department of Commerce building.

19. Classify the triangle by its sides and its angles.

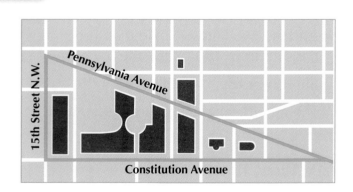

20. <u>Writing in Math</u> The measures of two angles of a triangle are 23° and 67°. Is the triangle an acute triangle, a right triangle, or an obtuse triangle? Explain your answer using geometric definitions in your explanation.

C Extensions

The sides of a right triangle have special names. The **legs** are the two sides that form the right angle. The third side is the **hypotenuse.**

Create a right triangle on a geoboard or draw one on dot paper. You may use a ruler and protractor to help answer the questions.

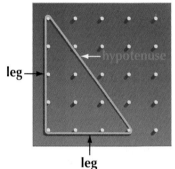

21. Which is the longest side, the hypotenuse or one of the legs?

22. Classify all the angles in your right triangle. Which is the largest?

 **Mixed Review and Test Prep**

 Take It to the NET
Test Prep
www.scottforesman.com

23. Give a definition for a pentagon.

24. Mrs. Johns lives 7 miles from her office. She drives to and from her office each day, 5 days a week. How many miles is this each week?

A. 10 **B.** 14 **C.** 35 **D.** 70

Discovery CHANNEL SCHOOL — Discover Math in Your World

 Take It to the NET
Video and Activities
www.scottforesman.com

The Red Pyramid

Considered to be second in size to the Great Pyramid of Cheops, the Red Pyramid stands 341 feet tall, with a square base measuring 722 feet on each of its four sides.

1. How many triangles would you see if you walked all the way around the base of the Red Pyramid? How far would you walk?

2. Do you think each face of the Red Pyramid is an equilateral, scalene, or isosceles triangle?

Key Idea
Quadrilaterals can be classified by the properties of their angles and sides.

Vocabulary
• parallelogram
• trapezoid
• rectangle
• rhombus
• square

Materials
• ruler
• protractor

Classifying Quadrilaterals

LEARN

How do you classify quadrilaterals?

Quadrilaterals can be classified by their angles or pairs of sides. Remember that a quadrilateral is any polygon with 4 sides.

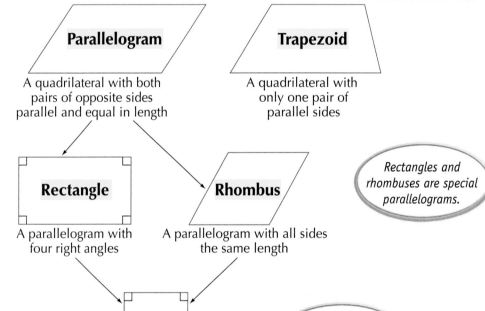

Parallelogram

A quadrilateral with both pairs of opposite sides parallel and equal in length

Trapezoid

A quadrilateral with only one pair of parallel sides

Rectangle

A parallelogram with four right angles

Rhombus

A parallelogram with all sides the same length

Rectangles and rhombuses are special parallelograms.

Square

A rectangle with all sides the same length

A square is a special rectangle. It is also a special rhombus.

WARM UP

Find the missing angle measure.

1.

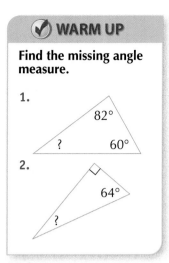

82°

?   60°

2.

64°

?

Activity

What is the sum of the measures of the angles of a quadrilateral?

a. Which quadrilaterals have all right angles? What is the sum of the measures of the four angles in each of those quadrilaterals?

b. Draw a large quadrilateral that has no right angles. What do you predict is the sum of the measures of the four angles?

c. Check your prediction by using a protractor to measure each of the angles. What is the sum of the measures?

d. Draw two more large quadrilaterals. In each quadrilateral, measure the angles. What is the sum of the measures?

How can you find a missing angle measure in a quadrilateral?

Example

Find the missing angle measure.

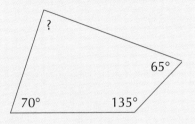

The sum of the measures of the angles of a quadrilateral is 360°.

360			
70	135	65	?

Add the known angle measures.

70 + 135 + 65 = 270

Subtract 270 from 360 to find the measure of the fourth angle.

360 − 270 = 90

The missing angle measure is 90°.

✔ Talk About It

1. How can you check the answer to the example?

2. Could the quadrilateral in the example be named by any of the five different names for quadrilaterals on the preceding page? Explain.

Take It to the NET
More Examples
www.scottforesman.com

CHECK ✔

For another example, see Set 6-6 on p. 385.

Classify each quadrilateral. Be as specific as possible.

1.

2.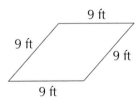
9 ft
9 ft
9 ft
9 ft

3.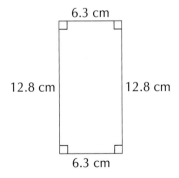
6.3 cm
12.8 cm   12.8 cm
6.3 cm

The measures of three angles of a quadrilateral are given. Find the measure of the fourth angle.

4. 95°, 150°, 35°

5. 60°, 120°, 60°

6. 143°, 90°, 78°

7. **Reasoning** Write a definition for a rhombus and for a parallelogram. How are they alike? How are they different?

A Skills and Understanding

Classify each quadrilateral. Be as specific as possible.

8.
10 m
8.3 m   8.3 m
10 m

9.
5 in.
5 in.   5 in.
5 in.

10.

The measures of three angles of a quadrilateral are given.
Find the measure of the fourth angle.

11. 54°, 100°, 120°   **12.** 150°, 30°, 30°   **13.** 90°, 106°, 117°

14. Reasoning Are any quadrilaterals regular polygons?
Use definitions to support your answer.

B Reasoning and Problem Solving

15. Can a quadrilateral have four acute
angles? Explain.

16. Which quadrilaterals have 2 pairs of
parallel sides?

Math and Music

Guitars are often decorated with geometric
shapes. Some musicians have elaborate
custom designs created for their guitar.

17. **Writing in Math** Use mathematical terms
from this lesson to describe the polygons
that decorate each guitar.

A.
B.
C.
D.

C Extensions

18. If you split a rectangle into two triangles,
what type of triangles do you get? What
if you split a rhombus? a square?

Mixed Review and Test Prep

Take It to the NET
Test Prep
www.scottforesman.com

19. What is the value of the underlined digit in 1<u>8</u>6,234,009?

20. How many obtuse angles are there in an obtuse triangle?

A. 0   **B.** 1   **C.** 2   **D.** 3

Enrichment

Drawing Geometric Figures

Materials: ruler, protractor

You can use a ruler and protractor to draw lines, angles, and polygons.

1. Trace $\overleftrightarrow{LM}$ at the right. Follow the steps to draw $\overleftrightarrow{AB} \perp \overleftrightarrow{LM}$.

Step 1 Label point B on $\overleftrightarrow{LM}$ between points L and M.

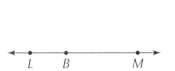

Step 2 Use a protractor and B as the vertex. Draw $\angle LBA$ with a measure of $90°$.

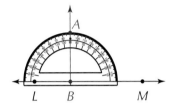

Step 3 Draw $\overleftrightarrow{AB}$. $\overleftrightarrow{AB} \perp \overleftrightarrow{LM}$ at point B.

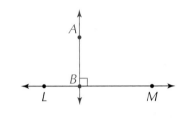

2. Trace $\overleftrightarrow{SW}$ at the right. Show points S, T and W. Follow the steps to draw $\overleftrightarrow{KL} \parallel \overleftrightarrow{ST}$.

Step 1 Use a protractor and S as the vertex. Draw an angle. Label it $\angle TSK$.

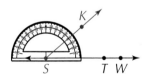

Step 2 With T as the vertex draw an angle with the same measure as $\angle TSK$ and $\overrightarrow{TW}$ as a side.

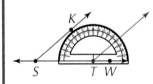

Step 3 With a ruler, measure $\overline{SK}$. Draw $\overline{TL}$ with the same length.

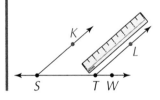

Step 4 Draw $\overleftrightarrow{KL}$. $\overleftrightarrow{KL} \parallel \overleftrightarrow{ST}$.

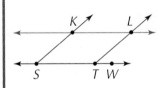

3. Follow the steps below to draw parallelogram $ABCD$.

Step 1 Draw a line. Label points A and B, so $\overline{AB}$ is 3 inches long.

Step 2 At point A, use a protractor to draw $\angle BAD$ with a measure of $60°$. Locate point D so that $\overline{AD}$ is 2 inches long.

Step 3 At point B, draw $\angle ABC$ with a measure of $120°$. Locate point C so that $\overline{BC}$ is 2 inches long.

Step 4 Draw $\overline{DC}$ to complete parallelogram $ABCD$.

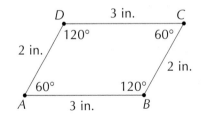

Use a ruler and protractor to draw these figures.

4. Draw a rectangle that is 4 in. long and 3 in. wide.

5. Draw a square with sides that are 5 cm long.

6. Draw an equilateral triangle with each side 6 cm long.

7. Draw a right triangle with each shorter side 3 inches long.

Activate Prior Knowledge

Activating prior knowledge when you read in math can help you use the **problem-solving strategy**, *Solve a Simpler Problem,* in the next lesson.

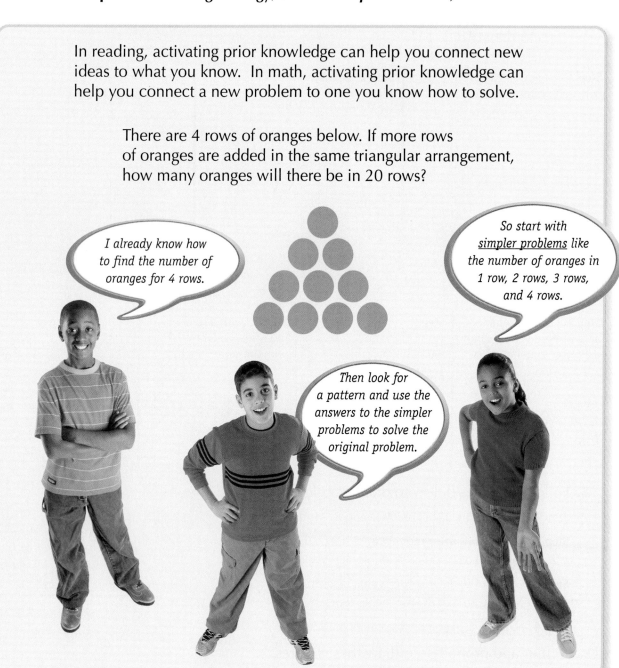

In reading, activating prior knowledge can help you connect new ideas to what you know. In math, activating prior knowledge can help you connect a new problem to one you know how to solve.

There are 4 rows of oranges below. If more rows of oranges are added in the same triangular arrangement, how many oranges will there be in 20 rows?

I already know how to find the number of oranges for 4 rows.

So start with simpler problems like the number of oranges in 1 row, 2 rows, 3 rows, and 4 rows.

Then look for a pattern and use the answers to the simpler problems to solve the original problem.

1. How many oranges are there in 1 row? 2 rows? 3 rows? 4 rows?

2. How can these simpler problems help you solve the original problem?

For 3–5, use the diagram at the right and the problem below.

A row of connected offices is being built along one side of a hallway. There will be one door leading into each office from the hallway and one door between neighboring offices. How many doors will there be for a row of 12 offices?

3. Write simpler problems like this one that you already know how to solve.

4. How many doors are there for 1 office? 2 offices? 3 offices?

5. **Writing in Math** Explain how you can use these simpler problems to help you solve the original problem.

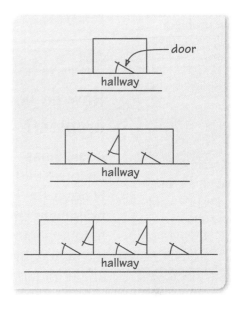

For 6–8, use the diagram at the right and the problem below.

A stop sign is shaped like a regular octagon. What is the sum of the measures of the angles of an octagon?

6. You can make a simpler problem by breaking apart the octagon as shown. What type of polygons has the octagon been broken into?

7. What do you know about the sum of the measures of the angles in each of these simpler polygons?

8. **Writing in Math** Explain how you can use these simpler problems to help you solve the original problem.

Problem-Solving Strategy

Reading Helps!

Making analogies

can help you with...

the problem-solving strategy, *Solve a Simpler Problem*.

Key Idea
Learning how and when to solve a simpler problem can help you solve problems.

Think It Through
I need to **use what I know** about polygons to solve simpler problems.

Solve a Simpler Problem

LEARN

How do you solve a simpler problem?

Angle Sums One of the most famous buildings in the United States is the Pentagon. The building is shaped like a regular pentagon. What is the sum of the measures of the angles of a pentagon?

Read and Understand

What do you know? The Pentagon is shaped like a regular pentagon. Each angle has the same measure.

What are you trying to find? Find the sum of the measures of the angles.

Plan and Solve

What strategy will you use?

How to Solve a Simpler Problem

Step 1 Break apart or change the problem into one that is simpler to solve.
Step 2 Solve the simpler problem.
Step 3 Use the answers to the simpler problem to solve the original problem.

Solve a simpler problem.

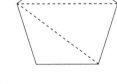

I can divide the pentagon into triangles.

The sum of the measures of the angles in each triangle is 180°.

$180 + 180 + 180 = 540$

Answer: The sum of the measures of the angles in the pentagon is 540°.

Look Back and Check

Is your work correct? Yes, there are three triangles and the sum of the angle measures in each is 180°. I added correctly to get 540°.

✔ Talk About It

1. How was the Angle Sums problem broken apart into a simpler problem?

2. What is the measure of each angle in a regular pentagon?

3. Use the strategy to find the sum of the measures of the angles of a hexagon.

When might you solve a simpler problem?

Summer Reading There are 12 books listed on the summer reading list. William is supposed to read 2 books from the list. How many different pairs of books are possible?

Simpler Problem Use letters to represent the books. Suppose there are just 2 books on the list. How many different pairs are possible? What if there are 3 books on the list? 4 books? 5 books?

Look for a pattern. Then continue the pattern to 12 books.

> **When to Solve a Simpler Problem**
>
> Think about solving a simpler problem when:
> **You can break the problem into simpler cases that are easier to solve.**
>
> • In the Angle Sums problem, break the pentagon into triangles. You know the number of degrees in each triangle, so you can solve the original problem.
>
> • In the Summer Reading problem, find the number of pairs for 2 books, 3 books, and so on. Then look for a pattern to find the number of pairs for 12 books.

| 2 books: 1 pair | 3 books: 3 pairs | 4 books: 6 pairs | 5 books: 10 pairs |

Number of books	2	3	4	5	6	7	8	9	10	11	12
Number of pairs	1	3	6	10	15	21	28	36	45	55	66

+2 +3 +4 +5 +6 +7 +8 +9 +10 +11

CHECK ✔

For another example, see Set 6-7 on p. 386.

1. Solve the simpler problem. Use the solution to help you solve the original problem.

   Seating Arrangement Six small square tables seating one person on a side are pushed together to make one long table. How many people could be seated at this long table?

   Simpler Problem How many people can be seated at 1 table? 2 tables pushed end to end? 3 tables pushed end to end? What is the pattern?

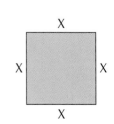
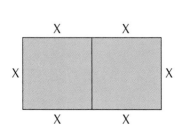

A Using the Strategy

In 2–3, solve the simpler problem. Use the solution to help you solve the original problem.

2. What is the sum of the whole numbers from 1 to 100?

Simpler Problem Pair the numbers as shown below. What is the sum of each pair? What is the sum of all 49 pairs? Which unpaired numbers need to be added in?

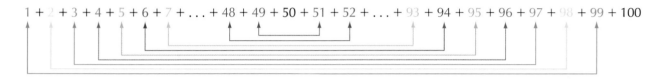

$1 + 2 + 3 + 4 + 5 + 6 + 7 + \ldots + 48 + 49 + 50 + 51 + 52 + \ldots + 93 + 94 + 95 + 96 + 97 + 98 + 99 + 100$

3. A **diagonal** is a line segment that connects two vertices of a polygon that are not already connected by a side. How many diagonals does a 10-sided polygon have?

Simpler Problem How many diagonals does a triangle have? a quadrilateral? a pentagon? a hexagon? What is the pattern?

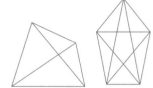

4. Eileen has 5 blouses and 5 skirts. How many different outfits are possible?

5. At a ball game, the first fan through the gate gets a free pennant, the second fan gets a water bottle, the third fan gets a trading card, and the fourth fan gets a pen. This pattern repeats over and over again for every four fans. What prize does the 33rd fan get?

B Mixed Strategy Practice

Solve each problem.

6. At Green Ridge Amusement Park, how many free tickets will the Neiderhorn family get if they purchase 60 tickets?

Green Ridge Amusement Park

Tickets $0.85
12 for $10

2 free tickets with every purchase of 12 tickets

7. Eric gave a clerk $50. He bought 3 hats for $7.95 each and an umbrella for $12.47. What change should he receive?

8. Nadine has 3 coins with a total value less than 50¢. If exactly two coins are the same, what are the possible total values of her coins?

 **Math and Art**

Kristina is crocheting squares for a quilt. When she puts them together, she wants a blue square in the center. The first "ring" of squares surrounding the center square will be orange. The second ring of squares will be green. Kristina is planning to have 8 rings of squares.

9. How many squares should she crochet for the eighth ring?

10. How many squares will she need in all?

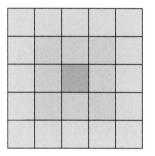

11. **Writing in Math** On their vacation, the Gomez family drove twice as many miles on Tuesday as they did on Monday. Then on Wednesday, they drove three times as many miles as they did on Tuesday. If they drove 360 miles on Wednesday, how many miles did they drive on Monday? Explain how you found your answer.

 **Mixed Review and Test Prep**

Take It to the NET
Test Prep
www.scottforesman.com

Find each quotient.

12. 368 ÷ 23   **13.** 22.54 ÷ 7   **14.** 2,418 ÷ 6   **15.** 3,366 ÷ 66

16. How many pairs of parallel sides does a trapezoid have? Draw an example.

17. If a 12-ounce package of cheese costs $3.36, what is the cost per ounce?

18. The measures of two angles of a triangle are 72° and 48°. Find the measure of the third angle.

A. 30°   **B.** 60°   **C.** 80°   **D.** 120°

STRATEGIES

- **Show What You Know**
  Draw a Picture
  Make an Organized List
  Make a Table
  Make a Graph
  Act It Out or Use Objects
- **Look for a Pattern**
- **Try, Check, and Revise**
- **Write an Equation**
- **Use Logical Reasoning**
- **Solve a Simpler Problem**
- **Work Backward**

Choose a tool

 Mental Math

TEST TALK

Think It Through
Stuck? I won't give up. I can:
- Reread the problem.
- Tell what I know.
- Identify key facts and details.
- Tell the problem in my own words.
- Show the main idea.
- Try a different strategy.
- Retrace my steps.

Problem-Solving Skill

Key Idea
There are specific things you can do to write a good description in math.

Writing to Describe

LEARN

How do you write a good description?

When you write to describe, you need to use geometric terms to describe geometric figures.

Shapes Opal sorted some shapes into two groups. Use geometric terms to describe one characteristic of each group.

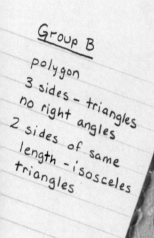

Group B
polygon
3 sides – triangles
no right angles
2 sides of same length – isosceles triangles

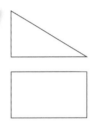   

Group A   Group B

Writing a Math Explanation

- Brainstorm characteristics describing each group using geometric terms.

- Look over your list for geometric terms that describe one characteristic of each group.

- Use these geometric terms correctly to describe each group.

Group A	Group B
polygon	polygon
3, 4, 5 sides	3 sides – triangles
right angles	no right angles
no regular polygons	2 sides of same length – isosceles triangles

All of the shapes in Group A have at least one right angle.

All of the shapes in Group B are isosceles triangles.

Think It Through

- I can **use brainstorming** to help me prepare to write.

- I'll use **math terms** accurately.

✔ Talk About It

1. Which math terms were used in the written description of each group? Why do you think these were chosen?

2. Are these the only descriptions possible? Explain.

CHECK ✓

Roberto sorted some polygons into two groups. Use geometric terms to describe a characteristic in each group.

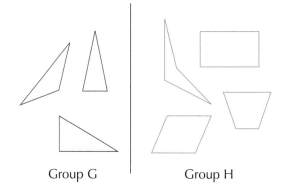

1. Make a table with characteristics of the two groups.

2. Which characteristics are not common to both groups?

3. Write your descriptions.

Group G   Group H

PRACTICE

For more practice, see Set 6-8 on p. 390.

Solve each problem. You may use a table to help plan your description.

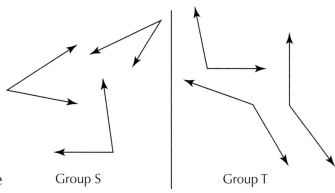

4. Opal sorted some angles into two groups. Use geometric terms to describe a characteristic in each group.

5. Use geometric terms to describe three properties of rectangles.

6. Use mathematical terms to describe the numbers in each set.

Group S   Group T

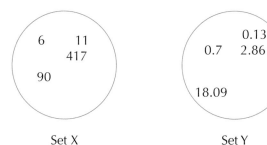

Set X   Set Y

7. Delia created two patterns. Use mathematical terms to describe a characteristic of each set.

Set 1: 6, 12, 18, 24, 30

Set 2: 5, 7, 11, 13, 17

8. Use geometric terms to describe three properties of this triangle.

9. Use geometric terms to describe three properties of this polygon.

Do You Know How?

Do You Understand?

Polygons (6-4)

Name each polygon.

1. **2.** **3.**

A Which polygon shown appears to be regular? Why?

B What do you look for when you are deciding the name for the polygon?

Classifying Triangles (6–5)

Classify each triangle by its sides and by its angles.

4. 3 cm 3 cm 3 cm **5.** 4 cm 4 cm **6.** 3 cm 3.5 cm 1 cm
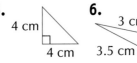

C An equilateral triangle is also isosceles. Explain why.

D If you know the measures of two angles of a triangle, how do you find the measure of the third angle?

Classifying Quadrilaterals (6-6)

Classify each quadrilateral. Be specific.

7. 7 cm 7 cm 7 cm 7 cm **8.** 6 in. 4 in. **9.** 6 in. 4 in. 4 in. 3 in.
 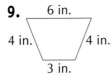

E Are all squares rectangles? Are all rectangles squares? Explain.

F If you know the measures of three angles of a quadrilateral, how do you find the measure of the fourth angle?

Solve a Simpler Problem (6-7)

10. Each team in a baseball league plays each of the other teams once. How many games will occur if the league has 8 teams?

G Make a table showing the number of games that will occur for 1 to 5 teams. How does this help you solve Exercise 10?

Writing to Describe (6-8)

11. Use geometric terms to name characteristics of this group of objects.
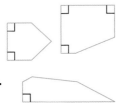

H How does a table help you describe the characteristics of a group?

MULTIPLE CHOICE

Use the figure at the right.

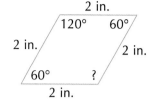

1. Which name does NOT apply? (6-6)

   A. quadrilateral   **C.** square

   B. rhombus   **D.** parallelogram

2. Which is the missing angle measure? (6-6)

   A. 60°   **B.** 120°   **C.** 240°   **D.** 180°

FREE RESPONSE

Classify each triangle by its sides and then by its angles. (6-5)

3. 3 ft 3 ft 30° 30°

4. 3 in. 1 in. 3.2 in.

5. 8 cm 8 cm 8 cm

6. 6 cm 2 cm 7 cm

Classify each figure. Be as specific as possible. (6-4, 6-6)

7. 10 in. 4 in.

8. 4 cm 2 cm 130° 50° 50° 130° 2 cm 4 cm

9.

10.

11. How many 1 × 1 squares are shown in the quilt at the right? How many 2 × 2 squares are shown? How many squares of any size are shown? (6-7)

Think It Through

• Sometimes **making a table** will help you solve a problem.

• Often you can **use the numbers in a table to find a pattern.**

Writing in Math

Explain why each description is impossible. (6-8)

12. A right obtuse triangle

13. An equilateral scalene triangle

14. A triangle with two obtuse angles

15. A rhombus with 2-inch and 4-inch sides

16. Draw six polygons. Try to divide them into two groups. Use geometric terms to describe the characteristics of each group. (6-8)

Vocabulary
• similar figures
• congruent figures

Congruence and Similarity

LEARN

✓ **WARM UP**
Draw an example of each figure.

1. square

2. trapezoid

3. right triangle

4. circle

How do you describe figures with the same shape?

Penelope used a machine at a camera store to make copies of a vacation photo. She made one copy that was the same size and another one four times as great.

Similar figures are figures that have the same shape. They may or may not have the same size. **Congruent figures** have the same size and shape.

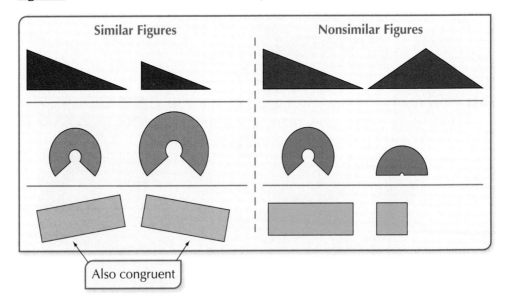

Also congruent

✓ Talk About It

1. Which of Penelope's vacation photos are congruent rectangles? Which photos are similar, but not congruent rectangles?

2. When are two similar figures also congruent?

How can you relate the angles and sides of polygons?

Similar Polygons

- Matching angles have the same measure.

    and

- The lengths of the sides in one polygon can be multiplied by the same number to give the lengths of the sides in the other polygon. (In this case, multiply by 2.)

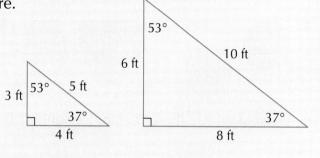

Congruent Polygons

- Matching angles have the same measure.

    and

- Matching sides have the same length.

✔ Talk About It

3. Can an obtuse triangle and a right triangle ever be similar? congruent? Explain.

4. Reasoning Is a 2 ft by 4 ft rectangle similar to a 6 ft by 20 ft rectangle? Explain.

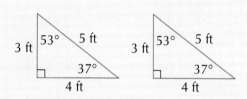
Take It to the NET
More Examples
www.scottforesman.com

CHECK ✔

For another example, see Set 6-9 on p. 386.

Do the figures in each pair appear to be similar? If so, are they also congruent?

1.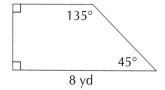

2.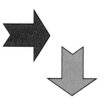

3.

4.

5. Reasoning Are these trapezoids congruent? Explain.

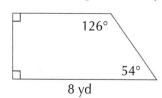

PRACTICE

A Skills and Understanding

Do the figures in each pair appear to be similar? If so, are they also congruent?

6.
7.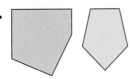
8.
9.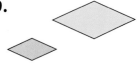

10. Reasoning Are these rectangles similar? Explain.

12 cm   2 cm
4 cm   6 cm

B Reasoning and Problem Solving

Is each situation an example of congruent or similar figures? Explain your reasoning.

11. Your school pictures come in wallet size as well as a larger print.

12. Your teacher gave everyone in class a gold star.

Math and Art

Wall murals are found on many walls, both indoors and outdoors. Usually an artist first paints a small original picture. Then an enlargement is painted on the wall.

13. A mural is 12 times as wide and 12 times as tall as the original painting. If the dimensions of the original painting are 2 ft by 3 ft, what are the dimensions of the mural?

14. **Writing in Math** If two triangles are congruent, and one is a right triangle, is the other a right triangle? Explain.

C Extensions

15. Draw a large scalene triangle. Join the midpoints of the sides with line segments. How would you describe the four smaller triangles? Try several examples.

Mixed Review and Test Prep

Take It to the NET
Test Prep
www.scottforesman.com

16. What is the sum of the measures of the angles of an octagon?

17. If the diameter of a wheel is 24 inches long, how long is the radius?

A. 48 inches   **B.** 24 inches   **C.** 12 inches   **D.** 8 inches

Enrichment

Constructing Bisectors and Angles

Materials: straightedge, compass

To **construct** geometric figures, you use a straightedge and a compass rather than a ruler and a protractor.

1. Congruent angles have the same measure. Trace ∠M. Follow these steps to construct an angle congruent to ∠M.

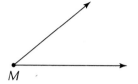

Step 1 Draw a ray with endpoint B. With endpoint M, as center, use your compass to draw an arc that intersects both sides of ∠M at points N and P. With the same opening and endpoint B as center, draw an arc that intersects the ray at point D.

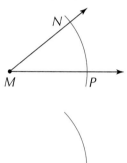

Step 2 Open your compass to length $\overline{NP}$. With D as center, draw an intersecting arc. Label point C.

Step 3 Draw $\overrightarrow{BC}$. ∠B and ∠M have the same measure. They are congruent angles.

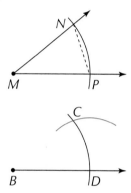
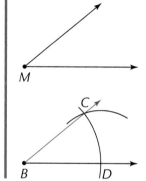

2. A **perpendicular bisector** divides a segment into two equal parts and is perpendicular to the segment. Trace $\overline{UV}$. Construct the perpendicular bisector of $\overline{UV}$.

Step 1 Set your compass to any opening greater than half the length of $\overline{UV}$. With U as center, draw an arc.

Step 2 With the same compass opening and V as center, draw an intersecting arc at points L and M.

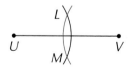

Step 3 Draw $\overleftrightarrow{LM}$. $\overleftrightarrow{LM}$ is the perpendicular bisector of $\overline{UV}$.

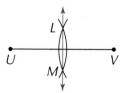

3. An **angle** bisector separates an angle into two equal parts. Trace ∠G. Construct the bisector of ∠G. Describe each step in words.

Step 1

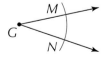

Step 2

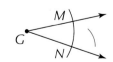

Step 3

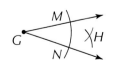

Step 4

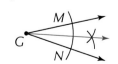

Key Idea
The size and shape of a figure do not change when it is slid, flipped, or turned.

Vocabulary
• transformations
• slide (translation)
• flip (reflection)
• turn (rotation)

Materials
• polygons
  or  tools

Transformations

LEARN

How can you move a figure?

For thousands of years beautiful designs, such as this quilt pattern, have been created by sliding, turning, and flipping figures. These **transformations** do not change the size or shape of a figure, so the completed design contains many congruent figures.

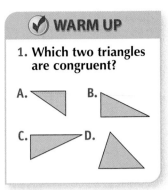

A **slide**, or **translation**, moves a figure in a straight direction.	A **flip**, or **reflection**, of a figure gives its mirror image.	A **turn**, or **rotation**, moves a figure about a point.
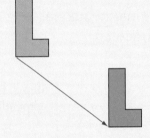	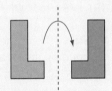	

Turns can be measured in degrees. Here are some common turns.

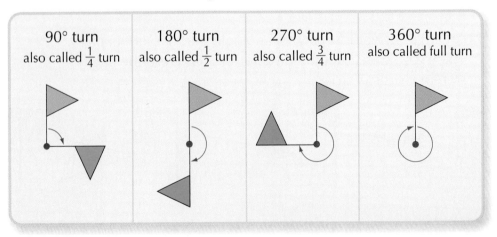

90° turn	180° turn	270° turn	360° turn
also called $\frac{1}{4}$ turn	also called $\frac{1}{2}$ turn	also called $\frac{3}{4}$ turn	also called full turn

The turns shown at the bottom of page 364 are clockwise (like the movement of a clock's hands). Counterclockwise turns are in the opposite direction.

✔ **Talk About It**

1. In the quilt design shown on page 364, give some examples of congruent triangles.

2. Why do you think $\frac{1}{4}$ turns, $\frac{1}{2}$ turns, $\frac{3}{4}$ turns, and full turns are so named?

3. Look at the turn of the letter L pictured on page 364. Is this a clockwise turn or a counterclockwise turn?

4. **Reasoning** In the quilt pattern, are triangles A and B related by a slide, a flip, or a turn? Triangles C and D? Triangles D and E?

Think It Through
I need to **visualize** when I analyze drawings of transformations.

Activity

How can I draw patterns?

a. This pattern was created with transformations starting with shape A. What transformation was used to move from shape A to shape B? shape B to shape C? and so on through shape I?

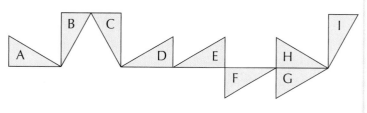

b. Work with a partner. Choose a polygon. Trace around it. Apply a transformation and trace around it again. Continue at least 8 more times. Show your partner your pattern and ask your partner to describe the transformations you used.

CHECK ✔

For another example, see Set 6-10 on p. 387.

Tell whether the figures in each pair are related by a slide, a flip, or a turn. If a turn, describe it.

1.

2.

3.

4.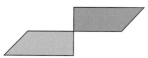

5. **Reasoning** Maria said the figures at the right are related by a 90° turn. Paul said they are related by a 270° turn. Who is right? Explain.

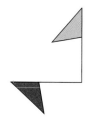

A Skills and Understanding

Tell whether the figures in each pair are related by a slide, reflection, or turn. If a turn, tell what type of turn.

6.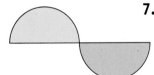

7.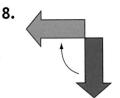

8.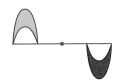

9.

10. Reasoning Sue told Ajay that these figures are related by a 180° turn. Ajay asked in which direction, clockwise or counterclockwise. Sue said it doesn't matter. Is Sue right? Explain.

B Reasoning and Problem Solving

11. As the hour hand on a clock moves from 12:00 to 3:00, what kind of turn is this? From 12:00 to 6:00? From 12:00 to 9:00? From 12:00 noon to 12:00 midnight?

12. If the figure at the right is reflected over the dashed line and then rotated 90° clockwise, which figure below shows the result?

A.

B.

C.

D.

Math and Social Studies

A good sense of direction is helpful for reading maps and following routes. Before beginning each turn, suppose you are facing north. Which way will you be facing after you make each turn?

13. 90° clockwise   **14.** 90° counterclockwise   **15.** 180°

16. Writing in Math Kyle said the figures below are related by a flip. Laura said they are related by a 180° turn. Georgette said they're related by a slide. Who is right? Explain.

C Extensions

Some polygons can fit together tightly leaving no gaps. Such an arrangement of figures, often used to tile floors, is called a **tessellation.** The tessellations shown here use only regular polygons.

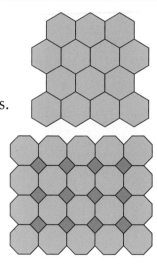

17. Which regular polygons were used to make each tessellation?

18. Which other regular polygons can be used *alone* to make a tessellation? Draw each tessellation. You may use a set of polygons to help.

19. Draw a tessellation that uses regular hexagons and equilateral triangles. You may use a set of polygons to help.

 **Mixed Review and Test Prep**

Take It to the NET
Test Prep
www.scottforesman.com

20. Can an obtuse triangle and an acute triangle be similar? Explain.

21. What type of figure is a chord?

    A. angle   **B.** ray   **C.** line segment   **D.** line

Learning with Technology

The Geometry Drawing eTool and Transformations

You can use the Geometry Drawing eTool to move figures. Draw a scalene triangle. Copy your triangle and place the copy over the original. Slide the new triangle to translate it. Then, flip the triangle.

1. Compare the original triangle to the new triangle. How is it the same? How is it different?

For the transformation known as a **glide reflection,** a figure is slid and then reflected. With the Coordinate Grid background selected, draw a trapezoid to the left of the *y*-axis. Slide the trapezoid up, and flip it vertically.

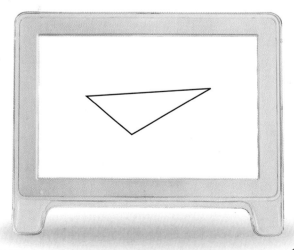

2. Continue using glide reflection to make a set of 10 trapezoid glide reflections along the *y*- and *x*-axes.

3. Use any shape and create a pattern that uses glide reflections.

Key Idea
Some figures can be split in half so that one side reflects onto the other side.

Vocabulary
• symmetric figure
• line of symmetry

Materials
• scissors

TEST TALK

Think It Through
I can **use objects** to help me create symmetric designs.

Symmetry

LEARN

Activity

How can you describe and create symmetric figures?

✓ **WARM UP**

Draw an example of each figure. Then draw a flip.

1. rectangle
2. trapezoid
3. right triangle
4. obtuse triangle

An artist designed the trademark at the right for a sporting goods company. Many trademarks are **symmetric figures.** This means they can be folded into two congruent parts that fit on top of each other. The fold line is a **line of symmetry.**

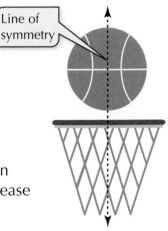

Line of symmetry

You can follow the steps below to create a design with two lines of symmetry.

a. Fold a sheet of paper in half. Then fold it in half again the other way (so the second crease is perpendicular to the first).

b. Draw a path that starts on one folded edge and ends at the other folded edge, as shown below.

c. Cut along the curve. Then open up the folded paper.

The figure you made should be symmetric with two lines of symmetry.

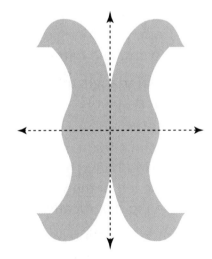

d. How many congruent parts are there in the figure you made?

e. Are the congruent parts related by slides, reflections, or turns?

How many lines of symmetry does each figure have? You may trace the figure and fold your paper to check.

1.
2.
3.
4.
5.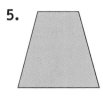

6. **Reasoning** Which hexagon has more lines of symmetry? Explain.

PRACTICE

For more practice, see Set 6-11 on p. 391.

A Skills and Understanding

How many lines of symmetry does each figure have? You may trace the figure and fold your paper to check.

7.
8.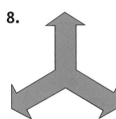
9.
10.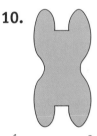
11.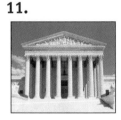

12. **Reasoning** Which quadrilateral has the most lines of symmetry? Explain.

B Reasoning and Problem Solving

Part of a symmetric trademark is shown. Make a tracing of each along with the line(s) of symmetry. Then complete the drawing.

13.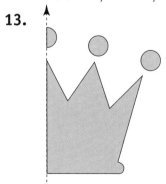
14.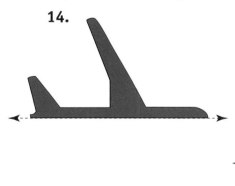
15.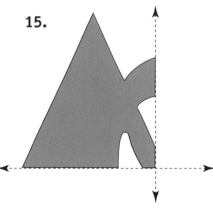

Math and Science

Your body, trees, bugs, and fruit are among the many examples of nearly symmetric figures in nature. Explain why each object below is not exactly symmetric.

16.

17.

18.

19.

20. **Writing in Math** Francine thinks that the lines of symmetry for a rectangle pass through the midpoints of the sides. Do you think she is right? Explain your thinking.

TEST TALK

Think It Through
I can **draw a picture** to help me examine geometric relationships.

C Extensions

When a figure rotates onto itself in less than a full turn, the figure has **rotational symmetry.** The figure at the right has rotational symmetry because a $\frac{1}{4}$ turn rotates the figure onto itself.

Tell if each figure below has rotational symmetry. If so, what is the smallest turn that will rotate the figure onto itself?

21.
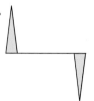

22.

23.

24.

25.

 Mixed Review and Test Prep

 Take It to the NET
Test Prep
www.scottforesman.com

26. Which has the greater product, 6×75 or 0.6×75?

27. Which two triangles appear to be similar?

A.

B.

C.

D.

Enrichment

Constructing Triangles

Materials: straightedge, compass

You use a straightedge and a compass to construct triangles.

1. Trace $\overline{XY}$ at the right. Follow these steps to construct equilateral triangle *ABC* with sides the length of $\overline{XY}$.

Step 1 Open the compass to length $\overline{XY}$. Keep this opening for each step.

Step 2 Draw a line and label point *A*. With *A* as center, draw an arc that intersects the line at *B*. $\overline{AB}$ is congruent to $\overline{XY}$.	**Step 3** With *A* as center, draw an arc.	**Step 4** With *B* as center, draw an intersecting arc at *C*.	**Step 5** Draw $\overline{AC}$ and $\overline{BC}$ to complete the triangle.

 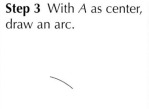

2. Trace $\overline{DE}$, $\overline{DF}$ and $\overline{EF}$ at the right. Follow the steps to construct triangle *DEF* with sides of these lengths.

Step 1 Draw a line and label point *D*. Open your compass to length $\overline{DE}$. With *D* as center, draw an arc intersecting the line at point *E*.

Step 2 Open your compass to length $\overline{DF}$. With *D* as center, draw an arc.

Step 3 Open your compass to length $\overline{EF}$. With *E* as center, draw an intersecting arc. Label the intersection point *F*.

Step 4 Draw $\overline{DF}$ and $\overline{EF}$ to complete triangle *DEF*.

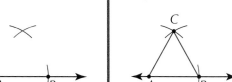

3. Trace $\angle R$, $\overline{RS}$, and $\overline{RT}$ at the right. Construct triangle *RST* with this angle and these side measures.

Step 1 Draw a line and label point *R*. With *R* as vertex, construct an angle congruent to $\angle R$.

Step 2 Open your compass to length $\overline{RS}$. With *R* as center, draw an arc that intersects one ray of $\angle R$ at point *S*. You may wish to extend the rays of $\angle R$.

Step 3 Open your compass to length $\overline{RT}$. With *R* as center, draw an arc that intersects the other ray of $\angle R$ at point *T*.

Step 4 Draw $\overline{ST}$ to complete triangle *RST*.

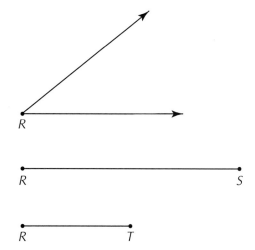   

Problem-Solving Applications

Skyscraper In many ways, the Hong Kong and Shanghai Bank leads the way in innovative high-rise designs. For instance, a "sun scoop" uses mirrors to reflect sunlight into a 12-story atrium. The popularity of this building has inspired the creation of other imaginative buildings around the world.

Trivia Even though this building has some of the most modern technology, its construction used some of the most ancient technology. The scaffolding was made with bamboo.

1 Name three geometric features visible in the structure of the bank building and describe their locations.

2 Cross braces appear like giant Xs. How many lines of symmetry does the cross brace have in the picture to the left?

3 The sun scoop has two sets of mirrors. The outside set has 480 mirrors. The inside set has 225 mirrors. Use front-end estimation and adjust to estimate the total number of mirrors in the sun scoop.

4 **Writing in Math** Write your own word problem using any of the facts or pictures in this lesson. Write its answer in a complete sentence.

5 At 5 levels, rows of triangles stretch across the building. Classify the triangles by their angles and sides. Are all the triangles congruent?

Using Key Facts

6 This bank building is about 9.5 times as tall as the basement is deep. How tall is this building?

Key Facts
Hong Kong and Shanghai Bank
• Total floor space   1,067,467 sq. ft
• Basement depth   61.7 ft
• Bank vault   over 55 tons
• Escalators   62
• Elevators   28
• Teller stations   116

7 **Decision Making** Suppose you were to design a new school that could hold at least 250 students. How many floors would it have? How many classrooms would be on each floor? If each classroom can have 25 students, what is the largest number of students that could attend the school?

Good News/ Bad News Many people believe that the bank succeeded in their goal of creating the best bank building in the world. Unfortunately, success comes at a great cost. When it was built, this was the most expensive building in the world!

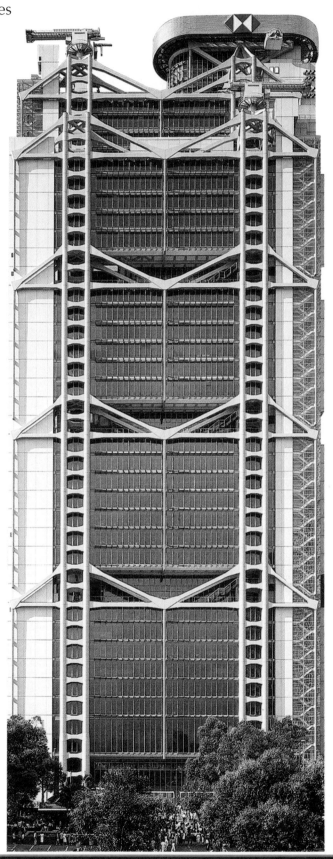

Do You Know How?

Do You Understand?

Similarity and Congruence (6-9)

Do the figures in each pair appear to be similar? If so, are they also congruent?

1.   **2.**   **3.**

Ⓐ Explain how you decide whether or not two figures are congruent.

Ⓑ Are all congruent figures similar? Are all similar figures congruent? Explain.

Transformations (6-10)

Tell whether the figures in each pair are related by a slide, a flip, or a turn.

4.   **5.**   **6.**

Ⓒ Explain how you decided how the two figures in each exercise were related.

Ⓓ Draw a right triangle. Then draw a 180° turn of this triangle.

Ⓔ Describe a 360° turn.

Symmetry (6-11)

How many lines of symmetry does each figure have?

7.   **8.**

9.   **10.**

Ⓕ Explain how you can check whether a line is a line of symmetry.

Ⓖ Do rectangles and squares have the same number of lines of symmetry? Explain.

MULTIPLE CHOICE

1. Which figure has exactly two lines of symmetry? (6-11)

A.   **B.**   **C.**   **D.**

2. Which two figures do not appear to be congruent? (6-9)

A.   **B.**   **C.**   **D.**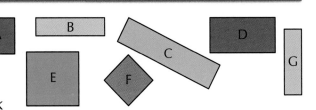

FREE RESPONSE

Use the figures at the right. (6-9)

3. Which pairs of figures are similar?

4. Which pairs of figures are congruent?

Before each turn, the minute hand on a clock is on 12. What number will the hand be on after each turn? (6-10)

5. $\frac{1}{4}$ turn   **6.** $\frac{1}{2}$ turn   **7.** $\frac{3}{4}$ turn   **8.** full turn

9. On a blueprint, a rectangular living room is 9 inches long by 6 inches wide. The actual room is 20 times this length and width. What are the dimensions of the room? (6-9)

10. Suppose you want to make a symmetric drawing. If you are given half of a drawing and the line of symmetry, would you flip, slide or turn your half to make the second half? Use a drawing to explain your answer. (6-11)

Think It Through
Sometimes **drawing a picture** can help you solve a problem.

Writing in Math

11. The letters at the right are capital block letters. Write your first name in block letters. Show the number of lines of symmetry in each letter of your name. (6-11)

A	B	C	D	E	F	G
H	I	J	K	L	M	N
O	P	Q	R	S	T	U
V	W	X	Y	Z		

Test-Taking Strategies

Understand the question.

Get information for the answer.

Plan how to find the answer.

Make smart choices.

Use writing in math.

Improve written answers.

Improve Written Answers

You can follow the tips below to learn how to improve written answers on a test. It is important to write a clear answer and include only information needed to answer the question.

1. Tanya placed these triangles on her desk.

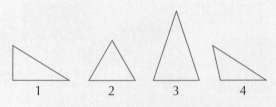

1   2   3   4

She knows that each triangle has three sides. On the lines below, use geometric terms to describe another characteristic of each triangle.

Triangle 1 _____

Improve Written Answers

• Check if your answer is complete.

*In order to **get as many points as possible,** I must write a description of each triangle.*

• Check if your answer makes sense.

*Have I used **mathematical terms** correctly to describe each triangle? Have I written my description on the right lines?*

• Check if your explanation is clear and easy to follow.

*I should reread each description to check that I have **accurately and clearly** described the triangle. Have I included only the information called for? I only need to describe one characteristic of each triangle.*

The rubric below is a scoring guide for Test Questions 1 and 2.

Scoring Rubric

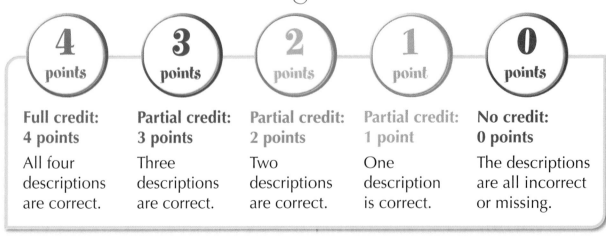

4 points	**3** points	**2** points	**1** point	**0** points
Full credit: 4 points	**Partial credit: 3 points**	**Partial credit: 2 points**	**Partial credit: 1 point**	**No credit: 0 points**
All four descriptions are correct.	Three descriptions are correct.	Two descriptions are correct.	One description is correct.	The descriptions are all incorrect or missing.

Irving used the scoring rubric on page 376 to score a student's answer to Test Question 1. The student's paper is shown below.

Triangle 1 <u>This is a right triangle.</u>

_____

Triangle 2 <u>All three sides of the</u>

<u>triangle have the same length.</u>

Triangle 3 <u>This is a scalene triangle.</u>

_____

Triangle 4 <u>This triangle has 3 acute</u>

<u>angles.</u>

Think It Through

The first two descriptions are correct. The last two descriptions are incorrect. Triangle 3 is not scalene. It has two sides that are the same length, so it's an isosceles triangle. Triangle 4 doesn't have 3 acute angles. One of the angles is an obtuse angle. Since only two descriptions are correct, the answer gets 2 points.

Now it's your turn.

Score the student's paper. If it does not get 4 points, rewrite it so that it does.

2. Roger placed these quadrilaterals on his desk.

1   2   3   4

He knows that each quadrilateral has four sides. Use geometric terms to describe another characteristic of each quadrilateral.

Quadrilateral 1 <u>This quadrilateral</u>

<u>has line symmetry.</u>

Quadrilateral 2 <u>All four sides of the</u>

<u>quadrilateral have the same length.</u>

Quadrilateral 3 <u>This is a rectangle.</u>

_____

Quadrilateral 4 <u>Opposite sides are</u>

<u>parallel.</u>

Central angle sounds related to "center."

The vertex of a **central angle** is the center of a circle. (p. 336)

Self Check

Use geometric terms to describe figures. (Lessons 6-1, 6-3)

Lines and parts of lines	**Pairs of lines**	**Circles and related figures**

Lines and parts of lines

Point: K •K

Line: $\overleftrightarrow{NS}$ •———•
N S

Line segment: $\overline{VW}$
midpoint: G •——•——•
V G W

Ray: $\overrightarrow{AB}$ •———→
A B

Plane PQR

Pairs of lines

Parallel

Intersecting

Perpendicular

Circles and related figures

Center: C

Radius: $\overline{CD}$

Diameter: $\overline{EF}$

Chord: $\overline{JM}$

Central angle: $\angle DCE$

Circle C

1. Name a line segment, ray, and perpendicular lines in this diagram.
2. Draw a circle. Then draw a chord in the circle.

"Oct-" means 8, as in octopus or octave.

An **octagon** has 8 sides. (p. 340)

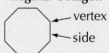

Self Check

Find angle measures and name figures. (Lessons 6-2, 6-4, 6-5, 6-6)

Without using a **protractor,** find the missing angle measure.

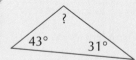

The angle measures in a triangle add up to 180° and in a quadrilateral, 360°.

The missing angle measure is 106 **degrees,** or 106°.

Identify figures.

Acute angle

exterior side
interior
vertex   side Z

Regular octagon

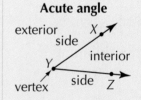

vertex
side

angles: acute, right, obtuse, straight

polygons: triangle, quadrilateral, pentagon, hexagon, octagon, regular polygon

triangles: equilateral, isosceles, scalene, right, acute, obtuse

quadrilaterals: trapezoid, parallelogram, rectangle, rhombus, square

3. The measures of 2 angles of a triangle are 35° and 72°. Find the measure of the third angle and tell what type of angle it is.

My sister and I look similar, but she's taller.

Similar figures *have the same shape. They may or may not have the same size. (p. 360)*

Self Check

Compare and transform figures (Lessons 6-9, 6-10, 6-11)

Similar figures
Same shape

Congruent figures
Same size and shape

Line of symmetry

Symmetric figure

Slide or
Translation

Flip or
Reflection

Turn or
Rotation

4. Are the orange quadrilaterals above related by a slide, a flip, or a turn?

Self Check

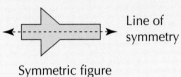

Earth rotates once every 24 hours.

A rotation *turns a figure. (p. 364)*

Solve problems by solving a simpler problem or by writing to describe. (Lessons 6-7, 6-8)

Solving a simpler problem might help you solve a more complex problem.

How many straws are needed to make an 8-car train?

3-car "train"
made with straws

Solve a simpler problem.

| 1 car | 2 cars | 3 cars |
| 4 straws | 7 straws | 10 straws |

The pattern is add 3. Continue the pattern to 8 cars.

An 8-car train needs 25 straws.

When you prepare to write a description, brainstorm first.

Use geometric terms to describe two properties of parallelograms.

4 sides, quadrilateral
opposite sides parallel
angle measures add up to 360°

A parallelogram has 4 sides. It has opposite sides parallel.

5. How many straws are needed to make a "double-decker" 5-car train?

Answers: 1. Sample answers: $\overleftrightarrow{VN}$; $\overleftrightarrow{VA}$; $\overleftrightarrow{HR}$ and $\overleftrightarrow{DP}$ 2. Sample answer: ◯ 3. 73°; acute 4. flip 5. 27 straws

MULTIPLE CHOICE

Choose the correct letter for each answer.

1. Which two lines are perpendicular?

A.    C.

B.   D.

2. Classify the angle.

A. acute   C. right

B. obtuse   D. straight

3. Which angle below measures 90°?

A.    C.

B.   D.

4. What name is given to any line segment that connects two points on a circle?

A. radius   C. chord

B. diameter   D. center

5. The diameter of a circle measures 16 inches. How long is its radius?

A. 4 in.   C. 16 in.

B. 8 in.   D. 32 in.

6. Which polygon has 5 sides?

A. quadrilateral   C. octagon

B. hexagon   D. pentagon

7. Which is a triangle with two sides the same length and an interior angle measuring 100°?

A. acute scalene   C. obtuse isosceles

B. acute isosceles D. obtuse scalene

8. Find the measure of ∠A.

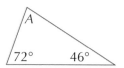

A. 44°   C. 72°

B. 62°   D. 82°

9. Which statement is **true?**

A. All parallelograms are rectangles.

B. All rhombuses are rectangles.

C. All trapezoids are parallelograms.

D. All squares are rhombuses.

10. The measures of three of the angles of a quadrilateral are 92°, 134°, and 40°. What is the measure of the fourth angle?

A. 54°

B. 94°

C. 114°

D. 266°

11. A square table seats two people on each side. How many people can be seated at the longest table that can be formed by pushing four of these square tables together?

A. 32 people

B. 24 people

C. 20 people

D. 16 people

TEST TALK

Think It Through

• I should **look for key words** in the problem.

• I can **eliminate** unreasonable answers.

12. If this figure is flipped over the dotted line and then rotated 180°, which figure below shows the result?

A.   **C.**

B.   **D.**

13. How many lines of symmetry does this figure have?

A. 0   **C.** 2

B. 1   **D.** 4

FREE RESPONSE

Use the diagram below. Name the following:

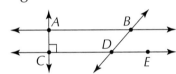

14. three points   **15.** two line segments

16. three lines   **17.** two rays

18. two parallel line segments

19. two intersecting rays that are not perpendicular

20. Draw circle D with diameter $\overline{AB}$, chord $\overline{LM}$, and central angle ADE that measures 80°.

Name each polygon. Then tell if it appears to be a regular polygon.

21.   **22.**

Classify each triangle by its sides and then by its angles.

23.   **24.**

Classify each quadrilateral. Be as specific as possible.

25.   **26.**

Tell whether the figures in each pair are related by a slide, a flip, or a turn. If a turn, describe it.

27.   **28.**

Writing in Math

29. Explain how you can tell if a figure is symmetric.

30. If two triangles are similar and one is an obtuse scalene triangle, is the other one also an obtuse scalene triangle? Explain.

31. Use geometric terms to describe three properties of this polygon.

TEST TALK

Think It Through

- I can **make a model** to explain my thinking.
- I need to make sure my model supports my answer.

Number and Operation

MULTIPLE CHOICE

1. Find 3.6 − 2.15.

   A. 1.9   **C.** 1.45

   B. 1.55   **D.** 1.11

2. What is $6.72 ÷ 2.4?

   A. $0.24   **C.** $2.80

   B. $2.40   **D.** $28

3. Which number has the digit 6 in the ten-thousands place?

   A. 6,146,218   **C.** 642,180

   B. 1,562,806   **D.** 16,063

FREE RESPONSE

4. Multiply 17 and 43.

5. List all the factors of 75.

6. Turkey sells for $4.98 a pound. Patricia made sandwiches for a luncheon. She purchased 7.5 pounds of turkey. What was the total cost for the turkey?

Think It Through

I should **make my answers brief but complete.**

Writing in Math

7. Explain the difference between a prime number and a composite number.

8. Describe how to round 64.97 to the nearest tenth.

Geometry and Measurement

MULTIPLE CHOICE

9. Which two lines are parallel?

10. An angle measuring 80° would be classified as what type of angle?

   A. acute   **C.** straight

   B. right   **D.** obtuse

11. Which drawing shows this figure turned 180°?

FREE RESPONSE

12. Find the measure of the fourth angle of a quadrilateral if three of the angles measure 86°, 92°, and 100°.

13. What is the name of a three-sided polygon with three unequal side lengths?

Writing in Math

14. Describe how you can tell if two figures are similar but not congruent.

Data Analysis and Probability

MULTIPLE CHOICE

15. Which number is the mode in the stem-and-leaf plot?

Stem	Leaf
1	0 0 4 5
2	1 3 5 7
3	0 1 3 5
4	
5	2 4 5

A. 5

B. 10

C. 27

D. 29

16. What is the probability of tossing a number less than 3 on a cube numbered 1–6?

A. $\frac{1}{6}$

B. $\frac{1}{3}$

C. $\frac{1}{2}$

D. $\frac{3}{1}$

FREE RESPONSE

17. How much higher was the average temperature in July than in June?

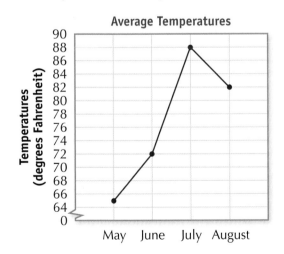

Average Temperatures

Writing in Math

18. In a set of data, can the mean, median, and mode be the same value? Use an example to explain your answer.

Algebra

MULTIPLE CHOICE

19. Which expression represents 3 less than a number *n*?

A. $3 - n$

B. $3n$

C. $n - 3$

D. $n + 3$

20. Solve $a + 6 = 24$.

A. $a = 30$

B. $a = 18$

C. $a = 16$

D. $a = 4$

FREE RESPONSE

21. Josh and Marissa are playing a game. Find the rule Marissa is using.

When Josh says 3, Marissa says 12.

When Josh says 5, Marissa says 20.

When Josh says 12, Marissa says 48.

22. Find $x + 7$ when $x = 14$.

Writing in Math

23. Mr. Kaster looked at the following table and said that the rule is "Add 40." Is he correct? Explain.

Input	Output
10	50
20	100
30	150
40	200

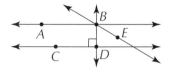
Set 6-1 (pages 328–331)

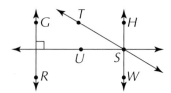

Name the following:

one point:	Point A
two line segments:	$\overline{AB}$, $\overline{CD}$
two rays:	$\overrightarrow{DC}$, $\overrightarrow{BE}$
two lines:	$\overleftrightarrow{CD}$, $\overleftrightarrow{EB}$
two parallel lines:	$\overleftrightarrow{CD} \parallel \overleftrightarrow{AB}$
two perpendicular lines:	$\overleftrightarrow{BD} \perp \overleftrightarrow{CD}$

Remember intersecting lines pass through the same point. If they form a right angle, they are perpendicular lines.

1. three points   **2.** two lines

3. a line segment   **4.** three rays

5. two perpendicular lines

6. two parallel lines

7. two intersecting but not perpendicular lines

Set 6-2 (pages 332–335)

Classify the angle as acute, right, obtuse, or straight. Then measure the angle.

An **acute angle** has a measure between 0° and 90°. The measure of the angle is less than 90°, so it is an acute angle.

Using a protractor, the angle measures 75°.

Remember you can use a protractor to measure and draw angles.

1.   **2.**

3.   **4.**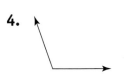

Set 6-3 (pages 336–337)

Identify the following:

the center:	Point C
two radii:	$\overline{CW}$, $\overline{CR}$
a diameter:	$\overline{RT}$
a chord:	$\overline{AB}$
three central angles:	$\angle RCT$, $\angle RCW$, $\angle WCT$

Remember that a diameter is a chord, but a chord is not necessarily a diameter.

1. the center

2. two radii

3. a diameter

4. a chord

5. three central angles

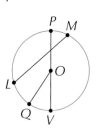

Name the polygon. Tell if it appears to be a regular polygon.

The polygon has 6 sides. It is a **hexagon.**

The side lengths are equal and the angles are of equal measure. It is a **regular polygon.**

Remember the name of the polygon tells how many sides the polygon has. A regular polygon has sides of equal length and angles of equal measure.

1.

2.

3.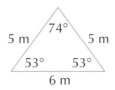

4.

Classify the triangle by its sides and then by its angles.

Two of the sides are the same length. The triangle is an **isosceles triangle.**

All the angles are less than 90°, or acute angles. The triangle is an **acute triangle.**

Remember equilateral, isosceles, and scalene describe a triangle by its sides, and right, acute, and obtuse describe a triangle by the measure of its angles.

1.

2.

3.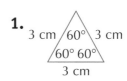

4.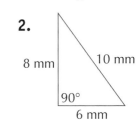

Classify the quadrilateral. Then find the missing angle measure.

The quadrilateral has two sets of parallel lines with all sides the same length. It is a rhombus.

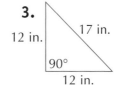

The sum of the angles of a quadrilateral equal 360°.

360° − (60° + 60° + 120°) = 120°

So, the missing angle measure is 120°.

Remember that quadrilaterals are four-sided polygons. They can be classified by their angles or pairs of sides.

Classify each quadrilateral. Be as specific as possible. Then find the missing angle measure.

1.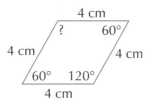

2.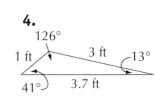

Set 6-7 (pages 352–355)

To solve a simpler problem, follow these steps.

Step 1: Break apart or change the problem into one that is simpler to solve.

Step 2: Solve the simpler problem.

Step 3: Use the answers to the simpler problem to solve the original problem.

Remember you can draw pictures to help you see a pattern or relationship between the simpler problem and the original problem.

1. Mario has 6 T-shirts. He needs to choose 3 T-shirts to take on a camping trip. How many different combinations of 3 T-shirts can he choose?

2. What is the sum of the angles of an octagon?

Set 6-8 (pages 356–357)

Use geometric terms to describe a characteristic in each group.

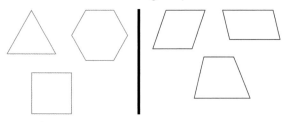

    Group A   Group B

All the shapes in Group A are regular polygons.

All the shapes in Group B are quadrilaterals.

Remember brainstorming can help you with writing to describe.

1. Use geometric terms to describe how these two polygons are the same and how they are different.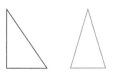

2. Use geometric terms to describe three properties of this polygon.

Set 6-9 (pages 360–363)

Do the figures appear to be similar? If so, are they also congruent?

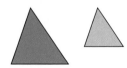

The two figures are the same shape, but not the same size.

The figures are similar, but not congruent.

Remember congruent figures have the same size and shape.

1.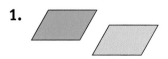

2.

3.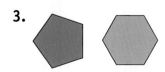

Tell whether the figures below are related by a slide, a flip, or a turn. If a turn, describe it.

The figures are mirror images of each other. Therefore, the figures are related by a flip.

Remember turns move a figure about a point and can be measured in degrees.

1.

2.

3.

4.

Tell how many lines of symmetry the figure has.

The figure has 1 line of symmetry.

Remember that for a figure to be symmetric, two halves need to be congruent.

1.

2.

3. 4. S

Set 6-1 (pages 328–331)

Use the diagram at the right to name each of the following.

1. three points

2. two lines

3. two perpendicular lines

4. two line segments

5. two parallel rays

6. three rays

7. two intersecting but not perpendicular lines

8. How many points are needed to draw a line?

Set 6-2 (pages 332–335)

Classify each angle as acute, right, obtuse, or straight. Then measure each angle. (Hint: Trace each angle and draw longer sides if necessary.)

1.

2.

3.

4.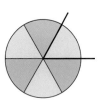

Draw an angle with each measure.

5. 15°   6. 135°   7. 95°   8. 170°

9. Measure the highlighted angles in the picture.

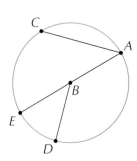

Set 6-3 (pages 336–337)

Use circle *B* to identify each of the following.

1. the diameter

2. a radius

3. a chord

4. two central angles

5. the center

6. A soup can has a diameter of 3.5 inches. How long is the radius?

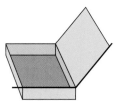

Set 6-4 (pages 340–341)

Name each polygon. Then tell if it appears to be a regular polygon.

1.   **2.**   **3.**   **4.**

5. Name the sides of the polygon below. Name the vertices.

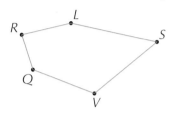

Set 6-5 (pages 342–345)

Classify each triangle by its sides and then by its angles.

1.    **2.**   **3.**

The measures of two angles of a triangle are given. Find the measure of the third angle.

4. 125°, 15°   **5.** 80°, 50°   **6.** 45°, 110°   **7.** 18°, 72°

8. The measures of two angles of a triangle are 73° and 42°. Is the triangle an acute, a right, or an obtuse triangle? Explain your answer.

Set 6-6 (pages 346–349)

Classify each quadrilateral. Be as specific as possible.

1.    **2.** 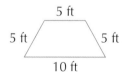   **3.**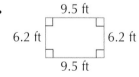

The measures of three angles of a quadrilateral are given. Find the measure of the fourth angle.

4. 90°, 90°, 110°   **5.** 98°, 76°, 82°   **6.** 105°, 45°, 45°

7. Are all rhombuses squares? Are all squares rhombuses? Explain.

Set 6-7 (pages 352–355)

Solve each problem. You may use a simpler problem
to help you solve the original problem.

1. Mrs. Ortiz wants to bake two types of cookies for
   the bake sale. She has 5 different recipes to
   choose from. How many different cookie
   combinations are possible?

2. What is the sum of all the odd numbers
   from 1 to 100?

Set 6-8 (pages 356–357)

Solve each problem. You may use a brainstorming table
to help plan your description.

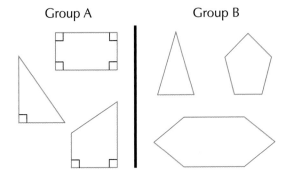

Group A   Group B

1. Use geometric terms to describe how rectangles and
   parallelograms are related.

2. Use geometric terms to describe a characteristic
   in each group.

Set 6-9 (pages 360–363)

Do the figures in each pair appear to be similar? If so, are
they also congruent?

1.    2.    3.

4. Heart-shaped pendants are sold in small, medium,
   and large sizes. Is this an example of congruent or
   similar figures? Explain your reasoning.

Take It to the NET
More Practice
www.scottforesman.com

Set 6-10 (pages 364–367)

Tell whether the figures in each pair are related by a flip, slide, or turn. If a turn, describe it.

1.

2.

3.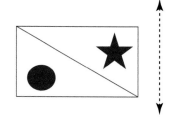

4. Draw what the figure at the right would look like if it were flipped over the dotted line and then rotated $\frac{3}{4}$ turn clockwise.

Set 6-11 (pages 368–371)

How many lines of symmetry does each figure have? You may trace the figure and fold your paper to check.

1.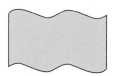

2.

3.

4.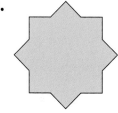

Part of a symmetric figure is shown. Trace each drawing along with the line(s) of symmetry. Then complete the figure.

5.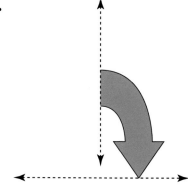

6.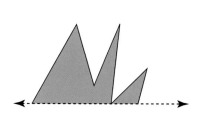

7.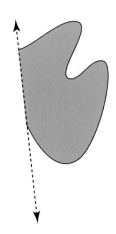

Fraction Concepts

DIAGNOSING READINESS

A Vocabulary
(pages 8–11, 66–67)

Choose the best term from the box.

1. In the number sentence $2 \times 8 = 16$, 2 and 8 are called __?__.

2. In 0.324, the 4 is in the __?__ place.

3. In 0.86, the 6 has a value of 6 __?__.

4. The number 8.6 is read as eight and six __?__.

Vocabulary

- **tenths** *(p. 8)*
- **factors** *(p. 66)*
- **hundredths** *(p. 8)*
- **thousandths** *(p. 8)*

B Division
(pages 152–155, 214–217)

5. $28 \div 6$

6. $88 \div 9$

7. $56 \div 4$

8. $72 \div 13$

9. $65 \div 12$

10. $75 \div 10$

11. $132 \div 54$

12. $640 \div 25$

13. If 87 photos are put into an album with 6 photos on each page, how many pages can be completely filled? How many photos are left for the page that is not filled?

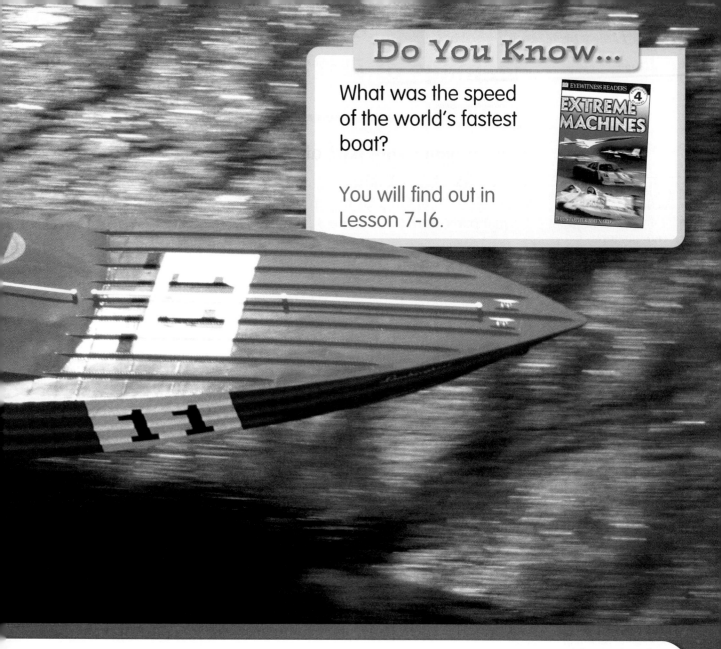

Do You Know...

What was the speed of the world's fastest boat?

You will find out in Lesson 7-16.

DK EYEWITNESS READERS

EXTREME MACHINES

CHRISTOPHER MAYNARD

C Place Value

(pages 8–11)

Write each number in standard form.

14. sixty-hundredths

15. two and four tenths

16. six thousandths

17. one and two hundredths

D Number Theory

(pages 162–167)

List all the factors for each number.

18. 10   **19.** 18   **20.** 50

21. 28   **22.** 70   **23.** 17

Write whether each number is prime or composite.

24. 13   **25.** 20   **26.** 45

Key Idea
A fraction can name part of a whole, a location on a number line, or part of a set.

Vocabulary
• fraction
• numerator
• denominator

Meanings of Fractions

 LEARN

How can you name part of a whole?

A fifth-grade class is landscaping the schoolyard as a project. A rectangular region is divided into 3 equal parts, and 2 out of the 3 parts are planted with flowers.

A **fraction** can be used to name part of a whole region.

$$\frac{2}{3}$$

The **numerator** tells how many of the equal parts are being planted with flowers.

The **denominator** tells the number of equal parts the whole region is divided into.

✔ **Talk About It**

1. What fraction names the part of the region above that is NOT planted with flowers?

2. **Reasoning** In the squares shown at the right, how many parts are shaded in each? Does $\frac{2}{3}$ name the shaded part for each square? Explain.

How can a fraction name a point on a number line?

Any segment can represent a whole amount. By dividing the segment into equal parts, you can use fractions to represent points on a number line.

Example A

What point is shown on the number line?

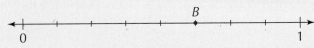

There are 8 equal segments between 0 and 1. Point B is $\frac{5}{8}$ of the way between 0 and 1. So the fraction $\frac{5}{8}$ names point B.

✔ **Talk About It**

3. Where would you locate the point for $\frac{7}{8}$ on the number line in Example A?

4. What fraction is shown by point A? point B?

 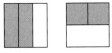

How can you name part of a set?

Sometimes a fraction is used to name a part of a set.

Example B

What fraction of the set of tools are shovels?

$\frac{9}{15}$ ← number of shovels
← number of tools

Example C

Draw counters to show two fifths, $\frac{2}{5}$, of a set shaded.

One Way	Another Way
Calvin showed single counters.	Trisha showed groups of counters.

✔ Talk About It

5. In Example B, what fraction of the set of tools are not shovels?

Take It to the NET
More Examples
www.scottforesman.com

6. Explain how Trisha's drawing shows $\frac{2}{5}$.

CHECK ✓

For another example, see Set 7-1 on p. 450.

Write the fraction that names the shaded part or point on a number line.

1.

2.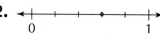

3.

In 4–6, draw a model to show each fraction.

4. $\frac{3}{7}$ as part of a set

5. $\frac{5}{8}$ as part of a whole

6. $\frac{4}{10}$ as a point on a number line

7. **Number Sense** Draw pictures to show $\frac{3}{8}$ as part of a whole in two different ways.

A Skills and Understanding

Write the fraction that names the shaded part or point on a number line.

8.

9.

10.

11.

12.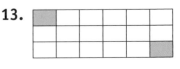

13.

In 14–16, draw a model to show each fraction.

14. $\frac{7}{9}$ as part of a whole

15. $\frac{5}{12}$ as part of a set

16. $\frac{2}{6}$ as a point on a number line

17. Number Sense If $\frac{2}{3}$ of a region is shaded, what part is not shaded?

B Reasoning and Problem Solving

18. Algebra Find the value of n, if $\frac{n}{7} = 1$.

19. Kathy has 5 blue toy ponies and 2 pink ones. What fraction of her ponies are pink?

20. Reasoning Karl had 10 car models. Seven were sports cars and 3 were sedans. Then he got 2 truck models. What fraction of his models are sports cars now?

21. Reasoning The diagrams at the right show how two equal-sized square-shaped gardens were planted with red flowers by two classes. What fraction names the part of each garden that is planted? Could the garden be divided in other ways so that the same part is planted? Explain.

Class 1   Class 2

22. Writing in Math Is the explanation below correct? If not, tell why and write a correct response.

Draw a square and shade $\frac{3}{4}$.

I divided the square into 4 parts and shaded 3 of them. So, $\frac{3}{4}$ of the square is shaded.

C Extensions

What fraction of each measuring cup is full?

23.

24.

25.

26. Reasoning If a measuring cup is one quarter filled with milk, what fraction represents the amount of milk needed to finish filling the cup?

Mixed Review and Test Prep

Take It to the NET
Test Prep
www.scottforesman.com

Tell how the light figure was moved to the position of the dark figure. Write slide, flip, or turn.

27.

28.

29.

30. What is the product of 1.8×2.4?

A. 1.08   **B.** 4.32   **C.** 10.8   **D.** 43.2

Learning with Technology

The Fraction eTool

Use the Fraction eTool to show parts of a whole. Place a fraction strip or wedge into the workspace. Enter 8 for the denominator and color 3 parts of the strip or wedge. What fraction can be used to name the shaded region? Use fraction strips or wedges to name these shaded regions.

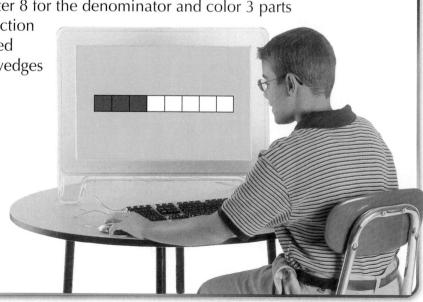

1. Denominator: 4
Color 3 parts

2. Denominator: 12
Color 7 parts

3. Denominator: 16
Color 9 parts

4. Denominator: 3
Color 2 parts

All text pages available online and on CD-ROM.

Fractions and Division

LEARN

How can you divide 3 objects into equal parts?

Example A

Anna, Tim, Mark, and Deb are sharing 3 quesadillas. What fractional amount does each one get?

Find $3 \div 4$.

What You Think

Divide each quesadilla into 4 equal parts.

Each person gets 1 piece from each quesadilla. So, each person gets 3 pieces. This is the same as $\frac{3}{4}$ of one quesadilla.

| Anna | Tim |
| Mark | Deb |

What You Write

$3 \div 4 = \frac{3}{4}$

Each person gets $\frac{3}{4}$ of a quesadilla.

Example B

Find $4 \div 6$.

$4 \div 6 = \frac{4}{6}$

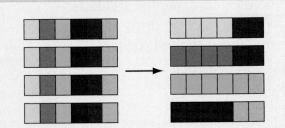

✔ **Talk About It**

1. Explain why one piece from each quesadilla in Example A is the same as $\frac{3}{4}$ of one quesadilla.

Give each answer as a fraction.

1. 9 ÷ 10　　**2.** 1 ÷ 3　　**3.** 5 ÷ 7　　**4.** 5 ÷ 12　　**5.** 3 ÷ 5

6. Reasoning Each of two pies was cut into 3 equal pieces. One piece from each pie was eaten. What part of a whole pie was eaten?

PRACTICE

For more practice, see Set 7-2 on p. 454.

(A) Skills and Understanding

Give each answer as a fraction.

7. 2 ÷ 9　　**8.** 6 ÷ 11　　**9.** 1 ÷ 2　　**10.** 7 ÷ 8　　**11.** 1 ÷ 4

12. Reasoning Each of four equal square cakes is divided into 5 equal pieces. What part of a whole cake is shown by the shaded pieces?

13. Number Sense If $x \div 7 < 1$, what whole numbers could x be?

(B) Reasoning and Problem Solving

Use the graph for 14–16. The runners ran the same distance each day.

14. What fraction shows how far Carly ran in one day?

15. Number Sense Who ran more than one mile a day?

16. **Writing in Math** Explain how you can find the fraction to show how far Mindy ran each day.

Ten Days of Practice

(Bar graph — Total Miles Ran)
Carly: 8　　Mindy: 7　　Katie: 11

Legend:
- Carly
- Mindy
- Katie

Mixed Review and Test Prep

Take It to the NET
Test Prep
www.scottforesman.com

Write the fraction that names the blue part of each.

17.

18.

19.

20. Which of the following shows a flip of the triangle at the right?

　　A.　　**B.** 　　**C.**　　**D.**

Think It Through
I know that $3\frac{2}{7}$ means $3 + \frac{2}{7}$, and $3 + \frac{2}{7} = \frac{21}{7} + \frac{2}{7} = \frac{23}{7}$.

Mixed Numbers

LEARN

What is a mixed number?

Shelly has 20 small quilt squares. For every 9 squares, she can sew a quilt pattern called a 9-patch. How many 9-patches does she have?

$$20 \div 9 = \frac{20}{9} = 2\frac{2}{9}$$

An **improper fraction** has a numerator greater than or equal to its denominator. A **mixed number** has a whole number and a fraction.

✔ **Talk About It**

1. What improper fraction describes the number of 9-patches?

2. What mixed number describes the number of 9-patches?

How do you change between improper fractions and mixed numbers?

Example A

Write $\frac{14}{5}$ as a mixed number.

$\frac{14}{5} = 14 \div 5$

• Divide the numerator by the denominator.

• Write the remainder as a fraction.

$$\begin{array}{r} 2\frac{4}{5} \\ 5\overline{)14} \\ -10 \\ \hline 4 \end{array}$$

So, $\frac{14}{5} = 2\frac{4}{5}$.

Example B

Write $3\frac{2}{7}$ as an improper fraction.

• Multiply the denominator by the whole number. $3 \times 7 = 21$

• Add the numerator. $21 + 2 = 23$

• Use the same denominator.

$\frac{23}{7}$ ← sum $(3 \times 7) + 2$
      ← same denominator

So, $3\frac{2}{7} = \frac{23}{7}$.

✔ **Talk About It**

3. Why do you multiply 3 and 7 in Example B?

CHECK ✓

Write an improper fraction and a mixed number for each model.

1.

2.

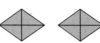

Write each improper fraction as a mixed number or each mixed number as an improper fraction.

3. $\frac{8}{3}$ **4.** $\frac{10}{7}$ **5.** $2\frac{4}{6}$ **6.** $8\frac{4}{5}$

7. Number Sense Andy said that $\frac{12}{2}$ is not an improper fraction because $12 \div 2 = 6$. Is he correct? Explain.

PRACTICE

For more practice, see Set 7-3 on p. 454.

A Skills and Understanding

Write an improper fraction and a mixed number for each model.

8.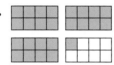

9.

Write each improper fraction as a mixed number.

10. $\frac{7}{2}$ **11.** $\frac{5}{3}$ **12.** $\frac{37}{10}$ **13.** $\frac{26}{5}$ **14.** $\frac{19}{7}$ **15.** $\frac{10}{3}$

Write each mixed number as an improper fraction.

16. $1\frac{9}{10}$ **17.** $3\frac{4}{9}$ **18.** $5\frac{1}{6}$ **19.** $4\frac{1}{2}$ **20.** $4\frac{1}{4}$ **21.** $6\frac{3}{5}$

22. Reasoning Can an improper fraction equal one? Can it be less than 1? Explain.

B Reasoning and Problem Solving

23. Ken has 37 quilt squares. How many 9-patches does he have?

24. Algebra If $4\frac{3}{5} = \frac{n}{5}$, how do you know $n > 20$?

25. Writing in Math Carrie has 48 quilt squares. How many complete 9-patches can she make? Explain your answer.

Mixed Review and Test Prep

Take It to the NET
Test Prep
www.scottforesman.com

Give each answer as a fraction.

26. $4 \div 15$ **27.** $7 \div 10$ **28.** $5 \div 6$ **29.** $9 \div 20$

30. Which fraction represents the part shaded?

A. $\frac{2}{3}$ **B.** $\frac{3}{5}$ **C.** $\frac{5}{3}$ **D.** $\frac{7}{2}$

Key Idea
Thinking about benchmark fractions can help you estimate fractional amounts.

Vocabulary
• benchmark fractions

Estimating Fractional Amounts

How can you estimate fractional amounts?

A fifth-grade class is making book shelves. The first board shown below is a whole board. Another board has been cut. About what fraction of the cut board is left?

Think about benchmark fractions. **Benchmark fractions** include $\frac{1}{4}, \frac{1}{3}, \frac{1}{2}, \frac{2}{3},$ and $\frac{3}{4}$. A length representing the whole board could be cut into 2, 3, or 4 equal pieces to represent these benchmark fractions.

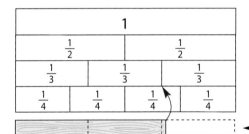

← about $\frac{2}{3}$

About $\frac{2}{3}$ of the board is left.

Example A
About what fraction of the shelf is painted?

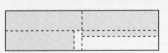

About $\frac{3}{4}$ of the shelf is painted.

Example B
About what fraction of the pie has been eaten?

About $\frac{1}{2}$ of the pie has been eaten.

✓ Talk About It

1. What is the benchmark fraction in Example A? Example B?

2. Draw a rectangle and shade about $\frac{1}{3}$ of it.

Estimate the shaded part of each.

1. **2.** **3.**

4. Reasoning Is about the same part of each rectangle shaded? Is about the same amount of area shaded in each? Explain.

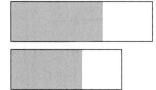

PRACTICE

For more practice, see Set 7-4 on p. 454.

Ⓐ Skills and Understanding

Estimate the shaded part of each.

5. **6.** **7.**

8. **9.** **10.**

11. Reasoning If about $\frac{1}{4}$ of a board is left, about what part was used?

Ⓑ Reasoning and Problem Solving

Estimate the fraction of the 20 most populated countries in the world that are located in each region.

12. Asia

13. Africa and North American combined

14. **Writing in Math** Draw two line segments that are different lengths. Shade about $\frac{3}{4}$ of each. Are the shaded parts the same length? Explain.

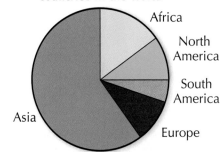

Locations of the 20 Most Populated Countries in the World

Africa

North America

South America

Europe

Asia

Mixed Review and Test Prep

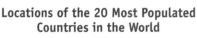

Take It to the NET
Test Prep
www.scottforesman.com

Write each improper fraction as a mixed number.

15. $\frac{39}{8}$ **16.** $\frac{7}{4}$ **17.** $\frac{17}{7}$ **18.** $\frac{14}{3}$ **19.** $\frac{99}{10}$ **20.** $\frac{19}{2}$

21. Which equals $8 \div 15$?

A. $\frac{7}{15}$ **B.** $\frac{8}{15}$ **C.** $2\frac{1}{8}$ **D.** $\frac{15}{8}$

 All text pages available online and on CD-ROM.

Fractions and Mixed Numbers on the Number Line

✓ **WARM UP**

Write each improper fraction as a mixed number.

1. $\frac{7}{4}$ 2. $\frac{14}{5}$

3. $\frac{3}{3}$ 4. $\frac{8}{7}$

LEARN

How can you locate fractions and mixed numbers on a number line?

Remember that you can divide the length from 0 to 1 into equal parts and locate fractions on the number line.

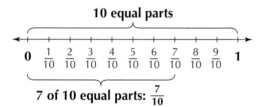

10 equal parts

$0 \quad \frac{1}{10} \quad \frac{2}{10} \quad \frac{3}{10} \quad \frac{4}{10} \quad \frac{5}{10} \quad \frac{6}{10} \quad \frac{7}{10} \quad \frac{8}{10} \quad \frac{9}{10} \quad 1$

7 of 10 equal parts: $\frac{7}{10}$

Example A

What fraction represents point A?

There are 8 equal parts between 0 and 1. Point A shows 3 of the 8 equal parts. So, $\frac{3}{8}$ represents point A.

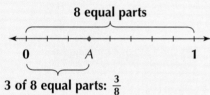

8 equal parts

$0 \qquad A \qquad 1$

3 of 8 equal parts: $\frac{3}{8}$

Numbers are in order on a number line from the least on the left to the greatest on the right. So, you can use a number line to order fractions and mixed numbers.

Example B

Locate points for $2\frac{1}{7}$, $1\frac{5}{7}$, and $\frac{13}{7}$ on a number line. Then order them from least to greatest.

$0 \quad \frac{1}{7} \quad \frac{2}{7} \quad \frac{3}{7} \quad \frac{4}{7} \quad \frac{5}{7} \quad \frac{6}{7} \quad 1 \quad 1\frac{1}{7} \quad 1\frac{2}{7} \quad 1\frac{3}{7} \quad 1\frac{4}{7} \quad 1\frac{5}{7} \quad 1\frac{6}{7} \quad 2 \quad 2\frac{1}{7} \quad 2\frac{2}{7} \quad 2\frac{3}{7} \quad 2\frac{4}{7} \quad 2\frac{5}{7} \quad 2\frac{6}{7} \quad 3$

$0 \quad \frac{1}{7} \quad \frac{2}{7} \quad \frac{3}{7} \quad \frac{4}{7} \quad \frac{5}{7} \quad \frac{6}{7} \quad \frac{7}{7} \quad \frac{8}{7} \quad \frac{9}{7} \quad \frac{10}{7} \quad \frac{11}{7} \quad \frac{12}{7} \quad \frac{13}{7} \quad \frac{14}{7} \quad \frac{15}{7} \quad \frac{16}{7} \quad \frac{17}{7} \quad \frac{18}{7} \quad \frac{19}{7} \quad \frac{20}{7} \quad \frac{21}{7}$

$1\frac{5}{7} < \frac{13}{7} < 2\frac{1}{7}$

✓ **Talk About It**

1. The number of equal parts between 0 and 1 in Example A is 8. In Example B, why are there only 7 equal parts between 0 and 1?

2. Describe how you would locate $2\frac{3}{4}$ on a number line.

1. What fraction or mixed number represents point *M*? Point *N*?

0   M   1   N   2

Draw a number line to show each set of numbers. Then order the numbers from least to greatest.

2. $\frac{4}{9}, \frac{3}{9}, \frac{2}{9}$

3. $\frac{10}{8}, 1\frac{4}{8}, 1\frac{3}{8}$

4. $2\frac{6}{12}, \frac{22}{12}, 1\frac{8}{12}, \frac{11}{12}$

5. Number Sense If a number line is divided into 4 equal segments between 0 and 1, what do you know about the points for $\frac{1}{2}$ and $\frac{2}{4}$?

PRACTICE

For more practice, see Set 7-5 on p. 455.

A Skills and Understanding

What fraction or mixed number represents each point?

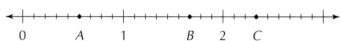
0   A   1   B   2   C

6. Point *A*   **7.** Point *B*   **8.** Point *C*

Draw a number line to show each set of numbers. Then order the numbers from least to greatest.

9. $\frac{4}{5}, \frac{3}{5}, \frac{1}{5}$

10. $\frac{13}{8}, \frac{2}{8}, 1\frac{3}{8}$

11. $2\frac{5}{8}, 2\frac{4}{8}, \frac{22}{8}$

12. $1\frac{6}{9}, \frac{4}{9}, \frac{19}{9}$

13. $2\frac{3}{10}, 1\frac{4}{10}, \frac{12}{10}$

14. $1\frac{5}{6}, \frac{13}{6}, 2\frac{2}{6}$

15. Number Sense Explain how you can easily tell that $12\frac{7}{8}$ is to the right of $10\frac{2}{5}$ on a number line.

B Reasoning and Problem Solving

16. Draw a number line to show the yards of material each student bought. Then order the lengths from least to greatest.

Student	Yards of Material
Ashley	$1\frac{1}{8}$
Pedro	$1\frac{5}{8}$
Mindy	$\frac{7}{8}$

17. Writing in Math What fraction represents point *Y*? Explain.

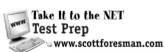
0   1

18. Estimate the shaded part.

19. Round 4.73895 to the nearest hundredth.

A. 4.7   **B.** 4.73   **C.** 4.739   **D.** 4.74

Problem-Solving Skill

Key Idea
Some problems have extra information, and some do not have enough information to solve them.

Extra or Missing Information

LEARN

How do you know if you have enough information to solve a problem?

Cabinet Knobs Orlando needs to buy knobs for new kitchen cabinets. A package of 4 knobs costs $8.95. Orlando buys 7 packages. What is the total cost of the knobs, not including tax?

Read and Understand

Step 1: What do you know?

• Tell what you know in your own words.

Orlando buys packages of knobs.

• Identify key details and facts.

Orlando buys 7 packages.
A package of 4 knobs costs $8.95.

Step 2: What are you trying to find?

• Tell what the question is asking.

• Show the main idea.

You want to know the total cost for the knobs, not including tax.

7 Packages

Plan and Solve

There is enough information to solve the problem.

Since 7 × $8.95 = $62.65, the total cost of the knobs, not including tax, is $62.65.

Look Back and Check

Is the answer reasonable?

Since 7 × $9 = $63, $62.65 is reasonable.

✔ Talk About It

1. What is the extra information in the Cabinet Knobs problem?

Decide if each problem has extra or missing information.
Solve if you have enough information.

1. The installation instructions for Orlando's cabinets say to use one knob for cabinet drawers under 18 inches wide and two knobs for drawers 18 inches wide or more. How many knobs does he need in all?

2. A package contains 3 large paintbrushes and 2 small paintbrushes. The package costs $19.98. What fraction of the brushes in the package are large brushes?

PRACTICE

For more practice, see Set 7-6 on p. 455.

Decide if each problem has extra or missing information.
Solve if you have enough information.

3. Kim buys a book, a video, and a radio. The video costs $12.65, and the book costs $7.49. The radio costs three times as much as the video. How much does the radio cost?

4. Pete charges $30 per hour to install kitchen cabinets. He installed 15 cabinets for a client. How much money did Pete earn?

For 5–6, use the table at the right.

5. The small brass knobs are sold in packages of 3. Each package sells for $14.99. How many packages of small brass knobs were sold in March?

6. In March, how many more brushed chrome knobs were sold than polished chrome knobs?

March Sales

Type of Knob	Number Sold
small brass	1,104
large brass	1,236
antique glass	689
brushed chrome	2,475

7. In *Children of the Longhouse,* there were 50 men attending when the League of Five Nations met. Nine of these were of the Fleet Nation, three were of the Bear Nation, six were of the Coyote Nation, and twelve were of the Crow Nation. How many were of the Deer Nation?

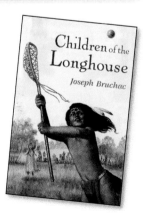

8. Mrs. Majko bought 12 bushes that cost $13.95 apiece and 8 trees that cost $16.95 apiece. What was the total cost of the bushes and trees, not including tax?

9. **Writing in Math** For 1–8, if there is missing information, write what is needed and then solve the problem.

Do You Know How? | Do You Understand?

Meanings of Fractions (7-1), Estimating Fractional Amounts (7-4)

Write a fraction for the shaded part.

1. ☐☐☐☐☐☐☐☐   **2.** ●● ○ / ● ●

Estimate the shaded part of each.

3. ■■■■■   **4.** [shaded box]

A Explain how you found the numerator and the denominator in Exercise 1.

B Tell which benchmark fractions you used to determine your estimating in Exercises 3 and 4.

Fractions and Division (7-2)

Give each answer as a fraction.

5. $1 \div 6$ **6.** $2 \div 9$ **7.** $7 \div 11$

C Tell how you found each fraction.

D Show Exercise 6 with a drawing.

Mixed Numbers (7-3)

Write as a mixed number.

8. $\frac{51}{10}$ **9.** $\frac{32}{9}$

Write as an improper fraction.

10. $5\frac{6}{7}$ **11.** $4\frac{1}{5}$

E Tell how you found each mixed number.

F Which operations do you use to change a mixed number to an improper fraction?

Fractions and Mixed Numbers on the Number Line (7-5)

What fraction or mixed number should be written at each point?

12. point F **13.** point H **14.** point G

G Tell how you identified each point.

H Should $1\frac{1}{7}$ be to the left or the right of point G on the number line? Explain.

Problem-Solving Skill: Extra or Missing Information (7-6)

Decide if the problem has extra or missing information. Solve if you can.

15. Tori needs 35 beads to make necklaces for her friends. Eight beads come in each package. One package costs $1.19. Tori bought 4 packages. Will she have enough beads?

I Tell what you know. Identify the key facts and details. What are you trying to find?

J Decide whether you have enough information to answer the question. Explain.

MULTIPLE CHOICE

1. Which fraction names the shaded part? (7-1)

A. $\frac{3}{4}$ B. $\frac{4}{3}$ C. $\frac{3}{7}$ D. $\frac{4}{7}$

2. Which fraction is the best estimate for the shaded part? (7-4)

A. $\frac{1}{4}$ B. $\frac{1}{3}$ C. $\frac{2}{3}$ D. $\frac{11}{12}$

Think It Through
It is important to **understand vocabulary,** like the word *estimate.*

FREE RESPONSE

Give each answer as a fraction. (7-2)

3. $3 \div 10$ **4.** $11 \div 12$ **5.** $1 \div 5$ **6.** $3 \div 8$

Write each improper fraction as a mixed number. (7-3)

7. $\frac{22}{4}$ **8.** $\frac{17}{2}$ **9.** $\frac{26}{6}$ **10.** $\frac{49}{8}$

Write each mixed number as an improper fraction. (7-3)

11. $4\frac{9}{10}$ **12.** $7\frac{1}{3}$ **13.** $9\frac{2}{7}$ **14.** $7\frac{5}{6}$

Draw a number line to show each set of numbers. Then order the numbers from least to greatest. (7-5)

15. $\frac{5}{4}, 1\frac{3}{4}, \frac{3}{4}$ **16.** $\frac{5}{7}, \frac{1}{7}, \frac{8}{7}$ **17.** $\frac{7}{3}, 1\frac{1}{3}, \frac{2}{3}$

For 18–19, use the information at the right. Decide if the problem has extra or missing information. Solve if you have enough information. (7-6)

18. Wilbur has $15. Will he have enough money to buy everyone in his family an admission ticket?

19. Lisa has $7. Carolyn has $8. Will Lisa have enough money for an admission ticket and the dolphin show?

TICKET PRICES

ITEM	PRICE
Admission	$3.25
Tram	$1.50
Dolphin Show	$2.25

Writing in Math

20. Write a problem about pizza with an answer of $\frac{4}{9}$. (7-1)

21. Explain what steps you can use to change a mixed number to an improper fraction. (7-3)

Understanding Equivalent Fractions

LEARN

Activity

How can you model the same fraction in more than one way?

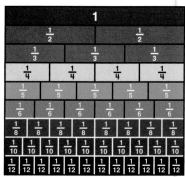

a. Use fraction strips to show $\frac{2}{3}$ and $\frac{8}{12}$.

b. Are $\frac{2}{3}$ and $\frac{8}{12}$ the same part of the red strip?

c. Use fraction strips to find another fraction equivalent to $\frac{2}{3}$ and $\frac{8}{12}$. What fraction is it?

d. Use the fraction strips to find as many fractions as you can that are equivalent to $\frac{9}{12}$.

How can you name a part in more than one way?

Equivalent fractions name the same part of a whole, part of a set, or a location on a number line.

Example A	Example B
Name the shaded part of the rectangle in 3 different ways.	Name the red part of the set in 3 different ways.

Example A: $\frac{1}{4}$ $\frac{2}{8}$ $\frac{4}{16}$

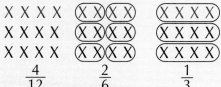

Example B: $\frac{4}{12}$ $\frac{2}{6}$ $\frac{1}{3}$

✔ Talk About It

1. In Example A, are there other fractions that would show the same shaded part? Explain.

2. If 18 buttons out of a set of 24 are red, name at least 2 different fractions to show the part of the set that is red.

Take It to the NET
More Examples
www.scottforesman.com

Write two fractions that name each shaded part or point on a number line.

1.    **2.**    **3.**

4. Reasoning If 6 out of 9 counters in a set are red, what fraction names the part of the set that is NOT red?

PRACTICE

For more practice, see Set 7-7 on p. 455.

A Skills and Understanding

Write two fractions that name each shaded part or point on a number line.

5.

6.

7.

8.

9.

10.

B Reasoning and Problem Solving

11. Write two fractions for the red part of the apples.

12. One pizza was divided into 6 equal pieces. Judy ate 2 of them. Another pizza of the same size was divided into 12 equal pieces. Tim ate 4 of them. Who ate more pizza? Explain.

13. **Writing in Math** Explain how you could draw a picture to show $\frac{3}{4} = \frac{6}{8}$.

Mixed Review and Test Prep

Take It to the NET
Test Prep
www.scottforesman.com

Estimate the shaded part of each.

14.   **15.**   **16.**

17. Find $1,008 \div 28$.

    A. 34   **B.** 35 R18   **C.** 36   **D.** 36 R4

 All text pages available online and on CD-ROM.

Key Idea
A fraction has many different names.

Vocabulary
• equivalent fractions (p. 410)

Equivalent Fractions

WARM UP

1. 8 × 9   2. 7 × 4

3. 6 × 9   4. 7 × 8

LEARN

How do you find equivalent fractions?

Two people measured the length of a barracuda tooth. One wrote $\frac{3}{8}$ inch, and the other wrote $\frac{6}{16}$ inch. Both were correct.

You can multiply or divide the numerator and denominator of a fraction by the same nonzero number to get equivalent fractions.

INCHES

$$\frac{3}{8} \xrightarrow{\times 2} = \frac{6}{16}$$ $$\frac{3}{5} \xrightarrow{\times 3} = \frac{9}{15}$$ $$\frac{12}{15} \xrightarrow{\div 3} = \frac{4}{5}$$ $$\frac{20}{25} \xrightarrow{\div 5} = \frac{4}{5}$$

Sometimes you need to change a fraction to an equivalent fraction with a different numerator or denominator.

Example A	Example B
Find the missing numerator.	Find the missing denominator.
$\frac{2}{5} = \frac{}{10}$	$\frac{15}{24} = \frac{5}{}$
You know both denominators.	You know both numerators.
Think: What number times 5 equals 10?	Think: What number can 15 be divided by to get 5?
Multiply 2 and 5 by 2.	Divide 15 and 24 by 3.
$\frac{2}{5} \xrightarrow{\times 2} = \frac{}{10}$ So, $\frac{2}{5} = \frac{4}{10}$.	$\frac{15}{24} \xrightarrow{\div 3} = \frac{5}{}$ So, $\frac{15}{24} = \frac{5}{8}$.

✓ Talk About It

1. Name two other fractions equivalent to $\frac{1}{5}$.

2. How could you use division to show that $\frac{2}{3}$ and $\frac{8}{12}$ are equivalent fractions?

3. Explain how to find the missing number in $\frac{7}{8} = \frac{14}{}$ to make the fractions equivalent.

Name two equivalent fractions for each fraction.

1. $\frac{5}{6}$ **2.** $\frac{1}{10}$ **3.** $\frac{3}{8}$ **4.** $\frac{10}{20}$ **5.** $\frac{5}{20}$

Find the missing number to make the fractions equivalent.

6. $\frac{3}{7} = \frac{\blacksquare}{28}$ **7.** $\frac{8}{24} = \frac{1}{\blacksquare}$ **8.** $\frac{6}{21} = \frac{\blacksquare}{7}$ **9.** $\frac{3}{4} = \frac{24}{\blacksquare}$

10. Number Sense Explain why $\frac{4}{10}$ and $\frac{3}{5}$ are not equivalent fractions.

PRACTICE

For more practice, see Set 7-8 on p. 455.

Ⓐ Skills and Understanding

Name two equivalent fractions for each fraction.

11. $\frac{2}{3}$ **12.** $\frac{5}{8}$ **13.** $\frac{2}{5}$ **14.** $\frac{8}{16}$ **15.** $\frac{3}{12}$

Find the missing number to make the fractions equivalent.

16. $\frac{7}{10} = \frac{21}{\blacksquare}$ **17.** $\frac{5}{\blacksquare} = \frac{20}{36}$ **18.** $\frac{\blacksquare}{6} = \frac{6}{36}$ **19.** $\frac{\blacksquare}{63} = \frac{7}{9}$

20. Number Sense Are $\frac{6}{9}$ and $\frac{8}{12}$ equivalent fractions? Explain.

Ⓑ Reasoning and Problem Solving

21. Two quarters of a basketball game are over. Now it is halftime. Explain how this could be.

22. A clock shows that $\frac{5}{60}$ and $\frac{1}{12}$ are equivalent fractions. Explain.

23. <u>**Writing in Math**</u> In a survey of 100 people, 50 people said they liked Brand X best. Explain why half the people liked Brand X best.

Think It Through
My answer should be brief but complete.

Mixed Review and Test Prep

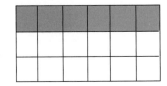
Take It to the NET
Test Prep
www.scottforesman.com

Write each mixed number as an improper fraction.

24. $3\frac{5}{6}$ **25.** $4\frac{4}{7}$ **26.** $1\frac{2}{5}$ **27.** $9\frac{2}{3}$

28. Which fraction does NOT name the shaded part of the figure?

A. $\frac{6}{18}$ **B.** $\frac{1}{3}$ **C.** $\frac{3}{9}$ **D.** $\frac{1}{4}$

Vocabulary
• factor (p. 66)
• common factors
• greatest common
  factor (GCF)

Think It Through
I can **make an
organized list** to
solve the problem.

Greatest Common Factor

LEARN

Activity

How many are on each team?

There are 18 boys and 24 girls who will be
divided into teams. Each team will consist of either all boys
or all girls. Each team will have an equal number of players.

a. Name all possible teams of only boys (1 team of
18 boys, 2 teams of 9 boys, and so on).

b. Name all possible teams consisting of only girls.

c. What is the largest number of people that each
team can have?

d. Suppose there are 12 boys and 15 girls. What is the
greatest number of people each team can have? Explain.

How can you find the greatest common factor?

Common factors of two numbers are factors that
are the same.

The **greatest common factor (GCF)** of two numbers
is the greatest number that is a factor of both.

Example

Find the greatest common factor of 18 and 24.

STEP 1 List the factors of 18 and 24.

18: 1, 2, 3, 6, 9, 18
24: 1, 2, 3, 4, 6, 8, 12, 24

STEP 2 Circle pairs of common factors and find the GCF.

18: 1, 2, 3, 6, 9, 18
24: 1, 2, 3, 4, 6, 8, 12, 24

The greatest common factor of 18 and 24 is 6.

✓ Talk About It

1. Name all the common factors for 18 and 24.

2. Is 3 also a greatest common factor of
18 and 24? Explain.

For another example, see Set 7-9 on p. 452.

Find the GCF of each pair of numbers.

1. 16, 24 **2.** 25, 40 **3.** 4, 28 **4.** 30, 36 **5.** 12, 18

6. Number Sense What is the GCF of 67 and 67?

PRACTICE

For more practice, see Set 7-9 on p. 456.

A Skills and Understanding

Find the GCF of each pair of numbers.

7. 12, 30 **8.** 27, 45 **9.** 25, 36 **10.** 16, 40 **11.** 15, 42

12. 10, 14 **13.** 6, 15 **14.** 9, 21 **15.** 8, 20 **16.** 16, 17

17. Number Sense Can the GCF of 24 and 40 be greater than 24? Explain.

B Reasoning and Problem Solving

18. A pet shop owner has received 36 parakeets and 20 cockatiels that will be put into cages with an equal number of birds in each cage. Each cage must contain all birds of the same type. What is the largest number of birds that could be put in each cage?

19. Reasoning If the greatest common factor of two numbers is 4 and each number is between 20 and 30, what are the two numbers?

20. **Writing in Math** What is the least common factor of any two nonzero whole numbers? Explain.

Mixed Review and Test Prep

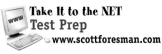
Take It to the NET
Test Prep
www.scottforesman.com

Find the missing number to make the fractions equivalent.

21. $\frac{8}{9} = \frac{\blacksquare}{72}$ **22.** $\frac{20}{32} = \frac{5}{\blacksquare}$ **23.** $\frac{\blacksquare}{5} = \frac{18}{45}$ **24.** $3\frac{2}{7} = 3\frac{10}{\blacksquare}$

25. **Writing in Math** Decide if the problem has extra or missing information. Explain. Solve if you have enough information.

Katrina buys 4 yards of ribbon that is $\frac{1}{2}$-inch wide. How much does she spend?

26. Which of the following is a prime number?

A. 47 **B.** 51 **C.** 85 **D.** 91

Fractions in Simplest Form

LEARN

How can you write a fraction in simplest form?

Floors, ceilings, and walls can be covered with tiles.

Todd and Martha are putting up 20 ceramic tiles. Of the 20 tiles, 12 are decorated. So, $\frac{12}{20}$ of the tiles are decorated. The picture also shows that $\frac{3}{5}$ are decorated.

A fraction is in **simplest form** if the numerator and denominator have no common factors other than 1.

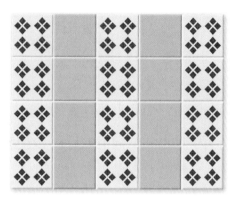

Example

Write $\frac{12}{20}$ in simplest form.

One Way
Divide by common factors until the only common factor is 1.

Since 12 and 20 are both even, divide both by 2.

$$\frac{12 \div 2}{20 \div 2} = \frac{6}{10}$$

But, both 6 and 10 can be divided by 2.

$$\frac{6 \div 2}{10 \div 2} = \frac{3}{5}$$

Another Way
Divide by the GCF.

Find the GCF:
12: 1, 2, 3, 4, 6, 12
20: 1, 2, 4, 5, 10, 20
The GCF of 12 and 20 is 4.

$$\frac{12 \div 4}{20 \div 4} = \frac{3}{5}$$

✓ **Talk About It**

1. Are $\frac{12}{20}$ and $\frac{3}{5}$ equivalent fractions? Explain.

2. How can you tell $\frac{3}{5}$ is in simplest form?

3. **Reasoning** Name two different fractions that are equivalent to $\frac{3}{4}$ when written in simplest form.

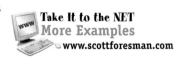

Take It to the NET
www More Examples
www.scottforesman.com

Write each fraction in simplest form.

1. $\frac{9}{21}$ **2.** $\frac{12}{30}$ **3.** $\frac{7}{42}$ **4.** $\frac{12}{54}$ **5.** $\frac{10}{14}$

6. Number Sense Explain how you can tell that $\frac{7}{8}$ is in simplest form.

PRACTICE

For more practice, see Set 7-10 on p. 456.

 Skills and Understanding

Write each fraction in simplest form.

7. $\frac{4}{8}$ **8.** $\frac{8}{10}$ **9.** $\frac{10}{20}$ **10.** $\frac{15}{25}$ **11.** $\frac{10}{50}$

12. $\frac{8}{32}$ **13.** $\frac{20}{30}$ **14.** $\frac{6}{54}$ **15.** $\frac{7}{42}$ **16.** $\frac{11}{33}$

17. $\frac{8}{22}$ **18.** $\frac{16}{18}$ **19.** $\frac{24}{40}$ **20.** $\frac{16}{24}$ **21.** $\frac{45}{72}$

22. $\frac{18}{20}$ **23.** $\frac{35}{100}$ **24.** $\frac{16}{48}$ **25.** $\frac{9}{12}$ **26.** $\frac{7}{21}$

27. Number Sense Explain how you can tell that $\frac{85}{90}$ is not in simplest form without finding all the factors of the numerator and denominator.

B **Reasoning and Problem Solving**

Math and Social Studies

What fraction of the states have these highest elevations? Give each fraction in simplest form.

28. over 10,000 ft

29. between 1,000 and 10,000 ft

30. **Writing in Math** Tracy said she knows $\frac{12}{17}$ is in simplest form because 17 is prime. Is she correct? Explain.

Data File

Highest Elevation	Number of States in the U.S.
Under 1,000 ft	5
1,000 to 10,000 ft	32
Over 10,000 ft	13

Mixed Review and Test Prep

Take It to the NET
Test Prep
www.scottforesman.com

Find the GCF of each pair of numbers.

31. 17, 22   **32.** 40, 100   **33.** 4, 10   **34.** 36, 42   **35.** 6, 27

36. Use the order of operations to evaluate $(12 + 36) \div (12 - 4)$.

     A. 0   **B.** 6   **C.** 8   **D.** 12

Key Idea
There are different ways to compare fractions.

Materials
• fraction strips or tools

Think It Through
I can **draw a picture** to show fraction strips.

Understanding Comparing Fractions

LEARN

Activity

How can you tell which fraction is greater?

WARM UP
Compare. Write >, <, or = for each ●.

1. 0.4 ● 0.7
2. 0.23 ● 0.2
3. 0.82 ● 0.78
4. 0.751 ● 0.715

a. Use fraction strips to show each pair of fractions. Decide which fraction is greater. Then write > or < for each ●.

Compare $\frac{3}{8}$ and $\frac{5}{8}$. ⟶ $\frac{3}{8}$ ● $\frac{5}{8}$

Compare $\frac{2}{3}$ and $\frac{1}{3}$. ⟶ $\frac{2}{3}$ ● $\frac{1}{3}$

Compare $\frac{7}{10}$ and $\frac{4}{10}$. ⟶ $\frac{7}{10}$ ● $\frac{4}{10}$

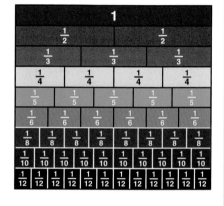

b. Describe a rule that tells how to compare two fractions with the same denominator.

c. Use fraction strips to show each pair of fractions. Decide which fraction is greater. Then write > or < for each ●.

Compare $\frac{1}{3}$ and $\frac{1}{2}$. ⟶ $\frac{1}{3}$ ● $\frac{1}{2}$

Compare $\frac{3}{8}$ and $\frac{3}{10}$. ⟶ $\frac{3}{8}$ ● $\frac{3}{10}$

Compare $\frac{5}{12}$ and $\frac{5}{8}$. ⟶ $\frac{5}{12}$ ● $\frac{5}{8}$

d. Describe a rule that tells how to compare two fractions with the same numerator.

e. Use the fraction strips to find four fractions equivalent to $\frac{1}{2}$. In every case, how is the denominator related to the numerator?

f. Write > or < for each ●. Use the first two comparisons to help you with the third one in each row.

$\frac{4}{10}$ ● $\frac{1}{2}$ ⟶ $\frac{1}{2}$ ● $\frac{5}{6}$ ⟶ $\frac{4}{10}$ ● $\frac{5}{6}$

$\frac{5}{8}$ ● $\frac{1}{2}$ ⟶ $\frac{1}{2}$ ● $\frac{3}{10}$ ⟶ $\frac{5}{8}$ ● $\frac{3}{10}$

$\frac{1}{3}$ ● $\frac{1}{2}$ ⟶ $\frac{1}{2}$ ● $\frac{3}{4}$ ⟶ $\frac{1}{3}$ ● $\frac{3}{4}$

g. Describe a rule that tells how to use $\frac{1}{2}$ to compare two fractions.

For another example, see Set 7-11 on p. 452.

Write >, <, or = for each ●. You may use fraction strips or drawings to help.

1. $\frac{2}{3}$ ● $\frac{2}{8}$ **2.** $\frac{7}{12}$ ● $\frac{5}{12}$ **3.** $\frac{1}{3}$ ● $\frac{6}{10}$ **4.** $\frac{9}{12}$ ● $\frac{3}{4}$

5. Reasoning Do you get the same amount of pizza when you eat $\frac{1}{4}$ of a medium pizza or $\frac{1}{4}$ of a large one? Explain.

PRACTICE

For more practice, see Set 7-11 on p. 456.

A **Skills and Understanding**

Write >, <, or = for each ●. You may use fraction strips or drawings to help.

6. $\frac{1}{6}$ ● $\frac{1}{8}$ **7.** $\frac{7}{10}$ ● $\frac{3}{10}$ **8.** $\frac{3}{8}$ ● $\frac{3}{4}$ **9.** $\frac{5}{12}$ ● $\frac{1}{2}$

10. $\frac{7}{12}$ ● $\frac{7}{10}$ **11.** $\frac{2}{3}$ ● $\frac{1}{6}$ **12.** $\frac{3}{4}$ ● $\frac{6}{8}$ **13.** $\frac{1}{2}$ ● $\frac{4}{6}$

14. $\frac{4}{12}$ ● $\frac{1}{3}$ **15.** $\frac{5}{8}$ ● $\frac{6}{8}$ **16.** $\frac{2}{10}$ ● $\frac{2}{3}$ **17.** $\frac{5}{6}$ ● $\frac{3}{10}$

18. Number Sense Explain how you can tell that $\frac{31}{64}$ is less than $\frac{1}{2}$.

B **Reasoning and Problem Solving**

Who ran farther:

19. Carrie or Karl?   **20.** Janie or Jordan?

21. Jordan or Jim?   **22.** Jim or Karl?

23. Algebra If $\frac{n}{18} < \frac{1}{2}$, what whole numbers could equal n?

24. <u>Writing in Math</u> Explain how you could decide if $\frac{15}{34}$ or $\frac{15}{28}$ is greater.

Name	Distance Ran
Carrie	$\frac{1}{2}$ mile
Karl	$\frac{2}{3}$ mile
Jim	$\frac{3}{8}$ mile
Janie	$\frac{9}{10}$ mile
Jordan	$\frac{3}{10}$ mile

Mixed Review and Test Prep

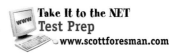

Take It to the NET
Test Prep
www.scottforesman.com

Write each fraction in simplest form.

25. $\frac{12}{16}$ **26.** $\frac{6}{9}$ **27.** $\frac{18}{32}$ **28.** $\frac{21}{28}$ **29.** $\frac{25}{75}$

Find the GCF of each pair of numbers.

30. 12, 34   **31.** 30, 32   **32.** 18, 31   **33.** 22, 33   **34.** 14, 100

35. Solve the equation $9x = 45$.

   A. $x = 5$ **B.** $x = 6$ **C.** $x = 36$ **D.** $x = 405$

Vocabulary
• common denominator

Comparing and Ordering Fractions and Mixed Numbers

✓ WARM UP
Find the missing number to make the fractions equivalent.

1. $\frac{1}{3} = \frac{\square}{27}$

2. $\frac{7}{28} = \frac{1}{\square}$

3. $\frac{18}{\square} = \frac{3}{5}$

LEARN

How can you compare and order fractions?

How can you compare $\frac{2}{6}$ and $\frac{2}{3}$? Here's what Lynda and Jason thought.

The numerators are the same. Each sixth is smaller than each third, so $\frac{2}{6} < \frac{2}{3}$.

I know $\frac{2}{6}$ is less than $\frac{1}{2}$ and $\frac{2}{3}$ is greater than $\frac{1}{2}$. So $\frac{2}{6} < \frac{2}{3}$.

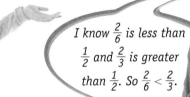

Fractions have a **common denominator** when their denominators are the same.

Example A

Compare $\frac{5}{8}$ and $\frac{4}{6}$. Find a common denominator to compare.

One Way

Find a common denominator.

8: 8, 16, ⃝24, 32, 40
6: 6, 12, 18, ⃝24, 30

Use 24 as the common denominator.

$$\frac{5}{8} \overset{\times 3}{=} \frac{15}{24} \qquad \frac{4}{6} \overset{\times 4}{=} \frac{16}{24}$$

$\frac{15}{24} < \frac{16}{24}$, so $\frac{5}{8} < \frac{4}{6}$.

Another Way

Multiply the denominators.

$$8 \times 6 = 48$$

Use 48 as the common denominator.

$$\frac{5}{8} \overset{\times 6}{=} \frac{30}{48} \qquad \frac{4}{6} \overset{\times 8}{=} \frac{32}{48}$$

$\frac{30}{48} < \frac{32}{48}$, so $\frac{5}{8} < \frac{4}{6}$.

Write $\frac{1}{9}$, $\frac{2}{9}$, $\frac{1}{12}$, and $\frac{1}{3}$ in order from least to greatest.

$\frac{1}{12} < \frac{1}{9}$ because the numerators are the same and 12 > 9.

$\frac{1}{9} < \frac{2}{9}$ because the denominators are the same and 1 < 2.

$\frac{2}{9} < \frac{1}{3}$ because $\overset{\times 3}{\frac{1}{3}} = \frac{3}{9}$ and $\frac{2}{9} < \frac{3}{9}$.

So, $\frac{1}{12} < \frac{1}{9} < \frac{2}{9} < \frac{1}{3}$.

✔ Talk About It

1. How did Lynda and Jason compare $\frac{2}{6}$ and $\frac{2}{3}$?

2. Explain how you could use a common denominator to compare $\frac{2}{6}$ and $\frac{2}{3}$.

3. If you know $\frac{2}{9} > \frac{1}{12}$, does that mean $\frac{1}{12} < \frac{2}{9}$?

How can you compare and order mixed numbers?

Example C

Write $1\frac{1}{4}$, $1\frac{1}{6}$, and $2\frac{1}{8}$ in order from least to greatest.

STEP 1	STEP 2	STEP 3
Compare the whole number parts first.	When the whole numbers are the same, compare the fraction parts.	Write the mixed numbers in order.
$1 < 2$	$\frac{1}{6} < \frac{1}{4}$	$1\frac{1}{6} < 1\frac{1}{4} < 2\frac{1}{8}$
So, $1\frac{1}{4} < 2\frac{1}{8}$.	So, $1\frac{1}{6} < 1\frac{1}{4}$.	
Also, $1\frac{1}{6} < 2\frac{1}{8}$.		

✔ Talk About It

4. Do you need to change $\frac{1}{4}$ to $\frac{2}{8}$ to compare $1\frac{1}{4}$ and $2\frac{1}{8}$? Explain.

5. Keisha said $\frac{1}{6} < \frac{1}{4}$ because something with 6 equal pieces has smaller pieces than something the same size with 4 equal pieces. Is she correct?

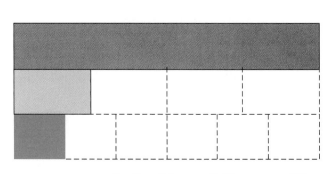

Compare. Write >, <, or = for each ◯.

1. $\frac{3}{7}$ ◯ $\frac{3}{10}$ **2.** $\frac{5}{6}$ ◯ $\frac{3}{4}$ **3.** $1\frac{1}{6}$ ◯ $1\frac{4}{15}$ **4.** $2\frac{1}{3}$ ◯ $2\frac{4}{6}$

Order the numbers from least to greatest.

5. $\frac{2}{3}, \frac{1}{5}, \frac{1}{4}, \frac{3}{10}$ **6.** $\frac{3}{4}, \frac{5}{12}, \frac{1}{3}, \frac{3}{8}$ **7.** $3\frac{5}{6}, 2\frac{2}{3}, 2\frac{2}{9}$

8. Number Sense Explain why $7\frac{12}{17} < 10\frac{3}{19}$.

PRACTICE

For more practice, see Set 7-12 on p. 456.

Ⓐ Skills and Understanding

Compare. Write >, <, or = for each ◯.

9. $\frac{4}{5}$ ◯ $\frac{3}{4}$ **10.** $\frac{7}{8}$ ◯ $\frac{5}{6}$ **11.** $2\frac{1}{4}$ ◯ $2\frac{2}{12}$ **12.** $\frac{4}{20}$ ◯ $\frac{2}{10}$

13. $\frac{2}{3}$ ◯ $\frac{13}{18}$ **14.** $\frac{1}{5}$ ◯ $\frac{2}{7}$ **15.** $\frac{14}{15}$ ◯ $\frac{9}{10}$ **16.** $3\frac{5}{8}$ ◯ $3\frac{2}{3}$

Order the numbers from the least to greatest.

17. $\frac{2}{3}, \frac{7}{12}, \frac{7}{9}, \frac{3}{4}$ **18.** $2\frac{4}{9}, 2\frac{3}{10}, 1\frac{3}{5}$ **19.** $\frac{1}{2}, \frac{7}{10}, \frac{3}{8}, 1$

20. $3\frac{4}{33}, 3\frac{6}{11}, 2\frac{1}{2}$ **21.** $\frac{3}{4}, \frac{1}{6}, \frac{2}{9}, \frac{13}{20}$ **22.** $\frac{5}{6}, \frac{1}{4}, \frac{5}{9}, \frac{1}{8}$

23. Number Sense Explain why $\frac{7}{18} > \frac{7}{20}$.

Ⓑ Reasoning and Problem Solving

☀ Math and Everyday Life

Carpenters often use objects such as bolts and drill bits. Both types of objects are commonly labeled with their diameters in fractions of an inch.

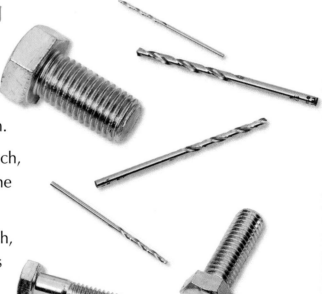

24. A carpenter has 5 different sizes of bolts: $\frac{3}{8}$ inch, $\frac{1}{4}$ inch, $\frac{5}{16}$ inch, $\frac{3}{4}$ inch, and $\frac{1}{2}$ inch. Order the sizes from least to greatest.

25. The carpenter has 5 drill bits: $\frac{7}{64}$ inch, $\frac{1}{16}$ inch, $\frac{1}{8}$ inch, $\frac{1}{32}$ inch, and $\frac{3}{32}$ inch. Order the sizes from least to greatest.

26. 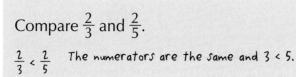 **Writing in Math** Is the explanation below correct? If not, tell why and write a correct response.

> Compare $\frac{2}{3}$ and $\frac{2}{5}$.
>
> $\frac{2}{3} < \frac{2}{5}$ The numerators are the same and $3 < 5$.

Think It Through

I can **use logical reasoning** to solve a problem.

C Extensions

Compare. Write > or < for each ⬤.

27. $\frac{7}{8}$ ⬤ $\frac{5}{6}$ **28.** $\frac{11}{12}$ ⬤ $\frac{8}{9}$ **29.** $\frac{14}{15}$ ⬤ $\frac{9}{10}$ **30.** $\frac{2}{3}$ ⬤ $\frac{6}{7}$

31. In 27–30, what pattern do you notice about the numerator and denominator for each fraction? Describe a rule you could use to compare two fractions when the numerator of each is one less than its denominator.

Mixed Review and Test Prep

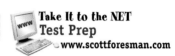

Take It to the NET
Test Prep
www.scottforesman.com

Write >, <, or = for each ⬤. You may use fraction strips or drawings to help.

32. $\frac{7}{10}$ ⬤ $\frac{1}{2}$ **33.** $\frac{2}{3}$ ⬤ $\frac{1}{10}$ **34.** $\frac{3}{4}$ ⬤ $\frac{3}{6}$ **35.** $\frac{5}{12}$ ⬤ $\frac{6}{8}$

36. Which of the following fractions is in simplest form?

A. $\frac{15}{25}$ **B.** $\frac{16}{20}$ **C.** $\frac{7}{18}$ **D.** $\frac{14}{21}$

Practice Game

Race to 1

Players: 2–3
Materials: Race to 1 Game Board; 7 markers; Fraction Cards, Set A

Mix and then place the cards facedown. Place a marker in the first cell of each row of the game board. Players take turns drawing the top card and moving one or more markers to the amount shown on the card. For example, if the card with fraction $\frac{3}{8}$ is drawn, the player may move a marker 3 places in the eighths row or 1 place in the fourths row and 1 place in the eighths row. A player who completes a row exactly keeps the marker. If a player cannot determine a play, the turn is lost. The game continues until all of the rows have been completed. The winner is the player who collects the most markers.

Do You Know How?

Do You Understand?

Understanding Equivalent Fractions (7-7), Equivalent Fractions (7-8)

Write two fractions that name each point on the number line.

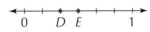

1. Point D **2.** Point E

Find the missing number to make the fractions equivalent.

3. $\dfrac{\blacksquare}{9} = \dfrac{3}{27}$ **4.** $\dfrac{7}{8} = \dfrac{49}{\blacksquare}$

5. $\dfrac{\blacksquare}{5} = \dfrac{9}{15}$ **6.** $\dfrac{5}{12} = \dfrac{\blacksquare}{36}$

A Tell how you found each equivalent fraction in Exercise 3 and 4.

B Explain how you decided whether to multiply or divide.

Greatest Common Factor (7-9), Fractions in Simplest Form (7-10)

7. Find the GCF of 14 and 42.

Write each fraction in simplest form.

8. $\dfrac{12}{36}$ **9.** $\dfrac{6}{16}$

10. $\dfrac{25}{70}$ **11.** $\dfrac{8}{10}$

12. $\dfrac{25}{50}$ **13.** $\dfrac{15}{45}$

C Tell how you could find the GCF of 6 and 16 and use it to put $\dfrac{6}{16}$ in simplest form.

D Explain how you can tell that $\dfrac{2}{11}$ is in simplest form.

**Understanding Comparing Fractions (7-11),
Comparing and Ordering Fractions and Mixed Numbers (7-12)**

Compare. Write >, <, or = for each ◯.

14. $\dfrac{8}{13}$ ◯ $\dfrac{3}{13}$ **15.** $\dfrac{3}{8}$ ◯ $\dfrac{4}{5}$

16. $\dfrac{9}{17}$ ◯ $\dfrac{9}{23}$ **17.** $\dfrac{2}{3}$ ◯ $\dfrac{5}{6}$

18. $2\dfrac{7}{9}$ ◯ $2\dfrac{3}{4}$ **19.** $3\dfrac{2}{7}$ ◯ $3\dfrac{3}{10}$

20. $3\dfrac{1}{4}$ ◯ $3\dfrac{1}{8}$ **21.** $5\dfrac{4}{10}$ ◯ $5\dfrac{2}{5}$

E Tell how you compared the fractions in Exercise 16.

F Explain how the fraction $\dfrac{1}{2}$ can help you compare two fractions.

MULTIPLE CHOICE

1. Which are two equivalent fractions that name the shaded part? (7-7)

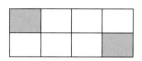

   A. $\frac{1}{2}, \frac{4}{8}$ **B.** $\frac{1}{4}, \frac{2}{8}$ **C.** $\frac{2}{8}, \frac{1}{2}$ **D.** $\frac{2}{8}, \frac{2}{10}$

Think It Through
For multiple-choice questions, **eliminate wrong answers.**

2. Which list shows $3\frac{5}{18}$, $\frac{19}{6}$, and $3\frac{7}{9}$ in order from least to greatest? (7-12)

   A. $\frac{19}{6}, 3\frac{7}{9}, 3\frac{5}{18}$ **B.** $3\frac{7}{9}, 3\frac{5}{18}, \frac{19}{6}$ **C.** $3\frac{5}{18}, \frac{19}{6}, 3\frac{7}{9}$ **D.** $\frac{19}{6}, 3\frac{5}{18}, 3\frac{7}{9}$

SHORT RESPONSE

Find the missing number to make the fractions equivalent. (7-8)

3. $\frac{4}{\blacksquare} = \frac{32}{40}$ 4. $2\frac{5}{7} = 2\frac{\blacksquare}{42}$ 5. $3\frac{18}{\blacksquare} = 3\frac{3}{4}$ 6. $\frac{18}{54} = \frac{\blacksquare}{9}$

Find the GCF of each pair of numbers. (7-9)

7. 15, 18   8. 5, 9   9. 27, 72   10. 36, 100

Write each fraction in simplest form. (7-10)

11. $\frac{8}{20}$ 12. $\frac{14}{63}$ 13. $\frac{21}{24}$ 14. $\frac{6}{22}$

Compare. Write >, <, or = for each ●. (7-11, 7-12)

15. $\frac{6}{7}$ ● $\frac{6}{11}$ 16. $\frac{11}{20}$ ● $\frac{5}{12}$ 17. $\frac{6}{7}$ ● $\frac{8}{9}$ 18. $4\frac{3}{7}$ ● $4\frac{2}{5}$

Use the table at the right for 19–20. (7-11, 7-12)

19. Which piece of fabric is shorter, the blue or the white?

20. Order the lengths of fabric from the least to the greatest.

Yards of Fabric

Color	Yards
Blue	$2\frac{2}{3}$
Green	$2\frac{1}{2}$
Red	$2\frac{3}{4}$
White	$2\frac{4}{9}$
Yellow	$\frac{1}{6}$

Writing in Math

21. Explain why the GCF of 8 and 9 is 1. (7-9)

22. How do you decide whether $\frac{15}{40}$ is in simplest form? (7-10)

Think It Through
• I can write many equivalent fractions for any fraction.
• I can look for equivalent fractions that have a denominator such as 10, 100, or 1,000.

Fractions and Decimals

LEARN

How can you write a fraction as a decimal?

About $\frac{6}{10}$ of the world's population live in Asia, and $\frac{13}{100}$ live in Africa. Fractions with denominators like 10 or 100 can easily be written as decimals.

Sometimes the word name for a fraction and place value are helpful.

$$\frac{6}{10} = 0.6 \qquad \frac{13}{100} = 0.13$$

Example A

Write $\frac{17}{1,000}$ as a decimal.

The word name for $\frac{17}{1,000}$ is seventeen thousandths.

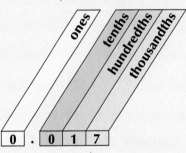

So, $\frac{17}{1,000} = 0.017$.

Many fractions do not have a denominator such as 10, 100, or 1,000, but can easily be written as an equivalent fraction with such a denominator.

Example B

Write $\frac{4}{5}$ as a decimal.

$$\frac{4}{5} = \frac{4 \times 2}{5 \times 2} = \frac{8}{10} = 0.8$$

Example C

Write $\frac{3}{20}$ as a decimal.

$$\frac{3}{20} = \frac{3 \times 5}{20 \times 5} = \frac{15}{100} = 0.15$$

✔ **Talk About It**

1. In Example A, how do you know $\frac{17}{1,000}$ is 0.017 and not 0.17?

2. In Example B, could you multiply both the numerator and denominator by 20 instead of 2 to change the fraction to a decimal? What decimal would you get?

How can you use division to change a fraction to a decimal?

Remember that $\frac{4}{5}$ means $4 \div 5$. So, you could also use division to change $\frac{4}{5}$ to a decimal.

Example D

Write $\frac{4}{5}$ as a decimal.

$\frac{4}{5} = 4 \div 5$

$$5\overline{)4.0} \quad \begin{array}{r} 0.8 \\ \hline 4.0 \\ -4\,0 \\ \hline 0 \end{array}$$

Insert a decimal point after 4 and write zeros as needed.

So, $\frac{4}{5} = 0.8$.

Example E

Write $\frac{3}{4}$ as a decimal.

$\frac{3}{4} = 3 \div 4$

$$\begin{array}{r} 0.75 \\ 4\overline{)3.00} \\ -2\,8 \\ \hline 20 \\ -20 \\ \hline 0 \end{array}$$

Insert a decimal point after 3 and write zeros as needed.

So, $\frac{3}{4} = 0.75$.

✔ Talk About It

3. How would you check your answers in Examples D and E?

4. Why were the zeros written in each dividend when dividing?

5. **Reasoning** If $\frac{40}{5} = 8$ and $\frac{4}{5} = 0.8$, predict the decimal equivalent for $\frac{4}{50}$. Use division to check your answer.

It is helpful to remember decimal equivalents for the following benchmark fractions.

$\frac{1}{4} = 0.25$

$\frac{1}{2} = 0.5$

$\frac{3}{4} = 0.75$

CHECK ✔

For another example, see Set 7-13 on p. 453.

Write a decimal and a fraction in simplest form for the shaded portion of each model.

1.

2.

3.

In 4–5, write each decimal as a fraction or mixed number in simplest form.
In 6–7, write each fraction or mixed number as a decimal.

4. 0.4   5. 3.08   6. $\frac{9}{30}$ 7. $2\frac{3}{20}$

8. **Number Sense** How are the fractions that are equivalent to 0.4 and 0.04 alike, and how are they different?

Ⓐ Skills and Understanding

Write a decimal and a fraction in simplest form for the shaded portion of each model.

9.  **10.**   **11.**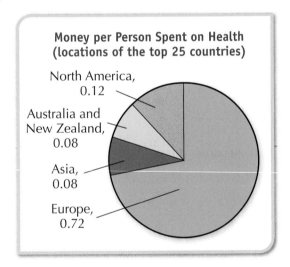

Write each decimal as a fraction or mixed number in simplest form.

12. 0.75   **13.** 0.45   **14.** 1.875   **15.** 8.54   **16.** 0.95

Write each fraction or mixed number as a decimal.

17. $\frac{7}{20}$ **18.** $\frac{1}{10}$ **19.** $5\frac{1}{8}$ **20.** $4\frac{1}{2}$ **21.** $8\frac{7}{10}$

22. Number Sense Use fractions to show why 0.9 = 0.90.

Ⓑ Reasoning and Problem Solving

Math and Social Studies

The circle graph shows where the 25 countries are located that spend the most per person on health.

What fraction of the countries are in

23. North America?

24. Europe?

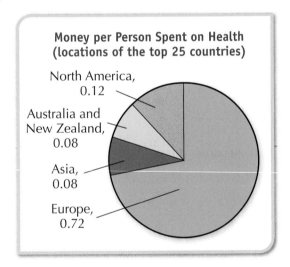

Money per Person Spent on Health (locations of the top 25 countries)
North America, 0.12
Australia and New Zealand, 0.08
Asia, 0.08
Europe, 0.72

25. **Writing in Math** Is the explanation below correct? If not, tell why and write a correct response.

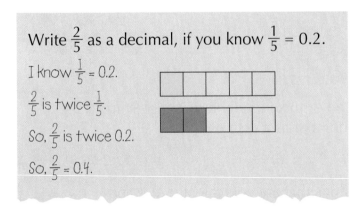

Write $\frac{2}{5}$ as a decimal, if you know $\frac{1}{5} = 0.2$.

I know $\frac{1}{5} = 0.2$.

$\frac{2}{5}$ is twice $\frac{1}{5}$.

So, $\frac{2}{5}$ is twice 0.2.

So, $\frac{2}{5} = 0.4$.

Think It Through
I can **use logical reasoning.**

C Extensions

When you change some fractions to decimals, you could keep dividing forever. You can write these fractions as rounded decimals. For example, to write $\frac{1}{3}$ as a decimal to the nearest hundredth, divide until you get the digit in the thousandths place. Then use this to round to the nearest hundredth.

$$
\begin{array}{r}
0.333 \\
3\overline{)1.000} \\
-9 \\
\hline
10 \\
-9 \\
\hline
10 \\
-9 \\
\hline
1
\end{array}
$$

So, $\frac{1}{3} \approx 0.33$.

$\approx$ means "is about equal to."

Write each fraction as a decimal to the nearest hundredth.

26. $\frac{2}{3}$ **27.** $\frac{4}{9}$ **28.** $\frac{5}{6}$ **29.** $\frac{1}{12}$

Mixed Review and Test Prep

Take It to the NET
Test Prep
www.scottforesman.com

What fraction or mixed number should be written at each point?

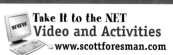

0   A   1   B   C   2

30. Point A   **31.** Point B   **32.** Point C

33. Which of the following equals $2\frac{4}{7}$?

    A. $\frac{7}{18}$ **B.** $\frac{7}{17}$ **C.** $\frac{17}{7}$ **D.** $\frac{18}{7}$

Discovery CHANNEL SCHOOL

Discover Math in Your World

Take It to the NET
Video and Activities
www.scottforesman.com

The Long and Short of It

Grand pianos come in a variety of lengths from $4\frac{1}{2}$ feet long to $9\frac{1}{2}$ feet long. To celebrate the 300th anniversary of the invention of the piano, a famous piano company created a piano that is 6 feet 2 inches long ($6\frac{1}{6}$ feet).

1. Write the length of the longest and shortest grand pianos as decimals.

2. For the piano that was created to celebrate the 300th anniversary, write the length as a decimal rounded to the nearest hundredth.

Key Idea
A point on a number line can represent a number that has both a fraction and a decimal name.

TEST TALK

Think It Through
I know that any fraction can be written as a decimal.

Fractions and Decimals on the Number Line

LEARN

How can you locate fractions and decimals on the same number line?

Rachel skated $\frac{7}{8}$ mile, Ayla skated 1.4 miles, and Tom skated $1\frac{1}{4}$ miles. Who skated the farthest?

WARM UP

Draw a number line to show each set of numbers. Then order the numbers from least to greatest.

1. 0.6, 0.74, 0.83

2. $1\frac{3}{5}$, $1\frac{1}{5}$, $\frac{4}{5}$

Example A

Show $\frac{7}{8}$, 1.4, and $1\frac{1}{4}$ on the same number line.

STEP 1

Write each fraction or mixed number as a decimal.

$\frac{7}{8} = 7 \div 8$

$= 0.875$

$$\begin{array}{r} 0.875 \\ 8\overline{)7.000} \\ -\ 6\ 4 \\ \hline 60 \\ -\ 56 \\ \hline 40 \\ -\ 40 \\ \hline 0 \end{array}$$

Since $\frac{1}{4} = 0.25$, $1\frac{1}{4} = 1.25$.

STEP 2

Place the numbers on the number line.

The point for $\frac{7}{8}$ or 0.875 is between 0.8 and 0.9.

The point for 1.25 is between 1.2 and 1.3.

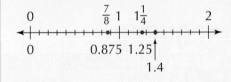

Since 1.4 is farthest to the right on the number line, Ayla skated the farthest.

Example B

Write a fraction or mixed number in simplest form and a decimal that name point *A*.

The number line is separated into fifths. Point *A* is at $1\frac{3}{5}$, and $\frac{3}{5}$ can be changed to 0.6 by dividing. So, $1\frac{3}{5} = 1 + 0.6 = 1.6$.

✔ **Talk About It**

1. In Example A, do $1\frac{1}{4}$ and 1.25 name the same point?

Show each set of numbers on the same number line.
Then order the numbers from least to greatest.

1. 0.6, $\frac{4}{5}$, $\frac{3}{10}$, $\frac{72}{100}$

2. $2\frac{4}{20}$, 0.95, $\frac{18}{20}$, 1.375

3. $1\frac{1}{20}$, 0.7, $1\frac{9}{20}$, 0.625

4. Write a mixed number in simplest form and a decimal that name point M.

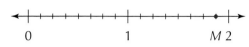

5. Number Sense Is 2.6 to the right or the left of $2\frac{1}{2}$ on a number line? Explain.

PRACTICE

For more practice, see Set 7-14 on p. 457.

Ⓐ Skills and Understanding

Show each set of numbers on the same number line.
Then order the numbers from least to greatest.

6. 0.7, $\frac{3}{5}$, $\frac{9}{12}$, $\frac{5}{8}$

7. 2.15, $\frac{1}{8}$, $1\frac{8}{25}$, $1\frac{7}{20}$

8. $\frac{30}{100}$, 1.55, $\frac{18}{50}$, $1\frac{8}{25}$

Write a fraction or mixed number in simplest form and a decimal that name each point.

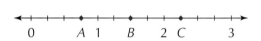

9. Point A

10. Point B

11. Point C

12. Number Sense A number line is labeled by tenths including 1.1, 1.2, 1.3, and 1.4. Between which two points should you place $1\frac{1}{8} = 1.125$?

Ⓑ Reasoning and Problem Solving

13. George has $1\frac{3}{4}$ pounds of apples, 1.8 pounds of peaches, and $1\frac{5}{8}$ pounds of oranges. Show these amounts on a number line. George has the most (by weight) of which fruit?

14. **Writing in Math** Write a mixed number in simplest form and a decimal that names point A. Explain your answer.

Take It to the NET
Test Prep
www.scottforesman.com

Mixed Review and Test Prep

15. Write 3.36 as a mixed number in simplest form.

16. Find $97.68 ÷ 6.

A. $11.28

B. $16.28

C. $16.38

D. $1628

Draw Conclusions

Drawing conclusions when you read in math can help you use the **problem-solving strategy, *Use Logical Reasoning,*** in the next lesson.

In reading, drawing conclusions can help you make sense of things as you think through a story. In math, drawing conclusions can help you use logical reasoning as you think through a problem.

Brett, Lucy, Dina, and Antonio are using red, blue, orange, and green markers. Each person is using a different color. Lucy does not have the blue marker. The color of Antonio's marker begins with the letter "g." Brett is using red. What color marker does each person have?

First I'll make a chart to record the given information.

To fill in the rest of the chart, look at each column and row and <u>draw conclusions</u>.

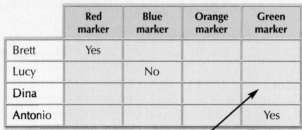

	Red marker	Blue marker	Orange marker	Green marker
Brett	Yes			
Lucy		No		
Dina				
Antonio				Yes

If there is a *Yes,* then you can conclude that the other cells in that row and column have to be *No.*

Continue to <u>use logical reasoning</u> to complete all the cells and solve the problem.

1. How can you draw the conclusion that Dina has the blue marker?

2. In each row and column of the completed chart, how many cells should say *Yes?*

For 3–5, use the problem below.

Josefa, Melissa, Sandy, and Rebecca are lining up. Rebecca is second in line. Sandy is in front of Rebecca. Josefa is not last in line. What is the order of the girls in line?

	First in Line	Second in Line	Third in Line	Fourth in Line
Josefa				No
Melissa				
Sandy	Yes			
Rebecca		Yes		

3. Why can you draw the conclusion that Sandy is not third in line?

4. Why can you draw the conclusion that Melissa is not first in line?

5. **Writing in Math** Could Melissa be fourth in line? Why or why not?

For 6–7, use the problem below.

Suzanne, Marty, Elizabeth, and Jason are using different sports equipment. Each person is using either a bat and ball, a jump rope, a hockey stick and puck, or a badminton racket and birdie. Marty is using the jump rope. Jason is not using the badminton racket and birdie. Suzanne is not using the bat and ball or the badminton racket and birdie. What equipment is each person using?

	Bat and ball	Jump rope	Hockey stick and puck	Badminton racket and birdie
Suzanne	No			No
Marty		Yes		
Elizabeth				
Jason				No

6. Why can you draw the conclusion that Suzanne is not using the jump rope?

7. **Writing in Math** Could Elizabeth be using the hockey puck and stick? Why or why not?

Problem-Solving Strategy

Reading Helps!

Drawing conclusions
can help you with...

the problem-solving strategy,
Use Logical Reasoning.

Use Logical Reasoning

LEARN

How do you use the logical reasoning strategy?

Volunteer Work Barry, Brenda, Burt, and Babette each volunteered for a different job. The jobs were clothes donations, can recycling, newspaper recycling, and food donations. Neither girl volunteered for newspapers. What did Brenda and Barry do when Burt worked at can recycling and Babette was at the clothes donations?

Read and Understand

What do you know? Four students each worked at different jobs. You know the students' names and jobs.

What are you trying to find? Find which job each student had.

Plan and Solve

What strategy will you use?

Strategy: Use logical reasoning.

	Clothes donations	Can recycling	Newspaper recycling	Food donations
Barry				
Brenda			No	
Burt		Yes		
Babette	Yes		No	

How to Make a Chart

Step 1: Make a chart with the needed labels.

Step 2: Fill in the chart with information given.

Step 3: Use what you are given and reasoning to make conclusions.

If there is a Yes, then all the other cells in that row and column have to be No.

	Clothes donations	Can recycling	Newspaper recycling	Food donations
Barry	No	No		
Brenda	No	No	No	
Burt	No	Yes	No	No
Babette	Yes	No	No	No

If Brenda has a No in three locations, then she has to be at food donations. Then Barry has to be at newspaper recycling.

Answer: Barry–newspaper; Brenda–food recycling; Burt–can recycling; Babette–clothes donations

Look Back and Check

Is your work reasonable? Yes, I filled in the information I was given. I made the right conclusions.

✔ Talk About It

1. In the Volunteer Work Problem, how did you decide that Brenda was at food donations and Barry was at newspaper recycling?

2. When a Yes is placed in a particular cell, what gets placed in the other cells in that row and in that column? Why?

3. Why does using a chart make it easier to use logical reasoning?

When might you use the logical reasoning strategy?

Musical Instruments Nancy, Martha, Steve, and Randy each play a different instrument. The instruments they play, not necessarily in this order, are trumpet, flute, clarinet, and trombone. Randy is playing the trumpet, and Martha is not playing the trombone. If Steve is playing the clarinet, what instrument is each playing?

When to Use Logical Reasoning

Think about using logical reasoning when:
- You are given several people or categories that are matched using given rules, and
- You can use known facts to reason out unknown facts.

First fill in what you know.

	trumpet	flute	clarinet	trombone
Nancy				
Martha				No
Steve			Yes	
Randy	Yes			

Then complete the chart.

	trumpet	flute	clarinet	trombone
Nancy	No	No	No	Yes
Martha	No	Yes	No	No
Steve	No	No	Yes	No
Randy	Yes	No	No	No

✔ Talk About It

4. What facts were you given in the problem that can be filled in on the chart to start?

5. How did you know that Nancy played the trombone?

CHECK ✓

For another example, see Set 7-15 on p. 453.

Use the chart and logical reasoning to finish solving the problem.

1. Heather, Mackenzie, Zach, and Paul participate in either swimming, tennis, baseball, or hockey. Mackenzie plays tennis. Heather cannot swim. If Zach plays baseball, in what sport does each participate?

	swimming	tennis	baseball	hockey
Heather	No			
Mackenzie		Yes		
Zach			Yes	
Paul				

A Using the Strategy

Use the chart and logical reasoning to finish solving each problem.

2. Chris, Todd, Becky, and Lee Ann work for a builder. One is a painter, one is a plumber, one is a carpenter, and one is an electrician. Chris and Todd will not paint. The carpenter's first name begins with L. Chris is not the electrician. Who has each job?

	painter	plumber	carpenter	electrician
Chris	No			No
Todd	No			
Becky				
Lee Ann			Yes	

3. Ally, Mia, and Lucia live in either Biloxi, Miami, or Dallas. Mia does not live in Texas. Lucia does not live in Florida. Ally lives in Mississippi. In what city does each live?

	Biloxi	Miami	Dallas
Ally			
Mia			
Lucia			

4. Paula, Nancy, and Ricki like either math, history, or art best. Ricki dislikes art. Nancy knows the students who like art and math best. Which student liked each subject best?

	math	history	art
Paula			
Nancy			
Ricki			

5. Mark, Ian, Tia, and Jill visited either Canada, Mexico, France or China. Mark has never been to Asia or Europe. He knows the person who visited Canada. Jill has not visited Canada or France. Ian has not been to France. Who visited each country?

	Canada	Mexico	France	China
Mark				
Ian				
Tia				
Jill				

Math and Everyday Life

Detectives often use logical reasoning to solve crimes. At a crime scene, a detective found four suspects—the butler, the gardener, the driver, and the cook. The names of the suspects were Al, Betty, Clare, and Dino.

6. Through detective work, a detective found that Dino could not drive, and Al and Dino did not know where the gardening tools were kept. Clare did not realize that her uniform was splashed with cooking grease. Who was the butler?

	butler	gardener	driver	cook
Al				
Betty				
Clare				
Dino				

B Mixed Strategy Practice

Solve each problem.

7. Kurt bought two items costing a total of $100. One item cost $10 more than the other. What was the cost of each item?

8. What is the sum of the angle measures for a hexagon? (HINT: The sum of the angle measures of a triangle is 180°.)

9. Nicole is buying two new sweaters. Four colors are available—white, black, red, and blue. How many two-color combinations can she pick?

10. Jane and Ellen are joggers. They recorded the number of miles they jogged each week for five weeks. Which person improved more?

Jane

Week 1	Week 2	Week 3	Week 4	Week 5
2	3	5	7	10

Ellen

Week 1	Week 2	Week 3	Week 4	Week 5
5	6	5	7	6

11. <u>Writing in Math</u> In using logical reasoning to solve a problem, Manuel always sets up a chart. When he sees a *Yes* in one cell, how can that help him in writing *Yes* or *No* in other cells?

STRATEGIES

- **Show What You Know**
  Draw a Picture
  Make an Organized List
  Make a Table
  Make a Graph
  Act It Out or Use Objects
- **Look for a Pattern**
- **Try, Check, and Revise**
- **Write an Equation**
- **Use Logical Reasoning**
- **Solve a Simpler Problem**
- **Work Backward**

Choose a tool

Mental Math

TEST TALK

Think It Through

Stuck? I won't give up. I can:
- Reread the problem.
- Tell what I know.
- Identify key facts and details.
- Tell the problem in my own words.
- Show the main idea.
- Try a different strategy.
- Retrace my steps.

Mixed Review and Test Prep

Take It to the NET
Test Prep
www.scottforesman.com

Write a fraction or mixed number in simplest form for each labeled point on the number line.

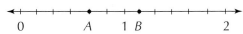

12. Point *A*   **13.** Point *B*

14. What decimal names $1\frac{7}{20}$?

15. What is the greatest common factor of 32 and 48?

A. 2   **B.** 4   **C.** 8   **D.** 16

Problem-Solving Applications

Extreme Machines The pursuit of speed has driven people to create extreme machines in many shapes and sizes. Their vehicles range from the supersonic car Thrust SSC down to modified lawnmowers!

Trivia The fastest humans did not travel in a car, boat, or plane. They traveled in the space capsule of Apollo 10. On their way from the moon, they sped through space at 24,791 miles per hour!

❶ Is there a line of symmetry in the shape of the Le Mans car shown on the left? In the Thrust SSC shown above?

Using Key Facts

❷ Order the vehicles in the Key Facts chart from the slowest to the fastest.

❸ Drag bikes race for only $\frac{1}{4}$ mile but they need about $\frac{1}{2}$ mile to stop! Draw a diagram of a 1-mile racetrack. Show the distance that the bikes race and the distance they need to stop.

Key Facts Fastest Speeds in 2002	
Vehicle	**Speed**
•Car	763 mph
•Helicopter	249 mph
•Ice sled	248 mph
•Levitating train	343 mph
•Motorcycle	322 mph
•Truck	407 mph

4 Some powerboats can accelerate from 0 to 100 miles per hour in about 12 seconds. What fraction of a minute is that time? Write your answer in simplest form.

5 In 2002, the world's fastest truck was a jet-powered fire truck. It roared down a track at 407 miles per hour. That year, the fastest boat could skim the water at about 0.78 times the truck's speed. How fast was the world's speediest boat? Round your answer to the nearest tenth.

6 Decision Making Choose three vehicles from the Key Facts chart that you woud like to see or ride. What type of graph would be best to compare the speeds of these vehicles? Make the graph of your choice.

7 Writing in Math Write your own word problem that uses information from this lesson. Write the answer to your problem in a complete sentence.

Good News/Bad News *Driving extreme machines may by thrilling, but controlling them at high speeds takes a lot of strength, knowledge, and daring.*

Do You Know How?

Do You Understand?

Fractions and Decimals (7-13)

Write a decimal and a fraction in simplest form for the shaded part.

1.

2.

Write each decimal as a fraction or mixed number in simplest form.

3. 0.28   —   **4.** 1.8

Write each as a decimal.

5. $4\frac{1}{25}$

6. $\frac{9}{20}$

Ⓐ Tell how you found each decimal and fraction in Exercises 1 and 2.

Ⓑ Explain how you found the fraction in Exercise 3.

Fractions and Decimals on the Number Line (7-14)

Write a fraction or mixed number in simplest form and a decimal that name each point.

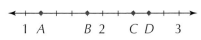

7. Point *C*   **8.** Point *B*

9. Point *D*   **10.** Point *A*

Ⓒ Tell how you found each decimal.

Ⓓ Explain how the number line shows that 1.2 < 1.8.

Problem-Solving Strategy: Use Logical Reasoning (7-15, 7-16)

Use the chart and logical reasoning to solve the problem.

11. Bob, Sue, and Matt take either piano, golf, or ballet lessons. Sue cannot read music. Neither Sue nor Matt like to dance. Who takes piano?

	piano	golf	ballet
Bob			
Sue	No		
Matt			

Ⓔ Tell what you know. Identify the key facts and details. What are you trying to find?

Ⓕ Explain how you solved the problem.

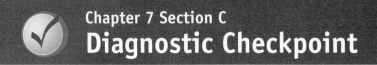
MULTIPLE CHOICE

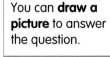

1. On a number line, which decimal would you put between $\frac{2}{5}$ and $\frac{35}{50}$? (7-14)

You can **draw a picture** to answer the question.

   A. 0.2   **B.** 0.32   **C.** 0.625   **D.** 0.71

2. Which shows 6.08 as a mixed number in simplest form? (7-13)

   A. $\frac{2}{25}$ **B.** $6\frac{8}{100}$ **C.** $6\frac{4}{5}$ **D.** $6\frac{2}{25}$

FREE RESPONSE

Write a decimal and a fraction in simplest form for the shaded portion of each model. (7-13)

3.   **4.**   **5.**

Write each decimal as a fraction or mixed number in simplest form. (7-13)

6. 0.5   **7.** 7.125   **8.** 1.24   **9.** 0.46

Write each fraction or mixed number as a decimal. (7-13)

10. $\frac{8}{25}$ **11.** $4\frac{9}{10}$ **12.** $\frac{3}{8}$ **13.** $5\frac{1}{20}$

Show each set of numbers on the same number line. Then order the numbers from least to greatest. (7-14)

14. 0.875, $\frac{11}{20}$, $\frac{2}{5}$ **15.** $1\frac{7}{10}$, $1\frac{1}{4}$, $\frac{2}{5}$, 1.65

16. Nick, Amy, and Maria play either softball, tennis, or badminton. Amy's sport does not require a ball. Nick's sport does not require a net. Use the chart and logical reasoning to find who plays each sport. (7-15, 7-16)

	softball	tennis	badminton
Nick			
Amy			Yes
Maria			

Writing in Math

17. Explain how a mixed number and a decimal can name the same point on a number line. (7-14)

18. Explain how to write 4.7 as a mixed number. (7-13)

Test-Taking Strategies

Understand the question.

Get information for the answer.

Plan how to find the answer.

Make smart choices.

Use writing in math.

Improve written answers.

Plan How to Find the Answer

After you understand a test question and get needed information, you need to plan how to find the answer. Think about problem-solving skills and strategies and computation methods.

1. The chart below shows the lengths of some famous horse races held in the United States each year.

FAMOUS HORSE RACE LENGTHS

Race	Length (in miles)
Belmont Stakes	1.5
Golden Gate Derby	$1\frac{1}{16}$
Kentucky Derby	1.25
Preakness Stakes	$1\frac{3}{16}$
Santa Anita Derby	$1\frac{1}{8}$

The Belmont Stakes, Kentucky Derby, and Preakness Stakes make up a special series of races called the Triple Crown. Which Triple Crown race is the **longest**?

A. Belmont Stakes

B. Kentucky Derby

C. Preakness Stakes

D. Santa Anita Derby

Understand the question.

I need to find out which Triple Crown race is the longest.

Get information for the answer.

The text tells me that the Triple Crown races are the Belmont Stakes, the Kentucky Derby, and the Preakness Stakes. The chart shows the length of each race.

Plan how to find the answer.

- Think about problem-solving skills and strategies.

  All of the lengths are mixed numbers or decimals. I can change the decimals to mixed numbers. Then use common denominators to compare the numbers.

- Choose computation methods.

  I'll still use paper and pencil since changing all the fractions to have a common denominator requires several computations.

2. The salt content in the Dead Sea is about $\frac{30}{100}$. The Dead Sea is so salty that no fish or plants can live in it.

Which of the following is NOT another way to write $\frac{30}{100}$?

A. $\frac{3}{10}$

B. $\frac{15}{50}$

C. 0.03

D. 0.30

Think It Through

I need to find the number that is NOT another name for the amount of salt in the Dead Sea. The text tells me that the salt content of the Dead Sea is $\frac{30}{100}$. I can check each response to see if the number is equal to $\frac{30}{100}$. I can use paper and pencil or mental math to find a fraction for the number with a denominator of 100.

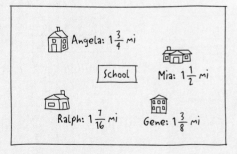

Now it's your turn.

For each problem, describe a plan for finding the answer.

3. Asia and Africa are the two largest continents. About $\frac{3}{10}$ of Earth's land is in Asia and about $\frac{1}{5}$ of Earth's land is in Africa. Which value below represents the amount of Earth's land in Africa?

A. about 0.20

B. about 0.25

C. about 0.40

D. about 0.50

4. Who lives closest to school?

Angela: $1\frac{3}{4}$ mi

School   Mia: $1\frac{1}{2}$ mi

Ralph: $1\frac{7}{16}$ mi   Gene: $1\frac{3}{8}$ mi

A. Angela

B. Gene

C. Mia

D. Ralph

Self Check

A mixed salad has a combination of ingredients. A **mixed number** is a combination of a whole number and a fraction. (p. 400)

Use **fractions** and **mixed numbers** to represent portions. (Lessons 7-1, 7-3)

Fraction	Mixed Number

Write a fraction to represent the shaded portion.

$$\frac{\text{numerator}}{\text{denominator}} = \frac{\text{shaded parts}}{\text{parts in all}} = \frac{2}{5}$$

So, $\frac{2}{5}$ of the rectangle is shaded.

How many circles are shaded?

2 whole circles are shaded, and $\frac{1}{4}$ of another circle is shaded.

So, $2\frac{1}{4}$ circles are shaded.

1. Write a fraction to represent the portion of the rectangle that is **not** shaded.

At my school, if you wear a hat to class, you are dressed "improperly" because you don't look a certain way. If a fraction has a numerator larger than its denominator, it is called an **improper fraction** because it doesn't look a certain way. (p. 400)

Self Check

You can **write fractions and mixed numbers in different ways.** (Lessons 7-2, 7-3, 7-6, 7-7, 7-13)

A Mixed Number as an Improper Fraction	A Fraction as a Decimal

Multiply the denominator by the whole number. Add the numerator. Write the sum as the numerator. Use the same denominator.

$$3\frac{2}{5} = \frac{5 \times 3 + 2}{5} = \frac{17}{5}$$

So, $3\frac{2}{5}$ written as an improper fraction is $\frac{17}{5}$.

Divide the numerator by the denominator.

$$\frac{4}{5} = 4 \div 5$$

So, $\frac{4}{5}$ written as a decimal is 0.8.

2. Write $1\frac{3}{4}$, $3\frac{1}{4}$, and $\frac{2}{5}$ in two different ways.

Friends with a lot in common tend to have the same interests. Fractions with a **common denominator** have the same denominator. (p. 420)

You can **compare fractions and mixed numbers** in different ways.

(Lesson 7-4, 7-10, 7-11, 7-12, 7-14)

Compare $1\frac{3}{8}$ and $1\frac{5}{6}$.

Use Benchmark Fractions

Compare the whole numbers. If they are equal, compare each fraction part to $\frac{1}{2}$.

$$\frac{3}{8} < \frac{1}{2}$$

$$\frac{5}{6} > \frac{1}{2}$$

$\frac{3}{8} < \frac{5}{6}$. So, $1\frac{3}{8} < 1\frac{5}{6}$.

Use Equivalent Fractions

Find a **common denominator**.

8: 8, 16, **24**, 32, 40, ...
6: 6, 12, 18, **24**, 30, ...

Write equivalent fractions with the common denominator. Compare.

$$\frac{3}{8} = \frac{9}{24} \qquad \frac{5}{6} = \frac{20}{24}$$

$\frac{9}{24} < \frac{20}{24}$. So, $1\frac{3}{8} < 1\frac{5}{6}$.

3. Compare $\frac{5}{12}$ and $\frac{5}{9}$, and compare $2\frac{1}{2}$ and $2\frac{2}{5}$.

I think computation problems with small numbers are simple. A fraction in **simplest form** is written with the smallest numbers possible. (p. 416)

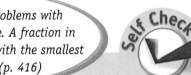

Use given information and logical reasoning to solve problems.

(Lesson 7-5, 7-8, 7-9, 7-15)

A fraction's numerator and denominator are two of these numbers: 6, 8, or 12. If written in simplest form, it would be $\frac{2}{3}$. What is the fraction?

Write all the proper fractions that have those numbers. Then write each fraction in **simplest form** by dividing its numerator and denominator by their **greatest common factor**.

$\frac{6}{8}$ 6: 1, **2**, 3, 6
8: 1, **2**, 4, 8

$\frac{6}{12}$ 6: 1, 2, 3, **6**
12: 1, 2, 3, 4, **6**, 12

$\frac{8}{12}$ 8: 1, 2, **4**, 8
12: 1, 2, 3, **4**, 6, 12

$$\frac{6}{8} = \frac{6 \div 2}{8 \div 2} = \frac{3}{4}$$

$$\frac{6}{12} = \frac{6 \div 6}{12 \div 6} = \frac{1}{2}$$

$$\frac{8}{12} = \frac{8 \div 4}{12 \div 4} = \frac{2}{3}$$

When written in simplest form, $\frac{8}{12}$ is $\frac{2}{3}$. So, the fraction is $\frac{8}{12}$.

4. Why are $\frac{8}{6}$, $\frac{12}{6}$, and $\frac{12}{8}$ not possible answers to this problem?

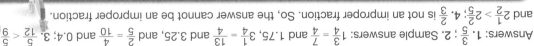
Answers: 1. $\frac{3}{5}$; 2. Sample answers: $1\frac{3}{4} = \frac{7}{4}$, $3\frac{1}{4} = \frac{13}{4}$ and 1.75, and 3.25, and $\frac{2}{5} = \frac{4}{10}$ and 0.4; 3. $\frac{5}{12} < \frac{5}{9}$ and $2\frac{1}{2} > 2\frac{2}{5}$; 4. $\frac{3}{2}$ is not an improper fraction. So, the answer cannot be an improper fraction.

Chapter 7 Key Vocabulary and Concept Review   445

MULTIPLE CHOICE

Choose the correct letter for each answer.

1. Which fraction names the shaded part of the figure below?

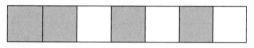

A. $\frac{3}{7}$ C. $\frac{1}{2}$

B. $\frac{4}{7}$ D. $\frac{7}{4}$

2. Which fraction equals 0.3?

A. $\frac{3}{1000}$ C. $\frac{3}{10}$

B. $\frac{1}{30}$ D. $\frac{1}{3}$

3. Which mixed number equals $\frac{15}{6}$?

A. $3\frac{1}{2}$ C. $2\frac{6}{15}$

B. $2\frac{1}{2}$ D. $2\frac{3}{15}$

4. What fraction names the shaded part of this set?

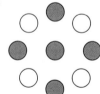

A. $\frac{9}{5}$ C. $\frac{5}{9}$

B. $\frac{5}{8}$ D. $\frac{4}{9}$

5. Which number represents point A on the number line?

A. $1\frac{7}{10}$ C. $\frac{7}{10}$

B. $1\frac{8}{10}$ D. $\frac{8}{10}$

6. Which fraction is NOT in its simplest form?

TEST TALK

Think It Through
- I should **watch for words** like not or except.
- I need to **read each answer carefully.**

A. $\frac{3}{4}$

B. $\frac{9}{17}$

C. $\frac{11}{22}$

D. $\frac{1}{6}$

7. Which is the most reasonable estimate for the part of this figure that is shaded?

A. $\frac{1}{4}$ C. $\frac{3}{4}$

B. $\frac{1}{2}$ D. $\frac{3}{1}$

8. Which equals $\frac{2}{7}$?

A. $7 \div 2$ C. $5 \div 7$

B. $2 \div 5$ D. $2 \div 7$

9. If $\frac{3}{17} = \frac{6}{\blacksquare}$, then $\blacksquare$ equals

A. 2   C. 35

B. 34   D. 51

10. The diameters of three buttons are 0.25 inch, $\frac{3}{8}$ inch, and $\frac{5}{16}$ inch. Which shows these diameters ordered from least to greatest?

A. $\frac{3}{8}, \frac{5}{16}, 0.25$ C. $0.25, \frac{5}{16}, \frac{3}{8}$

B. $0.25, \frac{3}{8}, \frac{5}{16}$ D. $\frac{5}{16}, 0.25, \frac{3}{8}$

11. What is the GCF of 18 and 63?

    A. 2   **C.** 9

    B. 3   **D.** 36

12. Which statement is **true?**

    A. $\frac{10}{16} = \frac{15}{20}$ **C.** $1\frac{3}{5} = \frac{4}{5}$

    B. $\frac{22}{7} = 3\frac{1}{7}$ **D.** $\frac{8}{14} = \frac{1}{2}$

13. In his aquarium, Mike has 3 angelfish and 9 goldfish. What fraction of the total fish are angelfish?

    A. $\frac{3}{4}$ **C.** $\frac{3}{11}$

    B. $\frac{1}{3}$ **D.** $\frac{1}{4}$

FREE RESPONSE

Write each mixed number as an improper fraction.

14. $3\frac{3}{8}$ **15.** $6\frac{7}{11}$

Write each fraction or mixed number as a decimal.

16. $\frac{1}{20}$ **17.** $9\frac{2}{5}$

Write >, <, or = for each ●.

18. $\frac{5}{6}$ ● $\frac{5}{7}$ **19.** $4\frac{6}{9}$ ● $4\frac{2}{3}$

20. $\frac{1}{6}$ ● $\frac{1}{5}$ **21.** $5\frac{3}{10}$ ● $5\frac{7}{20}$

Write the location of each point as a decimal and a fraction or mixed number in simplest form.

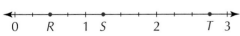

22. point *R*   **23.** point *S*

24. Use the chart and logical reasoning to solve the problem.

Jake, Alan, and Marie like either pie, cake, or pudding best. Jake does not like cake or pudding. Marie is a friend of the people who like pie or cake best. Which person likes each dessert best?

	pie	cake	pudding
Jake		No	No
Alan			
Marie			

Writing in Math

25. Write a decimal and a fraction in simplest form for the shaded portion. Explain.

26. Decide if the Swimming problem has extra or missing information. Explain. Then solve it if there is enough information.

Swimming In a 50-meter pool, Kelly swam 1.3 km and Cindy swam 1.35 km. Who swam farther?

27. Explain how to write $\frac{6}{30}$ in simplest form.

Think It Through
- I will **describe my steps in order.**
- My explanations should be **brief but complete.**

Number and Operation

MULTIPLE CHOICE

1. Which equals $\frac{3}{8}$?

A. $8 \div 3$ **C.** $3 \div 11$

B. $3 \div 8$ **D.** 3×8

2. Toby bought 6 pounds of chocolates for $38.88. What was the cost of 1 pound of the chocolates?

A. $3.24   **C.** $6.48

B. $5.48   **D.** $8.28

3. What is thirty-five hundredths written as a fraction in simplest form?

A. $\frac{35}{1000}$ **C.** $\frac{7}{20}$

B. $\frac{7}{25}$ **D.** $\frac{100}{35}$

FREE RESPONSE

4. What number represents point A on the number line?

5. What is the sum of 58,709 and 7,465?

Writing in Math

6. Draw two different pictures to show $\frac{5}{6}$ as part of a whole. Explain how each drawing shows the fraction.

Geometry and Measurement

MULTIPLE CHOICE

7. Which rectangle has an area of 25 square feet?

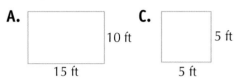

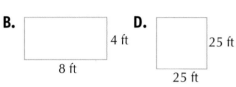

A. 10 ft, 15 ft   **C.** 5 ft, 5 ft

B. 4 ft, 8 ft   **D.** 25 ft, 25 ft

8. Which is **not** a polygon?

A. square   **C.** cylinder

B. rhombus   **D.** trapezoid

FREE RESPONSE

9. Classify this triangle by its sides and angles.

5 in.   4 in.   3 in.

10. Aaron has three ropes. Rope A is $4\frac{1}{3}$ yards long, rope B is 15 feet long, and rope C is 4.5 yards long. Which rope is the longest?

Writing in Math

11. Line segments $\overline{AB}$, $\overline{AC}$, $\overline{BD}$, and $\overline{CD}$ have equal lengths. $\overline{AB}$ is parallel to $\overline{CD}$. $\overline{AC}$ and $\overline{BD}$ are perpendicular to $\overline{AB}$ and $\overline{CD}$. Name the geometric figure that these four line segments form when the ends are attached. Explain how you know.

Think It Through

I can **draw a picture** to help me understand a problem.

TEST TALK

Data Analysis and Probability

MULTIPLE CHOICE

12. If you spin this spinner twice, how many possible outcomes are there?

A. 8 outcomes

B. 16 outcomes

C. 32 outcomes

D. 64 outcomes

13. You spin the spinner in problem 12 once. What is the probability of the pointer landing on a number greater than 3?

A. $\frac{1}{4}$

B. $\frac{3}{8}$

C. $\frac{1}{2}$

D. $\frac{5}{8}$

FREE RESPONSE

Use the line graph for 14–16.

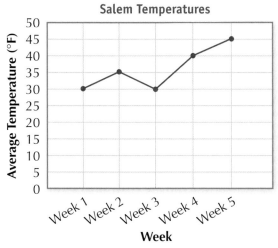

14. What was the range of temperatures in Salem during the five weeks?

15. What is the median temperature shown on the graph?

Writing in Math

16. Do you think a line graph is the best way to display this data? Explain.

Algebra

MULTIPLE CHOICE

17. If $\frac{7}{12} = \frac{\blacksquare}{84}$, then $\blacksquare$ equals

A. 14

C. 49

B. 42

D. 56

18. Which shows the first step taken when evaluating this expression?
$50 - 4(2 + 3) \div 2$

A. $50 - 4$

C. $2 + 3$

B. 4×2

D. $3 \div 2$

19. Which equation does not have the solution $n = 16$?

A. $n \div 2 = 8$

C. $3n = 48$

B. $73 - n = 67$

D. $n + 89 = 105$

FREE RESPONSE

20. Complete the table and describe the rule you used.

In	$\frac{1}{4}$	$\frac{1}{2}$	$\frac{3}{4}$	1
Out	0.25	0.5		1.0

21. Paula bought five postcards for $3.78, which included $0.18 tax. If each postcard was the same price, how much did each postcard cost before tax?

Writing in Math

22. Explain how you could use the Distributive Property to find 3×24.

Set 7-1 (pages 394–397)

Write the fraction that names the shaded part.

Number of shaded moons ⟶ 4
Total number of moons ⟶ 8

Remember that the denominator is the number below the fraction bar. It represents the total number of equal parts or total number of items.

Write the fraction that names the shaded part.

1.    **2.** [image of bar]

Set 7-2 (pages 398–399)

Find 3 ÷ 5.

$3 \div 5 = \dfrac{3}{5}$

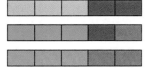

Remember that you can draw a picture to divide.

Give each answer as a fraction.

1. 7 ÷ 9   **2.** 10 ÷ 11

3. 1 ÷ 7   **4.** 3 ÷ 13

Set 7-3 (pages 400–401)

Write $\dfrac{42}{9}$ as a mixed number.

$\dfrac{42}{9} = 42 \div 9$

Divide the numerator by the denominator. Write the remainder as a fraction.

$$\begin{array}{r} 4\frac{6}{9} \\ 9\overline{)42} \\ -36 \\ \hline 6 \end{array}$$

So, $\dfrac{42}{9} = 4\dfrac{6}{9}$

Remember that an improper fraction has a numerator greater than or equal to its denominator.

Write each improper fraction as a mixed number.

1. $\dfrac{15}{8}$ **2.** $\dfrac{20}{7}$

3. $\dfrac{46}{5}$ **4.** $\dfrac{17}{3}$

Set 7-4 (pages 402–403)

Estimate the shaded part of the rectangle.

Compare the rectangle to benchmark fractions.

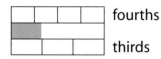 fourths

thirds

About $\dfrac{1}{3}$ of the rectangle is shaded.

Remember that benchmark fractions include $\dfrac{1}{4}, \dfrac{1}{3}, \dfrac{1}{2}, \dfrac{2}{3},$ and $\dfrac{3}{4}$.

Estimate the shaded part of each.

1.    **2.**

3.   **4.**

What fraction or mixed number should be written at Point *L*?

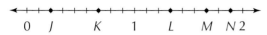

$$0 \quad J \quad\quad K \quad\quad 1 \quad\quad L \quad\quad M \quad N \; 2$$

Between 1 and 2 there are 9 equal parts. Point *L* is at $1\frac{3}{9}$ or $1\frac{1}{3}$.

So, $1\frac{1}{3}$ should be written at Point *L*.

Remember that fractions and mixed numbers can name points on a number line.

Use the number line on the left. What fraction or mixed number should be written at each point?

1. Point *J* **2.** Point *K*

3. Point *M* **4.** Point *N*

Decide if the problem has extra or missing information. Solve if you have enough information.

Marty has 5 bags of fruit. Each bag has 3 types of fruit. How many oranges does Marty have?

Identify what you know: 5 bags, 3 types of fruit. **Identify the question:** How many oranges does Marty have?

Can you solve? No, it does not tell how many oranges are in each bag.

Remember that some problems have too much information.

1. Ana has $35.65. She went to the store and bought bread, milk, and soup. How much change did she get back?

2. Karen bought 6 books at the book fair. Each book cost $3.95, and each bookmark cost $1.25. How much did Karen spend on books?

Write two fractions that name the shaded part.

The shaded part is half of the rectangle. Each half is divided into 3 equal parts. So, 3 out of 6 equal parts are shaded.

Both $\frac{1}{2}$ and $\frac{3}{6}$ name the shaded part.

Remember that more than one fraction can name part of a whole, part of a set, or a location on a number line.

1.

2.
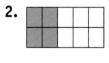

Write the missing number to make the fractions equivalent.

$$\frac{\square}{6} = \frac{40}{48} \longrightarrow \frac{\square}{6} \overset{\times\,8}{\underset{\times\,8}{=}} \frac{40}{48}$$

So, $\frac{5}{6} = \frac{40}{48}$.

Remember that you multiply or divide both the numerator and the denominator to find equivalent fractions.

1. $\frac{1}{\square} = \frac{7}{49}$ **2.** $\frac{\square}{45} = \frac{3}{9}$

3. $2\frac{4}{\square} = 2\frac{2}{3}$ **4.** $3\frac{8}{11} = 3\frac{64}{\square}$

Set 7-9 (pages 414–415)

Find the GCF of 8 and 36.

8: (1,) (2,) (4,) 8

36: (1,) (2,) 3, (4,) 6, 9, 12, 18, 36

Common factors of 8 and 36 are 1, 2, and 4. The GCF is 4.

Remember the GCF is the *greatest* factor common to the numbers.

1. 14, 35   2. 27, 54

3. 9, 20   4. 32, 40

5. 5, 18   6. 10, 35

Set 7-10 (pages 416–417)

Write $\frac{9}{24}$ in simplest form.

Find the GCF of 9 and 24.

9: (1,) (3,) 9

24: (1,) 2, (3,) 4, 6, 8, 12, 24

The GCF of 9 and 24 is 3.

$$\frac{9 \div 3}{24 \div 3} = \frac{3}{8}$$

Remember the simplest form can also be found by dividing by common factors until the only common factor is 1.

1. $\frac{10}{34}$ 2. $\frac{15}{50}$

3. $\frac{8}{18}$ 4. $\frac{4}{21}$

5. $\frac{12}{27}$ 6. $\frac{27}{72}$

Set 7-11 (pages 418–419)

Compare. Write >, <, or = for ⬤.

$\frac{9}{14}$ ⬤ $\frac{1}{3}$

These fractions do not have the same denominator or the same numerator, so compare them to $\frac{1}{2}$.

$$\frac{9}{14} > \frac{1}{2} \quad \text{and} \quad \frac{1}{2} > \frac{1}{3}$$

So, $\frac{9}{14} > \frac{1}{3}$.

Remember if two fractions have the same denominator, the one with the greater numerator is greater.

1. $\frac{5}{8}$ ⬤ $\frac{7}{8}$ 2. $\frac{4}{9}$ ⬤ $\frac{4}{7}$

3. $\frac{7}{12}$ ⬤ $\frac{1}{2}$ 4. $\frac{8}{12}$ ⬤ $\frac{2}{3}$

5. $\frac{2}{6}$ ⬤ $\frac{3}{6}$ 6. $\frac{9}{10}$ ⬤ $\frac{9}{12}$

Set 7-12 (pages 420–423)

Compare. Write >, <, or = for ⬤.

$\frac{8}{9}$ ⬤ $\frac{4}{5}$

Use 45 as the common denominator.

$\frac{8}{9} = \frac{40}{45}$ $\frac{4}{5} = \frac{36}{45}$

$\frac{40}{45} > \frac{36}{45}$, so $\frac{8}{9} > \frac{4}{5}$

Remember when comparing mixed numbers, first compare the whole number parts, then if needed, compare the fraction parts.

1. $\frac{3}{7}$ ⬤ $\frac{4}{9}$ 2. $\frac{3}{9}$ ⬤ $\frac{2}{6}$

3. $4\frac{8}{10}$ ⬤ $4\frac{6}{7}$ 4. $\frac{3}{8}$ ⬤ $\frac{1}{3}$

5. $6\frac{3}{8}$ ⬤ $6\frac{6}{8}$ 6. $\frac{8}{10}$ ⬤ $\frac{18}{25}$

Set 7-13 (pages 426–429)

Write a decimal and a fraction in simplest form for the shaded portion.

Name the fraction. $\frac{6}{40}$

Simplify. $\frac{3}{20}$

Find the decimal. Divide.

So, $\frac{3}{20}$ = 0.15.

$$\begin{array}{r} 0.15 \\ 20\overline{)3.00} \\ -2\ 0 \\ \hline 1\ 00 \\ -1\ 00 \\ \hline 0 \end{array}$$

Remember to add zeros in the dividend when needed.

1.
2.
3.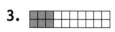
4.

Set 7-14 (pages 430–431)

Write a mixed number in simplest form and a decimal that name Point B.

$$\overset{\longleftrightarrow}{\underset{2\quad A\qquad B\,C\,3\qquad D\quad E\quad 4}{\rule{0pt}{0pt}}}$$

The number line is separated into eighths. Point B is at $2\frac{6}{8}$.

$2\frac{6}{8} = 2\frac{3}{4} = 2.75$

Both $2\frac{3}{4}$ and 2.75 name Point B.

Remember to include the whole number in your answers.

Use the number line on the left to name each point with a fraction in simplest form and a decimal.

1. Point A 2. Point C

3. Point D 4. Point E

Set 7-15 (pages 434–437)

Solve.

Tyrone, Tosha, and Lea collect either stamps, shells, or postcards. Lea's collection cannot be put into a book. Tyrone does not collect stamps. Who collects each item?

Use the chart and logical reasoning. Fill in what you know and finish completing the chart.

	stamps	shells	postcards
Tyrone	No	No	Yes
Tosha	Yes	No	No
Lea	No	Yes	No

Tyrone collects postcards, Tosha collects stamps, and Lea collects shells.

Remember that if Yes occurs in a cell, you can write No in the other cells for that row and column.

1. What clue allows you to write Yes for Lea in the shells column?

2. Suppose the second clue had been "Tosha does not collect postcards." Would the answer change?

Set 7-1 (pages 394–397)

Write the fraction that names the shaded part of each.

1.

2.

3.

4. Greg bought 15 apples. Four of the apples were green, and 11 of the apples were red. What fraction names the green part?

Set 7-2 (pages 398–399)

Give each answer as a fraction.

1. $7 \div 15$ **2.** $6 \div 7$ **3.** $4 \div 12$ **4.** $3 \div 11$

5. $1 \div 7$ **6.** $3 \div 10$ **7.** $4 \div 9$ **8.** $10 \div 20$

9. Erin has 5 yards of ribbon to make 16 decorations. How much ribbon should she use for each decoration?

Set 7-3 (pages 400–401)

Write each mixed number as an improper fraction.

1. $5\frac{1}{2}$ **2.** $3\frac{4}{7}$ **3.** $1\frac{3}{6}$ **4.** $3\frac{2}{3}$

5. $2\frac{2}{5}$ **6.** $5\frac{2}{3}$ **7.** $6\frac{1}{4}$ **8.** $9\frac{1}{10}$

9. Vernon is making a dessert. The recipe calls for $1\frac{1}{8}$ cups of almonds. How many eighths is that? Write this number as an improper fraction.

Set 7-4 (pages 402–403)

Estimate the shaded part of each.

1.

2.

3.

4. Porter used a little less than $\frac{1}{3}$ of the nails. About what part of the nails are left?

Take It to the NET
More Practice
www.scottforesman.com

Set 7-5 (pages 404–405)

What fraction or mixed number should
be written at each point?

$$0 \quad A \qquad B \quad 1 \quad C \qquad D \quad 2$$

1. Point A **2.** Point B

3. Point C **4.** Point D

Draw a number line to show each set of numbers. Then order the numbers
from least to greatest.

5. $1\frac{4}{7}, \frac{5}{7}, \frac{10}{7}$ **6.** $\frac{4}{5}, 1\frac{3}{5}, \frac{9}{5}$ **7.** $1\frac{3}{10}, \frac{15}{10}, \frac{7}{10}$

Set 7-6 (pages 406–407)

Decide if the problem has extra or missing information. Solve
if you have enough information.

1. Danika is making bracelets for the craft fair. Each
bracelet needs 34 beads and 9 inches of string. How
many beads will she need to make 5 bracelets?

2. Mason has 36 books that he needs to put into moving
boxes. How many boxes will Mason need in order to
pack all the books?

Set 7-7 (pages 410–411)

Write two fractions that name each shaded part.

1.    **2.** 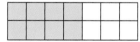   **3.** ▭

Set 7-8 (pages 412–413)

Find the missing number to make the fractions equivalent.

1. $\frac{5}{9} = \frac{\blacksquare}{45}$ **2.** $\frac{35}{40} = \frac{\blacksquare}{8}$ **3.** $2\frac{9}{\blacksquare} = 2\frac{36}{40}$ **4.** $\frac{40}{\blacksquare} = \frac{5}{7}$

5. $\frac{\blacksquare}{35} = \frac{1}{5}$ **6.** $\frac{4}{6} = \frac{\blacksquare}{48}$ **7.** $\frac{5}{12} = \frac{10}{\blacksquare}$ **8.** $3\frac{\blacksquare}{8} = 3\frac{24}{64}$

9. Thomas is taking a math test. There are 21 problems
on the test. If he is $\frac{2}{3}$ of the way through the test, how
many problems has he finished?

Set 7-9 (pages 414–415)

Find the GCF of each pair of numbers.

1. 12, 46   **2.** 24, 100   **3.** 36, 48   **4.** 28, 30

5. 9, 38   **6.** 40, 42   **7.** 20, 32   **8.** 6, 14

9. Joshua has 18 pencils and 42 erasers. He wants to put them in groups. What is the greatest number that can be in each group if the groups of pencils must be the same size as the groups of erasers?

Set 7-10 (pages 416–417)

Write each fraction in simplest form.

1. $\dfrac{10}{34}$ **2.** $\dfrac{20}{100}$ **3.** $\dfrac{36}{54}$ **4.** $\dfrac{3}{63}$

5. Marcy is working on her homework. She thinks that $\dfrac{45}{95}$ is in simplest form. Without finding all the factors, how do you know she is incorrect?

Set 7-11 (pages 418–419)

Write >, <, or = for each ●. You may use fraction strips or drawings to help.

1. $\dfrac{5}{8}$ ● $\dfrac{5}{12}$ **2.** $\dfrac{1}{4}$ ● $\dfrac{2}{8}$ **3.** $\dfrac{5}{6}$ ● $\dfrac{2}{3}$ **4.** $\dfrac{3}{10}$ ● $\dfrac{2}{10}$

5. Charles swam $\dfrac{7}{8}$ mile. Mary swam $\dfrac{7}{12}$ mile. Who swam farther?

Set 7-12 (pages 420–423)

Compare. Write >, <, or = for each ●.

1. $\dfrac{3}{5}$ ● $\dfrac{6}{10}$ **2.** $5\dfrac{1}{9}$ ● $5\dfrac{2}{5}$ **3.** $\dfrac{2}{7}$ ● $\dfrac{1}{6}$ **4.** $1\dfrac{7}{9}$ ● $1\dfrac{3}{4}$

Order the numbers from the least to the greatest.

5. $\dfrac{3}{5}, \dfrac{2}{5}, \dfrac{3}{7}, \dfrac{4}{9}$ **6.** $\dfrac{4}{5}, \dfrac{4}{7}, \dfrac{9}{10}, \dfrac{7}{8}$ **7.** $2\dfrac{2}{9}, 2\dfrac{1}{5}, 1\dfrac{2}{3}$

8. Each student is given the same book to read. Bret read $\dfrac{4}{5}$ of the book. Cale read $\dfrac{2}{3}$ of the book. Cheri read $\dfrac{5}{6}$ of the book. Who read the most?

Take It to the NET
More Practice
www.scottforesman.com

Set 7-13 (pages 426–429)

Write each decimal as a fraction or mixed number in simplest form.

1. 0.12
2. 8.68
3. 0.875
4. 1.1

Write each fraction or mixed number as a decimal.

5. $2\frac{7}{10}$
6. $\frac{9}{20}$
7. $\frac{61}{100}$
8. $4\frac{1}{4}$

9. Six out of sixteen people chose orange juice for breakfast. What is this amount in decimal form?

Set 7-14 (pages 430–431)

Show each set of numbers on the same number line. Then order the numbers from least to greatest.

1. 1.85, $1\frac{2}{5}$, $1\frac{7}{10}$
2. 0.29, $\frac{1}{5}$, $\frac{9}{20}$

3. $1\frac{3}{5}$, 1.55, $1\frac{4}{25}$, 0.625
4. $\frac{8}{25}$, $\frac{3}{8}$, $\frac{7}{20}$, 0.3

5. Makena's paper airplane flew 8.5 yards. Whitney's flew $8\frac{2}{3}$ yards, Michael's flew $8\frac{1}{4}$ yards, and Denaya's flew $8\frac{1}{6}$ yards. Whose airplane flew the farthest?

Set 7-15 (pages 434–437)

Solve.

1. Rhonda, Rhea, and Rae like either rock, rap, or jazz. The person who likes jazz has the shortest name. Rhea does not like rap. Who likes each type of music?

	rock	rap	jazz
Rhonda			
Rhea			
Rae			

2. John, Rob, Jenny, and Rachael are on teams for either soccer, baseball, bowling, or swimming. The person who bowls is the tallest of the four. Jenny does not swim. Rob is the shortest. John is taller than both Jenny and Rachael. Jenny does not play soccer. Rachael does not swim. Who is on each team?

	soccer	baseball	bowling	swimming
John				
Rob				
Jenny				
Rachael				

Fraction Operations

DIAGNOSING READINESS

A Vocabulary

(pages 394–397, 400–401, 410–411)

Choose the best term from the box.

1. In the fraction $\frac{3}{5}$, 3 is the ___?___ of the fraction and 5 is the ___?___ of the fraction.

2. Fractions that name the same part of a whole are ___?___.

3. ___?___ have a whole number and a fraction.

Vocabulary

- **mixed numbers** *(p. 400)*
- **denominator** *(p. 394)*
- **improper fractions** *(p. 400)*
- **numerator** *(p. 394)*
- **equivalent fractions** *(p. 410)*

B Mixed Numbers

(pages 400–401)

Write each as a mixed number.

4. $\frac{12}{7}$ **5.** $\frac{10}{3}$ **6.** $\frac{23}{10}$

7. $\frac{17}{11}$ **8.** $\frac{17}{12}$ **9.** $\frac{26}{25}$

Write each as an improper fraction.

10. $1\frac{3}{5}$ **11.** $4\frac{1}{2}$ **12.** $2\frac{9}{10}$

13. $5\frac{2}{3}$ **14.** $2\frac{5}{16}$ **15.** $4\frac{3}{10}$

16. How can you use division to change $\frac{16}{3}$ to a mixed number?

Do You Know...

What country has the longest shoreline?

You will find out in Lesson 8-16.

SHORELINE
See the natural world of a shoreline as never before!

C Fractions in Simplest Form

(pages 416–417)

Write each fraction in simplest form.

17. $\frac{3}{6}$ **18.** $\frac{10}{15}$ **19.** $\frac{3}{9}$

20. $\frac{14}{21}$ **21.** $\frac{4}{20}$ **22.** $\frac{9}{54}$

23. $\frac{9}{24}$ **24.** $\frac{20}{50}$ **25.** $\frac{12}{20}$

26. How does finding the greatest common factor help you write a fraction in simplest form?

D Common Denominators

(pages 420–423)

Compare. Write >, <, or = for each ⬤.

27. $\frac{3}{4}$ ⬤ $\frac{1}{12}$ **28.** $\frac{1}{3}$ ⬤ $\frac{5}{9}$ **29.** $\frac{1}{5}$ ⬤ $\frac{2}{10}$

30. Order the following fractions from least to greatest: $\frac{5}{12}, \frac{3}{4}, \frac{1}{6}, \frac{2}{3}$.

31. How does writing fractions with a common denominator help you compare the fractions?

Vocabulary
- numerator (p. 394)
- denominator (p. 394)
- common denominator (p. 420)

TEST TALK

Think It Through
I need **data from the map** to solve the problem.

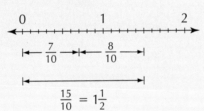

Adding and Subtracting Fractions with Like Denominators

LEARN

How do you add or subtract fractions with like denominators?

The map shows a trail. How far is it from the lake to the stables and then to the cabin?

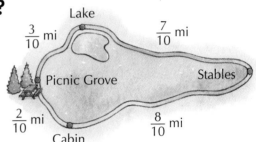

Lake — $\frac{3}{10}$ mi — $\frac{7}{10}$ mi — Stables

Picnic Grove

$\frac{2}{10}$ mi — $\frac{8}{10}$ mi

Cabin

Example A

Find $\frac{7}{10} + \frac{8}{10}$.

One Way
Use a model.

0   1   2

$\frac{7}{10}$ $\frac{8}{10}$

$\frac{15}{10} = 1\frac{1}{2}$

Another Way
Use paper and pencil.

$$\begin{array}{r} \frac{7}{10} \\ + \frac{8}{10} \\ \hline \end{array}$$

Add the numerators. Write the sum over the common denominator. Simplify the sum.

$\frac{15}{10} = 1\frac{5}{10} = 1\frac{1}{2}$

It is $1\frac{1}{2}$ miles from the lake to the stables and then to the cabin.

Example B

Find $\frac{7}{10} - \frac{3}{10}$.

Subtract the numerators. Write the difference over the common denominator. Simplify the difference.

$$\frac{7}{10} - \frac{3}{10} = \frac{4}{10} = \frac{2}{5}$$

✔ **Talk About It**

1. How can you use a number line to show the difference in Example B?

2. In Example A, why is the sum of $\frac{7}{10} + \frac{8}{10}$ not equal to $\frac{15}{20}$?

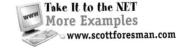
Take It to the NET
More Examples
www.scottforesman.com

Add or subtract. Simplify, if possible.

1. $\frac{6}{7} + \frac{6}{7}$ **2.** $\frac{3}{9} + \frac{5}{9} + \frac{1}{9}$ **3.** $\frac{7}{12} - \frac{5}{12}$ **4.** $\frac{6}{9} - \frac{2}{9}$

5. Number Sense When does the sum of two fractions equal 1?

PRACTICE

For more practice, see Set 8-1 on p. 522.

Ⓐ Skills and Understanding

Add or subtract. Simplify, if possible.

6. $\begin{array}{r} \frac{3}{4} \\ -\frac{1}{4} \\ \hline \end{array}$ **7.** $\begin{array}{r} \frac{3}{6} \\ +\frac{2}{6} \\ \hline \end{array}$ **8.** $\begin{array}{r} \frac{11}{16} \\ +\frac{5}{16} \\ \hline \end{array}$ **9.** $\begin{array}{r} \frac{9}{12} \\ -\frac{5}{12} \\ \hline \end{array}$ **10.** $\begin{array}{r} \frac{4}{5} \\ +\frac{3}{5} \\ \hline \end{array}$

11. $\frac{7}{8} - \frac{2}{8}$ **12.** $\frac{4}{9} + \frac{3}{9}$ **13.** $\frac{7}{10} - \frac{4}{10}$ **14.** $\frac{6}{7} + \frac{5}{7}$ **15.** $\frac{5}{11} - \frac{1}{11}$

16. $\frac{1}{12} + \frac{3}{12} + \frac{5}{12}$ **17.** $\frac{5}{9} + \frac{1}{9} + \frac{1}{9}$ **18.** $\frac{1}{4} + \frac{3}{4} + \frac{2}{4}$ **19.** $\frac{1}{8} + \frac{3}{8} + \frac{5}{8}$

20. $\frac{1}{6} + \frac{2}{6} + \frac{3}{6}$ **21.** $\frac{1}{2} + \frac{1}{2} + \frac{1}{2}$ **22.** $\frac{2}{3} + \frac{1}{3} + \frac{1}{3}$ **23.** $\frac{1}{10} + \frac{7}{10} + \frac{3}{10}$

24. Reasoning Suppose two fractions are both less than 1. Can their sum be greater than 1? Can the sum be greater than 2? Explain.

Ⓑ Reasoning and Problem Solving

For 25–27, use the trail map on page 460.

25. How far is it from the picnic grove to the stables by way of the cabin?

26. Which is farther from the stables, the lake or the cabin? How much farther?

27. **Writing in Math** Marta rode a total distance of 1 mile. Between which locations shown on the camp map did she ride? Explain your answer.

🦉 Mixed Review and Test Prep

Take It to the NET
Test Prep
www.scottforesman.com

Write a fraction or a mixed number for each point.

28. Point *A*   **29.** Point *B*   **30.** Point *C*

31. How many different ways can Mari, Al, Jose, and Kim stand in a row?

A. 4   **B.** 6   **C.** 8   **D.** 24

Key Idea
To add or subtract fractions with unlike denominators, first find a common denominator.

Vocabulary
• equivalent fractions (p. 410)

Materials
• fraction strips or

 tools

Think It Through
I can **use models** to solve problems.

Understanding Adding and Subtracting with Unlike Denominators

WARM UP

Compare. Write >, <, or = for each ⬤.

1. $\frac{7}{9}$ ⬤ $\frac{2}{3}$ 2. $\frac{1}{4}$ ⬤ $\frac{1}{3}$

3. $\frac{5}{6}$ ⬤ $\frac{2}{3}$ 4. $\frac{3}{5}$ ⬤ $\frac{6}{10}$

LEARN

Activity

How can fraction strips help you add and subtract fractions with unlike denominators?

Two beads are laid end to end. One is $\frac{3}{4}$ inch long and the other is $\frac{1}{8}$ inch long. What is the combined length?

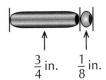

$\frac{3}{4}$ in. $\frac{1}{8}$ in.

Step 1 Use fraction strips to show $\frac{3}{4} + \frac{1}{8}$.

Step 2 Exchange $\frac{1}{4}$ strips with $\frac{1}{8}$ strips to find a fraction for $\frac{3}{4}$ with a denominator of 8.

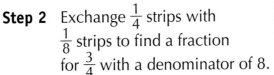

Step 3 How many $\frac{1}{8}$ strips are there? What is $\frac{3}{4} + \frac{1}{8}$?

Use fraction strips to find each sum.

a. $\frac{1}{8} + \frac{1}{2}$ **b.** $\frac{1}{6} + \frac{1}{3}$ **c.** $\frac{2}{3} + \frac{1}{12}$

Step 4 To find $\frac{2}{3} - \frac{1}{6}$, first use $\frac{1}{3}$ strips to show $\frac{2}{3}$.

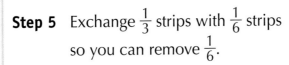

Step 5 Exchange $\frac{1}{3}$ strips with $\frac{1}{6}$ strips so you can remove $\frac{1}{6}$.

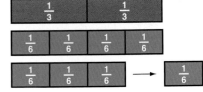

Step 6 How many $\frac{1}{6}$ strips are left? What is $\frac{2}{3} - \frac{1}{6}$?

Use fraction strips to find each difference.

d. $\frac{1}{2} - \frac{1}{12}$ **e.** $\frac{2}{3} - \frac{1}{2}$ **f.** $\frac{3}{4} - \frac{1}{3}$

g. How did you use equivalent fractions to show the sum and difference above?

Find each sum or difference. Simplify the answer, if possible.
You may use fraction strips or draw pictures to help.

1. $\frac{5}{6} - \frac{1}{3}$　　**2.** $\frac{1}{3} + \frac{1}{6}$　　**3.** $\frac{5}{6} - \frac{1}{12}$　　**4.** $\frac{2}{5} + \frac{3}{10}$　　**5.** $\frac{1}{8} + \frac{1}{4} + \frac{1}{2}$

6. Number Sense Which equivalent fraction for $\frac{1}{4}$ would
you use to subtract $\frac{1}{4}$ from $\frac{5}{12}$?

PRACTICE

For more practice, see Set 8-2 on p. 522.

Ⓐ Skills and Understanding

Find each sum or difference. Simplify the answer, if possible.
You may use fraction strips or draw pictures to help.

7. $\frac{1}{5} - \frac{1}{10}$　　**8.** $\frac{5}{8} + \frac{1}{4}$　　**9.** $\frac{5}{6} - \frac{1}{4}$　　**10.** $\frac{1}{5} + \frac{1}{2}$　　**11.** $\frac{3}{4} - \frac{1}{6}$

12. $\frac{1}{2} - \frac{1}{8}$　　**13.** $\frac{1}{2} + \frac{3}{10}$　　**14.** $\frac{1}{2} + \frac{1}{4}$　　**15.** $\frac{11}{12} - \frac{3}{4}$　　**16.** $\frac{1}{3} + \frac{5}{12}$

17. Reasoning Draw a picture to show that $\frac{5}{6} - \frac{1}{3} = \frac{1}{2}$.

Ⓑ Reasoning and Problem Solving

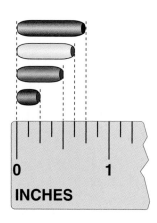

Use the drawing at the right for 18–21.

18. How long are two red beads together?

19. What is the combined length of 1 yellow, 1 red,
and 1 purple bead placed end-to-end?

20. How much longer is the red bead than the
blue bead?

21. Writing in Math Draw a string of beads that have
a total length of 2 inches. Explain your drawing.

Mixed Review and Test Prep

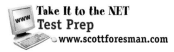
Take It to the NET
Test Prep
www.scottforesman.com

Add or subtract. Simplify the answer, if possible.

22. $\frac{3}{5} + \frac{4}{5}$　　**23.** $\frac{7}{10} - \frac{3}{10}$　　**24.** $15.7 + 2.45$　　**25.** $56.87 - 23.4$

26. Four boys ordered a pizza. Who ate the most pizza
if Jason ate $\frac{1}{6}$ of it, Lenny ate $\frac{1}{12}$ of it, Marc ate $\frac{5}{12}$ of
it, and Bart ate $\frac{1}{3}$ of it?

A. Lenny　　　**B.** Jason　　　**C.** Marc　　　**D.** Bart

Vocabulary
• multiple
• least common multiple (LCM)
• divisible (p. 162)
• least common denominator (LCD)

Think It Through
I can **make organized lists** to find the least common multiple and least common denominator.

Least Common Denominator

LEARN

How can you find the least common denominator of two fractions?

To find a common denominator of two fractions, it is helpful to know about **multiples** and the **least common multiple (LCM)**. You can find the nonzero multiples of any number by multiplying the number by 1, 2, 3, 4, and so on. The least common multiple of two numbers is the least number that is a multiple of both numbers.

Example A

Find the least common multiple of 3 and 4.

First find the common nonzero multiples of 3 and 4.

Multiples of 3: 3, 6, 9, **12**, 15, 18, 21, **24,** . . .
Multiples of 4: 4, 8, **12**, 16, 20, **24,** . . .

24 is a common multiple of 3 and 4.

12 is the least common multiple of 3 and 4.

12 is also the least number that is divisible by 3 and 4.

The **least common denominator (LCD)** of two fractions is the least common multiple of the denominators.

Example B

Find the least common denominator of $\frac{1}{8}$ and $\frac{5}{12}$.

Multiples of 8: 8, 16, **24,** 32, 40, **48.** . .
Multiples of 12: 12, **24,** 36, **48.** . .

24 is the **least common denominator** of $\frac{1}{8}$ and $\frac{5}{12}$.

✔ **Talk About It**

1. In Example B, why is 24 the least common denominator of $\frac{1}{8}$ and $\frac{5}{12}$?

2. What is the least common multiple of 10 and 4? What is the LCD of $\frac{1}{4}$ and $\frac{1}{10}$?

1. Find the least common multiple of 5 and 12.

Find the LCD for each pair of fractions.

2. $\frac{7}{10}$ and $\frac{1}{2}$ **3.** $\frac{2}{7}$ and $\frac{1}{3}$ **4.** $\frac{3}{4}$ and $\frac{5}{6}$ **5.** $\frac{1}{8}$ and $\frac{1}{6}$ **6.** $\frac{3}{8}$ and $\frac{5}{12}$

7. Number Sense In Exercise 2, Tanya said that since 10 is a multiple of 2, then 10 is the LCD. Is this true for any pair of numbers where one number is a multiple of the other?

PRACTICE

For more practice, see Set 8-3 on p. 522.

Ⓐ Skills and Understanding

Find the LCM of each pair of numbers.

8. 4 and 5   **9.** 8 and 12   **10.** 3 and 10   **11.** 6 and 8   **12.** 7 and 9

Find the LCD for each pair of fractions.

13. $\frac{3}{8}$ and $\frac{3}{4}$ **14.** $\frac{1}{3}$ and $\frac{5}{12}$ **15.** $\frac{11}{15}$ and $\frac{3}{5}$ **16.** $\frac{1}{6}$ and $\frac{1}{2}$ **17.** $\frac{2}{3}$ and $\frac{4}{9}$

18. $\frac{3}{4}$ and $\frac{1}{6}$ **19.** $\frac{5}{6}$ and $\frac{7}{10}$ **20.** $\frac{5}{8}$ and $\frac{7}{12}$ **21.** $\frac{1}{6}$ and $\frac{2}{9}$ **22.** $\frac{5}{8}$ and $\frac{5}{6}$

23. Mental Math Can you find the greatest common multiple for 3 and 4?

Ⓑ Reasoning and Problem Solving

Use the coins at the right for 24–25.

24. What is the combined width of a dime and quarter? Can you add any of the other diameters as they are given? Explain.

25. Use the LCD for the diameters of a penny and a nickel to compare their widths.

26. <u>**Writing in Math**</u> Eric says that you can always find the LCD for two fractions by multiplying their denominators. Do you agree? Why or why not?

$d = \frac{4}{5}$ in.

$d = \frac{9}{10}$ in.

$d = \frac{3}{4}$ in.

$d = \frac{7}{10}$ in.

 **Mixed Review and Test Prep**

 **Take It to the NET**
Test Prep
www.scottforesman.com

27. Find $\frac{1}{2} + \frac{3}{8}$.

| $\frac{1}{2}$ | | | $\frac{1}{8}$ | $\frac{1}{8}$ | $\frac{1}{8}$ |

| $\frac{1}{8}$ | $\frac{1}{8}$ | $\frac{1}{8}$ | $\frac{1}{8}$ | $\frac{1}{8}$ | $\frac{1}{8}$ | $\frac{1}{8}$ |

28. Algebra Solve $68 + n = 125$?

A. 193   **C.** 67

B. 183   **D.** 57

Key Idea
To add or subtract fractions with unlike denominators, find equivalent fractions with a common denominator, and then add or subtract.

Start He

1. How many people v house, apartment,

Numb

INCLUDE i
• foster
• people
  no other
• people l
  even

DO NOT I
• colle
• peo
  mer
Ar

Think It Through
I can also **use fraction strips to model** the problem.

$\frac{1}{4}$	

$\frac{1}{5}$	$\frac{1}{5}$

466

3. P

Adding and Subtracting Fractions with Unlike Denominators

WARM UP
Write in simplest form.

1. $\frac{20}{25}$ 2. $\frac{8}{20}$ 3. $\frac{9}{27}$

4. $1\frac{2}{6}$ 5. $\frac{9}{3}$ 6. $2\frac{4}{8}$

LEARN

How can you use the LCD to add or subtract fractions with unlike denominators?

The United States Constitution provides that a census, or population count, be taken in the United States every 10 years. The most recent census was completed in 2000. About 281 million people live in the United States.

Data File

U.S. Population by Age in 2000

Age Group	Approximate Fraction of Population
Under age 18	$\frac{1}{4}$
Ages 18 to 44	$\frac{2}{5}$
Ages 45 to 64	$\frac{9}{40}$
65 or over	$\frac{1}{8}$

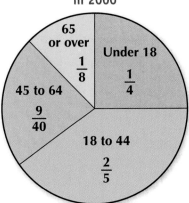

U.S. Population by Age in 2000

Example A

What fraction of the United States population was younger than age 45 in 2000?

Find $\frac{1}{4} + \frac{2}{5}$.

STEP 1

Find the LCM of the denominators.

$\frac{1}{4}$ Multiples of 4:
   4, 8, 12, 16, **20**, ...

$\frac{2}{5}$ Multiples of 5:
   5, 10, 15, **20**, 25, ...

So, the LCD is 20.

STEP 2

Write equivalent fractions with a denominator of 20.

$$\frac{1}{4} \xrightarrow{\times 5} \frac{5}{20} \qquad \frac{2}{5} \xrightarrow{\times 4} \frac{8}{20}$$

STEP 3

Add. Simplify, if necessary.

$$\begin{array}{r} \frac{1}{4} = \frac{5}{20} \\ + \frac{2}{5} = + \frac{8}{20} \\ \hline \frac{13}{20} \end{array}$$

About $\frac{13}{20}$ of the population was younger than age 45.

Example B

Find $\frac{5}{6} - \frac{8}{15}$.

STEP 1	STEP 2	STEP 3
Find the LCM.	Write equivalent fractions with a denominator of 30.	Subtract. Simplify, if possible.

STEP 1

$\frac{5}{6}$ Multiples of 6:
6, 12, 18, 24, **30**, . . .

$\frac{8}{15}$ Multiples of 15:
15, **30**, . . .

So, the LCD is 30.

STEP 2

$$\frac{5}{6} = \frac{25}{30} \qquad \frac{8}{15} = \frac{16}{30}$$

STEP 3

$$\begin{array}{r} \frac{5}{6} = \frac{25}{30} \\ -\frac{8}{15} = -\frac{16}{30} \\ \hline \frac{9}{30} = \frac{3}{10} \end{array}$$

Example C

Find $\frac{3}{8} + \frac{1}{6} + \frac{3}{4}$.

STEP 1	STEP 2	STEP 3
Find the LCM.	Write equivalent fractions.	Add. Simplify, if possible.

STEP 1

Multiples of 8: 8, 16, **24**, . . .

Multiples of 6: 6, 12, 18, **24**, . . .

Multiples of 4: 4, 8, 12, 16, 20, **24**, . . .

So, the LCD is 24.

STEP 2

$$\frac{3}{8} = \frac{9}{24}$$

$$\frac{1}{6} = \frac{4}{24}$$

$$\frac{3}{4} = \frac{18}{24}$$

STEP 3

$$\frac{9}{24} + \frac{4}{24} + \frac{18}{24} = \frac{31}{24} = 1\frac{7}{24}$$

✔ Talk About It

1. How is the LCD used in the Examples? How is the LCD used to add or subtract fractions with unlike denominators?

2. **Number Sense** In Example A, would you get the same sum if you used 40 as a common denominator instead of the LCD? Explain.

CHECK ✔

For another example, see Set 8-4 on p. 519.

Add or subtract. Simplify, if possible.

1. $\frac{2}{9}$
$+\frac{2}{3}$

2. $\frac{3}{4}$
$+\frac{1}{6}$

3. $\frac{4}{5}$
$-\frac{3}{10}$

4. $\frac{5}{6}$
$-\frac{1}{5}$

5. $\frac{13}{16}$
$-\frac{1}{2}$

6. **Number Sense** Without adding, how can you tell if the sum of $\frac{1}{5}$ and $\frac{1}{4}$ is greater or less than 1? Explain.

A Skills and Understanding

Add or subtract. Simplify, if possible.

7. $\dfrac{7}{10}$
$-\dfrac{1}{4}$

8. $\dfrac{5}{8}$
$+\dfrac{5}{6}$

9. $\dfrac{1}{2}$
$-\dfrac{1}{6}$

10. $\dfrac{3}{11}$
$+\dfrac{1}{2}$

11. $\dfrac{7}{12}$
$+\dfrac{2}{3}$

12. $\dfrac{2}{3} - \dfrac{1}{4}$ **13.** $\dfrac{3}{5} - \dfrac{1}{3}$ **14.** $\dfrac{11}{12} - \dfrac{5}{8}$ **15.** $\dfrac{5}{9} - \dfrac{2}{5}$ **16.** $\dfrac{7}{8} + \dfrac{1}{12}$

17. $\dfrac{7}{8} - \dfrac{2}{3}$ **18.** $\dfrac{1}{2} + \dfrac{3}{8} + \dfrac{3}{4}$ **19.** $\dfrac{2}{5} + \dfrac{1}{3} + \dfrac{5}{6}$ **20.** $\dfrac{1}{2} + \dfrac{1}{4} + \dfrac{1}{5}$ **21.** $\dfrac{7}{10} + \dfrac{1}{5} + \dfrac{1}{10}$

22. Reasoning Claire says you can multiply the denominators in $\dfrac{3}{5} + \dfrac{4}{10}$ and get a common denominator of 50. Is she correct? If so, does this always work? Explain.

B Reasoning and Problem Solving

Math and Social Studies

The ancient Egyptians used fractions more than 3,000 years ago! But they used only unit fractions, or fractions with a numerator of 1. The one exception was $\dfrac{2}{3}$. All other fractions were written as the sum of unit fractions that are all different. For example, $\dfrac{5}{12}$ would be written as $\dfrac{1}{3} + \dfrac{1}{12}$, or $\dfrac{1}{4} + \dfrac{1}{6}$.

Write each modern fraction as an Egyptian fraction.

23. $\dfrac{3}{4}$ **24.** $\dfrac{5}{6}$ **25.** $\dfrac{3}{8}$ **26.** $\dfrac{7}{12}$

27. What modern fraction is equal to this Egyptian fraction: $\dfrac{1}{2} + \dfrac{1}{5} + \dfrac{1}{10}$?

28. **Writing in Math** Is the explanation and answer below correct? If not, tell why and write a correct response.

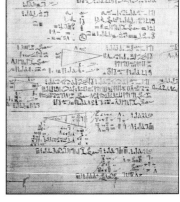

This papyrus, dating to 1650 BC, is often referred to as the Ahmes Papyrus in honor of the scribe who wrote it.

> Explain the steps for finding $\dfrac{2}{3} + \dfrac{1}{4}$.
>
> First, I use the LCD to write equivalent fractions with a common denominator.
>
> I add the numerators and write the sum over the common denominator.
>
> Then I simplify the sum.
>
> $\dfrac{2}{3} = \dfrac{2}{12}$ $\dfrac{1}{4} = \dfrac{1}{12}$
>
> $\dfrac{2}{12} + \dfrac{1}{12} = \dfrac{3}{12} = \dfrac{1}{4}$

Think It Through
- I should **show my work clearly** so that others can understand it.
- I will **write my steps in order.**

C Extensions

Find the greatest common factor (GCF) and the least common multiple (LCM) for each pair of numbers.

29. 4 and 6   **30.** 10 and 15   **31.** 12 and 15   **32.** 18 and 30

33. The first row of the table below has been completed. Use your results from 29–32 to help complete the rest of the table.

a	b	$a \times b$	GCF of a and b	LCM of a and b	$\left(\dfrac{\text{GCF of}}{a \text{ and } b}\right) \times \left(\dfrac{\text{LCM of}}{a \text{ and } b}\right)$
8	12	96	4	24	96
4	6	24			
10	15	150			
12	15	180			
18	30	540			

34. If you know the GCF of two numbers a and b, how could you easily find the LCM of a and b?

Mixed Review and Test Prep

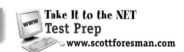
Take It to the NET
Test Prep
www.scottforesman.com

Find the LCD for each pair of fractions.

35. $\dfrac{7}{10}$ and $\dfrac{4}{7}$ **36.** $\dfrac{4}{9}$ and $\dfrac{1}{6}$ **37.** $\dfrac{3}{11}$ and $\dfrac{4}{33}$ **38.** $\dfrac{11}{12}$ and $\dfrac{5}{9}$

39. What is the mean of these ticket prices: $8, $5, $2, $10, $10?

    A. $35   **B.** $10   **C.** $8   **D.** $7

Practice Game

Decimals Are Fractions Too!

Players: 2
Materials: Fraction Cards, Set B
            Game Board: Decimals Are Fractions Too!
            25 markers for each player in 2 colors

Mix the cards and place them face down. In turn, the players turn over the top card and try to match the fraction to a decimal on the game board. If the player makes a match, he or she places a marker on the decimal shown. Only one marker may be placed in a turn. If the player does not find a match, the turn is over. Play continues in this manner until one player covers 5 decimals in a row horizontally, vertically, or diagonally. This player is the winner of the game.

Do You Know How?

Do You Understand?

Adding and Subtracting Fractions with Like Denominators (8-1)

Add or subtract. Simplify, if necessary.

1. $\frac{5}{9} + \frac{1}{9}$

2. $\frac{7}{8} - \frac{3}{8}$

3. $\frac{11}{12}$
$-\frac{5}{12}$

4. $\frac{3}{5}$
$\frac{1}{5}$
$+\frac{4}{5}$

Ⓐ Explain how to add fractions with like denominators.

Ⓑ How do you subtract fractions with like denominators?

Least Common Denominator (8-3)

Write each pair of fractions with their LCD.

5. $\frac{7}{12}$ and $\frac{1}{4}$

6. $\frac{5}{7}$ and $\frac{1}{2}$

7. $\frac{3}{4}$ and $\frac{1}{6}$

8. $\frac{5}{6}$ and $\frac{3}{8}$

Ⓒ How do you know when a number is the LCD of two fractions?

Ⓓ What number is always a common denominator of two fractions?

Understanding Adding and Subtracting with Unlike Denominators (8-2)
Adding and Subtracting Fractions with Unlike Denominators (8-4)

Add or subtract. Simplify, if necessary. You may use fraction strips or draw pictures to help.

9. $\frac{3}{8}$
$+\frac{1}{4}$

10. $\frac{9}{10}$
$-\frac{3}{4}$

11. $\frac{4}{5} + \frac{1}{2}$

12. $\frac{8}{15} - \frac{1}{3}$

13. $\frac{1}{2}$
$\frac{1}{4}$
$+\frac{1}{8}$

14. $\frac{2}{5}$
$\frac{3}{10}$
$+\frac{3}{5}$

Ⓔ How can you tell if one of the denominators is a common denominator?

Ⓕ Explain how using a common denominator greater than the LCD to add or subtract fractions will affect the answer.

Ⓖ Without adding, can you tell if $\frac{3}{5} + \frac{1}{2}$ is greater than 1? Explain.

MULTIPLE CHOICE

1. Which fraction shows the difference $\frac{7}{12} - \frac{1}{4}$ in simplest form? (8-4)

    A. $\frac{5}{6}$ **B.** $\frac{4}{12}$ **C.** $\frac{1}{3}$ **D.** $\frac{6}{8}$

2. Which number is NOT a common denominator of $\frac{5}{6}$ and $\frac{5}{9}$? (8-3)

    A. 36   **B.** 54   **C.** 15   **D.** 18

FREE RESPONSE

Add or subtract. Simplify, if possible. You may use fraction strips or draw pictures to help. (8-1 through 8-4)

3. $\frac{1}{7} + \frac{3}{7}$

4. $\frac{5}{9} - \frac{2}{9}$

5. $\frac{11}{12} + \frac{1}{6}$

6. $\frac{9}{10} - \frac{1}{3}$

7. $\frac{4}{5} - \frac{1}{4}$

8. $\frac{5}{8} + \frac{1}{2}$

9. $\frac{5}{6} - \frac{1}{4}$

10. $\frac{13}{20} - \frac{3}{10}$

11. $\frac{1}{15} + \frac{2}{3} + \frac{1}{5}$

12. Tony walked $\frac{1}{2}$ mile to Ed's house and then $\frac{3}{4}$ mile to the park. How far did Tony walk in all? (8-4)

13. Jen had $\frac{7}{8}$ of a pound of walnuts. She used $\frac{1}{2}$ of a pound for a cake. How many pounds of walnuts were left? (8-4)

> **TEST TALK**
>
> **Think It Through**
> To find the least common denominator of fractions, I need to **find the least common multiple of the denominators.**

Writing in Math

14. What is the LCD of the seven fractions shown on the map? Explain how you know it is the LCD. (8-3)

15. Which is larger, Asia or Africa? Explain how you know. (8-3)

16. Write and solve a problem about the total land area of three continents. (8-4)

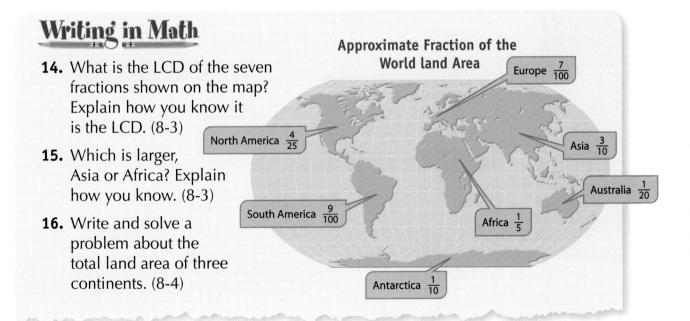

Approximate Fraction of the World land Area

Europe $\frac{7}{100}$

North America $\frac{4}{25}$

Asia $\frac{3}{10}$

Australia $\frac{1}{20}$

South America $\frac{9}{100}$

Africa $\frac{1}{5}$

Antarctica $\frac{1}{10}$

Key Idea
Before you can add or subtract mixed numbers, you need to understand how to rename them.

Vocabulary
• mixed number (p. 400)

Materials
• fraction strips

Understanding Adding and Subtracting Mixed Numbers

LEARN

Activity

How can fraction strips help you add and subtract mixed numbers?

a. Use fraction strips to show $1\frac{3}{5} + 1\frac{4}{5}$.

b. Combine the $\frac{1}{5}$ strips. Then combine the 1 strips.

c. How many $\frac{1}{5}$ strips are there? Exchange five $\frac{1}{5}$ strips for a 1 strip.

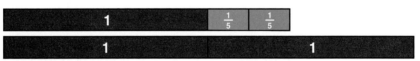

d. What is the sum $1\frac{3}{5} + 1\frac{4}{5}$?

e. To find $2\frac{1}{4} - 1\frac{3}{4}$, first use fraction strips to show $2\frac{1}{4}$.

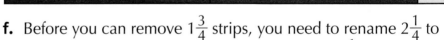

f. Before you can remove $1\frac{3}{4}$ strips, you need to rename $2\frac{1}{4}$ to show more fourths. Exchange a 1 strip for four $\frac{1}{4}$ strips.

g. Remove $1\frac{3}{4}$. What is the difference $2\frac{1}{4} - 1\frac{3}{4}$?

h. Why did you have to exchange fraction strips in both problems? How did each exchange show renaming mixed numbers or improper fractions?

For another example, see Set 8-5 on p. 519.

CHECK ✓

Find each sum or difference. Simplify the answer, if necessary.
You may use fraction strips or draw pictures to help.

1. $3\frac{3}{4} + 1\frac{3}{4}$ **2.** $5\frac{5}{8} + 1\frac{7}{8}$ **3.** $2\frac{1}{3} - 1\frac{2}{3}$ **4.** $8\frac{1}{9} - 3\frac{7}{9}$

5. Number Sense If you want to subtract $4\frac{5}{7}$ from 10, how
should you rename 10?

PRACTICE

For more practice, see Set 8-5 on p. 523.

(A) Skills and Understanding

Find each sum or difference. Simplify the answer, if necessary.
You may use fraction strips or draw pictures to help.

6. $6\frac{1}{7} + 7\frac{5}{7}$ **7.** $9\frac{5}{6} + 4\frac{1}{6}$ **8.** $3\frac{1}{8} - 1\frac{7}{8}$ **9.** $7 - 3\frac{4}{9}$

10. $2 + 4\frac{1}{3}$ **11.** $5\frac{7}{8} + \frac{3}{8}$ **12.** $4\frac{6}{7} - 1\frac{3}{7}$ **13.** $8 - 2\frac{3}{11}$

14. Number Sense How can you tell without subtracting
that $4\frac{1}{3} - 1\frac{2}{3}$ is less than 3?

(B) Reasoning and Problem Solving

15. How much longer is the
crayon than the eraser?

16. A pencil 5 in. long is placed
end-to-end next to the crayon.
What is the overall length?

17. **Writing in Math** Explain how
you would use fraction strips
to model the problem in
problem 15.

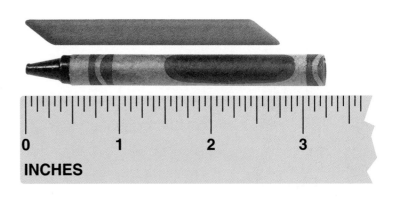

INCHES

Mixed Review and Test Prep

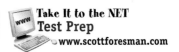

Take It to the NET
Test Prep
www.scottforesman.com

Add or subtract.

18. $1,278 + 692$ **19.** $2,081 - 1,568$ **20.** $231.7 + 88.9$ **21.** $47 - 3.62$

22. Mary bought $\frac{1}{2}$ yd of blue ribbon, $\frac{2}{3}$ yd of white ribbon, and $\frac{5}{6}$ yd
of red ribbon. How much ribbon did she buy?

     A. $\frac{1}{2}$ yd   **B.** $\frac{2}{3}$ yd   **C.** 2 yd   **D.** $2\frac{1}{6}$ yd

All text pages available online and on CD-ROM.

Key Idea
You can use rounding to estimate sums and differences of mixed numbers.

TEST TALK

Think It Through
- When a number is less than halfway between two numbers, I **use the lesser whole number.**
- When a number is halfway or more than halfway between two numbers, I **use the greater whole number.**

Estimating Sums and Differences of Mixed Numbers

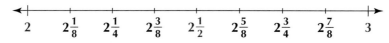

LEARN

How can you estimate with mixed numbers?

To estimate with mixed numbers, round the numbers to the nearest whole number.

$$2 \quad 2\frac{1}{8} \quad 2\frac{1}{4} \quad 2\frac{3}{8} \quad 2\frac{1}{2} \quad 2\frac{5}{8} \quad 2\frac{3}{4} \quad 2\frac{7}{8} \quad 3$$

To the nearest whole number:

$2\frac{1}{4}$ rounds to 2. $2\frac{1}{2}$ rounds to 3. $2\frac{3}{4}$ rounds to 3.

Example

The Gomez family is driving from Albuquerque, NM, to Denver, CO. Use the times on the map to estimate the total driving time.

$$3\frac{1}{3} + 1\frac{1}{2} + 1\frac{3}{4}$$

$$\downarrow \qquad \downarrow \qquad \downarrow$$

$$3 + 2 + 2 = 7$$

Round each mixed number to the nearest whole number. Then add.

It will take about 7 hours to drive from Albuquerque to Denver.

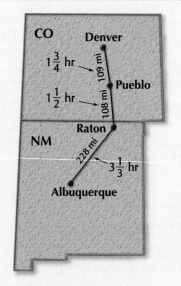

CO
Denver
$1\frac{3}{4}$ hr
109 mi
Pueblo
$1\frac{1}{2}$ hr
108 mi
Raton
NM
228 mi
$3\frac{1}{3}$ hr
Albuquerque

✔ **Talk About It**

1. In the Example, is the actual driving time more or less than 7 hours? Explain how you know.

2. In the Example, suppose the driving from Albuquerque to Raton is $3\frac{2}{3}$ hr. Explain how the estimate would change.

3. **Number Sense** How can you tell if a fraction is greater than, less than, or equal to $\frac{1}{2}$?

CHECK ✓

Estimate. First round to the nearest whole number.

1. $2\frac{1}{2} + 4\frac{5}{8}$ **2.** $8\frac{1}{3} - 2\frac{3}{4}$ **3.** $6\frac{1}{3} + 3\frac{1}{4} + 5\frac{1}{8}$ **4.** $9\frac{3}{8} - 1\frac{1}{2}$

5. Number Sense Name four mixed numbers that round to 3 when first rounded to the nearest whole number.

PRACTICE

For more practice, see Set 8-6 on p. 523.

A Skills and Understanding

Estimate. First round to the nearest whole number.

6. $6\frac{9}{10} + 3\frac{2}{3}$ **7.** $12\frac{1}{4} - 7\frac{4}{5}$ **8.** $4\frac{1}{8} - 1\frac{2}{3}$ **9.** $2\frac{1}{2} - \frac{7}{8}$

10. $5\frac{1}{4} + 5\frac{1}{5} + 2$ **11.** $2\frac{1}{2} + 1\frac{1}{3} + 3\frac{7}{12}$ **12.** $6\frac{1}{4} + 3\frac{2}{3} + 7\frac{4}{5}$ **13.** $3\frac{8}{11} + 5\frac{1}{3} + 1\frac{3}{5}$

14. Number Sense An estimated sum of two mixed numbers is about 6. One of the numbers is $3\frac{5}{8}$. What might be the other number? How do you know?

B Reasoning and Problem Solving

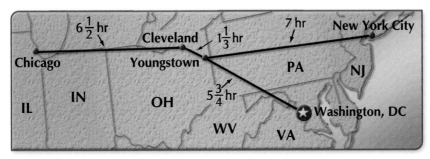

15. Estimate the driving times between Chicago and New York City and between Chicago and Washington, D.C.

16. **Writing in Math** Estimate the difference between the two shortest driving times on the map. Explain how you got your answer.

🦉 Mixed Review and Test Prep

Take It to the NET
Test Prep
www.scottforesman.com

Solve for *n*.

17. $14 + n = 22$ **18.** $7n = 63$ **19.** $n - 9 = 2$

20. What is the product of 2.7×1.9?

   A. 0.513   **B.** 5.13   **C.** 51.3   **D.** 513

21. **Writing in Math** How can you use fraction strips to show $1\frac{3}{4} - \frac{1}{2}$?

📖 All text pages available online and on CD-ROM.   **Section B Lesson 8-6**   **475**

Key Idea
You can add mixed numbers the same way you add whole numbers and fractions.

Adding Mixed Numbers

LEARN

How is adding mixed numbers like adding fractions and whole numbers?

Trail mix provides a high-energy food for activities like camping and hiking. Luke used the recipe at the right to make trail mix.

Trail Mix Recipe

$1\frac{3}{4}$ lb dried bananas $1\frac{1}{2}$ lb dried pineapple

$1\frac{3}{8}$ lb raisins $1\frac{5}{8}$ lb peanuts

$1\frac{1}{2}$ lb mixed nuts $\frac{3}{4}$ lb sunflower seeds

Think It Through
- I can break the mixed numbers apart to **solve two simpler problems.**
- I can **use estimation to check** if the exact answer is reasonable.

Example

How many pounds of dried bananas and raisins did Luke use?

Find $1\frac{3}{4} + 1\frac{3}{8}$.

STEP 1

Write equivalent fractions with the LCD.

$$1\frac{3}{4} = 1\frac{6}{8}$$
$$+ 1\frac{3}{8} = + 1\frac{3}{8}$$

STEP 2

Add the fractions.

$$1\frac{3}{4} = 1\frac{6}{8}$$
$$+ 1\frac{3}{8} = + 1\frac{3}{8}$$
$$\frac{9}{8}$$

STEP 3

Add the whole numbers. Simplify the sum, if necessary.

$$1\frac{3}{4} = 1\frac{6}{8}$$
$$+ 1\frac{3}{8} = + 1\frac{3}{8}$$
$$2\frac{9}{8} = 3\frac{1}{8}$$

So, Luke used $3\frac{1}{8}$ pounds of bananas and raisins.

✔ Talk About It

1. Estimate the sum found in the Example. Is the estimate close to the actual answer? Why is it helpful to compare an exact answer to an estimate?

2. How many pounds of peanuts and mixed nuts did Luke use? Show this sum on a number line.

3. **Reasoning** How is adding mixed numbers like adding fractions and whole numbers?

Estimate the sum first. Then add. Simplify, if necessary.

1. $3\frac{1}{6}$
$+ 5\frac{2}{3}$

2. $3\frac{1}{4}$
$+ 2\frac{7}{8}$

3. $11\frac{3}{4}$
$+ 7\frac{3}{4}$

4. $14\frac{7}{10}$
$+ 12\frac{3}{15}$

5. $22\frac{1}{2}$
$+ 17\frac{3}{5}$

6. Number Sense Can the sum of two mixed numbers be less than 1? Use examples to explain why or why not.

PRACTICE

For more practice, see Set 8-7 on p. 523.

Ⓐ Skills and Understanding

Estimate the sum first. Then add. Simplify, if necessary.

7. $3\frac{5}{8}$
$+ 4\frac{1}{2}$

8. $4\frac{1}{2}$
$+ 1\frac{6}{7}$

9. $17\frac{1}{3}$
$+ 5\frac{3}{5}$

10. $9\frac{7}{8}$
$+ 2\frac{7}{8}$

11. $30\frac{1}{2}$
$+ 12\frac{2}{3}$

12. $2\frac{3}{4} + 7\frac{3}{5}$ 　 **13.** $8\frac{2}{5} + 4\frac{3}{7}$ 　 **14.** $4\frac{1}{2} + 3\frac{8}{9}$ 　 **15.** $15 + 6\frac{2}{5}$ 　 **16.** $5\frac{6}{7} + 8\frac{1}{7}$

17. Mental Math What is the sum of $3\frac{1}{4}$ and $6\frac{3}{4}$?

Ⓑ Reasoning and Problem Solving

18. Luke's pop-up tent weighs $3\frac{7}{8}$ pounds, and his sleeping bag weighs $1\frac{1}{2}$ pounds. What is the total weight of both items?

19. Luke's backpack weighs $5\frac{1}{2}$ pounds. While hiking, he attaches his sleeping bag and tent to his backpack. How much weight does he have to carry altogether?

20. **Writing in Math** Brent says that the sum of two mixed numbers is always a mixed number. Do you agree? Explain.

🦉 Mixed Review and Test Prep

Take It to the NET
Test Prep
www.scottforesman.com

Estimate each sum or difference.

21. $12\frac{2}{3} + 5\frac{1}{4}$ 　 **22.** $15\frac{1}{8} - 4\frac{3}{4}$ 　 **23.** $9\frac{1}{2} + 4\frac{1}{10}$ 　 **24.** $31\frac{1}{4} - 10\frac{7}{8}$

25. What is $20 - 1.9$?

A. 19.1 　 **B.** 18.9 　 **C.** 18.1 　 **D.** 1

Subtracting Mixed Numbers

✓ **WARM UP**

1. $\frac{3}{4} - \frac{5}{8}$ 2. $\frac{2}{3} - \frac{1}{5}$

3. $\frac{6}{7} - \frac{3}{14}$ 4. $\frac{7}{10} - \frac{1}{4}$

LEARN

How do you subtract a mixed number from a mixed number?

Sheila collects butterflies and moths. She measured two wingspans as shown below.

Tiger Swallowtail $3\frac{3}{4}$ inches

← Buckeye $1\frac{7}{8}$ inches →

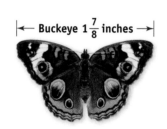

Example A

What is the difference between the wingspan measurements?

Find $3\frac{3}{4} - 1\frac{7}{8}$.

STEP 1	STEP 2	STEP 3
Write equivalent fractions with the LCD.	Rename $3\frac{6}{8}$ to show more eighths.	Subtract the fractions. Then subtract the whole numbers. Simplify the difference.

Think:
$$3\frac{6}{8} = 2 + 1 + \frac{6}{8}$$
$$= 2 + \frac{8}{8} + \frac{6}{8}$$

STEP 1
$$3\frac{3}{4} = 3\frac{6}{8}$$
$$-1\frac{7}{8} = -1\frac{7}{8}$$

STEP 2
$$3\frac{3}{4} = 3\frac{6}{8} = 2\frac{14}{8}$$
$$-1\frac{7}{8} = -1\frac{7}{8} = -1\frac{7}{8}$$

STEP 3
$$3\frac{3}{4} = 3\frac{6}{8} = 2\frac{14}{8}$$
$$-1\frac{7}{8} = -1\frac{7}{8} = -1\frac{7}{8}$$
$$1\frac{7}{8}$$

The difference between the wingspan measurements is $1\frac{7}{8}$ inches.

Think It Through
I can **use estimation** to see if the exact answer is reasonable.

✓ **Talk About It**

1. In Example A, why do you have to rename to subtract?

How do you subtract a mixed number from a whole number?

Example B

Find $7 - 1\frac{7}{8}$.

STEP 1	STEP 2
Rename 7 to show eighths.	Subtract the fractions. Then subtract the whole numbers.

$$7 \quad = \quad 6\frac{8}{8}$$
$$-\,1\frac{7}{8} = -\,1\frac{7}{8}$$

$$7 \quad = \quad 6\frac{8}{8}$$
$$-\,1\frac{7}{8} = -\,1\frac{7}{8}$$
$$\qquad\quad = \quad 5\frac{1}{8}$$

✔ **Talk About It**

2. In Example B, why do you have to rename 7?

3. How could you check the answer in Example B?

Take It to the NET
www More Examples
www.scottforesman.com

CHECK ✓

For another example, see Set 8-8 on p. 520.

Estimate the difference first. Then subtract. Simplify, if necessary.

1. $\quad 6\frac{1}{3} = \quad 6\frac{4}{12} = \quad 5\frac{12}{12}$
$\quad -2\frac{3}{4} = -2\frac{9}{12} = -2\frac{9}{12}$
$\qquad\qquad\qquad\qquad\qquad 3\frac{}{12}$

2. $\quad 9 \quad = \quad 8\frac{}{10}$
$\quad -2\frac{7}{10} = -2\frac{7}{10}$
$\qquad\qquad\qquad\quad 6\frac{}{10}$

3. $\quad 9\frac{3}{4}$
$\quad -2\frac{1}{8}$

4. $\quad 6\frac{1}{3}$
$\quad -2\frac{3}{5}$

5. Number Sense Can the difference of two mixed numbers be less than 1? Use examples to explain why or why not.

PRACTICE

For more practice, see Set 8-8 on p. 523.

A Skills and Understanding

Estimate the difference first. Then subtract. Simplify, if necessary.

6. $\quad 4\frac{1}{2} = \quad 4\frac{2}{4} = \quad 3\frac{}{4}$
$\quad -1\frac{3}{4} = -1\frac{3}{4} = -1\frac{3}{4}$
$\qquad\qquad\qquad\qquad\qquad 2\frac{}{4}$

7. $\quad 5 \quad = \quad 4\frac{}{8}$
$\quad -1\frac{3}{8} = -1\frac{3}{8}$
$\qquad\qquad\qquad\quad 3\frac{}{8}$

8. $\quad 7\frac{3}{10}$
$\quad -2\frac{4}{5}$

9. $\quad 4\frac{1}{3}$
$\quad -2\frac{3}{4}$

Estimate the difference first. Then subtract. Simplify, if necessary.

10. $6\frac{1}{3}$
$- 5\frac{2}{3}$

11. $4\frac{2}{5}$
$- 1\frac{3}{4}$

12. 8
$- 2\frac{4}{5}$

13. $4\frac{1}{6}$
$- 1\frac{3}{8}$

14. $21\frac{1}{2}$
$- 11\frac{1}{3}$

15. $4\frac{1}{8} - 1\frac{1}{2}$

16. $9 - 4\frac{3}{7}$

17. $15\frac{1}{6} - 4\frac{4}{9}$

18. $15\frac{1}{9} - 8$

19. $14\frac{2}{3} - 5\frac{1}{7}$

20. $6\frac{3}{4} - 1\frac{7}{8}$

21. $3\frac{3}{5} - \frac{7}{10}$

22. $4\frac{5}{6} - 4\frac{1}{3}$

23. $9\frac{1}{2} - 6\frac{3}{4}$

24. $9\frac{3}{7} - 1\frac{9}{14}$

25. Reasoning Sandra added $\frac{2}{3}$ to both 10 and $5\frac{1}{3}$ to find $10 - 5\frac{1}{3}$.
Does her strategy work? Explain why or why not.

B Reasoning and Problem Solving

Math and Science

Which has the greater wingspan?
How much greater?

26. Dog Face or Cloudless Sulphur

27. Io or Luna

28. Io or Cloudless Sulphur

29. The Hercules moth's wingspan is
14 inches. How much wider is this
than the wingspan of the Luna?

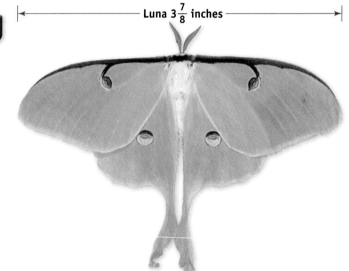
Luna $3\frac{7}{8}$ inches

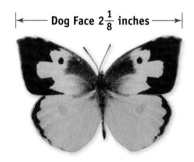
Dog Face $2\frac{1}{8}$ inches

Cloudless Sulphur $2\frac{3}{8}$ inches

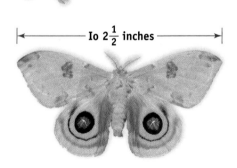
Io $2\frac{1}{2}$ inches

30. <u>Writing in Math</u> Is the explanation below correct? If not, tell
why and write a correct response.

Explain how to find $5 - 1\frac{3}{4}$.

I know that $5 - 1 = 4$. But $\frac{3}{4}$ are still left. So the answer is $4\frac{3}{4}$.

(C) Extensions

You can use inverse operations to solve equations that contain mixed numbers.

To solve, use the inverse operation. The inverse operation of addition is subtraction.

$n + 2\frac{1}{4} = 5$

$n = 5 - 2\frac{1}{4}$

$n = 2\frac{3}{4}$

Solve for *n*.

31. $n + 1\frac{3}{8} = 2\frac{1}{4}$

32. $6\frac{2}{3} = n - 8\frac{1}{6}$

33. $3\frac{3}{4} + n = 5\frac{1}{2}$

Mixed Review and Test Prep

Take It to the NET
Test Prep
www.scottforesman.com

Multiply or divide.

34. 245×52

35. 306×17

36. $588 \div 28$

37. $1,320 \div 66$

38. Find $6\frac{3}{5} + 2\frac{2}{3}$.

39. Find $23.4 \div 100$.

A. $9\frac{4}{15}$ **C.** $8\frac{5}{8}$

A. 234   **C.** 23.4

B. $8\frac{19}{30}$ **D.** $8\frac{4}{15}$

B. 2.34   **D.** 0.234

Learning with Technology

Using a Calculator to Add and Subtract Mixed Numbers

You can use a fraction calculator to add and subtract mixed numbers.

To find $6\frac{4}{15} + 3\frac{11}{18}$,

Press: 6 [Unit] 4 [n] 15 [d] [+] 3 [Unit] 11 [n] 18 [d] [ENTER =]

or

Press: 6 [Unit] 4 [/] 15 [+] 3 [Unit] 11 [/] 18 [=] , depending on your calculator.

Display:  $6\frac{4}{15} + 3\frac{11}{18} = 9\frac{79}{90}$

For 1–4, use a calculator to add or subtract.

1. $4\frac{7}{13} + 2\frac{1}{9}$

2. $11\frac{7}{24} + 5\frac{3}{16}$

3. $10\frac{5}{12} - 4\frac{7}{8}$

4. $45\frac{9}{14} - 15\frac{5}{21}$

Reading For Math Success

Identify Steps in a Process

Identifying the steps in a process can help you use the **problem-solving skill, *Work Backward,*** in the next lesson.

In reading, identifying the steps in a process can help you organize what you read. In math, it can help you work backward to solve problems in which you know the result of a series of steps.

Kyle had some money in his wallet. He added $3.00, which he earned for mowing the lawn. Then he bought a notebook for $3.75 and a pen for $1.20. After his purchases, he had $6.75 left in his wallet. How much did Kyle begin with?

First I'll identify the steps in the problem.

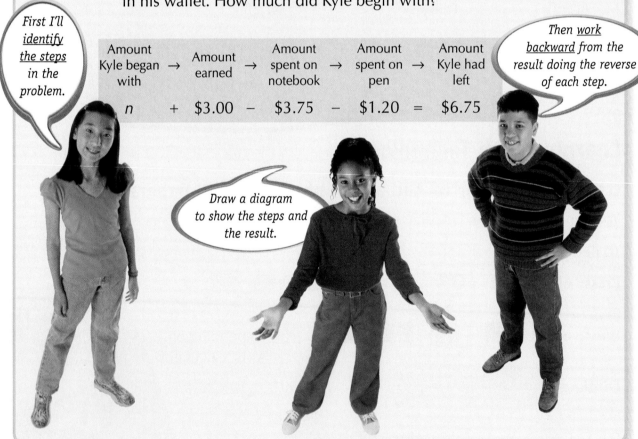

Amount Kyle began with		Amount earned		Amount spent on notebook		Amount spent on pen		Amount Kyle had left
n	+	$3.00	−	$3.75	−	$1.20	=	$6.75

Then <u>work backward</u> from the result doing the reverse of each step.

Draw a diagram to show the steps and the result.

1. How many steps from the starting number were taken to get the result $6.75?

2. As you work backward, how can you reverse the step where Kyle bought the pen?

For 3–5, use problem below.

Pam bought a roll of ribbon. She used $2\frac{3}{4}$ feet of ribbon on each of the two gifts she wrapped. Then she used $4\frac{1}{2}$ feet for an art project and 2 feet to make a scrapbook. There are 12 feet of ribbon left. How much ribbon was on the roll when Pam bought it?

3. Draw a diagram to show the steps involved in the problem.

4. Now work backward. How can you reverse the step where Pam used the ribbon to wrap gifts?

5. <u>Writing in Math</u> Explain the steps you would use to find the amount of ribbon on the roll Pam bought.

For 6–8, use the problem below.

Oscar finished his homework at 8:30 P.M. He recorded how much time he spent on each subject. When did Oscar start his homework?

1. Reading 45 minutes
2. Science 50 minutes
3. Math 40 minutes

6. Draw a diagram to show the steps involved in the problem.

7. Now work backward. How can you reverse the step where Oscar did his science homework?

8. <u>Writing in Math</u> Explain the steps you would use to solve the problem.

For 9–10, use the problem below.

Lizzie spilled some ink on her bank statement. How much money was in her account after the transaction she made on May 5?

9. Draw a diagram to show the steps involved in the problem.

10. <u>Writing in Math</u> What steps would you use to solve the problem?

Tri-County National Bank

Elizabeth Habib   Account No. 0002076

Date	Transaction	Balance
May 5		
May 16	Withdrawal: $20	
May 20	deposit: $30	
May 27	deposit: $10	$130

Problem-Solving Strategy

Key Idea
Learning how and when to work backward can help you solve problems.

Work Backward

LEARN

How do you work backward to solve a problem?

Tunnel Vision It took workers 5 weeks to dig a 10-mile tunnel. How much had the workers completed after the first 3 weeks of digging?

During the fourth week, the workers dug $2\frac{1}{2}$ miles. The next week, the workers dug $1\frac{1}{4}$ miles to complete the tunnel.

Read and Understand

What do you know?

The workers completed a 10-mile tunnel in 5 weeks. During week 4, they dug $2\frac{1}{2}$ miles. During week 5, they dug $1\frac{1}{4}$ miles.

What are you trying to find?

How many miles of tunnel did the workers dig in the first 3 weeks?

Plan and Solve

What strategy will you use?

Strategy: Work Backward

The number of miles they dug in the first 3 weeks is not known.

distance dug in the first 3 weeks = n miles

How to Work Backward

Step 1 Identify the unknown initial amount.

Step 2 Draw a picture to show each change, starting with the initial amount.

Step 3 Start at the end result. Work backward, using the inverse of each change.

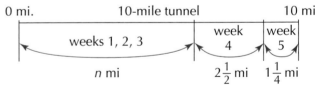

$10 - 1\frac{1}{4} - 2\frac{1}{2} = n; \qquad n = 6\frac{1}{4}$

Answer: The workers dug $6\frac{1}{4}$ miles of tunnel during the first 3 weeks.

Look Back and Check

Is your answer reasonable?

Yes, because when I work forward from the initial amount, I get the end result.

$6\frac{1}{4}$ mi $+ 2\frac{1}{2}$ mi $+ 1\frac{1}{4}$ mi $= 10$ mi

✔ Talk About It

1. Why do you subtract to solve the problem when the distance increased?

2. How would the solution to the problem change if a landslide filled in $\frac{3}{4}$ mi of the distance dug in Week 4?

When might you work backward?

Baking Carole has $1\frac{1}{4}$ cups of flour left over from the bag she bought. She used $3\frac{3}{4}$ cups of flour to make bread and 1 cup to make pretzels. To make biscuits, she used twice the amount of flour she used to make pretzels. How much flour was in the bag Carole bought?

When to Work Backward

Think about working backward when:
You know the end result of a series of steps.
- The workers completed a 10-mile tunnel after 5 weeks of digging.
- Carole has $1\frac{1}{4}$ cups of flour left over after making bread, pretzels, and biscuits.

You want to know what happened at the beginning of a series of steps.
- How many miles of the tunnel did they dig in the first 3 weeks?
- How much flour did Carole start with?

Step 1 The initial amount of flour in the bag is unknown.

Step 2

Initial amount of flour		Flour used in bread		Flour used in pretzels		Flour used in biscuits		Flour left over
n	−	$3\frac{3}{4}$	−	1	−	2	=	$1\frac{1}{4}$

Step 3 $1\frac{1}{4} + 2 + 1 + 3\frac{3}{4} = n,\ n = 8$

Answer: There were 8 cups of flour in the bag Carole bought.

✔ Talk About It

3. Why does Step 3 show the inverse operation of each change described in the problem?

4. Why is working backward a good strategy for solving this problem?

CHECK ✔

For another example, see Set 8-9 on p. 520.

Solve this problem by working backward. Write the answer in a complete sentence.

n = The initial amount of money Calvin had when he left home.

n	→	$2 \times n$	→	$2 \times (2 \times n)$	=	$24
Money when Calvin left home		Money after first job		Money after second job		Money when Calvin returned home

1. Calvin earned money shoveling snow in his neighborhood. When he got paid for his first job, he doubled the amount of money he had when he left home. When he got paid for his second job, he doubled the amount of money he had after his first job. When Calvin got home, he had $24. How much money did he have when he left home?

A Using the Strategy

Solve this problem by working backward. Write the answer in a complete sentence.

n = The initial amount of jojoba oil Mara added.

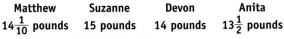

$$\boxed{n} + \boxed{2\frac{1}{3}} + \boxed{1\frac{1}{4}} + \boxed{1\frac{5}{12}} = \boxed{8}$$

2. Mara followed a recipe she found on the Internet to make her own perfume. She started by adding jojoba oil to a small bottle.

Then she added $2\frac{1}{3}$ ounces of sandalwood oil, $1\frac{1}{4}$ ounces of musk oil, and $1\frac{5}{12}$ ounces of frankincense oil. Mara made a total of 8 ounces of perfume. How much jojoba oil did she use?

Solve each problem by working backward. Write the answers in complete sentences. Use the Soccer Practice problem for 3–5.

3. What time did the scrimmage game start?

4. What time did the practice start?

5. **Decision Making** The Tigers' coach wants to have a scrimmage game for $\frac{2}{3}$ hour at the end of Tuesday's practice. If she wants to spend the same amount of time on the other activities and have practice end at 7:00 P.M., should she tell the players to show up earlier or later than they did on Monday? Explain.

> **Soccer Practice** The Tigers' soccer practice ended at 7:00 P.M. on Monday. The team began practice by stretching and running for $\frac{1}{3}$ hour. Then they practiced dribbling and shooting for $\frac{1}{2}$ hour. During the last $\frac{3}{4}$ hour, the team played a scrimmage game.

 Math and Science

Babies grow very fast during their first year. In fact, a baby gains an average of $2\frac{1}{5}$ pounds each month for the first three months after birth. All of the babies in this photo are 3 months old. How much did each baby probably weigh at birth?

Matthew $14\frac{1}{10}$ pounds   Suzanne 15 pounds   Devon 14 pounds   Anita $13\frac{1}{2}$ pounds

6. Matthew   **7.** Suzanne

8. Devon   **9.** Anita

10. Most babies' heads grow 4 inches in circumference during their first year. The head usually grows $\frac{1}{2}$ inch every month for the first four months after birth. How much does a baby's head usually grow in circumference between the ages of 4 months and 1 year?

B Mixed Strategy Practice

Solve each problem. Write the answer in a complete sentence.

11. Asia is about three times the size of Antarctica. Together, the two continents make up about $\frac{2}{5}$ of Earth's land. What fraction of Earth's land does Antarctica make up?

12. A hardware store has two kinds of screws on sale: flat head and round head. Each screw comes in three sizes: $\frac{1}{4}$ inch, $\frac{1}{2}$ inch, and $\frac{3}{4}$ inch. How many different screws are on sale at the store?

13. Between which two consecutive months from July through December did the number of visitors at Great Smoky Mountains National Park change the most?

GREAT SMOKY MOUNTAINS NATIONAL PARK VISITATION, 2000	
Month	Number of Visitors
July	$2\frac{4}{5}$ million
August	$2\frac{1}{10}$ million
September	$1\frac{9}{10}$ million
October	$2\frac{3}{10}$ million
November	$1\frac{7}{10}$ million
December	$1\frac{3}{10}$ million

STRATEGIES

- **Show What You Know**
  Draw a Picture
  Make an Organized List
  Make a Table
  Make a Graph
  Act It Out or Use Objects
- **Look for a Pattern**
- **Try, Check, and Revise**
- **Write an Equation**
- **Use Logical Reasoning**
- **Solve a Simpler Problem**
- **Work Backward**

Choose a tool
Mental Math

TEST TALK

Think It Through

Stuck? I won't give up. I can:
- Tell what I know.
- Identify key facts and details.
- Tell the problem in my own words.
- Show the main idea.
- Try a different strategy.
- Retrace my steps.

Mixed Review and Test Prep

Take It to the NET
Test Prep
www.scottforesman.com

Estimate the difference first. Then subtract. Simplify, if necessary.

14. $3\frac{1}{8} - 1\frac{3}{4}$ 15. $6 - 5\frac{3}{7}$ 16. $12\frac{1}{5} - 7\frac{4}{9}$ 17. $10\frac{5}{11} - 9$ 18. $15\frac{2}{3} - 10\frac{1}{7}$

19. **Writing in Math** A glass patio door is $\frac{5}{8}$-inch thick. The door is made of two panes of safety glass with air between them for greater insulation. The pane on the inside of the door is $\frac{3}{16}$-inch thick. The air space is $\frac{3}{8}$-inch thick. How thick is the outside pane of the door? Explain how you solved this problem.

Do You Know How?

Do You Understand?

Estimating Sums and Differences of Mixed Numbers (8-6)

Estimate each sum. Round to the nearest whole number.

1. $1\frac{7}{8} + 10\frac{3}{4}$ **2.** $14\frac{1}{2} + 2\frac{1}{3}$

3. $4\frac{1}{3} + 1\frac{11}{12}$ **4.** $3\frac{9}{10} + \frac{5}{6}$

A How can you tell when a fraction is less than $\frac{1}{2}$? Greater than $\frac{1}{2}$?

B How do you round when a mixed number is halfway between two whole numbers?

Understanding Adding and Subtracting Mixed Numbers (8-5)
Adding Mixed Numbers (8-7)
Subtracting Mixed Numbers (8-8)

Add or subtract. Simplify, if necessary. You may use fraction strips or draw pictures to help.

5. $3\frac{1}{10} - 2\frac{1}{5}$ **6.** $2\frac{1}{6}$ **7.** $5\frac{9}{10} + 4\frac{1}{4}$

$+ 1\frac{7}{8}$

8. $11 - 2\frac{7}{9}$ **9.** $9\frac{1}{2}$ **10.** $12\frac{3}{8} + 3\frac{7}{16}$

$- 4\frac{1}{5}$

C Explain when you need to simplify a mixed number answer. Give an example.

D Explain when you have to rename before you can subtract mixed numbers. Give an example.

Problem-Solving Strategy: Work Backward (8-9)

11. John has $7 left from the money his father gave him at the baseball game. He spent $8 on food and $10 on a T-shirt. How much money did John's father give him?

12. A winter storm began on Friday and by Monday morning there were 7 inches left. On Saturday, it melted 3 inches, and on Sunday it snowed another 4 inches. How much did it snow on Friday?

E What strategy did you use to solve Exercise 11?

F Is your answer to Exercise 11 reasonable? Explain how you know.

G Explain how you solved Exercise 12.

MULTIPLE CHOICE

1. Which shows the difference $6\frac{4}{9} - 2\frac{2}{3}$? (8-8)

   A. $4\frac{2}{9}$ **B.** $3\frac{7}{9}$ **C.** $4\frac{7}{9}$ **D.** $4\frac{2}{6}$

2. Which shows the best estimate of $3\frac{3}{5} + 2\frac{3}{8} + 4\frac{1}{8} + 4\frac{9}{10}$? (8-6)

   A. 13   **B.** 15   **C.** 16   **D.** 14

FREE RESPONSE

Estimate each sum or difference. Round to the nearest whole number. (8-6)

3. $4\frac{4}{5} + 3\frac{2}{7}$ **4.** $5\frac{3}{5} - 2\frac{1}{3}$ **5.** $3\frac{11}{13} + 4\frac{1}{4} + \frac{4}{7}$

Add or subtract. Simplify, if necessary. You may use fraction strips or draw pictures to help. (8-5, 8-7, 8-8)

6. $2\frac{1}{8}$ **7.** $8\frac{3}{7}$ **8.** $7\frac{2}{3}$ **9.** $6\frac{3}{4}$

   $+ 3\frac{3}{4}$ $- 5\frac{5}{7}$ $+ 5\frac{1}{2}$ $+ 8\frac{1}{3}$

10. $8\frac{3}{10} - 5\frac{3}{4}$ **11.** $13\frac{1}{7} - 6\frac{1}{2}$ **12.** $3\frac{5}{6} + 8\frac{1}{4}$ **13.** $8\frac{1}{10} + 2\frac{3}{5} + 3\frac{1}{2}$

14. Montell's family made a 1,500-mile trip in 3 days. On Day 3, they traveled 750 miles. On Day 2, they stopped at an amusement park, so they only traveled 200 miles. How many miles did they travel on Day 1? (8-9)

15. The Storm had a net gain of 10 yards in 4 plays, for a first down. During the last three plays, they passed for 7 yards, lost 5 yards, and ran for 6 yards. How many yards did the Storm gain on their first play? (8-9)

Think It Through
When working backward, remember to **use the inverse operations** of each change.

Writing in Math

16. Describe a sum of two distances on the map that equals 3 miles. (8-7)

17. What is the shortest route to go from the campground to the general store? Explain how you know. (8-7)

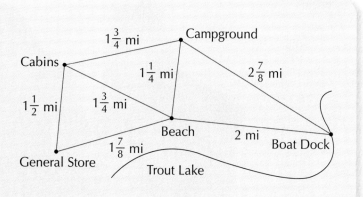

Key Idea
You can use multiplication to find a fraction of a whole number.

Materials
• counters or

 tools

Think It Through
• I can **use objects** to model the problem.
• I can break the problem into parts to **solve simpler problems**.

Multiplying Fractions by Whole Numbers

✔ WARM UP
1. 15×0.3 2. 10×0.2
3. 0.2×4 4. 20×0.5
5. 8×0.25 6. 0.7×6

LEARN

Activity

How can you use counters to find a fraction of a whole number?

A fruit salad recipe calls for $\frac{2}{3}$ of a dozen oranges and $\frac{3}{4}$ pound of grapes. How many oranges and how many ounces of grapes do you need to make the salad? A pound is 16 ounces.

a. Use 12 counters to show a dozen oranges. Separate them into three equal groups.

b. Find $\frac{1}{3}$ of 12. $\frac{1}{3}$ of 12 = ▨.

c. Find $\frac{2}{3}$ of 12. $\frac{2}{3}$ of 12 = ▨.

d. $\frac{2}{3}$ of a dozen oranges is how many oranges?

e. Use 16 counters to show 16 ounces. $\frac{3}{4}$ of 16 = ▨. So, $\frac{3}{4}$ pound of grapes is how many ounces?

f. How did finding $\frac{1}{3}$ of 12 help you find $\frac{2}{3}$ of 12? What fraction of 16 did you find first to help you find $\frac{3}{4}$ of 16?

g. Use counters to find each answer.

$\frac{1}{8}$ of 16 $\frac{5}{8}$ of 16 $\frac{7}{8}$ of 16 $\frac{1}{4}$ of 12 $\frac{3}{4}$ of 12

$\frac{1}{7}$ of 14 $\frac{3}{7}$ of 14 $\frac{6}{7}$ of 14 $\frac{1}{5}$ of 15 $\frac{4}{5}$ of 15

How can you use mental math to find a fraction of a whole number?

When you find a fraction of a whole number, you are multiplying a whole number by a fraction. Thinking about division of whole numbers can help you find the product mentally.

Example A

Find $\frac{1}{5} \times 20$. Use mental math.

$\frac{1}{5}$ of 20 gives the same result as dividing 20 by 5.

$20 \div 5 = 4$

So, $\frac{1}{5}$ of 20 = 4.

Example B

Find $\frac{3}{5} \times 20$. Use mental math.

Think: $\frac{3}{5}$ is 3 times as much as $\frac{1}{5}$.

$\frac{1}{5}$ of 20 = 4. Multiply 4 by 3.

So, $\frac{3}{5}$ of 20 = 12.

Example C

There are 32 cookies in the cookie jar. If $\frac{5}{8}$ of them are oatmeal, how many oatmeal cookies are there?

Find $\frac{5}{8} \times 32$.

Think: $\frac{5}{8}$ is five times $\frac{1}{8}$.

$\frac{1}{8}$ of 32 is 4.   Think: $32 \div 8 = 4$

$5 \times 4 = 20$, so $\frac{5}{8} \times 32 = 20$.

There are 20 oatmeal cookies.

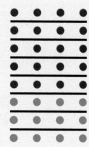

✔ Talk About It

1. In Example B, why do you multiply 4×3?

2. How does thinking about division help you find $\frac{1}{3}$ of 18 mentally?

3. **Number Sense** If you know that $\frac{1}{4} \times 28 = 7$, how do you find $\frac{3}{4} \times 28$?

For another example, see Set 8-10 on p. 520.

CHECK ✓

Find each product.

1. $\frac{1}{4}$ of 20   2. $\frac{2}{3}$ of 15   3. $\frac{1}{6} \times 18$ 4. $\frac{5}{7} \times 21$ 5. $24 \times \frac{3}{4}$

6. **Number Sense** Explain how you found $24 \times \frac{3}{4}$ mentally.

PRACTICE

For more practice, see Set 8-10 on p. 524.

Ⓐ Skills and Understanding

Find each product.

7. $\frac{1}{2}$ of 40   8. $\frac{1}{5}$ of 25   9. $\frac{2}{5}$ of 30   10. $\frac{3}{4}$ of 24   11. $\frac{5}{8}$ of 16

12. $\frac{4}{7} \times 14$ 13. $\frac{2}{3} \times 27$ 14. $\frac{2}{9} \times 90$ 15. $\frac{1}{4} \times 36$ 16. $\frac{2}{5} \times 40$

17. $50 \times \frac{7}{10}$ 18. $28 \times \frac{3}{7}$ 19. $\frac{7}{9} \times 45$ 20. $\frac{1}{6} \times 54$ 21. $\frac{8}{9} \times 27$

22. $\frac{1}{3} \times 126$ 23. $\frac{2}{3} \times 126$ 24. $\frac{1}{4} \times 96$ 25. $\frac{3}{4} \times 96$ 26. $\frac{1}{9} \times 108$

27. $\frac{5}{9} \times 108$ 28. $\frac{8}{9} \times 108$ 29. $\frac{1}{12} \times 168$ 30. $\frac{7}{12} \times 168$ 31. $\frac{11}{12} \times 168$

32. **Reasoning** If $\frac{2}{3}$ of a whole number is 10, what is that whole number? Explain how you found the answer.

Ⓑ Reasoning and Problem Solving

33. **Patterns** Copy and complete the table by writing the product of each expression in the box below it. Use patterns to find each product.

$\frac{1}{7} \times 91$	$\frac{2}{7} \times 91$	$\frac{3}{7} \times 91$	$\frac{4}{7} \times 91$	$\frac{5}{7} \times 91$	$\frac{6}{7} \times 91$	$\frac{7}{7} \times 91$
■	■	■	■	■	■	■

Find each product.

34. four-fifths of thirty

35. three-eighths of sixteen

36. one-fourth of one hundred

37. two-thirds of twenty-one

38. **Reasoning** How could you use the product of $\frac{1}{3} \times 90$ to find the product of $\frac{1}{6} \times 90$?

39. **Number Sense** Colby says that when you multiply a nonzero whole number by a fraction less than 1, the product is always less than the whole number. Do you agree? Why or why not?

Think It Through

I can **predict** solutions to the problem. Then I can use the given information to **verify** if they are correct.

Math and Social Studies

To help conserve natural resources and protect the environment, people in the United States recycle about 50 million tons of garbage each year. Use the circle graph to find how many tons of these materials are recycled each year.

U.S. Recycling, by Material

Metals $\frac{1}{10}$

Yard Waste $\frac{1}{5}$

Plastic and Glass $\frac{2}{25}$

Paper $\frac{1}{2}$

Other $\frac{3}{25}$

40. Yard waste

41. Paper

42. Metals

43. Plastic and glass

44. **Writing in Math** Explain how finding $\frac{1}{6}$ of 36 can help you find $\frac{5}{6}$ of 36.

Mixed Review and Test Prep

Take It to the NET
Test Prep
www.scottforesman.com

Add or subtract. Simplify, if possible.

45. $\frac{1}{9} + \frac{5}{9}$

46. $\frac{3}{10} + \frac{1}{4}$

47. $\frac{3}{5} + \frac{1}{2}$

48. $\frac{7}{8} - \frac{1}{4}$

49. $\frac{6}{7} - \frac{1}{2}$

50. $3\frac{3}{4} + 2\frac{1}{3}$

51. $5\frac{1}{2} + 1\frac{3}{8}$

52. $10\frac{2}{3} - 4\frac{1}{2}$

53. $7\frac{1}{4} - 1\frac{5}{8}$

54. Jill spent $12 for two books and $16.98 for one CD. She paid $1.74 in taxes and received $9.28 in change. How much money did she give the clerk?

A. $40.28

B. $40.00

C. $30.72

D. $28.98

Enrichment

Two Puzzles

1. A builder wants to subdivide a plot of land shaped like the one below into 4 equal lots of the same shape and size. How can this be done?

2. A cook wants to slice a cheese cylinder into 8 equal pieces. How can this be done by using only 3 straight slices?

All text pages available online and on CD-ROM.

Vocabulary
• benchmark (p. 402)
• compatible numbers (p. 22)

Think It Through

• I can **choose** different **methods** to estimate.

• I know that when I **use compatible numbers,** I can often do the computation mentally.

• I know that when I **use a benchmark** the computation will be easier.

Estimating Products of Fractions

LEARN

What are some ways to estimate a product of fractions?

Lucille lives $\frac{5}{8}$ of a mile from school. In three weeks, she walked that distance 36 times. Estimate the number of miles she walked. Estimate $\frac{5}{8} \times 36$.

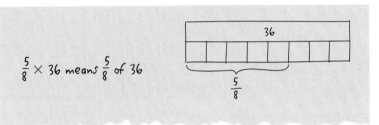

$\frac{5}{8} \times 36$ means $\frac{5}{8}$ of 36

Example

Estimate $\frac{5}{8} \times 36$.

You can use compatible numbers to estimate products that involve fractions.

One Way

Think: 8 is not a factor of 36. But 8 is a factor 32, and 32 is close to 36.

$\frac{1}{8} \times 32 = 4$, and

$\frac{5}{8} \times 32 = 20$

So, $\frac{5}{8}$ of 36 is about 20.

One estimate is about 20 miles.

Another Way

Change the fraction to the closest **benchmark.** Remember that benchmarks are numbers like $\frac{1}{2}$ and 1.

Think: $\frac{5}{8}$ is close to $\frac{1}{2}$.

$\frac{1}{2} \times 36 = 18$

So, $\frac{5}{8}$ of 36 is about 18.

Another estimate is about 18 miles.

✔ **Talk About It**

1. In the Example, what other compatible numbers could you use to estimate the product?

2. Which method would you use to estimate $\frac{7}{8} \times 6$?

Estimate each product.

1. $8 \times \frac{9}{10}$　　　**2.** $\frac{3}{5} \times 12$　　　**3.** $10 \times \frac{1}{9}$　　　**4.** $\frac{1}{3} \times 17$　　　**5.** $\frac{4}{5} \times 62$

6. Reasoning How will finding $\frac{1}{6}$ of 30 help you estimate $\frac{5}{6}$ of 29?

PRACTICE

For more practice, see Set 8-11 on p. 524.

A Skills and Understanding

Estimate each product.

7. $\frac{3}{8} \times 33$　　**8.** $\frac{1}{4} \times 37$　　**9.** $36 \times \frac{2}{7}$　　**10.** $\frac{3}{4} \times 15$　　**11.** $61 \times \frac{7}{9}$

12. $\frac{1}{2} \times 25$　　**13.** $\frac{2}{3} \times 19$　　**14.** $\frac{9}{10} \times 22$　　**15.** $\frac{2}{9} \times 73$　　**16.** $50 \times \frac{3}{7}$

17. $\frac{6}{7} \times 100$　　**18.** $16 \times \frac{4}{5}$　　**19.** $\frac{3}{10} \times 44$　　**20.** $\frac{8}{9} \times 50$　　**21.** $10 \times \frac{5}{8}$

22. Number Sense Do you think the actual product of $\frac{1}{9} \times 75$ is greater than or less than 8? Explain your answer.

B Reasoning and Problem Solving

23. One lap around the school track is $\frac{1}{4}$ mile. If Eddie runs 6 laps around the track and then $2\frac{1}{2}$ miles home, about how far will he run in all?

24. Carol lives $\frac{3}{7}$ of a mile from school. She walks to and from school 5 times a week. About how many miles does she walk each week in all?

25. Sheri has 3 hats, 4 sweaters, and 2 pairs of jeans. How many different outfits can she make of one hat, one sweater, and a pair of jeans?

26. <u>Writing in Math</u> Explain how finding $\frac{1}{8}$ of 40 helps you estimate $\frac{7}{8}$ of 39.

Mixed Review and Test Prep

Take It to the NET
Test Prep
www.scottforesman.com

Find each product.

27. $\frac{1}{6}$ of 24　　　**28.** $\frac{3}{7}$ of 14　　　**29.** $\frac{2}{3} \times 18$　　　**30.** $20 \times \frac{4}{5}$

31. Find the mode of this data set: 6, 9, 10, 13, 8, 6, 9, 6, 7, 6

　　A. 6　　　　　**B.** 8　　　　　**C.** 9　　　　　**D.** 80

Key Idea
You can multiply
two fractions to
find a fraction of
a fraction.

Materials
• square sheets
  of paper
• red and yellow
  colored pencils
  or tools

Think It Through
• I can **make a
  model** to show
  the problem.
• I can **look for
  patterns** in the
  products to find a
  multiplication rule.

Multiplying Fractions

LEARN

Activity

How can you use a model to find the product of two fractions?

You can use paper folding to find $\frac{1}{2}$ of $\frac{3}{4}$.

a. Fold a square sheet of paper vertically in half.

b. Fold the paper vertically in half again. Each section is what fraction of the sheet of paper?

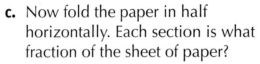

c. Now fold the paper in half horizontally. Each section is what fraction of the sheet of paper?

d. Shade $\frac{3}{4}$ of the vertical sections red and $\frac{1}{2}$ of the horizontal sections yellow.

e. The part that is shaded both red and yellow shows $\frac{1}{2} \times \frac{3}{4}$.
What is $\frac{1}{2} \times \frac{3}{4}$?

f. Fold paper to find each product.

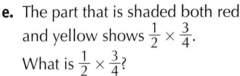
$$\frac{1}{2} \times \frac{1}{2} = \frac{}{} \quad \frac{1}{2} \times \frac{1}{4} = \frac{}{} \quad \frac{1}{4} \times \frac{1}{4} = \frac{}{} \quad \frac{3}{4} \times \frac{3}{4} = \frac{}{} \quad \frac{1}{2} \times \frac{5}{8} = \frac{}{}$$

g. Use the pictures to find the products.

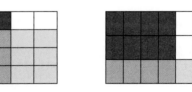
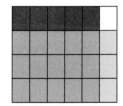

$$\frac{3}{4} \times \frac{1}{3} = \frac{}{} \qquad \frac{1}{3} \times \frac{4}{5} = \frac{}{} \qquad \frac{3}{4} \times \frac{5}{6} = \frac{}{}$$

h. Study the numerators and denominators in each problem in parts e and f. What pattern do you see between the fractions multiplied and their products?

How do you multiply fractions using paper and pencil?

	Example A	Example B
	Find $\frac{2}{3} \times \frac{3}{5}$.	Find $\frac{4}{9} \times 12$.
STEP 1	Multiply the numerators. $\frac{2}{3} \times \frac{3}{5} = \frac{\mathbf{2 \times 3}}{} = \frac{6}{}$	Write the whole number as an improper fraction. $\frac{4}{9} \times 12 = \frac{4}{9} \times \frac{\mathbf{12}}{\mathbf{1}}$
STEP 2	Multiply the denominators. $\frac{2}{3} \times \frac{3}{5} = \frac{2 \times 3}{\mathbf{3 \times 5}} = \frac{6}{15}$	Multiply the numerators. Then multiply the denominators. $\frac{4}{9} \times \frac{12}{1} = \frac{\mathbf{4 \times 12}}{\mathbf{9 \times 1}} = \frac{48}{9}$
STEP 3	Simplify the product. $\frac{2}{3} \times \frac{3}{5} = \frac{2 \times 3}{3 \times 5} = \frac{6}{15} = \mathbf{\frac{2}{5}}$	Simplify the product. $\frac{4}{9} \times \frac{12}{1} = \frac{\mathbf{4 \times 12}}{\mathbf{9 \times 1}} = \frac{48}{9} = 5\frac{3}{9} = \mathbf{5\frac{1}{3}}$
	So, $\frac{2}{3} \times \frac{3}{5} = \frac{2}{5}$.	So, $\frac{4}{9} \times 12 = 5\frac{1}{3}$.

✔ Talk About It

1. In Example B, how did you change the problem so that you could multiply a fraction by a fraction?

2. **Mental Math** How can you find the product of $\frac{4}{4} \times \frac{2}{7}$ mentally?

Take It to the NET
More Examples
www.scottforesman.com

CHECK ✔

For another example, see Set 8-12 on p. 521.

Choose the multiplication problem that each model represents.
HINT: Blue and yellow mixed together yield green.

1.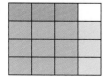

    a. $\frac{3}{4} \times \frac{3}{4}$ **b.** $\frac{4}{4} \times \frac{3}{4}$

2.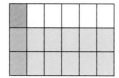

    a. $\frac{2}{6} \times \frac{1}{3}$ **b.** $\frac{2}{3} \times \frac{1}{6}$

3.

    a. $\frac{4}{5} \times \frac{1}{4}$ **b.** $\frac{3}{4} \times \frac{1}{5}$

Find each product. Simplify, if necessary.

4. $\frac{3}{4} \times \frac{5}{6}$ **5.** $15 \times \frac{1}{7}$ **6.** $\frac{3}{4} \times \frac{1}{4} \times 2$ **7.** $\frac{3}{8} \times \frac{2}{3}$ **8.** $\frac{1}{6} \times \frac{5}{6}$ **9.** $\frac{1}{3} \times \frac{1}{4} \times \frac{3}{4}$

10. Number Sense $\frac{2}{9} \times \frac{7}{8} = \frac{7}{36}$. What is $\frac{7}{8} \times \frac{2}{9}$? How do you know without multiplying?

A Skills and Understanding

Write the multiplication problem that each model represents.

11.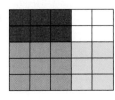

12.

13.

Find each product. Simplify, if necessary.

14. $\frac{3}{7} \times \frac{2}{3}$ **15.** $\frac{1}{8} \times \frac{2}{5}$ **16.** $\frac{3}{8} \times \frac{1}{2}$ **17.** $\frac{2}{3} \times \frac{3}{4}$ **18.** $\frac{2}{3} \times \frac{5}{6}$ **19.** $\frac{5}{7} \times \frac{1}{2}$

20. $\frac{5}{8} \times \frac{1}{5}$ **21.** $\frac{1}{4} \times \frac{1}{6}$ **22.** $\frac{3}{4} \times \frac{3}{9}$ **23.** $\frac{2}{3} \times \frac{7}{8}$ **24.** $\frac{2}{5} \times \frac{2}{3}$ **25.** $\frac{5}{6} \times \frac{3}{4}$

26. $\frac{1}{2} \times \frac{2}{5} \times \frac{2}{3}$ **27.** $\frac{1}{2} \times \frac{1}{2} \times \frac{1}{2}$ **28.** $\frac{7}{10} \times \frac{5}{7} \times \frac{1}{5}$ **29.** $\frac{1}{3} \times \frac{3}{4} \times \frac{1}{2}$

30. Algebra If $\frac{1}{2} \times$ ▨ $= \frac{1}{4}$, what is ▨?

B Reasoning and Problem Solving

Math and Art

Origami is the Japanese art of paper folding. Many origami figures start from a 4-inch-by-4-inch square of paper.

31. Suppose you fold a paper vertically in half two times.

    a. What fraction of the sheet of paper is each section?

    b. How does the folded sheet of paper show $\frac{1}{2} \times \frac{1}{2}$?

    c. If you then fold it horizontally in half, what fraction of the sheet of paper is each section now? What product does the folded sheet of paper show now?

32. The origami figure at right is a regular octagon. If each side is $\frac{2}{3}$ inch long, how can you use multiplication to find its perimeter?

33. **Writing in Math** Is the explanation below correct? If not, tell why and write a correct response.

> Find $\frac{1}{3}$ of $\frac{1}{5}$.
> I write $\frac{1}{3} \times \frac{1}{5}$. Then I multiply the numerators and denominators. So, $\frac{1}{3} \times \frac{1}{5} = \frac{1}{15}$.

This origami figure was created from several sheets of folded paper.

C Extensions

You can sometimes simplify fractions before you multiply by dividing by common factors of the numerator and denominator.

Find $\frac{2}{3} \times \frac{5}{8}$.

Think: The numerator of $\frac{2}{3}$ and the denominator of $\frac{5}{8}$ have a common factor of 2.

Divide by the common factor, 2.

$$\frac{2}{3} \times \frac{5}{8} = \frac{\overset{1}{\cancel{2}}}{3} \times \frac{5}{\underset{4}{\cancel{8}}} = \frac{1}{3} \times \frac{5}{4}$$

Multiply the numerators. Multiply the denominators.

$$\frac{1}{3} \times \frac{5}{4} = \frac{5}{12}$$

So, $\frac{2}{3} \times \frac{5}{8} = \frac{5}{12}$.

Simplify first. Then find each product.

34. $\frac{3}{4} \times \frac{1}{6}$ **35.** $\frac{1}{15} \times \frac{5}{7}$ **36.** $\frac{2}{3} \times \frac{3}{8}$ **37.** $\frac{4}{5} \times \frac{3}{16}$ **38.** $\frac{3}{4} \times \frac{4}{9}$ **39.** $\frac{3}{10} \times \frac{5}{6}$

 **Mixed Review and Test Prep**

 **Take It to the NET**
Test Prep
www.scottforesman.com

Estimate each product.

40. $25 \times \frac{7}{8}$ **41.** $\frac{5}{6} \times 19$ **42.** $\frac{5}{8} \times 30$ **43.** $48 \times \frac{4}{5}$ **44.** $37 \times \frac{1}{4}$

45. Parking at the airport costs $2.50 for the first hour and $1.75 for each additional hour. How much would it cost to park for 4 hours?

A. $9.50 **B.** $7.75 **C.** $7.00 **D.** $4.25

DISCOVERY CHANNEL SCHOOL

Discover Math in Your World

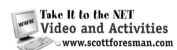 **Take It to the NET**
Video and Activities
www.scottforesman.com

Disappearing Lands

The wetlands of Louisiana cover about 3.5 million acres. During the 60-year period leading up to 1990, the Mississippi River delta lost more than 1,000 square miles of land.

1. If $\frac{2}{5}$ of all coastal wetlands in the continental United States are in Louisiana and $\frac{4}{5}$ of the U.S. wetlands loss occur in Louisiana, what part of the U.S. wetlands loss occurs in Louisiana?

2. Louisiana is currently losing wetlands at the rate of about 35 square miles each year. At this rate, estimate how many square miles are lost each month ($\frac{1}{12}$ of a year).

All text pages available online and on CD-ROM.

Multiplying Mixed Numbers

WARM UP
Rewrite as an improper fraction.

1. $4\frac{1}{3}$ 2. $9\frac{1}{2}$ 3. $1\frac{7}{8}$

4. $3\frac{3}{4}$ 5. $2\frac{3}{10}$ 6. $5\frac{2}{3}$

LEARN

How can you find the product of mixed numbers?

When multiplying two mixed numbers, it sometimes helps to estimate first.

Example A

The area of a forest preserve is $1\frac{1}{4}$ miles wide and $3\frac{3}{4}$ miles long. Estimate $1\frac{1}{4} \times 3\frac{3}{4}$.

$1\frac{1}{4} \times 3\frac{3}{4} =$ Round each mixed number to the nearest whole number.

$1 \times 4 = 4.$ So, $1\frac{1}{4} \times 3\frac{3}{4}$ is about 4.

To multiply mixed numbers, change each to an improper fraction and multiply as you would with fractions.

Example B

Central Park in New York City is $\frac{1}{2}$ mile wide and $2\frac{1}{2}$ miles long. Multiply $\frac{1}{2}$ by $2\frac{1}{2}$ to find the area.

STEP 1	STEP 2	STEP 3
Write the mixed number as an improper fraction.	Multiply as you would multiply fractions.	Simplify the product.
$2\frac{1}{2} = \frac{(2 \times 2) + 1}{2} = \frac{5}{2}$	$\frac{1}{2} \times \frac{5}{2} = \frac{1 \times 5}{2 \times 2} = \frac{5}{4}$	$\frac{1}{2} \times \frac{5}{2} = \frac{5}{4} = 1\frac{1}{4}$

So, Central Park covers $1\frac{1}{4}$ square miles.

✔ **Talk About It**

1. In Example A, name the two improper fractions you would use and find the product.

2. **Number Sense** Explain how you would use improper fractions to multiply $8 \times 2\frac{3}{4}$.

Estimate the product. Then copy and complete the multiplication.

1. $2\frac{2}{3} \times 9 = \frac{\square}{3} \times \frac{9}{1}$

2. $4\frac{1}{2} \times 1\frac{1}{3} = \frac{\square}{2} \times \frac{\square}{3}$

3. $3\frac{1}{2} \times 1\frac{1}{4} = \frac{\square}{2} \times \frac{\square}{4}$

4. Number Sense Give a number for n so that $1\frac{1}{2} \times n$ is more than $1\frac{1}{2}$.

PRACTICE

For more practice, see Set 8-13 on p. 525.

A Skills and Understanding

Estimate the product. Then copy and complete the multiplication.

5. $3\frac{4}{5} \times 10 = \frac{\square}{5} \times \frac{10}{1}$

6. $3\frac{1}{8} \times 1\frac{2}{5} = \frac{\square}{8} \times \frac{\square}{5}$

7. $1\frac{3}{4} \times 1\frac{3}{5} = \frac{\square}{4} \times \frac{\square}{5}$

Estimate. Then find each product. Simplify.

8. $1\frac{1}{5} \times 6\frac{1}{2}$

9. $2\frac{4}{7} \times 7$

10. $\frac{3}{4} \times 5\frac{1}{6}$

11. $2 \times 4\frac{3}{4}$

12. $2\frac{5}{6} \times 3$

13. $4\frac{1}{3} \times 1\frac{2}{3}$

14. $6\frac{1}{8} \times 2\frac{2}{7}$

15. $5 \times 5\frac{4}{5}$

16. $4\frac{2}{3} \times 2\frac{1}{2}$

17. $2\frac{1}{2} \times 3\frac{1}{3} \times \frac{4}{5}$

18. Number Sense How could you use multiplication to find $1\frac{5}{8} + 1\frac{5}{8} + 1\frac{5}{8}$?

B Reasoning and Problem Solving

Use the recipe at the right for 19–21.

19. Kelly wants to make half of this pancake recipe. How much of each ingredient will she use?

20. Reasoning Suppose Kelly wants to make $\frac{1}{3}$ the recipe. Does this make sense? Explain.

21. <u>Writing in Math</u> The Lost Valley campers will make $2\frac{1}{2}$ times this recipe for a pancake supper. Rewrite the recipe showing the amount of each ingredient they will use.

PANCAKES

$5\frac{1}{4}$ cups pancake mix

4 eggs

$4\frac{1}{2}$ tablespoons butter

$3\frac{2}{3}$ cups milk

Mixed Review and Test Prep

Take It to the NET
www **Test Prep**
www.scottforesman.com

Multiply. Be sure your answer is in simplest form.

22. $\frac{3}{4} \times \frac{5}{6}$

23. $\frac{1}{3} \times \frac{2}{3}$

24. $\frac{9}{10} \times \frac{5}{6}$

25. $\frac{4}{5} \times \frac{5}{8}$

26. $\frac{1}{2} \times \frac{5}{9}$

27. What is the LCM of 9 and 15?

A. 135 **B.** 45 **C.** 24 **D.** 3

Key Idea
If you want to separate a whole number into equal groups of a fraction, you can divide the whole number by the fraction.

Materials
• fraction strips
• inch ruler marked in eighths

TEST TALK

Think It Through
I can **use a model** to solve the problem.

Understanding Division with Fractions

LEARN

Activity

How can I use models to show division of fractions?

Paula has completed the 3-inch strip of a beaded belt shown. The beads are $\frac{1}{4}$ inch long, and the bands of color are $\frac{1}{2}$ inch wide.

Use fraction strips and a ruler to find these answers.

a. First, use fraction strips for 1 and $\frac{1}{4}$. Lay three 1 strips end to end. Then lay $\frac{1}{4}$ strips end to end until you have enough to match three 1 strips. How many $\frac{1}{4}$ strips do you need?

b. Now use the ruler shown at the right. How many $\frac{1}{4}$-inch beads are in 1 inch? In 2 inches? In 3 inches? So, $3 \div \frac{1}{4} = \blacksquare$.

c. Next use strips for $\frac{1}{2}$ and 1. Lay the $\frac{1}{2}$ strips end to end until the length matches the three 1 strips. How many are needed?

d. How many $\frac{1}{2}$-inch bands of color are in 1 inch? In 2 inches? In 3 inches? So, $3 \div \frac{1}{2} = \blacksquare$.

e. Use your ruler to draw a 6-inch line segment. How many $\frac{3}{4}$-inch segments are in 6 inches? So, $6 \div \frac{3}{4} = \blacksquare$.

f. Use your ruler to draw a 6-inch line segment. How many $\frac{3}{8}$-inch segments are in 6 inches? So, $6 \div \frac{3}{8} = \blacksquare$.

g. How is dividing 6 by $\frac{3}{4}$ different from multiplying 6 by $\frac{3}{4}$?

✓ WARM UP
1. 3.2×10
2. 0.9×100
3. 10×0.2
4. $0.3 \times 1,000$
5. 32.45×10
6. 3.44×100

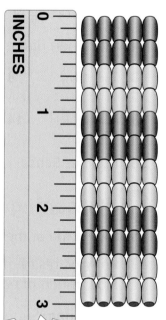

INCHES
0
1
2
3

Use the picture to find each quotient.

1. How many $\frac{1}{3}$s are in 3? $3 \div \frac{1}{3} = $ ▨ .

2. How many $\frac{2}{3}$s are in 4? $4 \div \frac{2}{3} = $ ▨ .

3. Reasoning Explain how you could draw pictures to find $9 \div \frac{2}{3}$.

PRACTICE

For more practice, see Set 8-14 on p. 525.

Ⓐ Skills and Understanding

Use the picture to find each quotient.

4. How many $\frac{1}{5}$s are in 1? $1 \div \frac{1}{5} = $ ▨ .

5. How many $\frac{2}{5}$s are in 4? $4 \div \frac{2}{5} = $ ▨ .

Find each quotient. You can draw pictures to help you.

6. $4 \div \frac{1}{2}$ **7.** $5 \div \frac{1}{4}$ **8.** $2 \div \frac{1}{5}$ **9.** $1 \div \frac{1}{8}$ **10.** $3 \div \frac{1}{10}$

11. $3 \div \frac{3}{4}$ **12.** $6 \div \frac{2}{3}$ **13.** $9 \div \frac{3}{8}$ **14.** $15 \div \frac{3}{5}$ **15.** $10 \div \frac{5}{8}$

16. Reasoning When you are dividing by a fraction with a numerator of 1, explain how you can find the quotient.

Ⓑ Reasoning and Problem Solving

Use the chart at the right for 17–18. A measure written in $\frac{4}{4}$ time has 4 beats.

17. In $\frac{4}{4}$ time, how many half notes are in 5 measures?

18. In $\frac{4}{4}$ time, how many quarter notes are in 3 measures?

Notes in $\frac{4}{4}$ time		
Symbol	**Name**	**Beats**
𝅝	whole	4
𝅗𝅥	half	2
𝅘𝅥	quarter	1

19. <u>**Writing in Math**</u> Write a word problem that can be solved by dividing 9 by $\frac{3}{4}$.

🦉 Mixed Review and Test Prep

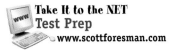
Take It to the NET
www **Test Prep**
www.scottforesman.com

20. Find $3\frac{3}{4} \times 1\frac{2}{3}$ in simplest form.

21. Which type of graph is best for displaying the change of data over time?

    A. line graph   **B.** line plot   **C.** circle graph   **D.** double bar graph

Problem-Solving Skill

Key Idea
Some problems can be solved by using an operation.

Choose an Operation

LEARN

How can you decide what the main idea of a problem is?

Blood Facts Blood is constantly moving throughout the circulatory system. The Data File at right shows approximately how all that blood is usually distributed.

To help solve a problem, draw a picture of the action in a problem. The picture shows the main idea and helps you **choose the needed operation.**

Data File

Average Blood Distribution	
Blood Vessel or Organ	Fraction of Blood
Veins	$\frac{13}{20}$
Arteries	$\frac{1}{10}$
Heart	$\frac{1}{10}$
Lungs	$\frac{1}{10}$
Capillaries	$\frac{1}{20}$

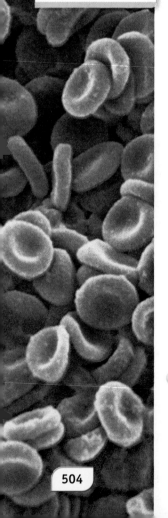

Think It Through
I can **draw a picture** to show the main idea.

Example A	Example B
What part of the total amount of blood in the body is usually in the veins and arteries?	People with type A blood make up about $\frac{2}{5}$ of the population. In a group of 25 students, how many would you expect to have type A blood?

Read and Understand

Show the main idea.

Total amount of blood	
$\frac{13}{20}$	$\frac{1}{10}$

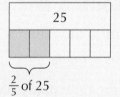

$\frac{2}{5}$ of 25

Plan and Solve

Choose an operation.

Add to combine unequal fractional parts.

$$\frac{13}{20} + \frac{1}{10}$$

$$\frac{13}{20} + \frac{2}{20} = \frac{15}{20} = \frac{3}{4}$$

Multiply $\frac{2}{5}$ by 25 to find $\frac{2}{5}$ of 25.

$$\frac{2}{5} \times 25$$

$$\frac{2}{5} \times \frac{25}{1} = \frac{50}{5} = 10$$

✔ **Talk About It**

1. Give the answer to each problem above in a complete sentence.

2. **Number Sense** In Example A, how could you use your answer to find what part of the total blood is NOT in the veins or arteries?

For another example, see Set 8-15 on p. 521.

Copy and complete the picture to help you choose an operation. Then solve the problem.

1. A container holds 5 quarts when filled. Now it contains $3\frac{3}{4}$ quarts of water. How much more water must be added to fill the container?

For more practice, see Set 8-15 on p. 525.

Draw a picture to show the main idea.
Then choose an operation to solve the problem.
Use the Data File at right to answer 2–4.

2. There are 16 ounces in 1 pound. How many pounds does an average person's skin weigh?

3. What is the combined weight of an average person's two lungs?

4. How much more does the average brain weigh than the average lung?

5. Of the 206 bones in an adult human body, 26 are located in each foot. How many bones in an adult body are NOT in the feet?

6. Water makes up about $\frac{7}{10}$ of a person's total body weight. Kelly weighs 120 pounds. About how many pounds of Kelly's weight are water?

7. On average, people blink 9,365 times a day, and each blink lasts 0.15 second. How many minutes a day does an average person spend blinking? Round your answer to the nearest minute.

8. In *Salsa Stories,* Abuelo uses sawdust on the floor for his carpet making. For the painting of one carpet he needs 20 sacks of sawdust. If each sack weighs $3\frac{1}{2}$ pounds, what is the weight of the sawdust he needs for each carpet?

9. **Writing in Math** Write and solve a story problem to match each picture.

Data File

Largest Human Organs

Organ	Average Weight (oz)
Skin	96
Liver	55
Brain	$49\frac{7}{10}$
Lungs (each)	$19\frac{1}{4}$

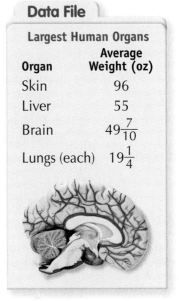

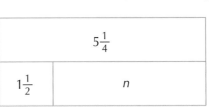

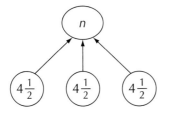

	$5\frac{1}{4}$	
$1\frac{1}{2}$		n

DK Problem-Solving Applications

Shoreline Animals As you walk along a shore, an entirely different world lies just out of view. Just under the water live animals unlike anything on land. If you are patient and wait for the tide to go out, you may be able to see some of these unique creatures.

Trivia Scallops can swim even though they lack flippers. When they clap their shells together, they create jets of water that propel them forward.

1 Australia has about 16,100 miles of coastline. Russia has about 1.46 times as much coastline, Canada has about 9.5 times as much, and the United States has about 0.77 times as much coastline as Australia. Which country has the most coastline? How much coastline do these 4 countries have altogether?

2 **Decision Making** It may take about 12 king scallops or 58 queen scallops to weigh one pound. Would you use mental math, paper and pencil, or a calculator to compute the difference between these two quantities?

3 The peacock worm may be about 12 inches long. It lives in the sand and makes a tube of mud that may be up to 4 inches above the sand. What fraction of the worm's length is the height of the tube?

Using Key Facts

4 How many more legs than antennae do hermit crabs have?

Key Facts
Common Hermit Crab

- 2 pairs of antennae
- 5 pairs of legs
- $5\frac{7}{8}$-inch leg span

5 Some people consider the coconut crab to be the largest hermit crab. Its leg span may be over 5 times the leg span of the common hermit crab. What is the leg span of the largest hermit crab?

6 King ragworms may grow to be 36 inches long. Some smaller ragworms live with hermit crabs in the crabs' shells. These may grow to be $\frac{1}{4}$ the size of the king ragworm. What is the length of the smaller worms?

7 **Writing in Math** Write your own word problem that involves fractions. Write its answer in a complete sentence.

Good News/Bad News
Unfortunately, a hermit crab may lose a leg in a battle with another animal. The good news is that the hermit crab will soon regrow its missing leg.

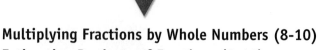

Do You Know How?

Do You Understand?

Multiplying Fractions by Whole Numbers (8-10)
Estimating Products of Fractions (8-11)

Find each product.

1. $\frac{1}{8}$ of 24   **2.** $\frac{5}{6}$ of 12   **3.** $\frac{2}{3} \times 18$

Estimate each product.

4. $\frac{4}{9} \times 35$ **5.** $\frac{3}{5} \times 44$ **6.** $3\frac{3}{4} \times 7$

A Explain how you would find $\frac{3}{4} \times 16$.

B Tell which method you used in Exercises 5 and 6. Explain why.

Multiplying Fractions (8-12)
Multiplying Mixed Numbers (8-13)

Find each product. Be sure your answer is in simplest form.

7. $\frac{2}{3} \times \frac{3}{5}$ **8.** $\frac{4}{9} \times \frac{3}{4}$ **9.** $\frac{5}{7} \times \frac{1}{3}$

10. $4\frac{1}{2} \times 6$ **11.** $1\frac{3}{4} \times \frac{1}{2}$ **12.** $2\frac{1}{3} \times 3\frac{3}{4}$

C Explain how you solved Exercise 7.

D What is the first thing you do when you multiply mixed numbers?

Understanding Division with Fractions (8-14)

Find each quotient. You can draw pictures to help you.

13. $2 \div \frac{1}{8}$ **14.** $3 \div \frac{1}{2}$ **15.** $3 \div \frac{3}{4}$

E Draw a picture to show how many $\frac{2}{3}$s are in 6. What is $6 \div \frac{2}{3}$?

Problem-Solving Skill: Choose an Operation (8-15)

16. In 2000, there were approximately 281 million people living in the United States. About $\frac{5}{8}$ of the people were ages 18 to 64. About $\frac{1}{8}$ of the people were ages 65 and older. What part of the total population was under age 18?

F Draw a picture to show the main idea in Exercise 16.

G Explain how you would find the number of people living in the United States between the ages 18 to 64.

MULTIPLE CHOICE

1. Which fraction shows the product $\frac{3}{4} \times \frac{8}{9}$ in simplest form? (8-12)

A. $\frac{24}{36}$ **B.** $\frac{4}{6}$ **C.** $\frac{2}{3}$ **D.** $\frac{11}{13}$

2. Eight lengths of ribbon, each $1\frac{3}{4}$ feet long, is how many feet of ribbon? (8-13)

A. 56 feet   **B.** 14 feet   **C.** 9 feet   **D.** $3\frac{3}{4}$ feet

FREE RESPONSE

Estimate each product. (8-11)

3. $14 \times \frac{3}{5}$ **4.** $\frac{3}{4} \times 11$ **5.** $4\frac{7}{8} \times 3\frac{1}{8}$ **6.** $10\frac{1}{3} \times 8$ **7.** $20 \times \frac{6}{7}$

Multiply. Be sure your answer is in simplest form. (8-10, 8-12, 8-13)

8. $\frac{1}{5} \times \frac{2}{3}$ **9.** $\frac{1}{2} \times \frac{3}{4}$ **10.** $\frac{3}{7} \times \frac{1}{3}$ **11.** $\frac{3}{5} \times \frac{5}{6}$

12. $10 \times \frac{1}{5}$ **13.** $\frac{2}{3} \times 18$ **14.** $\frac{1}{2} \times 34$ **15.** $\frac{1}{10} \times 18$

16. $1\frac{1}{3} \times 9$ **17.** $2\frac{4}{5} \times 3\frac{1}{2}$ **18.** $1\frac{1}{2} \times 6\frac{1}{3}$ **19.** $1\frac{2}{3} \times 2\frac{3}{5}$

Think It Through
To multiply mixed numbers, I need to first **change them to improper fractions.**

Use the rectangles at the right to help you find each quotient. (8-14)

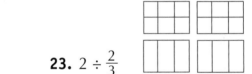

20. $1 \div \frac{1}{6}$ **21.** $2 \div \frac{1}{6}$ **22.** $2 \div \frac{1}{3}$ **23.** $2 \div \frac{2}{3}$

24. In 2000, $\frac{3}{25}$ of U.S. states had areas under 10,000 square miles; $\frac{13}{50}$ of U.S. states had areas between 10,000 and 50,000 sq mi; and $\frac{23}{50}$ of U.S. states had areas between 50,000 and 100,000 sq mi. What fraction of U.S. states had areas over 100,000 sq mi? (8-15, 8-16)

25. In 2000, $\frac{3}{5}$ of all U.S. states had populations under 5 million. What fraction of U.S. states had populations over 5 million? How many states had populations over 5 million? (8-15)

Writing in Math

26. Copy and shade the picture at the right to find $\frac{2}{3} \times \frac{1}{2}$. Explain what the different types of shading represent. (8-12)

27. Explain how you can find $\frac{4}{7}$ of 14 mentally. (8-10)

Test-Taking Strategies

Understand the question.

Get information for the answer.

Plan how to find the answer.

Make smart choices.

Use writing in math.

Improve written answers.

Plan How to Find the Answer

After you understand a test question and get needed information, you need to plan how to find the answer. Think about problem-solving skills and strategies and computation methods.

1. Tammy found this table showing that the number of calories a person uses in various activities depends on the person's weight.

Calories Used in One Minute			
	Weight		
Activity	**100 lb**	**120 lb**	**150 lb**
Bicycling	$2\frac{3}{5}$	$2\frac{9}{10}$	$3\frac{1}{2}$
Skating	$4\frac{2}{5}$	5	$5\frac{4}{5}$
Jogging	$8\frac{1}{10}$	$9\frac{1}{5}$	$10\frac{4}{5}$
Running	$10\frac{2}{5}$	$12\frac{4}{5}$	15

Tammy weighs 119 pounds. About how many calories does she use when jogging for 15 minutes?

A. 119 calories

B. 138 calories

C. 1,104 calories

D. 1,785 calories

Understand the question

I need to find about how many calories Tammy uses jogging for 15 minutes.

Get information for the answer.

The text tells me that Tammy weighs 119 pounds, which is about 120 pounds, and that she is jogging for 15 minutes. I can read the column in the table for 120 pounds to find that Tammy uses about $9\frac{1}{5}$ calories for each minute she jogs.

Plan how to find the answer.

- Think about problem-solving skills and strategies.

  I can multiply to find the answer.

- Choose computation methods.

  I need to find $15 \times 9\frac{1}{5}$. Since I need to change the mixed number to an improper fraction to multiply, I will use paper and pencil. I can use mental math to check my answer by estimating the product.

2. The circle graph below shows what parts of the total group of students have natural brown, blond, black, or red hair.

Hair Color

ESTIMATE the fraction of all the students who have natural brown hair. Then explain how you made your estimate.

Think It Through

I need to find an estimate for the fraction of all the students who have natural brown hair. The circle graph shows the part of the total population that has each hair color. To estimate the fractional amount, I can compare the size of the graph section labeled "Brown" to the benchmark fractions: $\frac{1}{4}$, $\frac{1}{3}$, $\frac{1}{2}$, and $\frac{3}{4}$.

Now it's your turn.

For each problem, describe a plan for finding the answer.

3. The dotted line shows Andrew's route as he rowed across Silver Lake.

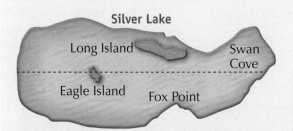

When Andrew got to Eagle Island, he had gone $\frac{3}{4}$ mile. Estimate the distance across the lake taking Andrew's route. Explain how you made your estimate.

4. In the wild, giant pandas spend about $\frac{1}{2}$ of the day eating bamboo. They sleep about $\frac{2}{5}$ of the day.

Which operation would be best to use if you want to find the total part of each day a giant panda spends eating and sleeping?

A. addition

B. subtraction

C. multiplication

D. division

Least means smallest.

The least common multiple (LCM) *of two numbers is the smallest number that is a multiple of both.*

Add and subtract fractions. (Lessons 8-1, 8-2, 8-3, 8-4)

Add or subtract fractions with **like denominators.**

Add or subtract the numerators. Write the answer over the common denominator. Simplify if possible.

$$\frac{11}{12} + \frac{5}{12} = \frac{16}{12} = 1\frac{4}{12} = 1\frac{1}{3}$$

Add or subtract fractions with **unlike denominators.**

Use the **least common denominator** to write equivalent fractions.

$$\begin{array}{r} \frac{5}{6} = \frac{10}{12} \\ -\frac{3}{4} = -\frac{9}{12} \\ \hline \frac{1}{12} \end{array}$$

Find the **LCM:**
Multiples of 6: 6, **12, ...**
Multiples of 4: 4, 8, **12, ...**

*And the **least common denominator (LCD)** of two fractions is the least common multiple of the denominators.* (p. 264)

1. Find $\frac{11}{15} - \frac{7}{15}$ and $\frac{9}{10} + \frac{2}{3}$.

"*Re" means to do something again, as in rewrite.*

*When you **rename** a mixed number, you use a different way to name the same amount.* (p. 472)

Add and subtract mixed numbers. (Lessons 8-5, 8-7, 8-8)

Write equivalent fractions with the LCD. First, add or subtract the fractions. Then add or subtract the whole numbers. Simplify if possible.

$$\begin{array}{r} 5\frac{3}{5} = 5\frac{9}{15} \\ + 2\frac{2}{3} = + 2\frac{10}{15} \\ \hline 7\frac{19}{15} = 8\frac{4}{15} \end{array}$$

$$\begin{array}{r} 9\frac{1}{2} = 9\frac{7}{14} \\ - 4\frac{3}{7} = - 4\frac{6}{14} \\ \hline 5\frac{1}{14} \end{array}$$

$$\begin{array}{r} 6\frac{1}{4} = 6\frac{3}{12} = 5\frac{15}{12} \\ - 1\frac{1}{3} = -1\frac{4}{12} = -1\frac{4}{12} \\ \hline 4\frac{11}{12} \end{array}$$

Rename $6\frac{3}{12}$ to show more twelfths. Think:

$$6\frac{3}{12} = 5 + 1 + \frac{3}{12}$$
$$= 5 + \frac{12}{12} + \frac{3}{12}$$
$$= 5\frac{15}{12}$$

2. Find $1\frac{1}{4} + 1\frac{5}{6}$, $4\frac{5}{6} - 2\frac{3}{8}$, and $6\frac{4}{9} - 3\frac{2}{3}$.

Remember, **compatible numbers** are numbers that are easy to work with. (p. 494)

Self Check

Multiply and divide with fractions. (Lessons 8-10, 8-11, 8-12, 8-13, 8-14)

Estimate $\frac{5}{6} \times 31$.

Use **compatible numbers.**

$\frac{1}{6} \times 30 = 5$, and

$\frac{5}{6} \times 30 = 25$.

So, $\frac{5}{6} \times 31$ is about 25.

When multiplying with fractions, change whole or mixed numbers to improper fractions. Multiply the numerators. Multiply the denominators. Simplify.

$20 \times \frac{2}{3} = \frac{20}{1} \times \frac{2}{3}$

$= \frac{40}{3}$

$= 13\frac{1}{3}$

$3\frac{1}{8} \times 1\frac{1}{5} = \frac{25}{8} \times \frac{6}{5}$

$= \frac{150}{40}$

$= 3\frac{30}{40} = 3\frac{3}{4}$

Find $3 \div \frac{1}{4}$.

Use pictures.

There are twelve $\frac{1}{4}$s in 3.

So $3 \div \frac{1}{4} = 12$.

---

3. Estimate $\frac{3}{5} \times 24$, and find $2\frac{1}{6} \times \frac{3}{10}$ and $4 \div \frac{1}{6}$.

Self Check

Work backward or choose an operation to solve problems. (Lessons 8-9, 8-15)

Work backward from the end result, using the opposite operation of each change.

Mia exercised for 2 hours. After she jogged, she swam for $\frac{3}{4}$ hour and biked for $\frac{1}{2}$ hour. How long did she jog?

$n = 2 - \frac{1}{2} - \frac{3}{4}$

$n = \frac{3}{4}$

She jogged for $\frac{3}{4}$ hr.

Show the main idea to help choose an operation.

Brianna bought 24 feet of lamp wire. She used $\frac{1}{3}$ of the wire to fix a lamp. How many feet of wire did she use?

24		
$\frac{1}{3}$ of 24		

Multiply.

$\frac{1}{3} \times 24 = 8$

Brianna used 8 feet of wire.

*You **work backward** when you start with the end result and figure out what happened at the beginning. (p. 485)*

---

4. Polly lives 4 miles from the library. She takes the bus for $3\frac{1}{4}$ miles and walks the rest of the way. How far does she walk?

Answers: 1. $\frac{4}{15}$; $1\frac{17}{30}$ 2. $3\frac{1}{12}$; $2\frac{11}{24}$; $2\frac{7}{9}$ 3. Sample estimate: 15; $\frac{13}{20}$; 24 4. $\frac{3}{4}$ mile

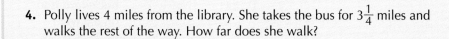
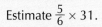

MULTIPLE CHOICE

Choose the correct letter for each answer.

1. What is $\frac{7}{8} + \frac{3}{8}$?

   A. $\frac{1}{2}$ **C.** $1\frac{1}{4}$

   B. $\frac{5}{8}$ **D.** $1\frac{4}{5}$

2. Mark walks $\frac{4}{5}$ mile to school. Jack walks $\frac{1}{5}$ mile less than Mark. How far does Jack walk to school?

   A. 1 mile   **C.** $\frac{1}{2}$ mile

   B. $\frac{3}{5}$ mile   **D.** $\frac{1}{5}$ mile

3. Find $\frac{3}{10} - \frac{1}{5}$.

   A. $\frac{1}{10}$ **C.** $\frac{5}{10}$

   B. $\frac{2}{5}$ **D.** $\frac{4}{5}$

4. What is the LCD of $\frac{5}{6}$ and $\frac{3}{4}$?

   A. 4   **C.** 18

   B. 12   **D.** 24

5. Add $\frac{5}{6}$ and $\frac{1}{8}$.

   A. $\frac{23}{24}$ **C.** $\frac{1}{4}$

   B. $\frac{3}{7}$ **D.** $\frac{1}{8}$

6. Find $5\frac{1}{3} - 3\frac{2}{3}$.

   A. $1\frac{1}{3}$ **C.** $2\frac{1}{3}$

   B. $1\frac{2}{3}$ **D.** $2\frac{2}{3}$

7. The length of Nick's garden is $4\frac{3}{5}$ ft. The width of the garden is $1\frac{1}{2}$ ft less than the length. How wide is Nick's garden?

   A. $3\frac{2}{3}$ ft   **C.** $3\frac{1}{10}$ ft

   B. $3\frac{3}{10}$ ft   **D.** $2\frac{1}{10}$ ft

8. Estimate to the nearest whole number. $4\frac{1}{3} + 5\frac{5}{6} + 7\frac{1}{8}$

   A. 16   **C.** 18

   B. 17   **D.** 19

9. Add $1\frac{5}{8}$ and $2\frac{1}{4}$.

   A. $3\frac{7}{16}$ **C.** $3\frac{3}{4}$

   B. $3\frac{1}{2}$ **D.** $3\frac{7}{8}$

10. Multiply $\frac{5}{6}$ and 48.

   A. 8   **C.** 38

   B. 30   **D.** 40

11. $\frac{3}{8}$ of 82 is about ____.

   A. 10

   B. 20

   C. 30

   D. 60

TEST TALK

Think It Through
- I can **work backward from an answer.**
- I can **eliminate** unreasonable answers.

12. Louie has a piece of rope that is $\frac{2}{3}$ yd long. He used $\frac{1}{2}$ of the piece of rope to make a knot. How long is the rope used to make the knot?

A. $\frac{1}{6}$ yd   **C.** $\frac{1}{3}$ yd

B. $\frac{1}{4}$ yd   **D.** $\frac{11}{12}$ yd

13. What is $2 \div \frac{1}{3}$? You can draw a picture to help.

A. $\frac{1}{6}$ **C.** $1\frac{1}{2}$

B. $\frac{2}{3}$ **D.** 6

FREE RESPONSE

Add or subtract. Simplify the answer, if possible.

14. $\frac{3}{7} + \frac{5}{7}$

15. $\frac{4}{5} - \frac{1}{8}$

16. $3\frac{3}{4} - 1\frac{5}{6}$

17. $4\frac{1}{5} + \frac{7}{10}$

18. $16 - 2\frac{4}{9}$

19. $\frac{13}{16} + \frac{3}{8} + \frac{1}{4}$

Estimate.

20. $4\frac{9}{11} - 1\frac{3}{4}$

21. $\frac{6}{7} \times 50$

Find each product. Simplify, if necessary.

22. $16 \times \frac{5}{8}$

23. $\frac{3}{7} \times \frac{1}{6}$

24. $1\frac{3}{4} \times 1\frac{2}{7}$

Find the LCD of each pair of fractions.

25. $\frac{5}{6}$ and $\frac{3}{10}$

26. $\frac{1}{3}$ and $\frac{3}{4}$

27. $\frac{1}{8}$ and $\frac{3}{5}$

28. $\frac{2}{9}$ and $\frac{1}{6}$

29. Christy used a full bag of flour. She made two batches of muffins. Each batch used $2\frac{1}{4}$ c of flour. Then she used $1\frac{1}{2}$ c flour to make pancakes and the remaining $2\frac{1}{6}$ c to make banana bread. How much flour is in a full bag?

30. Find $4 \div \frac{1}{2}$. You can draw a picture to help.

Writing in Math

31. Explain how to use compatible numbers to estimate the product of a whole number and a fraction. Give an example.

32. Explain how knowing $\frac{1}{5}$ of 45 can help you find $\frac{3}{5}$ of 45.

33. Write and solve a story problem to match the picture.

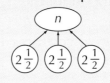

TEST TALK

Think It Through
- I can **work backward** to solve a problem.
- My answers should be **brief but complete.**

Number and Operation

MULTIPLE CHOICE

1. Find $\frac{6}{7} + \frac{1}{2}$.

  A. $\frac{3}{7}$ **C.** 1

  B. $\frac{7}{9}$ **D.** $1\frac{5}{14}$

2. What is the product of 18 and $\frac{5}{9}$?

  A. 2   **C.** 10

  B. 5   **D.** 16

3. Which fraction is equivalent to $\frac{4}{5}$?

  A. $\frac{8}{15}$ **C.** $\frac{8}{9}$

  B. $\frac{12}{15}$ **D.** $\frac{9}{10}$

4. Which decimal is equivalent to $\frac{3}{5}$?

  A. 0.06   **C.** 0.3

  B. 0.03   **D.** 0.6

FREE RESPONSE

5. Find $\frac{3}{9} \times \frac{1}{4}$.

6. Find the LCM of 4 and 6.

7. Fabric is on sale for $3 a yard. Mrs. Nickel bought $5\frac{2}{3}$ yards of fabric. What was the total cost for the fabric?

Writing in Math

8. Explain how to use compatible numbers to estimate $17 \times \frac{3}{8}$.

9. Explain what it means for a fraction to be in simplest form.

Geometry and Measurement

MULTIPLE CHOICE

10. Which angle is acute?

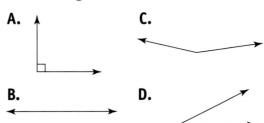

11. Which type of triangle has two equal sides and an angle measuring more than 90°?

  A. right scalene   **C.** obtuse isosceles

  B. acute scalene   **D.** acute isosceles

12. Which drawing shows this figure flipped across the dotted line?

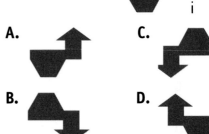

FREE RESPONSE

13. Find the measure of the third angle of a triangle if two of the angles measure 32° and 58°. Classify the triangle by its angles.

Writing in Math

14. List the similarities and differences between a trapezoid and a rhombus.

Data Analysis and Probability

15. Liza pulled a marble from the bag without looking. What is the probability she pulled a blue marble?

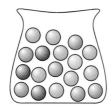

A. $\frac{1}{6}$ **C.** $\frac{1}{3}$

B. $\frac{3}{10}$ **D.** $\frac{1}{2}$

16. What is the mean of this data set?

12, 15, 7, 18, 15, 9, 11, 17

A. 13   **C.** 15

B. 13.5   **D.** 18

FREE RESPONSE

17. What fraction of the total number of students ate pizza for lunch?

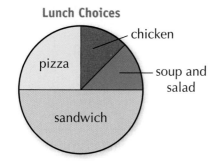

Lunch Choices

Writing in Math

18. What type of graph would be best to show how toy sales for a company increased and decreased during 2003? Explain your answer.

Algebra

MULTIPLE CHOICE

19. The LCM of two numbers is 12. Which pair could be the two numbers?

A. 3 and 6

B. 2 and 6

C. 3 and 4

D. 3 and 9

20. Find $1\frac{1}{6} - \frac{3}{4}$.

A. $\frac{1}{3}$ **C.** $1\frac{7}{12}$

B. $\frac{5}{12}$ **D.** $1\frac{11}{12}$

FREE RESPONSE

21. Solve $p + 10 = 15$.

22. Simplify the expression.

$$20 - 3 \times 2 + 1$$

Think It Through

- I need to remember to **follow the order of operations.**
- My answer should be **brief but complete.**

Writing in Math

23. Explain why addition and subtraction are called inverse operations.

24. Explain how to find ▪.

$$\frac{5}{6} = \frac{▪}{18}$$

Set 8-1 (pages 460–461)

Find $\frac{5}{8} + \frac{7}{8}$.

$\frac{5}{8} + \frac{7}{8} = \frac{12}{8}$ Add the numerators.
Write the sum over the common denominator.

$\qquad = 1\frac{4}{8} = 1\frac{1}{2}$ Simplify the sum.

Remember when adding or subtracting fractions with like denominators, the denominator does not change.

1. $\frac{1}{7} + \frac{5}{7}$ **2.** $\frac{3}{4} - \frac{1}{4}$

3. $\frac{9}{10} - \frac{3}{10}$ **4.** $\frac{5}{12} + \frac{11}{12}$

5. $\frac{5}{11} + \frac{2}{11} + \frac{4}{11}$ **6.** $\frac{3}{8} + \frac{3}{8} + \frac{7}{8}$

7. $\frac{1}{10} + \frac{1}{10} + \frac{1}{10}$ **8.** $\frac{1}{12} + \frac{5}{12} + \frac{7}{12}$

Set 8-2 (pages 462–463)

Find $\frac{3}{4} - \frac{5}{12}$.

Step 1: Use fraction strips to show $\frac{3}{4}$.

$\frac{1}{4}$	$\frac{1}{4}$	$\frac{1}{4}$

Step 2: Exchange $\frac{1}{4}$ strips with $\frac{1}{12}$ strips so you can remove $\frac{5}{12}$.

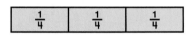

Step 3: Count the number of $\frac{1}{12}$ strips that are left. Simplify the difference.

$\frac{3}{4} - \frac{5}{12} = \frac{4}{12} = \frac{1}{3}$

Remember to add or subtract unlike fractions, you need to use equivalent fractions. Equivalent fractions name the same value. Use fraction strips or drawings to help you find equivalent fractions.

1. $\frac{1}{2} + \frac{1}{4}$ **2.** $\frac{7}{8} - \frac{1}{4}$

3. $\frac{4}{5} + \frac{3}{10}$ **4.** $\frac{5}{6} - \frac{5}{12}$

5. $\frac{5}{8} + \frac{3}{4}$ **6.** $\frac{2}{3} + \frac{5}{6}$

7. $\frac{9}{10} - \frac{3}{5}$ **8.** $\frac{1}{4} - \frac{1}{6}$

Set 8-3 (pages 464–465)

Find the least common denominator (LCD) of $\frac{3}{10}$ and $\frac{1}{6}$.

Multiples of 10: 10, 20, **30**, 40, 50 …

Multiples of 6: 6, 12, 18, 24, **30**, 36, …

30 is the least common multiple of 6 and 10.

So, 30 is the least common denominator of $\frac{3}{10}$ and $\frac{1}{6}$.

Remember the least common multiple of two numbers is the least number that is a multiple of both numbers.

1. $\frac{1}{2}$ and $\frac{3}{5}$ **2.** $\frac{1}{8}$ and $\frac{5}{12}$

3. $\frac{1}{4}$ and $\frac{5}{6}$ **4.** $\frac{7}{9}$ and $\frac{7}{12}$

5. $\frac{1}{6}$ and $\frac{4}{9}$ **6.** $\frac{3}{4}$ and $\frac{1}{7}$

7. $\frac{3}{8}$ and $\frac{1}{5}$ **8.** $\frac{1}{3}$ and $\frac{1}{5}$

Find $\frac{5}{6} + \frac{3}{4}$.

Step 1: Find the LCD

The LCD is 12.

Step 2: Use the LCD to write equivalent fractions.

$$\frac{5}{6} = \frac{10}{12} \qquad \frac{3}{4} = \frac{9}{12}$$

Step 3: Add the equivalent fractions. Simplify, if possible.

$$\frac{10}{12} + \frac{9}{12} = \frac{19}{12} = 1\frac{7}{12}$$

Remember when writing an equivalent fraction, multiply the numerator and denominator by the same number.

1. $\frac{3}{4} - \frac{1}{8}$ **2.** $\frac{5}{9} + \frac{2}{5}$

3. $\frac{7}{8} - \frac{2}{3}$ **4.** $\frac{4}{5} - \frac{1}{3}$

5. $\frac{3}{5} + \frac{1}{4} + \frac{3}{8}$ **6.** $\frac{2}{7} + \frac{1}{2} + \frac{2}{3}$

7. $\frac{4}{5} + \frac{3}{10} + \frac{3}{4}$ **8.** $\frac{5}{6} + \frac{1}{8} + \frac{5}{12}$

Find $1\frac{1}{4} + 1\frac{3}{4}$.

Use fraction strips to show $1\frac{1}{4} + 1\frac{3}{4}$.

Combine the 1 strips. Then combine the $\frac{1}{4}$ strips.

$$1\frac{1}{4} + 1\frac{3}{4} = 2\frac{4}{4} = 3$$

Remember sometimes you need to rename mixed numbers to add or subtract them.

1. $5 - 2\frac{3}{8}$ **2.** $7\frac{1}{5} + 4\frac{3}{5}$

3. $4\frac{5}{6} - 2\frac{1}{6}$ **4.** $5\frac{5}{8} + 4\frac{7}{8}$

5. $1\frac{5}{9} + 4\frac{4}{9}$ **6.** $6\frac{3}{10} - 2\frac{9}{10}$

Estimate $2\frac{1}{4} + 5\frac{7}{8}$.

$2\frac{1}{4} + 5\frac{7}{8}$ Round each mixed number to the nearest whole number. Then add.

$$2 + 6 = 8$$

Remember you can use a number line to round mixed numbers.

1. $7\frac{6}{7} - 3\frac{1}{8}$ **2.** $3\frac{1}{5} + 3\frac{5}{6}$

3. $5\frac{1}{2} - 4\frac{1}{3}$ **4.** $6\frac{1}{4} + 2\frac{3}{5} + 1\frac{7}{9}$

Find $2\frac{1}{3} + 3\frac{5}{6}$.

$$2\frac{1}{3} = 2\frac{2}{6}$$
$$+ 3\frac{5}{6} = 3\frac{5}{6}$$
$$\overline{\phantom{+3\frac{5}{6}}}$$
$$5\frac{7}{6} = 6\frac{1}{6}$$

Step 1: Write equivalent fractions with the LCD.

Step 2: Add the fractions.

Step 3: Add the whole numbers. Simplify the sum, if necessary.

Remember you can add mixed numbers the same way you add whole numbers and fractions.

1. $5\frac{1}{2} + 2\frac{3}{8}$ **2.** $12\frac{3}{10} + 4\frac{2}{5}$

3. $1\frac{3}{4} + 2\frac{5}{8}$ **4.** $9\frac{2}{3} + 7\frac{5}{9}$

Set 8-8 (pages 478–481)

Find $5\frac{1}{5} - 3\frac{1}{2}$.

$5\frac{1}{5} = 5\frac{2}{10} = 4\frac{12}{10}$

$-\ 3\frac{1}{2} = 3\frac{5}{10} = 3\frac{5}{10}$

$\overline{\phantom{-\ 3\frac{1}{2} = 3\frac{5}{10} = }}$

$1\frac{2}{10} = 1\frac{1}{5}$

Step 1: Write equivalent fractions with the LCD.

Step 2: Rename $5\frac{2}{10}$ to show more tenths.

Step 3: Subtract the fractions. Then subtract the whole numbers. Simplify the difference.

Remember subtracting mixed numbers often requires renaming.

1. $7\frac{5}{6} - 3\frac{2}{3}$ **2.** $9 - 2\frac{3}{8}$

3. $5\frac{1}{4} - 1\frac{1}{3}$ **4.** $3\frac{3}{7} - 1\frac{1}{2}$

5. $4\frac{2}{3} - 2\frac{5}{8}$ **6.** $10\frac{3}{4} - 6\frac{11}{12}$

Set 8-9 (pages 484–487)

To work backward, follow these steps.

Step 1: Identify the unknown initial amount.

Step 2: List each change, starting with the initial amount.

Step 3: Start at the end result. Work backward using the inverse of each change.

Remember addition and subtraction are inverse operations.

1. Josie worked on her English paper for $\frac{2}{3}$ hour. Then she spent $\frac{1}{2}$ hour on math homework. After that, she spent $\frac{3}{4}$ hour on the computer. If she logged off the computer at 8:00, what time did she start working on her English paper?

Set 8-10 (pages 490–493)

Find $\frac{3}{5} \times 35$.   Think: $\frac{3}{5}$ is $3 \times \frac{1}{5}$

$\frac{1}{5}$ of 35 is 7.   Think: $35 \div 5 = 7$

$3 \times 7 = 21$, so $\frac{3}{5} \times 35 = 21$

Remember thinking about division can help you multiply.

1. $\frac{5}{6} \times 36$ **2.** $\frac{2}{7}$ of 42

3. $\frac{3}{10}$ of 70   **4.** $\frac{2}{3} \times 21$

5. $\frac{7}{12} \times 60$ **6.** 81 of $\frac{7}{9}$

Set 8-11 (pages 494–495)

Estimate $\frac{5}{6} \times 44$.

One way

Use compatible numbers.

$\frac{1}{6} \times 42 = 7$, and $\frac{5}{6} \times 42 = 35$.

So, $\frac{5}{6} \times 44$ is about 35.

Another way

Change $\frac{5}{6}$ to the nearest benchmark.

$1 \times 44 = 44$

So, $\frac{5}{6} \times 44$ is about 44.

Remember you can use benchmarks or compatible numbers to estimate products of fractions.

1. $\frac{3}{5} \times 27$ **2.** $\frac{5}{8} \times 39$

3. $\frac{7}{9} \times 65$ **4.** $\frac{1}{4} \times 33$

Find $\frac{3}{8} \times \frac{2}{3}$.

$\frac{3}{8} \times \frac{2}{3} = \frac{6}{24}$

$\qquad = \frac{1}{4}$

Step 1: Multiply the numerators
Step 2: Multiply the denominators
Step 3: Simplify the product.

Remember you can write whole numbers as improper fractions with a denominator of 1.

1. $\frac{7}{8} \times \frac{3}{4}$ **2.** $9 \times \frac{4}{5}$

3. $\frac{1}{3} \times \frac{3}{10}$ **4.** $\frac{1}{2} \times \frac{3}{4} \times \frac{2}{3}$

5. $\frac{5}{12} \times \frac{2}{3}$ **6.** $\frac{4}{7} \times 6$

Find $2\frac{1}{3} \times 1\frac{1}{4}$.

$2\frac{1}{3} \times 1\frac{1}{4} = \frac{7}{3} \times \frac{5}{4}$

$\qquad \frac{7}{3} \times \frac{5}{4} = \frac{35}{12}$

$\qquad\qquad = 2\frac{11}{12}$

Step 1: Write the mixed numbers as improper fractions.
Step 2: Multiply as you would multiply fractions.
Step 3: Simplify the product.

Remember to write a mixed number as an improper fraction, multiply the whole number by the denominator and add the numerator. The number in the denominator remains the same.

1. $2\frac{2}{5} \times 8$ **2.** $1\frac{5}{6} \times 1\frac{1}{3}$

3. $3\frac{3}{8} \times 5\frac{1}{2}$ **4.** $4\frac{1}{4} \times 7$

Find $2 \div \frac{1}{5}$.

Use fraction strips to break 2 into $\frac{1}{5}$s.

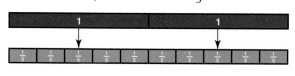

$2 \div \frac{1}{5} = 10$

Remember you can use pictures to help you find quotients.

1. $7 \div \frac{1}{4}$ **2.** $10 \div \frac{2}{3}$

3. $6 \div \frac{1}{3}$ **4.** $8 \div \frac{4}{5}$

5. $9 \div \frac{3}{7}$ **6.** $5 \div \frac{1}{8}$

A video store says that $\frac{3}{5}$ of the movies people rented yesterday were new releases. If the video store rented 55 movies yesterday, how many were new releases?

Multiply $\frac{3}{5}$ by 55 to find the number of new releases.

$\frac{3}{5} \times 55 = \frac{3}{5} \times \frac{55}{1} = \frac{165}{5} = 33$

The video store rented 33 new releases.

Remember to read the problem carefully and then choose which operation to use.

1. Peter gave away 4 apple pies. He gave each friend a slice of pie. Each slice was $\frac{1}{8}$ of a pie. How many slices of pie did Peter give to his friends?

Set 8-1 (pages 460–461)

Add or subtract. Simplify, if possible.

1. $\frac{3}{8} + \frac{7}{8}$

2. $\frac{5}{6} - \frac{1}{6}$

3. $\frac{1}{9} + \frac{7}{9}$

4. $\frac{11}{12} - \frac{3}{12}$

5. $\frac{8}{10} + \frac{3}{10}$

6. $\frac{3}{11} + \frac{1}{11} + \frac{5}{11}$

7. $\frac{3}{7} + \frac{4}{7} + \frac{2}{7}$

8. $\frac{13}{16} - \frac{3}{16}$

9. $\frac{3}{16} + \frac{5}{16}$

10. $\frac{11}{20} - \frac{3}{20}$

11. $\frac{1}{8} + \frac{3}{8} + \frac{5}{8}$

12. $\frac{9}{25} - \frac{2}{25}$

13. One hiking trail is $\frac{4}{6}$ mile long and another is $\frac{3}{6}$ mile long. If Tammy hikes both trails, how far will she have hiked?

Set 8-2 (pages 462–463)

Find each sum or difference. Simplify the answer, if possible. You may use fraction strips or draw pictures to help.

1. $\frac{1}{4} + \frac{3}{8}$

2. $\frac{7}{8} - \frac{1}{2}$

3. $\frac{1}{3} + \frac{5}{12}$

4. $\frac{1}{3} - \frac{1}{6}$

5. $\frac{3}{16} + \frac{3}{4}$

6. $\frac{5}{6} - \frac{2}{3}$

7. $\frac{9}{10} - \frac{3}{5}$

8. $\frac{5}{6} + \frac{3}{4}$

9. $\frac{3}{4} + \frac{3}{8}$

10. $\frac{5}{8} - \frac{1}{4}$

11. $\frac{1}{10} + \frac{1}{5} + \frac{1}{10}$

12. $\frac{15}{16} - \frac{1}{8}$

Set 8-3 (pages 464–465)

Find the least common denominator for each pair of fractions.

1. $\frac{5}{6}$ and $\frac{1}{4}$

2. $\frac{3}{16}$ and $\frac{3}{8}$

3. $\frac{1}{2}$ and $\frac{7}{9}$

4. $\frac{2}{7}$ and $\frac{1}{3}$

5. $\frac{5}{12}$ and $\frac{2}{3}$

6. $\frac{5}{8}$ and $\frac{3}{10}$

7. $\frac{4}{9}$ and $\frac{1}{12}$

8. $\frac{1}{5}$ and $\frac{3}{4}$

9. $\frac{1}{12}$ and $\frac{1}{4}$

10. $\frac{2}{3}$ and $\frac{1}{24}$

11. $\frac{3}{10}$ and $\frac{1}{4}$

12. $\frac{5}{16}$ and $\frac{2}{3}$

Set 8-4 (pages 466–469)

Add or subtract. Simplify, if possible.

1. $\frac{3}{5} + \frac{1}{3}$

2. $\frac{5}{6} + \frac{7}{12}$

3. $\frac{7}{8} - \frac{1}{5}$

4. $\frac{9}{10} - \frac{5}{6}$

5. $\frac{5}{8} + \frac{5}{12}$

6. $\frac{13}{16} - \frac{1}{4}$

7. $\frac{1}{3} + \frac{3}{5} + \frac{7}{10}$

8. $\frac{3}{8} + \frac{1}{6} + \frac{3}{4}$

9. $\frac{3}{8} + \frac{1}{3}$

10. $\frac{7}{16} - \frac{3}{8}$

11. $\frac{9}{20} + \frac{1}{10} + \frac{1}{5}$

12. $\frac{5}{12} + \frac{1}{3} + \frac{1}{2}$

13. What do you add to $\frac{1}{5}$ to get $\frac{1}{2}$?

Take It to the NET
www More Practice
www.scottforesman.com

Set 8-5 (pages 472–473)

Find each sum or difference. Simplify the answer, if necessary. You may use fraction strips or draw pictures to help.

1. $2\frac{1}{8} + 5\frac{3}{8}$ 　　**2.** $6\frac{1}{6} - 3\frac{5}{6}$ 　　**3.** $4\frac{1}{3} - 3\frac{2}{3}$ 　　**4.** $7\frac{3}{7} + 5\frac{5}{7}$

5. $2\frac{1}{12} - 1\frac{11}{12}$ 　　**6.** $9 - 6\frac{1}{5}$ 　　**7.** $1\frac{5}{9} + 1\frac{7}{9}$ 　　**8.** $3\frac{3}{5} + 2\frac{4}{5}$

9. A piece of wood that is $2\frac{1}{2}$ feet long is cut from a 6-foot board. What is the length of the remaining piece?

Set 8-6 (pages 474–475)

Estimate each sum or difference. Round to the nearest whole number.

1. $5\frac{2}{5} + 4\frac{1}{3}$ 　　**2.** $10\frac{7}{8} - 7\frac{3}{10}$ 　　**3.** $2\frac{2}{3} + 2\frac{1}{6}$ 　　**4.** $8\frac{1}{12} - 2\frac{6}{7}$

5. $3\frac{1}{4} - 1\frac{5}{6}$ 　　**6.** $3\frac{8}{9} + 4\frac{3}{4} + 1\frac{1}{5}$ 　　**7.** $5\frac{7}{8} + 7\frac{2}{11} + 3$ 　　**8.** $6\frac{4}{5} - 3\frac{7}{9}$

9. Franco ran $3\frac{3}{10}$ miles on Monday and $2\frac{3}{4}$ miles on Tuesday. Estimate the total number of miles he ran in the two days.

10. A $6\frac{3}{4}$-inch length is cut from a ribbon that is $19\frac{1}{2}$ inches long. Estimate how much ribbon is left.

Set 8-7 (pages 476–477)

Estimate the sum first. Then add. Simplify, if necessary.

1. $8\frac{3}{4} + 5\frac{1}{6}$ 　　**2.** $1\frac{5}{8} + 1\frac{1}{3}$ 　　**3.** $3\frac{6}{7} + 1\frac{1}{2}$ 　　**4.** $4\frac{3}{5} + 2\frac{3}{10}$

5. $7\frac{5}{12} + 6\frac{3}{4}$ 　　**6.** $2\frac{5}{6} + 9\frac{3}{8}$ 　　**7.** $12 + 4\frac{5}{16}$ 　　**8.** $2\frac{9}{10} + 2\frac{1}{4}$

9. $1\frac{7}{8} + 2\frac{1}{4}$ 　　**10.** $3\frac{3}{16} + 1\frac{3}{8}$ 　　**11.** $5\frac{2}{3} + 1\frac{3}{4}$ 　　**12.** $4\frac{1}{24} + 5\frac{1}{16}$

13. Mrs. Kern placed $2\frac{1}{4}$ lb of bananas and $3\frac{3}{8}$ lb of grapes into a basket. If the basket weighs $\frac{1}{2}$ lb by itself, how much did the basket with the fruit weigh?

Set 8-8 (pages 478–481)

Estimate the difference first. Then subtract. Simplify, if necessary.

1. $5\frac{1}{6} - 2\frac{2}{3}$ 　　**2.** $2\frac{7}{8} - 1\frac{1}{2}$ 　　**3.** $12\frac{3}{4} - 7$ 　　**4.** $8 - 3\frac{3}{7}$

5. $9\frac{3}{10} - 4\frac{4}{5}$ 　　**6.** $6\frac{5}{6} - \frac{3}{4}$ 　　**7.** $3\frac{1}{2} - 1\frac{7}{8}$ 　　**8.** $4\frac{7}{10} - 2\frac{5}{6}$

9. One tree is $19\frac{1}{2}$ feet tall. Another tree nearby is $16\frac{3}{4}$ feet tall. What is the difference in their heights?

Set 8-9 (pages 484–487)

Solve each problem by working backward. Write each answer in a complete sentence.

1. Gracie has $1\frac{5}{6}$ ft of ribbon left over. She used $2\frac{1}{3}$ ft to wrap a gift and $\frac{3}{4}$ ft to decorate a picture frame. To tie the end of her braid, she used $\frac{1}{2}$ ft of the ribbon. How many feet of ribbon did Gracie start with?

2. Tracy has a flower that is $1\frac{5}{6}$ ft tall. She planted the flower 5 weeks ago. If the flower grew $\frac{1}{4}$ ft each week, how tall was the flower when Tracy planted it?

Set 8-10 (pages 490–493)

Find each product.

1. $\frac{1}{4}$ of 24

2. $\frac{5}{6}$ of 42

3. $\frac{7}{9}$ of 54

4. $\frac{3}{5}$ of 30

5. $21 \times \frac{2}{3}$

6. $\frac{8}{9} \times 117$

7. $\frac{3}{8} \times 96$

8. $\frac{5}{7} \times 70$

9. $\frac{2}{3} \times 24$

10. $\frac{5}{6} \times 12$

11. $\frac{5}{12} \times 60$

12. $25 \times \frac{2}{5}$

13. At a school play, $\frac{3}{4}$ of the tickets sold were student tickets. If 300 tickets were sold, how many were student tickets?

14. On a 25-question test, Stephen answered $\frac{4}{5}$ of the questions correctly. How many questions did he answer correctly?

Set 8-11 (pages 494–495)

Estimate each product.

1. $\frac{3}{4} \times 25$

2. $\frac{3}{7} \times 16$

3. $\frac{1}{9} \times 44$

4. $\frac{3}{8} \times 38$

5. $\frac{2}{3} \times 20$

6. $\frac{5}{6} \times 43$

7. $30 \times \frac{11}{12}$

8. $29 \times \frac{3}{7}$

9. $\frac{1}{2} \times 19$

10. $9 \times \frac{1}{4}$

11. $26 \times \frac{1}{5}$

12. $38 \times \frac{1}{3}$

13. About how much does a $\frac{3}{4}$-pound steak cost if steak sells for $9 a pound?

14. Jeffrey has 7 boards. Each board is $\frac{5}{8}$ yard long. About how many yards of board does Jeffrey have?

Take It to the NET
More Practice
www.scottforesman.com

Set 8-12 (pages 496–499)

Find each product. Simplify, if necessary.

1. $\frac{2}{3} \times \frac{4}{5}$ **2.** $\frac{3}{7} \times \frac{3}{5}$ **3.** $\frac{7}{8} \times \frac{1}{4}$ **4.** $\frac{1}{3} \times \frac{2}{7}$

5. $\frac{1}{9} \times \frac{1}{2}$ **6.** $\frac{1}{6} \times \frac{1}{5} \times 12$ **7.** $\frac{5}{6} \times \frac{3}{8} \times 4$ **8.** $\frac{11}{12} \times \frac{3}{4}$

9. Draw a model that represents $\frac{2}{5}$ of $\frac{1}{10}$.

Set 8-13 (pages 500–501)

Estimate. Then find each product. Simplify, if necessary.

1. $3\frac{1}{6} \times 1\frac{1}{3}$ **2.** $5\frac{2}{5} \times 2\frac{7}{12}$ **3.** $1\frac{7}{8} \times 2\frac{3}{5}$ **4.** $4\frac{1}{4} \times \frac{7}{9}$

5. $2\frac{1}{5} \times 3\frac{3}{4}$ **6.** $\frac{5}{6} \times 1\frac{1}{8}$ **7.** $9 \times 6\frac{2}{3}$ **8.** $12 \times 1\frac{1}{5}$

9. To make a gallon of punch, Jacquelyn needs $2\frac{3}{4}$ pints of orange juice. If Jacquelyn wants to make $4\frac{1}{2}$ gallons of punch, how many pints of orange juice will she need?

Set 8-14 (pages 502–503)

Use the picture to find the quotient.

1. How many $\frac{5}{6}$ are in 5?

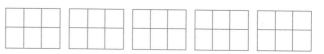

Find each quotient. You can draw pictures to help you.

2. $7 \div \frac{1}{5}$ **3.** $3 \div \frac{1}{8}$ **4.** $4 \div \frac{2}{7}$ **5.** $18 \div \frac{9}{10}$

Set 8-15 (pages 504–505)

Draw a picture to show the main idea. Then choose an operation to solve the problem.

1. Kevin is training for a biathlon. Today he biked $12\frac{3}{4}$ miles and ran $3\frac{3}{10}$ miles. How many miles did he bike and run today?

2. For a batch of 12 muffins, a recipe calls for $2\frac{1}{3}$ cups of flour. Martina needs to bake 36 muffins for a bake sale. How many cups of flour does she need?

CHAPTER 9
Measurement

A Vocabulary
(Grade 4)

Choose the best term from the box.

1. The __?__ is the distance around a polygon.

2. The __?__ is the number of square units needed to cover a polygon.

3. A meter is a __?__ unit of length.

4. A yard is a __?__ unit of length.

Vocabulary

- **metric** *(Grade 4)*
- **area** *(Grade 4)*
- **perimeter** *(Grade 4)*
- **customary** *(Grade 4)*

B Changing Units of Length
(Grade 4)

5. 1 ft = ▇ in. 6. 1 yd = ▇ in.

7. 1 yd = ▇ ft 8. 1 mi = ▇ ft

9. 1 cm = ▇ mm 10. 1 m = ▇ mm

11. 1 m = ▇ cm 12. 1 km = ▇ m

13. Which is easier, to change meters to kilometers or yards to inches? Explain.

Do You Know...

What size shoe would the Statue of Liberty wear?

You will find out in Lesson 9-16.

Amazing **BUILDINGS**
See inside great buildings of the world – from castles and cathedrals, to palaces and monuments

Illustrated by Paolo Donati
Written by Philip Wilkinson

C Multiplying and Dividing by 10, 100, and 1,000
(pages 84–85, 230–231)

14. 4.6×100 **15.** 23.71×100

16. $7.04 \times 1,000$ **17.** 0.05×10

18. $583 \div 100$ **19.** $91.5 \div 10$

20. $456 \div 1,000$ **21.** $0.5 \div 10$

22. If you divide by 100, is the quotient greater than or less than the dividend?

D Multiplication and Division
(pages 88–91, 214–217, 234–237, 490–493, 500–501)

23. 5×3.14 **24.** 4×16.5

25. $4 \times 3\frac{1}{4}$ **26.** $\frac{1}{2} \times 4 \times 7$

27. $64 \div 16$ **28.** $3.9 \div 3$

29. $150 \div 50$ **30.** $180 \div 12$

31. Explain how to use multiplication to check the quotient of a division problem.

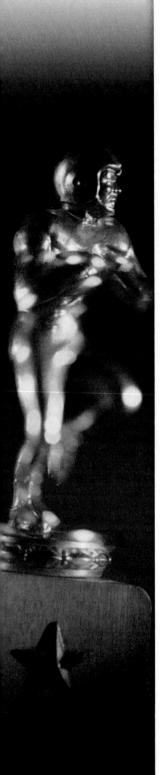

Customary Units of Length

LEARN

How can you change between one customary unit of length and another?

Customary units of length include inches, feet, yards, and miles. Lengths can be changed from one customary unit of length to another by multiplying or dividing.

Data File

Customary Units of Length

12 inches (in.) = 1 foot (ft)

36 inches = 3 feet = 1 yard (yd)

5,280 feet = 1,760 yards = 1 mile (mi)

Example A

A professional football field must be 120 yards long, including both end zones. What is the field's length in feet?

To change larger units to smaller units, multiply.

1 yard = 3 feet

1 ft	1 ft	1 ft
1 yd		

120 yards = 120 × 3 feet

120 yards = 360 feet

A football field is 360 feet long.

Example B

A football trophy is 22 inches tall. What is the trophy's height in feet?

To change smaller units to larger units, divide.

12 inches = 1 foot

1 in.	1 in.	1 in.	1 in.	1 in.	1 in.	1 in.	1 in.	1 in.	1 in.	1 in.	1 in.
1 ft

$$\begin{array}{r} 1 \text{ foot} \\ 12\overline{)22} \\ -12 \\ \hline 10 \text{ extra inches} \end{array}$$

The trophy is 1 foot 10 inches tall.

✔ Talk About It

1. In Example A, why do you multiply by 3?

2. To change 30 feet to yards, would you multiply 30 by 3 or divide 30 by 3? Explain.

3. **Number Sense** Why is the answer in Example B in feet *and* inches? Is there a way to give the answer using only feet? Explain.

How do you add and subtract measurements?

The goalpost crossbar on a football field is exactly 10 feet above the ground. Antoine wants to be able to jump up and touch it. When he stretches his arms as far as possible, he can reach 6 feet 8 inches.

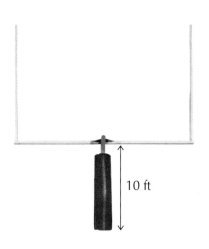

10 ft

Think It Through

• I should **add** to **combine** measurements.

• I should **subtract** to find the **difference** between measurements.

Example C

Antoine can jump 1 ft 7 in. from the ground. If he stretches his arms while he jumps, can he touch the crossbar?

$$
\begin{array}{r}
6 \text{ ft} \quad 8 \text{ in.} \\
+ 1 \text{ ft} \quad 7 \text{ in.} \\
\hline
7 \text{ ft } 15 \text{ in.}
\end{array}
$$

15 in. > 1 ft
You need to rename the answer.

15 in. = 1 ft 3 in.
7 ft + 1 ft 3 in. = 8 ft 3 in.

8 ft 3 in. < 10 ft. So, Antoine cannot touch the crossbar.

Example D

How much more would Antoine have to be able to jump to reach the crossbar?

$$
\begin{array}{r}
9 \text{ ft 12 in.} \\
\cancel{10 \text{ ft 0 in.}} \\
- 8 \text{ ft 3 in.} \\
\hline
1 \text{ ft 9 in.}
\end{array}
$$

0 < 3
You need to rename to subtract.
10 ft = 9 ft 12 in.

So, Antoine would need to jump another 1 foot 9 inches to reach the crossbar.

✔ Talk About It

4. In Example C, why do you have to rename your answer?

5. In Example D, why is subtraction the right operation to use?

6. **Estimation** About how tall do you think Antoine is? Why?

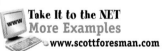

Take It to the NET
More Examples
www.scottforesman.com

For another example, see Set 9-1 on p. 584.

CHECK ✔

Copy and complete.

1. 12 ft = ___ yd **2.** 7 yd = ___ in. **3.** 48 in. = ___ ft **4.** 9 ft 6 in. = ___ in.

5. 21 ft 8 in.
  + 10 ft 7 in.

6. 6 ft 9 in.
  − 2 ft 11 in.

7. 4 yd 2 ft
  + 1 yd 2 ft

8. Number Sense In Exercise 6, why do you have to rename units?

Ⓐ Skills and Understanding

Copy and complete.

9. 18 yd = ___ in. **10.** 24 ft = ___ yd **11.** 56 ft = ___ yd ___ ft. **12.** 2 mi = ___ yd

13. 156 ft = ___ yd **14.** 3 mi = ___ ft **15.** 12 ft 7 in. = ___ in. **16.** 10 yd = ___ in.

17. 10 in.
    + 5 ft 4 in.

18. 9 yd 1 ft
    − 4 yd 2 ft

19. 1 mi 880 yd
    +   880 yd

20. 30 ft 9 in.
    − 19 ft 4 in.

21. 15 ft + 2 yd **22.** 1 ft 7 in. − 11 in. **23.** 2 mi − 1,500 yd **24.** 8 yd 1 ft + 1 yd 1 ft

25. Reasoning Mary is 5 ft 9 in. tall. Is she taller or shorter than 2 yards?

Ⓑ Reasoning and Problem Solving

Calculator When Walter Payton retired, he held the record for the most yards gained rushing in his professional football league. Use the data at the right.

26. How many miles did Payton gain rushing in his career?

27. What is the average number of yards he gained rushing in each game?

28. On high school football fields, the distance between the goalpost uprights is 23 ft 4 in. In professional football, the distance is 18 ft 6 in. How much farther apart are the high school goalpost uprights?

29. **Writing in Math** Terrence found the number of feet in 5 miles below. Do you agree with his method? Explain. If not, describe the process you would use.

    5 × 1,760 = 8,800 feet

Gained 16,726 yards in his career. Played in 190 games.

🦋 Math and Science

Many sports teams have chosen animals for their mascots. This table shows the average lengths of some of those animals.

Animals Chosen as Mascots	
Animal	**Average Length (in.)**
Grizzly Bear	84
Dolphin	72
Jaguar	80
Lion	110

30. What is the average length of each animal in feet and inches?

31. Arnold's soccer team has a dolphin as a mascot. The mascot is 7 feet long. Is this mascot longer or shorter than a real dolphin? What is the difference in their lengths?

C Extensions

Write the fraction equivalents for these units of measurement.

32. 1 in. = ___ ft **33.** 1 ft = ___ yd **34.** 1 yd = ___ mi **35.** 1 in. = ___ yd

36. A building has 5 floors. A painter needs to know the height of the building. Since the building is too tall to measure, the painter measures the height of the first floor and finds it is $9\frac{1}{2}$ feet tall. If each floor is the same height, what is the height of the building?

Mixed Review and Test Prep

Take It to the NET
Test Prep
www.scottforesman.com

Find each quotient. You can draw pictures to help.

37. $3 \div \frac{1}{2}$ **38.** $4 \div \frac{3}{4}$ **39.** $3 \div \frac{1}{12}$ **40.** $7 \div \frac{7}{8}$

41. Algebra Give the next two fractions in this pattern. $\frac{1}{2}, \frac{1}{4}, \frac{1}{8}, \frac{1}{16}$

A. $\frac{1}{18}, \frac{1}{20}$ **B.** $\frac{1}{32}, \frac{1}{64}$ **C.** $\frac{1}{24}, \frac{1}{32}$ **D.** $\frac{1}{8}, \frac{1}{4}$

Enrichment

Measuring Tools and Units of Measure

Often more than one measuring instrument can be used to measure the same thing. For example, you could measure your height with a ruler, a yardstick, or a tape measure.

1. Why is a tape measure more appropriate than a ruler for measuring waist size?

2. Look up the meaning of the word *odometer*. Why is an odometer more appropriate than a ruler in some cases?

3. Mechanics use an instrument called a gap gauge to measure spark plug gap. Why do you think they need a special instrument for measuring spark plug gap?

Use a dictionary to look up each unit and then decide which are units of length. Write *yes* if the unit is a unit of length. Otherwise, write *no*.

4. acre **5.** furlong **6.** nautical mile

7. parsec **8.** hectare **9.** light-year

Key Idea
If you need more precise measurements of length, you can use fractions of an inch.

Materials
• inch ruler

Measuring with Fractions of an Inch

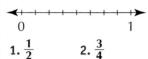
LEARN

How can you use fractions to measure more precisely?

Since an inch ruler is divided into equal parts, you can use fractions to measure lengths.

> On this **ruler,** each mark between two whole inches is $\frac{1}{16}$ inch.

Example

Find the length of the nail to the nearest inch, nearest $\frac{1}{2}$ inch, nearest $\frac{1}{4}$ inch, and nearest $\frac{1}{8}$ inch.

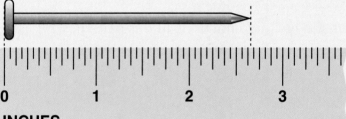

Nearest inch: 3 in.

Nearest $\frac{1}{2}$ inch: $2\frac{1}{2}$ in.

Nearest $\frac{1}{4}$ inch: $2\frac{3}{4}$ inch

Nearest $\frac{1}{8}$ inch: $2\frac{5}{8}$ in.

Activity

Will using different fraction units always give you different measurements?

a. Find the height of the doll-house mirror shown at the right to the nearest inch, nearest $\frac{1}{2}$ inch, nearest $\frac{1}{4}$ inch, and nearest $\frac{1}{8}$ inch. Write each fraction in simplest form.

b. Do some of the measurements from **part a** seem to be the same? Explain.

c. Measure the length of at least two other objects to the nearest inch, nearest $\frac{1}{2}$ inch, nearest $\frac{1}{4}$ inch, and nearest $\frac{1}{8}$ inch.

d. If a carpenter is building a doll house, would it be close enough to measure the parts to the nearest inch? Explain.

Measure each segment to the nearest inch, $\frac{1}{2}$ inch, $\frac{1}{4}$ inch, and $\frac{1}{8}$ inch.

1. ├────────────────────────┤ **2.** ├──────────┤

Use your ruler to draw a segment of each length.

3. $\frac{7}{8}$ in.   **4.** $1\frac{3}{4}$ in.   **5.** $2\frac{1}{4}$ in.   **6.** $3\frac{1}{8}$ in.   **7.** $1\frac{7}{8}$ in.

8. Reasoning If a landscaper is measuring the width of a flower bed, would it be helpful to measure to the nearest $\frac{1}{8}$ inch? Explain.

Ⓐ Skills and Understanding

Measure each segment to the nearest inch, $\frac{1}{2}$ inch, $\frac{1}{4}$ inch, and $\frac{1}{8}$ inch.

9. ├────────────────────┤   **10.** ├──────────────────────┤

Use your ruler to draw a line segment of each length.

11. $\frac{3}{8}$ in.   **12.** $2\frac{3}{4}$ in.   **13.** $1\frac{1}{2}$ in.   **14.** $4\frac{1}{4}$ in.   **15.** $3\frac{7}{8}$ in.

16. Reasoning To the nearest $\frac{1}{2}$ inch, a board is 4 inches wide. Is it reasonable that its actual width is $3\frac{3}{8}$ inches? Explain.

Ⓑ Reasoning and Problem Solving

17. Real objects are 12 times as large as objects in a doll house. What would be the real-world dimensions of the doll-house painting at the right?

18. **Writing in Math** Describe how you would find the length of an object to the nearest $\frac{1}{2}$ inch if the actual length of the object is between $2\frac{1}{2}$ inches and 3 inches long.

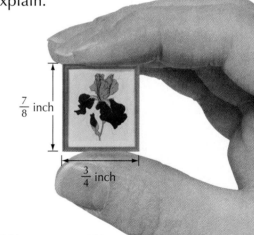

$\frac{7}{8}$ inch

$\frac{3}{4}$ inch

Mixed Review and Test Prep

Take It to the NET
Test Prep
www.scottforesman.com

Write as a fraction or mixed number in simplest form.

19. 1.5   **20.** 0.7   **21.** 2.75   **22.** 0.375

23. Which measurement is longer than 10 feet?

   A. 3 yards   **B.** 120 inches   **C.** 4 yards   **D.** 108 inches

Metric Units of Length

 LEARN

What units are used to measure length in the metric system?

Measurements in the metric system are based upon the **meter** (m). Other commonly used metric units are the **centimeter** (cm), **millimeter** (mm), and **kilometer** (km).

> 1 meter = 100 centimeters
> 1 meter = 1,000 millimeters
> 1,000 meters = 1 kilometer

1 meter	1 centimeter	1 millimeter	1 kilometer
about the length of a bat	about the length of an ant	about the thickness of a dime	about the length of 4 city blocks

Example A

Write mm, cm, m, or km to complete the following sentence.

A paper clip is about 5 ___ long, and a door is about 2 ___ high.

A paper clip is 5 cm long, and a door is about 2 meters high.

Example B

What metric unit of length would be most appropriate to measure the distance between two cities?

The kilometer is the most appropriate since the other units are so small.

Example C

What is the length to the nearest centimeter and to the nearest millimeter? The smallest units represent millimeters.

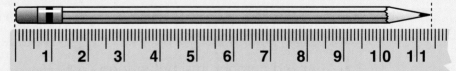

CENTIMETERS

Nearest centimeter: 11 cm   Nearest millimeter: 114 mm

✔ **Talk About It**

1. Where is 0 centimeters on the ruler in Example C?

Which unit would be most appropriate for each measurement? Write mm, cm, m, or km.

1. thickness of a window pane

2. length of a car

3. length of a river

Measure each segment to the nearest centimeter and to the nearest millimeter.

4. |————————|

5. |————|

6. Reasoning Henry says that his ballpoint pen is 17 meters long. Is this reasonable? Explain.

PRACTICE

For more practice, see Set 9-3 on p. 588.

A Skills and Understanding

Which unit would be most appropriate for each measurement? Write mm, cm, m, or km.

7. distance across an ocean   **8.** length of a soccer field   **9.** thickness of a nail

Measure each segment to the nearest centimeter and to the nearest millimeter.

10. |————————————| **11.** |————————————|

Complete each sentence with mm, cm, m, or km.

12. A swimming pool is about 50 ▨ long.   **13.** A man is about 180 ▨ tall.

14. Connections What fraction of a kilometer is a meter?

B Reasoning and Problem Solving

15. In a jumping competition, Michael jumped 2 meters and Ricardo jumped 213 centimeters. Who won?

16. <u>**Writing in Math**</u> Sally said that the width of the fingernail on her smallest finger is about 1 cm. Explain if this is reasonable.

Mixed Review and Test Prep

Take It to the NET
Test Prep
www.scottforesman.com

Measure to the nearest inch, $\frac{1}{2}$ inch, $\frac{1}{4}$ inch, and $\frac{1}{8}$ inch.

17. |————————| **18.** |————————————————|

19. Which of the following is seven billion, four hundred five million, sixty-nine thousand written in standard form?

A. 7,004,569   **B.** 7,450,690,000   **C.** 7,400,569,000   **D.** 7,405,069,000

Key Idea
You can change between metric measurements by multiplying or dividing by 10, 100, or 1,000.

Vocabulary
- kilometer (p. 534)
- hectometer
- dekameter
- meter (p. 534)
- decimeter
- centimeter (p. 534)
- millimeter (p. 534)

Think It Through
I can **use mental math** to multiply or divide by numbers such as 10, 100, or 1,000.

Converting Metric Units Using Decimals

LEARN

✓ **WARM UP**

Use mental math to divide or multiply.

1. 5.6×100

2. $7.15 \div 10$

3. $190 \div 1,000$

How can you change from one metric unit to another?

Like our number system, the metric system is based on 10. Every metric unit is 10 times as much as the next smaller unit.

1 kilometer	1 hectometer	1 dekameter	1 meter	1 decimeter	1 centimeter	1 millimeter
1,000 m	100 m	10 m	1 m	0.1 m	0.01 m	0.001 m

The metric units of length above can be represented by symbols as shown below. To change from larger units to smaller units, you multiply. To change from smaller units to larger units, you divide.

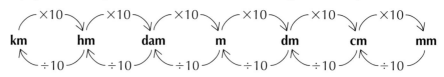

$\times 10$ km → hm → dam → m → dm → cm → mm $\div 10$

Example A

The baton that runners pass in Olympic relay races is 29 centimeters long. What is the baton's length in millimeters?

To change larger units to smaller units, multiply.

29 cm = ___ mm

Think: 1 cm = 10 mm

$29 \times 10 = 290$

29 cm = 290 mm

The baton is 290 mm long.

Example B

The world record for the pole vault is a little more than 600 centimeters. What is the record pole vault height in meters?

To change smaller units to larger units, divide.

600 cm = ___ m

Think: 100 cm = 1 m

$600 \div 100 = 6$

600 cm = 6 m

The height is a little more than 6 m high.

✓ **Talk About It**

1. In Example A, why do you multiply the 29 cm by 10?

2. In Example B, why do you divide the 600 cm by 100?

3. **Number Sense** Can 4 kilometers be changed to meters? Why or why not?

How can you change between metric units when decimals are involved?

Your tibia and femur are the longest bones in your body. Their lengths are measured in metric units.

Example C

How many millimeters long are most people's shinbones?

To change larger units to smaller units, multiply.

43.03 cm = ___ mm

Think: 1 cm = 10 mm

43.03 × 10 = 430.3

43.03 cm = 430.3 mm

So, most people's shinbones are 430.3 mm long.

Example D

How many centimeters long are most people's thighbones?

To change smaller units to larger units, divide.

505 mm = ___ cm

Think: 10 mm = 1 cm

505 ÷ 10 = 50.5

505 mm = 50.5 cm

So, most people's thighbones are 50.5 cm long.

The average femur, or thighbone, is 505 mm long.

The average tibia, or shinbone, is 43.03 cm long.

✔ Talk About It

4. In each example, why does the decimal point in the measurement move the way it does?

5. Estimation To the nearest centimeter, what are the lengths of an average tibia and femur?

6. Number Sense How could you use multiplication in Example D instead of division? (Hint: 1 mm = 0.1 cm)

Take It to the NET
More Examples
www.scottforesman.com

Find each equal measure.

1. 843 cm = ___ m **2.** 58.1 m = ___ mm **3.** 7.5 dm = ___ m **4.** 6.29 m = ___ km

5. Number Sense Start with 20 cm. Copy and complete this chart with equal measures. What is the same about all of the measures? What is different?

___ mm	20 cm	___ dm	___ m

PRACTICE

For more practice, see Set 9-4 on p. 588.

Ⓐ Skills and Understanding

Find each equal measure.

6. 75 m = ___ dam **7.** 1.6 m = ___ cm **8.** 85 hm = ___ m **9.** 260 mm = ___ cm

10. 5.3 km = ___ m **11.** 0.2 dm = ___ mm **12.** 1 m = ___ cm **13.** 156 cm = ___ m

14. Number Sense Start with 5.3 dm. Copy and complete this chart with equal measures.

___ mm	___ cm	5.3 dm	___ m

15. Number Sense Harry says that 5.28 cm is the same length as 528 m. Do you agree? Explain.

Ⓑ Reasoning and Problem Solving

🏊 Math and Social Studies

In the first modern Olympic games held in 1896, swimmers raced in the ice-cold ocean! Today's swimmers compete in temperature-controlled 50-meter pools.

16. How many pool lengths do competitors have to swim in each race?

17. Which race is one hectometer long?

18. Which race is 1.5 kilometers long?

19. Estimation During the 2000 Summer Olympics, a new world record of 3 minutes and 41 seconds was set for the 400 m freestyle. About how long did it take the swimmer to complete each length of the pool during that race?

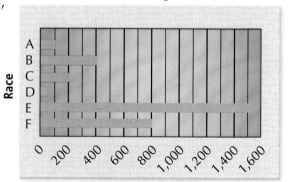

Freestyle Olympic Swimming Race Lengths

Distance (in meters)

Use the table for Problems 20–22.

20. What is the longest bone in each of your arms?

21. What is the shortest bone in each of your arms?

22. Your ulna and radius are both in your lower arms. What is the difference in their lengths in centimeters?

23. <u>**Writing in Math**</u> Alonzo found the number of centimeters in 6.5 meters below. Do you agree with his method? Why or why not?

> *6.5 × 100 = 650*
> *6.5 m = 650 cm*

Data File

HUMAN ARM BONES	
Bone	**Average Length**
Humerus	3.646 dm
Radius	26.42 cm
Ulna	282 mm

C Extensions

In the United States, we use both the customary and metric systems of measurement. You will often have to understand how the two systems compare. Choose a reasonable metric unit to complete each sentence.

24. 1 inch is about 2.5 ___.   **25.** 1 mile is about 1.6 ___.   **26.** 1 yard is about 1 ___.

Mixed Review and Test Prep

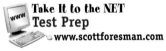

Take It to the NET
Test Prep
www.scottforesman.com

27. 25×16 **28.** $148 \div 4$ **29.** 87×32 **30.** $361 \div 19$

31. Which measurement is shorter than 15 decimeters?

    A. 1 meter   **B.** 150 centimeters   **C.** 1,500 millimeters   **D.** 1 dekameter

Practice Game

Match Them

Players: 2 or 3   **Materials:** Metric Cards

Mix the cards and place them face down in four rows of six each. The first player turns over two cards. If the cards show equivalent measures, the player keeps both cards and takes another turn. If the cards do not show equivalent measures, the cards are returned to their original position face down in the array, and the next player takes a turn. The game ends when all the cards have been correctly matched. The winner is the player with the most cards at the end of the game.

3.76 m   700 m

Algebra

Key Idea
You can find the distance around any polygon by adding the lengths of its sides.

Vocabulary
• perimeter
• formula

Think It Through
I can **use a formula** to find the **perimeter** of a square or rectangle.

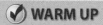 **WARM UP**

Find each sum.

1. 25 + 12 + 9 + 17 + 5
2. 3.7 + 4.8 + 6.5 + 9.3
3. 119 + 75 + 84 + 238
4. 6 + 9 + 7 + 2 + 8 + 9

Finding Perimeter

LEARN

How can you find the distance around a shape?

You can find the **perimeter,** or the distance around the outside of any polygon, by adding all the lengths of its sides.

Example A

A fountain in a pool is surrounded by a low fence.

Find the perimeter of the fence.

Perimeter = the sum of the side lengths

$P = 5.3 + 3.8 + 1.7 + 1.7 + 4.3 + 2.8 = 19.6$ m

So, the perimeter of this fence is 19.6 m.

5.3 m

2.8 m

3.8 m

4.3 m

1.7 m   1.7 m

Sometimes it is possible to use a **formula,** or a general rule, to find the perimeter.

Example B

Find the perimeter of the square.

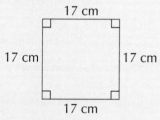

17 cm

17 cm   17 cm

17 cm

Perimeter = 4 × side

$P = 4 \times s$ s = side

$P = 4 \times 17 = 68$ cm

Example C

Find the perimeter of the rectangle.

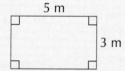

5 m

3 m

Perimeter = (2 × length) + (2 × width)

$P = (2 \times \ell) + (2 \times w)$

$P = (2 \times 5) + (2 \times 3)$ ℓ = length
w = width

$P = 10 + 6 = 16$ m

✔ Talk About It

1. **Algebra** In Example A, does it matter in which order you add the lengths of the sides? Explain.

2. **Number Sense** Thomas said that the perimeter of this triangle is 20 cm. What was his error? Explain.

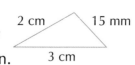

2 cm   15 mm

3 cm

For another example, see Set 9-5 on p. 585.

CHECK ✓

Find the perimeter of each figure.

1.
4 cm
4 cm
2 cm
2 cm
3 cm
3 cm

2.
10 ft
4 ft
4 ft
10 ft

3.
6 in. 5 in.
10 in.
5 in.
4 in.
8 in.
6 in.

4. Estimation What is a good estimate for the perimeter of your desk? Name a tool you could use to find the perimeter. Explain your answer.

PRACTICE

For more practice, see Set 9-5 on p. 589.

Ⓐ Skills and Understanding

Find the perimeter of each figure.

5.
5 ft   5 ft
8 ft

6.
2 in.
2 in.
4.3 in.
3 in.
6 in.
7.5 in.

7.
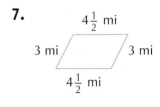
$4\frac{1}{2}$ mi
3 mi
3 mi
$4\frac{1}{2}$ mi

8. Number Sense The perimeter of an equilateral triangle is 15 yd. What is the length of each of its sides?

Ⓑ Reasoning and Problem Solving

9. You use exactly 30 feet of fencing to surround a rectangular-shaped garden. What are all the possible whole-number lengths and widths of that garden?

10. Number Sense If the length and width of a rectangle measuring 4 feet by 5 feet are doubled, is its perimeter also doubled? Explain your reasoning.

11. **Writing in Math** Describe two different methods you could use to find the perimeter of a square whose sides each measure 1.5 meters.

Mixed Review and Test Prep

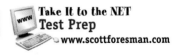
Take It to the NET
Test Prep
www.scottforesman.com

Find each equal measure.

12. 4 cm = ___ m   **13.** 4.3 km = ___ m   **14.** 2.1 cm = ___ mm   **15.** 250 m = ___ km

16. What is the mean of this data set of years?

8, 9, 7, 4, 9, 5

A. 9 years   **B.** 7.5 years   **C.** 7 years   **D.** 5 years

Algebra

Key Idea
The circumference, diameter, and radius of a circle have special relationships that can help you measure circles.

Vocabulary
• circumference
• diameter (p. 336)
• radius (p. 336)
• pi

Materials
• 5 circular objects
• string
• metric ruler
• calculator

Think It Through
I can **look for patterns** to describe relationships between the measurements.

Finding Circumference

LEARN

Activity

How are the measurements of a circle related to one another?

You know how to find the perimeter of figures that have straight sides. But a circle does not have sides. So, you need to use a different method to find the **circumference** of a circle.

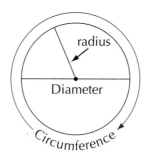

The circumference measures the distance around a circle.

a. Find 5 circular objects that you can measure, such as a can, a clock, a plate, a bicycle tire, and so on.

b. For each object, measure the diameter of the circle to the nearest mm. Make sure that your diameter goes through the center of the circle.

c. Wrap string around the outside of each object. Then use a ruler to measure the length of the string to the nearest mm. This is the circumference of the circle.

d. Record your measurements in a table like this one and look for patterns. You can use a calculator to find $C \div d$ in each case.

e. What pattern do you see between your measurements of the diameters and the circumferences?

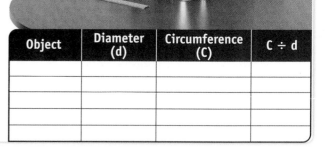

Object	Diameter (d)	Circumference (C)	C ÷ d

Is the relationship between diameter and circumference true for ALL circles?

For any circle, the circumference is always *about* 3.14 times the diameter. Because this value is always the same, ancient mathematicians gave it a special name, **pi** (pronounced like *pie*). Pi is represented by the Greek letter π. However, 3.14 is only an approximate value of π. The digits in π actually go on forever: 3.141592....

$$\pi \approx 3.14159\,26535\,89793\,23846\,26433\,83279$$

Because the relationship between the circumference and diameter of a circle is always the same, you can use a formula to describe it.

> **FORMULA FOR CIRCUMFERENCE**
>
> Circumference = π × Diameter
> $C = \pi \times d$

Example A

Find the circumference.

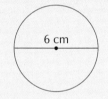

6 cm

$C = \pi \times d$

$C \approx 3.14 \times 6$

$C \approx 18.84$ cm

Example B

Find the circumference.

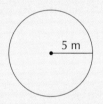

5 m

Remember: diameter = 2 × radius

$C = \pi \times 2 \times r$ or $C = 2 \times \pi \times r$

$C \approx 2 \times 3.14 \times 5$

$C \approx 31.4$ m

Think It Through
I should remember that there are two different formulas for finding circumference.

≈ means "approximately equal to." Remember that 3.14 is an approximate value for π.

✔ Talk About It

1. Why can $C = \pi \times d$ or $C = 2 \times \pi \times r$ be used to find circumference?

2. Reasoning Why do you think people use 3.14 as an estimate for π?

CHECK ✓

For another example, see Set 9-6 on p. 585.

Find each circumference. Use 3.14 for π.

1.

9 cm

2.

100 cm

3.

3 in.

4. Number Sense If you know the radius of a circle, how do you find its diameter?

A Skills and Understanding

Find each circumference. Use 3.14 for π.

5.

8 ft

6.
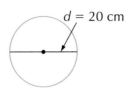
$d = 20$ cm

7.

2.5 m

8. $d = 6$ cm **9.** $r = 7$ ft **10.** $d = 1$ in. **11.** $r = 11$ mm

12. Estimation A circle has a diameter of 7 inches. Is its circumference more or less than 21 inches? Explain.

B Reasoning and Problem Solving

The diameter of each tire on Jabari's bike is 2 feet.

13. About how far will the bike move with one complete turn of its wheels?

14. About how many times do the tires turn if Jabari rides his bike 1 mile? (Remember: 1 mile = 5,280 ft)

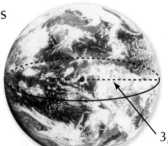
2 ft

15. **Writing in Math** Raphael wrote the statement below. Do you agree? Why or why not?

> When you use 3.14 to find the circumference of a circle, your answer will never be exact.

Math and Science

For thousands of years, people have used approximations of π to estimate the circumferences of circular objects. Use the diagram to identify each of the measurements below as the diameter or circumference of Earth or its moon.

1,080 miles
3,963.5 miles

16. 7,927 mi **17.** 2,160 mi

18. 6,782.4 mi **19.** 24,890.78 mi

20. Estimation About how many times as large is the circumference of Earth than the circumference of its moon?

C Extensions

Because the digits in π go on forever, people sometimes use the improper fraction $\frac{22}{7}$ for its value instead of 3.14. Find the circumference of each circle using $\frac{22}{7}$ for π.

21. $d = 2$ m   **22.** $r = 3$ ft   **23.** $d = 5$ cm

 **Mixed Review and Test Prep**

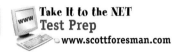
Take It to the NET
Test Prep
www.scottforesman.com

Find the perimeter of each regular polygon.

24. square with $s = 6.8$ cm   **25.** pentagon with $s = 7$ ft   **26.** hexagon with $s = 19$ in.

Write <, >, or = for each ●.

27. 6.3 ● 6.29   **28.** 7.2 ● 7.20   **29.** 0.08 ● 0.8

30. Algebra Find the rule for this pattern: 45, 38, 31, 24, 17,…

   A. add 7   **B.** subtract 9   **C.** subtract 7   **D.** add 9

Discovery

CHANNEL

SCHOOL™

Discover Math in Your World

Lift Off

Take It to the NET
Video and Activities
www.scottforesman.com

Two of the main parts of the space shuttle can be used again. These are the orbiter and the solid rocket boosters. A third main part is the external fuel tank, which must be replaced with each new launch.

For 1–3, use 3.14 for π.

1. The external fuel tank has a diameter of 823 cm. What is the circumference of the fuel tank?

2. The payload bay, which is part of the orbiter, isabout 18 m long and has a circumference of about 14.4 m. Estimate the diameter to the nearest meter.

3. The solid rocket boosters are the largest solid propellant motors ever built. Each booster is 116 feet long with a radius of 6 ft. It contains over 1 million pounds of propellant. What is the circumference of each booster?

Do You Know How?

Do You Understand?

Customary Units of Length (9-1); Measuring with Fractions of an Inch (9-2)

Find each equal measure.

1. 38 in. = ___ ft ___ in.

2. 27 yd = ___ ft   **3.** 2 mi = ___ yd

Add or subtract.

4. 9 ft + 2 yd   **5.** 2 ft 5 in. − 10 in.

6. Measure the line segment below to the nearest inch, $\frac{1}{2}$ inch, $\frac{1}{4}$ inch, and $\frac{1}{8}$ inch.

_____

A Explain why and how you renamed units to solve Exercise 5.

B Explain how to measure the length of the line segment below to the nearest inch, $\frac{1}{2}$ inch, $\frac{1}{4}$ inch, and $\frac{1}{8}$ inch.

_____

Metric Units of Length (9-3); Converting Metric Units Using Decimals (9-4)

Choose a reasonable metric unit for each measurement.

7. The distance between two cities

8. The length of your math textbook

Find each equal measure.

9. 35 mm = ___ cm

10. 2.5 km = ___ m

11. 18 m = ___ dm

C Explain how you chose the most appropriate units of measure for Exercise 7.

D When changing between units of measurement, how do you know whether to multiply or divide?

E Emily is 1.4 m tall. Julie is 138 cm tall. Who is taller? Explain how you know.

Finding Perimeter (9-5); Finding Circumference (9-6)

Find each perimeter.

12. A rectangle with a width of 7 ft and a length of 12 ft

13. A regular hexagon with a side of 4 in.

Find each circumference. Use 3.14 for π.

14. d = 5 cm   **15.** r = 2 ft

16. r = 3 yd   **17.** d = 10 mm

F Explain how you could use formulas to find the perimeters in Exercises 12 and 13.

G The perimeter of a square is 12 inches. What is the length of each of its sides? Explain how you know.

MULTIPLE CHOICE

1. Shawn has a rope that is 12 feet 4 inches long. He cuts off a piece that is 1 foot 10 inches long. How much rope does he have left over? (9-1)

   A. 10 ft 6 in.   **B.** 11 ft 6 in.   **C.** 12 ft 2 in.   **D.** 14 ft 2 in.

2. Which figure has a perimeter of 15 meters? (9-5)

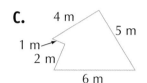

   A. 4 m / 4 m / 4 m / 4 m   **B.** 5 m / 2.5 m / 2.5 m / 5 m   **C.** 4 m / 5 m / 1 m / 2 m / 6 m   **D.** 7 m / 1 m / 1 m / 7 m

FREE RESPONSE

Find each equal measure. (9-1, 9-4)

3. 7.9 mm = ___ cm   4. 30 ft = ___ in.   5. 1 mi 5 yd = ___ ft   6. 19 km = ___ m

Find each circumference. Use 3.14 for π. (9-6)

7.
6 ft

8.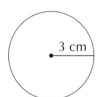
3 cm

9.
7 in.

10.
10 mm

11. Find the width and length to the nearest inch, $\frac{1}{2}$ inch, $\frac{1}{4}$ inch, and $\frac{1}{8}$ inch. (9-2)

Writing in Math

12. What is the perimeter of the square at the right? Explain two different ways you can find the perimeter of this square. (9-5)

3.5 dm / 3.5 dm / 3.5 dm / 3.5 dm

13. If you know the radius of a circle, how can you find its circumference? (9-6)

14. What customary and metric units of length would you use to measure the height of the ceiling in your classroom? Explain your choices. (9-1, 9-3)

Vocabulary
• area

Materials
• geoboard or dot paper or
 tools

Think It Through
• When I **measure area,** I always use **square units.**
• I can **draw a picture** or **make a model** to find the area of a figure.

Finding Area

LEARN

Activity

How can you use counting to find the area of a shape?

When you found the perimeter and circumference of figures, you were finding the distance around the figures. **Area** is the number of square units needed to cover a surface or figure.

You can use a geoboard or dot paper to make a shape and then count square units to find its area.

This is 1 square unit.   This is $\frac{1}{2}$ square unit.

Step 1 Make each of these figures on a geoboard or draw them on dot paper.

Step 2 Count the number of whole square units and half square units each figure covers to find its area. Record your results.

Step 3 On another piece of dot paper, draw shapes with these areas:

• 6 square units

• 2 square units

• $3\frac{1}{2}$ square units

a. What strategy did you use to find the areas? Did you do the same thing for each figure?

b. Sara counted all the $\frac{1}{2}$ square units first and then all the whole square units. Michael did the opposite. Did they get the same areas? Why or why not?

c. **Reasoning** Brianna looked at Figure C and said she could find the area by subtracting 1 square unit from 9 square units. Can you use a similar process with any of the other figures? Explain.

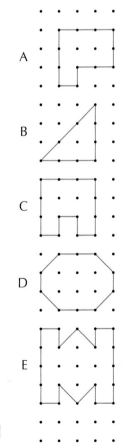

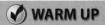

For another example, see Set 9-7 on p. 585.

Find the area of each figure.

1. **2.** **3.**

4. On dot paper, draw a shape with an area of $3\frac{1}{2}$ square units.

5. **Number Sense** Scott finds the areas of the figures above by counting all the half squares first and dividing that count by 2. Then he adds that quotient to the number of whole squares. Does his method work? Why or why not?

PRACTICE

For more practice, see Set 9-7 on p. 589.

A Skills and Understanding

Find the area of each figure.

6. **7.** **8.**

On dot paper, draw a shape with each given area.

9. $2\frac{1}{2}$ square units   **10.** 7 square units   **11.** $5\frac{1}{2}$ square units   **12.** 10 square units

13. **Number Sense** How many square units are in a square with sides of 3 units each?

B Reasoning and Problem Solving

Draw each polygon on dot paper.

14. a rectangle, an area of 6 square units   **15.** a triangle, an area of 2 square units

16. a triangle, an area of 1 square unit   **17.** a square, an area of 9 square units

18. **Writing in Math** Explain how area is different from perimeter.

Mixed Review and Test Prep

Take It to the NET
Test Prep
www.scottforesman.com

Write each fraction as a mixed number in simplest form.

19. $\frac{4}{3}$ **20.** $\frac{7}{2}$ **21.** $\frac{29}{6}$ **22.** $\frac{18}{4}$

23. If the radius of a circle is 4 cm, what is its circumference?

 All text pages available online and on CD-ROM.

Algebra

Key Idea
You can use formulas to find the areas of squares and rectangles.

Think It Through
I always **measure area** in **square units** like square feet (ft^2) or square meters (m^2).

Areas of Squares and Rectangles

LEARN

How can you find the areas of squares and rectangles without counting?

When a figure is very large, it would take a long time to count all the square units to find its area. If the figure is a square or rectangle, there are simple formulas you can use instead.

A square that measures 1 foot on each side is a square foot, or 1 ft^2.

1 ft

1 ft

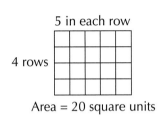

5 in each row

4 rows

Area = 20 square units

Example A

Find the area of the high school basketball court.

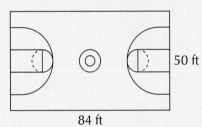

50 ft

84 ft

The court is a rectangle, so its opposite sides are equal.

A = length × width = ℓ × w

A = 84 feet × 50 feet

A = 4,200 square feet
    = 4,200 ft^2

Example B

Find the area of the baseball infield.

90 ft   90 ft

90 ft   90 ft

The infield is a square, so all of its sides are equal.

A = side × side = s^2

A = 90 feet × 90 feet
    = (90 feet)^2

A = 8,100 square feet
    = 8,100 ft^2

✔ Talk About It

1. Which two dimensions do you measure when you find the area of a rectangle?

2. **Connections** Can you use the formula for the area of a rectangle to find the area of a square? Explain.

Find the area of each figure.

1.
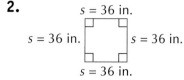
ℓ = 17 m
w = 9 m

2.
s = 36 in.
s = 36 in.   s = 36 in.
s = 36 in.

3.
120 ft
60 ft

4. a square with a side of 16 cm

5. a rectangle with sides 7 yd and 11 yd

6. Estimation What is a good estimate for the area of your classroom? Explain how you found your estimate.

PRACTICE

For more practice, see Set 9-8 on p. 590.

Ⓐ Skills and Understanding

Find the area of each figure.

7.
$4\frac{1}{2}$ yd
$4\frac{1}{2}$ yd

8.
ℓ = 9.8 cm
w = 2 cm

9.
200 ft
85 ft

10. a rectangle with sides 3.6 m and 9.5 cm

11. a square with a side of 27 miles

12. Number Sense How many square feet are in a square yard? How many square centimeters are in a square meter?

Ⓑ Reasoning and Problem Solving

13. What are the perimeter and area of a professional football field?

14. What are the perimeter and area of each striped end zone of the field?

15. **Writing in Math** Explain which has the greater area, an 8-meter square or a 7-by-9-meter rectangle.

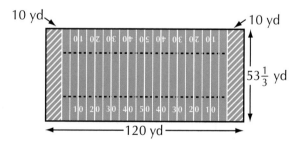
10 yd   10 yd
$53\frac{1}{3}$ yd
— 120 yd —

Mixed Review and Test Prep

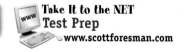
Take It to the NET
Test Prep
www.scottforesman.com

On dot paper, draw a shape with each area.

16. 8 square units

17. $6\frac{1}{2}$ square units

18. $12\frac{1}{2}$ square units

19. Which would be best to display data that changes over time?

    A. bar graph   **B.** line graph   **C.** circle graph   **D.** stem-and-leaf plot

Algebra

Key Idea
You can use the formula for the area of a rectangle to find a formula for the area of a parallelogram.

Vocabulary
• base
• height

Materials
• grid paper
• ruler
• scissors

Think It Through
• I know that **rectangles** and **parallelograms** both have **parallel opposite sides.**
• I can **make a model** or **use a formula** to find the areas of parallelograms.

Areas of Parallelograms

LEARN

Activity

How can you use rectangles to find the areas of parallelograms?

a. Copy this parallelogram on grid paper. It has a **base** of 6 units and a **height** of 3 units.

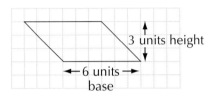

3 units height

← 6 units →
base

b. Cut out the parallelogram and draw a dotted line to form a right triangle.

c. Cut out the triangle and move it to the opposite side of the parallelogram.

d. What shape did you create? What are its base and height? What is its area? Use counting to find the area of your original parallelogram.

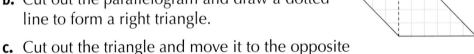

3 units

6 units

How can you use a formula to find the area of a parallelogram?

Example

To find the area of a parallelogram, adapt the formula for the area of a rectangle—just substitute base and height for length and width.

A = **base** × **height**

$A = b \times h$

$A = 7$ ft × 4 ft = 28 ft^2

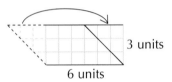

4 ft

← 7 ft →

4 ft

← 7 ft →

✔ **Talk About It**

1. **Connections** In the Example, which parts of the parallelogram and the rectangle are congruent?

 **CHECK** ✓

For another example, see Set 9-9 on p. 586.

Find the area of each parallelogram.

1.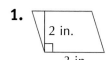
2 in.
3 in.

2.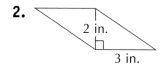
2 in.
3 in.

3.
4 ft
1 ft

4. Reasoning If you cut any piece from a parallelogram and attach it to another side, do you change the figure's area? Explain.

PRACTICE

For more practice, see Set 9-9 on p. 590.

Ⓐ Skills and Understanding

Find the area of each parallelogram.

5.
4.5 cm
2 cm

6.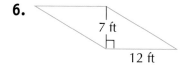
7 ft
12 ft

7.
16 m
3.7 m

8. Reasoning Why is finding the area of a parallelogram like finding the area of a rectangle?

Algebra Find the missing measurement for each parallelogram.

9. $A = 48$ in^2, $b = 8$ in.; $h = $ ___

10. $A = 54$ m^2, $b = $ ___, $h = 9$ m

11. $A = 37.5$ cm^2, $b = 5$ cm, $h = $ ___

12. $A = $ ___, $b = 12$ yd, $h = 16$ yd

13. On grid paper, draw four different parallelograms that have a base of 5 units and a height of 4 units. Label each parallelogram with its area.

14. Which of these figures has the greatest area: a 5-ft-by-10-ft rectangle, a parallelogram with a 6-ft base and an 8-ft height, or a 4-ft square?

15. **Writing in Math** Shawn says the area of this parallelogram is 20 in^2. Is he correct? If not, tell why and explain how to find the correct area.

4 in. 5 in.
4 in.

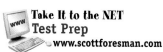 **Mixed Review and Test Prep**

Take It to the NET
www **Test Prep**
www.scottforesman.com

Find each sum.

16. $2.695 + 13.4$ **17.** $0.79 + 5.8$ **18.** $1.6 + 8.5 + 0.2$ **19.** $3.709 + 16.94$

20. Which unit can be used to measure the area of a figure?

A. centimeters **B.** meters **C.** square inches **D.** feet

 All text pages available online and on CD-ROM.

Algebra

Key Idea
You can use the relationship between triangles and parallelograms to find the area of a triangle.

Think It Through
- I need to know the **base** and the **height** of a triangle to find its area.
- I can **use a formula** to find the **area of a triangle.**

Areas of Triangles

LEARN

Activity

How can you use parallelograms to find the areas of triangles?

a. Copy this triangle on grid paper. It has a base of 6 units and a height of 4 units.

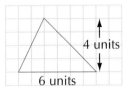

b. Cut out your triangle. Then draw and cut out a triangle congruent to your triangle.

c. You can rotate one triangle and translate it to make a parallelogram.

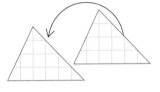 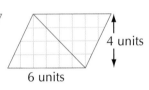

d. What is the base and height of the parallelogram that you created? What is its area? What is the area of one of the triangles?

How can you use a formula to find the area of a triangle?

Example

To find the area of a triangle, adapt the formula for the area of a parallelogram—just multiply by $\frac{1}{2}$.

Area = $\frac{1}{2} \times$ base $\times$ height

$A = \frac{1}{2} \times b \times h$

$A = \frac{1}{2} \times 7$ cm $\times 5$ cm $= 17.5$ cm^2

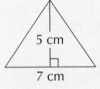

✓ Talk About It

1. In the Example, how do you know that the area of the triangle is exactly half the area of the parallelogram?

2. **Number Sense** Instead of multiplying by $\frac{1}{2}$, Kim divided by 2 to find the area of the triangle. Does her method work? Why or why not?

For another example, see Set 9-10 on p. 586.

Find the area of each triangle.

1.

6 in.
6 in.

2.

3 m
4 m

3.

4 yd
2 yd

4. Reasoning Triangle A has a base of 6 cm and a height of 9 cm. Triangle B has a base of 9 cm and a height of 6 cm. Which triangle has the greater area? Explain.

PRACTICE

For more practice, see Set 9-10 on p. 590.

Ⓐ Skills and Understanding

Find the area of each triangle.

5.

5 ft
4 ft

6.
7.2 cm
12 cm

7.
$3\frac{1}{2}$ yd
$6\frac{1}{2}$ yd

8. Number Sense Carlos says the area of this traffic sign is 600 in². Do you agree? Why or why not?

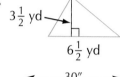
30″
YIELD
20″ 30″ 30″ 30″

Ⓑ Reasoning and Problem Solving

Algebra Find the missing measurement for each triangle.

9. $A =$ _____, $b = 8.1$ mm, $h = 16$ mm

10. $A =$ _____, $b = 23$ yd, $h = 9$ yd

11. $A = 24$ ft², $b =$ _____, $h = 6$ ft

12. $A = 30$ in², $b = 5$ in., $h =$ _____

Use triangles and rectangles to find the area of each figure.

13.

3 cm
4 cm
2 cm

14.

6 ft
6 ft   3 ft

15. <u>Writing in Math</u> How are the areas of triangles, rectangles, and parallelograms related? Use examples as part of your explanation.

🕷 Mixed Review and Test Prep

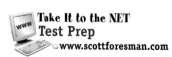 **Take It to the NET**
Test Prep
www.scottforesman.com

Classify each angle measure as acute, right, or obtuse.

16. 117°   **17.** 90°   **18.** 37°   **19.** 45°

20. What is the area of a parallelogram with base 5 m and a height of 7.5 m?

   A. 37.5 m   **B.** 12.5 m   **C.** 12.5 m²   **D.** 37.5 m²

Understand Graphic Sources: Pictures

Understanding graphic sources such as pictures when you read in math can help you use the **problem-solving strategy, *Draw a Picture,*** in the next lesson.

In reading, understanding pictures can help you understand what you read. In math, understanding pictures can help you solve problems.

Skip's Garden

10 yd

15 yd

= flowers

= shrubs

= vegetables

Some pictures have a title to give a general idea of what the picture shows.

You can get information from labels and symbols.

Pictures sometimes have a key that explains what the symbols represent.

1. Which two sections of Skip's garden have the same dimensions?

2. What is planted in the section of the garden that measures 3 yards by 15 yards?

For 3–5, use the picture at the right.

3. What does this picture show?

4. How many statues are there in the park?

5. **Writing in Math** How would you use the information in the picture to find the distance between the two flagpoles?

Veteran's Memorial Park

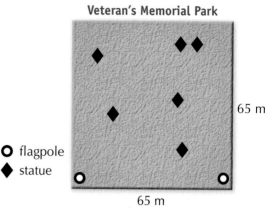

○ flagpole
◆ statue

65 m

65 m

For 6–8, use picture at the right.

6. What does this picture show?

7. How much do students pay for tickets?

8. **Writing in Math** Inez bought a ticket for $28. Could her seat be in section 10? Why or why not?

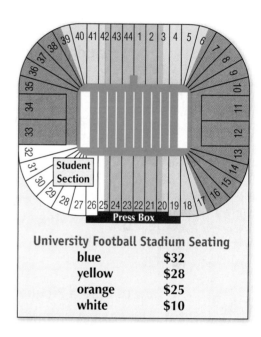

University Football Stadium Seating

blue	$32
yellow	$28
orange	$25
white	$10

For 9–12, use the picture at the right.

9. Which region of the United States is shown?

10. What is the weather forecast for Atlanta?

11. Which cities will be partly sunny? How do you know?

12. **Writing in Math** Compare the weather forecasts for Orlando and Miami. How are they alike? How are they different?

October 10 Weather Forecast
for Southeast United States

Problem-Solving Strategy

Key Idea
Learning how and when to draw a picture can help you solve problems.

Draw a Picture

LEARN

How can you use a picture to help solve a problem?

Dog Pen Tia has 12 one-meter sections of fencing to enclose a rectangular pen for her dog. She wants the pen to have the greatest possible (maximum) area. What dimensions should the pen have?

Read and Understand

What do you know?

Tia has 12 one-meter fence sections to enclose a rectangle. Each side will be a whole number of meters.

What are you trying to find?

The rectangle with a 12-meter perimeter that has the greatest area

Plan and Solve

What strategy will you use?

Strategy: Draw a Picture

How to Draw a Picture

Step 1 Use the given information to decide what to draw.

Step 2 Draw the picture on a grid or dot paper for accuracy.

Step 3 Label all the parts and dimensions of your drawing.

Step 4 Use the drawing to solve the problem.

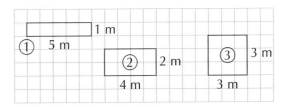

Area of ①: $5 \times 1 = 5$ m^2

Area of ②: $4 \times 2 = 8$ m^2

Area of ③: $3 \times 3 = 9$ m^2

Answer: The pen should be 3 m wide by 3 m long.

Look Back and Check

Is your answer reasonable?

Yes, the square's perimeter is 12 meters and it has the greatest area.

✔ Talk About It

1. What is the same about all the rectangles you drew? What is different?

For another example, see Set 9-11 on p. 586.

1. Use the picture to solve the Pool Deck problem. Write the answer in a complete sentence.

    Pool Deck A circular swimming pool has a radius of 3 meters. Maya wants to build a deck around the pool that is 1 meter wide. What will be the outside circumference of the deck?

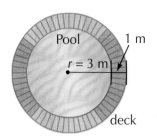

PRACTICE

For more practice, see Set 9-11 on p. 590.

Solve. Write your answer in a complete sentence.

2. Amie's square flower garden covers 25 ft² of her backyard. She built a wall around the garden that is 1 foot thick. What is the perimeter of the outside border of the wall?

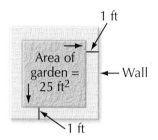

3. Paul has 16 ft² of material to make a rectangular quilt. The silk for the quilt's border is expensive, so he wants the quilt to have the least possible (minimum) perimeter. If Paul uses all 16 ft², what dimensions should he use for the quilt?

4. Suppose Paul had 9 ft² of material. If he uses all 9 ft², what dimensions should Paul use so the quilt has the least perimeter?

5. Jolita needs an area of 36 square yards to plant vegetables. The fencing she is using to enclose the area costs $3 per foot. What is the least amount Jolita must spend to fence the planting area?

6. Mrs. Chin's kitchen is 8 feet long and 6 feet wide. She wants to expand the kitchen to have more space. If she doubles the dimensions of the room, how will the area change? How will the perimeter change?

7. At a picnic, Albert, Brenda, Carlos, and Denise are sitting along one side of a table. In how many different orders could the four friends be sitting?

8. **Writing in Math** Andy says that rectangles with the same perimeter can have different areas. Nina says that rectangles with the same area can have different perimeters. Who do you think is right? Explain.

STRATEGIES

- **Show What You Know**
  Draw a Picture
  Make an Organized List
  Make a Table
  Make a Graph
  Act It Out or Use Objects
- **Look for a Pattern**
- **Try, Check, and Revise**
- **Write an Equation**
- **Use Logical Reasoning**
- **Solve a Simpler Problem**
- **Work Backward**

Choose a tool

Mental Math

Do You Know How?

Do You Understand?

Finding Area (9-7), Areas of Squares and Rectangles (9-8)

Find each area.

1.
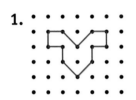

2.
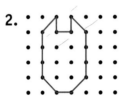

3.
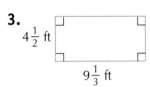
$4\frac{1}{2}$ ft
$9\frac{1}{3}$ ft

4.
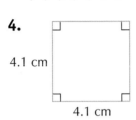
4.1 cm
4.1 cm

A Explain why you can use a formula to find the areas in Exercises 3 and 4, but you cannot in Exercises 1 and 2.

B The school playground has a rectangular sandbox measuring 12 ft by 9 ft. The park playground has a rectangular sandbox measuring 10 ft by 11 ft. Which sandbox has the greater area? Explain how you know.

Areas of Parallelograms (9-9)
Areas of Triangles (9-10)

Find each area.

5.
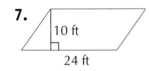
7 mm
2 mm

6.
5 in.
8 in.

7.
10 ft
24 ft

8.
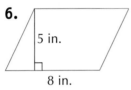
1.25 cm
4 cm

C Explain how the formula for finding the area of a triangle is related to the formula for finding the area of a parallelogram.

D Parallelogram *A* has a base of 15 ft and a height of 12 ft. Parallelogram *B* has a base of 14 ft and a height of 13 ft. Which parallelogram has the lesser area? Explain how you know.

Problem-Solving Strategy: Draw a Picture (9-11)

9. Draw pictures to solve the Vegetable Garden problem.

   Vegetable Garden Leigh has 40 feet of fencing to mark the perimeter of her rectangular vegetable garden. What length and width will give her garden the greatest area?

E Explain how you decided what to draw. How did your pictures help you find the answer?

F When might drawing a picture be helpful in solving a problem?

MULTIPLE CHOICE

1. Find the area of this figure. (9-7)

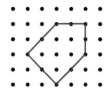

A. 6 square units   **C.** 10 square units

B. 8 square units   **D.** 12 square units

2. What is the area of a triangle with a base of 12 ft and a height of 6.5 ft? (9-10)

A. 78 ft^2 **B.** 78 ft   **C.** 39 ft^2 **D.** 39 ft

FREE RESPONSE

Find each area. (9-8, 9-9, 9-10)

3.

$4\frac{1}{2}$ ft

$4\frac{1}{2}$ ft

4.

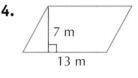

7 m

13 m

5.

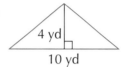

4 yd

10 yd

6.

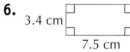

3.4 cm

7.5 cm

For 7–8, use the Dinner Party problem. (9-8, 9-11)

Dinner Party Holly rented 16 square tables for a dinner party. Each table can seat 2 people on each side. Holly wants to arrange the tables in a rectangle to make one large table.

7. Draw pictures to show all the different rectangles Holly could make with the tables she has.

8. Which arrangement would have the largest perimeter so that the most people could sit around the table?

Writing in Math

9. If you know the area and height of a parallelogram, how can you find its base? (9-9)

10. Explain why you can use the formula for the area of a rectangle to find the area of a square. (9-8)

11. Draw a picture of a triangle that has an area of 8 in^2 on grid paper. Label the lengths of its base and height. Explain how you know that the area is 8 in^2. (9-10)

Think It Through
I can **draw pictures** to help explain my thinking.

TEST TALK

Think It Through
I can **multiply or divide** to change between units of time.

Time

LEARN

How do you convert one unit of time to another?

Jin-Souk just had a party to celebrate her graduation. Her father videotaped the party. The video camera's battery lasted for 7,260 seconds!

✓ **WARM UP**

1. 5 × 365
2. 4,800 ÷ 60
3. 365 × 60
4. 1,460 ÷ 365

Data File

Units of Time
60 seconds (s) = 1 minute (min)
60 minutes = 1 hour (h)
24 hours = 1 day (d)
7 days = 1 week (wk)
12 months (mo) = 1 year (yr)
52 weeks = 1 year
365 days = 1 regular year
366 days = 1 leap year
100 years = 1 century

Example A

How many hours did the video camera battery last?

To change from smaller units to larger units, divide.

7,260 seconds = ___ minutes

Think: 60 seconds = 1 minute

7,260 ÷ 60 = 121 minutes

121 minutes = ___ hours

121 ÷ 60 = 2 h, 1 extra min

The video camera battery lasted 2 hours and 1 minute!

Example B

How many days old is Tyrone if he is 11 years today, and 3 years of his life were leap years?

To change from larger units to smaller units, multiply.

8 regular years = ___ days

Think: 1 regular year = 365 days

8 × 365 days = 2,920 days

3 leap years = ___ days

3 × 366 days = 1,098 days

2,920 d + 1,098 d = 4,018 d

Tyrone is 4,018 days old.

✓ **Talk About It**

1. **Reasoning** In Example B, why do you need to know how many days were in 8 regular years?

2. **Number Sense** In Example A, why do you have to divide twice?

3. **Connections** Why is it impossible to complete this statement? 1 month = ___ days

Find each equal measure.

1. 360 s = ___ min

2. 23 wk = ___ d

3. 72 h = ___ d

4. 75 h = ___ s

5. 2 centuries = ___ yr

6. 5 d = ___ s

7. Number Sense A leap year occurs every 4 years. If a leap year occurred last year, when will the next leap year occur?

PRACTICE

For more practice, see Set 9-12 on p. 591.

Ⓐ Skills and Understanding

Find each equal measure.

8. 48 h = ___ d

9. 5 min = ___ s

10. 10,080 min = ___ wk

11. 2 yr = ___ wk

12. 7,200 s = ___ h

13. 3 centuries = ___ yr

14. 5 h 30 min = ___ s

15. 2 yr = ___ d

16. 91 d = ___ wk

17. Reasoning Brian says there are exactly 4 weeks in a month. Do you agree? Explain.

Ⓑ Reasoning and Problem Solving

18. Calculator Darren is 5,781,600 minutes old, and Saundra is 46,896,000 seconds old. Who is older? By how much time?

19. Calculator The common male housefly has a very short lifespan—only 1,468,800 seconds. How many days does it live?

20. **Writing in Math** Do you agree with the way Pam found the number of days in 129,600 seconds? If not, tell why and find the correct answer.

> 129,600 ÷ 60 = 2,160
> 2,160 ÷ 24 = 90
> 129,600 seconds = 90 days

Mixed Review and Test Prep

Take It to the NET
Test Prep
www.scottforesman.com

Find each equal measure.

21. 150 mm = ___ cm

22. 9.4 km = ___ m

23. 0.28 dm = ___ cm

24. What is the area of a triangle with a 7-in. base and a 9-in. height? Draw a picture to help.

A. 63 in.

B. 63 in^2

C. 31.5 in^2

D. 16 in.

All text pages available online and on CD-ROM.

Key Idea
You can add and subtract units of time.

Vocabulary
• elapsed time

Elapsed Time

LEARN

How can you find how much time passes between two events?

The Acela Express is the fastest train in the United States. To use the train's schedule, you need to know how to find the difference between two times, or **elapsed time.**

✓ **WARM UP**

1. 3 h = _____ min

2. 78 min = _____ h
   _____ min

3. 119 min = _____ h
   _____ min

4. 12 h = _____ min

Example A

How long does the trip from Boston to New Haven take?

One way to find elapsed time is to subtract.

End Time − Start Time = Elapsed Time

$$\begin{array}{r} 8\text{ h} \quad 78\text{ min} \\ \cancel{9\text{ h }18\text{ min}} \\ -\ 7\text{ h }20\text{ min} \\ \hline 1\text{ h }58\text{ min} \end{array}$$

18 min < 20 min
You need to rename to subtract.
9 h 18 min = 8 h 78 min

The trip takes 1 hour 58 minutes.

Data File

Acela Express Schedule
Train #2155

City	Time
Boston, MA	7:20 A.M.
Providence, RI	7:50 A.M.
New Haven, CT	9:18 A.M.
New York, NY	10:42 A.M.
Stop in NY	
Depart NY	11:00 A.M.
Metropark, NJ	11:26 A.M.
Philadelphia, PA	12:09 P.M.
Baltimore, MD	1:09 P.M.
Washington, D.C.	1:43 P.M.

Example B

How long does the trip from New York to Baltimore take?

Another way to find elapsed time is to count up on a number line. This is a good method to use when both A.M. and P.M. are involved.

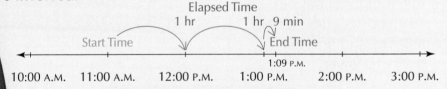

Elapsed Time
1 hr   1 hr 9 min
Start Time   End Time
                        1:09 P.M.
10:00 A.M. 11:00 A.M. 12:00 P.M. 1:00 P.M. 2:00 P.M. 3:00 P.M.

1 h + 1 h + 9 min = 2 h 9 min

The trip takes 2 hours 9 minutes.

✓ **Talk About It**

1. **Reasoning** Which method do you prefer for finding elapsed time, using subtraction or a number line? Why?

How can you use elapsed time to find when an event began or ended?

For another example, see Set 9-13 on p. 587.

Example C

Carl boarded the Acela Express in Providence and rode for 1 hour and 28 minutes. In which city did he arrive?

You can **add** to find the end time.

Start Time + Elapsed Time = End Time

$$
\begin{array}{l}
7 \text{ h } 50 \text{ min} \\
+ 1 \text{ h } 28 \text{ min} \\
\hline
8 \text{ h } 78 \text{ min} = 9 \text{ h } 18 \text{ min}
\end{array}
$$

Rename 78 min as 1 h 18 min.

Carl ended his trip at 9:18 A.M., so he arrived in New Haven.

Example D

Lisa rode the Acela Express for 34 minutes to reach Washington, D.C. From which city did she depart?

You can **subtract** to find the start time.

End Time − Elapsed Time = Start Time

$$
\begin{array}{l}
1 \text{ h } 43 \text{ min} \\
- 0 \text{ h } 34 \text{ min} \\
\hline
1 \text{ h } 9 \text{ min}
\end{array}
$$

Lisa started her trip at 1:09 P.M., so she departed from Baltimore.

✔ Talk About It

2. In Example D, why is the elapsed time shown as 0 h 34 min?

3. Reasoning How could you count up on a number line to solve Examples C and D?

CHECK ✓

Find each elapsed time.

1. 5:00 A.M. to 7:17 A.M.

2. 2:20 P.M. to 4:18 P.M.

3. 11:15 A.M. to 1:50 P.M.

4.
P.M. P.M.

5.

6.
A.M. P.M.

Find each start time or end time using the given elapsed time.

7. Start Time: 6:12 P.M.
Elapsed Time: 4 h

8. End Time: 3:05 A.M.
Elapsed Time: 1 h 28 min

Add or subtract.

9.
$$
\begin{array}{l}
3 \text{ h } 20 \text{ min} \\
+ 2 \text{ h } 35 \text{ min}
\end{array}
$$

10.
$$
\begin{array}{l}
7 \text{ h } 55 \text{ min} \\
- 2 \text{ h } 45 \text{ min}
\end{array}
$$

11.
$$
\begin{array}{l}
5 \text{ h } 7 \text{ min } 18 \text{ s} \\
+ 3 \text{ h } 4 \text{ min } 15 \text{ s}
\end{array}
$$

12. Number Sense When you add or subtract units of time, how do you know when you have to rename?

Ⓐ Skills and Understanding

Find each elapsed time.

13. 7:45 A.M. to 10:23 A.M.   **14.** 6:18 P.M. to 11:00 P.M.   **15.** 9:15 A.M. to 2:30 P.M.

16.
A.M.   A.M.

17.
P.M.   P.M.

18.
A.M.   P.M.

Find each start time or end time using the given elapsed time.

19. Start: 6:58 A.M.
Elapsed: 3 h 40 min

20. End: 5:36 P.M.
Elapsed: 4 h 9 min

21. Start: 11:30 A.M.
Elapsed: 2 h 25 min

Add or subtract.

22. 5 h 10 min
+ 2 h 20 min

23. 6 h 12 min
− 1 h 15 min

24. 8 h 1 min 15 s
+ 2 h 6 min 50 s

25. 17 h
− 5 h 40 min

26. 3 h 15 min
+ 4 h 48 min

27. 6 h 32 min
− 5 h 37 min

28. 9 h 12 min 3 s
+ 7 h 52 min 8 s

29. 36 h
− 4 h 25 min

30. What time will it be 2 hours and 12 minutes after 7:14 P.M.?

31. What time will it be 4 hours and 50 minutes before 11:18 A.M.?

32. Number Sense Look at the Acela Express schedule on page 564. How long is the train stopped in New York, NY?

Ⓑ Reasoning and Problem Solving

🌐 Math and Social Studies

The United States lies in 6 different time zones. At 5:00 P.M. a concert was broadcast live from San Francisco. It lasted 3 hr 30 min. Use the time zone map to find what time the concert began and ended in each city.

33. Dallas   **34.** New Orleans

35. Honolulu   **36.** New York

37. Find a state that lies in more than one time zone. What are all the possible start times for the concert in that state?

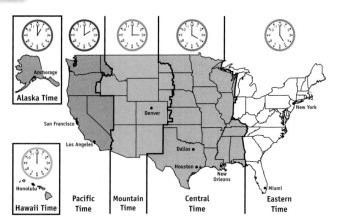

38. Reasoning Describe two methods you could use to find how long the Acela Express takes to travel from Philadelphia, PA, to Washington, D.C.

39. What is the shortest elapsed time between cities on the Acela schedule?

40. Number Sense The Acela Express travels at 150 miles per hour. If the train traveled nonstop between Boston and Washington, D.C., estimate how long the trip would take.

41. <u>**Writing in Math**</u> Is Lynn's subtraction at the right correct? If not, explain why and show the correct subtraction.

> **Boston to Washington, D.C.**
> 463 miles

$$
\begin{array}{r}
4\text{ h}\quad 35\text{ min} \\
\cancel{5\text{ h } 25\text{ min}} \\
-\ 2\text{ h } 31\text{ min} \\
\hline
2\text{ h}\quad 4\text{ min}
\end{array}
$$

C Extensions

Instead of counting up on a number line to deal with A.M. and P.M., you can rename units of time in a special way. Rename P.M. hours by adding them to 12:00. The subtraction to the right shows the elapsed time from 7:20 A.M. to 1:43 P.M. 1:43 is renamed as 13:43.

$$
\begin{array}{r}
13\text{ h } 43\text{ min} \\
\cancel{1\text{ h } 43\text{ min p.m.}} \\
-\ 7\text{ h } 20\text{ min a.m.} \\
\hline
6\text{ h } 23\text{ min}
\end{array}
$$

Use this method to find each elapsed time.

42. 9:05 A.M. to 2:40 P.M.　　**43.** 5:15 A.M. to 1:12 P.M.

Mixed Review and Test Prep

Take It to the NET Test Prep
www.scottforesman.com

44. 540 min = ___ h　　**45.** 3,000 s = ___ min　　**46.** 72 mo = ___ yr

47. Which multiplication property is illustrated in $5 \times 4 = 4 \times 5$?

A. Associative　　**B.** Identity　　**C.** Commutative　　**D.** Distributive

Learning with Technology

Time eTool

Before using the Time eTool, copy the table and record each missing time. Then use the Time eTool to check your answers.

Starting Time	Elapsed Time	Ending Time
3:15 P.M.	2 h 35 min	
	5 h 27 min	7:52 P.M.
9:22 A.M.		6:44 P.M.
12:03 P.M.	15 h 42 min	
	6 h 59 min	3:00 A.M.

Think It Through
I know that a **negative** temperature is **less than zero** degrees on either scale.

Temperature

LEARN

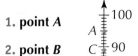
How do you read temperatures and find changes in temperatures?

Like other measurements, temperature can be expressed in different units. In the customary system, temperature is read in degrees **Fahrenheit** (°F). In the metric system, temperature is read in degrees **Celsius** (°C).

Example A

A bearded lizard needs a "hot spot" in its cage that stays about 95°F. What is that temperature in degrees Celsius?

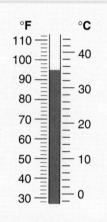

Find the temperature on one scale and read across to find the other.

95°F is the same as 35°C.

Example B

Inside and outside temperatures are shown on the two thermometers. What is the temperature difference on each scale?

In Fahrenheit, 68° − 23° = 45° difference.

In Celsius, you need to find the difference between 20° and −5°. From 20° to 0° is 20°. Then it is another 5 degrees down to −5 degrees.

20 degrees + 5 degrees = 25 degrees difference.

✓**Talk About It**

1. **Reasoning** Which temperature is colder, 80°F or 50°C? Explain.

2. **Number Sense** In Example B, why do you add to find a difference in temperature?

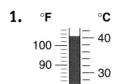

For another example, see Set 9-14 on p. 587.

Write each temperature in Celsius and Fahrenheit.

1. 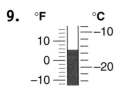 **2.** 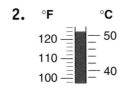 **3.**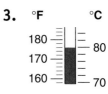

Find each change in temperature.

4. 12°F to 56°F   **5.** 5°C to 41°C   **6.** 101°F to 2°F   **7.** 0°C to 31°C

8. Reasoning Which is greater, a change of 10°C or a change of 10°F? Explain.

 PRACTICE

For more practice, see Set 9-14 on p. 591.

(A) Skills and Understanding

Write each temperature in Celsius and Fahrenheit.

9. 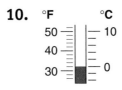 **10.** 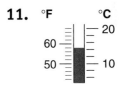 **11.**

Find each change in temperature.

12. 22°C to 31°C   **13.** 46°F to 8°F   **14.** 18°F to −4°F

15. Number Sense What is the difference between the boiling (212°F, 100°C) and freezing (32°F, 0°C) points of water in the Fahrenheit scale? In the Celsius scale?

(B) Reasoning and Problem Solving

16. Number Sense Normal body temperature for humans is 98.6°F. About what is it in °C?

17. **Writing in Math** Phil says that in either scale, a negative temperature outside means icy conditions. Explain why you agree or disagree.

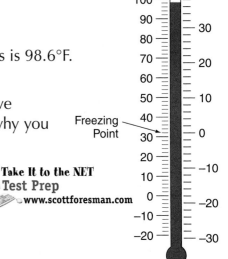

Freezing Point

Mixed Review and Test Prep

**Take It to the NET
Test Prep**
www.scottforesman.com

Find each elapsed time.

18. 6:30 A.M. to 11:19 A.M.   **19.** 9:05 A.M. to 3:45 P.M.

20. Choose the greatest fraction.

   A. $\frac{8}{9}$ **B.** $\frac{18}{19}$ **C.** $\frac{28}{29}$ **D.** $\frac{38}{39}$

All text pages available online and on CD-ROM.

Problem-Solving Skill

Reading Helps!
Identifying steps in a process
can help you with...
Writing to Explain.

Key Idea
Writing to explain can help you when you are asked to explain how you solved a problem.

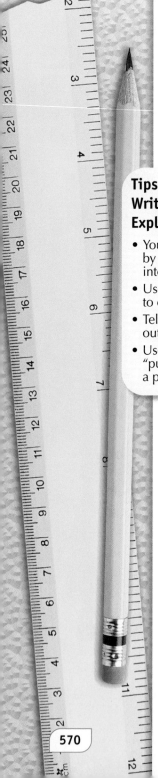

Writing to Explain

LEARN

How do you write a good explanation?

Broken Ruler Write and explain how you would use the broken ruler below to measure the length of the pencil to the nearest $\frac{1}{4}$ inch.

Tips for Writing Good Explanations

- You can explain a process by breaking the process into steps.
- Use pictures and words to explain.
- Tell about things to watch out for or be careful about.
- Use words like "find" and "put" when explaining a process.

These steps explain how to measure the pencil using this broken ruler.

1. Find a nice end point. I will use the mark at 2 inches. The end is gone, so we need a point to use for the end.

2. Put the end point of the ruler—the 2—at one end of the pencil. Make sure the ruler and the pencil are right beside each other.

3. Find the place on the ruler for the other end of the pencil.

4. Find the quarter inch places on the ruler that the pencil length is between.

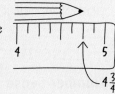

5. Find which quarter inch the pencil is closer to.

Here it is $4\frac{3}{4}$.

6. Now be careful. Remember, you started at 2. So, the real length is $4\frac{3}{4} - 2$ or $2\frac{3}{4}$ inches.

✔ Talk About It

1. What "process" is being explained here?

2. Why did the explanation above tell you to be careful?

3. Is there any part of the explanation you think could be clearer? Explain.

1. Explain in writing how to use the ruler on the preceding page to measure to the nearest $\frac{1}{8}$ inch rather than the nearest $\frac{1}{4}$ inch.

PRACTICE

For more practice, see Set 9-15 on p. 591.

Write to explain.

cup

2. How could you use the measuring cup to find the capacity of the container?

3. Suppose a classmate had never heard of the metric system. Use metric lengths to explain in writing to this classmate how the metric system is organized.

4. How could you find the area of this irregular building lot shown at the right?

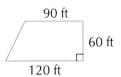

90 ft

60 ft

120 ft

5. How could you estimate the height of this building made of concrete blocks if the only measuring instrument you have is a ruler?

6. Describe whether you need to find area or perimeter for each situation. Then tell what measuring instrument you would use and give an appropriate unit of measure to describe the results of your measurements.

   a. You are going to purchase wall-to-wall carpeting to cover your room.

   b. You are enclosing a yard with fencing.

   c. You are covering the top of a table with square mosaic tiles.

7. A tunnel in an ant farm is shown, but the label on the glass covers some of the ants. Estimate the total number of ants that would be shown in the tunnel if the label were not there. Explain how you made your estimate.

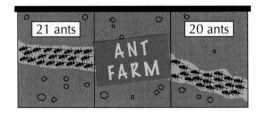

21 ants   20 ants

ANT FARM

8. The anaconda snake is one of the longest snakes in the world. In a picture, the snake is $2\frac{3}{4}$ inches. The picture was drawn using a scale of 1 in. = 8 ft. Estimate the actual length of the snake. Explain how you made your estimate.

Problem-Solving Applications

Statue of Liberty Originally named "Liberty Enlightening the World," the statue was a gift from France to celebrate the United States' 100th birthday. The statue has welcomed millions of people into the United States and has become a symbol of the nation.

Trivia The sculptor first created a 4-foot-tall statue whose face was modeled after his mother. This was enlarged to 9 feet, then to 36 feet, and finally to 151 feet. Each step required thousands of measurements!

1 The statue is made with more than 300 rectangular copper sheets. The average width of a sheet is about 4 feet. The average area is 32 square feet. What is the average length of a copper sheet?

2 One of the statue's fingernails is a rectangle with a perimeter of about 46 inches. One side of the fingernail measures 10 inches. What is the length of each of the other sides?

Key Facts
Statue of Liberty

• Steel frame weight	125 tons
• Copper sheeting weight	100 tons
• Copper sheeting thickness	$\frac{3}{32}$ in.
• Height of head	17 ft 3 in.
• Width of eye	2 ft 6 in.
• Width of mouth	3 ft
• Length of nose	4 ft 6 in.

Good News/Bad News *Visitors can get a great view of the city and harbor from the windows in the statue's crown. Unfortunately, they have to climb 354 steps to get there!*

3 To find the standard U.S. women's shoe size, measure the person's foot in inches and subtract 7.33. Multiply the result by 3 and then add 1.5. The Statue of Liberty's foot is about 25 feet long. What size shoe would the Statue of Liberty wear?

Using Key Facts

4 A penny is about $\frac{1}{16}$ inch thick. Is the copper sheeting on the statue thicker or thinner than a penny?

5 What is the combined weight of the statue's copper and steel?

6 **Writing in Math** Write your own measurement problem using any of the information given in this lesson. Answer your problem with a complete sentence.

7 **Decision Making** On your trip to the Statue of Liberty, you have $40.00 to spend on three souvenirs for yourself, your family, and a friend. What would you buy? How much money would you have left over?

Statue of Liberty Souvenir	Price
10-inch replica	$11.50
T-shirt	$10.99
Pen	$4.95
Mug	$7.50
Poster	$2.49

Review

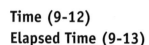

Do You Know How?

Do You Understand?

Time (9-12)
Elapsed Time (9-13)

Find each equal measure.

1. 17 wk = ___ d   **2.** 480 s = ___ min

3. 84 mo = ___ yr   **4.** 3 d = ___ min

Find the elapsed time.

5. 7:00 A.M. to 9:27 A.M.

6. 11:45 A.M. to 2:34 P.M.

Ⓐ In which exercise did you have to multiply or divide twice to change between units of measurement? Why was this necessary?

Ⓑ Explain how to find the start time if you are given the elapsed time and end time.

Temperature (9-14)

Write each temperature in Celsius and Fahrenheit.

7. 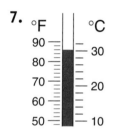   **8.**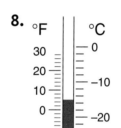

Find each change in temperature.

9. 31°C to 16°C   **10.** 48°F to 54°F

11. 97°F to 79°F   **12.** 18°C to 23°C

Ⓒ Which operation did you use to find each change of temperature in Exercises 9–12? Why did you choose that operation?

Ⓓ The average temperature in Jacksonville, Florida, in March is 62°F. During the same month in Miami, Florida, the average temperature is 22°C. Which city has the warmer average temperature in March? Explain how you know. You may use the thermometer shown in Exercise 7 in your explanation.

Problem-Solving: Writing to Explain (9-15)

13. Tim's soccer practice today was 17 minutes longer than usual. Usually, practice lasts 1 hr 20 min. If Tim's practice started at 11:30 A.M. today, what time did it end?

Ⓔ List the steps you used to find the answer.

Ⓕ Explain another way you could have solved Exercise 13.

MULTIPLE CHOICE

1. The museum tour lasted 1 hour and 25 minutes. How many seconds long was the tour? (9-12)

A. 85 s   **C.** 3,625 s

B. 1,560 s   **D.** 5,100 s

2. Find the elapsed time from 10:50 A.M. to 12:10 P.M. (9-13)

A. 1 h 20 min   **C.** 2 h 40 min

B. 1 h 40 min   **D.** 3 h

FREE RESPONSE

Find each change in temperature. You may use the thermometer to help you. (9-14)

3. 13°F to 25°F   **4.** 25°C to −5°C   **5.** −10°F to 2°F

6. 50°C to 23°C   **7.** 32°F to 88°F   **8.** −8°C to 18°C

9. Write the temperature shown on the thermometer in Celsius and Fahrenheit. (9-14)

Change each measurement. (9-12)

10. 63 d = ___ wk   **11.** 4 hr = ___ s   **12.** 144 mo = ___ yr

Add or subtract. (9-13)

13.   4 h 29 min
    + 1 h 38 min

14.   7 h 15 min
    − 4 h 20 min

15.   3 h 1 min 8 s
    + 2 h 7 min 59 s

Writing in Math

16. How many seconds are in 5 days? Explain how you found your answer. (9-12, 9-15, 9-16)

17. Explain how you would rename to subtract 5 h 14 min from 8 h. (9-13)

18. If you were given two different temperatures, one in degrees Celsius and one in degrees Fahrenheit, explain how you could determine which one was warmer. (9-14, 9-15)

Test-Taking Strategies

Understand the question.

Get information for the answer.

Plan how to find the answer.

Make smart choices.

Use writing in math.

Improve written answers.

Plan How to Find the Answer

After you understand a test question and get needed information, you need to plan how to find the answer. Think about problem-solving skills and strategies and computation methods.

1. The picture below shows a square picnic shelter surrounded by a rectangular playground.

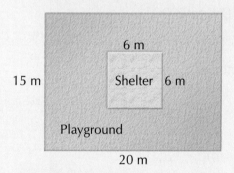

What is the area of the playground? (The picnic shelter is not part of the playground.)

Understand the question.

I need to find the area of the playground.

Get information for the answer.

The text tells me that the picnic shelter is a square, that the playground is a rectangle, and that the picnic shelter is not part of the playground. The picture shows me the dimensions of the picnic shelter and the dimensions of the playground and picnic shelter combined.

Plan how to find the answer.

• Think about problem-solving skills and strategies.

Since both shapes are rectangles, I can use a formula to find their areas. A = length × width

*To solve, I can break apart the problem into **simpler problems.***

First, I will multiply 15 m × 20 m to find the area of the playground and picnic shelter combined. Then I will multiply 6 m × 6 m to find the area of just the picnic shelter. Finally, I will subtract the area of the picnic shelter from the combined area to find the area of the playground. I will make sure to label my answer in square meters.

• Choose computation methods.

Since the problem involves several steps, I will use paper and pencil.

2. The reticulate python snake of Asia is one of the longest snakes in the world. The actual snake is about 160 times the length of the snake pictured below.

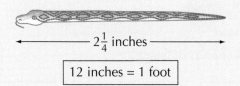

$2\frac{1}{4}$ inches

12 inches = 1 foot

About how many feet long is a reticulate python snake?

A. 30 inches

B. 360 inches

C. 30 feet

D. 360 feet

Think It Through

I can see that the pictured snake is $2\frac{1}{4}$ inches long. The text tells me that the actual snake is 160 times this length. The question asks for the actual length in feet. First, I will multiply to find the actual length in inches. Then I will divide by 12 to find the actual length in feet. I will use paper and pencil to do the computations.

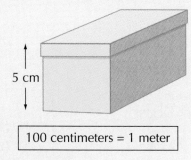

Now it's your turn.

For each problem, describe a plan for finding the answer.

3. A professional baseball home plate is shown below.

12 in.   12 in.

$8\frac{1}{2}$ in. $8\frac{1}{2}$ in.

17 in.

12 inches = 1 foot

What is the perimeter of the home plate in **feet and inches**?

A. 4 feet

B. 4 feet 10 inches

C. 5 feet 2 inches

D. 58 inches

4. How many of the boxes shown below can be stacked into a space that is 2.5 meters tall?

5 cm

100 centimeters = 1 meter

A. 5 boxes

B. 10 boxes

C. 50 boxes

D. 250 boxes

I can change 1 dollar to 100 cents. I can change 1 meter to 100 **centimeters**. *(p. 534)*

Self Check

You can **find equal measures** using **different units of length.**
(Lessons 9-1, 9-2, 9-3, 9-4)

Find the equal measure.
7 m = _____ cm

1 meter = 100 **centimeters**

7 × 100 = 700 **Multiply** to change larger units to smaller units.
7 m = 700 cm

Find 5 ft 8 in. + 3 ft 6 in.

Line up the units and add.

Rename 14 inches.

5 ft 8 in.
+ 3 ft 6 in.
———————
8 ft 14 in. = 8 ft + 1 ft + 2 in. = 9 ft + 2 in.

5 ft 8 in. + 3 ft 6 in. = 9 ft 2 in.

1. Copy and complete 50 hm = $\frac{?}{}$ m = $\frac{?}{}$ dm = $\frac{?}{}$ cm = $\frac{?}{}$ mm, and find 3 ft – 1 ft 4 in.

Self Check

You can sometimes **use formulas** to find **perimeter.** (Lessons 9-5, 9-6, 9-11)

A pie is shaped like a circle. **Pi (π)** *describes the relationship between the* **diameter** *of a circle and its* **circumference.** *(p. 542)*

Find the **perimeter** of the figure.

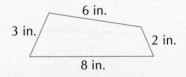
6 in.
3 in.
2 in.
8 in.

Perimeter = the sum of the side lengths

$P = 6 + 2 + 8 + 3$

$P = 19$ in.

Find the **perimeter** of the rectangle.

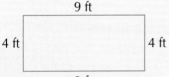
9 ft
4 ft   4 ft
9 ft

$P = (2 × \ell) + (2 × w)$
$P = (2 × 9) + (2 × 4)$
$P = 18 + 8$
$P = 26$ ft

Find the **circumference** of the circle.

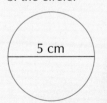
5 cm

$C = π × $ **diameter**
$C = 3.14 × 5$
$C = 15.7$ cm

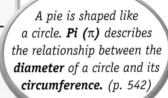

2. Find the perimeter of a rectangle with sides of 8 m and 7 m, and find the circumference of a circle with a diameter of 2 in.

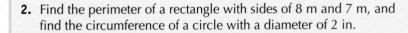

In my kitchen, some of the square floor tiles are covered by an area rug.

You can sometimes **use formulas** to find **area.** (Lessons 9-7, 9-8, 9-9, 9-10, 9-11)

Find the **area** of the rectangle.

12 ft

6 ft

Area = length × width

A = ℓ × w

A = 6 × 12

A = 72 ft²

Find the **area** of the parallelogram.

8 m

7 m

Area = base × height

A = b × h

A = 8 × 7

A = 56 m²

Find the **area** of the triangle.

5 in.

4 in.

Area = $\frac{1}{2}$ × base × height

A = $\frac{1}{2}$ × b × h

A = $\frac{1}{2}$ × 4 × 5

A = 10 in²

3. Find the area of a triangle with a 10-ft base and a 9-ft height, and the area of a square with sides of length 4 cm.

Draw a picture **to solve a problem.** (Lessons 9-11, 9-12, 9-13, 9-14, 9-15)

Soccer practice started at 11:30 A.M. and ended at 1:20 P.M. How long was soccer practice?

Draw a number line to show the problem. Then count up to find the **elapsed time.**

11:00 A.M.   12:00 A.M.   1:00 P.M.   2:00 P.M.

1 h   30 min   20 min

1 h + 30 min + 20 min = 1 h + 50 min

Soccer practice was 1 h 50 min.

4. The class started at 8:29 A.M. and ended at 9:05 A.M. How long was the class?

Answers: 1. 5,000 m, 50,000 dm, 500,000 cm, and 5,000,000 mm AND 1 ft 8 in.; 2. 30 m and 6.28 in.; 3. 45 ft² and 16 cm²; 4. Class was 36 minutes.

Chapter 9 Key Vocabulary and Concept Review   579

MULTIPLE CHOICE

Choose the correct letter for each answer.

1. Complete 180 in. = ___ ft.

   A. 10   **C.** 15

   B. 12   **D.** 18

2. Find 7 yd 1 ft − 5 yd 2 ft.

   A. 1 yd 2 ft   **C.** 12 yd 7 ft

   B. 2 yd 1 ft   **D.** 14 yd 1 ft

3. What is the length of this line segment to the nearest $\frac{1}{2}$ inch?

INCHES

   A. 1 in.   **C.** $1\frac{1}{2}$ in.

   B. $1\frac{1}{4}$ in.   **D.** 2 in.

4. Which unit would be most appropriate to measure the length of a swimming pool?

   A. millimeter   **C.** meter

   B. centimeter   **D.** kilometer

5. Complete 9.7 dm = ___ m.

   A. 0.097   **C.** 97

   B. 0.97   **D.** 970

6. What is the perimeter of this figure?

   A. 16.2 cm

   B. 16.2 cm^2

   C. 19.2 cm

   D. 19.2 cm^2

4.3 cm
3.7 cm
2.5 cm
6.8 cm
1.9 cm

7. What is the temperature in °F and °C?

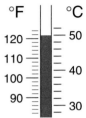

   A. 120°F; 50°C

   B. 50°C; 120°F

   C. 122°F; 50°C

   D. 122°C; 50°F

8. What is the area of a square with each side measuring $3\frac{1}{2}$ inches?

   A. $9\frac{1}{4}$ in^2 **C.** $12\frac{1}{4}$ in^2

   B. $9\frac{1}{2}$ in^2 **D.** 14 in^2

9. Find the circumference. Use 3.14 for π.

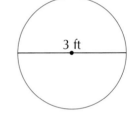

3 ft

   A. 9.32 ft

   B. 9.42 ft

   C. 18.64 ft

   D. 18.84 ft

10. Which of the following is NOT a formula for the area of a polygon?

   A. $A = \ell \times w$

   B. $A = \frac{1}{2} \times b \times h$

   C. $A = b \times h$

   D. $A = (2 \times \ell) + (2 \times w)$

11. The base of a right triangle is 8 cm long. It has a height of 2.4 cm. What is the area of the triangle?

   A. 5.2 cm^2

   B. 9.6 cm^2

   C. 10.4 cm^2

   D. 19.2 cm^2

TEST TALK

Think It Through
I can **draw a picture** to show the problem.

12. What is the area of the parallelogram?

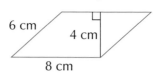

A. 18 cm

C. 32 cm²

B. 24 cm²

D. 48 cm²

13. What is the area of the figure?

A. 5 square units

B. 7 inches

C. 7 squares

D. 8 square units

FREE RESPONSE

Find each equal measure.

14. 2 d = __ min

15. 4.8 km = __ m

16. 18 ft = __ yd

17. 120 mm = __ cm

18. 3,600 s = __ h

19. 2 yd 1 ft = __ in.

Find each elapsed time.

20. 9:27 A.M. to 11:05 A.M.

21. 6:45 P.M. to 10:00 P.M.

Find each change in temperature.

22. 27°F to 35°F

23. 33°C to 18°C

Find the perimeter and area of each figure.

24.

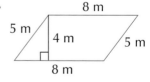

25.

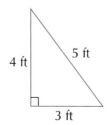

26. The square and the hexagon below have the same perimeter. The hexagon is made up of sides of equal measure. How long is each side of the hexagon?

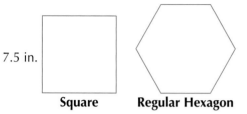

Square   Regular Hexagon

Writing in Math

27. Explain the difference between the perimeter of a figure and the area of a figure.

28. Draw a picture to solve this problem.

A square stage is surrounded by a dance floor whose outside border is a rectangle. The stage measures 12 ft on each side. The outside border of the dance floor is 20 ft by 35 ft. What is the area of the dance floor only?

29. Solve this problem and show your computations. Then explain how you found your answer.

The average body temperature for most lizards is between 88°F and 95°F. The average body temperature for most rattlesnakes is between 59°F and 99°F. Which animal has the greater range of average body temperatures? By how much?

Think It Through
• I will **write my steps in order.**
• I will **make my answer brief but complete.**

Number and Operation

MULTIPLE CHOICE

1. What is 237.258 rounded to the nearest hundredth?

    A. 200   **C.** 237.26

    B. 237   **D.** 237.3

2. Estimate $68 \times 24 \times 3$.

    A. 1,400   **C.** 4,200

    B. 3,600   **D.** 6,300

3. Find the greatest common factor for 12 and 30.

    A. 2   **C.** 4

    B. 3   **D.** 6

FREE RESPONSE

4. Write these fractions in order from least to greatest.

$$\frac{2}{3} \quad \frac{4}{5} \quad \frac{1}{3} \quad \frac{1}{2}$$

5. Five friends earned a total of $90.65 shoveling snow off their neighbors' driveways. If they divide the money equally, how much will each friend get?

6. Find $89,204 - 27,351$.

Writing in Math

7. Explain how to estimate the sum of $4\frac{2}{3}$ and $2\frac{1}{8}$. Then solve the problem and explain how you can use your estimate to see if your exact answer is reasonable.

Geometry and Measurement

MULTIPLE CHOICE

8. What is the area of this triangle?

    A. 7 in^2

    B. 14 in^2

    C. 24 in^2

    D. 48 in^2

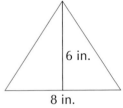

6 in.

8 in.

9. Which of the following does NOT equal 10 meters?

    A. 1 dam   **C.** 100 cm

    B. 100 dm   **D.** 10,000 mm

FREE RESPONSE

10. Christine used a rectangular piece of plywood measuring 4 ft by 8 ft to build the floor of her tree house. What are the area and perimeter of the floor?

11. Find 2 h 8 min 35 s + 1 h 20 min 41 s.

12. A train left one station at 11:40 A.M. and arrived at the next station at 1:30 P.M. How long did the trip take?

Writing in Math

13. Thomas made a kite by sewing two congruent triangles together to form a parallelogram. The base of each triangle is 15 in. and the height is 7 in. What is the area of the kite Thomas made? How did you find your answer?

Think It Through
I can **draw pictures** to model problems.

Data Analysis and Probability

MULTIPLE CHOICE

14. The sides of a number cube are labeled 1–6. If you toss the cube once, which of the following is the least likely outcome?

A. It will land on an even number.

B. It will land on a number divisible by 3.

C. It will land on an odd number.

D. It will land on a prime number.

15. You flip a fair coin once. What is the probability that it will land heads up?

A. $\frac{1}{4}$

B. $\frac{1}{2}$

C. 1

D. 2

FREE RESPONSE

Use the bar graph for Items 16–17.

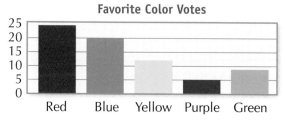

Favorite Color Votes

16. How many people voted for either purple or blue?

17. Which color had twice as many votes as yellow?

Writing in Math

18. What is the average age of the students in your class? Explain your answer.

Algebra

MULTIPLE CHOICE

19. Evaluate the expression $\frac{72}{n}$ for $n = 12$.

A. 6

B. 7

C. 12

D. 864

20. What is the next number in this pattern? 3, 9, 27, 81, ____

A. 243

C. 2,187

B. 729

D. 6,561

21. Which of the following statements is NOT true for the equation $4n = 25$?

A. n must be less than 4.

B. n must be less than 25.

C. 25 divided by 4 must equal n.

D. 25 divided by n must equal 4.

FREE RESPONSE

22. What is the rule for this table?

In	$\frac{1}{2}$	1	$1\frac{1}{2}$	2
Out	$\frac{1}{4}$	$\frac{1}{2}$	$\frac{3}{4}$	1

23. A town park is 15 yards wide and n yards long. Write an expression to show how to find the perimeter of the park.

Writing in Math

24. Explain the meaning of each part of the equation $C = \pi \times d$.

Set 9-1 (pages 528–531)

Find 8 ft 3 in. − 6 ft 10 in.

Set up the problem. Rename units, if necessary. Then subtract.

$$\begin{array}{l} \overset{7 \text{ ft, }15 \text{ in.}}{\cancel{8} \text{ ft } \cancel{3} \text{ in.}} \\ -\ 6 \text{ ft } 10 \text{ in.} \\ \hline \quad 1 \text{ ft } 5 \text{ in.} \end{array}$$ 3 in. < 10 in.
So, you need to rename to subtract.
Think: 1 ft = 12 in.

Remember to line up the correct units.

1. 12 yd 2 ft
  − 9 yd 1 ft

2. 4 ft 11 in.
  + 7 ft 3 in.

3. 10 ft − 3 ft 8 in.

4. 1 yd 2 ft + 16 ft

5. 25 yd 1 ft + 6 yd 1 ft

Set 9-2 (pages 532–533)

Find the length to the nearest inch, $\frac{1}{2}$ inch, $\frac{1}{4}$ inch, and $\frac{1}{8}$ inch.

0 Inches 1   2

To the nearest:

inch = 1 in.

$\frac{1}{4}$ inch = $1\frac{2}{4}$ = $1\frac{1}{2}$ in.

$\frac{1}{2}$ inch = $1\frac{1}{2}$ in.

$\frac{1}{8}$ inch = $1\frac{3}{8}$ in.

Remember to write your measurements in fractions using simplest form.

1. Find the length to the nearest $\frac{1}{4}$ inch.

2. Find the length to the nearest $\frac{1}{8}$ inch.

Set 9-3 (pages 534–535)

Choose a reasonable metric unit for the length of a school bus

The meter is the most appropriate since millimeters and centimeters are too small, and kilometers are too large.

Remember that commonly used metric units are the millimeter (mm), centimeter (cm), meter (m) and kilometer (km).

1. length of a hair brush

2. width of a screw

Set 9-4 (pages 536–539)

Find the equal measure.

1.6 cm = ___ m

Think: 100 cm = 1 m

$1.6 \div 100 = 0.016$

1.6 cm = 0.016 m

To change larger units to smaller units, multiply. To change smaller units to larger units, divide.

Remember that the decimal point moves to the left when you divide by 10 and to the right when you multiply by 10.

1. 5.8 m = ___ cm

2. 247 m = ___ km

3. 6.1 dm = ___ mm

Set 9-5 (pages 540–541)

Find the perimeter.

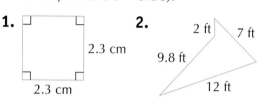

P = perimeter
ℓ = length
w = width

Remember that to find the perimeter of a square you can use the formula for rectangles or the one for squares ($P = 4 \times s$, where s = side).

5 m

8 m

One Way: Use a formula.

$P = (2 \times \ell) + (2 \times w)$

$P = (2 \times 8) + (2 \times 5) = 16 + 10 = 26$ m

Another Way: Add the side lengths.

$P = 8 + 5 + 8 + 5 = 26$ m

1.

2.3 cm

2.3 cm

2.

2 ft   7 ft

9.8 ft

12 ft

3. 14 in.   14 in.

27 in.

Set 9-6 (pages 542–545)

Find the circumference.

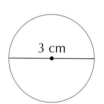

3 cm

C = circumference
Use 3.14 for π.
d = diameter

Remember that the diameter of a circle is twice the radius of that circle.

1.

2 in.

2.

3 m

Use the formula $C = \pi \times d$.

$C \approx 3.14 \times 3 = 9.42$ cm

3. a circle with a radius of 4 ft

4. a circle with a diameter of 7 yd

Set 9-7 (pages 548–549)

Find the area.

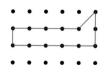

Count the number of whole square units and half square units to find the area.

Area = $5\frac{1}{2}$ square units

Remember that two half square units equal one whole square unit.

1.    **2.**

Set 9-8 (pages 550–551)

Find the area.

3 ft

3 ft

A = area
s = side
s² = side × side

Remember that the formula for the area of a rectangle is $A = \ell \times w$, where ℓ = length and w = width.

Use the formula. $A = s^2$

$A = 3^2 = 3 \times 3 = 9$ ft²

1.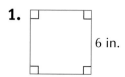

6 in.

6 in.

2.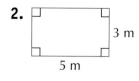

3 m

5 m

Set 9-9 (pages 552–553)

Find the area.

5 in.

7 in.

> A = area
> b = base
> h = height

Use the formula $A = b \times h$.

$A = 7 \times 5 = 35\ \text{in}^2$

Remember that area is always measured in square units, such as square feet (ft^2).

1.

9 ft

12 ft

2.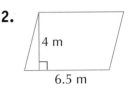

4 m

6.5 m

Set 9-10 (pages 554–555)

Find the area.

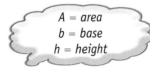

6 m

4 m

> A = area
> b = base
> h = height

Use the formula $A = \frac{1}{2} \times b \times h$.

$A = \frac{1}{2} \times 4 \times 6 = 12\ \text{m}^2$

Remember that the base is one side of the triangle. Its height is perpendicular to that base.

1.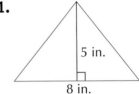

5 in.

8 in.

2.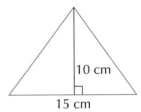

10 cm

15 cm

Set 9-11 (pages 558–559)

When you draw a picture to solve a problem, follow these steps:

Step 1: Use the given information to decide what to draw.

Step 2: Draw the picture on grid or dot paper for accuracy.

Step 3: Label all the parts and dimensions.

Step 4: Use the drawing to solve the problem.

Remember it can help to draw a picture when a problem involves measurement or geometry.

Draw a picture to solve the Garden problems.

Garden Tyler wants his rectangular garden to have the greatest area possible. What should be the dimensions of the garden if Tyler has

1. 24 feet of fencing?

2. 12 feet of fencing?

3. 40 feet of fencing?

Set 9-12 (pages 562–563)

1 h = 60 min, so
3 h = 3 × 60 min

Find the equal measure.

3 h = ___ s

1 h = 60 min and 1 min = 60 s

3 × 60 = 180 min

180 × 60 = 10,800 s

So, 3 h = 10,800 s

Remember that to change between units, you may have to multiply or divide more than once.

1. 24 mo = ___ yr **2.** 600 s = ___ min

3. 84 d = ___ wk **4.** 4 h = ___ s

5. 144 h = ___ d **6.** 156 wk = ___ h

Set 9-13 (pages 564–567)

Find the elapsed time.

2:36 P.M. to 7:15 P.M.

Subtract the end time from the start time.

$$\begin{array}{r} 6\,h \quad 75\,min \\ \cancel{7\,h\ 15\,min} \\ -\ 2\,h\ 36\,min \\ \hline 4\,h\ 39\,min \end{array}$$

Remember to check your units before you subtract and after you add to see if you need to rename.

1. 9:05 P.M. to 11:14 P.M.

2. 4:27 A.M. to 5:00 A.M.

3. 7:32 A.M. to 8:50 A.M.

4. 10:48 A.M. to 1:04 P.M.

Set 9-14 (pages 568–569)

Find the change in temperature in °F.

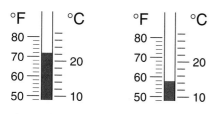

The temperature dropped from 72°F to 58°F.

72 − 58 = 14°F decrease

Remember to subtract the low temperature from the high temperature to find the change.

1. 47°C to 16°C **2.** 12°C to 20°C

3. 89°F to 100°F **4.** 0°F to 41°F

5. 116°F to 107°F **6.** 9°C to −1°C

Set 9-15 (pages 570–571)

When you are asked to explain how you found an answer, follow these steps:

Step 1: Solve the problem, showing all your computations. Check your work.

Step 2: Identify the steps you followed to find the answer.

Step 3: Use a diagram, such as a flow chart, to help prepare what to write.

Step 4: Write your steps in order.

Remember to show your work clearly so that others can understand it.

1. Find the area of a triangle with a base of five feet and a height of four feet. Explain how you found your answer.

2. The school play lasted 1 hour and 45 minutes. It ended at 9:20 P.M. What time did the play start? Explain how you found your answer.

Set 9-1 (pages 528–531)

Find each equal measure.

1. 84 in. = ___ ft

2. 4 mi = ___ yd

3. 21 ft = ___ yd

Add or subtract.

4. 7 ft 9 in. – 2 ft 11 in.

5. 4 yd 2 ft + 5 yd 2 ft

6. Tammy bought 8 yards of material. She used 3 yd 2 ft of it to make a dress. How much material did she have left over?

Set 9-2 (pages 532–533)

Find the length and width of each rectangle to the nearest inch, $\frac{1}{2}$ inch, $\frac{1}{4}$ inch, and $\frac{1}{8}$ inch.

1.

2.

3. Find the width and height of this postage stamp to the nearest $\frac{1}{8}$ inch.

Set 9-3 (pages 534–535)

Choose a reasonable metric unit for each measurement.

1. The width of a bottle cap

2. The distance from Boston to New York City

Measure each segment to the nearest centimeter and to the nearest millimeter.

3. ├──────────────┤

4. ├─────────────────────┤

5. Competitors must swim 32 times across a pool to swim a 1,600-meter race. How many times do they have to swim across the pool to complete a 400-meter race?

Set 9-4 (pages 536–539)

Find each equal measure.

1. 2.5 m = ___ cm

2. 138 mm = ___ dm

3. 0.9 km = ___ m

4. The Nature Center trail is 4.5 kilometers long. There is a marker every 500 meters along the trail, as well as one at the beginning and one at the end. How many markers are along the entire trail?

Take It to the NET
More Practice
www.scottforesman.com

Set 9-5 (pages 540–541)

Find the perimeter of each figure.

1.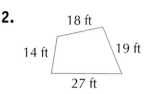

2.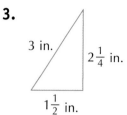

3.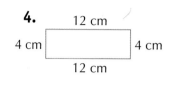

4.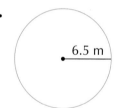

5. a 9 ft-by-10 ft rectangle

6. a square with sides measuring 2.5 cm

7. a regular hexagon with 8-meter sides

8. a regular octagon with 12-inch sides

9. The perimeter of a rectangular park is 218 yards. The park is 44 yards wide. What is the length of the park?

Set 9-6 (pages 542–545)

Find each circumference. Use 3.14 for π.

1.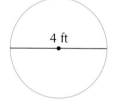

2.

3.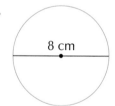

4.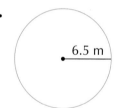

5. $d = 2$ in.

6. $r = 1.5$ km

7. $r = 9$ yd.

8. $d = 7$ mm

9. A carousel on the Ocean City boardwalk has a radius of 12.5 ft. What is the circumference of the carousel?

Set 9-7 (pages 548–549)

Find the area of each figure.

1.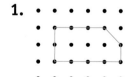

2.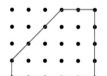

3.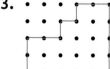

4.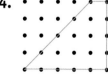

5. A figure drawn on dot paper has an area of 24 square units. It only covers whole and half square units. If it covers 19 whole square units, how many half square units does it cover?

Set 9-8 (pages 550–551)

Find the area of each figure.

1. a square with a side of 25 ft

2. a rectangle with sides of 9 yd and 12 yd

3. a 16 m-by-15 m rectangle

4. a rectangle with sides of 4.7 cm and 6.5 cm

5. a rectangle with sides of 7 mi and 9 mi

6. a square with a side of 3.5 km

7. The area of a rectangle is 36 ft². If it is 9 ft long, how wide is it?

Set 9-9 (pages 552–553)

Find the area of each parallelogram.

1.
11 ft
10 ft

2.
6 m
3.5 m

3.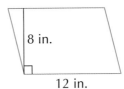
8 in.
12 in.

4.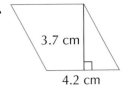
3.7 cm
4.2 cm

5. The area of a parallelogram is 143 yd². If its base is 11 yd long, what is its height?

Set 9-10 (pages 554–555)

Find the area of each triangle.

1.
8 in.
6 in.

2.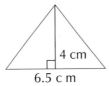
4 cm
6.5 c m

3.
9 ft
10 ft

4.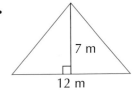
7 m
12 m

5. The base of a right triangle is 4 cm and its height is 9 cm. What is the area of the triangle?

Set 9-11 (pages 558–559)

Draw a picture to solve each problem.

1. John's square backyard patio has an area of 144 ft². He wants to cover the patio with an outdoor carpet. He wants the carpet to have the least perimeter possible. What should be the dimensions of John's outdoor carpet if the dimensions must be in whole feet?

2. Anita rides her bike the same distance every Saturday. From her house, she rides 4.5 miles north, then 3 miles west, then 4.5 miles south. How many miles does Anita have to ride to get back home? in which direction? How many miles does she ride in all?

Take It to the NET
More Practice
www.scottforesman.com

Set 9-12 (pages 562–563)

Find each equal measure.

1. 7 h = ___ min

2. 12 d = ___ s

3. 6 yr = ___ mo

4. 26 wk = ___ yr

5. 8 wk = ___ h

6. 120 h = ___ d

7. Bill worked 7 hours a day for 14 days. How many minutes did he work in all?

Set 9-13 (pages 564–567)

Find each elapsed time.

1. 6:15 P.M. to 8:07 P.M.

2. 11:48 A.M. to 2:20 P.M.

3. 9:36 A.M. to 10:12 A.M.

4. 3:45 P.M. to 5:20 P.M.

Find each start time or end time using the given elapsed time of the event.

5. Start: 4:20 P.M.; Elapsed Time: 1 h 55 min

6. End: 11:15 A.M.; Elapsed Time: 29 min

7. School starts at 7:50 A.M. and ends at 3:15 P.M. How long is each school day?

Set 9-14 (pages 568–569)

Find each change in temperature.

1. 16°F to 73°F

2. 28°C to 9°C

3. 8°F to −10°F

4. 17°C to 21°C

5. 30°C to −12°C

6. −9°F to 55°F

7. What temperature is shown on the thermometer in °F and °C?

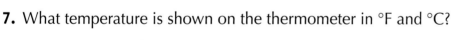

Set 9-15 (pages 570–571)

Solve each problem. Show your computations. Then explain how you found your answer.

1. On one day in Florida, it was 71°F in Miami. Jacksonville's temperature on that day was 5°F cooler than in Miami. The temperature in Key West was 12°F warmer than in Jacksonville. What was the temperature that day in Key West?

2. Tamara spent a total of 2 hours and 35 minutes studying for the math test. Brian spent a total of 9,420 seconds studying. Who spent more time studying for the test?

Measuring Solids

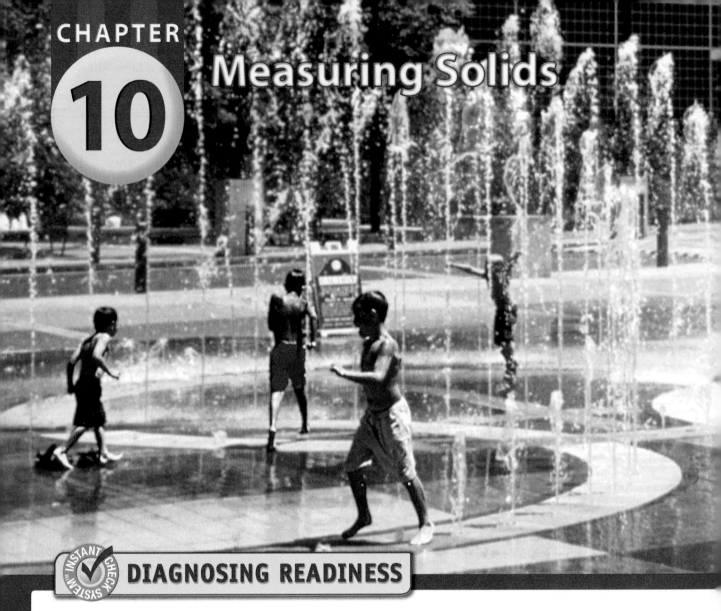

DIAGNOSING READINESS

A Vocabulary
(pages 360–363, 528–531, 534–535)

Choose the best term from the box.

1. Polygons that have the same size and shape are __?__.

2. Polygons that have the same shape but not the same size are __?__.

3. A __?__ is a metric unit of length.

4. A __?__ is a customary unit of length.

Vocabulary
- **meter** *(p. 534)*
- **congruent** *(p. 360)*
- **yard** *(p. 528)*
- **similar** *(p. 362)*

B Classifying Polygons
(pages 340–349)

Classify each polygon. Be as specific as possible.

5.
2 in.
2 in. □ 2 in.
2 in.

6.
3 cm | 5 cm
4 cm

7.
3 m △ 3 m
3 m

8.
3 ft
2 ft ▱ 2 ft
3 ft

9.
1 in. 1 in.
1 in. ⬡ 1 in.
1 in. 1 in.
1 in.

10.
2.5 m
1.5 m ⬔ 2 m
1 m

11. What is a regular polygon?

Do You Know...

How much does a gallon of water weigh?

You will find out in Lesson 10-11.

RUSSELL ASH
INCREDIBLE COMPARISONS

C Finding Area

(pages 548–555)

Find the area.

12.

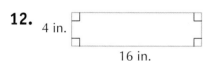

4 in.
16 in.

13.
2.2 cm 2 cm
6 cm

14.
6 m 7.8 m
5 m

15. 5 in.
3 in.
8 in.

16. What is the area of a square dog pen with sides of length 20 feet?

17. What is the difference between the perimeter and the area of a polygon?

D Order of Operations

(pages 172–173)

18. $(3 \times 8) \times 10$

19. $3 \times (8 \times 10)$

20. $(\frac{1}{2} \times 8) \times 12$

21. $\frac{1}{2} \times (8 \times 12)$

22. $3 \times (8 + 5)$

23. $(3 \times 8) + 5$

24. $15 - (2 \times 4)$

25. $(15 - 2) \times 4$

26. If the parentheses in Exercise 18 are removed, the answer remains the same. What other exercises share this property?

Vocabulary
• polyhedron (pl. polyhedra)
• solid figure
• face
• edge
• vertex
• prism
• cylinder
• cone
• pyramid
• sphere

Think It Through
I can **use models** of different solids to determine the vertices, edges, and faces.

Solid Figures

LEARN

What is a solid figure?

A **polyhedron** is a three-dimensional **solid figure** with flat surfaces. Solid figures are also called solids.

• The flat surfaces are called **faces.** The outline of each face is a polygon.
• The line segment where two faces intersect is called an **edge.**
• The point where edges intersect is called a **vertex.**

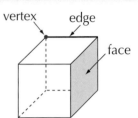

✓ **WARM UP**

Classify each polygon.

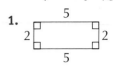

Example A

For the polyhedron shown at the right, name the vertices, edges, and faces.

vertices: *A, B, C, X, Y,* and *Z*
edges: $\overline{AB}, \overline{AC}, \overline{BC}, \overline{XY}, \overline{XZ}, \overline{YZ}, \overline{AX}, \overline{BY},$ and $\overline{CZ}$
faces: $\triangle ABC, \triangle XYZ,$ and quadrilaterals *ABYX, BYZC,* and *AXZC*

Some solid figures also have curved surfaces. Solid figures with curved surfaces are not polyhedrons.

EXAMPLES OF SOLID FIGURES

Prism	Cylinder	Cone	Pyramid
Solid with two congruent parallel bases and faces that are parallelograms	Solid with two circular bases that are congruent and parallel	Solid with one circular base. The points on this circle are joined to one point outside the base.	Solid with a base that is a polygon. The edges of the base are joined to a point outside the base.

✓ **Talk About It**

1. Use Example A to help name the vertices, edges, and faces of the pyramid shown in the chart above.

2. **Reasoning** This circle is one view of a solid. Can you tell just from this picture whether you are looking at a cylinder or a cone? Explain.

3. Reasoning Another solid figure is the **sphere.** It has a point that is exactly in the center. What do you know about the distance from any point on the sphere to the center?

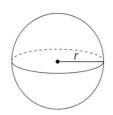

How can you tell one solid from another?

Features of a solid figure can help you identify it. Notice that a prism or a pyramid can be named by the type of base it has.

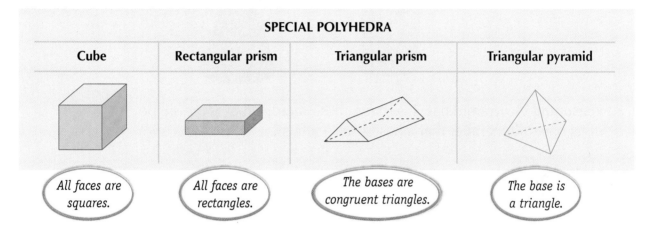

SPECIAL POLYHEDRA

Cube	Rectangular prism	Triangular prism	Triangular pyramid
All faces are squares.	All faces are rectangles.	The bases are congruent triangles.	The base is a triangle.

Below are examples of things found in the world around us that are solids.

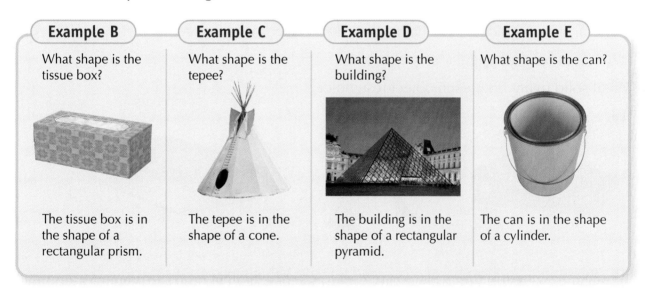

Example B

What shape is the tissue box?

The tissue box is in the shape of a rectangular prism.

Example C

What shape is the tepee?

The tepee is in the shape of a cone.

Example D

What shape is the building?

The building is in the shape of a rectangular pyramid.

Example E

What shape is the can?

The can is in the shape of a cylinder.

✔ Talk About It

4. Look at Examples B, C, D, and E. Name other objects in the real world that have similar shapes. Tell why the objects you named are similar.

5. How many faces does a triangular prism have? A triangular pyramid?

6. Reasoning A solid is made from 4 equilateral triangles. What is it?

Take It to the NET
More Examples
www.scottforesman.com

Use the solid figure shown at the right for 1–3.

1. Name the vertices.   **2.** Name the edges.   **3.** Name the faces.

4. Does a cylinder have any vertices? Explain your answer.

What solid figure does each object resemble?

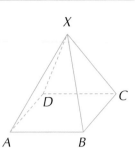

5.

6.

7.

8. Reasoning A pyramid has 7 vertices and 7 faces. What is the shape of its base? Remember that a base is also a face.

A Skills and Understanding

Use the solid pictured at the right for 9–11.

9. Name the vertices.   **10.** Name the edges.   **11.** Name the faces.

12. Is a cube a rectangular prism? Explain.

What solid figure does each object resemble?

13.

14.

15.

16. Reasoning A prism has 9 edges and 5 faces. What type of prism is it? Be as specific as possible.

B Reasoning and Problem Solving

Use the drawing at the right for 17–20. Describe the part of the drawing that suggests each solid named.

17. triangular prism   **18.** rectangular prism

19. cone   **20.** cylinder

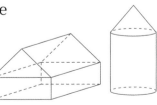

Math and Social Studies

People and organizations build monuments, such as the ones shown at the right, to remember heroes and events. A **sphere,** or ball, is placed inside the top of one structure.

21. Describe the faces of the structure that holds the sphere. What kind of solid figure is represented?

22. **Writing in Math** Margaret said that a pyramid must have a square base. Is she correct? Explain.

C Extensions

23. Think of cutting apart and unwrapping this cylinder to get two circles and one rectangle. One dimension of the rectangle is 3 in. What is the other dimension? Hint: Think about the circumference of a circle. Use 3.14 for π.

10 in.

3 in.

Cut and unwrap.

Mixed Review and Test Prep

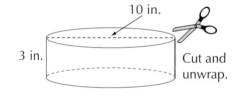

Take It to the NET
Test Prep
www.scottforesman.com

Find each area.

24. Square with $s = 4.5$ cm

25. Parallelogram with $b = 12$ m, $h = 3.7$ m

26. Triangle with $b = 6.2$ in., $h = 11$ in.

27. Which best describes a triangle with congruent sides?

    A. right   **B.** equilateral   **C.** obtuse   **D.** square

28. **Writing in Math** Describe how you would find the increase in the temperature from the morning temperature of $-2°F$ to the 6:00 P.M. temperature of $+38°F$.

Discovery CHANNEL SCHOOL

Discover Math in Your World

Take It to the NET
Video and Activities
www.scottforesman.com

Solid Ice

Ice is water in the solid state. It is a crystalline substance composed of hydrogen and oxygen. The most basic form of an ice crystal is a hexagonal prism.

hexagonal prism

1. Name the polygons that make up a hexagonal prism.

2. How many faces does a hexagonal prism have? How many vertices?

Vocabulary
• net

Materials
• grid paper
• scissors
• tape
• cubes

Think It Through
I can **act it out** by copying, cutting, folding, and taping the net.

Views of Solid Figures

LEARN

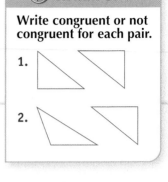
Activity

In what ways can you picture a solid?

A box is shown at the right. From this view, you see the top and two faces of it. You cannot see the bottom or the other faces of it.

A **net** is a plane figure which when folded gives a solid figure. Think about unfolding a box to make a net for a rectangular solid.

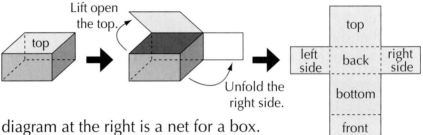

Lift open the top.

Unfold the right side.

The diagram at the right is a net for a box.

Step 1 On grid paper, make a copy of this net. Be sure to copy the dotted lines, as well as the solid lines.

Step 2 Cut out your copy along the solid lines.

Step 3 Crease along the dotted lines.

Step 4 Fold the figure so that the six rectangles become the six faces of a box. Tape along the edges to hold the faces in position.

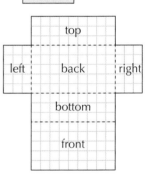

a. The box you made is 9 units long, 3 units wide, and 5 units high. Explain how you can find these dimensions from the drawing on the grid paper.

b. On another piece of grid paper, draw a net for a square pyramid. Be sure to include the dotted lines that are the fold lines. Cut out the net and make the pyramid.

c. A net has 6 squares. What solid will be formed from it?

d. Reasoning Is this figure a net for a cube? Explain.

Activity

Can views from different angles help picture a solid?

This diagram shows a rectangular prism with three different viewers.

The viewers are at the front, at one side, and above the solid. The viewer at the top looks straight down and sees a rectangle 4 units by 3 units.

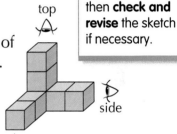

top

side

front

a. Describe the rectangle the viewer in the front sees.

b. Which viewer sees a rectangle that is 3 units long and 2 units wide? Explain how you decided.

c. Reasoning Make a sketch of a rectangular prism that these viewers observe. Use the diagram above as a model or draw your own model.

- front: rectangle 4 units long and 2 units wide
- side: rectangle 4 units long and 2 units wide
- top: rectangle 4 units long and 4 units wide

Think It Through
I can **try** a sketch, then **check and revise** the sketch if necessary.

The solid pictured at the right is made of cubes. Sketches of the front view, the side view, and the top view are shown.

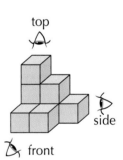

top

side

front

front view   side view   top view

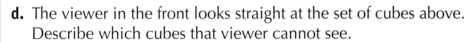

d. The viewer in the front looks straight at the set of cubes above. Describe which cubes that viewer cannot see.

e. The solid shown at the right is made of cubes. Build the solid with cubes. Then sketch the front view, the side view, and the top view.

f. Reasoning How many cubes in the solid at the right are not visible to the viewer in the front? at the top? from the side?

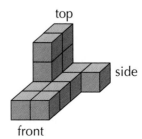

top

side

front

CHECK ✓

For another example, see Set 10-2 on p. 638.

1. What solid does this net represent?

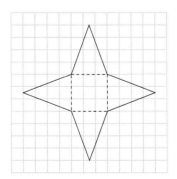

2. Draw front, side, and top views of the solid made from unit cubes.

top

side

front

3. Reasoning In Exercise 2, how many blocks are NOT visible to the front viewer?

A Skills and Understanding

What solid does each net represent?

4.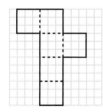

5.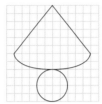

6.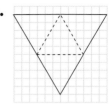

Draw front, side, and top views of each stack of unit blocks.

7.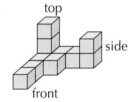

8.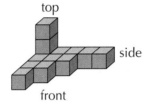

9.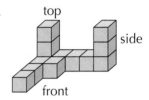

10. Reasoning Could the figure below be a net for a cube? Explain.

11. Reasoning How many blocks are not visible from the top view?

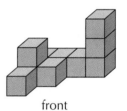

front

B Reasoning and Problem Solving

Think about looking at this kitchen from different views.

12. Make a rough sketch of the kitchen looking directly down from above. Label the sink, refrigerator, and range.

13. Make a rough sketch of the view you see if you are looking directly into the kitchen from the wall to the left of the entry.

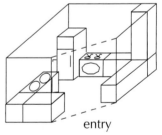

entry

Math and Science

Use the information at the right for 14–15.

14. The weight was evenly distributed across three zones. To the nearest ton, how much did each zone support?

15. "Push jacks" were used to move the lighthouse 5 ft at a time. How many "pushes" did it take to move the lighthouse to its new location?

The all-brick Cape Hatteras Lighthouse, located in North Carolina, weighs 4,400 T and is the tallest in the United States. In 1999 it was moved 2,850 ft to its new site.

16. **Writing in Math** A student says this diagram could not be a net for a cube. Do you agree? Explain.

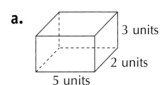

C Extensions

17. On grid paper draw a net for each solid shown at the right.

a. 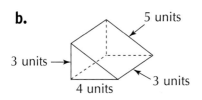 3 units, 2 units, 5 units

b. 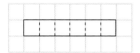 5 units, 3 units, 4 units, 3 units

Mixed Review and Test Prep

Take It to the NET
Test Prep
www.scottforesman.com

Estimate each product.

18. $\frac{1}{2} \times 49$

19. $\frac{2}{3} \times 58$

20. $\frac{7}{12} \times 100$

21. $3\frac{1}{5} \times 4\frac{7}{8}$

22. $12 \times 5\frac{1}{7}$

23. $6\frac{9}{10} \times 7\frac{1}{10}$

24. Which is the correct name of this object?

   A. cylinder   **C.** triangular prism

   B. cone   **D.** pyramid

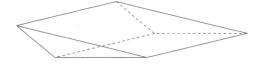

25. **Writing in Math** Explain how you would decide if a solid figure is a rectangular prism, a triangular prism, a square pyramid, or a triangular pyramid.

Learning with Technology

The Geometry Drawing eTool and Solid Figures

You can use the Geometry Drawing eTool to draw prisms. With the geoboard workspace selected, draw a scalene triangle. Then, make a copy of the scalene triangle and place it directly below the first triangle. Connect the vertices of the two triangles with line segments.

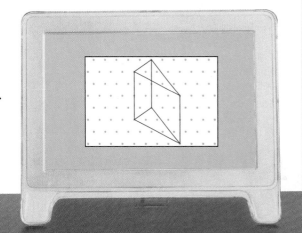

1. Is the drawn solid a triangular prism? How can you tell?

Draw the following prisms.

2. rectangular prism

3. cube

Vocabulary
• surface area

Materials
• grid paper

Think It Through

• I can **get information from the picture.**

• I can **use logical reasoning** to find the formula for surface area.

Surface Area

LEARN

Activity

How can you find a formula for the surface area of a rectangular prism?

WARM UP

Find the area of each rectangle with length ℓ and width w.

1. ℓ: 8 m and w: 16 m

2. ℓ: 6 ft and w: 10 ft

The **surface area (SA)** of a rectangular prism is the sum of the areas of all its faces. The box at the right is a rectangular prism.

9 in.

10 in.

14 in.

The diagram at the right below is a net for this box. The amount of wrapping paper you need for a package depends on the surface area.

Step 1 Copy this diagram. Label all the lengths and widths of the rectangles.

Step 2 Use the measurements to find the areas of the six rectangles. What is their sum?

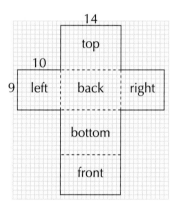

14

top

10

9 | left | back | right

bottom

front

a. Which pairs of faces are congruent?

b. Explain why the expression below gives the surface area of the box. Use the expression to find the area of the box.

2 × (area of **front**) + 2 × (area of **top**) + 2 × (area of **left**)

c. Write a formula for surface area *(SA)* of a rectangular prism with length ℓ, width w, and height h.

d. Use the formula to find the surface area of the prisms below.

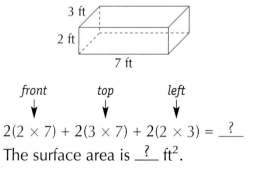

3 ft

2 ft

7 ft

3 cm

3 cm

3 cm

Note that 2 × (2 × 7) can be written as 2(2 × 7).

front *top* *left*

$2(2 \times 7) + 2(3 \times 7) + 2(2 \times 3) = \underline{\ ?\ }$

The surface area is $\underline{\ ?\ }$ ft².

front *top* *left*

$2(\underline{\ ?\ }) + 2(\underline{\ ?\ }) + 2(\underline{\ ?\ }) = \underline{\ ?\ }$

The surface area is $\underline{\ ?\ }$ cm².

e. Find the surface area of a cube with each edge 9 ft.

f. **Reasoning** Which box needs more wrapping paper? Show your work.

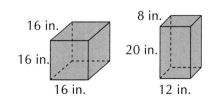

16 in.

16 in.

16 in.

8 in.

20 in.

12 in.

CHECK ✓   *For another example, see Set 10-3 on p. 638.*

Find the surface area of each rectangular prism.

1.   2.5 cm
   5 cm
      5 cm

2.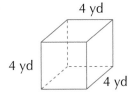
   2 in.   4 in.
        6 in.

3.   7 ft
        7 ft
   7 ft

4. Reasoning A cube has a surface area of 96 cm². What is the length of each edge?

PRACTICE   *For more practice, see Set 10-3 on p. 641.*

A Skills and Understanding

Find the surface area of each rectangular prism.

5.   2 cm
   3.5 cm
   4.5 cm

6.   4 yd
   4 yd
        4 yd

7. $2\frac{1}{2}$ in.
   $2\frac{1}{2}$ in.
        6 in.

8. Reasoning A box has a surface area of 150 ft². Each face has the same area. What do you know about the dimensions of the box?

B Reasoning and Problem Solving

An aquarium can be used as a hamster cage if it is covered with a wire top. Use the information at the right for 9–11.

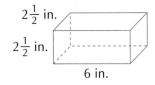
16 in.
24 in.   16 in.

9. Estimation Estimate the area of the five glass faces.

10. How much glass was used to make the aquarium?

11. How much mesh wire is needed for the top of the cage?

12. Writing in Math Fred claims he can find the surface area of a rectangular prism with this expression. Is he right? Explain.

2(area of back) + 2(area of left) + 2(area of bottom)

Mixed Review and Test Prep

Take It to the NET
Test Prep
www.scottforesman.com

Write as a fraction or mixed number in lowest terms.

13. 0.45   **14.** 1.6   **15.** 0.04   **16.** 0.15   **17.** 0.85

18. For which solid would you make a net with exactly five faces?

   A. cube   **B.** rectangular prism   **C.** triangular pyramid   **D.** square pyramid

 All text pages available online and on CD-ROM.

Visualize

Visualizing when you read in math can help you use the **problem-solving strategy,** *Act it Out or Use Objects,* in the next lesson.

In reading, visualizing can help you "see" what is happening in a story. In math, visualizing can help you "see" what is happening in a problem so that you can act it out or use objects to solve the problem.

Brian is painting a square wall. He is using a 5-by-5 checkerboard design with alternating red and black squares. If he places red squares in the corners, how many black squares will there be?

When I visualize the problem, I see a checkers game board, but smaller.

I'll act it out and use objects. I'll use 1-cm paper or plastic squares in 2 colors.

Then arrange the squares in a checkerboard pattern.

1. How many squares are needed to make the 5-by-5 design?

2. Can all the corners be the same color in a 4-by-4 checkerboard pattern? Explain.

For 3–5, use the problem below.

Karyn has 32 small cubes. She wants to glue together some of the small cubes to make as large a cube as possible. How many small cubes will she use?

3. Visualize the problem. Describe what you see.

4. Now act it out and use objects by representing the problem with small cubes.

5. **Writing in Math** Can Karyn use exactly 4 smaller cubes to make a larger cube? Explain.

For 6–8, use the problem below.

Chika wants to build a rectangular dog pen with an area of 36 square feet. Three sides will be enclosed by a fence, and the fourth side will be the side of her garage. She wants to know if a square pen will require the least amount of fencing.

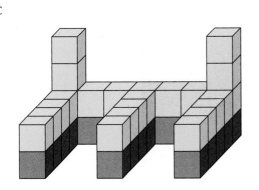

6. Visualize the problem. Describe what you see.

7. Now act it out and use objects by representing the problem with plastic or paper squares.

8. **Writing in Math** How much fencing is required for a square pen? Explain how you found your answer.

For 9–11, use the problem below.

The "castle" at a playground is made of 1-foot plastic blocks, as shown at the right. What is the area of the part that is covered by the castle.

9. Which part of the castle do you need to "see" when you visualize the area covered by the castle?

10. Now act out the problem and use objects by representing the problem with small cubes.

11. **Writing in Math** Did you need to use 1-foot cubes to model the problem? Explain.

Problem-Solving Strategy

Key Idea
Learning how and when to use objects can help you solve problems.

Materials
• cubes or square tiles
• squares of paper

Use Objects

LEARN

How can objects be used to model a problem?

Patio Designs Mr. Santo is going to construct a patio using the design at the right, but his patio will have 5 square blocks in the middle row. How many blocks will he need to make the patio?

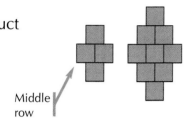

Middle row

Read and Understand

What do you know?

To have 2 blocks in the middle, 4 blocks are needed. To have 3 blocks in the middle, 9 blocks are needed.

What are you trying to find?

Find the total number of blocks needed when there are 5 blocks in the middle.

Plan and Solve

What strategy will you use?

Strategy: Use Objects
Use cubes or square tiles to make models.

How to Use Objects

Step 1 Choose objects.
Step 2 Show the known information.
Step 3 Use the objects to solve the problem.

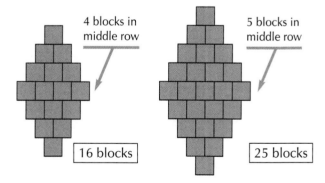

4 blocks in middle row

5 blocks in middle row

16 blocks

25 blocks

Answer: When there are 5 blocks in the middle row, a total of 25 blocks are needed.

Look Back and Check

Is your answer reasonable?

Yes, the pattern continues in the models of the two patios and I counted the blocks correctly.

✔ Talk About It

1. For the **Patio Designs** problem, compare the number of blocks in the middle with the total number of blocks needed. Explain the pattern.

2. Reasoning Without making a model, how many blocks would you need for a patio with 7 blocks in the middle? With 10 blocks in the middle?

CHECK ✓

For another example, see Set 10-4 on p. 639.

1. The Painted Cube The picture represents 27 centimeter cubes that were glued together to form a larger cube. Then all 6 faces of the larger cube were painted.

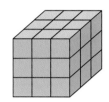

a. Use cubes to make a model of the painted cube.

b. How many of the 27 cubes will have paint on 1 face? On 2 faces? On 3 faces? On 0 faces?

PRACTICE

For more practice, see Set 10-4 on p. 642.

Using Name Cards to Solve a Problem Write each name on a slip of paper: Juan, Lu, Wanda, Carol, and Todd. Put the name cards in the correct order to solve the problem.

2. Five friends are waiting in line to get on the roller coaster. Use the clues to determine in what order the five people are standing.

> There is a person in front and behind Juan.
> Carol is second in line.
> The same number of people are in front of Lu and behind him.
> There are 2 people between Juan and Wanda.

Folding Paper to Solve a Problem Fold a sheet of paper in half, then in half again, and so on to solve the problem.

3. After one fold, there are two sections. How many sections are there after 2 folds? After 3 folds? After 4 folds? If you could fold the paper 6 times, how many sections would you have?

4. Sean has 3 pairs of jeans, 3 T-shirts, and 2 jackets. How many outfits can he make of a pair of jeans, a T-shirt, and a jacket?

5. **Writing in Math** Four people can sit at a table. If two tables are put together, 6 people can be seated. How many tables are needed to make a long table that will seat 20 people? Explain how you solved the problem.

STRATEGIES

- **Show What You Know**
  Draw a Picture
  Make an Organized List
  Make a Table
  Make a Graph
  Act It Out or Use Objects
- **Look for a Pattern**
- **Try, Check, and Revise**
- **Write an Equation**
- **Use Logical Reasoning**
- **Solve a Simpler Problem**
- **Work Backward**

Choose a tool

Mental Math

TEST TALK

Think It Through

Stuck? I won't give up. I can:
- Reread the problem.
- Tell what I know.
- Identify key facts and details.
- Tell the problem in my own words.
- Show the main idea.
- Try a different strategy.
- Retrace my steps.

 All text pages available online and on CD-ROM.

Do You Know How?

Do You Understand?

Solid Figures (10-1)

Identify each solid. Be as specific as possible.

1.   **2.**   **3.**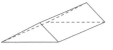

Give the number of each in the triangular prism.

4. faces   **5.** edges   **6.** vertices

A How are a cylinder and a cone alike?

B How are a cone and a pyramid alike?

Views of Solid Figures (10-2)

What solid does the net represent? Be as specific as possible.

7.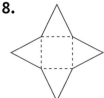

8.

C When you look at a net, how can you tell if it represents a pyramid?

D In Exercise 8, how do the number of sides of the base compare to the number of triangular faces?

Surface Area (10-3)

Find the surface area of each solid.

9. 3 in.   12 in.   10 in.

10. 4 cm   4 cm   4 cm   4 cm

E In Example 9, how many rectangles are 3 in. by 12 in.? 3 in. by 10 in.? 12 in. by 10 in.?

F Explain how you found the surface area of the cube in Exercise 10.

Problem-Solving Strategy: Use Objects (10-4)

11. You can make one square with 4 toothpicks, two squares with 7 toothpicks, and so on. How many toothpicks do you need to make 6 squares in a row?

G How can using objects help you to solve Exercise 11?

Chapter 10 Section A
Diagnostic Checkpoint

MULTIPLE CHOICE

1. A square prism has how many vertices? (10-1)

   A. 6 **B.** 2 **C.** 4 **D.** 8

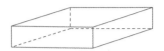

2. You can see all of the blocks in the figure at the right. Which shows the top view of the solid? (10-2)

   A. **B.** **C.** **D.**

FREE RESPONSE

Name the solid that each net makes. Be as specific as possible. (10-2)

3. 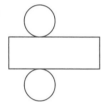 4. 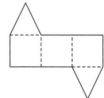 5.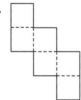

For 6–9, choose the appropriate polygon to complete the sentence. (10-1)

6. Each face of a prism is a __?__. 7. Each base of a triangular prism is a __?__.

8. Each face of a cube is a __?__. 9. Each face of a triangular pyramid is a __?__.

10. Each edge of a box is 2 ft long. Is 25 square feet of wrapping paper enough to cover the box? (10-3)

11. A gallon of paint will cover about 400 ft². Is one gallon enough to cover the sides of a building that is 30 ft wide, 50 ft long, and 20 ft high? Explain. (10-3)

TEST TALK

Think It Through
Sketching a figure and labeling the dimensions might help you find the surface area.

Writing in Math

12. The triangles at the right form a pattern. If this pattern of triangles were to continue, how many objects would be in the fifth triangle? Explain how you found your answer. (10-4)

13. Bethany has 4 siblings. Bethany is neither the oldest nor the youngest. Jamie is the second oldest. There are three siblings that are older than Cody and younger than Erin. Brandon is younger than Bethany. List the five siblings in order from youngest to oldest. Explain how you can determine if your answer is reasonable. (10-4)

Algebra

Key Idea
What you know about area can help you find volume of solid figures.

Vocabulary
• volume
• cubic unit

Materials
• cubes

Think It Through
• I can **make a model** to solve the problem.
• I can **look for a pattern** while I am building.

Volume

LEARN

Activity

How do you measure how much space something occupies?

Volume is a measure of the space inside a solid figure. You can measure the volume of a solid figure by counting how many cubic units are needed to fill it.

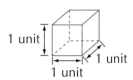

> The volume of a cube 1 unit on each edge is 1 **cubic unit,** or 1 unit³.

You can use unit cubes to build a rectangular prism and measure the volume. The volume of each cube is 1 cubic unit.

Step 1 Lay out 4 cubes in a row. Lay out 4 cubes right next to these cubes. Lay out another set of 4 cubes next to these. These are rows 1, 2, and 3.

Step 2 Stack 2 more cubes on top of each cube already laid out.

a. How many cubes are used altogether? What is the volume of the rectangular prism you made?

b. What if you had stacked 4 more cubes on top of each cube already laid out in Step 1? What would be the volume?

You can also find the volume of a rectangular prism using a formula.

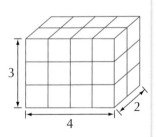

Formula for the Volume of a Rectangular Prism

If a rectangular prism has base area B and height h, then volume V is given by $V = B \times h$.

For any rectangular prism: $V = (\text{length} \times \text{width}) \times \text{height}$

$$V = (\ell \times w) \times h \text{ or } V = B \times h \text{ or } V = Bh$$

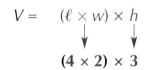

$$V = (\ell \times w) \times h$$
$$(4 \times 2) \times 3$$

The volume of the prism at the right is 24 units³.

In the prism above,
ℓ = 4 units
w = 2 units
h = 3 units

The base layer is 4 by 2 and the height is 3.

Step 3 Estimate first. Then use the formula to find the volume of each rectangular prism for **c–f.** Use unit cubes to verify each answer.

c. A rectangular prism with $B = 25$ in^2 and $h = 3$ in.

d. The base of a rectangular prism is a rectangle with a length of 5 ft and a width of 4 ft. The height of the solid is 9 ft.

e.
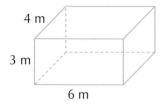
4 m
3 m
6 m

f.
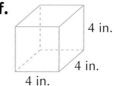
4 in.
4 in.
4 in.

g. A rectangular prism has a volume of 45 yd^3. The base area is 9 yd^2. What is the height of the prism?

h. The figure at the right is a cube. What is the area of the base? What is the volume of the cube? Does $a \times a \times a$ (also written as a^3) give the number of cubic units in the cube? Explain.

a
a
a

CHECK ✓

For another example, see Set 10-5 on p. 639.

Use unit cubes, make a drawing, or use the formula to find the volume of each rectangular prism for **1–6.**

1. base area: 120 mm^2
height: 6 mm

2. base area: 49 ft^2
height: 7 ft

3. base area: 65 in^2
height: 2.5 in.

4.

3 yd
1 yd
5.5 yd

5.
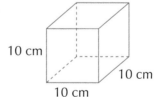
10 cm
10 cm
10 cm

6.
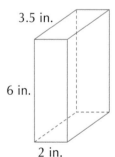
3.5 in.
6 in.
2 in.

7. The rectangular prism below is made up of blocks each 1 ft on a side. What is the volume of the solid?

8. Algebra The base of a rectangular prism is a rectangle with a length of 8 m and a width of 4 m. The volume is 64 m^3. What is the height of the prism?

A Skills and Understanding

Find the volume of each rectangular prism.

9. base area: 40.4 cm²
height: 5 cm

10. base area: 64 in²
height: 8 in.

11. base area: 1,250 m²
height: 20 m

12.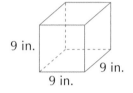
9 in.
9 in.
9 in.

13. 9 mm
7.5 mm
15 mm

14. 3 yd
6 yd
6 yd

15. base: square 5 in. on a side
height: twice the length of the base

16. base: rectangle 5.5 cm by 3.2 cm
height: half the short side of the base

17. Algebra A rectangular solid has volume 96 yd³. The base area is 16 yd². What is the height of the solid?

B Reasoning and Problem Solving

18. Matt built five rectangular prisms with unit cubes. Each prism had a base that was 4 by 5 units. If he started with 2 layers and continued to add a layer each time he built a new prism, how many cubes did he use for the largest prism?

Math and Everyday Life

Garden soil is sold by the pound or by the cubic foot. Use the information at the right for **19.**

19. Algebra Ms. Evans wants to build a raised flower bed. She purchased 1,600 ft³ of soil. The base of the flower bed will have an area of 800 ft².

a. If she uses all of the soil she purchased, how high above the ground will the top of the flower bed be?

b. What is the least amount of money that she could have paid for the soil she purchased? Assume that soil can only be purchased in quantities of 100, 500, 1,000 or 2,000 ft³.

Garden Soil	
Volume (ft³)	Cost
100	$4.99
500	$20.00
1,000	$37.50
2,000	$54.99

20.  Hernando's work to find the volume of this rectangular prism is shown at right. Is he correct? Explain.

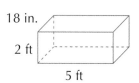

18 in.

2 ft

5 ft

$V = 2 \times 5 \times 1.5$
$V = 15$ cubic feet

C Extensions

21. Estimation Estimate the volume of the water in the pool at the right by following the steps below.

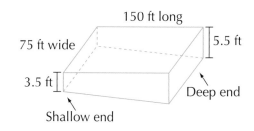

150 ft long

75 ft wide

5.5 ft

3.5 ft

Deep end

Shallow end

Step 1 Underestimate the volume by using 150 ft by 75 ft by 3.5 ft deep.

Step 2 Overestimate the volume by using 150 ft by 75 ft by 5.5 ft deep.

Step 3 Estimate the pool's volume by finding half of the sum of the volumes from Steps 1 and 2. Is the estimate reasonable?

Mixed Review and Test Prep

Take It to the NET
Test Prep
www.scottforesman.com

Find the mean of each set of numbers.

22. 3, 3, 9, 9, and 11

23. 6, 2, 8, 10, 11, and 11

24. Which represents the surface area of this rectangular prism?

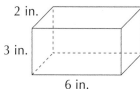

2 in.

3 in.

6 in.

A. $(2 \times 3) + (3 \times 6) + (2 \times 6)$

C. $2 + 3 + 6$

B. $2 \times 3 \times 6$

D. $2(2 \times 3) + 2(3 \times 6) + 2(2 \times 6)$

Enrichment

Volume of a Cylinder and Cone

Materials: Nets of a cone and a cylinder having congruent bases and equal heights

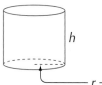

h

h

r

Connections The volume of any cylinder can be found using the general formula $V = Bh$, where B is the area of the base and h is the height. Follow the steps at the right to explore how the volume of a cone is related to the volume of a cylinder with the same height and base.

Step 1 Cut out the cone and cylinder and make the solid.

Step 2 Carefully fill the cone with beans. Pour the beans from the cone into the cylinder. Repeat until the cylinder is filled. Be sure to record the number of times that you fill the cone.

1. Reasoning Write a formula that could be used to find the volume of a cone if you know the radius of the base and the height. (Hint: The area of a circle is $\pi \times r \times r$.)

2. Use your formulas to find the volumes of a cylinder and a cone both having a height of 6 in. and a base radius of 2 in.

Vocabulary
• capacity
• teaspoon
• tablespoon
• fluid ounce
• cup
• pint
• quart
• gallon

Customary Units of Capacity

LEARN

How can you measure liquid?

Capacity is a measure of an amount of liquid. Many different units can be used to measure capacity.

A common measuring device for capacity is a measuring cup, but many other devices can be used.

Data File

Unit	Relationship
teaspoon (tsp)	1 tsp = $\frac{1}{3}$ tbsp
tablespoon (tbsp)	1 tbsp = 3 tsp
fluid ounce (fl oz)	1 fl oz = 2 tbsp
cup (c)	1 c = 8 fl oz
pint (pt)	1 pt = 2 c
quart (qt))	1 qt = 2 pt
gallon (gal)	1 gal = 4 qt

Example A

$\square$ gal = 10 qt

Think: 1 gal = 4 qt
10 ÷ 4 = 2 R2
10 qt = 2 gal 2 qt or $2\frac{1}{2}$ gal

Example B

4 qt 1 pt = $\square$ pt

Think: 1 qt = 2 pt
(2 × 4) + 1 = 8 + 1
4 qt 1 pt = 9 pt

You can add and subtract units of capacity just as you can add and subtract units of length.

Example C

$\begin{array}{r} 5 \text{ gal } 1 \text{ qt} \\ -3 \text{ gal } 3 \text{ qt} \\ \hline \end{array}$ = $\begin{array}{r} 4 \text{ gal } 5 \text{ qt} \\ -3 \text{ gal } 3 \text{ qt} \\ \hline 1 \text{ gal } 2 \text{ qt} \end{array}$

Example D

$\begin{array}{r} 3 \text{ pt } 1 \text{ c} \\ +3 \text{ pt } 1 \text{ c} \\ \hline 6 \text{ pt } 2 \text{ c} \\ 7 \text{ pt} \end{array}$ **Think:** 2 c = 1 pt
Add 1 pt to 6 pt.

✔ Talk About It

1. In Example A, why is 2 R2 equal to 2 gal 2 qt or $2\frac{1}{2}$ gal?

2. In Example C, why do you change 5 gal 1 qt to 4 gal 5 qt?

3. Reasoning Which unit (or units) of capacity would be reasonable to measure each capacity?

a. milk carton   **b.** medicine bottle   **c.** car's gas tank
d. drinking glass   **e.** thimble   **f.** swimming pool

Copy and complete.

1. 96 pt = ▮ qt   **2.** 5 gal = ▮ pt   **3.** 2 qt 1 pt = ▮ pt   **4.** 5 pt = ▮ qt ▮ pt

Write each answer in simplest form.

5.   6 qt 2 pt   **6.**   5 tbsp 1 tsp   **7.**   3 qt   **8.**   5 gal 1 pt
     $+$ 2 qt 4 pt $-$ 2 tbsp 2 tsp $+$ 2 gal 3 qt $-$ 2 pt

9. Mental Math How many quarts are in $\frac{1}{2}$ gallon?

PRACTICE

For more practice, see Set 10-6 on p. 642.

Ⓐ Skills and Understanding

Copy and complete.

10. 35 pt = ▮ c   **11.** 18 qt = ▮ pt   **12.** 9 pt = ▮ qt ▮ pt   **13.** 7 gal 2 qt = ▮ qt

Write each answer in simplest form.

14.   3 gal 2 qt   **15.**   5 c 2 fl oz   **16.**   1 pt   **17.**   5 c 2 fl oz
     $+$ 3 gal 3 qt $-$ 3 c 9 fl oz $+$ 4 qt 1 pt $-$ 7 fl oz

18. Estimation Estimate the number of pints in $49\frac{3}{4}$ cups.

19. Reasoning Does it make sense to use cups to find the capacity of a fishpond? Explain.

Ⓑ Reasoning and Problem Solving

Use the information at the right for 20–22.

20. How many gallons of orange juice are needed for 60 servings?

21. Estimation About how many gallons of orange sherbet are needed for 60 servings?

22. Writing in Math This is Darla's work to find how many quarts of water are needed for 60 servings. Is she correct? Explain.

12 Servings of Punch	
Ingredients	**Quantity**
Chilled orange juice	2 pt
Cold water	1 c
Orange sherbet	1 qt

$5 c = 2 pt 1 c$
$2 pt 1 c = 1 qt 1 c$

🦉 Mixed Review and Test Prep

Take It to the NET
www **Test Prep**
www.scottforesman.com

Write the prime factorization.

23. 49   **24.** 256   **25.** 77   **26.** 105   **27.** 210

28. Which represents the volume of a rectangular prism?

   A. $\ell + w + h$ **B.** $6 \times \ell$ **C.** $\ell \times w \times h$ **D.** $\ell \times (w + h)$

Vocabulary
• milliliter
• liter

Materials
• metric measuring cup

Metric Units of Capacity

What are some metric units of capacity?

Two common metric units of capacity are the **milliliter** (mL) and **liter** (L).

A milliliter is about 20 drops of water.

A liter is a little more than a quart.

$$1 \text{ L} = 1{,}000 \text{ mL}$$
$$1 \text{ mL} = 0.001 \text{ L}$$

To change from milliliters to liters, divide by 1,000.
To change from liters to milliliters, multiply by 1,000.

Example A

450 mL =   L

Think: 1,000 mL = 1 L

$450 \div 1{,}000 = 0.450$

450 mL = 0.450 L

Example B

2.3 L =   mL

Think: 1 L = 1,000 mL

$2.3 \times 1{,}000 = 2{,}300$

2.3 L = 2,300 mL

✔ **Talk About It**

1. In Example B, why do you multiply?

2. **Number Sense** Which container, A or B, has more solution in it? Explain.

A   B

1.24 L   1,245 mL

Activity

How do you measure with metric units?

a. Select at least 3 different containers. For example, you might select a drinking glass, a pitcher, and a milk carton. Make a table like the following. Use a metric measuring cup to measure each capacity to the nearest milliliter.

Container	Estimated capacity	Actual capacity in mL

b. Name each capacity in liters.

WARM UP
Multiply or divide.
1. 32 × 100
2. 83 ÷ 10
3. 0.04 × 1,000
4. 0.04 ÷ 1,000

Copy and complete.

1. 4.2 mL = ▇ L   **2.** 1.4 L = ▇ mL   **3.** 18 mL = ▇ L   **4.** 800 L = ▇ mL

5. Mental Math There are 1,022 kiloliters (kL) of solution in a huge vat. How many liters is this? Hint: Think about the relationship between kilometers and meters.

PRACTICE

For more practice, see Set 10-7 on p. 643.

Ⓐ Skills and Understanding

Copy and complete.

6. 0.3 mL = ▇ L   **7.** 222 mL = ▇ L   **8.** 222 L = ▇ mL   **9.** 0.003 L = ▇ mL

10. 28.8 mL = ▇ L   **11.** 0.5 mL = ▇ L   **12.** 1,800 mL = ▇ L   **13.** 1.007 L = ▇ mL

14. Estimation Which capacity is most reasonable for each object?

a. cup of soup	**b.** soup spoon	**c.** thermos bottle	**d.** barrel of oil
200 mL or 2 L	10 mL or 1 L	1.5 L or 15 L	170 L or 170 mL

Ⓑ Reasoning and Problem Solving

15. If one dose of medicine is given by a teaspoon that holds 18 mL, how many full doses does a bottle holding 355 mL contain?

16. A child receives one tsp of medication (20 mL) every 4 h starting at 8:00 A.M. How many mL does the child receive from 8:00 A.M. to 8:00 P.M. including the 8:00 A.M. and 8:00 P.M. doses?

17. A cubic centimeter will hold 1 mL of water. How many milliliters will an aquarium hold if the aquarium is 40 cm long, 20 cm wide, and 30 cm high? How many liters does the aquarium hold?

18. If you were filling a 1-L container by pouring liquid from a 125-mL measuring cup, how many times would you have to fill the cup?

19. <u>Writing in Math</u> Does 1 kL = 1,000,000 mL? Explain.

Doses of medication are often given by teaspoon. There are, however, different quantities that a teaspoon will hold.

Mixed Review and Test Prep

Take It to the NET
Test Prep
www.scottforesman.com

Evaluate.

20. $(3 + 5) \times 5$ **21.** $(25 + 75) \div 2$ **22.** $3(2 + 7) - 5$ **23.** $10 \div (2 + 3)$

24. How many pints are in $2\frac{1}{2}$ gallons?

   A. 25   **B.** 20   **C.** 10   **D.** 8

Do You Know How?

Do You Understand?

Volume (10-5)

Find the volume of each rectangular solid.

1.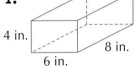

4 in.
8 in.
6 in.

2.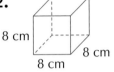

8 cm
8 cm
8 cm

3. The volume of the box at the right is 100 cm³. What is the height?

5 cm
5 cm

A Explain how you found the answer to Exercise 1.

B The area of an object measures the amount of surface it covers. What does the volume of an object measure?

C Explain how you found the height of the box in Exercise 3.

Customary Units of Capacity (10-6)

Copy and complete.

4. 6 gal = ▨ qt   **5.** 14 qt = ▨ c

6. 12 fl oz = ▨ c   **7.** 10 pt = ▨ qt

8. 3 qt = ▨ pt   **9.** 7 pt = ▨ qt ▨ pt

Add or subtract.

10. 6 qt 1 pt
       + 2 qt 1 pt

11. 8 gal
       − 3 gal 2 qt

D In Exercises 4–9, explain how you determined when to multiply and when to divide.

E Explain the difference between volume and capacity.

F What are two things you would measure in gallons?

Metric Units of Capacity (10-7)

Copy and complete.

12. 30 L = ▨ mL   **13.** 4.3 L = ▨ mL

14. 4,000 mL = ▨ L   **15.** 500 mL = ▨ L

16. 0.6 L = ▨ mL   **17.** 2,700 mL = ▨ L

G To change from millimeters to liters, do you multiply or divide by 1,000? Explain how you know.

H What are two things you would measure in milliliters?

MULTIPLE CHOICE

1. Which is the same as 3.5 gallons? (10-6)

   A. 50 c   **B.** 28 pt   **C.** 10 qt   **D.** 128 fl oz

2. Which shows the volume of the box? (10-5)

5 ft
7.5 ft
4 ft

   A. 150 ft^2 **B.** 175 ft^3 **C.** 175 ft^2 **D.** 150 ft^3

FREE RESPONSE

Copy and complete. (10-6, 10-7)

3. 5 qt =   pt   **4.** 9 gal =   qt   **5.** 7 c =   pt

6. 4 pt =   c   **7.** 1 qt =   pt   **8.** 12 fl oz =   c   fl oz

9. 23 L =   mL   **10.** 0.07 L =   mL   **11.** 250 mL =   L

Add or subtract. (10-6)

12.   6 qt 1 pt
     + 5 qt 1 pt

13.   3 pt
     − 1 pt 1c

14.   7 gal 2 qt
     − 4 gal 3 qt

Find the volume of each rectangular solid. (10-5)

15. base area: 8 m^2
    height 3.2 m

16. length 21 in.
    width: 12 in.
    height: 8 in.

17. length: 2.5 cm
    width: 1.4 cm
    height: 10 cm

Think It Through

- To change a **smaller unit to a larger unit,** I **divide.**

- To change a **larger unit to a smaller unit,** I **multiply.**

Writing in Math

18. A box is 10 cm high and has a volume of 240 cm^3. Find three possible lengths and widths of the base. Explain how you found the dimensions. (10-5)

19. Cortez is building a tree house shaped like a box. The base is a square; the height is 5 ft; and the volume is 180 ft^3. What are the dimensions of the base? Explain how you can check your answer for reasonableness. (10-5)

Vocabulary
- weight
- ounce
- pound
- ton

Customary Units of Weight

LEARN

✓ **WARM UP**
Multiply or divide.
1. 96×12 2. $96 \div 12$
3. $5\frac{1}{4} \times 16$ 4. $8 \div 16$

How can you measure how light or heavy something is?

Weight is a measure of how light or heavy something is. Commonly used units of weight in the customary system are **ounces** (oz), **pounds** (lb), and **tons** (T).

16 oz = 1 lb
2,000 pounds = 1 ton

rose

about 1 ounce

a man's shoe

about 1 lb

500 bricks

about 1 ton

Example A

lb = 1.2 T

Think: 1 T = 2,000 lb

$1.2 \times 2,000 = 2,400$

2,400 lb = 1.2 T

Example B

40 oz =   lb

Think: 16 oz = 1 lb

$40 \div 16 = 2$ R8

40 oz = 2 lb 8 oz or $2\frac{1}{2}$ lb

Example C

$$\begin{array}{r} 3 \text{ lb } 2 \text{ oz} = \\ - 1 \text{ lb } 8 \text{ oz} = \end{array} \quad \begin{array}{r} 2 \text{ lb } 18 \text{ oz} \\ - 1 \text{ lb } 8 \text{ oz} \\ \hline 1 \text{ lb } 10 \text{ oz} \end{array}$$

Example D

$$\begin{array}{r} 3 \text{ T } 1,000 \text{ lb} \\ + 5 \text{ T } 1,300 \text{ lb} \\ \hline 8 \text{ T } 2,300 \text{ lb} \\ 9 \text{ T } 300 \text{ lb} \end{array}$$

Think: 2,000 lb = 1 T
Add 1 T to 8 T.
300 lb are left.

✓ **Talk About It**

1. In Example A, why do you multiply?

2. Discuss the types of measuring instruments you know about that measure weight.

3. **Reasoning** Which unit of weight would you use to measure each weight?

   a. a truck   **b.** a large sack of dog food   **c.** a tomato

Take It to the NET
More Examples
www.scottforesman.com

Copy and complete.

1. 0.5 T = ▓ lb   **2.** 3.5 lb = ▓ oz   **3.** 5,000 lb = ▓ T   **4.** 20 oz = ▓ lb

Write each answer in simplest form.

5.   5 lb 8 oz
    + 3 lb 4 oz

6.   30 T   500 lb
    − 28 T 1,500 lb

7.   6 lb 8 oz
    + 1 lb 9 oz

8.   35 T
    − 30 T 1,675 lb

9. Estimation Estimate the number of tons in 5,980 lb.

PRACTICE

For more practice, see Set 10-8 on p. 643.

Ⓐ Skills and Understanding

Copy and complete.

10. 0.1 T = ▓ lb   **11.** 168 oz = ▓ lb   **12.** 1600 lb = ▓ T   **13.** 0.5 lb = ▓ oz

Write each answer in simplest form.

14.   8 lb 9 oz
    + 8 lb 8 oz

15.   18 T   180 lb
    − 12 T 1,180 lb

16.   12 oz
    + 6 lb 4 oz

17.   3 T 1,000 lb
    −   2,675 lb

18. Estimation Estimate the number of pounds in 66 oz.

Ⓑ Reasoning and Problem Solving

19. Sam bought 3 lb of tomatoes, $2\frac{1}{2}$ lb of green beans, and 8 oz of broccoli at the market. How much did the contents of the bag weigh after it was packed with the vegetables?

Estimation About how many birds of each type would it take to weigh 1 pound?

Bird	Weight
American Crow	15.8 oz
Mourning Dove	4.2 oz
American Robin	2.7 oz
Baltimore Oriole	1.2 oz

20. crow   **21.** dove   **22.** robin   **23.** oriole

24. <u>Writing in Math</u> Explain how would you change $1\frac{1}{4}$ lb to ounces.

🕷 Mixed Review and Test Prep

Take It to the NET
www Test Prep
www.scottforesman.com

Multiply.

25. $\frac{1}{2} \times 2\frac{1}{2}$ **26.** $\frac{1}{4} \times 3\frac{2}{3}$ **27.** $1\frac{1}{5} \times 1\frac{1}{5}$ **28.** $12 \times 3\frac{5}{6}$ **29.** $2\frac{3}{4} \times 1\frac{1}{3}$

30. How many milliliters are in 5 liters?

    A. 0.5 mL   **B.** 50 mL   **C.** 500 mL   **D.** 5,000 mL

Key Idea
Weight and mass
are different.

Vocabulary
• mass
• gram
• kilogram
• milligram

Materials
• pan balance
• unit cubes
  (grams)

Think It Through
• I can **compare the masses** to order the objects.
• I need to **choose an operation** to change units.

Metric Units of Mass

LEARN

Activity

What is mass and how is it measured?

Mass measures the quantity of matter in an object. The **milligram** (mg), **gram** (g), and **kilogram** (kg) are common metric units of mass.

When someone goes into space, weight decreases, but mass stays the same. An astronaut in space is weightless, but still has a mass of 150 kg. Use a pan balance to learn about mass.

Step 1 Choose 4 objects, such as an eraser, a pen, a small book, and a CD.

Step 2 Place one object on a pan. On the other pan, place unit cubes (grams) until the pans balance. Record the mass by adding the mass of the cubes used.

Step 3 Repeat Step 2 for the other objects.

a. Which object has the greatest mass? The least mass?

b. Order the objects from the least mass to the greatest mass.

WARM UP

Multiply or divide.

1. 100 × 4.8

2. 674.3 ÷ 10

3. 1,000 × 55.6

1,000 mg = 1 g
1,000 g = 1 kg

How can you change units of mass?

To change a measurement from one unit to another, multiply or divide by a power of 10.

Example A

3.1 kg =   g

Think: 1 kg = 1,000 g

3.1 × 1,000 = 3,100

3.1 kg = 3,100 g

Example B

456 mg =   g

Think: 1,000 mg = 1 g

456 ÷ 1,000 = 0.456

456 mg = 0.456 g

✔ **Talk About It**

1. In Example B, why do you divide?

2. Number Sense List 735 mg, 8 kg, and 345 g from least to greatest.

Take It to the NET
More Examples
www.scottforesman.com

Copy and complete.

1. 285 mg = ▮ g   **2.** 0.45 g = ▮ kg   **3.** 2.34 kg = ▮ g   **4.** 84 g = ▮ mg

5. 1.3 g = ▮ kg   **6.** 0.03 kg = ▮ g   **7.** 1,320 mg = ▮ g   **8.** 0.4 kg = ▮ mg

9. Number Sense List 0.3 mg, 320 kg, and 3,204 g from least to greatest.

PRACTICE

For more practice, see Set 10-9 on p. 643.

(A) Skills and Understanding

Copy and complete.

10. 0.008 kg = ▮ g   **11.** 1.8 kg = ▮ g   **12.** 349 g = ▮ kg   **13.** 0.001 kg = ▮ g

14. 23.8 g = ▮ kg   **15.** 200 kg = ▮ g   **16.** 188 mg = ▮ g   **17.** 1.23 kg = ▮ mg

18. Number Sense List 0.83 mg, 8,300 g, and 320.5 kg from least to greatest.

(B) Reasoning and Problem Solving

In many parts of the world, postal rates for letters are based on grams, not ounces. Use the table of rates at the right for 19–20.

19. Reasoning Using the pattern in the table, what would it cost to mail letters with masses of 140 g, 160 g, and 180 g?

2002 Postal Rates for Letters Mailed in Bermuda		
More than	No more than	Cost
0 g	20 g	$0.35
20 g	40 g	$0.45
40 g	60 g	$0.55
60 g	80 g	$0.65
80 g	100 g	$0.75

20. Which costs more, mailing one letter with a mass of 100 g or mailing two letters each with a mass of 50 g? Explain.

21. Matt wants to carpet an area for his weightlifting equipment. The area is 4 ft by $6\frac{1}{2}$ ft. How much carpeting must he purchase?

22. <u>Writing in Math</u> Would it be better to express the mass of a person in milligrams, grams, or kilograms? Explain.

Mixed Review and Test Prep

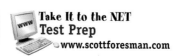

Take It to the NET
Test Prep
www.scottforesman.com

To the nearest tenth, find the circumference of each circle. Use 3.14 for π.

23. radius of 15 in.

24. diameter of 12 in.

25. Which correctly represents 2.3 m in centimeters?

   A. 0.023 cm   **C.** 230 cm

   B. 0.23 cm   **D.** 2300 cm

26. Which correctly represents 2.5 lb in ounces?

   A. 0.15625 oz   **C.** 40 oz

   B. 5.25 ft   **D.** 80 oz

All text pages available online and on CD-ROM.

Problem-Solving Skill

Reading Helps!

Making judgments

can help you with...

identifying whether you need an exact answer or estimate.

Key Idea
Sometimes you need an exact answer to solve a problem, and sometimes an estimate is enough.

Exact Answer or Estimate

LEARN

When do you need to measure and when is an estimate enough?

The real-world situation tells whether you need to measure or if you can estimate to solve a problem. If an estimate is all that is needed, you can often estimate using mental math.

Example A

Ms. Lynch wants to find the largest mirror that will fit on this door. The mirror is to be the same distance from each edge of the door and must fit inside the handle.

36 in.

76 in.

4 in.

Example B

Greg was told certain shrubs should be planted more than two feet apart. He wants to plant four shrubs along this fence.

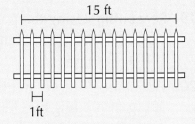

15 ft

1 ft

Read and Understand

What do you know?	The mirror must fit inside the handle and be the same distance from each edge.	Four shrubs need to be planted. They need to be planted more than 2 feet apart.
What are you trying to find?	The dimensions of the largest mirror that will fit on the door	Where the shrubs should be planted so they are at least 2 feet apart

✔ Talk About It

1. Find the greatest dimensions for the mirror. Check to see if your answer is reasonable. Why is an exact answer needed?

2. Show one way to locate the four shrubs. Check to see if your answer is reasonable. Why can you estimate?

3. **Reasoning** What helps you decide whether you need an exact answer or an estimate?

Tell whether an exact answer or an estimate is needed. Then solve the problem and check to see if your answer is reasonable.

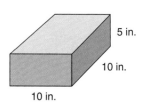

1. Angie has the box shown at the right that she wants to wrap. She plans to use plain brown paper that comes in rolls 20 in. wide by 3 yards long. Is one roll enough?

5 in.
10 in.
10 in.

PRACTICE   *For more practice, see Set 10-10 on p. 643.*

Tell whether an exact answer or an estimate is needed. Then solve each problem and check to see if your answer is reasonable.

2. Potting soil is sold by the cubic foot. Max wants to fill a 2 ft by 3 ft by 2 ft raised bed with soil. How much potting soil does he need to buy?

3. **Reasoning** Andy counts the number of bricks from the ground to the roof of the town hall in his town. He knows one brick is 3 in. high and the bricks start 15 inches up from the ground. About how tall is the building? Explain how you found your answer.

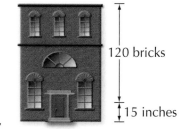

120 bricks

15 inches

4. In the picture at the right, if the bricks started at the ground, how many more rows of bricks would be needed?

5. A fenced-in area for Dr. Steele's dog Millie will be 3 feet wide and 18 feet long. How much fencing will he need to fence the area for his dog?

6. Mae's mother plans to make a flower garden using the plans shown at the right. If she wants to use sod for the grassy area, how many square feet of sod must she purchase?

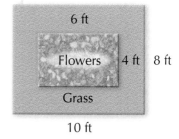

6 ft
Flowers   4 ft   8 ft
Grass
10 ft

7. Mae's mother wants to put lighting around the flower area of the garden. She wants to place the lights so that they are at least 2 ft apart. How many lights are needed?

8. Gina's bedroom is 10 ft wide and 12 ft long. The ceiling is 8 ft high. She wants to paint the walls of her bedroom and the ceiling a pale yellow. To do that, she will need two coats of paint.

   a. If a gallon of paint covers 400–450 sq. ft, will 1 gallon of paint be enough? If not, how much should she buy?

   b. The paint costs $12.99 a gallon. How much will the paint for Gina's room cost?

Writing in Math Tell the appropriate unit of measure for each blank. Explain how you made your decision.

9. The notebook is 12 ___ long.

10. The wheelbarrow weighs 12 ___.

11. It took Tony 12 ___ to tie his shoes.

12. The bottle holds 12 ___ of juice.

Problem-Solving Applications

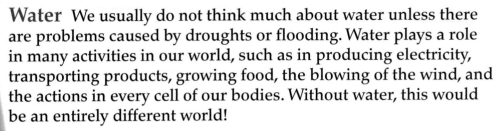

Water We usually do not think much about water unless there are problems caused by droughts or flooding. Water plays a role in many activities in our world, such as in producing electricity, transporting products, growing food, the blowing of the wind, and the actions in every cell of our bodies. Without water, this would be an entirely different world!

Trivia Each second, the Amazon River releases about 6 million cubic feet of water into the Atlantic Ocean. Within only 2 hours, it could supply enough water for everyone in the world to take a bath.

North Sea

❶ The Pacific Ocean contains more water than all of the world's other seas and oceans put together. A cubic tank big enough to hold it would have sides about 551 miles long. What is the volume of the Pacific Ocean? Round your answer to the nearest ten million.

Using Key Facts

❷ Which body of water is closest to twice the depth of the Gulf of Mexico? Half the depth of the Atlantic Ocean?

Gulf of Mexico

South China Sea

Caribbean Sea

Indian Ocean

Atlantic Ocean

Pacific Ocean

Empire State Building

Key Facts
Water Depths

Area	Greatest Depth
• North Sea	660 m
• Gulf of Mexico	3,871m
• South China Sea	5,016 m
• Caribbean Sea	7,535 m
• Indian Ocean	7,725 m
• Atlantic Ocean	8,648 m
• Pacific Ocean	11,033 m

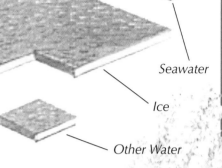

Seawater

Ice

Other Water

3 **Decision Making** Seawater makes up over $\frac{97}{100}$ of all the water on Earth. Ice makes up over $\frac{2}{100}$ of the world's water. All other water accounts for less than $\frac{1}{100}$ of the total supply. This data could be shown with a table or a graph. Which way would be best? Explain your choice. Show the data with the method you chose.

4 A gallon of water weighs about 133 ounces. How many pounds does a gallon of water weigh? Round your answer to the nearest thousandth. Write the word name for this weight.

5 The highest recorded wave occurred when a landslide along a bay in Alaska pushed water 518 meters up the opposite shore. The highest wind-generated wave was about $\frac{1}{15}$ this height. How tall was this wind-generated wave? Round your answer to the nearest tenth.

6 **Writing in Math** Write your own word problem using any of the information given on these pages. Solve it and write the answer in a complete sentence.

Good News/Bad News The Three Gorges Dam is under construction on the Yangtze River in China. Its huge reservoir may be about 400 miles long and store billions of cubic yards of water. This dam will protect millions of acres of land from floods and generate huge amounts of electricity. However, the reservoir will submerge hundreds of towns, villages, and factories, and dozens of archaeological sites.

Do You Know How?

Do You Understand?

Customary Units of Weight (10-8)

Copy and complete.

1. 48 oz = ▦ lb   **2.** 3,000 lb = ▦ T

3. 9 lb = ▦ oz   **4.** 3 T = ▦ lb

5. 46 oz = ▦ lb ▦ oz

6. 9,000 lb = ▦ T ▦ lb

Add or subtract.

7.   5 lb 6 oz   **8.**   2 T
   + 3 lb 8 oz   − 1 T 400 lb

Ⓐ What rule did you use to change from pounds to ounces in Exercise 3?

Ⓑ Name two things you would measure in tons.

Ⓒ Explain how you could estimate Exercise 6 to test your answer for reasonableness.

Metric Units of Mass (10-9)

Copy and complete.

9. 12 kg = ▦ g

10. 8,500 g = ▦ kg

11. 3.4 kg = ▦ g

12. 0.37 kg = ▦ g

13. 357 g = ▦ kg

14. 8 g = ▦ kg

15. 231 mg = ▦ g

16. 1.5 kg = ▦ mg

Ⓓ When you move a decimal point right 3 places, are you multiplying or dividing? By what power of 10?

Ⓔ Are weight and mass the same? Give an example to support your answer.

Problem-Solving Skill: Exact Answer or Estimate (10-10)

17. Mr. Thillens has a 50-foot roll of fencing. Does he have enough to enclose a rectangular pen 19 feet long and 11 feet wide?

18. Betsy has 12 feet of ribbon. How much ribbon will she have left after cutting fifteen 9-inch lengths of ribbon?

Ⓕ Did you estimate or find an exact answer for Exercise 17? Explain why.

Ⓖ Did you estimate or find an exact answer for Exercise 18? Explain why.

MULTIPLE CHOICE

1. Which is the same as 0.8 kg? (10-9)

　A. 800 g　　　**B.** 80 g　　　**C.** 0.008 g　　　**D.** 0.08 g

2. Which is the same as 44 oz? (10-8)

　A. 3 lb　　　**B.** 2 lb 14 oz　　　**C.** 2 lb 12 oz　　　**D.** 2 lb 10 oz

FREE RESPONSE

Copy and complete. (10-8, 10-9)

3. 90 g = ▧ kg　　　**4.** 0.42 kg = ▧ g　　　**5.** 2,500 g = ▧ kg

6. 3 lb = ▧ oz　　　**7.** 40 oz = ▧ lb　　　**8.** 1,000 lb = ▧ T

9. 3 T = ▧ lb　　　**10.** 150 oz = ▧ lb ▧ oz　　　**11.** 2,345 lb = ▧ T ▧ lb

A large packing box and a smaller box are shown below. (10-10)

1 ft 6 in.　8 in.　10 in.　30 in.　2 ft 8 in.　1 ft

Test Talk

Think It Through
I should **decide if an exact answer or an estimate is needed.**

12. Give the dimensions of the large packing box in inches.

13. Will two of the smaller boxes fit in the large box?

Writing in Math

School Supplies

Ballpoint Pens	$0.59 each
Binders	$2.99 each
Colored Pencils	$1.98 per box
Folders	$0.75 each
Notebook Paper	$0.99 per spiral
Pencils	$0.29 each

Scott wants to buy one box of colored pencils, two folders, and one spiral of notebook paper. He has $5.00 to spend. (10-10, 10-11)

14. Using the above example, write a question in which you can estimate to find the answer.

15. Using the above example, write a question in which you must find an exact answer.

Test-Taking Strategies

Understand the question.

Get information for the answer.

Plan how to find the answer.

Make smart choices.

Use writing in math.

Improve written answers.

Make Smart Choices

To answer a multiple-choice test question, you need to choose an answer from answer choices. The steps below will help you make a smart choice.

1. Amos has a 5-quart bucket that he uses to fill a 30-gallon fish tank. How many buckets of water does it take to fill the tank?

   A. 6 buckets

   B. 20 buckets

   C. 24 buckets

   D. 150 buckets

Understand the question.

I need to find the number of buckets of water it takes to fill a fish tank.

Get information for the answer.

*The numbers I need are given in the **text**.*

Plan how to find the answer.

*This looks like a **multiple-step** problem. First, I'll convert the capacity of the fish tank to quarts. There are 4 quarts in a gallon. $30 \times 4 = 120$, so **30 gallons = 120 quarts**. Now I should consider each answer choice.*

Make Smart Choices.

- Eliminate wrong answers.

- Check answers for reasonableness; estimate.

- Try working backward from the answer.

  I can use multiplication to see which answer choice is the same as 120 quarts.

  Start with answer choice A. 6 buckets = 6×5 quarts = 30 quarts. 30 quarts $\neq$ 120 quarts, so answer choice A is wrong.

  Try answer choice B. 20 buckets = 20×5 quarts = 100 quarts. 100 quarts $\neq$ 120 quarts, so answer choice B is wrong.

  Try answer choice C. 24 buckets = 24×5 quarts = 120 quarts. That works.

  The correct answer is C, 24 buckets.

2. Which of these measurements best describes the weight of a camera?

A. 12 pounds

B. 1.2 tons

C. 12 ounces

D. 120 pounds

Think It Through

I need to choose the measurement that best describes the weight of a camera. My cat weighs about 15 pounds, so answer choice A, 12 pounds, is too heavy and I should eliminate it. Answer choices B and D are even heavier, so I should eliminate them. That leaves answer choice C, which is reasonable because 12 ounces is a little less than a pound, and a jogging shoe weighs about a pound. Answer choice C, 12 ounces, is the best choice.

Now it's your turn.

For each problem, give the answer and explain how you made your choice.

3. How many 20-centimeter pieces of ribbon can be cut from this roll?

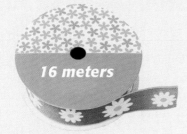

16 meters

A. 320 pieces

B. 100 pieces

C. 80 pieces

D. 8 pieces

4. Which of these measurements best describes the height of a stool?

A. 26 inches

B. 2.6 miles

C. 26 feet

D. 26 yards

Self Check

Surface contains the word "face." The flat polygon-shaped surfaces of a polyhedron are called **faces.** (p. 594)

Identify solid figures. (Lesson 10-1)

A **polyhedron** is a solid figure with all flat surfaces.

Solid figures that have curved surfaces are not polyhedra.

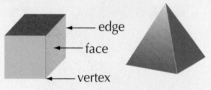

| Prism | Pyramid | Cylinder | Cone | Sphere |

1. What type of prism is shown at the right?

Squares are flat. We use **square units** to measure the area of a flat figure.

A cube is solid. We use **cubic units** to measure the volume of a solid figure. (p. 610)

Self Check

The **surface area** of a polyhedron is the sum of the areas of all its faces. (p. 602)

Find surface area and volume. (Lessons 10-2, 10-3, 10-5)

Find the surface area and volume of this rectangular prism.

3 m

4 m

5 m

A **net** helps you visualize all the faces.

Surface area = 2(5 × 4) +

2(5 × 3) +

2(4 × 3) =

94 m²

5 m

4 m

4 m

top

4 m

3 m   left   front   right

bottom   4 m

back   3 m

Use a formula to find **volume.**

$V = (\ell \times w) \times h$

$= (5 \times 4) \times 3$

$= 60$ m³   Remember to use **cubic units.**

2. Find the surface area and volume of a rectangular prism 6 ft by 2 ft by 7 ft.

Self Check

Compute with measures. (Lessons 10-6, 10-7, 10-8, 10-9)

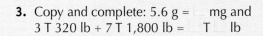

To change to a smaller unit, multiply. To change to a larger unit, divide.	Add or subtract.

273 mL = ___ L

273 ÷ 1,000 = 0.273

273 mL = 0.273 L

$$7 \text{ gal } 1 \text{ qt} = \quad 6 \text{ gal } 5 \text{ qt}$$
$$- 2 \text{ gal } 2 \text{ qt} = -2 \text{ gal } 2 \text{ qt}$$
$$\overline{\quad\quad\quad\quad\quad 4 \text{ gal } 3 \text{ qt}}$$

$$7 \text{ lb } 12 \text{ oz}$$
$$+ 3 \text{ lb } 9 \text{ oz}$$
$$\overline{10 \text{ lb } 21 \text{ oz} = 11 \text{ lb } 5 \text{ oz}}$$

Customary Units of Capacity
1 tbsp = 3 tsp 1 fl oz = 2 tbsp
1 c = 8 fl oz   1 pt = 2 c
1 qt = 2 pt   1 gal = 4 qt

Customary Units of Weight
1 lb = 16 oz
1 T = 2,000 lb

Metric Units of Capacity
1 L = 1,000 mL

Metric Units of Mass
1 g = 1,000 mg
1 kg = 1,000 g

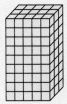

3. Copy and complete: 5.6 g = ___ mg and
3 T 320 lb + 7 T 1,800 lb = ___ T ___ lb

Self Check

Decide whether to estimate or give an exact answer. Use objects to solve problems. (Lessons 10-4, 10-10)

Sometimes you only to need find an estimate.	Acting out a problem with objects can help you solve it.

A pit shaped like a rectangular prism measures 2.8 yd by 3.1 yd by 3.9 yd. Are 24 cubic yards of sand enough to fill the pit?

Estimate by rounding. $3 \times 3 \times 4 = 36$

No, there is not enough sand.

Suppose each cube is a room of a building. How many rooms have 2 outside walls?

Use cubes. Count the cubes along the vertical edges.

36 rooms have 2 outside walls.

4. Are 6 cartons of juice, 2.2 quarts each, enough to fill a 3-gallon punchbowl?

Answers: 1. Triangular prism 2. 136 ft²; 84 ft³ 3. 5,600; 11 T 120 lb 4. Yes

MULTIPLE CHOICE

Choose the correct letter for each answer.

1. Which solid figure does this object resemble?

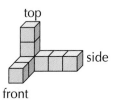

A. prism

B. cylinder

C. pyramid

D. cone

2.   2 gal 1 qt
    + 1 gal 3 qt

A. 3 gal 3 qt   **C.** 5 gal

B. 4 gal   **D.** 5 gal 1 qt

3. Which of the following is the top view of this solid made from unit cubes?

A.

B.

C.

D.

4. How do you find the surface area of a rectangular prism?

A. Find the product of its length, width, and height.

B. Find the sum of the areas of all its faces.

C. Multiply its base area by its height.

D. Multiply the areas of all its faces by 2.

5. A restaurant just received a shipment of 28 pints of ice cream. Each sundae gets 1 cup of ice cream. How many sundaes can be made with the ice cream shipment?

A. 7 sundaes   **C.** 56 sundaes

B. 14 sundaes   **D.** 112 sundaes

6. Find the surface area of this rectangular prism.

A. 29.5 ft²

B. 30 ft²

C. 59 ft²

D. 72 ft²

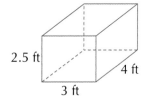

7. A box is filled with 3 layers of cubes. Each layer has 7 rows, and each row has 12 cubes. How many cubes are in the box?

A. 21 cubes   **C.** 84 cubes

B. 36 cubes   **D.** 252 cubes

8. Find the volume of this rectangular prism.

A. 21.2 cm³

B. 324 cm²

C. 291.6 cm³

D. 324 cm³

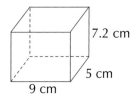

9. Which of the following statements is **not** true of a rectangular prism?

A. It has 6 faces that are rectangles.

B. It has 8 vertices.

C. It has 6 edges.

D. It has congruent parallel bases.

10. Which is a net for a triangular prism?

A.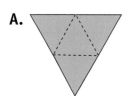

C.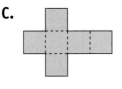

B.

D.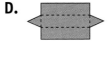

11. How many grams are in 0.5 kilogram?

A. 500 g

C. 500,000 g

B. 5,000 g

D. 1,000,000 g

12. Which of the following measures equals 4.2L?

A. 42 mL

B. 420 mL

C. 4,200 mL

D. 42,000 mL

FREE RESPONSE

Find the surface area and volume of each rectangular prism.

13.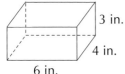
3 in.
4 in.
6 in.

14.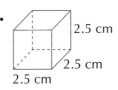
2.5 cm
2.5 cm
2.5 cm

Find each missing number.

15. 2.6 T = ▨ lb

16. 29 kg = ▨ g

17. 750 mL = ▨ L

18. 18 qt = ▨ pt

19. 88 oz = ▨ lb

20. 4 fl oz = ▨ tbsp

Write each answer in simplest form.

21.
  3 T 1,250 lb
+   1,019 lb

22.
  7 pt 1 c
+ 2 pt 1 c

23.
  12 gal
− 5 gal 3 qt

24.
  4 lb 12 oz
− 2 lb 14 oz

25. Tell whether an exact answer or an estimate is needed for the following problem. Then solve the problem.

Each bag contains 6,000 cubic inches of potting soil. A flower box is 36 inches long, 9 inches wide, and 10 inches tall. Is one bag of soil enough to fill the flower box?

Writing in Math

26. Explain how you could use objects to solve this problem.

Brenda wants to extend this pattern to form a larger pattern of bricks for her patio. She wants the middle row of the larger pattern to have 4 bricks. How many bricks will she need to make her pattern?

Middle row

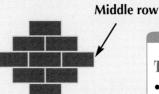

Think It Through
- I will **write my steps in order.**
- I will make my explanation **brief, but complete.**

27. A kitten has a mass of 2,500 grams. Explain how to change this measurement to kilograms.

28. How is the surface area of a rectangular prism different from its volume?

Number and Operation

MULTIPLE CHOICE

1. Mr. Lewis drove 283.8 miles in 6 hours. What was his average speed?

   A. 47.3 mph   **C.** 277.8 mph

   B. 48.8 mph   **D.** 298.8 mph

2. Which of the following fractions is NOT equivalent to $\frac{4}{10}$?

   A. $\frac{2}{5}$ **B.** $\frac{12}{30}$ **C.** $\frac{1}{2}$ **D.** $\frac{8}{20}$

3. What is the greatest common factor (GCF) of 6, 16, and 20?

   A. 1   **B.** 2   **C.** 4   **D.** 6

FREE RESPONSE

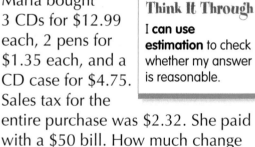

Think It Through

I **can use estimation** to check whether my answer is reasonable.

4. Maria bought 3 CDs for $12.99 each, 2 pens for $1.35 each, and a CD case for $4.75. Sales tax for the entire purchase was $2.32. She paid with a $50 bill. How much change did she get back?

5. List the prime numbers less than 20.

Writing in Math

6. Explain whether or not you have enough information to solve this problem. Tell any information that is needed or that is missing. Solve if you have enough information.

   Jamal reads every night before he goes to sleep. He read for 35 minutes on Thursday. How many minutes did Jamal read during the entire week?

Geometry and Measurement

MULTIPLE CHOICE

7. What is the surface area of this rectangular prism?

   A. 10 in^2

   B. 15 in^2

   C. 36 in^2

   D. 66 in^2

   4 in.

   3 in.

   3 in.

8. The school assembly started at 11:45 A.M. and ended at 1:20 P.M. How long did the assembly last?

   A. 1 h 35 min   **C.** 2 h 35 min

   B. 2 h 25 min   **D.** 10 hr 25 min

9. Which solid figure has a base that is a polygon and faces that are all triangles that meet at a common point?

   A. prism   **C.** cone

   B. cylinder   **D.** pyramid

FREE RESPONSE

10. A box of cereal is 14 inches tall, 7 inches long, and 2.5 inches wide. How many cubic inches of cereal can the box hold?

11. How many faces, edges, and vertices does a square pyramid have?

Writing in Math

12. Group the words below into two categories. Explain why you grouped them as you did.

cup	fluid ounce	ton
milligram	pound	liter
teaspoon	quart	gram
kilogram	milliliter	gallon

Data Analysis and Probability

MULTIPLE CHOICE

13. Donna's sock drawer contains 6 black socks, 8 blue socks, and 10 white socks. If she pulls out a sock at random, what is the probability that the sock will be white?

A. $\frac{1}{3}$

C. $\frac{1}{2}$

B. $\frac{5}{12}$

D. $\frac{2}{3}$

14. A data measure for the data set shown below is 13. Which measure is it?

13, 19, 12, 9, 12, 10, 16

A. range

C. mean

B. mode

D. median

FREE RESPONSE

Use the chart for Problems 15–17.

LARGEST U.S. STATES, BY AREA		
State	Surface Area (square miles)	
	Land	Water
Alaska	571,951	91,316
California	155,959	7,736
Montana	145,552	1,490
Texas	261,797	6,784

15. What is the total surface area of Texas?

16. Write the states in order from least total surface area to greatest total surface area.

Writing in Math

17. Which state's land area is about 6 times its water area? Explain your answer.

Algebra

MULTIPLE CHOICE

18. Which equation shows the relationship between a and b?

b	7	9	11	13
a	14	18	22	26

A. $b = a + 7$

C. $a = 14 - b$

B. $a = 2 \times b$

D. $b = a \times 2$

19. Which number goes in the ___ to complete the pattern?

$\frac{1}{4}, \frac{1}{2},$ ___ $, 1, 1\frac{1}{4}, 1\frac{1}{2}, \ldots$

A. $\frac{1}{8}$

C. $\frac{2}{4}$

B. $\frac{1}{3}$

D. $\frac{3}{4}$

20. Solve for the variable. $24 = x + 12$

A. $x = 1$

C. $x = 12$

B. $x = 2$

D. $x = 36$

FREE RESPONSE

21. The perimeter of a rectangle is 24 feet. Its length is twice its width. Explain how you could find the length and width, then solve.

Writing in Math

22. Explain how to evaluate the expression $\frac{7}{8} \times m$ for $m = \frac{1}{2}$. Evaluate the expression for the given value of the variable.

Set 10-1 (pages 594–597)

What solid figure does this object resemble?

Classify solid figures by their shape and their faces, edges, and vertices.

Surfaces: All polygons
So, it is a polyhedron.

Faces: Except for the base, all triangles with a common point
So, it is a pyramid.

Bases: 1 square base
So, it is a square pyramid.

Remember that a prism has 2 congruent parallel bases, and a pyramid only has 1 base.

1.

2.

3. Name the vertices, edges, and faces of this solid figure.

Set 10-2 (pages 598–601)

Draw front, side, and top views of this solid made from unit cubes.

Remember to consider blocks hidden from your view in your drawings.

1.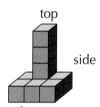

2.

3. What solid figure is represented by this net?

Set 10-3 (pages 602–603)

Find the surface area of this rectangular prism.

Use a formula.
$SA = 2\ell w + 2wh + 2\ell h$

SA = surface area
ℓ = length
w = width
h = height

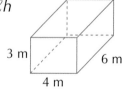

$SA = 2\ell w + 2wh + 2\ell h$
$SA = 2(4 \times 6) + 2(6 \times 3) + 2(4 \times 3)$
$SA = 48 + 36 + 24 = 108 \text{ m}^2$

Remember that surface area is always measured in square units, such as m² or in².

1.

2.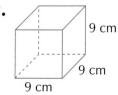

3. Each edge of a cube is 3 feet long. What is the surface area of the cube?

When you use objects to solve problems, follow these steps.

Step 1: Choose objects.

Step 2: Show the known information.

Step 3: Use the objects to solve the problem.

Remember to state clearly at the beginning what your objects represent in the problem.

1. Tom used bricks to build steps. How many bricks will he use to build 10 steps?

2 steps   3 steps

2. A carton is filled with boxes of rice. There are 3 layers of boxes. Each layer has 6 rows with 10 boxes in each. If 7 boxes of rice are removed, how many boxes are left in the carton?

Find the volume of this rectangular prism.

Use a formula.

$V = \ell \times w \times h$

V = volume
ℓ = length
w = width
h = height

8 ft
10 ft
7 ft

$V = \ell \times w \times h$
$V = 7 \times 10 \times 8 = 560 \text{ ft}^3$

Remember that volume is always measured in cubic units, such as cm^3 or yd^3.

1.

3 cm

4.5 cm

2 cm

2.

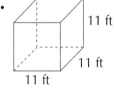

11 ft

11 ft

11 ft

3. A rectangular prism has a base area of 32 square inches. If the prism is 9 inches tall, what is its volume?

Find 9 gal 3 qt + 4 gal 2 qt.

```
  9 gal 3 qt
+ 4 gal 2 qt
 13 gal 5 qt
```

Think: 5 qt > 1 gal
Simplify your sum.
4 qt = 1 gal
5 ÷ 4 = 1 R1

13 gal 5 qt = 13 gal + 1 gal + 1 qt

13 gal 5 qt = 14 gal 1 qt

Remember to multiply to change from larger units to smaller units, and divide to change from smaller units to larger units.

1. 80 pt = ▮ qt

2. 3 gal = ▮ qt

3. 6 c = ▮ fl oz

4. 7 pt = ▮ qt ▮ pt

5.
```
  2 gal 2 qt
+ 1 gal 3 qt
```

6.
```
  4 c 3 fl oz
- 2 c 7 fl oz
```

Set 10-7 (pages 616–617)

Complete 275 mL = ▨ L.

Think: 1,000 mL = 1 L

$275 \div 1,000 = 0.275$

275 mL = 0.275 L

Remember to pay attention to decimal points when you change between units.

1. 0.3 mL = ▨ L
2. 16 L = ▨ mL
3. 2.9 L = ▨ mL
4. 148 mL = ▨ L
5. How many milliliters are in 0.25L?

Set 10-8 (pages 620–621)

Find 8 lb 3 oz − 5 lb 8 oz.

Think: 1 lb = 16 oz. So, 8 lb = 7 lb 16 oz.

$$\begin{array}{rcr} 8\text{ lb }3\text{ oz} &=& 7\text{ lb }19\text{ oz} \\ -\ 5\text{ lb }8\text{ oz} &=& -\ 5\text{ lb }\ \ 8\text{ oz} \\ \hline && 2\text{ lb }11\text{ oz} \end{array}$$

Remember that you may have to regroup units to subtract or to write your sum in simplest form.

1. 240 oz = ▨ lb
2. 0.8 T = ▨ lb
3. 3,000 lb = ▨ T
4. 2.5 lb = ▨ oz

5.
$$\begin{array}{r} 5\text{ lb }\ 7\text{ oz} \\ +\ 4\text{ lb }12\text{ oz} \end{array}$$

6.
$$\begin{array}{r} 6\text{ T }250\text{ lb} \\ -\ 1\text{ T }500\text{ lb} \end{array}$$

Set 10-9 (pages 622–623)

Complete 4.8 kg = ▨ g.

Think: 1 kg = 1,000 g

$4.8 \times 1,000 = 4,800$
4.8 kg = 4,800 g

Remember that you sometimes have to multiply or divide more than once to change between units.

1. 2.1 kg = ▨ g
2. 575 g = ▨ kg
3. 1,400 mg = ▨ g
4. 0.9 kg = ▨ mg
5. List 3,200 g, 0.32 mg, and 320 kg in order from least to greatest.

Set 10-10 (pages 624–625)

Tell whether an exact answer or an estimate is needed. Then solve the problem and check to see if your answer is reasonable.

Ken's box is 3.2 ft long on each edge. He wants to use the box to hold 20 cubes. Each cube is 1 ft long on each edge. Is his box large enough to hold all the cubes?

Think: I only need to know if the box is large enough. So, I only need an estimate.

Estimate the volume: $3 \times 3 \times 3 = 27$ ft^3.
27 ft^3 > 20 ft^3
So, the box is large enough.

Remember that words such as *at least,* *enough,* and *about* usually mean that you only need an estimate to solve.

1. One quart of paint will cover about 80 ft^2. Is one quart enough to paint a cube that is 5 ft long on each edge? If not, how much paint do you need?

2. If 1 quart of paint costs $8.99, how much will it cost to buy the paint needed to paint the cube described in Problem 1?

Chapter 10
More Practice

Take It to the NET
More Practice
www.scottforesman.com

Set 10-1 (pages 594–597)

What solid figure does each object resemble?

1.

2.

3.

4.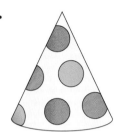

5. Name the vertices, edges, and faces of the solid figure at right. Name the figure.

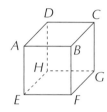

Set 10-2 (pages 598–601)

What solid does each net represent?

1.

2.

3.

Draw front, side, and top views of each stack of unit blocks.

4.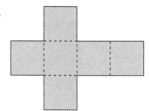

5.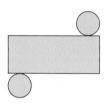

6.

7. How many cubes in the solid at the right are not visible to the viewer from the top?

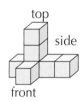

Set 10-3 (pages 602–603)

Find the surface area of each rectangular prism.

1.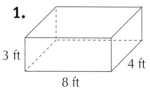
3 ft 4 ft 8 ft

2.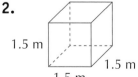
1.5 m 1.5 m 1.5 m

3.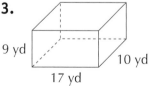
9 yd 10 yd 17 yd

4.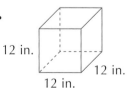
12 in. 12 in. 12 in.

5. Two 3-inch cubes were covered with a fuzzy material to make toys. How much material was needed to cover both of the cubes?

Set 10-4 (pages 606–607)

Use objects to solve. Write your answer in a complete sentence.

1. Five friends are lining up for a picture. Use the clues to determine in what order the five people are standing.

> There are 3 people between Mark and Sandy.
> Olga is second in line.
> Katherine is in the middle of the line.
> Brian and Sandy are next to each other.

2. A grocer has 5 crates of cereal boxes. Each crate has 3 layers, and each layer has 30 boxes of cereal. How many boxes of cereal are there?

Set 10-5 (pages 610–613)

Use unit cubes, make a drawing, or use the formula to find the volume of each rectangular prism.

1. base area: 50 cm^2
height: 7 cm

2. base area: 64 ft^2
height: 8 ft

3. base area: 100 in^2
height: 4 in

4.

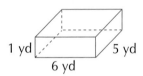

1 yd, 5 yd, 6 yd

5.

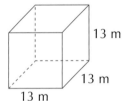

13 m, 13 m, 13 m

6.

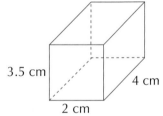

3.5 cm, 2 cm, 4 cm

7. The volume of a rectangular prism is 252 cm^3. The prism is 9 cm long and 7 cm wide. How tall is the prism? Explain how you found your answer.

Set 10-6 (pages 614–615)

Copy and complete.

1. 24 pt = ▒ c

2. 15 tsp = ▒ tbsp

3. ▒ qt = 10 gal

4. 3 qt 1 pt = ▒ pt

5. 40 fl oz = ▒ c

6. ▒ gal = 8 qt

7. 48 tbsp = ▒ fl oz

8. ▒ qt = 8 gal 3 qt

Write each answer in simplest form.

9. 2 gal 2 qt
+ 1 gal 3 qt

10. 3 gal 1 qt
− 1 gal 2 qt

11. 5 tbsp 2 tsp
+ _____ 8 tsp

12. 20 c 4 fl oz
− 9 c 6 fl oz

13. Arlene needs to fill her 10-gallon fish tank with water. She only has a measuring cup that holds 2 cups of water. How many times will she have to fill the measuring cup to fill the fish tank?

Take It to the NET
www More Practice
www.scottforesman.com

Set 10-7 (pages 616–617)

Copy and complete.

1. 0.5 mL = ▨ L   **2.** 115 mL = ▨ L   **3.** 115 L = ▨ mL   **4.** 0.08 L = ▨ mL

5. 23.5 mL = ▨ L   **6.** 0.1 mL = ▨ L   **7.** 2.004 L = ▨ mL   **8.** 6.9 mL = ▨ L

9. A lab beaker holds 100 milliliters. How many times would you have to fill the beaker to fill a container with a capacity of 0.5 liter?

Set 10-8 (pages 620–621)

Copy and complete.

1. 0.2 T = ▨ lb   **2.** 112 oz = ▨ lb   **3.** 3,800 lb = ▨ T   **4.** 0.4 lb = ▨ oz

Write each answer in simplest form.

5.   6 lb 9 oz
  + 6 lb 9 oz

6.   8 T
  − 5 T 200 lb

7.   15 oz
  + 2 lb 6 oz

8.   3 T 1,000 lb
  −   4,125 lb

9. A truck can safely carry 3 tons. The truck is loaded with 32 televisions. Each television weighs 175 pounds. Is it safe to drive the truck? Explain.

Set 10-9 (pages 622–623)

Copy and complete.

1. 0.007 kg = ▨ g   **2.** 1.3 kg = ▨ g   **3.** 479 g = ▨ kg   **4.** 0.02 kg = ▨ g

5. 51.9 g = ▨ kg   **6.** 217 mg = ▨ g   **7.** 0.5 g = ▨ mg   **8.** 1.64 kg = ▨ mg

9. A scientist measures the mass of three objects. Object A has a mass of 750 mg, object B has a mass of 7,500 g, and object C has a mass of 0.75 kg. List the objects in order from least to greatest mass.

Set 10-10 (pages 624–525)

Tell whether an exact answer or an estimate is needed. Then solve the problem and check to see whether your answer is reasonable.

1. Tyler built a sandbox that is 12 feet long, 8 feet wide, and 1 foot tall. He bought 100 cubic feet of sand at the hardware store. Does he have enough sand to fill the box?

2. Liza wants to make a bookshelf out of milk crates. Each crate costs $2.50. She plans to have 7 rows of crates in a stack, with 5 crates in each row. How much money will she spend in all for the bookshelf?

DIAGNOSING READINESS

A Vocabulary
(pages 400–401, 410–411)

Choose the best term from the box.

1. Fractions that name the same part of a whole are __?__.

2. Fractions that have numerators that are greater than or equal to the denominator are __?__.

3. Numbers that have a whole number and a fraction are called __?__.

Vocabulary
- **equivalent fractions** *(p. 410)*
- **mixed numbers** *(p. 400)*
- **improper fractions** *(p. 400)*

B Equivalent Fractions
(pages 410–411)

Give the missing numerator or denominator.

4. $\dfrac{1}{3} = \dfrac{3}{\blacksquare}$

5. $\dfrac{3}{8} = \dfrac{6}{\blacksquare}$

6. $\dfrac{2}{3} = \dfrac{\blacksquare}{15}$

7. $\dfrac{8}{12} = \dfrac{2}{\blacksquare}$

8. $\dfrac{6}{9} = \dfrac{\blacksquare}{3}$

9. $\dfrac{20}{40} = \dfrac{\blacksquare}{2}$

10. $\dfrac{5}{8} = \dfrac{\blacksquare}{16}$

11. $\dfrac{9}{12} = \dfrac{3}{\blacksquare}$

12. $\dfrac{4}{6} = \dfrac{\blacksquare}{24}$

13. Write five fractions equivalent to $\dfrac{2}{3}$.

Do You Know...

How many calories are in a tub of theater popcorn?

You will find out in Lesson 11-11.

MIRIAM POLUNIN
Healing
FOODS
A Practical Guide to Key Foods for Good Health

C Finding Patterns
(pages 106–107)

Copy and complete each table.
Then write a rule.

14.

Number of cartons	1	2	■	■	■
Number of eggs	12	24	36	■	■

15.

Number of pencils	2	4	6	■	■
Cost in dollars	0.50	1.00	■	2.00	■

D Fractions and Decimals (pages 426–429)

Write each decimal as a fraction or as a mixed number in lowest terms.

16. 0.25 **17.** 0.72 **18.** 0.4

19. 4.5 **20.** 2.75 **21.** 1.875

Write each fraction as a decimal.

22. $\frac{3}{10}$ **23.** $\frac{1}{5}$ **24.** $\frac{5}{8}$

25. $1\frac{9}{10}$ **26.** $1\frac{4}{5}$ **27.** $6\frac{1}{8}$

Key Idea
You have compared quantities using > and <. There are other ways to compare two quantities.

Vocabulary
• ratio

Think It Through

I need to remember that all ratios can be written as $\frac{a}{b}$ but not all ratios compare a part to the whole.

Understanding Ratios

LEARN

How can you use math to compare quantities?

A **ratio** is a comparison of like or unlike quantities. A ratio can compare *a part to a part, a part to the whole,* or *the whole to a part.*

The ratio of the number of Presidents with birthdays in January to the number of Presidents with birthdays in October can be written in three ways.

Data File

Number of Presidents with Birthdays in each Month			
January	4	July	4
February	4	August	4
March	4	September	1
April	4	October	6
May	2	November	5
June	1	December	3
		Total	**42**

4 to 6   4:6 $\frac{4}{6}$ ← You can think of this as a fraction or as division, $4 \div 6$

Example A	Example B	Example C
Write a ratio for the number of Presidents with birthdays in November to the number of Presidents with birthdays in September. 5 to 1 5:1 $\frac{5}{1}$	Write a ratio for the Presidents with birthdays in December to the total number of Presidents. 3 to 42 3:42 $\frac{3}{42}$	The ratios 5 to 42, 5:42, and $\frac{5}{42}$ compare two quantities shown in the Data File. What two quantities are being compared? Number of Presidents with birthdays in November to the total number of Presidents.

✔ **Talk About It**

1. Which ratios in the examples compare a part to a part? Which compare a part to the whole?

2. Even though you can write ratios to look like a fraction, do all ratios compare a part to the whole? Explain.

Take It to the NET
More Examples
www.scottforesman.com

Write each ratio in three other ways.

1. yellow shapes to blue shapes

2. blue shapes : all shapes

3. all shapes : green shapes

4. blue or green shapes to all shapes

5. **Reasoning** Is the ratio 42 to 6 the same as the ratio 6 to 42? Explain.

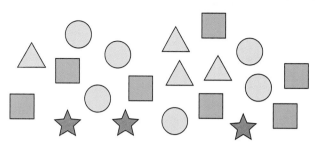

PRACTICE

For more practice, see Set 11-1 on p. 691.

(A) Skills and Understanding

Use the Data File at the right to write a ratio for each comparison.

6. number who were 2nd born to 3rd born

7. number who were 6th born to the total

8. number who were 5th born to 6th born

9. number of only children to total

10. **Number Sense** No President was 8th born. Does the ratio 42:0 make sense for this data?

Data File

Presidents by Birth Order

Birth order	Number of Presidents
eldest	11
2nd born	12
3rd born	5
5th born	2
6th born	2
7th born	1
youngest	6
only child	3
Total	**42**

(B) Reasoning and Problem Solving

A type of ball game played in New Guinea is played with 4 players, 5 balls, 4 hoops, and 1 rope. Write a ratio for each comparison.

11. number of balls to number of hoops

12. number of hoops to number of ropes

13. number of ropes to number of players

14. number of players to number of ropes

15. If 12 players are playing, how many balls, hoops, and ropes are needed?

16. **Writing in Math** The ratio of girls to the total number of students in a certain classroom is 16 to 25. What is the ratio of boys to girls in this classroom? Tell how you decided.

Mixed Review and Test Prep

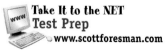

Take It to the NET
Test Prep
www.scottforesman.com

17. If a carpenter is replacing a broken windowpane, is an estimate enough or should the carpenter measure the window? Explain.

18. Which best describes a triangle with three congruent sides?

    A. rectangle   **B.** right   **C.** scalene   **D.** equilateral

Key Idea
Different ratios
can be used
to name the
same comparison.

Vocabulary
• equal ratios
• proportion
• terms

Equal Ratios

LEARN

What are equal ratios?

Equal ratios show the same comparison.

> **Orange juice directions:**
>
> **Mix 3 cans of cold water with 1 can of orange juice concentrate.**

The picture below shows why the ratios $\frac{3}{1}$, $\frac{6}{2}$, and $\frac{9}{3}$ are the same.

3 cans of water for 1 can of concentrate	6 cans of water for 2 cans of concentrate	9 cans of water for 3 cans of concentrate
$\frac{3}{1} = 3 \div 1 = 3$	$\frac{6}{2} = 6 \div 2 = 3$	$\frac{9}{3} = 9 \div 3 = 3$

In each case, there are 3 cans of water for each can of orange juice concentrate.

✔ Talk About It

1. What is another ratio equal to $\frac{3}{1}$? Think of drawing more cans to decide.

2. Could the equal ratios comparing cans of water to cans of orange concentrate be written as $\frac{1}{3} = \frac{2}{6} = \frac{3}{9}$? Explain.

How can you find equal ratios?

> **Example A**
>
> Write 18:24 in simplest form.
>
> $$18:24 = \frac{18}{24} = \frac{18 \div 6}{24 \div 6} = \frac{3}{4}$$
>
> Three of 4 dog owners surveyed let their pets sleep in the room with them.

★ DAILY NEWS ★

Tampa, FL: In a survey of 24 dog owners, 18 owners let their dogs sleep in the room with them.

You can use multiplication or division to find other ratios equal to $\frac{18}{24}$.

Example B

Write two other ratios equal to $\frac{18}{24}$.

Use multiplication.

		18×2	18×3
People who let dogs sleep in room	18	36	54
Total number of dog owners	24	48	72
		24×2	24×3

Equal ratios: $\frac{18}{24} = \frac{36}{48} = \frac{54}{72}$

Use division.

		$18 \div 2$	$18 \div 3$
People who let dogs sleep in room	18	9	6
Total number of dog owners	24	12	8
		$24 \div 2$	$24 \div 3$

Equal ratios: $\frac{18}{24} = \frac{9}{12} = \frac{6}{8}$

A statement that two ratios are equal is called a **proportion.** Since each ratio has two **terms,** a proportion has four terms.

Any two ratios from Examples A and B could be used to write a proportion since all are equal to $\frac{3}{4}$.

To tell if two ratios form a proportion, change each to simplest form. For example, both $\frac{5}{10}$ and $\frac{10}{20}$ equal $\frac{1}{2}$ in simplest form. So, $\frac{5}{10} = \frac{10}{20}$ is a proportion.

✔ Talk About It

3. Name one ratio other than those shown in Examples A and B that equals $\frac{3}{4}$.

4. Are the ratios 6:5 and 42:35 equal? Explain.

5. Could the ratios $\frac{6}{15}$ and $\frac{4}{12}$ be used to write a proportion? Explain.

Take It to the NET
More Examples
www.scottforesman.com

CHECK ✔

For another example, see Set 11-2 on p. 688.

Write each ratio in simplest form.

1. 15 to 50   **2.** 40:100   **3.** 6 to 18   **4.** 20 to 30   **5.** 49 to 21

Give two other ratios that are equal to each.

6. $\frac{6}{9}$ **7.** 5 to 3   **8.** 10:15   **9.** $\frac{7}{1}$ **10.** $\frac{24}{60}$

11. Number Sense How can you tell just by looking at these ratios that they are not equal: 13:6 and 13:7?

PRACTICE

A Skills and Understanding

Write each ratio in simplest form.

12. 36 to 18   **13.** 13:39   **14.** 24 to 60   **15.** 15 to 75   **16.** 72 to 60

Give two other ratios that are equal to each.

17. $\frac{1}{5}$ **18.** 5 to 8   **19.** 12:16   **20.** $\frac{4}{1}$ **21.** $\frac{30}{50}$

Are the ratios in each pair equal?

22. $\frac{5}{25}$ and $\frac{1}{5}$ **23.** $\frac{7}{9}$ and $\frac{2}{3}$ **24.** $\frac{5}{10}$ and $\frac{16}{40}$ **25.** $\frac{4}{12}$ and $\frac{24}{48}$ **26.** $\frac{64}{24}$ and $\frac{24}{9}$

27. Mental Math Are the ratios 18 to 5 and 35 to 5 equal? Explain.

B Reasoning and Problem Solving

Math and Everyday Life

28. A newspaper headline for the survey at the right says, "Three out of every 5 cats live only indoors." Is this correct? Explain.

29. Another newspaper headline for the survey at the right says, "There are about 3 cats that live indoors for every 1 that lives outdoors." Is this correct? Explain.

30. In a game, each player gets 6 numbered cards. Make a table to show how many cards are needed for 2, 3, 4, and 5 players. If 54 cards are available, how many people can play?

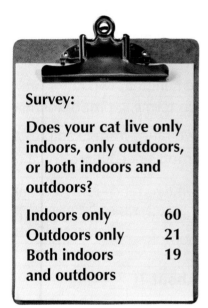

Survey:

Does your cat live only indoors, only outdoors, or both indoors and outdoors?

Indoors only	60
Outdoors only	21
Both indoors and outdoors	19

31. Think about extending the design at the right. How many stars would you expect to find in a diagram with 48 shapes in it? How many squares?

32. __Writing in Math__ Is the explanation below correct? If not, tell why and write a correct response.

How can you use division to decide whether the ratios $\frac{36}{9}$ and $\frac{48}{12}$ are equal?

I know that $\frac{36}{9}$ means 36 ÷ 9 and $\frac{48}{12}$ means 48 ÷ 12. Both quotients equal 4. So the ratios are equal.

C Extensions

Give two ratios for each picture.

33.

34.

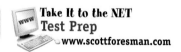

Mixed Review and Test Prep

Graph each ordered pair.

35. (1, 2)　　**36.** (3, 6)　　**37.** (2, 5)　　**38.** (2, 3)　　**39.** (3, 5)

40. Ms Donahue's class has 11 boys and 13 girls. Write the ratio of boys to the whole class in three different ways.

41. Without multiplying, which product is greater than 100?

A. 9.8×8.2　　**B.** 10.2×8.2　　**C.** 11.2×11.2　　**D.** 0.1×11.2

Learning with Technology

Using a Calculator to Find Equal Ratios

You can use your calculator to find equal ratios and to simplify ratios.
You can find an equal ratio for 18:24 (or $\frac{18}{24}$) as follows:

Press: 18 24 F⊃D F⊃D =

Display: N/D→n/d 75/100

The message N/D→n/d in the display means that the ratio shown is equal to 18:24, but not yet simplified. Pressing Simp = until N/D→n/d disappears from the display will give the ratio in simplest form. If you keep pressing Simp = , the final display will be 3/4. So the simplest form for 18:24 is 3:4 or $\frac{3}{4}$

For 1–3, use your calculator to find equal ratios for each.
Keep finding equal ratios until the last is in simplest form.

1. $\frac{68}{200}$　　**2.** $\frac{78}{300}$　　**3.** $\frac{375}{1000}$

All text pages available online and on CD-ROM.

Algebra

Key Idea
There is a pattern when equal ratios are graphed.

Materials
• grid paper
• timer

Think It Through
I can **look for a pattern in the way points fall on the graph.**

Graphs of Equal Ratios

LEARN

Activity

Are all the ratios the same?

Ratios equal to a given ratio form a pattern. You can see the pattern when you use graphing.

a. One skate in a pair of inline skates has 4 wheels. To make two skates, you would need 8 wheels. Copy and complete this table.

Number of skates	1	2	3	4	5	6
Number of wheels	4	8				

Each column gives an ordered pair. (number of skates, number of wheels)

b. On grid paper, make a coordinate diagram like this one. Label it as shown here.

c. On your paper, graph each ordered pair from the table.

d. In your own words, describe the pattern you see in your graph.

e. Connect the points in the graph. If the graph for the inline skates were extended, would the point for (9 skates, 36 wheels) be part of the pattern? Explain.

Breathing 12 times to 20 times per minute is common for adult humans. Suppose an adult breathes 12 times per minute. Copy and complete this table.

Minutes	1	2	3	4	5	6
Breaths	12	24				

f. Make a graph of the data from the table. Label the horizontal axis "Number of minutes" and the vertical axis "Number of breaths."

g. Describe the pattern in the graph. Would the point for (30 minutes, 450 breaths) be part of the pattern if the graph were extended? Explain.

1. A tricycle has three wheels. Copy and complete this table of equal ratios.

Number of tricycles	1	2	3	4	5	6
Number of wheels	3	6				

2. On a grid, graph the ordered pairs from the table. Connect them with a line.

3. If the line is extended, is the point for (10, 30) on the line?

PRACTICE

For more practice, see Set 11-3 on p. 691.

Ⓐ Skills and Understanding

4. A pentagon has five sides. Copy and complete this table of equal ratios.

Number of pentagons	1	2	3	4	5	6
Number of sides	5	10				

5. On a grid, graph the ordered pairs from the table. Connect them with a line.

6. If the line is extended, is the point for (12, 70) on the line?

7. Number Sense A student said that the points for (8, 6) and (10, 8) were both on his graph of equal ratios. Is he correct? Explain.

Ⓑ Reasoning and Problem Solving

8. Equal ratios were used to get line A at the right. Another set of equal ratios was used to get line B. Which line is for ratios equal to $\frac{1}{2}$ and which is for ratios equal to $\frac{1}{5}$? How did you decide?

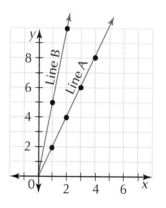

9. Give three equal ratios from the graph at the right.

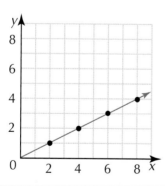

10. **Writing in Math** Is the graph at the right a graph of equal ratios? Explain.

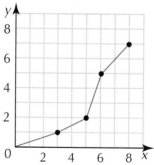

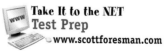

Mixed Review and Test Prep

Take It to the NET
Test Prep
www.scottforesman.com

11. 480 ÷ 24   **12.** 98 ÷ 7   **13.** 640 ÷ 20   **14.** 550 ÷ 50   **15.** 375 ÷ 25

16. Which ratio equals 10:15?

A. 1:5   **B.** 2 to 3   **C.** 2 to 5   **D.** 3:2

 All text pages available online and on CD-ROM.

Key Idea
A rate is a special kind of ratio.

Vocabulary
• rate
• unit rate

Materials
• clock or watch

TEST TALK

Think It Through
I can **make a table to record data** from the activity.

Rates

LEARN

Activity

Are all ratios the same?

a. How many times can you write your full name in 30 seconds? Work with a partner. Take turns. One person writes his or her name (so others can read it!), and the other keeps the time. Switch roles and repeat the process.

b. Write the ratio of *the number of times you wrote your name to 30 seconds.*

c. Assume you could write at the same pace. What would be the ratio of the number of times you can write your name to 1 minute? To 10 seconds? (Hint: Make a table of equal ratios.)

d. Think of other comparisons. What words might be written in each space?

35 ___ in 1 hour   78 ___ in 1 minute

What is a special kind of ratio?

A **rate** is a ratio that compares unlike units. A common rate is miles per hour. If the comparison is to 1 unit, the rate is called a **unit rate**.

Example

Give the unit rate for 22 laps in 5 minutes.

$$\frac{22 \text{ laps}}{5 \text{ minutes}} = \frac{? \text{ laps}}{1 \text{ minute}}$$

Since $\frac{22 \div 5}{5 \div 5} = \frac{4.4}{1}$, the unit rate is $\frac{4.4 \text{ laps}}{1 \text{ min}}$.

✔ Talk About It

1. Why were the top and bottom numbers in the example divided by 5?

2. What would you do to find the unit rate for 7.5 pounds for $3?

3. **Number Sense** Which is the better gas mileage: $\frac{24 \text{ miles}}{1 \text{ gallon}}$ or $\frac{130 \text{ miles}}{5 \text{ gallons}}$? How did you decide?

Tell the two units being compared in each rate.

1. 2 cans each day   **2.** $1.75 per ounce   **3.** 15 miles in 6 hours

Write each rate as a unit rate.

4. 15 books in 3 weeks   **5.** 24 cans in 2 boxes   **6.** 8 visits in 5 days

7. Number Sense Suppose your pulse is 26 beats in 15 seconds. What is the unit rate per one minute?

PRACTICE

For more practice, see Set 11-4 on p. 692.

Ⓐ Skills and Understanding

Tell the two quantities being compared in each rate.

8. 44 feet in 2 seconds   **9.** $6.25 for 5 pounds   **10.** 63 miles in 4 hours

Write each rate as a unit rate.

11. $2.40 for 12 pencils   **12.** 220 miles in 5 hours   **13.** $44 for 5 hours work

14. 255 miles for 10 gallons   **15.** 150 words in 4 minutes   **16.** $5,400 for 9 weeks work

17. Number Sense Kyle said, "I can write my name 35 times in 1 second." Does this rate make sense? Explain.

Ⓑ Reasoning and Problem Solving

18. Which rate statements make sense, and which do not? For those that do not, tell why.

   a. Fred ran the 26-mile marathon at a pace of 45 miles per hour.

   b. Jan can jump rope at 55 jumps per minute.

   c. The copy machine copies 125 pages a second.

19. <u>Writing in Math</u> For which type of juice is it easier to decide the better buy? Explain.

Apple Juice
$1.75 /6 cans

Orange Juice
$0.35 /1 can

Mixed Review and Test Prep

Take It to the NET
Test Prep
www.scottforesman.com

20. Copy and complete the table. Then graph the ratios on the same grid.

Number of cars	1	2	3	4	5	6
Number of tires	4	8				

21. Which gives the circumference of a circle?

   A. π × radius   **B.** π × diameter   **C.** 0.5 × π × radius   **D.** 0.5 × π × diameter

Do You Know How?

Do You Understand?

Understanding Ratios (11–1)

1. Write the ratio of boys to girls in class 5.

Grant School 5th Grade		
Class	Boys	Girls
1	12	11
2	10	14
3	9	13
4	12	9
5	11	13

2. Write the ratio of girls to boys in 5th grade.

3. Write the ratio of girls to all students in 5th grade.

A For Exercises 2 and 3, tell if the ratio represents *part to part, part to whole,* or *whole to part.*

B For which class is the ratio of boys to girls closest to 1:1?

Equal Ratios (11–2)

4. Write the ratio 12:27 in simplest form.

5. Give two other ratios equal to 2:5.

Are the ratios in each pair equal?

6. $\frac{3}{4}$ and $\frac{6}{12}$ 7. $\frac{6}{9}$ and $\frac{3}{2}$ 8. $\frac{3}{10}$ and $\frac{12}{40}$

C Are the ratios 12 to 15 and 4 to 5 equal? Explain.

D What is a proportion? Include an example of a proportion in your explanation.

Graphs of Equal Ratios (11–3)

9. A movie ticket costs $3. Copy and complete the table of equal ratios.

Number of movie tickets	1	2	3	4	5	6
Cost of movie tickets	$3	$6	■	■	■	■

10. On a grid, graph the ordered pairs from the table.

E If the line that contains the points from Exercise 10 were extended, would the point (9, 26) be on the line? Explain.

F Describe the pattern in the graph from Exercise 10.

Rates (11–4)

Write each as a unit rate.

11. Gerry bought 12 baseballs for $72.

12. Lucy made 2 quarts juice for 8 people.

G Is 45 miles in 2 hours a rate? Why or why not?

H Is 55 miles per hour a unit rate? Why or why not?

MULTIPLE CHOICE

1. Which ratio is equal to 8:14? (11–2)

   A. 14:8   **B.** 16:42   **C.** 4:7   **D.** 7:4

2. Which ratio is NOT equal to 4:6? (11–2)

   A. 2:3   **B.** 12:18   **C.** 16:24   **D.** 12:8

Think It Through
I should **read the problem carefully** and watch for words like **NOT**.

FREE RESPONSE

Are the ratios in each pair equal? (11–2)

3. $\frac{3}{5}$ and $\frac{12}{20}$ 4. $\frac{4}{7}$ and $\frac{14}{8}$ 5. $\frac{2}{3}$ and $\frac{4}{9}$ 6. $\frac{12}{16}$ and $\frac{3}{4}$

Use the table at the right for Exercises 7–10. Write each ratio, and then put it in simplest form. (11–1, 11–2)

Total Area in Square Miles	Number of U.S. States
Less than 25,000	10
25,000–49,999	9
50,000–74,999	14
75,000–99,999	9
100,000 or greater	8

7. U.S. states with less than 25,000 mi² to U.S. states with greater than 100,000 mi².

8. U.S. states with 50,000 mi²–74,999 mi² to all U.S. states.

9. Write a ratio about the area of U.S. states that is 1:1.

10. Write two ratios about the area of U.S. states that are equal.

11. Sound travels 13 miles in 1 minute in some situations. Copy and complete this table of equal ratios. (11–3)

Minutes	1	2	3	4	5	6
Miles	13	26				

12. On a grid, graph the ordered pairs from the table. (11–3)

13. If the line that contains the points from Exercise 12 were extended, would the point (8, 98) be on the line? Explain. (11–3)

Writing in Math

Fresh Fruit Mart

Peaches
9 for $1.98

Melons
69¢ each

Lemons
5 for 75¢

Oranges
6 for $1.50

Bananas
25¢ per lb

Apples
3 lb for 99¢

14. Which of the fruit prices are given as a unit rate? Explain. (11–4)

15. The Food Store is also running a sale on fruit. They are advertising 5 oranges for $1.40 and 10 peaches for $2.00. Which store has lower priced oranges? peaches? Explain. (11–4)

Understand Graphic Sources: Tables and Charts

Understanding graphic sources such as tables and charts when you read in math can help you use the **problem-solving strategy, *Make a Table,*** in the next lesson.

In reading, understanding tables can help you understand what you read. In math, understanding tables can help you solve problems.

This title tells you the table is about winners of the Indianapolis 500.

The entry 148 is in the column for speed and the row that shows the year 1996. So, in 1996, the winning speed was 148 miles per hour.

The other information in the *table* are the entries. They reveal specific information.

Indianapolis 500 Winners

Year	Driver	Average Speed (miles per hour)
1996	Buddy Lazier	148
1997	Arie Luyendyk	146
1998	Eddie Cheever, Jr.	145
1999	Kenny Brack	153
2000	Juan Montoya	168
2001	Helio Castroneves	154

The title of the *table* or *chart* tells you in general what it is about.

These headings tell you that the table shows the year, driver, and speed.

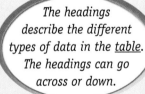

The headings describe the different types of data in the *table*. The headings can go across or down.

1. Who won the race in 1999?

2. How many of these winning speeds were greater than 150 miles per hour?

For 3–5, use the Animal Speed table at the right.

3. What information is given in the table?

4. **Writing in Math** Write a sentence that tells the information given in the last line of the table.

5. Which animal can run almost twice as fast as a rabbit?

Animal Speeds

Animal	Speed (miles per hour)
Cheetah	64
Squirrel	12
Rabbit	35
Elephant	25
Grizzly Bear	30
Lion	50

For 6–8, use The Four Oceans table at the right.

6. What is the area of the Atlantic Ocean?

7. Which ocean has an average depth of about 13,000 feet?

8. **Writing in Math** Is the order of the oceans from greatest area to least area the same as the order from greatest depth to least depth? Explain.

The Four Oceans

Ocean	Area (square miles)	Average depth (feet)
Pacific	64,000,000	13,215
Atlantic	31,815,000	12,880
Indian	25,300,000	13,002
Arctic	5,4440,200	3,953

For 9–12, use the chart below.

9. What do you think *currencies* means?

10. What type of information is given in this table?

11. How is the * symbol used?

12. **Writing in Math** Doreen thinks that one United States dollar is worth about one Euro. Is she right? Explain.

Prices in Other Currencies*

	Purse $30	Boom Box $58	Bicycle $140	Computer $900
United States				
Europe (Euro)	31	59	143	919
Hong Kong (Hong Kong Dollar)	234	452	1,092	7,020
Mexico (Peso)	306	591	1,427	9,173
Japan (Yen)	3,696	7,146	17,249	110,889

* Rates of exchange as of October, 2002.

Problem-Solving Strategy

Key Idea
Learning how and when to make a table can help you solve problems.

Make a Table

LEARN

How do you make and use a table to solve a problem?

Chains A link for a chain is made up of two triangles and three trapezoids. Links are put together to make a chain for decorating the classroom. Twelve triangles were used to make the chain. How many trapezoids were used?

1 Link

2 Links

3 Links

Read and Understand

Think It Through
Understanding graphic sources such as tables and charts will help me make a table to find the number of trapezoids used.

What do you know?   The number of each shape used for 1 link
The number of triangles used for the chain

What are you trying to find?   The number of trapezoids needed for the chain when 12 triangles are used

Plan and Solve

What strategy will you use?

Strategy: Make a Table

How to Make a Table

Step 1 Set up the table with the correct labels.

Step 2 Enter known data in the table.

Step 3 Look for a pattern. Extend the table.

Step 4 Find the answer in the table.

Number of Links					
Number of Trapezoids					
Number of Triangles					

Number of Links	1	2	3			
Number of Trapezoids	3	6	9			
Number of Triangles	2	4	6			

Number of Links	1	2	3	4	5	6
Number of Trapezoids	3	6	9	12	15	18
Number of Triangles	2	4	6	8	10	12

Number of Links	1	2	3	4	5	6
Number of Trapezoids	3	6	9	12	15	18
Number of Triangles	2	4	6	8	10	12

Answer: 18 trapezoids are used with 12 triangles.

Look Back and Check

Is your work correct?   Yes. Each link in the chain has 2 more triangles and 3 more trapezoids.

✔ Talk About It

1. What are the headings for the table on page 660?

2. What patterns do you see in the table on page 660?

3. What is the ratio of trapezoids to triangles in each link? Does the ratio of trapezoids to triangles change as the number of links increases? Explain.

For another example, see Set 11-5 on p. 689.

CHECK ✓

Copy and complete the table to solve each problem. Write the answer in a complete sentence.

1. Jewelry Misty designs jewelry using beads. The beads shown are for one pattern on a necklace. How many cylinders will she use if she uses 20 cubes?

Number of patterns	1	2		
Number of cubes	5	10		
Number of cylinders	2	4		

2. Bridges Rich plans to build a bridge for his train set. Shown is the first layer for two columns that will be connected. All the layers will be the same. If he uses 14 cubes, how many layers is he planning to build and how many rectangular prisms will he need?

Number of layers	1	2	3		
Number of cubes	2	4			
Number of prisms	6				

PRACTICE

For more practice, see Set 11-5 on p. 692.

Solve. Write the answer in a complete sentence.

3. Alvaro made clay monsters. For each monster face, he used 3 beads and 2 in. of green string. He used 45 beads. How much string was used?

Number of monsters	1	2	3		
Number of beads	3	6	9		
Length of string	2 in.	4 in.			

4. Alberto spends 13 h 45 min over a 3-week period doing homework. If he spends the same amount of time each day, 5 days a week, doing homework, how much time does he spend a day?

5. Ansley spent $3.50 for film and $18.49 for a CD. She also bought lunch. She started the day with $30. If she had at least $3 left, what is the most that she could have spent for lunch?

6. <u>Writing in Math</u> Describe a ratio that can be seen in the chain at the right.

STRATEGIES

- **Show What You Know**
  Draw a Picture
  Make an Organized List
  Make a Table
  Make a Graph
  Act It Out or Use Objects
- **Look for a Pattern**
- **Try, Check, and Revise**
- **Write an Equation**
- **Use Logical Reasoning**
- **Solve a Simpler Problem**
- **Work Backward**

Choose a tool

Mental Math

All text pages available online and on CD-ROM.

Key Idea
Equal ratios are
used to make
scale drawings.

Vocabulary
• scale drawing
• scale

Materials
• centimeter
  graph paper

Scale Drawings

LEARN

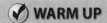
✔ WARM UP

Measure each length to
the nearest centimeter.

1. _____

2. _____

3. _____

Activity

How can you make a scale drawing?

A **scale** is a ratio that shows the
relationship between a length
in a drawing and the actual
object. Ratios are used to
make a **scale drawing**.

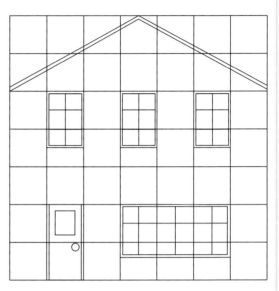

In the scale drawing at the
right, the scale is 1 cm:4 ft, or
1 cm = 4 ft. On the drawing,
the door is 2 cm high. So the
actual door is 8 feet high.

a. Make a scale drawing of
your classroom. Use the scale
2 cm:1 foot (2 cm = 1 foot).
The table of equal ratios
will help.

drawing (cm)	2	4	6	8	10	12	14	16	18	20	22	24	26	28	30
actual (ft)	1	2	3	4	5	6	7	8	9	10	11	12	13	14	15

drawing (cm)	32	34	36	38	40	42	44	46	48	50	52	54	56	58	60
actual (ft)	16	17	18	19	20	21	22	23	24	25	26	27	28	29	30

Follow these steps.

> **Step 1:** Measure the length of each side of your classroom
> to the nearest foot.
>
> **Step 2:** Use the table of equal ratios to find the length of
> the corresponding sides in the scale drawing.
>
> **Step 3:** Make the scale drawing. Tape together sheets of the
> centimeter graph paper as needed.
>
> **Step 4:** Write the scale on the drawing and label the
> drawing so others understand the drawing.

b. What is the scale for your drawing?

c. What scale might you use if you wanted the scale drawing
to be larger? Smaller?

d. Could you make a scale drawing of your classroom that
would fit on one sheet of centimeter graph paper? Explain.

In 1–2, refer to the scale drawing of the house on the preceding page.

1. Find the actual height of the building.

2. Find the actual width of the window on the first floor.

3. Number Sense Suppose the length of a wall in another scale drawing is 15 cm. Using the scale 1 cm: 3 ft, what is the actual length of this wall?

PRACTICE

For more practice, see Set 11-6 on p. 692.

Ⓐ Skills and Understanding

Refer to this scale drawing of a room.

4. What is the actual length of the room?

5. What is the actual width of the room?

6. Number Sense A student said that she can make a larger scale drawing of the classroom in the activity on page 662 by using a scale of 1 cm = 1 foot. Is she correct?

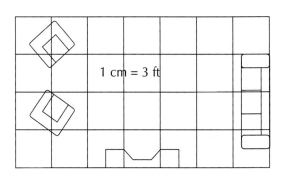

1 cm = 3 ft

Ⓑ Reasoning and Problem Solving

7. The scale for a map is 1 inch:5 miles (1 in. = 5 mi). How long would the distance on the map be for a straight road that is 20 miles long? Explain.

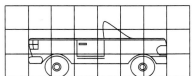

8. The scale drawing at the right uses the scale 1 in.:12 ft. How long is the real car? How did you decide?

9. A scale drawing of a tree is 7 inches tall. The actual tree is 28 feet tall. What scale was used?

10. <u>Writing in Math</u> Suppose you want to use the scale 3 cm = 1 foot to make a drawing of your room. How could you use a table of equal ratios to decide what length and width the drawing should be?

🦉 Mixed Review and Test Prep

Take It to the NET
Test Prep
www.scottforesman.com

11. Basil saved $10 in his first month of work. Each month after that he saved $10 more than he did in the preceding month. Make a table to find how much he saved in his sixth month of work.

12. Which represents 6:50 in simplest form?

    A. 12:100   **B.** 3:25   **C.** $\frac{6}{50}$ **D.** 2 to 25

Problem-Solving Skill

Key Idea
There are specific things you can do to write a good explanation in math.

Think It Through

When I write to explain, I should **identify steps in a process,** such as how I make a prediction based on data.

Writing to Explain

LEARN

How do you write a good explanation?

When you **write to explain** a prediction, you need to tell why something will happen.

Stop Sign Some friends wanted their town to put a stop sign at an intersection near their school. Use the data collected by the four people below to predict how many cars go through this intersection in one hour. Write and explain how you made your prediction.

Results of Traffic Survey		
Name	Number of Cars Passing by	Number of Minutes Cars Were Counted
Jack	10	7
Jo	42	4
Randy	30	6
Tina	21	3

Writing a Math Explanation

- Make sure your prediction is clearly stated.
- Use steps to make your explanation clear.
- Show and explain carefully how you used the numbers to make your prediction.

I predict that 300 cars go through the intersection in one hour. Below is how I made my prediction.

1. I added to find 103 cars in 20 minutes. 103 is about 100, so this gives the ratio $\frac{100}{20}$.

2. $\frac{100}{20} = \frac{5}{1}$, So, about 5 cars pass through the intersection in 1 minute.

3. There are 60 minutes in 1 hour. If 5 cars pass by in 1 minute, then 5 × 60 = 300 cars pass by in 1 hour.

✔ Talk About It

1. Is the explanation clear? Explain.

2. How does using a unit ratio help you find the total number of cars?

3. There are 3 twenty-minute periods in one hour. Explain how you can use this fact to find the answer another way.

1. The table shows the data collected by three employees to predict about how many people will enter an amusement park in one hour.

	Number of People Entering	Number of Minutes People Were Counted
Ruth	118	12
Ann	74	8
Max	82	10

Based on these results, predict how many people will enter the park in 1 hour. Explain how you made your prediction.

PRACTICE

For more practice, see Set 11-7 on p. 693.

Write to explain.

2. Gerald is taking a 3,000-mile car trip. Based on data shown at the right, predict how many gallons of gasoline he will use.

Number of Miles Driven	Gallons of Gasoline Used
479	16
436	14
597	19

3. You take your pulse and find 12 beats in 10 seconds. At this rate, is your pulse for 1 minute greater than or less than 100?

4. Reasonableness Write and explain whether each situation makes sense. If it does not, rewrite it so that it does make sense.

　a. Janie can write her name about 38 times in 1 second.

　b. If you buy two movie tickets, you get one free box of popcorn. Twelve children went to a movie. They got 24 free boxes of popcorn.

5. Dorothy is building a dog run. The run will be 6 feet wide. Copy and extend the table to show the number of feet of fencing needed for a run that is 9, 10, 11, or 12 feet long. Explain how the number of feet of fencing changes as the length changes.

Length in feet	6	7	8
Feet of **fencing**	24	26	28

6. The quilt at the right has symmetrical designs in each corner. Draw the design for the lower right corner. Explain why you made the drawing you did.

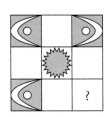

Do You Know How?

Do You Understand?

Problem-Solving Strategy: Make a Table (11–5)

1. Jennifer pays 7¢ sales tax on every dollar she spends. Make a table showing the tax on $1, $2, $3, and so on through $8 in spending. Write a rule for the table.

2. How much sales tax will Jennifer pay on an item that costs $20?

(A) How does making a table help you solve a problem?

(B) How did you find the answer to Exercise 2?

Scale Drawings (11–6)

The scale on a map is 2 cm:125 km.

3. What actual distance does 10 cm on the map represent?

4. What length on the map represents an actual distance of 375 km?

5. What actual distance does 1 cm on the map represent?

(C) Explain how you found the answer to Exercise 5.

(D) Would the scale of 4 cm:250 km be larger, smaller, or the same as the scale of 2 cm:125 km? Explain how you know.

Problem-Solving Skill: Writing to Explain (11–7)

6. The table shows the number of cars that went through the Northgate tollbooth at four times during the day.

	Number of Cars Passing Through	Number of Minutes Counted
Morning	47	5
Noon	60	6
Afternoon	51	6
Evening	44	4

Based on this data, predict how many cars go through the tollbooth in 1 hour. Explain how you made your prediction.

(E) What numbers given in the problem did you use to make your prediction?

(F) Did you use a unit ratio to help you make your prediction? If so, what unit ratio did you use.

MULTIPLE CHOICE

1. A model dinosaur is 4 feet long. The scale for the model is 2 ft:25 ft. Which is the actual length of the dinosaur? (11–6)

   A. 25 ft   **B.** 50 ft   **C.** 100 ft   **D.** 200 ft

2. A Seismosaurus might grow to a length of 150 feet. Using the scale 2 ft:25 ft, what is the length of a model of a 150-ft Seismosaurus? (11–6)

   A. 12 in.   **B.** 6 ft   **C.** 12 ft   **D.** 300 in.

FREE RESPONSE

A telephone company charges 9 cents a minute for long-distance calls.

3. Copy and complete the table. (11–5)

Length of Call (in min)	1	2	3	4	5	6	7	8	9	10
Cost of Call (in cents)	9	18	27							

4. How much would a 10-minute long-distance call cost? (11–5)

5. Explain how to find how much a 20-minute long-distance call would cost. (11–5)

A model train is built to the scale 1 in.:87 in. The length of the model railroad cars are given to the nearest inch. Find the actual length of the cars in inches. (11–6)

6. sleeper car: 11 in.   7. tank car: 7 in.   8. boxcar: 6 in.

9. If the actual length of a refrigerator car is 696 inches, what would be the length of the model refrigerator car? (11–6)

Writing in Math

10. Mrs. Karth drives her car for her job, and she kept track of the number of miles she drove in a 5-day work week. Based on this data, predict how many miles she will drive in 1 year of 300 working days. Explain how you made your prediction. (11-7)

Mrs. Karth's Mileage for 5 Days	
Day	**Miles Driven**
Monday	86
Tuesday	97
Wednesday	42
Thursday	53
Friday	73

Vocabulary
• percent

Materials
• grid paper

Think It Through
• I can **act it out** by making a new 10 by 10 square grid.

• I know that **part of a percent** is the number of units per 100.

Understanding Percent

LEARN

What does percent mean?

A **percent** is a ratio in which the first term is compared to 100. The percent is the number of hundredths that represent the part. Percent means *per hundred*.

✓ **WARM UP**
Write an equal ratio with a denominator of 100.

1. $\frac{1}{10}$ 2. $\frac{1}{2}$ 3. $\frac{1}{4}$

LOANS AS LOW 10%   Sales Tax is 7%   **Sale** All items 25% off

About 3 out of every 5 households in a certain community have a personal computer.

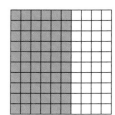

$\frac{3}{5} = \frac{60}{100} = 60\%$

3 out of 5 means $\frac{3}{5}$.

I can find an equivalent fraction with a denominator of 100.

We say "sixty percent."

Activity

How can percent be used?

The floor plan for a computer store is shown at the right. It is divided into 100 parts.

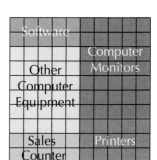

Software | Computer Monitors | Other | Computer Equipment | Sales Counter | Printers

a. Write the amount of space each section occupies as a fraction in lowest terms and as a percent.

b. Make a hundreds grid like the ones on this page. Mark sections to divide up the grid to show the following.

  15% is occupied by the sales counter.
  30% is occupied by computer monitors.
  20% is occupied by printers.
  The rest is occupied by software and other items.

c. For part **b,** how did you decide what the part occupied by software and other items should be?

d. Is it possible to make a floor plan with these percents? Explain.

  10% sales counter   40% monitors

  30% printers   30% software

CHECK ✓

Write the fraction in lowest terms and the percent that represents the shaded part of each figure.

1.

2.

3.

4.

5. Number Sense If a 10-by-10 grid has 100 squares that are completely shaded, what percent represents the shaded part?

PRACTICE

For more practice, see Set 11-8 on p. 693.

Ⓐ Skills and Understanding

Write the fraction in lowest terms and the percent that represents the shaded part of each figure.

6.

7.

8.

9.

10. Number Sense If $\frac{2}{8} = \frac{1}{4} = 25\%$, then what is $\frac{1}{8}$ as a percent?

Ⓑ Reasoning and Problem Solving

11. The picture at the right shows that 50% is not always the same amount. Explain why.

Each line segment shows 50%. Copy each line segment and draw the line segment that shows 100%.

12. ─────────────

13. ─────────────────────

14. ──

15. Writing in Math Which of these circle graphs does not make sense? Tell why.

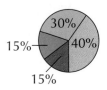

🕷 Mixed Review and Test Prep

Take It to the NET
Test Prep
www.scottforesman.com

16. 0.3×34.5 **17.** 0.5×2.4 **18.** 0.06×0.3 **19.** 9.7×6.08

20. Writing in Math Some park employees gathered data and found that 153 people entered the park in 10 minutes. Based on this data, predict how many people will enter the park in 1 hour. Explain.

Mental Math: Finding a Percent of a Number

LEARN

How can you find a percent of a number mentally?

When the denominator of a fraction is a factor of 100, it is easy to change the fraction to a percent. Here are some common percents.

$\frac{1}{10} = \frac{10}{100} = 10\%$	$\frac{1}{5} = \frac{20}{100} = 20\%$	$\frac{1}{4} = \frac{25}{100} = 25\%$	$\frac{1}{2} = \frac{50}{100} = 50\%$

Think It Through
I need to **use an equivalent fraction** for the percent.

The table shows some common percents and their fraction and decimal equivalents.

Percent	10%	20%	25%	$33\frac{1}{3}\%$	40%	50%	60%	$66\frac{2}{3}\%$	75%	80%	90%
Fraction	$\frac{1}{10}$	$\frac{1}{5}$	$\frac{1}{4}$	$\frac{1}{3}$	$\frac{2}{5}$	$\frac{1}{2}$	$\frac{3}{5}$	$\frac{2}{3}$	$\frac{3}{4}$	$\frac{4}{5}$	$\frac{9}{10}$
Decimal	0.1	0.2	0.25	$0.33\frac{1}{3}$	0.4	0.5	0.6	$0.66\frac{2}{3}$	0.75	0.8	0.9

In the table above, notice that the decimal for $\frac{1}{3}$ is written as $0.33\frac{1}{3}$. Often it is written as 0.333... or $0.\overline{3}$ to show that the digit keeps repeating when 1 is divided by 3.

Example A

Find $33\frac{1}{3}\%$ of 24.

$33\frac{1}{3}\% \times 24 = \frac{1}{3} \times 24$

$\qquad\qquad = 8$ Since 3 is a factor of 24, $\frac{1}{3}$ of 24 is easy to find.

Example B

Find 75% of 40.

$75\% \times 40 = \frac{3}{4} \times 40$

$\qquad\qquad = 30$ $40 \div 4 = 10$ and $10 \times 3 = 30$

✔ Talk About It

1. Why are the examples above easy to calculate mentally?

2. Is 20% of 63 easy to do mentally? Explain.

3. Name two other ways to write $0.66\frac{2}{3}$ to show that the digit keeps repeating when 2 is divided by 3.

Take It to the NET
www **More Examples**
www.scottforesman.com

For another example, see Set 11-9 on p. 690.

Find each using mental math.

1. 25% of 36   **2.** 10% of 200   **3.** 75% of 48   **4.** 60% of 50

5. Reasoning Order these numbers from least to greatest.

$$25\%, \frac{1}{3}, 0.45, 75\%, \frac{2}{3}, 0.8$$

6. Number Sense What rule can you use to find 10% of a number? Use 10% of 25 to explain.

PRACTICE

For more practice, see Set 11-9 on p. 693.

Ⓐ Skills and Understanding

Find each using mental math.

7. $66\frac{2}{3}\%$ of 66   **8.** 80% of 40   **9.** 20% of 25   **10.** 100% of 48

11. Reasoning Order these numbers from least to greatest.

$$60\%, \frac{1}{4}, 0.75, 28\%, \frac{1}{2}, 0.55$$

12. Number Sense If 1% of a number is 21, what is 2% of the number?

Ⓑ Reasoning and Problem Solving

Use a calculator as shown at the right for 13–16. Give decimal answers to the nearest tenth.

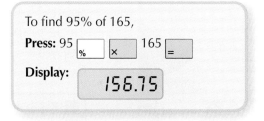

To find 95% of 165,
Press: 95 [%] [×] 165 [=]
Display: 156.75

13. 35% of 86   **14.** 3% of 1,250

15. 87% of 567   **16.** 34.5% of 186

17. Writing in Math In *Chess-Dream in a Garden*, there are 16 people on a side, just as a standard chess game has 16 pieces on a side. Each side has 8 pawns, 2 bishops, 2 knights, 2 rooks, 1 queen, and 1 king. As a percent, what part of the pieces are pawns, and what part are bishops? Explain how you decided.

🦉 Mixed Review and Test Prep

 Take It to the NET www **Test Prep** www.scottforesman.com

Estimate.

18. 9.8×99.8 **19.** 0.87×24.9 **20.** 98×0.49 **21.** 0.45×12

22. Which is NOT another name for $\frac{2}{5}$?

A. 40%   **B.** 0.4   **C.** $\frac{20}{50}$ **D.** 20%

All text pages available online and on CD-ROM.

Estimating Percents

LEARN

Activity

How can you label sections of a circle by using percents?

a. Copy the following circles that have all sections equal in size. Label each colored section with the correct fraction and percent.

b. Look at the circle graph shown at the right. Suppose the green section is labeled 63%. How do you know the label is wrong? What is a good estimate for the percent that is green? Yellow?

c. In a survey of 50 people, 25 named baseball as their favorite sport, 15 named basketball, and 10 named football. Which circle graph is the best way to show the results of the survey? Copy the graph and label each section with the correct sport. Explain how you decided.

☐ Baseball
☐ Basketball
☐ Football

How can you estimate the percent of a number?

Example A

If there are 825 seniors, about how many students are going to a 4-year college?

28% of 825 is about 25% of 800.

$25\% \text{ of } 800 = 25\% \times 800$

$= \frac{1}{4} \times 800$

$= 200$

About 200 seniors plan to go to a 4-year college.

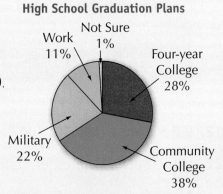

High School Graduation Plans

Work 11%
Not Sure 1%
Four-year College 28%
Community College 38%
Military 22%

About how many students plan to enter the military?
Refer to the graph in Example A on the preceding page.

22% of 825 is about 20% of 800.

20% of 800 = 20% × 800

$$= \frac{1}{5} \times 800$$

$$= 160$$

About 160 high school seniors plan to enter the military.

✔ Talk About It

1. What number was substituted for 28% in Example A? for 22% in Example B?

2. About how much is 11% of 825? Tell how you estimated.

3. **Number Sense** Is the exact answer in Example B greater than or less than 160? How can you decide without finding the exact answer?

CHECK ✔

For another example, see Set 11-10 on p. 690.

Estimate.

1. 21% of 130 **2.** $33\frac{1}{3}$% of 39 **3.** 49% of 650 **4.** 51% of 678 **5.** 74% of 36

6. **Estimation** Fran estimated 45% of 89 by finding 50% of 90. Will her estimate be greater than or less than the exact answer? Explain.

PRACTICE

For more practice, see Set 11-10 on p. 693.

A Skills and Understanding

Estimate.

7. 74% of 80 **8.** 9% of 50 **9.** 32% of 61

10. 49% of 184 **11.** 99% of 762 **12.** 11% 288

13. 32% of 85 **14.** 8% of 65 **15.** 53% of 300

16. **Number Sense** Lakeesha bought a new sweater. The sales tax is 8%. Is $4 a reasonable estimate for the amount of sales tax she must pay? Explain.

$39.95

B Reasoning and Problem Solving

Math and Everyday Life

A common restaurant tip is about 15% of the total bill. An easy way to estimate the tip is to estimate 10% of the bill, and then add half that amount.

If the bill is $18.85, you could think: 10% of $20 is $2 and half of $2 is $1. So $3 is a reasonable tip.

Estimate a reasonable tip for each restaurant bill.

17. $37.00   **18.** $8.89

19. $21.50   **20.** $43.75

Algebra Use mental math to replace *n*.

21. 10% of *n* is $20.   **22.** 50% of *n* is $600.

C Extensions

Many stores offer discounts on certain items.

Example: An item costing $18.95 is offered at a 5% discount. What is the amount of the discount to the nearest cent?

5% of $\$18.95 = 5\% \times \$18.95$

$\qquad = 0.05 \times \$18.95 = \$0.9475$ ◄─┤ Change the percent to a decimal and multiply. Round the product to the nearest cent.

The amount of the discount to the nearest cent is $0.95.

Find the amount of each discount to the nearest cent.

23. a 25% discount on an item costing $5.89

24. a 40% discount on an item costing $79.95

25. <u>Writing in Math</u> Explain how to estimate 27% of $98.

Mixed Review and Test Prep

Take It to the NET
Test Prep
www.scottforesman.com

Find by using mental math.

26. 20% of 45   **27.** 50% of 12   **28.** 75% of 24   **29.** $33\frac{1}{3}\%$ of 60

30. Which is the measure of an obtuse angle?

    A. 45°   **B.** 90°   **C.** 135°   **D.** 180°

31. Which is NOT equivalent to 4 ft?

    A. 0.5 yd   **B.** $\frac{4}{3}$ yd   **C.** 48 in.   **D.** 1 yd 1 ft

Enrichment

Using a grid to enlarge or reduce figures.

When a figure is drawn on a grid, it is easy to enlarge or reduce the figure. The segment lengths in the second figure below are twice as long as those in the first. Notice that $\frac{\text{length } AB}{\text{length } CD} = \frac{4 \text{ units}}{8 \text{ units}} = \frac{1}{2}$. When you compare any two corresponding lengths on the figures, the ratio is always 1:2.

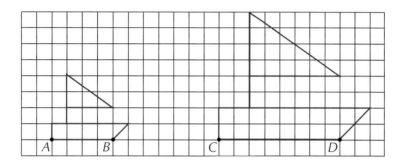

Copy the first figure above on another grid. Make an enlargement in which each corresponding length on the second figure is 3 times as long as each length on the first.

Discover Math in Your World

The Right Balance

It is recommended that no more than 30% of your calorie intake should be fat calories. Mae consumes about 2,200 total calories daily.

1. Use mental math to find the maximum amount of fat calories that Mae's daily food intake should contain.

2. A cookie package label says that one cookie contains 140 calories and that 70 calories in each cookie are fat calories. If Mae eats three cookies, has she exceeded the recommended amount of fat calories for the day? Explain.

All text pages available online and on CD-ROM.

Problem-Solving Applications

Food We get more than just energy from the food we eat. Food supplies our cells with a wide variety of chemicals they need to do their jobs. Food also gives our bodies the materials they need to repair and replace old cells. In fact, every few years, virtually all of our cells in our bodies are replaced by new ones!

Trivia The sandwich is named after John Montagu, the Earl of Sandwich. Although the combination of meat and bread was probably enjoyed long before his time, the Earl is often given credit for making the first sandwich in the mid-1700s with salted beef on toasted bread.

1 The picture shown here is a circle graph of what many nutritionists feel is a balanced diet. Estimate the percent of a person's diet that should be made with fruits and vegetables.

2 A quarter pound of roast beef has 25 grams of protein. How many grams of protein are in one ounce of roast beef? Round your answer to the nearest tenth.

3 Tabi kept track of all the food she ate during a week. She found that $\frac{2}{5}$ of her diet consisted of fruit and vegetables. What percent of her diet was made of all other types of foods combined?

Good News/Bad News As the world develops better farms and industries, more people can get better nutrition than ever before. Unfortunately, as societies modernize, it also becomes easier to eat too many processed foods that have few nutrients.

Using Key Facts

4 A large tub of theater popcorn may have over 16.7 times the calories of a regular serving of popcorn. How many calories are in a bucket of theater popcorn?

Key Facts
Calories in Common Foods

Food	Quantity	Calories
•Milk	240 mL	120
•Orange juice	250 mL	115
•Hamburger	85 g	240
•Hot dog	45 g	120
•Popcorn	840 mL	105
•Potato chips	11 chips	150
•Flavored yogurt	240 mL	230
•Applesauce	120 mL	100
•Banana	Medium	110

5 A piece of lasagna measuring 3 inches by 4 inches has 450 calories. What are possible dimensions of a piece that has 900 calories?

6 **Writing in Math** Write your own word problem that involves food. Solve it and write its answer in a complete sentence.

7 **Decision Making** When sitting, a person may use 70 calories per hour. Choose at least 3 foods from the Key Facts chart for a lunch. Estimate how many hours of inactivity would be needed to use the calories in your meal.

Do You Know How?

Do You Understand?

Understanding Percent (11–8)

Write the fraction in lowest terms and the percent that represents the shaded part of each figure.

1.

2.

3.

4.

Ⓐ Explain how you found the fraction in Exercise 3.

Ⓑ Copy and complete the shading of the figure to represent 65%.

Ⓒ If $\frac{2}{5}$ = 40%, then what is $\frac{1}{5}$ as a percent? Explain how you found your answer.

Mental Math: Finding a Percent of a Number (11–9)

Find each using mental math.

5. 60% of 25
6. 50% of 64
7. 20% of 45
8. 75% of 40
9. If 3% of a number is 15, what is 6% of the number?

Ⓓ Explain how you solved Exercise 8.

Ⓔ Would 25% of 97 be easy to do mentally? Explain.

Ⓕ Explain how you solved Exercise 9.

Estimating Percents (11–10)

Estimate.

10. 49% of 80
11. 21% of 35
12. 76% of 100
13. 62% of 150
14. Super Sports charges 9% sales tax. About how much sales tax would be added to a $250 pair of skis?

Ⓖ Tell what percents you used in place of the given percents in Exercises 10–11. Explain why you made the choices you did.

Ⓗ Is the exact answer to Exercise 14 greater than or less than your estimate? Explain how you know.

MULTIPLE CHOICE

1. Which figure represents $\frac{2}{5}$? (11–8)

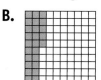

A. **B.** **C.** **D.**

2. Which number is closest to 74% of 80? (11–10)

A. 20   **B.** 60   **C.** 50   **D.** 70

FREE RESPONSE

Write the fraction in lowest terms and the percent that represents the shaded part of each figure. (11–8)

3.   **4.**   **5.**   **6.**

Find each using mental math. (11–9)

7. 50% of 20   **8.** 20% of 45   **9.** 10% of 300   **10.** 100% of 55

Estimate. (11–10)

11. 27% of 40   **12.** 51% of 120   **13.** 98% of 37   **14.** 32% of 70

Writing in Math

15. Explain how to shade a 10-by-10 grid to represent the percent of U.S. states bordering the Great Lakes. What is this percent? (11–8)

16. If there are twice as many U.S. states bordering the Mississippi River as there are U.S. states bordering the Pacific Ocean, explain how to find the fraction of U.S. states bordering the Mississippi River. Write this fraction as a percent. (11–8)

U.S States Bordering Bodies Of Water

Body of Water	Fraction of States
Pacific Ocean	$\frac{1}{10}$
Atlantic Ocean (including Gulf of Mexico)	$\frac{9}{25}$
Great Lakes	$\frac{4}{25}$

Test-Taking Strategies

Understand the question.

Get information for the answer.

Plan how to find the answer.

Make smart choices.

Use writing in math.

Improve written answers.

Improve Written Answers

You can follow the tips below to learn how to improve written answers on a test. It is important to write a clear answer and include only information needed to answer the question.

1. The table below shows the price of amusement park tickets. Complete the pattern in the table to find the price of 5 tickets.

Highcrest Amusement Park Tickets					
Number of Tickets	1	2	3	4	5
Price	$18	$36	$54	$72	–

Answer:_____

On the lines below, explain how the price changes as the number of tickets changes.

_____

Improve Written Answers

• Check if your answer is complete.

*In order to **get as many points as possible,** I must find the price of 5 tickets and I must explain how the price changes as the number of tickets changes.*

• Check if your answer makes sense.

I should check that my explanation works for every pair of numbers in the table. Then I should check that it works for the price I found for 5 tickets.

• Check if your explanation is clear and easy to follow.

*I should reread my explanation to be sure it is **accurate and clear.** I shouldn't include any unnecessary information.*

The rubric below is a scoring guide for Test Questions 1 and 2.

Scoring Rubric

4 points	**3** points	**2** points	**1** point	**0** points
Full credit: 4 points The answer and explanation are correct.	**Partial credit: 3 points** The answer is correct, but the explanation does not fully describe the relationship.	**Partial credit: 2 points** The answer is correct or the explanation is correct, but not both.	**Partial credit: 1 point** The answer is incorrect. The explanation shows partial understanding.	**No credit: 0 points** The answer and explanation are both incorrect or missing.

Daryl used the scoring rubric on page 680 to score a student's answer to Test Question 1. The student's paper is shown below.

Answer: _____$80_____

On the lines below, explain how the price changes as the number of tickets changes.

The price goes up $18 for

every additional ticket.

_____

Think It Through

The answer is wrong. The student probably made a computational error since the explanation seems fine. The correct answer is $90. Since the answer is wrong, but the explanation is right, this paper scores 2 points.

Now it's your turn.

Score the student's paper. If it does not get 4 points, rewrite it so that it does.

2. Jill needs to buy some racks to hold her CDs. The table shows how many CDs she'll be able to store in the racks.

Number of racks	1	2	3	4	5	6
Number of CDs	15	30	45	60	75	

Find the number of CDs Jill can store if she buys 6 racks. Explain how the number of CDs changes as the number of racks changes.

Jill can store 90 CDs. Each time the

number of racks changes by 1, the

number of CDs changes by 15.

_____

_____

An equation with two **equal ratios** is a **proportion**.
(p. 649)

Self Check

Write and graph equal ratios. (Lessons 11-1, 11-2, 11-6)

The **ratio** of vowels to consonants in FIGHTERS is $\frac{2}{6}$.
Find 2 ratios equal to $\frac{2}{6}$.

Multiply or divide both terms by the same nonzero number.

$\frac{2 \times 2}{6 \times 2} = \frac{4}{12}$ $\frac{2 \div 2}{6 \div 2} = \frac{1}{3}$

$\frac{2}{6} = \frac{4}{12}$ ← **proportion**

Graph the **terms** in the **equal ratios.**

$\frac{2}{6}$, $\frac{4}{12}$, $\frac{6}{18}$, and $\frac{1}{3}$.

You can see that the points lie on a line.

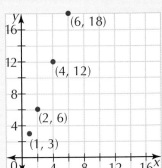

1. Find 3 ratios equal to the ratio of red dots to green. • • • • • • • • • • • • • • • •

Self Check

Unit means one.
A **unit rate** is a comparison to 1 unit.
(p. 654)

Find unit rates and use them to write to explain. (Lessons 11-4, 11-7)

Which is the better buy? Tell how you decided.

$2.96 for 8 pears $1.70 for 5 pears

Divide to find each **unit rate.**

$\frac{\$2.96}{8} = \frac{?}{1}$ unit rate = $\frac{\$0.37}{1 \text{ pear}}$

$\frac{\$1.70}{5} = \frac{?}{1}$ unit rate = $\frac{\$0.34}{1 \text{ pear}}$

The better buy is $1.70 for 5 pears. I figured out the unit rate for each and found that at $2.96 for 8 pears, each pear costs $0.37. But at $1.70 for 5 pears, each pear costs only $0.34.

2. Which is the better buy, 12 pencils for $1.68 or 20 pencils for $3.00?

There are 100 cents in a dollar.

Percent is a ratio in which the first term is compared to 100. (p. 668)

Self Check

Compute and estimate with percents. (Lessons 11-8, 11-9, 11-10)

Percent means *per hundred*.

40%

Find 25% of 68.

$25\% \text{ of } 68 = \frac{1}{4} \times 68$

$= 17$

Estimate 18% of 156.

Use compatible numbers.

18% of 156 is about 20% of 150.

$20\% \text{ of } 150 = \frac{1}{5} \times 150$

$= 30$

18% of 156 is about 30.

3. Find $33\frac{1}{3}\%$ of 60 and estimate 12% of 87.

The **scale** in a **scale drawing** is a ratio that compares the dimensions in the drawing to the dimensions of the real object.

Self Check

Make a table or use scales to solve problems. (Lessons 11-5, 11-6)

Make a table when quantities change using a pattern.

Rayanne jogged for 20 minutes. Every day she plans to jog 2 minutes more than on the previous day. How long will she jog on the seventh day?

Day	1	2	3	4	5	6	7
Time (min)	20	22	24	26	28	30	32

She will jog 32 minutes.

Use ratios when working with scale drawings.

The **scale** for the **scale drawing** of a room is 1 in.: 3 ft. If a room is 15 feet long, how long would it be on the drawing?

Write equal ratios. $\frac{1}{3} = \frac{?}{15}$

$\frac{1}{3} = \frac{5}{15}$

The room is 5 in. long on the drawing.

4. In the scale drawing described above, how long would a 9-foot couch be?

Answers: 1. Sample answer: $\frac{6}{8}$; $\frac{3}{4}$; $\frac{12}{16}$ 2. 12 pencils for $1.68 3. 20; sample estimate: 9 4. 3 in.

Chapter 11 Key Vocabulary and Concept Review   683

MULTIPLE CHOICE

Choose the correct letter for each answer.

1. Which ratio compares the number of blue squares to the number of circles?

 A. 2:2   **C.** 4:2

 B. 2:4   **D.** 2:6

2. Which ratio is equal to 9:4?

 A. $\frac{3}{2}$

 B. 4 to 9

 C. $\frac{8}{18}$

 D. 27:12

Think It Through
I can **eliminate** wrong answers.

3. Find the unit rate of 48 miles in 3 hours.

 A. $\frac{1 \text{ mi}}{12 \text{ hr}}$ **C.** $\frac{16 \text{ mi}}{1 \text{ hr}}$

 B. $\frac{18 \text{ mi}}{1 \text{ hr}}$ **D.** $\frac{32 \text{ mi}}{2 \text{ hr}}$

4. If a line through the points on the graph at the right were extended, which point would be on the line?

 A. (6, 12)

 B. (8, 24)

 C. (7, 20)

 D. (9, 28)

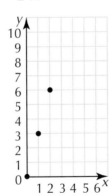

5. Which is the best buy?

 A. 5 oz for $3.90   **C.** 4 oz for $3.24

 B. 8 oz for $6.08   **D.** 12 oz for $9.00

6. Bo is decorating for a party. He hangs balloons in bunches of 4 purple balloons and 6 white balloons. If he hangs 12 bunches of balloons, how many white balloons are there?

 A. 2 balloons   **C.** 48 balloons

 B. 12 balloons   **D.** 72 balloons

7. What percent represents the shaded part of the figure?

 A. 4%   **C.** 40%

 B. 20%   **D.** 80%

8. Find 25% of 84.

 A. 21   **C.** 42

 B. 25   **D.** 63

9. Which fraction is equivalent to 20%?

 A. $\frac{1}{20}$ **C.** $\frac{1}{5}$

 B. $\frac{1}{10}$ **D.** $\frac{1}{2}$

10. Estimate 35% of 299.

 A. about 40   **C.** about 100

 B. about 50   **D.** about 150

11. Which ratio is 6:18 written in simplest form?

 A. $\frac{3}{1}$ **C.** 1 to 3

 B. $\frac{1}{9}$ **D.** 2:6

12. In a scale drawing, a boat is 3 inches long. The scale is 1 in.: 9 ft. What is the actual length of the boat?

 A. 3 inches   **C.** 27 inches

 B. 3 feet   **D.** 27 feet

13. Which of the following is a pair of equal ratios?

A. $\frac{3}{4}$; 8:6   **C.** 5 to 2; 2:5

B. $\frac{9}{3}$; 6:2   **D.** 2 to 12; $\frac{4}{16}$

For 14–15, use the table below.

Colors of Cars in the Mall Parking Lot					
Red	Black	White	Tan	Blue	Green
15	28	35	10	21	24

14. What is the ratio of green cars to red cars?

A. 5:6   **C.** 4:3

B. 3:2   **D.** 8:5

15. Which two quantities are being compared with the ratio 35:21?

A. blue cars to black cars

B. blue cars to white cars

C. white cars to blue cars

D. white cars to red cars

FREE RESPONSE

Write a ratio in simplest form for each comparison.

Data File

Shapes in Design

Shape	Number
square	8
triangle	12
circle	6
star	15

16. stars to squares

17. triangles to circles

18. stars to all shapes

19. circles to stars

Write each ratio in simplest form.

20. 16 to 18   **21.** 6:20

Give two other ratios that are equal to each.

22. 8 to 5   **23.** 12:40

Write each rate as a unit rate.

24. 207 miles on 9 gallons

25. $153 for 18 hours of work

26. A hexagon has 6 sides. Copy and complete the table of equal ratios. Then, on a grid, graph the ordered pairs from the table and connect them with a line.

Number of hexagons	1	2	3	4	5
Number of sides	6	12			

27. If the line in problem 26 is extended, is the point (8, 24) on the line?

Write the percent that represents the shaded part of each figure.

28.   **29.**

Find each using mental math.

30. $33\frac{1}{3}$% of 72   **31.** 60% of 50

Estimate.

32. 65% of 46   **33.** 49% of 99

Writing in Math

34. A map has a scale of 3 cm = 35 km. Explain how to find the actual distance between two cities that are 9 cm apart on the map.

35. Ted and his family are driving 600 miles on vacation. Based on the data below, predict how many gallons of gasoline the family will use. Explain how you made your prediction.

Number of Miles Driven	Gallons of Gasoline Used
136	7
107	6
153	8

Number and Operation

MULTIPLE CHOICE

1. Find 25% of 80.

  A. 20   **C.** 60

  B. 40   **D.** 320

2. Which ratio is equal to 6:10?

  A. 9:15   **C.** 5:3

  B. 2:5   **D.** 3:2

3. Find $152 \div 4$.

  A. 36   **C.** 38

  B. 37   **D.** 48

FREE RESPONSE

4. Add $\frac{5}{6}$ and $\frac{3}{4}$.

5. Order the following from least to greatest.

   42%, 0.3, $\frac{1}{4}$, 0.08, 75%, $\frac{3}{5}$

6. Jack earned $143.75 last week. He worked 23 hours last week. What is Jack's hourly wage?

Writing in Math

7. Explain how to use compatible numbers to estimate 34% of 59.

8. Which store has the better deal? Tell how you decided.

Geometry and Measurement

MULTIPLE CHOICE

9. What is the area of the parallelogram?

   12 ft

  A. 30 ft^2 **C.** 60 ft^2

  B. 34 ft^2 **D.** 72 ft^2

10. 3 yards = ___ feet

  A. 3   **C.** 9

  B. 6   **D.** 18

11. What is the volume of a cube with a side length of 5 cm?

  A. 15 cm^3 **C.** 125 cm^3

  B. 25 cm^3 **D.** 150 cm^3

FREE RESPONSE

12. Classify the triangle by its sides and by its angles.

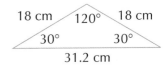

13. Draw circle B with diameter AC, chord RS and central angle ABS that measures 55°.

Writing in Math

14. Describe how to find the perimeter and area of a triangle.

Data Analysis and Probability

15. How many pairs of candidates are possible if the following people are running for president and vice-president of the student council?

Candidate

President	Vice President
Isabelle	Rich
Al	Denise
Joe	Kate

A. 8   **C.** 12

B. 9   **D.** 18

16. What is the median of this data set?

34, 22, 28, 30, 30, 24, 20, 24

A. 30   **C.** 26

B. 26.5   **D.** 14

17. What was the average temperature in July?

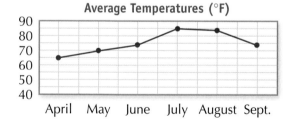

Average Temperatures (°F)

April   May   June   July   August   Sept.

Writing in Math

18. Describe the trend in the above graph. Predict what the average temperature will be in October. Explain your answer.

Algebra

19. Solve for the variable.
$$6y = 54$$

A. $y = 8$ **C.** $y = 48$

B. $y = 9$ **D.** $y = 60$

20. Solve for the variable.
$$b - 15 = 18$$

A. $b = 3$ **C.** $b = 23$

B. $b = 13$ **D.** $b = 33$

21. A tree in a scale drawing measures 4 cm. The scale is 2 cm = 3 ft. What is the actual height of the tree?

A. 4 ft   **C.** 8 ft

B. 6 ft   **D.** 12 ft

22. Solve for the variable.
$$\frac{s}{6} = 12$$

23. Write an algebraic expression for 5 more than a number.

Writing in Math

24. Complete the table of equal ratios. Then, graph the ordered pairs on a grid and connect them with a line. Is the point (3,10) on the line? Explain.

Number of boxes	2	4	6	8	10
Number of cans	8	16			

25. Explain how to evaluate the expression $x - 20$ if $x = 100$.

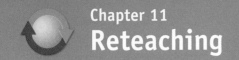

Set 11-1 (pages 646–647)

Write a ratio for diamonds to triangles three ways.

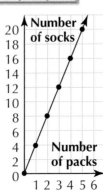

There are 5 diamonds and 4 triangles.

5:4   5 to 4 $\frac{5}{4}$

Remember that a ratio is a comparison of like or unlike quantities. The order of the terms is important.

1. blue shapes to green shapes

2. triangles to squares

3. red shapes to all shapes

4. red diamonds to other diamonds

Set 11-2 (pages 648–651)

Give two ratios equal to $\frac{20}{12}$.

One Way: Multiply.

$$\frac{20 \times 2}{12 \times 2} = \frac{40}{24} \qquad \frac{20 \times 3}{12 \times 3} = \frac{60}{36}$$

Another Way: Divide.

$$\frac{20 \div 2}{12 \div 2} = \frac{10}{6} \qquad \frac{20 \div 4}{12 \div 4} = \frac{5}{3}$$

Remember to find equivalent ratios, you must perform the same operation on each quantity.

1. $\frac{6}{10}$ **2.** 5:4   **3.** $\frac{15}{12}$

4. 2 to 8   **5.** $\frac{8}{14}$ **6.** 27:9

7. 35:40   **8.** $\frac{28}{14}$ **9.** $\frac{7}{11}$

Set 11-3 (pages 652–653)

There are 4 socks in a pack. Copy and complete the table. Then, on a grid, graph the ordered pairs from the table. If the line is extended, is the point (14, 26) on the line?

Number of Packs	1	2	3	4	5
Number of Socks	4	8			

No, the point (14, 26) would not be on the line, since $\frac{14}{26} = \frac{7}{13}$ and $\frac{1}{4}$ are not equal ratios.

Remember that equal ratios form a straight line when graphed.

1. Each page in a photo album holds 6 photos. Copy and complete this table of equal ratios.

Number of Pages	1	2	3	4	5	6
Number of Photos	6	12				

2. On a grid, graph the ordered pairs from the table. Connect the points with a line.

3. If the line were extended, would the point (16, 96) be on the line?

Set 11-4 (pages 654–655)

Write 315 miles in 6 hours as a unit rate.

Use equivalent fractions.

$$\frac{315 \text{ miles}}{6 \text{ hours}} = \frac{? \text{ miles}}{1 \text{ hour}} \qquad \frac{315 \div 6}{6 \div 6} = \frac{52.5}{1}$$

$$\text{Unit rate} = \frac{52.5 \text{ miles}}{1 \text{ hour}}$$

Remember that a unit rate is a comparison where the second term is 1 unit.

1. 44 miles in 8 days

2. 63 pages in 3 hours

3. $5.40 for 12 cans

4. $105 for 7 hours of work

5. 55 pages in 25 seconds

Set 11-5 (pages 660–661)

To make a table, follow these steps.

Step 1: Set up the table with the correct labels.

Step 2: Enter known data in the table.

Step 3: Look for a pattern. Extend the table.

Step 4: Find the answer in the table.

Remember to read the problem carefully and make sure the information in your table represents the problem.

1. Adam is training for a race. For every 3 minutes he runs, he walks for 4 minutes. Yesterday, he ran for 27 minutes. How many minutes did he walk?

Set 11-6 (pages 662–663)

A scale drawing for a tabletop is shown below on a centimeter grid. What is the actual length of the table?

$$\frac{1 \text{ cm}}{6 \text{ in.}} = \frac{3 \text{ cm}}{? \text{ in.}} \qquad \text{Write equal ratios.}$$

$$\frac{1 \times 3}{6 \times 3} = \frac{3}{18} \qquad \text{Find the missing number.}$$

The actual length of the table is 18 inches.

Scale: 1 cm : 6 in.

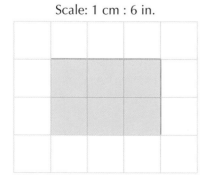

Remember to check that the labels are the same for each ratio in the proportion.

1. What is the actual width of the table?

2. The scale of a map is 1 in. = 28 m. A straight road on the map is 3.5 inches long. What is the actual length of the road?

3. A scale drawing of a statue is 3 inches tall. The actual statue is 21 feet tall. What scale was used?

Set 11-7 (pages 664–665)

The table shows the number of tickets sold for the first three days of a theater production. Based on these results, predict how many tickets will be sold in all if the production runs for 10 days.

Performance	1	2	3
Number of Tickets Sold	324	273	305

Since 324 + 273 + 305 = 902, about 900 tickets were sold in 3 days. Since $\frac{900}{3}$ = 300, about 300 people attended each performance. Since 10 × 300 = 3,000, I predict about 3,000 tickets will be sold in 10 days.

Remember to state your prediction clearly.

1. Suppose the production only runs for 7 days. Predict how many tickets will be sold in all.

2. If 284 tickets were sold at the third performance, rather than 305 tickets, would this change your prediction? Explain.

Set 11-8 (pages 668–669)

Write the fraction in lowest terms and the percent that represents the shaded part of the figure.

$\frac{24}{100} = \frac{6}{25}$

$= 24\%$

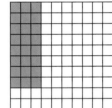

Remember that a percent is a comparison to 100.

1.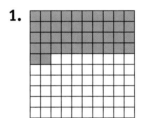

2.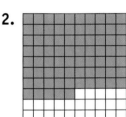

Set 11-9 (pages 670–671)

Find 20% of 60 using mental math.

You can use fraction equivalents.

$20\% = \frac{1}{5}$

$\frac{1}{5} \times 60 = 12$

So, 20% of 60 is 12.

This is easy to multiply mentally, because 5 is a factor of 60.

Remember it is easy to multiply a fraction and a number when the denominator of the fraction is a factor of the number.

1. 40% of 80
2. 25% of 24
3. $33\frac{1}{3}$% of 36
4. 75% of 56

Set 11-10 (pages 672–675)

Estimate 26% of 638.

26% × 638 is about 25% × 640.

$25\% = \frac{1}{4}$ $\frac{1}{4} \times 640 = 160$

So, 26% of 638 is about 160.

Remember you can use compatible numbers and fraction equivalents to estimate percents.

1. 24% of 48
2. 68% of 89
3. 74% of 361
4. 19% of 451
5. 11% of 292
6. 52% of 75

Take It to the NET
More Practice
www.scottforesman.com

Set 11-1 (pages 646–647)

Use the data file at the right to write a ratio for each comparison.

1. comedy to action   **2.** suspense to horror

3. action to all other movies   **4.** comedy to all movies

5. cartoon to comedy   **6.** all movies to suspense

7. Of the comedy movies rented, 25 were DVDs. Write a ratio comparing the number of comedy DVDs that were rented to the number of comedy tapes that were rented.

Data File	
Movie Rentals	
Movie type	# Rented
Comedy	45
Horror	38
Suspense	22
Action	60
Cartoon	35

Set 11-2 (pages 648–651)

Write each ratio in simplest form.

1. 10 to 8   **2.** 21:7   **3.** 24 to 9   **4.** 36:54

Give two other ratios that are equal to each.

5. $\frac{6}{20}$ **6.** $\frac{16}{10}$ **7.** 12 to 14   **8.** 32:48

Are the ratios in each pair equal?

9. $\frac{5}{6}$ and $\frac{12}{10}$ **10.** 35:7 and 5:1

11. $\frac{8}{15}$ and $\frac{15}{8}$ **12.** $\frac{18}{3}$ and $\frac{6}{1}$

13. 48 to 72 and 10 to 15   **14.** 60:54 and 36:30

Set 11-3 (pages 652–653)

1. Suppose each box contains 5 cans. Copy and complete this table of equal ratios.

Number of boxes	1	2	3	4	5	6
Number of cans	5	10				

2. On a grid, graph the ordered pairs from the table. Connect the points with a line.

3. If the line were extended, would the point for (12,70) be on the graph?

4. Give three equal ratios from the graph below.

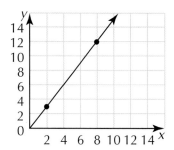

Set 11-4 (pages 654–655)

Tell the two units being compared in each rate.

1. 3 miles in 30 minutes   **2.** 2 cups per recipe   **3.** $6.25 an hour

Write each as a unit rate.

4. 12 laps in 10 minutes   **5.** $112.50 for 15 hours

6. 9 cups for 12 servings   **7.** $7.47 for 3 pounds

8. Ms. Jacobson bought 4 pounds of grapes for $4.76. What was
the unit price for the grapes?

Set 11-5 (pages 660–661)

Solve. Write each answer in a complete sentence.

1. Kitt makes flower arrangements.
For each arrangement she used
2 roses and 5 carnations. She used
30 carnations. How many
arrangements did she make?

Number of arrangements	1	2	3	4	5	6
Number of roses	2	4				
Number of carnations	5	10				

2. Josie uses 4 yards of fabric to
make dresses for 3 dolls. If she
used 16 yards of fabric, how
many dresses did she make?

Yards of fabric	4	8			
Number of dresses made	3	6			

3. Brian spent a total of 8 hours running this week. He ran a distance
of 42 miles. If he runs the same distance each hour, how many
miles does he run in an hour?

Set 11-6 (pages 662–663)

Refer to the scale drawing to the right.

1. The width of the sandbox in the drawing
is 1 cm. What is the actual length of the
sandbox?

2. What is the actual length and width of
the entire playground?

3. Tom drew a scale drawing of himself. In
the drawing he is 8 inches tall. If the scale
of the drawing is 2 in. = 1.5 ft, what is Tom's
actual height?

4. Two cities are located 150 miles apart. On a
map, the two cities are located 3 inches apart.
What is the scale of the map?

slides
area

swings
area

1 cm = 5 ft

sandbox

Take It to the NET
More Practice
www.scottforesman.com

Set 11-7 (pages 664–665)

1. The table shows the amount of money Mariah saved each week during a 4-week period. Based on these results, predict how much money she will save in a 10-week period. Explain how you made your prediction.

Week	1	2	3	4
Amount Saved	$47	$45	$59	$41

Set 11-8 (pages 668–669)

Write the fraction in lowest terms and the percent that represents the shaded part of each figure.

1.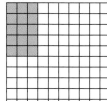

2.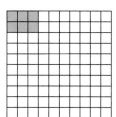

3.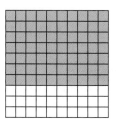

Set 11-9 (pages 670–671)

Find each using mental math.

1. 20% of 55	**2.** 25% of 96	**3.** 75% of 240
4. 10% of 530	**5.** $66\frac{2}{3}$% of 420	**6.** 80% of 600
7. 50% of 12	**8.** 25% of 72	**9.** 75% of 200
10. 60% of 15	**11.** 20% of 35	**12.** $33\frac{1}{3}$% of 162

13. If 10% of a number is 8, what is 20% of the number?

Set 11-10 (pages 672–675)

Estimate each.

1. 32% of 62	**2.** 21% of 74	**3.** 74% of 239
4. 18% of 123	**5.** 9% of 167	**6.** 67% of 89
7. 38% of 43	**8.** 65% of 601	**9.** 49% of 999

10. The bill for dinner was $38.15. If Mrs. Kennedy wants to leave an 18% tip, about how much should she leave?

Algebra: Integers, Equations, and Graphing

DIAGNOSING READINESS

Ⓐ Vocabulary
(Grade 4, pages 36–37, 66–67, 152–153)

1. In $4 + 5 = 9$, 9 is the __?__ of 4 and 5.

2. In $6 \times 3 = 18$, 6 and 3 are __?__ and 18 is the __?__.

3. In $32 \div 8 = 4$, 4 is the __?__.

4. In $8 - 3 = 5$, 5 is the __?__ of 8 and 3.

5. In $n - 8 = 12$, n is called a __?__.

> **Vocabulary**
>
> - **product** *(p. 66)*   - **difference** *(Grade 4)*
> - **factors** *(p. 66)*   - **sum** *(Grade 4)*
> - **quotient** *(p. 152)*   - **variable** *(p. 104)*

Ⓑ Writing Expressions
(pages 104–105)

Write each as an algebraic expression.

6. the sum of v and 18

7. 15 less than m

8. the quotient of k and 3

9. k decreased by 8

10. the product of 7 and t

11. h divided by 10

12. A table is x feet long. What is its length in inches?

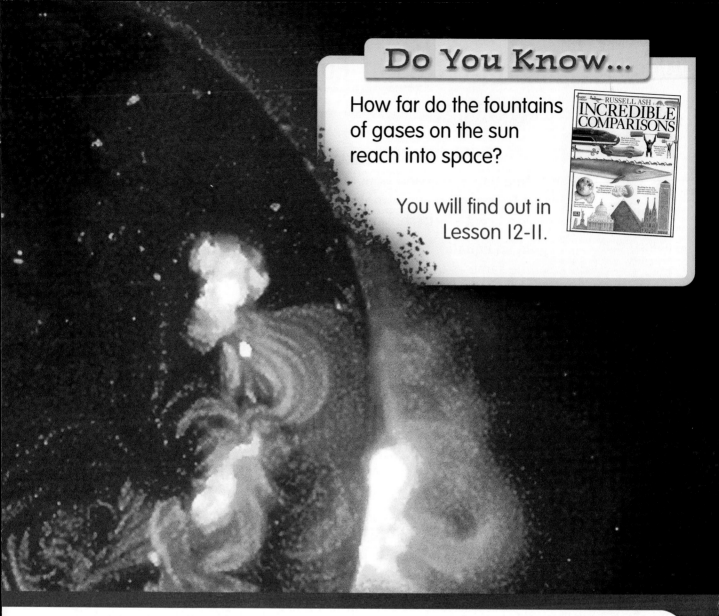

Do You Know...

How far do the fountains of gases on the sun reach into space?

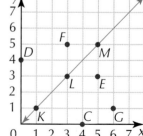

You will find out in Lesson 12-11.

C Solving Equations
(pages 108–109)

Solve each equation.

13. $6 + a = 36$

14. $k + 31 = 66$

15. $m - 18 = 70$

16. $s - 54 = 175$

17. $6 \times h = 54$

18. $63 = p \times 9$

19. $\frac{n}{4} = 8$

20. $72 \div w = 8$

21. Write an equation for "the sum of a number and 7 equals 28."

22. Write an equation for "the product of 3 and some number is 15."

D Graphing Ordered Pairs
(pages 174–175, 652–653)

23. Give the ordered pairs for points G, L, and M.

24. Name the point at (3, 5) and the point at (5, 3).

25. Are the points (0, 4) and (4, 0) the same? Explain.

26. If the line is extended, do you think (8, 8) would be on the line? Why or why not?

Algebra

Key Idea
In an equation, the expressions on each side have the same value.

Vocabulary
• equation (p. 108)
• properties of equality
• inverse operations (p. 133)

Properties of Equality

LEARN

What are the properties of equality?

Mia had 5 CDs and bought 2 more. Juan had 3 CDs and bought 4 more. You could write $5 + 2 = 3 + 4$ to show that each has the same number of CDs.

In an **equation,** the value of the expression on the left is the same as the value of the expression on the right.

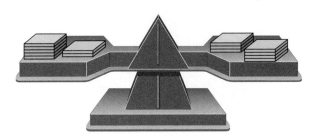

Properties of equality tell what you can do to both sides of an equation so that the sides stay equal.

Properties of Equality

Property	Example
Addition Property of Equality You can add the same number to both sides of an equation and the sides remain equal.	$8 + 4 = 7 + 5$ So, $8 + 4 + 3 = 7 + 5 + 3$
Subtraction Property of Equality You can subtract the same number from both sides of an equation and the sides remain equal.	$9 + 15 = 24$ So, $(9 + 15) - 4 = 24 - 4$
Multiplication Property of Equality You can multiply both sides of an equation by the same number and the sides remain equal.	$7 \times 6 = 14 \times 3$ So, $7 \times 6 \times 2 = 14 \times 3 \times 2$
Division Property of Equality You can divide both sides of an equation by the same number (except 0) and the sides remain equal.	$12 + 8 = 20$ So, $(12 + 8) \div 5 = 20 \div 5$

✅ Talk About It

1. Which property of equality is illustrated by each pair of equations?

   a. $4 \times 5 = 10 \times 2$
   So, $4 \times 5 + 12 = 10 \times 2 + 12$.

   b. $4 + 6 = 9 + 1$
   So, $(4 + 6) \div 5 = (9 + 1) \div 5$.

   c. $22 - 11 = 33 - 22$
   So, $5 + 22 - 11 = 5 + 33 - 22$.

   d. $9 + 5 = 5 + 9$
   So, $(9 + 5) \times 2 = (5 + 9) \times 2$.

2. The equation $5 + 2 = 3 + 4$ shows that Mia and Juan have the same number of CDs. What equation would show how many CDs each has after giving away 1 CD?

What are inverse operations?

Another idea you will use when solving equations is **inverse operations.** Addition undoes subtraction, and subtraction undoes addition. Division undoes multiplication, and multiplication undoes division. Inverse operations undo each other.

When you solve equations, you use properties of equality and inverse operations.

Before solving equations, you need to look at expressions with variables and decide how to get the variables alone.

Think It Through

When I need to get a variable alone, I need to remember to use inverse operations.

Example

For each expression, tell what inverse operation and what number to use to get n alone.

$n + 3$	$n - 3$	$n \times 7$	$n \div 8$
Subtraction undoes addition.	Addition undoes subtraction.	Division undoes multiplication.	Multiplication undoes division.
Subtract 3.	Add 3.	Divide by 7.	Multiply by 8.
		Remember: you can not divide by 0.	

✔ Talk About It

3. In the first expression above, what inverse operation is used to get n alone? What inverse operation is used in the third expression shown above?

4. Number Sense Why is $137 \div 14 \times 14$ easy to evaluate?

CHECK ✓

For another example, see Set 12-1 on p. 742.

Which property of equality is illustrated by each pair of equations?

1. $8 \times 6 = 3 \times 16$
So, $(8 \times 6) - 6 = (3 \times 16) - 6$.

2. $12 + 6 = 18$
So, $(12 + 6) \div 2 = 18 \div 2$.

3. $3 + 7 = 8 + 2$
So, $(3 + 7) \times 10 = (8 + 2) \times 10$.

4. $8 = 24 \div 3$
So, $8 + 7 = (24 \div 3) + 7$.

Tell what inverse operation and what number can be used to get n alone.

5. $n - 8$ **6.** $21 + n$ **7.** $43 \times n$ **8.** $n \div 12$

9. Reasoning In an expression, subtraction is used to get n alone. What operation was being performed in the original expression?

Ⓐ Skills and Understanding

Which property of equality is illustrated by each pair of equations?

10. $16 + 2 = 18$
So, $(16 + 2) - 8 = 18 - 8$.

11. $3 \times 4 = 4 \times 3$
So, $(3 \times 4) \div 6 = 4 \times 3 \div 6$.

12. $12 \div 6 = 2$
So, $(12 \div 6) + n = 2 + n$.

13. $10 - 5 = 5$
So, $(10 - 5) + 2 = 5 + 2$.

14. $8 + 6 = 6 + 8$
So, $(8 + 6) \div 2 = (6 + 8) \div 2$.

15. $18 \times 4 = 9 \times 8$
So, $(18 \times 4) + 6 = (9 \times 8) + 6$.

Tell what inverse operation and what number you would use to get *n* alone.

16. $n - 5$ **17.** $n \div 8$ **18.** $45 + n$ **19.** $25 \times n$

20. $4 \times n$ **21.** $n \times 18$ **22.** $n \div 14$ **23.** $n + 7$

24. Reasoning Multiplication is used to get *n* alone in an expression. What operation was being performed in the original expression?

Ⓑ Reasoning and Problem Solving

Reasoning Write the missing number that makes each equation true.

25. $5 \times 6 = (3 + 2) \times$ ⬤   **26.** $(12 - 2) \div 2 = 10 \div$ ⬤   **27.** $8 +$ ⬤ $= (4 \times 2) + 5$

28. $(4 \times 8) \div 2 = (8 \times 4) \div$ ⬤   **29.** $(8 \div 2) \times 5 =$ ⬤ $\times 5$ **30.** ⬤ $+ (8 - 4) = 5 + (8 - 4)$

31. $(18 \div 3) - 6 =$ ⬤ $- 6$ **32.** $(7 \times 4) - 1 = (7 \times 4) -$ ⬤   **33.** $13 - n = (12 + 1) -$ ⬤

Using the rule given, find the value of each variable.

Rule: Divide by 20	
80	4
120	*y*
n	7
400	*z*
2,000	100

34.
35.
36.

Rule: Subtract 35	
80	45
36	*y*
n	75
96	*z*
70	35

37.
38.
39.

Use the data file at the right for 40–42.

40. Nauru is how many square miles greater in area than Monaco?

41. Representations Carrie uses the data to make a bar graph. She decides to arrange the bars from left to right in decreasing heights. From left to right on the graph, how should the bars be labeled? Explain how you decided.

42. Estimation The areas of which two countries together are closest in size to the area of San Marino?

Data File

Smallest Countries

Country	Area (sq. mi)
Monaco	0.38
Nauru	8.19
San Marino	23.6
Tuvalu	10.0
Vatican City	0.17

Math and Everyday Life

43. Joel had $12 on Sunday. On Monday, Susan gave him $5. If Joel gave Frank $5 on Tuesday, how much money does Joel now have?

44. Cal walked 7 miles and then returned by a route that was 2 miles longer. How far did he walk in all?

45. **Writing in Math** Matt wrote the answer shown at the right to this question: "In the expression $4 + n$, what operation would you use to get n alone?" Is Matt's answer correct? Explain why or why not.

> You need to use subtraction because $4 + n = n + 4$ and the inverse operation for addition is subtraction.

C Extensions

Place parentheses to make each statement true.

46. $3 + 6 - 6 \times 4 \div 4 = 7 - 4$

47. $14 \div 2 + 8 \times 3 - 3 = 12 - 12$

 **Mixed Review and Test Prep**

Take It to the NET Test Prep
www.scottforesman.com

Estimate each amount.

48. 26% of 40

49. 52% of 60

50. 11% of 12

51. 77% of 200

52. If 45% of a class of 34 students wants pizza, about how many want pizza?

A. 34 students
B. 17 students
C. 10 students
D. 4 students

Practice Game

Graphs and Hidden Treasure

Number of players: 2
Materials: 10×10 grid

Each player has a 10×10 grid. Secretly, each player marks four points (vertices) on his or her grid to form a rectangle with an area of 12 square units. (Samples are shown at the right.) The rectangle represents a hidden treasure.

The object is for each player to locate the opponent's hidden treasure. Players take turns guessing ordered pairs to locate vertices. Each time a player guesses a vertex correctly, the player marks the point on his or her grid.

The winner is the player who locates all four vertices.

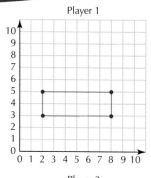
Player 1

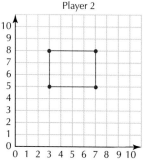
Player 2

Algebra

Key Idea
Using the properties of equality and inverse operations will help you solve addition and subtraction equations.

Vocabulary
• inverse operations (p. 133)

Think It Through
I can **draw a picture** to show the main idea.

Solving Addition and Subtraction Equations

LEARN

How can we use addition and subtraction to solve equations?

A group of runners is training for a marathon. Today's distance to run is 21 miles. After 6 miles the group will stop for water. How many more miles do they need to run to complete the distance?

21	
6	x

Let x = the number of miles runners need to complete.
$x + 6 = 21$

Example A

	What You **Think**	What You **Write**
STEP 1 Use an **inverse operation** and a property of equality to solve.	Subtract 6 from both sides and simplify.	$x + 6 = 21$ $x + 6 - 6 = 21 - 6$ $x = 15$ **Answer: The runners have 15 mi more to run.**
STEP 2 Check your work.	Substitute 15 for x. It checks.	$x + 6 = 21$ $15 + 6 = 21$ $21 = 21$

Example B

$y - 37 = 129$

$y - 37 + 37 = 129 + 37$

$y = 166$

Check: $y - 37 = 129$

$166 - 37 = 129$

$129 = 129$

✔ Talk About It

1. In Example B, what inverse operation was used to solve the equation?

2. **Number Sense** When solving the equation $y + 34 = 61$, is y greater than 30 or less than 30? How do you know without solving the equation?

WARM UP

Solve using mental math.

1. $75 + c = 100$

2. $100 - 35 = d$

3. $425 + y = 1,000$

4. $1,000 - 350 = e$

Solve and check each equation.

1. $x + 13 = 29$ **2.** $c - 45 = 61$ **3.** $654 = m + 147$ **4.** $n + 23 = 78$

5. $347 + t = 791$ **6.** $d - 34 = 79$ **7.** $p + 456 = 765$ **8.** $75 = n - 39$

9. Reasoning In the equation $s + (12 - 2) = 42$, what number do you subtract from both sides to solve the equation?

PRACTICE

For more practice, see Set 12-2 on p. 745.

Ⓐ Skills and Understanding

Solve and check each equation.

10. $x + 24 = 42$ **11.** $c - 68 = 78$ **12.** $91 = m + 19$ **13.** $n + 70 = 265$

14. $746 + t = 947$ **15.** $d - 58 = 12$ **16.** $p + 275 = 753$ **17.** $98 = n - 18$

18. Reasoning Why is it NOT necessary to use an inverse operation to find the value of n in the equation $32 + 31 = n$?

Ⓑ Reasoning and Problem Solving

Reasoning Use mental math to solve each equation.

19. $x + 13 = 33$ **20.** $c - 80 = 20$

21. $500 = m + 100$ **22.** $n + 50 = 100$

Use the information at the right for 23–24.

23. Mr. Mar's class plans to travel to the picnic in vans. How many vans are needed?

24. Mr. Mar's class has raised $213 from different projects and collected $27 in donations. How much more money do they need to cover the total cost?

Class Picnic Transportation And Costs

Number of people going: 35 people

Van capacity: 16 passengers

Total cost of picnic including vans: $500

25. **Writing in Math** Use estimation to find the approximate value of n in the equation $78 + n = 193$. Tell how you found your estimate.

🦉 Mixed Review and Test Prep

Take It to the NET
Test Prep
www.scottforesman.com

Evaluate.

26. $5 + 7 \div 7$ **27.** $(18 - 18) \times 5$ **28.** $23 - 18 + 18$ **29.** $12 \div 12 \times 8$

30. Which of the following can be used to get n alone in $n + 6$?

   A. Subtract 8   **B.** Subtract 6   **C.** Add 8   **D.** Add 6

Algebra

Key Idea
Using the properties of equality and inverse operations will help you solve multiplication and division equations.

Think It Through
I can **draw a picture** to show the main idea.

Solving Multiplication and Division Equations

LEARN

How can we use multiplication and division to solve equations?

A local youth baseball league plans to purchase 1,200 baseballs for the coming season. If there are 24 baseballs in one box, how many boxes will the league need to purchase?

1,200			
24	24	24	?

Let x = the number of boxes needed.
$24x = 1,200$

Example

		What You **Think**	What You **Write**
STEP 1	Use an inverse operation and a property of equality to solve.	Divide both sides by 24 and simplify. $\frac{24x}{24}$ means $24x \div 24$.	$24x = 1,200$ $\frac{24x}{24} = \frac{1,200}{24}$ $x = 50$ **Answer: The league needs to buy 50 boxes.**
STEP 2	Check your work.	Substitute 50 for x. It checks.	$24x = 1,200$ $24 \times 50 = 1,200$ $1,200 = 1,200$

✓ Talk About It

1. In Step 1, why must you divide both sides of the equation by 24?

2. In Step 2, why do you substitute 50 for x?

3. What inverse operation and what number would you use to solve $\frac{y}{36} = 4$?

4. **Number Sense** When solving $5x = 80$, is x greater than 10 or less than 10? How do you know without solving the equation?

Take It to the NET
www **More Examples**
www.scottforesman.com

Solve and check each equation. Remember $\frac{n}{5}$ means $n \div 5$.

1. $y \div 9 = 12$ **2.** $2 \times n = 91$ **3.** $85 = 17r$ **4.** $15 = \frac{s}{3}$

5. Reasoning Randy divides 48 by 6 to solve an equation for *y*. One side of the equation is 48. Write the equation.

Ⓐ Skills and Understanding

Solve and check each equation. Remember $\frac{n}{5}$ means $n \div 5$.

6. $y \div 4 = 14$ **7.** $6 \times n = 84$ **8.** $299 = 13 \times f$ **9.** $26 = s \div 6$

10. $9t = 702$ **11.** $\frac{w}{7} = 77$ **12.** $\frac{u}{4} = 36$ **13.** $45y = 135$

14. Reasoning Melinda multiplies 9 by 12 to solve an equation for *n*. One side of the equation is 9. Write the equation.

Ⓑ Reasoning and Problem Solving

Reasoning Use mental math to solve each equation.

15. $\frac{y}{5} = 10$ **16.** $\frac{x}{10} = 20$ **17.** $100 = 10t$ **18.** $20n = 600$

Use the data at the right for 19–20.

19. How many cases of each type of ball are needed?

20. Estimation All cases of balls cost the same price. Estimate the type of ball for which the least amount is spent in all.

21. **Writing in Math** Use estimation to decide if the value of *n* in $7n = 65$ is greater than 10 or less than 10. Tell how you decided.

Data File

Sports Equipment for Season

Equipment	Number needed	Number in case
Baseballs	100	48
Footballs	50	12
Soccer balls	50	12
Tennis balls	300	48

Mixed Review and Test Prep

Take It to the NET
Test Prep
www.scottforesman.com

Solve each equation.

22. $6 + n = 78$ **23.** $x - 120 = 92$ **24.** $n - 24 = 72$ **25.** $d + 59 = 87$

26. How many outfits of a shirt and shorts can be made from 3 shirts and 4 pairs of shorts?

   A. 3   **B.** 4   **C.** 12   **D.** 24

Identify the Main Idea

Identifying the main idea when you read in math can help you use the **problem-solving strategy, *Write an Equation,*** in the next lesson.

In reading, identifying the main idea helps you understand what the story is about. In math, the main idea for many story problems is **equal groups** or **part-part-whole** with something unknown.

Katrina walks the same distance every day. Last week she walked 38.5 miles. How many miles did she walk each day?

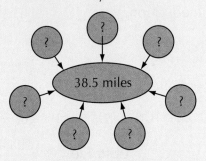

38.5 miles

Let m = the number of miles walked each day.

Number of equal groups		Amount per group		Total amount
7	×	m	=	38.5

The main idea here is equal groups with the amount per group unknown.

Randy bought a sweater and a book at the store. The book cost $5.95. Before tax, his bill was $23.55. How much did the sweater cost?

$23.55	
$5.95	?

Let c = the cost of the sweater.

Part		Part		Whole
5.95	+	c	=	23.55

The main idea here is part-part-whole with one part unknown.

1. Write a different equation for the first problem.

2. For each problem above, tell how you can solve the equation.

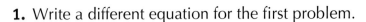

For 3–6, use the problem and picture below.

The buses are lined up to take 155 fifth graders on a field trip. If each bus will transport the same number of students, how many students will ride on each bus?

3. Identify the main idea.

4. Draw a picture to show the main idea.

5. Write an equation for the problem.

6. <u>Writing in Math</u> Tell how you can solve the equation.

For 7–10, use the problem below and the picture at the right.

Mick earns money mowing lawns. He earns $12 for each lawn he mows. He wants to save up to buy the bike in the ad. How many lawns will he have to mow to earn enough for the bike?

7. Identify the main idea.

8. Draw a picture to show the main idea.

9. Write an equation for the problem.

10. <u>Writing in Math</u> Tell how you can solve the equation.

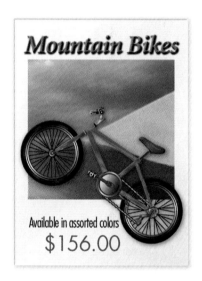

Mountain Bikes

Available in assorted colors

$156.00

For 11–14, use the problem below and the data at the right.

A grocer used two containers to pack the chicken salad for Mr. Baldi's deli order. One container held 1.6 pounds of chicken salad. How much was in the other container?

11. Identify the main idea.

12. Draw a picture to show the main idea.

13. Write an equation for the problem.

14. <u>Writing in Math</u> Write a different part-part-whole problem using data from the deli order.

Deli Order — Jim Baldi

1.4 lb Swiss cheese
2.2 lb corned beef
2.8 lb chicken salad
3 large dill pickles
1 dozen rolls

Problem-Solving Strategy

Reading Helps!

Identifying the main idea

can help you with...

the problem-solving strategy,
Write an Equation.

Algebra

Key Idea
Learning how and when to write an equation can help you solve problems.

Vocabulary
• variable (p. 100)

Write an Equation

LEARN

How do you write an equation to solve a problem?

Summer Savings Danielle got a job at a car wash earning $6 an hour, after taxes. How many hours does she have to work to earn $2,000 after taxes?

Read and Understand

What do you know?

Danielle earns $6 an hour, after taxes. She wants to earn a total of $2,000.

What are you trying to find?

The number of hours Danielle has to work to earn $2,000

Plan and Solve

What strategy will you use?

Strategy: Write an Equation

$2,000				
6	6	6		...

Let n = the number of hours of work

$6 an hour times the number of hours equals $2,000.

$$6 \times n = 2,000$$

$$(6 \times n) \div 6 = 2,000 \div 6 \quad \text{Divide both sides by 6.}$$

$$n = 333\frac{1}{3}$$

Answer: **Danielle has to work a little more than 333 hours to earn $2,000.**

How to Write an Equation

Step 1 Show the main idea in the problem.

Step 2 Use a letter to show what you are trying to find. This is called a **variable.**

Step 3 Write a number sentence.
Think: Use words first.

Step 4 Solve the number sentence.

Look Back and Check

Is your answer reasonable?

Yes. Use estimation to find out.

$6 \times 300 = 1,800$ and 1,800 is close to 2,000. So, 333 hours seems reasonable.

Talk About It

1. Explain how the picture shows Step 1, the main idea, in the problem on page 706.

2. What does *n* stand for in Step 2?

3. **Reasoning** Why do you use multiplication instead of addition to write the equation on page 706?

When might you write an equation?

Savings Challenge Russ saved $2,700 from his summer job to buy a used car. If Russ saved six times as much as Penny, how much did Penny save?

Penny's saving: ?   Russ's savings: $2,700

Let *n* = the amount Penny saved.

Russ saved six times the amount Penny saved, so let 6 × *n* = the amount Russ saved.

$$6 \times n = 2,700$$ ← The amount Russ saved (6 × *n*) is $2,700.

$$(6 \times n) \div 6 = 2,700 \div 6$$

$$n = 450$$

Think:

Smaller Amount	Times as Many	Larger Amount
■	× ■	= ■

When to Write an Equation

Think about writing an equation when:

The story has an unknown quantity
• Penny's amount is unknown.

The relationship between quantities involves one or more operations.
• Russ saved 6 times as much as Penny.

 **Talk About It**

4. What does *n* stand for? Why is 6 × *n* the amount Russ saved?

5. Give the answer to the problem in a complete sentence.

6. How would you check to see if $450 is correct?

CHECK ✓   *For another example, see Set 12-4 on p. 743.*

Use the picture to write an equation. Solve and check.

1. Jill saved $675 in 1 year. She saved $532 in the first 9 months. How much did she save the last 3 months?

   Let *x* = the amount Jill saved the last 3 months.

$675	
$532	*x*

2. Todd loaned his sister $32 and had $45 left. How much money did Todd have before he loaned his sister the money?

   Let *x* = the amount of money Todd had.

x	
$32	$45

ⓐ Using the Strategy

Using an Equation to Solve a Problem Use the picture shown to write an equation. Solve and check.

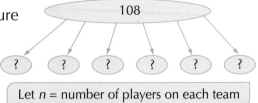

3. A town softball league has 108 players. There are 6 teams in the league. How many players are on each team?

Let n = number of players on each team

Writing an Equation to Solve a Problem Draw a picture to show the main idea for each problem. Then write an equation and solve it. Write the answer in a complete sentence.

Use the information at the right for 4–6.

4. You want to buy a taco and a medium drink. How much money do you need?

5. You buy four tacos. How much do you spend?

6. **Decision Making** You would like to buy a taco dinner and a large drink or 3 tacos. You have $9.00 to spend on the food and tip. You want to leave at least $1.00 for a tip. Which should you order? Explain.

Data File

Taco Diner
Price List

Item	Cost
Taco	$2.75
Taco Dinner	$5.75
Medium Drink	$0.99
Large Drink	$1.49

Math and Social Studies

Use the map at the right for 7–11.

7. How much farther is it from Yellowstone to Casper than from Casper to Rawlins?

8. If you average 50 miles per hour and make no stops along the way, about how long will it take to go from Rawlins to Cheyenne?

9. The Smith family makes two round trips between Rawlins and Casper. How many miles do they drive altogether?

10. What is the distance from Casper to Rawlins and then to Cheyenne?

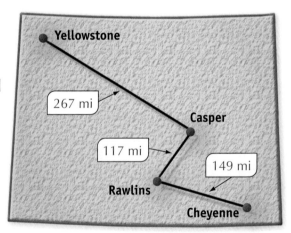

11. Your family plans to take a 2-day trip from Yellowstone to Cheyenne by the route shown. You are also planning to sightsee for at least 4 hours each day. If you average 50 miles per hour, about how long will it take to get from Yellowstone to Cheyenne including the sightseeing time?

12. **Number Sense** If you leave Casper at noon, would you have to average more or less than 50 miles per hour to reach Yellowstone by 5:00 P.M.?

B Mixed Strategy Practice

Solve each problem. Write the answer in a complete sentence. Use the Taco Diner price list on page 708.

13. You have $10.00 to spend and want to buy two tacos and two medium drinks. Do you have enough money? Explain how you decided.

14. A taco dinner consists of 2 tacos and a medium drink. How much money do you save buying the dinner than buying two tacos and a medium drink separately?

15. Colin usually practices his guitar an hour a day. On weekends he practices an extra half hour a day. About how many hours does he practice in a month?

16. The Steinman family drove 2,200 miles from San Diego to Chicago. The car's gasoline tank holds 20 gallons. Mrs. Steinman filled the tank 5 times. About how many miles per gallon did they average on the trip?

17. Bart's room is 10 feet by 13 feet. The ceiling is 8 ft high. One of the 13-feet-long walls has no windows or doors. How much wallpaper does he need to paper that wall?

18. **Writing in Math** Is the explanation below correct? If not, tell why and write a correct response.

> What are the next two pictures in the pattern?
>
>
>
> I think the next pictures in the pattern will be like the fourth and fifth pictures. The original figure is rotating clockwise by 90° each time.

STRATEGIES
- **Show What You Know**
  Draw a Picture
  Make an Organized List
  Make a Table
  Make a Graph
  Act It Out or Use Objects
- **Look for a Pattern**
- **Try, Check, and Revise**
- **Write an Equation**
- **Use Logical Reasoning**
- **Solve a Simpler Problem**
- **Work Backward**

Choose a tool   Mental Math

Mixed Review and Test Prep

Take It to the NET
Test Prep
www.scottforesman.com

Solve each equation.

19. $y \div 8 = 22$ 20. $5 \times n = 90$ 21. $120 = 5 \times f$ 22. $84 = s \div 7$

23. $6t = 480$ 24. $\frac{w}{9} = 108$ 25. $\frac{u}{3} = 42$ 26. $50y = 450$

27. A rectangle is 8 inches long. The perimeter is 24 inches. What is its width?

A. 40 inches   **B.** 16 inches   **C.** 8 inches   **D.** 4 inches

Do You Know How?

Do You Understand?

Properties of Equality (12-1)

Evaluate each expression.

1. $41 - 13 + 13$ **2.** $3 \times 2 + 4 - 4$

What inverse operation and what number would you use to get n alone?

3. $n + 15$ **4.** $n \div 4$

5. $n \times 6$ **6.** $n - 7$

Ⓐ What is the inverse operation of division? How do you know?

Ⓑ Without using a calculator, explain how you can quickly evaluate $6 \times 4 + 162 - 162$.

Solving Addition and Subtraction Equations (12-2)

Solve and check each equation.

7. $x + 65 = 125$ **8.** $m - 29 = 76$

9. $k - 147 = 62$ **10.** $425 = 181 + a$

Ⓒ Can x have any value in $x + 65$? Can x have any value in $x + 65 = 125$? Explain.

Solving Multiplication and Division Equations (12-3)

Solve and check each equation.

11. $\frac{n}{12} = 5$ **12.** $12n = 180$

13. $600 = 30d$ **14.** $26 = \frac{r}{3}$

Ⓓ Explain how you used inverse operations to solve Exercise 12.

Ⓔ When solving $3n = 315$, is n less than 100 or greater than 100? Explain how you know.

Problem-Solving Strategy: Write an Equation (12-4)

Draw a picture to show the main idea. Then write an equation and solve it.

15. Stan earns $6 an hour mowing lawns. How many hours does he have to work to earn $96?

16. After buying a $9.50 video, Darci had $3.75 left. How much money did she have before she bought the video?

Ⓕ Explain how to check your answer in Exercise 15 for reasonableness.

Ⓖ Describe a situation in which you would multiply a number by 7. Draw a picture to show the main idea.

Ⓗ When writing an equation, why do you tell what the variable represents?

MULTIPLE CHOICE

1. Which is the solution to $y - 13 = 65$? (12-2)

   A. $y = 845$ **B.** $y = 78$ **C.** $y = 52$ **D.** $y = 5$

2. Which describes what you do to both sides of $\frac{y}{12} = 108$ to solve for y? (12-1)

   A. Add 12   **B.** Divide by 12   **C.** Multiply by 12   **D.** Subtract 12

3. Which equation has a solution of 6? (12-2, 12-3)

   A. $n + 5 = 6$ **B.** $5 + n = 12$ **C.** $3 \times n = 24$ **D.** $n \div 2 = 3$

FREE RESPONSE

What inverse operation and what number would you use to get n alone? (12-1)

4. $n + 6$ 5. $8n$ 6. $n \div 4$

Solve and check each equation. (12-2, 12-3)

7. $r - 8 = 14$ 8. $k - 20 = 42$ 9. $x + 67 = 125$

10. $133 + h = 210$ 11. $49 = y - 39$ 12. $\frac{g}{9} = 51$

13. $12m = 72$ 14. $32b = 192$ 15. $54 = \frac{p}{3}$

> **TEST TALK**
>
> **Think It Through**
> I need to **use inverse operations** to undo operations and solve equations.

16. Use the picture to write an equation. Solve and check. (12-4)

    Brian rode his bike a total of 345 miles over the summer. He rode 275 miles in the first 7 weeks. How many miles did he ride in the last 3 weeks?

345 mi	
275 mi	x

17. Draw a picture to show the main idea. Then write an equation and solve it. (12-4)

    Jenna made $132 babysitting this month. If Jenna earns $6 an hour, how many hours did she babysit this month?

Writing in Math

For each equation, write a problem that can be solved by using the equation. Then write the answer in a complete sentence. (12-4)

18. $16 \times n = 96$ 19. $n - 75 = 36$

20. $5 + n = 8$ 21. $56 \div n = 8$

Algebra

Key Idea
A number line can be used to identify, represent, compare, and order integers.

Vocabulary
- integers
- positive integers
- negative integers
- opposites

Think It Through
- I can **use a number line** to represent integers.
- I need to **decide what a number represents** and if it is a positive or negative situation.

Understanding Integers

LEARN

What are integers and what situations can be represented with integers?

Temperatures that fall below 0° are written with a negative sign. For example, 2° below zero would be written as ⁻2°.

The numbers ⁺22 and ⁻67 are called **integers**. Integers are the whole numbers and their opposites, where 0 is its own opposite.

✔ **WARM UP**

Name the number for each point on the number line.

A B C
0 1 2

1. A   2. B   3. C

4. Is 2° below zero colder or warmer than 4° below zero? Explain.

Negative integers are less than 0. The symbol for negative five is ⁻5.

The number 0 is neither positive nor negative.

Positive integers are greater than 0. The symbol for positive six is ⁺6 or 6.

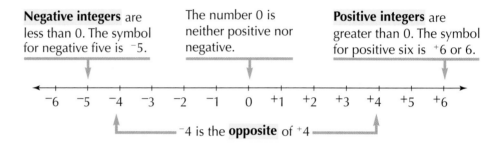

⁻6 ⁻5 ⁻4 ⁻3 ⁻2 ⁻1 0 ⁺1 ⁺2 ⁺3 ⁺4 ⁺5 ⁺6

⁻4 is the **opposite** of ⁺4

The tables below give an integer for each word description.

Word Description	Integer
A high temperature of 108°F	⁺108
30 feet below sea level	⁻30
A loss of 12 yards	⁻12

Word Description	Integer
A low temperature of 65°F below zero	⁻65
4 steps forward	⁺4
A deposit of $25	⁺25

✔ **Talk About It**

1. Name three examples of situations that can be represented by negative integers. Name three that can be represented by positive integers.

2. **Number Sense** What is the opposite of 7? of ⁻7?

3. On a number line, how many units from 0 would the points be located that represent 5 and ⁻5?

How do you compare and order integers?

Which is less, a temperature of ⁻8°F or ⁻10°F? Look at the number line below. Integers, just like whole numbers and fractions, increase in value as you move from left to right on the number line. You can see that ⁻10 < ⁻8. Therefore, ⁻10°F < ⁻8°F or ⁻8°F > ⁻10°F.

Think It Through
I can **draw a number line** to compare and order integers.

⁻10 ⁻9 ⁻8 ⁻7 ⁻6 ⁻5 ⁻4 ⁻3 ⁻2 ⁻1 0 ⁺1 ⁺2 ⁺3 ⁺4 ⁺5 ⁺6 ⁺7 ⁺8 ⁺9 ⁺10

You can use the number line to compare integers.

Example A

Compare. Use >, <, or = for .

⁻3   ⁺5

The integer ⁻3 is farther to the left on the number line than the integer ⁺5.

So, ⁻3 < ⁺5 or ⁺5 > ⁻3.

Example B

Compare. Use >, <, or = for .

⁻2   ⁻4

The integer ⁻2 is farther to the right on the number line than the integer ⁻4.

So, ⁻2 > ⁻4 or ⁻4 < ⁻2.

You can also use the number line to order integers.

Example C

Order the integers ⁻3, 0, ⁺6, and ⁻5 from least to greatest.

STEP 1 Locate the integers on a number line.

⁻7 ⁻6 ⁻5 ⁻4 ⁻3 ⁻2 ⁻1 0 ⁺1 ⁺2 ⁺3 ⁺4 ⁺5 ⁺6 ⁺7

STEP 2 Write the integers from left to right as they appear on the number line.

⁻5, ⁻3, 0, ⁺6

✔ Talk About It

4. In Example B, ⁻2 > ⁻4, but 4 > 2. Why?

5. Number Sense What might you do to order the numbers ⁻8, ⁻10, ⁺5, and ⁺8 without using a number line?

Write an integer for each word description.

1. 75 degrees above zero   **2.** 12 ft below sea level   **3.** a withdrawal of $25

Use the number line at the
right for 4–7. Write the
integer for each point.

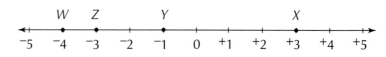

4. *W*   **5.** *X*   **6.** *Y*   **7.** *Z*

Compare. Use >, <, or = for each ⬤.

8. $^+5$ ⬤ $^-6$ **9.** $^-3$ ⬤ $^+3$ **10.** $^-12$ ⬤ $^-9$ **11.** $^-17$ ⬤ $^+17$

Write in order from least to greatest.

12. $^-1, 0, ^+8$ **13.** $^-5, ^-3, ^-7$ **14.** $^-8, 4, ^+6, ^-4$ **15.** $2, ^-2, ^-5, ^+5$

16. Reasoning A football team started at the 20-yard line. In the first two
plays, the team lost 4 yards and gained 4 yards. Did they end up where
they started? Explain your reasoning.

PRACTICE

For more practice, see Set 12-5 on p. 746.

Ⓐ Skills and Understanding

Write an integer for each word description.

17. A withdrawal of $10   **18.** A deposit of $2

19. A temperature drop of 15°   **20.** 14 ft below sea level

21. A loss of 6 yards   **22.** 10 degrees above zero

*Death Valley in California is the
lowest point in the United States.*

Use the number line at the
right for 23–26. Write the
integer for each point.

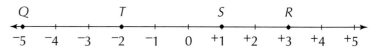

23. *Q*   **24.** *R*   **25.** *S*   **26.** *T*

Compare. Use >, <, or = for each ⬤.

27. $^-6$ ⬤ $^+6$ **28.** $^+30$ ⬤ $^-31$ **29.** $^+4$ ⬤ $^-12$ **30.** $^-12$ ⬤ $^-12$

31. $^-2$ ⬤ $^+4$ **32.** $^+6$ ⬤ $^-2$ **33.** $^-23$ ⬤ $^-28$ **34.** $^+52$ ⬤ $^+54$

Write in order from least to greatest.

35. $0, ^-4, ^+2$ **36.** $4, ^+2, ^-7$ **37.** $^+14, ^-8, ^-15$ **38.** $0, ^-4, ^+5$

39. $^-9, ^+4, ^+12, ^-10$ **40.** $^-1, ^-8, ^+2, ^-5$ **41.** $^-7, ^+4, ^-8, ^-5$ **42.** $^-2, ^+3, ^+2, ^-4$

43. Reasoning A number, *x*, is 4 units to the left of $^-5$ on
the number line. What is *x* and is it greater than or
less than $^-5$?

B Reasoning and Problem Solving

Math and Everyday Life

Use the Data File at the right for 44–45.

44. Name the players with the highest and lowest scores.

45. Name the players who scored less than 0.

46. Writing in Math Is the explanation below correct. If not, tell why and write a correct response.

> Which is less, ⁻13 or ⁻12?
> ⁻13 is less because it is farther to the left from 0 on the number line.

Dart Board Scores	
Player	**Score**
Brett	2
Ken	20
Heather	-7
Burr	-13
Chase	-18
Quinn	11
Stacey	9

C Extensions

Order each set of numbers from least to greatest.

47. $^-1, {}^+2, 0.35, \frac{1}{2}$

48. $^+3, {}^-2, 1.2, 50\%$

49. $^-3, {}^-2, {}^+5, 4\frac{3}{4}, 4.5, 100\%$

Mixed Review and Test Prep

Take It to the NET
Test Prep
www.scottforesman.com

50. 12×3.4

51. 6.2×40

52. 31.5×5

53. Colby scored 8 and 6 on two out of three throws. Which equation could NOT be used to find how many points he needs to score a total of 20 for 3 throws?

A. $20 - (8 + 6) = n$ **B.** $20 - 8 + 6 = n$ **C.** $8 + 6 + n = 20$ **D.** $20 - n = 8 + 6$

Learning with Technology

Spreadsheet/Data/Grapher eTool

Use a spreadsheet to order and compare integers. Enter these integers in Column A of the spreadsheet: ⁻7, ⁻3, 3, 7, 10, ⁻4, 6, 2, 5, ⁻6. Use the sort feature to order these integers from least to greatest. Now enter the number of units each integer is from 0 in column B.

1. Is ⁻7 greater than ⁻3? Is 7 greater than 3?

2. If one negative integer is more units from 0 than a second negative integer, is it less than or greater than the second integer? Does this same rule apply for positive integers?

	A	B
1	–7	7
2	–3	3
3	3	3
4	7	7
5	10	10
6	–4	4
7	6	6
8	2	2
9	5	5
10	–6	6

Algebra

Key Idea
You can use a number line to show the addition of integers.

Vocabulary
• positive integers (p. 712)
• negative integers (p. 712)

Materials
• number lines

Think It Through
I can **draw a picture of a number line** to show the main idea.

Adding Integers

LEARN

How do you add integers?

In two plays, a team had a loss of 7 yards and a gain of 6 yards. What was their total gain or loss? You could find ⁻7 + ⁺6.

To find ⁻7 + ⁺6, you can think of walking along a number line. Use the rule at the right.

Rule for adding integers on the number line: Always start at 0 and face the positive integers. Walk forward for **positive integers** and backward for **negative integers.**

Start at 0. Face positive integers. Walk backward 7 steps for ⁻7.

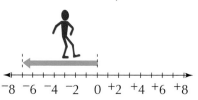

Then walk forward 6 steps for ⁺6.

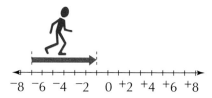

You stop at ⁻1. So, ⁻7 + ⁺6 = ⁻1

Example A

Find ⁺2 + ⁻4.

Start at 0. Move forward 2 units. Then move backward 4 units.

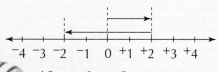

⁺2 + ⁻4 = ⁻2

Example B

Find ⁻3 + ⁻1.

Start at 0. Move backward 3 units. Then move backward 1 more unit.

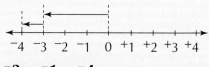

⁻3 + ⁻1 = ⁻4

✓ **Talk About It**

1. In Example A, how would the sum be different if the addends were ⁻2 and ⁺4? Explain how this would look on the number line.

2. **Representations** How would ⁺4 + ⁺5 look on a number line?

3. **Number Sense** The integers ⁺7 and ⁻7 are opposites. What statement can you make about the sum of any integer and its opposite?

Take It to the NET
More Examples
www.scottforesman.com

Add. Use a number line.

1. $^{+}1 + {}^{-}4$ **2.** $^{+}2 + {}^{+}2$ **3.** $^{-}6 + {}^{-}3$ **4.** $^{-}9 + {}^{+}7$

5. $^{-}2 + {}^{-}5$ **6.** $^{+}7 + {}^{-}2$ **7.** $^{-}4 + {}^{+}5$ **8.** $^{-}4 + {}^{-}2$

9. Number Sense Name two addends whose sum is 0.

PRACTICE

For more practice, see Set 12-6 on p. 746.

Ⓐ Skills and Understanding

Add. Use a number line.

10. $^{+}6 + {}^{-}4$ **11.** $^{+}1 + {}^{-}9$ **12.** $^{-}7 + {}^{-}2$ **13.** $^{-}3 + {}^{+}8$

14. $^{+}6 + {}^{+}3$ **15.** $^{-}3 + {}^{-}2$ **16.** $^{+}2 + {}^{-}4$ **17.** $^{+}5 + {}^{+}5$

18. Number Sense What is the sum of $^{+}7$, $^{-}7$, $^{+}15$, $^{-}1$, and $^{+}1$? Explain how you found your answer.

Ⓑ Reasoning and Problem Solving

Use the thermometer at the right for 19–21.

19. Tuesday's low temperature was $^{-}1°F$. On Wednesday, the low temperature was 4° colder. What was the low temperature on Wednesday?

20. Over a 3-day period, the temperature went from a high of 78°F to a high of 97°F. What was the increase over the 3-day period?

21. From the beginning of a day to the end of the day, the temperature increased 12°F. If the temperature at the end of the day was 8°F, what was the temperature at the beginning of the day?

22. <u>Writing in Math</u> Last week, Marcia deposited $25 and withdrew $50. Tell how you could find what she had at the start of the week if her balance is now $120?

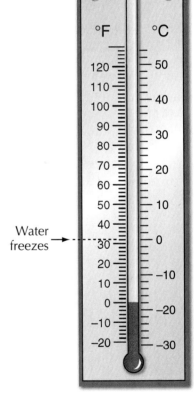

🦉 Mixed Review and Test Prep

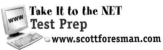

Take It to the NET
Test Prep
www.scottforesman.com

Write in order from least to greatest.

23. $^{-}3, {}^{-}6, {}^{+}5, 0$ **24.** $^{+}6, {}^{-}5, {}^{+}1, {}^{-}7$ **25.** $^{-}6, {}^{+}7, {}^{+}9, {}^{-}4$ **26.** $^{-}8, {}^{+}2, {}^{-}7, {}^{-}3$

27. Which of the following is NOT true?

     A. $^{-}6 < {}^{+}6$ **B.** $^{-}6 > {}^{-}7$ **C.** $^{-}6 > {}^{-}5$ **D.** $^{-}6 = {}^{-}6$

Algebra

Key Idea
You can use a number line to show the subtraction of integers.

Vocabulary
• positive integers (p. 712)
• negative integers (p. 712)

Materials
• number lines

Think It Through
I can **draw a picture of a number line** to show the main idea.

Subtracting Integers

> **LEARN**

How do you subtract integers?

Example A

Find $^+4 - ^-3$.

To subtract integers, you can think of walking along a number line. Start at 0. Face the positive integers.

| Walk forward 4 steps for $^+4$. | The subtraction sign (−) means *turn around*. | Then walk backward 3 steps for $^-3$. |

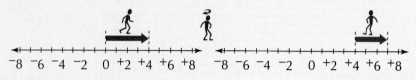

$^-8$ $^-6$ $^-4$ $^-2$ 0 $^+2$ $^+4$ $^+6$ $^+8$ $^-8$ $^-6$ $^-4$ $^-2$ 0 $^+2$ $^+4$ $^+6$ $^+8$

You stop at $^+7$. So $^+4 - ^-3 = ^+7$

The problem above shows how to subtract a negative integer from a positive integer. Other cases that exist are shown below.

Example B

Find $^+2 - ^+4$.

Start at 0. Face the positive integers.

| Walk forward 2 steps for $^+2$. | The subtraction sign (−) means *turn around*. | Then walk forward 4 steps for $^+4$. |

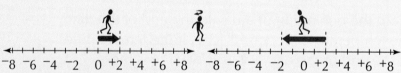

$^-8$ $^-6$ $^-4$ $^-2$ 0 $^+2$ $^+4$ $^+6$ $^+8$ $^-8$ $^-6$ $^-4$ $^-2$ 0 $^+2$ $^+4$ $^+6$ $^+8$

You stop at $^-2$. So $^+2 - ^+4 = ^-2$

Example C

Find $^-6 - ^-3$.

Start at 0. Face the positive integers.

| Walk backward 6 steps for $^-6$. | The subtraction sign (−) means *turn around*. | Then walk backward 3 steps for $^-3$. |

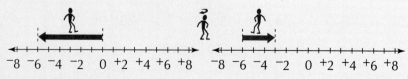

$^-8$ $^-6$ $^-4$ $^-2$ 0 $^+2$ $^+4$ $^+6$ $^+8$ $^-8$ $^-6$ $^-4$ $^-2$ 0 $^+2$ $^+4$ $^+6$ $^+8$

You stop at $^-3$. So $^-6 - ^-3 = ^-3$

The table at the right illustrates an important fact.

Subtracting an integer is the same as adding its opposite.

$^+4 - ^-3 = ^+7$	$^+4 + ^+3 = ^+7$
$^+2 - ^+4 = ^-2$	$^+2 + ^-4 = ^-2$
$^-6 - ^-3 = ^-3$	$^-6 + ^+3 = ^-3$

✔ Talk About It

1. In Example C, why does the arrow point to the right on the number line located on the right?

Take It to the NET
More Examples
www.scottforesman.com

CHECK ✔

For another example, see Set 12-7 on p. 744.

Rewrite each subtraction using addition. Then find the answer. Use a number line to check.

1. $^-8 - ^-4$ 2. $^+3 - ^+1$ 3. $^+5 - ^-2$ 4. $^+6 - ^-8$

5. **Reasoning** How are $^+6 - ^+9$ and $^+6 + ^-9$ alike? different?

PRACTICE

For more practice, see Set 12-7 on p. 746.

Ⓐ Skills and Understanding

Rewrite each subtraction using addition. Then find the answer. Use a number line to check.

6. $^-7 - ^-1$ 7. $^+4 - ^+3$ 8. $^+9 - ^-4$ 9. $^-4 - ^+9$

10. $^-9 - ^-5$ 11. $^+2 - ^+1$ 12. $^+7 - ^-4$ 13. $^+3 - ^-9$

14. $^-2 - ^-6$ 15. $^-4 - ^+8$ 16. $^+5 - ^+7$ 17. $^+1 - ^-5$

18. **Reasoning** Which is greater, $^+8 - ^-10$ or $^+8 + ^-10$?

Ⓑ Reasoning and Problem Solving

19. On a winter day, the high temperature was $^+3°F$ and the low temperature was $^-5°F$. What is the difference?

20. The temperature increased 13° over 4 hours. It is now 58°F. What was it 4 hours ago?

21. **Writing in Math** Explain how to use a number line to find $^-5 - ^-2$.

🦉 Mixed Review and Test Prep

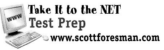
Take It to the NET
Test Prep
www.scottforesman.com

22. $^+8 + ^-5$ 23. $^-3 + ^+8$ 24. $^-2 + ^+9$ 25. $^-6 + ^-6$

26. Which is NOT true?

A. $^-7 < ^-5$ B $^-7 + ^+7 = 0$ C. $^+5 - ^-5 = 0$ D. $0 > ^-5$

Problem-Solving Skill

Algebra

Key Idea
There are specific things you can do to write a good explanation in math

Writing to Explain

LEARN

How do you write a good explanation?

When you **write to explain** a pattern, you will need to tell how a change in one quantity results in the change of another quantity.

New Books Becky used the News Flash information to make a table showing the number of new books published in 30 minutes, 60 minutes, and 90 minutes. Copy the table and use the pattern to extend the table to 180 minutes.

News Flash
Over 96,000 new books were published in 2000! That's 5.5 books every half hour, 11 books every hour, and 16.5 books every hour and a half.

Number of Minutes	30	60	90			
Number of New Books Published	5.5	11.0	16.5			

Explain how the number of books change as the number of minutes change.

TEST TALK

Think It Through

When I write to explain a pattern in a table, I must be sure to **tell how a change in one number results in the change in another number.**

Writing a Math Explanation

- Identify the quantities shown in the table.

- Tell how one quantity changes as the other quantity changes. Be specific. This is an explanation of the pattern.

Every 30 minutes, the number of books published increases by 5.5 books.

As the number of minutes increases by 30, the number of books published increases by 5.5. So, the number of books after 120 minutes is 16.5 + 5.5 or 22.0. The number after 150 minutes is 22.0 + 5.5 or 27.5, and the number after 180 minutes is 27.5 + 5.5 or 33.

✔ Talk About It

1. Neil wrote, "The pattern increases 30 minutes each time." Is he correct? Why or why not?

2. **Algebra** When Josh was asked to explain how to find the number of books published in 24 hours, he said he used the equation $y = 11x$. Write an explanation for Josh's method and give the answer.

Write to explain.

1. Six teams are playing in a tournament. Each team will play one game against each of the other teams. Copy the table and use the pattern to complete the table for 6 teams.

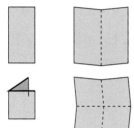

Number of teams	2	3	4		
Number of games	1	3	6		

Explain how the number of games changes as the number of teams changes.

PRACTICE

For more practice, see Set 12-8 on p. 747.

Write to explain.

2. Suppose you fold a piece of a paper in half, in half again, and then in half a third time. Copy the table and use the pattern to extend it to 6 folds.

Number of folds	1	2	3			
Number of sections	2	4	8			

Explain how the number of sections changes as the number of folds changes.

3. The diagram at the right is called a **Venn diagram.** Copy the diagram and put the numbers 14, 15, 16, and 18 in the correct locations. Explain why you put each number where you did.

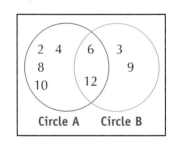

4. The graph shows the result of a survey of 36 students. Use these results to predict how many students out of the 200 attending the school picnic will order chocolate ice cream cones. Explain how you made your prediction.

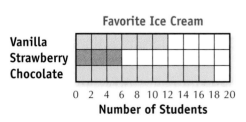

5. Explain how the figures at the right are alike. Explain how they are different.

Do You Know How?

Do You Understand?

Understanding Integers (12-5)

Write an integer for each word description.

1. 83° above zero   **2.** a loss of 10 yards

3. Write the integer for point A.

Compare. Use >, <, or = for each ⬤.

4. ⁻7 ⬤ ⁺7   **5.** 0 ⬤ ⁻3   **6.** ⁻5 ⬤ ⁻4

7. Order ⁻1, ⁺1, ⁻5 from least to greatest.

Ⓐ Give the opposite of each word description in Exercises 1 and 2.

Ⓑ Describe what happens as you go from right to left on the number line.

Ⓒ Explain how you ordered the integers in Exercise 7.

Adding Integers (12-6)

Add. Use a number line.

8. ⁺4 + ⁻3   **9.** ⁻2 + ⁺2   **10.** ⁻1 + ⁻5

11. 0 + ⁻4   **12.** ⁺3 + ⁺3   **13.** ⁻4 + ⁻2

Ⓓ Explain how you found the sum in Exercise 10.

Ⓔ What is the sum of any number and its opposite? Explain.

Subtracting Integers (12-7)

Subtract.

14. ⁻4 − ⁺1   **15.** ⁻3 − ⁺3   **16.** ⁻2 − ⁻2

17. 0 − ⁻3   **18.** ⁻6 − ⁺1   **19.** ⁺1 − ⁺5

Ⓕ Explain how to solve Exercise 16, using a number line.

Ⓖ Rewrite Exercises 17–19, using addition.

Problem-Solving Skill: Writing to Explain (12-8)

20. The table shows the length of each side of an equilateral triangle and its perimeter. Copy the table and use the pattern to complete it.

Length of side (in.)	1	2	3	4	5	6
Perimeter (in.)	3	6	9	■	■	■

Explain how the perimeter of the triangle changes as the length of the sides change.

Ⓗ What quantities shown in the table help you find a pattern?

Ⓘ How does making a table help you describe the pattern?

MULTIPLE CHOICE

1. Which shows ⁻2, ⁺5, and ⁻5 in order from least to greatest? (12-5)

A. ⁻5, ⁻2, ⁺5   **B.** ⁺5, ⁻2, ⁻5   **C.** ⁺5, ⁻5, ⁻2   **D.** ⁻2, ⁻5, ⁺5

2. What is ⁻4 − ⁻6? (12-7)

A. ⁻2   **B.** ⁺2   **C.** ⁻10   **D.** ⁺10

3. Which expression does NOT have a value of ⁻5? (12-6)

A. ⁻2 + ⁻3   **B.** ⁻4 + ⁻1   **C.** ⁻8 + ⁺3   **D.** ⁻8 + ⁻3

FREE RESPONSE

Write an integer for each word description. (12-5)

4. A profit of $125   **5.** 10°F below zero   **6.** 20 ft below sea level

Compare. Use >, <, or = for each ⚬. (12-5)

7. ⁻10 ⚬ ⁻5   **8.** ⁻3 ⚬ ⁺2   **9.** ⁺12 ⚬ ⁻12   **10.** ⁻5 ⚬ 0

Order the numbers from least the greatest. (12-5)

11. ⁻10, ⁻3, ⁺3, ⁻2   **12.** ⁻7, ⁺8, ⁻6, 0   **13.** ⁺2, ⁺7, ⁻5, ⁻3

Add or subtract. (12-6, 12-7)

14. ⁻4 + ⁺1   **15.** ⁻7 + ⁺3   **16.** ⁺5 + ⁻7   **17.** ⁺5 + ⁻5

18. ⁺7 − ⁻3   **19.** ⁺10 − ⁻10   **20.** ⁻9 − ⁻6   **21.** 0 − ⁻8

TEST TALK

Think It Through

I can **draw a picture of a number line** to help add and subtract integers.

Writing in Math

22. Decide if the statement is true or false. Use an example to help explain your answer.
If an integer *a* is greater than an integer *b,* then the opposite of integer *a* will be greater than the opposite of integer *b*. (12-5)

23. Use the table at the right.

a. Jeff has a summer baby-sitting job. He agreed to be paid the amounts shown in the table. If the pattern continues, how much will he earn on Day 12? Explain how the amount he earns changes as the number of days changes.

b. Did Jeff make a good decision agreeing to be paid this way? Why or why not?

Day	Earnings that day
1	2¢
2	4¢
3	8¢
4	16¢
5	32¢

Algebra

Key Idea
A coordinate grid can be extended to include both negative and positive numbers.

Vocabulary
• coordinate plane
• ordered pair (p. 174)
• x-value
• origin
• y-value

Materials
• grid paper

The Coordinate Plane

LEARN

How do you name a point located on a coordinate plane?

A coordinate grid that extends to include both negative and positive numbers is called a **coordinate plane.** A location on the coordinate plane is named by an **ordered pair** (x, y) of numbers.

The vertices of the square shown at the right are labeled W, X, Y, and Z. These points are represented by ordered pairs.

The ordered pair locating W is (⁻2, ⁺3).

The x-coordinate is ⁻2. The y-coordinate is ⁺3.   The origin is (0, 0).

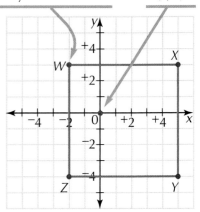

> The first number in an ordered pair represents the **x-value.** It tells how many units to the left or right of the **origin** a point is located.
>
> The second number in an ordered pair represents the **y-value.** It tells how many units up or down from the origin a point is located.

Example A

> For the square graphed above, name the ordered pair for each point given.
>
> Point X: (⁺5, ⁺3)   Point Y: (⁺5, ⁻4)   Point Z: (⁻2, ⁻4)

Think It Through
I need to be sure to **remember that order is important** when naming the ordered pair for a point.

✓ **Talk About It**

1. In the square shown above, if the vertex Z were located at (⁻4, ⁻3), would it be farther to the right or to the left of where it is now located?

2. **Representations** Study the ordered pairs naming the endpoints of each side of the square shown above. What is the same about the ordered pairs? What is different?

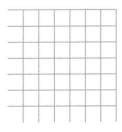

3. **Reasoning** A point is 2 units to the left of the y-axis and 4 units below the x-axis. Name the ordered pair that locates the point.

Name the ordered pair for each point.

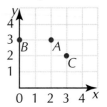

1. A   2. B   3. C

Draw a grid and locate and label each point.
4. R (3, 6)   5. S (6, 3)

How do you graph a point on a coordinate plane?

The method used to name the ordered pair that locates a point can be applied to graphing a point when you are given an ordered pair.

Example B

Graph Point *M* located by the ordered pair (⁻4, ⁺3).

Move 4 units to the left for the *x*-coordinate of ⁻4 and then 3 units up for the *y*-coordinate of ⁺3.

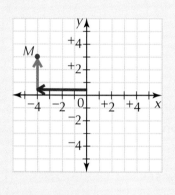

Example C

Graph Point *N* located by the ordered pair (⁻2, ⁻3).

Move 2 units to the left for the *x*-coordinate of ⁻2 and then 3 units down for the *y*-coordinate of ⁻3.

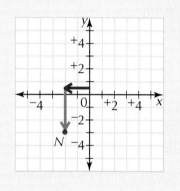

✔ Talk About It

4. In Example C above, if the *y*-coordinate were ⁺3, how would you graph the point?

5. Representations Look at the illustration at the right. What is the same about any points graphed to the left of the *y*-axis? What is different?

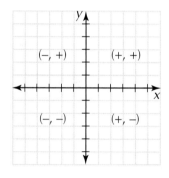

For another example, see Set 12-9 on p. 744.

CHECK ✔

Write the ordered pair for each point.

1. *A*   **2.** *B*   **3.** *C*   **4.** *D*   **5.** *E*

Name the point for each ordered pair.

6. (0, ⁻5)   **7.** (⁺4, ⁻1)   **8.** (⁺3, ⁺1)

9. (⁻1, ⁺4)   **10.** (⁺5, ⁻2)   **11.** (⁺3, ⁻4)

12. Representation What ordered pair names the point of intersection of the *x*- and *y*-axes?

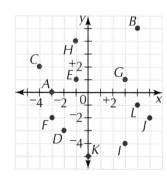

A Skills and Understanding

Write the ordered pair for each point.

13. M   **14.** N   **15.** O

16. P   **17.** Q   **18.** R

Name the point for each ordered pair.

19. ($^-$3, $^-$1)   **20.** ($^+$1, $^-$2)   **21.** ($^+$4, $^-$4)

22. ($^-$2, 0)   **23.** ($^+$2, $^+$4)   **24.** ($^-$2, $^+$3)

25. Representation Write the ordered pair that is located by starting at the origin and moving 4 units to the left.

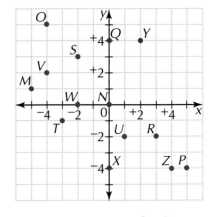

B Reasoning and Problem Solving

26. Kara walked three blocks east, two blocks north, three blocks south, and four blocks west. How many blocks and in what directions was she from the point where she started?

27. Lee Ann has 24 daisies and 16 carnations to arrange in vases. Each vase must contain both daisies and carnations and each arrangement must be exactly the same. All flowers must be used. What is the greatest number of arrangements she can make? How many of each flower will be in each arrangement?

Math and Social Studies

A coordinate grid could be placed over a map. A map of Florida is shown at the right. Use the map for 28–31.

28. What ordered pair would locate Tallahassee?

29. Which city is nearest to the ordered pair (2, $^-$4) on the map?

30. Which city is located at the origin?

31. **Writing in Math** Is Kate's explanation correct? If not, tell why and write a correct response.

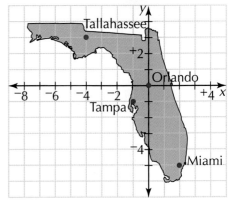

> How do you find the correct ordered pair for Tampa on the map?
>
> I start at the origin. Then I move 1 unit left and 1 unit down. So, the correct ordered pair is (1, 1).

C Extensions

Draw two coordinate planes. Use the coordinate planes to graph each set of points. Connect the points in order and then connect the last point to the first point. Name the geometric figure formed. Be as specific as possible.

32. ($^-$1, $^+$3), ($^-$3, $^-$3), ($^+$2, $^-$1)

33. ($^-$1, $^+$2), ($^+$3, $^+$2), ($^+$2, $^-$1), ($^-$2, $^-$1)

The two axes divide a coordinate plane into four **quadrants** that are labeled I, II, III, and IV. In which quadrant would each point below be located?

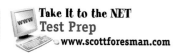

34. ($^-$2, $^-$3)

35. ($^+$5, $^-$6)

36. ($^-$3, $^+$8)

37. ($^+$8, $^+$6)

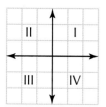

Mixed Review and Test Prep

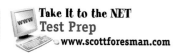
Take It to the NET
Test Prep
www.scottforesman.com

38. 4.2×0.04

39. $[18 - (6 \times 3)] \times 2$

40. $2.65 \div 5$

41. $^+5 - {}^-3$

42. Barry gives two friends 21 marbles each. If he has 235 marbles left, how many marbles did he have before he gave marbles to his friends?

A. 277

B. 256

C. 214

D. 193

43. **Writing in Math** What conclusions can you draw about the two patterns at the right? Clearly state what is the same and what is different. Use examples in your explanation.

Set A: 1, 3, 5, 7, 9, 11, …

Set B: 1, 3, 9, 27, 81, 243, …

Discovery CHANNEL SCHOOL — Discover Math in Your World

Take It to the NET
Video and Activities
www.scottforesman.com

It's Hot!

The average temperature on the sun's surface is approximately 8,700°F. Mercury's average surface temperature is 332°F. Earth's average surface temperature is 50°F. Pluto, the farthest planet from the sun, has an average surface temperature of $^-$355°F.

1. How much hotter is the average surface temperature of Earth than that of Pluto?

2. How much hotter is the average surface temperature of the sun than that of Mercury?

Algebra

Key Idea
Ordered pairs can be used to graph equations on a coordinate plane.

Vocabulary
• linear equation

Materials
• grid paper

CH PATRO
QUARTERS

Graphing Equations

LEARN

How do you graph an equation on a coordinate plane?

In Chicago, the Fahrenheit temperature in January averages 46 degrees cooler than the Fahrenheit temperature in Miami.

Chicago temperature   Miami temperature

$$y = x - 46$$

For any equation with two variables, such as $y = x - 46$, you can substitute any value for x and then find the corresponding value for y. The two values can be written as an ordered pair (x, y).

For example, in the equation $y = x - 46$, if $x = 70$, then $y = 70 - 46$, or 24.

The ordered pair is (70, 24).

To graph an equation on a coordinate plane, you need to create a **table of x- and y-values.** The ordered pairs from the table are used to graph points on the coordinate plane. You can then draw a line through the points to graph the equation.

Graph the equation $y = x - 4$.

Make a table of x- and y-values. Use at least three convenient values for x and find the corresponding values for y. Use the ordered pairs to locate points on the graph. Connect the points to graph the equation.

x	y
⁺4	0
⁺2	⁻2
0	⁻4

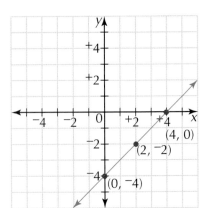

✔ Talk About It

1. In the table above, explain why the value of y is ⁻2 when x is ⁺2.

2. Why should you use at least three values for x when creating a table of values?

1. Which three ordered pairs might form a straight line?
   (⁻1, ⁺5)   (⁻1, 0)
   (⁻1, ⁻2)   (⁺4, ⁻1)

2. Draw a grid and locate each point. Then connect the points with a line segment.
   (⁺3, ⁻1)   (⁻2, ⁺1)

An equation such as $y = x + 2$ is called a **linear equation.** Its graph is a straight line.

In graphing a line, only 2 points are needed to determine the line location. But a third point is graphed to serve as a check.

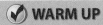

Take It to the NET
More Examples
www.scottforesman.com

For each equation, find the values of *y* when *x* = ⁻2, when *x* = 0, and when *x* = ⁺2. Then name the ordered pairs.

1. $y = x - 5$ **2.** $y = x + 4$ **3.** $y = 2 - x$

Graph each equation. First make a table using *x*-values of 0, ⁺1, and ⁺2.

4. $y = x + 3$ **5.** $y = x - {}^-2$ **6.** $y = x + x$

7. Reasoning Does the line for $y = x - 6$ pass through the point (6, 0)? Explain.

PRACTICE

For more practice, see Set 12-10 on p. 747.

Ⓐ Skills and Understanding

For each equation, find the values of *y* when *x* = ⁻1, when *x* = 0, and when *x* = ⁺1. Then name the ordered pairs.

8. $y = x + 2$ **9.** $y = x - {}^-4$ **10.** $y = 1 - x$

Graph each equation. First make a table using *x*-values of 0, ⁺1, and ⁺2.

11. $y = x + 1$ **12.** $y = x - 3$ **13.** $y = 4x$

14. Reasoning Is the point (4, ⁻1) on the same line as points (0, ⁻5), (1, ⁻4), and (2, ⁻3)? Explain how you decided.

Ⓑ Reasoning and Problem Solving

Use the sign at the right for 15–16.

15. Use $y = 3x$, where *x* is the cost of a 1-day ticket. Find the cost of three 1-day tickets.

16. You have a $10-off coupon for a single 1-week ticket. Find the cost of two 1-week tickets using the coupon.

17. <u>Writing in Math</u> If the ordered pairs (−2, 3), (0, 3), (5, 3), and (10, 3) were graphed, they would lie on a horizontal line. Do you think $x = 3$ or $y = 3$ is the correct equation to describe the line through the points? Explain.

🦉 Mixed Review and Test Prep

Take It to the NET
Test Prep
www.scottforesman.com

Write the ordered pair for each point.

18. *A* **19.** *E* **20.** *C* **21.** *H*

22. Which ordered pair locates Point *G*?

A. (⁻4, ⁺1) **B.** (⁺4, ⁻1)

C. (⁻4, ⁻1) **D.** (⁺4, ⁺1)

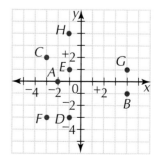

Problem-Solving Applications

Solar System Studying space may help us to improve our everyday lives. By studying the weather on other planets, we may be able to better understand our weather on Earth. Radio stations, power companies, and satellite communication companies also benefit from knowledge about the solar system.

Trivia The activity of the sun can affect the atmosphere on Earth. This, in turn, can affect radio broadcasting. This once caused police officers using their radios in California to be answered by dispatchers in Minnesota!

Pluto
Mercury
Mars
Venus
Earth

1 NASA reported that the temperature of Venus stays close to 464°C and that the temperature for Pluto may be about ⁻223°C. How much hotter is Venus than Pluto?

Neptune

2 If you were to walk on Mars, the air near your toes may have a temperature of 18°C, but the air at your head may be 27°C colder. What would be the temperature near your head?

Uranus

Using Key Facts

3 Find the range and median of the planets' diameters.

Saturn

Key Facts	
Planet	**Diameter** (to nearest thousand)
•Mercury	3,000 mi
•Venus	8,000 mi
•Earth	8,000 mi
•Mars	4,000 mi
•Jupiter	89,000 mi
•Saturn	75,000 mi
•Uranus	32,000 mi
•Neptune	31,000 mi
•Pluto	1,000 mi

Jupiter

4 If a model of the sun were as tall as an astronaut, the model of Jupiter would be about as big as the astronaut's helmet. Jupiter's radius is about 72,000 kilometers. The sun's radius is about 696,000 kilometers. What ratio, in simplest form, shows the ratio of Jupiter's radius to the sun's radius?

5 **Decision Making** Survey 6 people to find which planet they would like to explore as an astronaut. Decide what type of graph would best display your data. Make the graph of your choice. Include a title for your graph.

6 Prominences are fountains of gases on the sun that may rise with a speed of about 100 miles per second. At this rate, how long would it take a prominence to rise to a height equal to the diameter of Earth? To a height equal to 8 Earth diameters?

7 **Writing in Math** Use the information in this lesson to write your own word problem. Answer your question with a complete sentence.

Good News/Bad News *Space probes have enabled researchers to learn much about other planets. Unfortunately, the task of making and delivering probes is very complicated and many of the missions fail.*

Do You Know How?

Do You Understand?

The Coordinate Plane (12-9)

Write the ordered pair for each point.

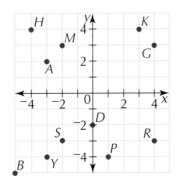

1. A   2. R

3. G   4. Y

Name the point for each ordered pair.

5. $(^-2,^+3)$ 6. $(^+3,^+4)$ 7. $(^+1,^-4)$

8. $(0,^-2)$ 9. $(^-2,^-3)$ 10. $(^-4,^+4)$

11. Which point is closest to the origin?

12. Which point is furthest from the origin?

A How can you tell if an ordered pair names a point below the x-axis?

B What do you know about the location of a point in which the first number of the ordered pair is a negative integer?

C To move from point R to point M, would you move in a positive or negative direction along the x-axis? How many units?

D To move from point S to point G, would you move in a positive or negative direction along the y-axis? How many units?

Graphing Equations (12-10)

For each equation, find the values of y when x = $^-$2, x = 0, and x = 2. Then name the ordered pairs.

13. $y = x + 4$ 14. $y = x - 1$

Graph each equation. First make a table of values of y when x = $^-$2, x = 0, and x = 2.

15. $y = 2 - x$ 16. $y = x - {}^-3$

17. Name 3 points on the line at the right.

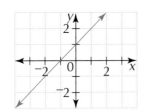

18. If the graph were extended, would the point (3, 4) be on the line?

E Is $(^+6,^+5)$ on the graph for $y = x - 1$? How can you tell?

F Tell how you could rewrite the equation in Exercise 16 using addition. Would rewriting the equation this way change your table of values? Explain.

G Explain how you determined your answer for Exercise 18.

H Could $y = x + 2$ be the equation for the graph in Exercises 17 and 18? Explain why or why not.

MULTIPLE CHOICE

1. Which is the ordered pair for point *M*? (12-9)

   A. ($^-$2, $^+$1)   **B.** ($^-$1, $^-$2)   **C.** ($^+$2, $^-$1)   **D.** ($^+$1, $^+$2)

2. Which point is NOT on the line $y = x + 4$? (12-10)

   A. (0, $^+$4)   **B.** ($^-$4, 0)   **C.** ($^-$2, $^+$2)   **D.** ($^+$2, $^+$2)

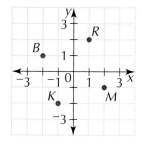

FREE RESPONSE

Give the ordered pair of each of these locations. (12-9)

3. the origin

4. 3 units to the right of the origin and 4 units up

5. 4 units to the left of origin

6. 1 unit to the left of the origin and 3 units down

For each equation, find the values of *y* when $x = ^-2$, $x = 0$, and $x = ^+2$. Then name the ordered pairs. (12-10)

7. $y = x + 5$ **8.** $y = 3 - x$ **9.** $y = x - ^-1$

Graph each equation. First make a table using *x*-values of $^-1$, 0, and $^+1$. (12-10)

10. $y = x + 4$ **11.** $y = x - 3$ **12.** $y = x$

13. If the graph of the line in Exercise 10 were extended, would the point ($^-$4, 0) be on the line? Explain why or why not. (12-10)

14. Will (2, $^-$2) be on the graph of the line in Exercise 12? Explain why or why not. (12-10)

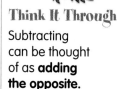

Think It Through
Subtracting can be thought of as **adding the opposite.**

Writing in Math

15. Give the ordered pairs for three points on the line at the top right. What do you think will always be true for any point on this line? (12-10)

16. Decide if the statement is true or false. Use the line at the bottom right to help explain your answer.

On a vertical line, all the ordered pairs will have the same *y*-coordinates. (12-10)

17. How could you use *x*-coordinates to find the length of a horizontal line segment in the coordinate plane? How could you use *y*-coordinates to find the length of a vertical line segment in the coordinate plane?

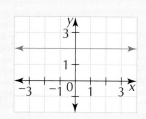

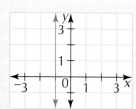

Test-Taking Strategies

Understand the question.

Get information for the answer.

Plan how to find the answer.

Make smart choices.

Use writing in math.

→ **Improve written answers.**

Improve Written Answers

You can follow the tips below to learn how to improve written answers on a test. It is important to write a clear answer and include only information needed to answer the question.

1. Matt's house is at (2, 5). Draw a point to show the location of (2, 5).

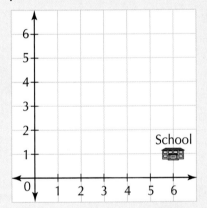

On the lines below, explain how you located the point at (2, 5).

_____

Improve Written Answers

- Check if your answer is complete.

  *In order to **get as many points as possible**, I must plot a point at (2, 5) and I must explain how I found the location of (2, 5).*

- Check if your answer makes sense.

  *I should follow the steps in my explanation and see if I wind up at the point I plotted. Is my **use of mathematical terms** correct?*

- Check if your explanation is clear and easy to follow.

  *I should reread my explanation to be sure it is **accurate and clear.** I shouldn't include any unnecessary information.*

The rubric below is a scoring guide for Test Questions 1 and 2.

Scoring Rubric

4 points	**3** points	**2** points	**1** point	**0** points
Full credit: 4 points	**Partial credit: 3 points**	**Partial credit: 2 points**	**Partial credit: 1 point**	**No credit: 0 points**
The point marked and the explanation are correct.	The point marked is correct, but the explanation is missing a small detail.	The point marked is correct or the explanation is correct, but not both.	The point marked is incorrect. The explanation shows partial understanding.	The point marked and the explanation are both incorrect or missing.

Anita used the scoring rubric on page 734 to score a student's answer to Test Question 1. The student's paper is shown below.

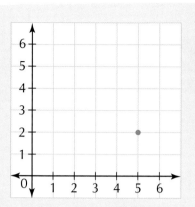

On the lines below, explain how you located the point at (2, 5).

I started at the origin, which is

(0, 0). Then I moved up 2 units.

Then I moved to the right 5 units.

Think It Through

The point and the explanation are both wrong. This student got the x-coordinate and y-coordinate switched. But the student knew that you should start at the origin and that the numbers in an ordered pair tell you how many units to move. So, since there's partial understanding, I'd give this answer 1 point.

Now it's your turn.

Score the student's paper. If it does not get 4 points, rewrite it so that it does.

2. Give the ordered pair that describes the location of the bank.

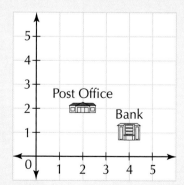

Explain how you determined the ordered pair.

The bank is at (4, 1). I found the

point by counting.

"Equal" is part of Properties of Equality.

The **properties of equality** *say that you can add, subtract, multiply, or divide both sides of an equation by the same number, and the sides stay equal. (But you can't divide by 0.)*

Self Check

Solve equations. (Lessons 12-1, 12-2, 12-3)

Use **Properties of Equality** and **inverse operations** to solve each equation.

$t + 17 = 83.$	$c - 72 = 19$	$216 = 8s$	$\frac{m}{6} = 49$
$t + 17 - \mathbf{17} = 83 - \mathbf{17}$	$c - 72 + \mathbf{72} = 19 + \mathbf{72}$	$\frac{216}{8} = \frac{8s}{8}$	$\frac{m}{6}\mathbf{(6)} = 49\mathbf{(6)}$
$t = 66$	$c = 91$	$27 = s$	$m = 294$

1. Solve $n - 34 = 52$ and $5y = 70$.

Self Check

Order, add, and subtract integers. (Lessons 12-5, 12-6, 12-7)

Integers are the whole numbers and their **opposites**. You can use a number line to picture **positive** and **negative integers**.

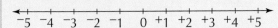

Find $^+1 + {}^-4$.

Picture the addition on a number line.

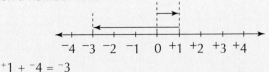

$^+1 + {}^-4 = {}^-3$

Order 0, $^-1$, $^+4$, and $^-5$ from least to greatest.

Refer to the number line.

From least to greatest, the integers are: $^-5$, $^-1$, 0, $^+4$.

Find $^+5 - {}^-2$.

Add the opposite of the integer being subtracted.

$^+5 - {}^-2 = {}^+5 + {}^+2 = {}^+7$

Positive and negative are opposites.

2. Order $^+2$, $^-6$, $^+7$, and $^-8$ from least to greatest and find $^-5 + {}^-4$, $^-8 - {}^-3$, and $^-6 + {}^+2$.

*Negative integers, $^-1$, $^-2$, $^-3$, and so on, are the **opposites** of positive integers, 1, 2, 3, and so on. (p. 710)*

Linear equation contains the word "line."

*The graph of a **linear equation** is a straight line. (p. 728)*

Self Check ✓

Graph points and equations on the coordinate plane. (Lessons 12-9, 12-10)

Graph the **linear equation** $y = x - 3$ on a **coordinate plane.**

Make **a table of x- and y- values.** Graph the **ordered pairs** in the table. Draw a line to connect the points.

x	y
0	⁻3
⁺2	⁻1
⁺4	⁺1

← To graph (⁺2, ⁻1), move 2 units to the right of the **origin** and 1 unit down.

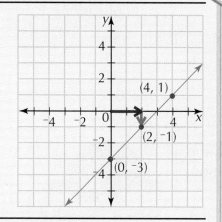

3. Is the point (⁻3, ⁻5) on the line for $y = x - 3$?

Self Check ✓

Write an equation or write to compare to solve problems. (Lessons 12-4, 12-8)

To write an equation, decide which operation is indicated by the main idea.

Tom drove 175 miles to a convention. This was seven times as far as his boss had to drive. How far did his boss drive?

Let x = the distance Tom's boss drove.

$7x = 175$

$\dfrac{7x}{7} = \dfrac{175}{7}$

$x = 25$

boss' distance: x

Tom's distance: 175 mi

Tom's boss drove 25 miles.

Tell how groups you are comparing are alike and how they are different.

Compare the sets of integers.

Set A: ⁻2, ⁻4, ⁻5, ⁻9

Set B: ⁻9, ⁻5, ⁻4, ⁻2

Both sets contain the same four negative integers. But in Set A, they are written from greatest to least, and in Set B, they are written from least to greatest.

4. A desk and chair cost $1,022. If the desk costs $738, how much is the chair?

Answers: 1. $n = 86$; $y = 14$ 2. ⁻8, ⁻6, ⁺2, ⁺7; ⁻9; ⁻5; ⁻4 3. No 4. $284

MULTIPLE CHOICE

Choose the correct letter for each answer.

1. What inverse operation must be used to get *n* alone in the expression $n \times 6$?

   A. addition   **C.** multiplication

   B. subtraction   **D.** division

2. Solve $81 = m + 9$.

   A. $m = 9$ **C.** $m = 81$

   B. $m = 72$ **D.** $m = 90$

3. What is the value of *c* in the equation $c - 4 = 42$?

Think It Through
- I should **watch for highlighted words.**
- I should **check to make sure my answer is reasonable.**

   A. 13

   B. 38

   C. 46

   D. 168

4. Solve $\frac{t}{8} = 16$.

   A. $t = 2$ **C.** $t = 24$

   B. $t = 8$ **D.** $t = 128$

5. Solve $7n = 98$.

   A. $n = 7$ **C.** $n = 91$

   B. $n = 14$ **D.** $n = 105$

6. Marcus biked a total of 276 miles in a month. He biked 168 miles the first 3 weeks. How far did he bike the last week?

   A. 56 miles   **C.** 92 miles

   B. 69 miles   **D.** 108 miles

7. Which list is in order from least to greatest?

   A. $0, {}^-1, {}^-2, {}^+4$ **C.** ${}^-2, {}^-3, 0, {}^+1$

   B. ${}^-4, {}^-2, {}^+1, {}^+3$ **D.** ${}^-1, 0, {}^+2, {}^-3$

8. Which word description could be used for the integer ${}^-5$?

   A. a deposit of $5

   B. a temperature of 5°F

   C. 5 feet below the water surface

   D. a gain of 5 yards

9. Which comparison is true?

   A. ${}^-4 > {}^-1$ **C.** ${}^-5 = {}^+5$

   B. ${}^-5 < {}^-2$ **D.** ${}^+3 < {}^-7$

10. Add ${}^-9$ and ${}^+5$.

   A. ${}^-4$ **C.** ${}^-14$

   B. ${}^+14$ **D.** ${}^+4$

11. At noon the temperature was 8°C. By 6:00 P.M., the temperature had risen 5°C. What was the temperature at 6:00 P.M.?

   A. 3°C   **C.** 13°C

   B. ${}^-3$°C   **D.** ${}^-13$°C

12. Find ${}^-5 - {}^-14$.

   A. ${}^-19$ **C.** ${}^+9$

   B. ${}^-9$ **D.** ${}^+19$

13. Hector is saving money to buy a printer that costs $89. He has saved $38. He drew the picture below to help him decide how much more he has to save.

Which equation could he write to find how much more he needs to save?

   A. $x + 38 = 89$ **C.** $38x = 89$

   B. $38 + 89 = x$ **D.** $x - 38 = 89$

For 14–15, use the coordinate grid.

14. Which point is located at ($^-$1, $^+$4)?

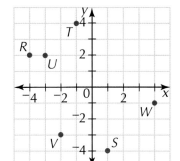

   A. R

   B. S

   C. T

   D. W

15. What is the ordered pair for point U?

   A. ($^+$2, $^-$3)   **C.** ($^-$3, $^+$2)

   B. ($^+$3, $^-$2)   **D.** ($^-$2, $^+$3)

16. The graph shows which equation?

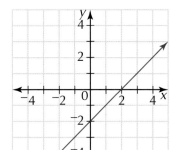

   A. $y = x + 2$

   B. $y = x - 2$

   C. $y = 2 - x$

   D. $y = x - 1$

FREE RESPONSE

Solve and check each equation.

17. $y - 67 = 15$ **18.** $15 + a = 31$

19. $18r = 54$ **20.** $\frac{q}{7} = 14$

21. Jocelyn must read a total of 60 pages. To find the average number of pages she will have to read each day in 3 days, she drew this picture.

60		
n	*n*	*n*

Write an equation to find the number of pages Jocelyn would have to read each day.

Write an integer for each word description.

22. 75 feet below sea level

23. a withdrawal of $15

Compare. Use >, <, or = for each ◯.

24. $^-$5 ◯ $^-$3   **25.** $^+$7 ◯ $^-$11

26. $^-$8 ◯ $^-$9   **27.** $^-$3 ◯ $^+$2

Add or subtract. Use a number line.

28. $^-$6 + $^-$9   **29.** $^+$4 − $^-$8

30. $^-$5 − $^-$6   **31.** $^-$7 + $^+$12

32. Graph the equation $y = x + 3$. First make a table using x-values of $^-$3, 0, and $^+$3.

Writing in Math

33. Explain how to locate a point with the ordered pair ($^-$3,$^+$1).

34. Describe how to solve the equation below. Then solve the equation.

$$m + 98 = 107$$

35. Compare the two sets of ordered pairs shown below. Graph the points on a coordinate grid and connect the points. Then describe how the two lines are alike and how they are different.

Set A	Set B
($^+$2, 0)	($^+$2, 0)
($^+$1, $^+$1)	($^+$1, $^-$1)
(0, $^+$2)	(0, $^-$2)
($^-$1, $^+$3)	($^-$1, $^-$3)

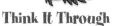

Think It Through

- My answers should be **brief but complete**.
- I should **check if my answer is clear and easy to follow**.

Number and Operation

MULTIPLE CHOICE

1. Find $^-7 + {}^+3$.

   A. $^-10$ **C.** $^+4$

   B. $^-4$ **D.** $^+10$

2. What is 25% of 60?

   A. 1.5   **C.** 240

   B. 15   **D.** 1,500

3. Which list is in order from greatest to least?

   A. $^-4, {}^+2, {}^-1, 0$ **C.** $^+3, 0, {}^-1, {}^-5$

   B. $^-3, {}^-5, {}^+2, {}^+7$ **D.** $^-1, {}^-4, +2, {}^+5$

FREE RESPONSE

4. Find $^-7 - {}^-5$.

5. Find $^-5 + {}^+8$.

6. Write three fractions equivalent to $\frac{4}{12}$.

7. Kris was playing a board game. She picked a card that had her move 5 spaces forward from start. The next card had her move 2 spaces back and the third card had her move 4 spaces forward. How many spaces was Kris from start?

Writing in Math

8. Explain the Addition Property of Equality. Give an example.

9. Hunter says that subtraction of a positive number is the same as addition of a negative number. Is he correct? Explain your answer.

Geometry and Measurement

MULTIPLE CHOICE

10. An angle with a measure of 85° is classified as

    A. right.   **C.** obtuse.

    B. acute.   **D.** straight.

11. A trapezoid must have all of the following EXCEPT

    A. four sides.

    B. four angles.

    C. four parallel sides.

    D. at least one obtuse angle.

12. Which drawing shows the figure turned 90° clockwise?

    A.   **C.**

    B.   **D.**

FREE RESPONSE

13. Find the measure of the fourth angle if three angles of a quadrilateral measure 76°, 97° and 62°.

14. Draw a right isosceles triangle.

Writing in Math

15. Describe what makes a figure a regular polygon.

Data Analysis and Probability

MULTIPLE CHOICE

16. What is the mode of the data set?

25, 32, 33, 41, 18, 25, 29

A. 7   **C.** 25

B. 18   **D.** 29

17. What is the mean of 6, 8, 10, and 12?

A. 10   **C.** 8

B. 9   **D.** 6

FREE RESPONSE

18. Look at the graph of temperatures. Did the temperature increase or decrease from 9:00 P.M. to 3:00 A.M.? By how much?

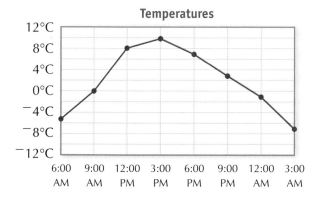

Writing in Math

19. Jessica is looking at a circle graph of favorite activities. The shaded area for dancing is $\frac{1}{3}$ of the circle. The shaded area for movies is $\frac{1}{4}$ of the circle. The shaded area for reading is $\frac{5}{12}$ of the circle. Jessica said the favorite activity is dancing. Is this correct? Explain your answer.

Algebra

MULTIPLE CHOICE

20. Solve for a.

$$a - 16 = 38$$

A. $a = 2$ **C.** $a = 45$

B. $a = 16$ **D.** $a = 54$

21. Which ordered pair makes this equation true?

$$y = x - 4$$

A. $(^-1, ^-5)$ **C.** $(^-2, ^+4)$

B. $(0, ^+2)$ **D.** $(^-5, ^-1)$

22. Find the value of b in the equation $\frac{b}{7} = 9$.

A. 9   **C.** 63

B. 16   **D.** 72

FREE RESPONSE

23. Solve for n.
$8n = 72$

24. Solve for n.
$n - 28 = ^-20$

25. Graph the equation $y = ^-4 + x$.

Writing in Math

26. Explain the difference between an equation and a linear equation. Explain how to graph a linear equation.

27. Explain how to use inverse operations and the properties of equality to solve an equation.

Set 12-1 (pages 696–699)

Tell what inverse operation and what number you would use to get n alone in the expression $n \times 3$.

Division can undo multiplication.

$n \times (3 \div 3) = ?$

$n \times 1 = n$

Dividing $n \times 3$ by 3 leaves just n.

Remember that inverse operations undo each other.

1. $12 + n$ **2.** $n - 10$

3. $n \div 5$ **4.** $14 \times n$

5. $n + 31$ **6.** $n \times 16$

7. $n \times 2 = 300$ **8.** $\frac{n}{22} = 5$

9. $n + 47 = 72$ **10.** $3n = 21$

11. Which property of equality is illustrated by this statement?
$15 + 7 = 22$, so $(15 + 7) - 5 = 22 - 5$

Set 12-2 (pages 700–701)

Solve and check the equation $x + 72 = 120$.

Step 1 Use an inverse operation to solve.

$x + 72 = 120$

$x + 72 - 72 = 120 - 72$ Subtract 72 from both

$x = 48$ sides and simplify.

Step 2 Check your work.

$x + 72 = 120$

$48 + 72 = 120$ Substitute 48 for x.

$120 = 120$ It checks.

Remember that you must perform the same operation to both sides of an equation to keep it equal.

1. $a + 35 = 98$ **2.** $b - 27 = 46$

3. $n - 104 = 118$ **4.** $56 + z = 71$

5. $g + 18 = 80$ **6.** $y - 16 = 7$

7. $f - 51 = 32$ **8.** $p + 67 = 142$

9. $n + 27 = 42$ **10.** $y - 63 = 41$

Set 12-3 (pages 702–703)

Solve and check the equation $y \div 6 = 7$.

Step 1 Use an inverse operation to solve.

$y \div 6 = 7$

$y \div 6 \times 6 = 7 \times 6$ Multiply both sides

$y = 42$ by 6 and simplify.

Step 2 Check your work.

$y \div 6 = 7$

$42 \div 6 = 7$

$7 = 7$ Substitute 42 for y. It checks.

Remember that division can be written as $n \div 3$ or $\frac{n}{3}$ and multiplication can be written as $3n$ or $3 \times n$.

1. $12g = 48$ **2.** $b \div 6 = 3$

3. $\frac{k}{5} = 8$ **4.** $t \div 9 = 14$

5. $r \times 7 = 63$ **6.** $25p = 175$

7. $\frac{x}{15} = 4$ **8.** $13 \times d = 104$

9. $n \div 15 = 8$ **10.** $77n = 231$

To write an equation to solve a problem, follow these steps.

Step 1: Show the main idea in the problem.

Step 2: Use a letter to show what you are trying to find. This is called a variable.

Step 3: Write a number sentence. Think: Use words first.

Step 4: Solve the number sentence.

Remember that you can write an equation when the story has an unknown quantity or if the relationship between quantities involves one or more operations.

1. Jermaine is 12 years old. He is 3 years younger than Angela. How old is Angela?

2. Cajun bought sneakers and a baseball hat at the sporting goods store. He spent a total of $54. If the sneakers cost $42, how much did the hat cost?

3. Mr. Mark is arranging his book collection. He places the books evenly on 4 shelves. If there are 15 books on each shelf, how many books are in Mr. Mark's collection?

Compare $^-3$ ⬤ $^-2$. Use >, <, or = for ⬤.

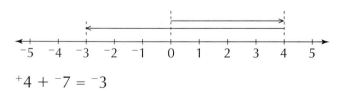

The integer $^-3$ is farther to the left on the number line than the integer $^-2$.

So, $^-3 < {}^-2$

Remember that integers increase as you move from left to right on a number line.

1. $^-6$ ⬤ $^+4$ 2. $^+5$ ⬤ $^-3$

3. $^-7$ ⬤ $^-10$ 4. $^-1$ ⬤ $^-8$

5. $^+12$ ⬤ $^-9$ 6. $^-5$ ⬤ $^-2$

7. $^-8$ ⬤ $^-13$ 8. $^-6$ ⬤ $^+9$

Find $^+4 + {}^-7$.

Start at 0. Move forward 4 units. Then move backward 7 units.

$^+4 + {}^-7 = {}^-3$

Remember that when adding on a number line, you move to the right for positive integers and to the left for negative integers.

1. $^+6 + {}^-4$ 2. $^-3 + {}^-4$

3. $^-5 + {}^+2$ 4. $^-1 + {}^-8$

5. $^+7 + {}^-10$ 6. $^-9 + {}^+12$

7. $^-11 + {}^-6$ 8. $^+2 + {}^-7$

Set 12-7 (pages 718–719)

Subtract $^-6 - ^-5$.

To subtract an integer, add the opposite of the integer being subtracted.

$^-6 - ^-5 \rightarrow ^-6 + ^+5$

$^-6 + ^+5 = ^-1$

Remember when using a number line to subtract integers, the subtraction sign means *turn around*.

1. $^+5 - ^+8$ **2.** $^-9 - ^+4$

3. $^-3 - ^-7$ **4.** $^+14 - ^-6$

Set 12-8 (pages 720–721)

When you write to explain a pattern, follow these steps.

Step 1: Find two pieces of information that will help you identify a pattern.

Step 2: Tell how one quantity changes as the other changes. Be specific.

Remember that studying a table might help you figure out a pattern.

1. The table shows the total amount Tammy spends for lunch. Copy and extend the table to show how much she spends in 4, 5, and 6 days. Explain how the total spent changes as the number of days changes.

Day	Total
1	$1.25
2	$2.50
3	$3.75

Set 12-9 (pages 724–727)

Write the ordered pair for Point B.

Point B is located 2 units to the left of the origin and 4 units up from the origin.

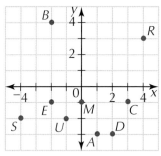

The ordered pair locating B is $(^-2, ^+4)$.

Remember that the first number in an ordered pair represents the x-value. The second number represents the y-value.

1. Point A   **2.** Point C

3. Point D   **4.** Point R

5. Point S   **6.** Point M

7. Name the point for the ordered pair $(^-2, ^-1)$.

Set 12-10 (pages 728–729)

Graph the equation $y = x + ^-5$.

Make a table of x- and y-values. Substitute at least 3 convenient values for x and find the corresponding values for y. Use the ordered pairs to locate points on the graph. Connect the points to graph the equation.

x	y
0	$^-5$
$^+2$	$^-3$
$^+4$	$^-1$

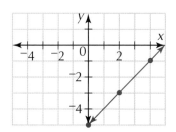

Remember to graph a line, only 2 points are needed, but a third point is graphed to serve as a check.

1. $y = ^+3 + x$ **2.** $y = x - ^-1$

3. $y = ^-2 + x$ **4.** $y = x + ^-1$

5. $y = ^+5 - x$ **6.** $y = ^+3 - x$

Chapter 12
More Practice

Take It to the NET
More Practice
www.scottforesman.com

Set 12-1 (pages 696–699)

Which property of equality is illustrated by each pair of equations?

1. $4 \times 5 = 5 \times 4$
$4 \times 5 - 6 = 5 \times 4 - 6$

2. $8 + 15 = 23$
$(8 + 15) \times 3 = 23 \times 3$

3. $24 \div 6 = 4$
$24 \div 6 + 1 = 4 + 1$

Tell what inverse operation and what number you would use to get n alone.

4. $n \div 32$ **5.** $n + 17$ **6.** $n - 29$ **7.** $6 \times n$

Use what you know about inverse operations to evaluate each expression.

8. $6 \times 11 \div 6$ **9.** $73 + 21 - 21$ **10.** $48 \div 8 - 5 + 5$

Set 12-2 (pages 700–701)

Solve and check each equation.

1. $t + 7 = 18$ **2.** $b - 26 = 44$ **3.** $82 = a + 14$ **4.** $5 = v - 7$

5. $c - 11 = 92$ **6.** $r + 105 = 276$ **7.** $v - 50 = 16$ **8.** $3 + p = 9$

9. Lorraine wants to buy a bike that costs $178. She has $82 in the bank and she earned $28 for baby-sitting last night. How much more money does Lorraine need to buy the bike?

Set 12-3 (pages 702–703)

Solve and check each equation. Remember $\frac{n}{5}$ means $n \div 5$.

1. $c \div 4 = 9$ **2.** $8b = 112$ **3.** $138 = 23 \times n$ **4.** $3 = p \div 5$

5. $f \times 16 = 400$ **6.** $\frac{m}{7} = 35$ **7.** $26s = 78$ **8.** $\frac{y}{3} = 42$

Set 12-4 (pages 706–709)

Draw a picture to show the main idea for each problem. Then write an equation and solve it. Write the answer in a complete sentence.

1. The flower shop has 180 roses. The flowers are arranged in 15 vases. How many roses are in each vase?

2. Danny biked 36 miles yesterday. If Danny biked 3 times as far as Jason, how far did Jason bike?

3. Ella had 25 baseball cards. She gave four to one friend and two to another friend. How many cards does she have now?

Set 12-5 (pages 712–715)

Write an integer for each word description.

1. A deposit of $9   **2.** 4 degrees below zero   **3.** A loss of $12

Use the number line at the right for 4–7.
Write the integer for each point.

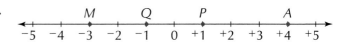

4. M **5.** A **6.** P **7.** Q

Compare. Use >, <, or = for each ◯.

8. $^+4$ ◯ $^-6$ **9.** $^-1$ ◯ $^-7$ **10.** $^-15$ ◯ $^+2$ **11.** $^-5$ ◯ $^-11$

12. $^+8$ ◯ $^+10$ **13.** $^-4$ ◯ $^-2$ **14.** $^+6$ ◯ $^+6$ **15.** $^-6$ ◯ 0

Write in order from least to greatest.

16. $0, ^-6, ^+8$ **17.** $^-3, ^+1, ^-7$ **18.** $^+9, ^-6, ^-1$ **19.** $^-2, ^-5, ^+1, ^-4$

20. $^+2, ^+1, ^-3$ **21.** $^-5, ^-6, ^+7$ **22.** $^-1, ^-5, ^-3$ **23.** $^+4, 0, ^-2, ^-8$

Set 12-6 (pages 716–717)

Add. Use a number line.

1. $^+8 + ^-4$ **2.** $^+3 + ^+4$ **3.** $^-7 + ^-9$ **4.** $^+2 + ^-5$

5. $^-1 + ^-8$ **6.** $^+4 + ^-10$ **7.** $^-5 + ^+8$ **8.** $^-12 + ^+6$

9. $^-2 + ^-16$ **10.** $^+10 + ^-10$ **11.** $^-9 + ^+4$ **12.** $^-6 + ^+8$

13. Will had $89 in his savings account. On Monday he
deposited $25. On Saturday, he withdrew $32 to buy
a pair of jeans. How much money does he have in his
account now?

Set 12-7 (pages 718–719)

Rewrite each subtraction using addition.

1. $^-8 - ^-6$ **2.** $^+17 - ^-9$ **3.** $^-12 - ^+23$ **4.** $^-15 - ^+4$

Subtract. Use a number line.

5. $^-10 - ^-4$ **6.** $^+9 - ^-3$ **7.** $^-5 - ^+4$ **8.** $^-1 - ^+3$

9. $^+7 - ^-9$ **10.** $^-3 - ^-4$ **11.** $^+12 - ^-8$ **12.** $^-6 - ^+9$

13. $^+5 - ^-10$ **14.** $^-7 - ^-8$ **15.** $^+8 - ^-8$ **16.** $^-10 - ^+7$

17. At noon, the temperature was 16°F. By midnight,
the temperature had dropped to $^-4$°F. What was
the temperature change from noon to midnight?

Take It to the NET
More Practice
www.scottforesman.com

Set 12-8 (pages 720–721)

Write to explain.

1. The table shows the total number of kilometers Mr. Jackson drove to and from work during the first 3 days of the week. Copy the table and use the pattern to extend it to Sunday. Explain how the total number of kilometers changes as the number of the day changes.

	Day	Miles
Mon.	1	22.5
Tue.	2	45
Wed.	3	67.5

Set 12-9 (pages 724–727)

Write the ordered pair for each point.

1. *C*   2. *H*   3. *E*

4. *F*   5. *A*   6. *J*

Name the point for each ordered pair.

7. ($^+$1, $^-$3)   8. ($^+$3, $^-$1)   9. ($^-$1, $^-$4)

10. ($^-$5, $^+$3)   11. ($^+$3, $^+$4)   12. (0, $^+$2)

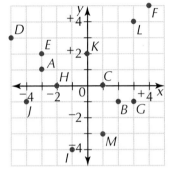

13. To get from Point *X* to Point *Y*, Harry moved 8 units right, then 5 units up. If Point *X* is located at ($^-$3, $^+$1) on a coordinate grid, where on the grid is Point *Y* located?

Set 12-10 (pages 728–729)

For each equation, find the values of *y* when *x* = $^-$2, when *x* = 0, and when *x* = $^+$2.

1. $y = x + {}^-4$ 2. $y = {}^+6 - x$ 3. $y = x - {}^+1$ 4. $y = {}^-2 + x$

5. $y = x + {}^+6$ 6. $y = {}^-7 - x$ 7. $y = x - {}^+5$ 8. $y = {}^-9 + x$

Graph each equation. First make a table using *x*-values of $^-$2, 0, and $^+$2.

9. $y = x + {}^+1$ 10. $y = x + {}^-2$ 11. $y = {}^-3 + x$ 12. $y = {}^+1 - x$

13. Darrell runs 6 miles each day. To find how far Darrell runs in 4 days, use the equation $y = 4x$, where *x* is the number of miles Darrell runs each day.

A

acute angle An angle whose measure is less than 90°. (p. 333)

acute triangle A triangle whose angles are all acute angles. (p. 342)

algebraic expression A mathematical phrase involving a variable or variables, numbers, and operations. (p. 100)
Example: x – 3

angle Two rays that have the same endpoint. (p. 332)

area The number of square units needed to cover a surface or figure. (p. 548)

Associative Property of Addition Addends can be regrouped and the sum remains the same. (p. 22)
Example: 1 + (3 + 5) = (1 + 3) + 5

Associative Property of Multiplication Factors can be regrouped and the product remains the same. (p. 66)
Example: 2 × (4 × 10) = (2 × 4) × 10

average The number found by adding all the data and dividing by the number of data. Also, called the *mean*. (p. 282)

axis Either of two lines drawn perpendicular to each other in a graph. (p. 262)

B

bar graph A graph that uses bars to show data. (p. 262)

base of a polygon The side of a polygon to which the height is perpendicular (p. 552)

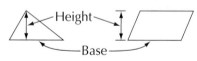

base of a solid The face of a solid that is used to name the solid (p. 595)

benchmark fractions The fractions $\frac{1}{4}$, $\frac{1}{3}$, $\frac{1}{2}$, $\frac{2}{3}$ and $\frac{3}{4}$. (p. 402)

C

capacity The amount a container will hold. (p. 614)

center The point from which all points in a circle are equally distant. (p. 336)

centimeter (cm) A metric unit of length. 100 centimeters equal 1 meter. (p. 534)

central angle An angle whose vertex is the center of the circle. (p. 336)

certain (event) An event that will always happen. (p. 296)

chord A line segment that connects two points on the circle. (p. 336)

circle A closed plane figure made up of all the points the same distance from one point called the center. (p. 336)

Center — Circle

circle graph A graph in the shape of a circle that shows what part of the whole each portion of the data represents. (p. 286)

circumference The distance around a circle. (p. 542)

common denominator A number that is the denominator of two or more fractions. (p. 420)

common factor A number that is a factor of two or more given numbers. (p. 414)

Commutative Property of Addition The order of addends can be changed and the sum remains the same. (p. 22)
Example: 3 + 7 = 7 + 3

Commutative Property of Multiplication The order of factors can be changed and the product remains the same. (p. 66)
Example: 3 × 5 = 5 × 3

compatible numbers Numbers which are easy to compute with mentally. (p. 22)

compensation Adjusting one number of an operation to make computations easier and balancing the adjustment by changing the other number. (p. 22)

composite number A whole number greater than one that has more than two factors. (p. 164)

cone Solid with one circular base, the points on the circle are joined to one point outside the base. (p. 594)

Base

congruent figures Figures that have the same size and shape. (p. 360)

coordinate plane A coordinate grid that extends to include both positive and negative numbers. (p. 724)

coordinates The two numbers in an ordered pair. (p. 174)

cubic unit (unit³) A cube 1 unit on each edge used to measure volume. (p. 610)

cup (c) A customary unit of capacity. 1 cup equals 8 fluid ounces. (p. 614)

cylinder A solid figure with two circular bases that are congruent and parallel. (p. 594)

data Collected information. (p. 260)

dekameter (dam) A metric unit of length equal to 10 meters. (p. 536)

decimeter (dm) A metric unit of length. 10 decimeters equal 1 meter. (p. 536)

degree (°) A unit of measure for angles. (p. 332)

degree Celsius (°C) A unit of measure for measuring temperature in the metric system. (p. 568)

degree Fahrenheit (°F) A unit of measure for measuring temperature in the customary system. (p. 568)

denominator The number below the fraction bar in a fraction. (p. 394)

diameter Any line segment through the center that connects two points on the circle. (p. 336)

difference The number that results from subtracting one number from another. (p. 104)

digits The symbols used to show numbers: 0, 1, 2, 3, 4, 5, 6, 7, 8, 9. (p. 4)

Distributive Property Multiplying a sum (or difference) by a number is the same as multiplying each number in the sum (or difference) by the number and adding (or subtracting) the products. (p. 70)
Example: $3 \times (10 + 4) = (3 \times 10) + (3 \times 4)$

dividend The number to be divided. (p. 152)

divisibility rules Rules that are used to find if a number is divisible by numbers such as 2, 3, 4, 5, 6, 9, or 10. (p. 162)

divisible A number is divisible by another number if there is no remainder after dividing. (p. 162)

divisor The number used to divide another number. (p. 152)

double bar graph A bar graph that displays two different shaded bars to compare the two sets of data. (p. 262)

edge A line segment where two faces meet in a solid figure. (p. 594)

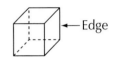
Edge

elapsed time The difference between two times. (p. 564)

equally likely (outcomes) Having the same chance of occurring. (p. 296)

equal ratios Ratios that show the same comparison. (p. 648)

equation A number sentence that uses an equal sign to show that two expressions have the same value. (p. 108)
Examples: $9 + 3 = 12$, $x - 5 = 10$

equilateral triangle A triangle whose sides all have the same length. (p. 342)

equivalent decimals Decimals which name the same amount. (p. 8)
Examples: $0.7 = 0.70$

equivalent fractions Fractions that name the same part of a whole region, length, or set. (p. 410)
Example: $\frac{1}{3} = \frac{2}{6}$

estimate To give an approximate value rather than an exact answer. (p. 204)

event A collection of one or more outcomes. (p. 296)

expanded form A way to write a number that shows the place value of each digit. (p. 4)
Example: $3,000 + 500 + 60 + 2$

exterior (of an angle) The points outside the rays that form an angle. (p. 332)

face A flat surface of a polyhedron. (p. 594)

Face

factor pair A pair of numbers whose product equals a given number. (p. 162)

factors Numbers that are multiplied to get a product. (p. 66)

flip (reflection) The change in the position of a figure that gives the mirror image of the figure. (p. 364)

fluid ounce (fl oz) A customary unit of capacity equal to 2 tablespoons. (p. 614)

formula An equation that states a rule. (p. 540)

fraction A symbol, such as $\frac{2}{3}$, $\frac{5}{1}$, or $\frac{8}{5}$, used to name a part of a whole, a part of a set, a location on a number line, or a division of whole numbers. (p. 394)

frequency table A table used to show the number of times something occurs. (p. 260)

front-end estimation A method of estimating by changing numbers to the place-value of their front digit and then finding the sum or difference. (p. 28)

gallon (gal) A unit for measuring capacity in the customary system. 1 gallon equals 4 quarts. (p. 614)

gram (g) A metric unit of mass equal to 1,000 milligrams. (p. 622)

greatest common factor (GCF) The greatest number that is a factor of two or more numbers. (p. 414)

hectometer (hm) Metric unit of length equal to 100 meters. (p. 536)

height The length of a segment from one vertex of a polygon perpendicular to the base. (p. 552)

hexagon A polygon with 6 sides. (p. 340)

hundredth One part of 100 equal parts of a whole. (p. 8)

Identity Properties The properties that state the sum of any number and 0 is that number (p. 22), and the product of any number and 1 is that number (p. 76)

impossible (event) An event that can never happen. (p. 297)

improper fraction A fraction whose numerator is greater than or equal to its denominator. (p. 400)

input/output table A table of values which shows one output value for each input value. (p. 106)

integers Whole numbers and their opposites. (p. 712)

interior (of an angle) The points between the two rays that form an angle. (p. 332)

intersecting lines Lines that pass through the same point. (p. 329)

interval (on a graph) The difference between adjoining numbers on an axis of a graph. (p. 263)

inverse operations Operations that undo each other. (p. 133)

isosceles triangle A triangle with at least two sides of the same length. (p. 342)

kilogram (kg) A metric unit of mass equal to 1,000 grams. (p. 622)

kilometer (km) A metric unit of length equal to 1,000 meters. (p. 534)

leaf The part of a stem-and-leaf plot that shows the ones digit of a number. (p. 270)

least common denominator (LCD) The least common multiple of the denominators of two fractions. (p. 464)

least common multiple (LCM) The smallest of the nonzero common multiples of two numbers. (p. 464)

line A set of points that goes on forever in two directions. (p. 328)

linear equation An equation whose graph is a straight line. (p. 728)

line graph A graph that connects points to show how data changes over time. (p. 266)

line of symmetry The fold line in a symmetric figure. (p. 368)

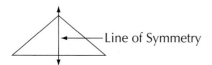
Line of Symmetry

line plot A display of responses along a number line with x's recorded above the response to indicate the number of times the response occurred. (p. 260)

line segment Part of a line having two endpoints. (p. 328)

liter (L) A metric unit of capacity equal to 1,000 milliliters. (p. 616)

mass The amount of matter in an object. (p. 622)

mean The number found by adding all the data and dividing by the number of data. Often called the average. (p. 282)

median The middle number in an ordered set of data. (p. 282)

meter (m) A metric unit of length equal to 100 centimeters. (p. 534)

midpoint The point halfway between the endpoints of a line segment. (p. 328)

milligram (mg) A metric unit of mass. 1,000 milligrams equal 1 gram. (p. 622)

milliliter (mL) A metric unit of capacity equal to 0.001 liters. (p. 616)

millimeter (mm) A metric unit of length. 1,000 millimeters equal 1 meter. (p. 534)

mixed number A number that has a whole-number part and a fractional part. (p. 400)

mode The data value that occurs most often in a set of data. (p. 282)

multiple The product of a given whole number and any other whole number (p. 464).

multiple of 10 A number that has 10 as a factor. (p. 202)

negative integers Integers that are less than zero. (p. 712)

net A plane figure which when folded gives the original shape of a solid. (p. 598)

numerator The number above the fraction bar in a fraction. (p. 394)

obtuse angle An angle whose measure is between 90° and 180°. (p. 333)

obtuse triangle A triangle in which one angle is an obtuse angle. (p. 342)

octagon A polygon with 8 sides. (p. 340)

opposites Numbers that are the same distance away from zero. (p. 712)

order of operations The order in which operations are done in calculations. Work inside parentheses is done first. Then multiplication ad division are done in order from left to right, and finally addition and subtraction are done in order from left to right. (p. 172)

ordered pair A pair of numbers used to locate a point on a graph. (p. 174)

origin The point where the two axes of the coordinate plane intersect. The origin is represented by the ordered pair (0, 0). (p. 724)

ounce (oz) A customary unit of weight. 16 ounces equal 1 pound. (p. 620)

outcome A result in an experiment. (p. 296)

overestimate The result of using larger numbers to estimate a sum or product. The estimate is larger than the actual answer. (p. 68)

parallel lines In a plane, lines that never cross and are the same distance apart. (p. 329)

parallelogram A quadrilateral with both pairs of opposite sides parallel. (p. 346)

partial product Products found by breaking one of the factors into ones, tens, hundreds, and so on, and then multiplying each of these by the other factor. (p. 73)

pentagon A polygon with 5 sides. (p. 340)

percent A ratio in which the first term is compared to 100. (p. 668)

perimeter The distance around the outside of any polygon. (p. 540)

period A group of 3 digits in a number. Periods are separated by a comma and start from the right of a number. (p. 4)

perpendicular lines Two lines that intersect to form right angles. (p. 329)

pi (π) The ratio of the circumference of a circle to its diameter. The decimal for π is 3.141592….
As approximations for π, 3.14 and $3\frac{1}{7}$ are often used. (p. 543)

pictograph A chart pictures or symbols to compare data that can be counted. (p. 288)

pint (pt) Customary unit of capacity equal to 2 cups. (p. 614)

place value The position of a digit in a number that is used to determine the value of the digit. (p. 4) *Example:* In 5,318, 3 is in the hundreds place. So the 3 has a value of 300.

plane An endless flat surface. (p. 328)

point Exact location in space (p. 328)

polygon A closed plane figure made up of line segments. (p. 340)

polyhedron A three-dimensional solid figure with flat surfaces. (p. 594)

positive integers Integers greater than zero. (p. 712)

pound (lb) A customary unit of weight equal to 16 ounces. (p. 620)

prime factorization Writing a number as a product of all of its prime factors. (p. 165)

prime number A whole number greater than 1 that has exactly two factors, itself and 1. (p. 164)

prism A solid figure with two congruent parallel bases and faces that are parallelograms. (p. 594)

probability The ratio of the number of ways an event can occur to the total number of possible outcomes. (p. 302)

product The number that is the result of multiplying two or more factors. (p. 66)

properties of equality Properties that tell what you can do to both sides of an equation so the sides stay equal. (p. 696)

proportion A statement that two ratios are equal. (p. 649)

protractor An instrument used to measure and draw angles. (p. 333)

pyramid A solid figure with a base that is a polygon and whose faces are triangles with a common vertex. (p. 594)

Q

quadrilateral A polygon with 4 sides. (p. 340)

quart (qt) A customary unit of capacity equal to 2 pints. (p. 614)

quotient The number other than the remainder that is the result of dividing. (p. 104)

R

radius Any line segment that connects the center of a circle to a point on the circle. (p. 336)

range The difference between the largest value and the smallest value in a data list. (p. 271)

rate A ratio that compares unlike units. (p. 654)

ratio A pair of numbers that shows a comparison of two quantities and can be written as 9:4, $\frac{9}{4}$, or 9 to 4. (p. 646)

ray Part of a line that has one endpoint and extends forever in only one direction. (p. 328)

rectangle A parallelogram with four right angles. (p. 346)

rectangular array An arrangement of objects in rows and columns so that each row has the same number of objects and each column has the same number of objects. (p. 164)

regular polygon A polygon which has sides of equal length and angles of equal measure. (p. 340)

remainder The number less than the divisor that remains after the division is complete. (p. 152)

rhombus A parallelogram with all sides the same length. (p. 346)

right angle An angle whose measure is 90°. (p. 333)

right triangle A triangle in which one angle is a right angle. (p 342)

rounding A process that tells which multiple of 10, 100, 1,000, etc. a number is closest to. (p. 26)

sample A representative part of a larger group. (p. 260)

sample space The set of all possible outcomes. (p. 300)

scale (in a drawing) A ratio that shows the relationship between lengths in a drawing and the actual object. (p. 662)

scale (in a bar graph) A series of numbers at equal distances along an axis on a graph. (p. 263)

scale drawing A drawing using relationships between lengths in the drawing and the actual object. (p. 662)

scalene triangle A triangle in which no sides have the same length. (p. 342)

sides (of an angle) The two rays that form the angle. (p. 332)

similar figures Figures that have the same shape. They may or may not have the same size. (p. 360)

Similar hexagons

simplest form A fraction in which the greatest common factor of the numerator and denominator is one. (p. 416)

slide (translation) The change in the position of a figure that moves it up, down, or sideways. (p. 364)

solid figure (also solid) A figure that has three dimensions and volume. (p. 594)

solution The value of the variable that makes an equation true. (p. 108)

sphere A solid figure with all points the same distance from the center point. (p. 595)

square A rectangle with all sides the same length. (p. 346)

standard form A number written with commas separating groups of three digits starting from the right. (p. 4)
Example: 3,458

stem The part of a stem-and-leaf plot that shows all but the last digit of a number. (p. 270)

stem-and-leaf plot A graph for organizing data that, with 2-digit data, groups together all data with the same number of tens. (p. 270)

straight angle An angle whose measure is 180°. (p. 333)

sum The number that is the result of adding two or more addends. (p. 104)

surface area (SA) The sum of the areas of all faces of a polyhedron. (p. 602)

survey A way to collect data to answer a question. (p. 260)

symmetric figure A figure that can be folded into two congruent parts that fit on top of each other. (p. 368)

table of values A table used to show how one quantity is related to another. (p. 176)

tablespoon (tbsp) A customary unit of capacity equal to 3 teaspoons. (p. 614)

teaspoon (tsp) A customary unit of capacity equal to $\frac{1}{3}$ tablespoon. (p. 614)

tenth One out of ten equal parts of a whole. (p. 8)

terms The two numbers being compared in a ratio. (p. 649)

thousandth One out of 1,000 equal parts of a whole. (p. 8)

ton (T) A customary unit of weight equal to 2,000 pounds. (p. 620)

transformation A move such as a slide, flip, or turn that does not change the size or shape of a figure. (p. 364)

trapezoid A quadrilateral that has exactly one pair of parallel sides. (p. 346)

tree diagram A diagram used to organize outcomes of an experiment. (p. 300)

trend The general direction in a data set. (p. 266)

triangle A polygon with 3 sides. (p. 340)

turn (rotation) The change in the position of a figure that moves it around a point. (p. 364)

underestimate The result of using smaller numbers to estimate a sum or product. The estimate is smaller than the actual answer. (p. 68)

unit rate A rate where the comparison is to 1 unit. (p. 654)

variable A letter, such as *n*, that stands for a number in an expression or an equation. (p. 100)

vertex (plural, vertices) (in an angle) The common endpoint in an angle. (p. 332)

vertex (in a polyhedron) A point where edges meet in a polyhedron. (p. 594)

volume The number of cubic units that fit inside a solid figure. (p. 610)

weight A measure of how light or how heavy something is. (p. 620)

word form A number written in words using place value. (p. 4)

x-value The first number in an ordered pair. (p. 724)

y-value The second number in an ordered pair. (p. 724)

Zero Property of Multiplication. In Multiplication, the product of a number and 0 is 0. (p. 76)
Example: $8 \times 0 = 0$ (p. 76)

Measures–Customary

Length
1 foot (ft) = 12 inches (in.)
1 yard (yd) = 3 feet, or 36 inches
1 mile = 5,280 feet, or 1,760 yards

Weight
1 pound (lb) = 16 ounces (oz)
1 ton (T) = 2,000 pounds

Capacity
1 cup (c) = 8 fluid ounces (fl oz)
1 pint (pt) = 2 cups
1 quart (qt) = 2 pints
1 gallon (gal) = 4 quarts

Time
1 minute (min) = 60 seconds (s)
1 hour (h) = 60 minutes
1 day (d) = 24 hours
1 week (wk) = 7 days
1 month (mo) = 28 to 31 days,
           or about 4 weeks
1 year (yr) = 12 months (mo),
           or 52 weeks,
           or 365 days

Measures–Metric

Length
1 meter (m) = 1,000 millimeters (mm)
1 meter = 100 centimeters (cm)
1 meter = 10 decimeters (dm)
1 centimeter (cm) = 10 millimeters
1 decimeter = 10 centimeters
1 kilometer (km) = 1,000 meters

Mass/Weight
1 gram (g) = 1,000 milligrams (mg)
1 kilogram (kg) = 1,000 grams

Capacity
1 liter (L) = 1,000 milliliters (mL)

Symbols

$=$	is equal to	π	pi (approximately 3.14)	$\overleftrightarrow{AB}$	line AB
$>$	is greater than	$°$	degree	$\overline{AB}$	line segment AB
$<$	is less than	$°C$	degree Celsius	$\overrightarrow{AB}$	ray AB
$\approx$	is approximately equal to	$°F$	degree Fahrenheit	$\angle ABC$	angle ABC
$\cong$	is congruent to	10^2	ten to the second power	$\triangle ABC$	triangle ABC
2:5	ratio of 2 to 5	$\parallel$	is parallel to	(3, 4)	ordered pair 3, 4
%	percent	$\perp$	is perpendicular to		

Formulas

$P = $ sum of lengths of all sides	Perimeter (general formula)	$A = s \times s$	Area of a square
$P = (2 \times \ell) + (2 \times w)$	Perimeter of a rectangle	$A = b \times h$	Area of a parallelogram
$P = 4 \times s$	Perimeter of a square	$A = \frac{1}{2} \times b \times h$	Area of a triangle
$A = \ell \times w$	Area of a rectangle	$C = \pi \times d$	Circumference of a circle
		$V = \ell \times w \times h$	Volume of a rectangular prism

CREDITS

Cover
Illustration: Drew Rose
Photograph: ©2002 J. H. Pete Carmichael

Text
Dorling Kindersley (DK) is an international publishing company specializing in the creation of high-quality reference content for books, CD-ROMs, online materials, and video. The hallmark of DK content is its unique combination of educational value and strong visual style. This combination allows DK to deliver appealing, accessible, and engaging educational content that delights children, parents, and teachers around the world. Scott Foresman is delighted to have been able to use selected extracts of DK content within this Scott Foresman Math program.

44–45: "Canberra" from *Ships* by Moira Butterfield. Copyright ©1994 by Dorling Kindersley Limited; 110–111: "Light and Heavy" from *Incredible Comparisons* by Russell Ash. Copyright ©1996 by Dorling Kindersley Limited; 180–181: "Running on Rails" from *Machines and How They Work* by David Burnie. Copyright ©1991 by Dorling Kindersley; 238–239: "Animal Speed" from *Incredible Comparisons* by Russell Ash. Copyright ©1996 by Dorling Kindersley Limited; 306–307: "World Population" from *The World in One Day* by Russell Ash. Text copyright ©1997 by Russell Ash. Compilation and illustration copyright ©1997 by Dorling Kindersley Limited; 372–373: "Hong Kong and Shanghai Bank" from *Architecture* by Neil Stevenson. Copyright ©1997 by Dorling Kindersley Limited; 438–439: *Extreme Machines* by Christopher Maynard. Copyright ©2000 by Dorling Kindersley Limited; 506–507: "Life on Shore" from *Shoreline* by Barbara Taylor. Copyright ©1993 by Dorling Kindersley Limited; 574–575: "Statue of Liberty" from *Amazing Buildings* by Philip Wilkinson. Text copyright ©1993 by Philip Wilkinson. Copyright ©1993 by Dorling Kindersley Limited; 626–627: "Water" from *Incredible Comparisons* by Russell Ash. Copyright ©1996 by Dorling Kindersley Limited; 676–677: "The Basic Healthy Diet" from *Healing Foods* by Miriam Polunin. Text copyright ©1997 by Miriam Polunin. Copyright ©1997 by Dorling Kindersley Limited; 732–733: "The Solar System" from *Incredible Comparisons* by Russell Ash. Copyright ©1996 by Dorling Kindersley Limited.

Illustrations
344, 460, 708 Phyllis Pollema-Cahill

Photographs
Every effort has been made to secure permission and provide appropriate credit for photographic material. The publisher deeply regrets any omission and pledges to correct errors called to its attention in subsequent editions.

Unless otherwise acknowledged, all photographs are the property of Scott Foresman, a division of Pearson Education.

Photo locators denoted as follows: Top (T), Center (C), Bottom (B), Left (L), Right (R), Background (Bkgd)

Chapter 1: 2 ©Volvox/Index Stock Imagery; 4 (BL) European Space Agency/Photo Researchers, Inc., (L) PhotoDisc, (TR) ©Antonio M. Rosario/Getty Images; 5 (CR) ©Antonio M. Rosario/Getty Images; 6 (L) SuperStock, (CR) Getty Images; 7 (CR) ©Mark E. Gibson Stock Photography, (CL) Hot Ideas/Index Stock Imagery; 8 Getty Images; 9 Getty Images; 10 ©Toyofumi Mori/Getty Images; 12 (BL) ©Jake Martin/Getty Images, (CL) Getty Images; 13 ©Dorling Kindersley; 18 (TR) Emil Buehler Naval Aviation Library, (L) ©John H. Clark/Corbis; 19 ©George H. H. Huey/Corbis; 21 Jeff Rotman/Photo Researchers, Inc.; 24 ©Bettmann/Corbis; 27 ©Janicek/Getty Images; 28 ©Neil Robinson/Getty Images; 31 Corbis; 33 (CR, TR) Getty Images, (BR) ©Dorling Kindersley; 36 (L) ©Mark E. Gibson Stock Photography, (CR) NASA/Science Source/Photo Researchers, Inc.; 37 ©Dorling Kindersley; 38 Corbis; 40 (L) Richard Heinzen/SuperStock, (Bkgd) Larry Larimer/Brand X Pictures; 41 ©Michal Heron/Corbis; 42 V.C.L./FPG International LLC; 43 ©Duomo/Corbis; 44 ©Dorling Kindersley; 47 Getty Images; 48 ©Michael T. Sedam/Corbis **Chapter 2:** 64 ©Jeff Hunter/Getty Images; 67 Richard Hutchings; 68 (L) Getty Images, (Bkgd) Corbis; 70 Brian Hagiwara/FoodPix; 72 Ray Dean/Photonica; 74 (CR) Getty Images, (BR) ©Antonio M. Rosario/Getty Images; 76 Getty Images; 77 ©Dorling Kindersley; 84 Michael Abbey/Photo Researchers, Inc.; 85 (CR) ©Lester V. Bergman/Corbis, (C) Pictor/Alamy.com; 86 (L) Brian Hagiwara/FoodPix, (CR) ©Comstock Inc.; 88 (L, BR) digitalvisiononline.com, (TR) Creatas; 90 ©Buddy Mays/Corbis; 92 ©Steven Weinberg/Getty Images; 94 Eyebyte/Alamy.com; 96 ©Comstock Inc.; 97 ©Jeremy Woodhouse/Getty Images; 100 ©Mike Powell/Allsport/Getty Images; 102 Joseph Nettis/Stock Boston; 104 ©Comstock Inc.; 107 Corbis; 108 ©Art Wolfe/Getty Images; 110 ©Dorling Kindersley; 111 ©Dorling Kindersley; 114 (CL) ©Dorling Kindersley, (L) Getty Images; 115 Getty Images; 120 Terry Wild Studio, Inc. **Chapter 3:** 130 ©Bryan F. Peterson/Corbis; 132 ©Yellow Dog Productions/Getty Images; 133 ©Ben Osborne/Getty Images; 135 Getty Images; 136 ©Barros & Barros/Getty Images; 137 Getty Images; 138 Getty Images; 143 ©Kevin Schafer/Corbis; 144 ©Tim Thompson/Corbis; 148 David Lorenz Winston/Brand X Pictures; 151 Getty Images; 152 Christi Carter/Grant Heilman Photography; 154 ©Buddy Mays/Corbis; 155 Chance Morgan; 156 Bob Crandall/Stock Boston; 157 Gary Conner/Index Stock Imagery; 158 Mike Dobel/Masterfile Corporation; 159 Corbis; 162 ©Color Day Production/Getty Images; 163 A. Ramey/PhotoEdit; 164 Bob Anderson/Masterfile Corporation; 166 Culver Pictures Inc.; 168 Mary Kate Denny/PhotoEdit; 174 (BL) ©Richard Cummins/Corbis, (L) ©Roger Ressmeyer/Corbis; 176 ©D. Boone/Corbis; 177 David Lissy/eStock Photo; 180 ©Dorling Kindersley; 190 Getty Images **Chapter 4:** 200 ©Frank Lane/Parfitt/Getty Images; 202 digitalvisiononline.com; 203 Andrew Wenzel/Masterfile Corporation; 204 ©Siede Preis/Getty Images; 206 (TR) ©Richard Hamilton Smith/Corbis, (CR) Natural Selection Stock Photography, Inc.; 210 Tim Davis/Photo Researchers, Inc.; 214 ©Gary Randall/Getty Images/FPG; 216 ©Jess Alford/Getty Images; 220 (BL) European Space Agency/Photo Researchers, Inc., (CR) Brand X Pictures; 221 ©Gail Shumway/Getty Images; 222 ©Steve Bloom/Getty Images; 223 Arthur Montes De Oca; 224 Bill Bachmann/PhotoEdit; 225 José Caldas/Reflexo; 230 Tetsu/Photonica; 231 ©William Manning/Corbis; 232 Laszlo Selly/FoodPix; 233 Burke/Triolo/Brand X Pictures; 236 Getty Images; 238 ©Dorling Kindersley; 239 ©Dorling Kindersley; 247 ©Ryan McVay/Getty Images **Chapter 5:** 258 digitalvisiononline.com; 262 ©Jim Cummins/Corbis; 266 ©Vittoriano Rastelli/Corbis; 268 Getty Images; 270 ©Lawrence Manning/Corbis; 272 Getty Images; 276 ©John Kelly/Getty Images; 282 digitalvisiononline.com; 285 ©Volvox/Index Stock Imagery; 286 ©Marcelo Coelho/Getty Images; 288 Getty Images; 292 ©Duomo/Corbis; 300 ©Allsport/Getty Images; 303 SuperStock; 306 ©Dorling Kindersley; 307 ©Dorling Kindersley **Chapter 6:** 326 ©Jacob Halaska/Index Stock Imagery; 328 (L) Allan Davey/Masterfile Corporation, (TC) Mark C. Burnett/Photo Researchers, Inc.; 330 ©David Butow/Corbis/SABA; 332 Frank Chmura/ImageState/Alamy.com; 337 ©Dorling Kindersley; 340 (L) ©Araldo de Luca/Corbis, (CR) Getty Images, (BC) Larry Stepanowicz/Visuals Unlimited, (BR) Don W. Fawcett/Photo Researchers, Inc., (T) Aneal S. Vohra/Unicorn Stock Photos, (C) ChromoSohm/Sohm/Photo Researchers, Inc., (CC) Aneal S. Vohra/Unicorn Stock Photos; 342 ©Richard Cummins/Corbis; 345 bygonetimes/Alamy.com; 346 (L) Large Composition A with Black, Red, Yellow and Blue. 1920. Oil on canvas, 91.5 x 92 cm. Mondrian, Piet (1872–1944). ©2003 Mondrian/Holtzman Trust/Artists Rights Society (ARS), New York. Photo: ©Alinari/Art Resource, NY; 352 (L) © William Cornett, (TR) Department of Defense; 360 ©Harold Sund/Getty Images; 362 Rudi Von Briel/PhotoEdit; 369 ©Peter Gridley/Getty Images; 370 (TL, T) Getty Images, (TC) Brian Hagiwara/FoodPix, (TR) digitalvisiononline.com; 372 (TR) Richard Bryant/Arcaid, (CL, BR) ©Ian Lambot; 373 Ian Lambot/Arcaid **Chapter 7:** 392 ©Oli Tennent/Getty Images; 394 ©Glen Allison/Getty Images; 395 (TR) ©Dorling Kindersley, (TRR) Hemera Technologies; 405 ©1997 Aaron Haupt/Stock Boston; 406 ©William Cornett; 412 2002/©Norbert Wu; 416 ©Historical Picture Archive/Corbis; 419 Bob Daemmrich/Stock Boston; 426 ©Walter Bibikow/Getty Images; 428 Daemmrich Photography; 429 Hemera Technologies; 433 (C, T) Getty Images, (B) Corbis; 435 Getty Images; 436 Doug Adams/Unicorn Stock Photos; 438 (TR, CL) ©Dorling Kindersley, (B) ©Sporting Pictures (UK) Ltd.; 439 The Times/Rex Features **Chapter 8:** 458 digitalvisiononline.com; 460 Mark Tomalty/Masterfile Corporation; 466 ©Spencer Grant/PhotoEdit; 468 Bridgeman Art Library/SuperStock; 474 ©David Olsen/Getty Images; 476 (L) Davis Barber/PhotoEdit, (TR) Felicia Martinez/PhotoEdit; 477 Brand X Pictures; 478 (L) ©Brian Kenney, (TR) M. H. Sharp/Photo Researchers, Inc., (T) ©David H. Ahrenholz; 480 (TR, TL) ©David H. Ahrenholz, (T) ©Brian Kenney, (TC) E. R. Degginger/Color-Pic, Inc.; 484 ©Connie Coleman/Getty Images; 486 ©Barbara Peacock/Getty Images; 487 ©David W. Hamilton/Getty Images; 498 Michael Newman/PhotoEdit; 499 ©W. Cody/Corbis; 500 ©Gary Cralle/Getty Images; 502 Jeff Greenberg/Index Stock Imagery; 503 Getty Images; 504 ©Yorgos Nikas/Getty Images; 505 Getty Images; 506 ©Dorling Kindersley; 507 ©Dorling Kindersley; 511 ©Keren Su/Getty Images **Chapter 9:** 526 ©Richard Hamilton Smith/Corbis; 528 Getty Images; 529 Getty Images; 530 ©Allen Dean Steele/Getty Images; 531 (B) ©Tim Davis/Getty Images, (BL) Brand X Pictures; 532 ©Steve Allen/Getty Images; 536 ©Steve Chenn/Corbis; 537 ©L. Bassett/Visuals Unlimited; 539 ©L. Bassett/Visuals Unlimited; 540 ©Jorg Greuel/Getty Images; 544 ©Steve Hix/Getty Images; 545 ©Bettmann/Corbis; 552 ©Mark L. Stephenson/Corbis; 554 ©Richard Bryant/Arcaid/Alamy.com; 555 Corbis; 558 ©Bill Losh/Getty Images; 562 ©Jose Luis Pelaez, Inc./Corbis; 564 ©Reuters NewMedia Inc./Corbis; 568 ©Shoot Pty. Ltd./Index Stock Imagery; 570 (L) ©Dorling Kindersley, (BL) ©Ernie Friedlander/Index Stock Imagery; 574 ©Dorling Kindersley; 575 ©Dorling Kindersley; 576 ©Dorling Kindersley; 577 ©Dorling Kindersley **Chapter 10:** 592 ©Jeff Greenberg/Index Stock Imagery; 595 (CL) ©Spike Mafford/Getty Images, (C) Richard Hutchings/Photo Researchers, Inc., (CC) ©My World/Getty Images, (CR) Getty Images; 596 (TL) ©Anthony Meshkinyar/Getty Images, (TC) Getty Images, (TR) Hemera Technologies, (CC) ©Mitch Hrdlicka/Getty Images, (CR) ©William Cornett; 597 ©Pat O'Hara/Corbis; 600 ©Bill Losh/Getty Images; 606 Terry Wild Studio, Inc.; 610 ©Digital Art/Corbis; 612 ©Walter Chandoha; 616 (CL) ©Joseph Harnish, (CC) ©William Cornett; 620 (L) Rebecca Shepherd/Alamy.com, (CL) Getty Images; 621 ©Giel/Getty Images; 622 Getty Images; 623 ©Don Klumpp/Getty Images; 626 ©Dorling Kindersley; 627 ©Dorling Kindersley; 631 Hemera Technologies **Chapter 11:** 644 Getty Images; 646 (L) Getty Images, (CR) ©Geoffrey Clements/Corbis; 647 Corbis; 648 Brian Sytnyk/Masterfile Corporation; 649 ©O. Alamany and E. Vicens/Corbis; 650 (CR) Getty Images, (CC) ©Dorling Kindersley; 651 (CR) Brand X Pictures, (TR) Getty Images; 657 (BL, B) Corbis, (BR, CC) Getty Images, (BC, BRB) ©Comstock Inc.; 659 (C, CR) ©Comstock Inc., (CL, CC) Getty Images, (BC) ©Robert Y. Ono/Corbis, (TL) ©Joel Sartore/NGS Image Collection; 664 ©Lester Lefkowitz/Corbis; 665 ©Peter Hendrie/Getty Images; 667 ©Comstock Inc.; 668 Paul Eekhoff/Masterfile Corporation; 670 Nora Good/Masterfile Corporation; 672 ©Frank Whitney/Getty Images; 674 ©Real Life/Getty Images; 675 (BR) Mark Tomalty/Masterfile Corporation; 676 ©Dorling Kindersley; 677 ©Dorling Kindersley **Chapter 12:** 694 Getty Images; 698 ©Travel Pix/Getty Images; 700 ©AFP/Corbis; 701 Brand X Pictures; 702 ©Olney Vasan/Getty Images; 703 Hemera Technologies; 705 ©David Young-Wolff/Getty Images; 706 ©Terje Rakke/Getty Images; 707 ©Cindy Lewis/Alamy.com; 712 ©Jan Tove Johansson/Getty Images; 713 ©Willard Clay/Getty Images; 714 ©Bill Ross/Corbis; 716 ©Joe McBride/Getty Images; 718 ©Thom Lang/Corbis; 719 ©Jean-Pierre Pieuchot/Getty Images; 720 Robert Holmes; 728 Getty Images; 729 Getty Images; 730 Gail Mooney/Masterfile Corporation; 732 ©Dorling Kindersley; 733 ©Dorling Kindersley

Rule, 84–85, 106–107, 162–163, 176–179

Ruler, 336–337, 342–349